GRADE

11

VOLUME 2

Printed in the U.S.A.

ISBN 978-0-358-41645-6

4 5 6 7 8 9 10 1468 29 28 27 26 25 24 23 22

4500856000

r11.20

(into) Literature™

Program Consultants:

Kylene Beers
Martha Hougen
Tyrone C. Howard
Elena Izquierdo
Carol Jago
Weston Kieschnick
Erik Palmer
Robert E. Probst

GRADE
11
VOLUME 2

Program Consultants

Kylene Beers

Nationally known lecturer and author on reading and literacy; coauthor with Robert Probst of *Disrupting Thinking, Notice & Note: Strategies for Close Reading,* and *Reading Nonfiction;* former president of the National Council of Teachers of English. Dr. Beers is the author of *When Kids Can't Read: What Teachers Can Do* and coeditor of *Adolescent Literacy: Turning Promise into Practice,* as well as articles in the *Journal of Adolescent and Adult Literacy.* Former editor of *Voices from the Middle,* she is the 2001 recipient of NCTE's Richard W. Halle Award, given for outstanding contributions to middle school literacy.

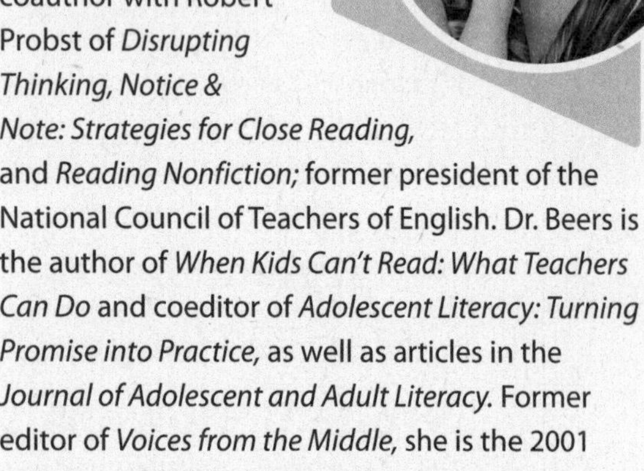

Martha Hougen

National consultant, presenter, researcher, and author. Areas of expertise include differentiating instruction for students with learning difficulties, including those with learning disabilities and dyslexia; and teacher and leader preparation improvement. Dr. Hougen has taught at the middle school through graduate levels. Dr. Hougen has supported Educator Preparation Program reforms while working at the Meadows Center for Preventing Educational Risk at The University of Texas at Austin and at the CEEDAR Center, University of Florida.

Tyrone C. Howard

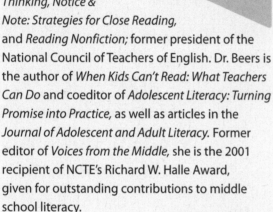

Veteran teacher, author, and professor in the Graduate School of Education and Information Studies at UCLA. Dr. Howard is the inaugural director of the UCLA Pritzker Center for Strengthening Children and Families, a campus-wide consortium examining academic, mental health, and social and emotional experiences and challenges for the most vulnerable youth populations. Dr. Howard has published over 75 peer-reviewed journal articles and several bestselling books, including, *Why Race & Culture Matters in Schools* and *Black Male(d): Peril and Promise in the Education of African American Males*. He is considered one of the premier experts on educational equity and access in the country.

Elena Izquierdo

Nationally recognized teacher educator and advocate for English language learners. Dr. Izquierdo is a linguist by training, with a Ph.D. in Applied Linguistics and Bilingual Education from Georgetown University. She has served on various state and national boards working to close the achievement gaps for bilingual students and English language learners. Dr. Izquierdo is a member of the Hispanic Leadership Council, which supports Hispanic students and educators at both the state and federal levels.

Carol Jago

Teacher of English with 32 years of experience at Santa Monica High School in California; author and nationally known lecturer; former president of the National Council of Teachers of English. Ms. Jago currently serves as Associate Director of the California Reading and Literature Project at UCLA. With expertise in standards assessment and secondary education, Ms. Jago is the author of numerous books on education, including *With Rigor for All* and *Papers, Papers, Papers*; and she is active with the California Association of Teachers of English, editing its scholarly journal *California English* since 1996. Ms. Jago also served on the planning committee for the 2009 NAEP Reading Framework and the 2011 NAEP Writing Framework.

Weston Kieschnick

Author, award-winning teacher, principal, instructional development coordinator, and dean of education. Mr. Kieschnick has driven change and improved student learning in multiple capacities over his educational career. Now, as an experienced instructional coach and Senior Fellow with the International Center for Leadership in Education (ICLE), Mr. Kieschnick shares his expertise with teachers to transform learning through online and blended models. He is the author of *Bold School: Old School Wisdom + New School Innovation = Blended Learning that Works* and co-author of *The Learning Transformation: A Guide to Blended Learning for Administrators*.

Erik Palmer

Veteran teacher and education consultant based in Denver, Colorado. Author of *Well Spoken: Teaching Speaking to All Students* and *Digitally Speaking: How to Improve Student Presentations.* His areas of focus include improving oral communication, promoting technology in classroom presentations, and updating instruction through the use of digital tools. He holds a bachelor's degree from Oberlin College and a master's degree in curriculum and instruction from the University of Colorado.

Robert E. Probst

Nationally respected authority on the teaching of literature; Professor Emeritus of English Education at Georgia State University. Dr. Probst's publications include numerous articles in *English Journal* and *Voices from the Middle,* as well as professional texts including (as coeditor) *Adolescent Literacy: Turning Promise into Practice* and (as coauthor with Kylene Beers) *Disrupting Thinking, Notice & Note: Strategies for Close Reading,* and *Reading Nonfiction.* He has served NCTE in various leadership roles, including the Conference on English Leadership Board of Directors, the Commission on Reading, and column editor of the NCTE journal *Voices from the Middle.*

UNIT 1

Foundations and Encounters

Page 1

ESSENTIAL QUESTIONS

What connects people to certain places?
What values and beliefs shape who we are?
What does it mean to be a stranger in a strange land?
What happens when cultures collide?

KEY LEARNING OBJECTIVES

- Determine and analyze theme
- Analyze plot
- Analyze and evaluate structure
- Determine central idea
- Synthesize information
- Paraphrase
- Compare themes

READER'S CHOICE

UNIT 1 TASKS

Ed

Go online for
Unit and Selection Videos
Interactive Annotation and Text Analysis
Selection Audio Recordings
SAT® Exam / ACT® Test Prep
Collaborative Writing — Writable

UNIT 2

Building a Democracy

Page 126

ESSENTIAL QUESTIONS

What does oppression look like?

How do we gain our freedom?

How can we share power and build alliances?

How do we reach our goals?

KEY LEARNING OBJECTIVES

- Analyze argument
- Determine and analyze themes
- Analyze media
- Analyze point of view
- Analyze and evaluate structure
- Analyze author's purpose
- Analyze and compare tone

READER'S CHOICE

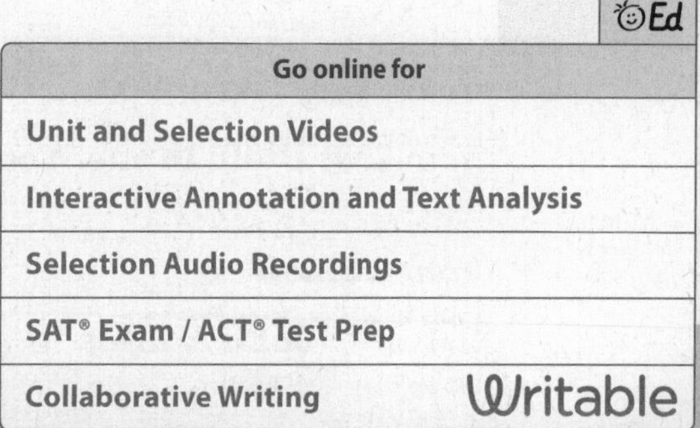
Go online for
Unit and Selection Videos
Interactive Annotation and Text Analysis
Selection Audio Recordings
SAT® Exam / ACT® Test Prep
Collaborative Writing
Writable

UNIT 3

The Individual and Society

Page 248

ESSENTIAL QUESTIONS

How can we be true to ourselves?
How do we relate to the world around us?
What do we secretly fear?
When should we stop and reflect on our lives?

KEY LEARNING OBJECTIVES

- Analyze structure and purpose
- Analyze figurative language
- Summarize
- Compare main ideas
- Analyze symbols
- Analyze mood
- Analyze allegory

COLLABORATE & COMPARE

Compare Themes

READER'S CHOICE

SHORT READS

Available online Ed

from **Nature**
from **Self-Reliance**
Essays by Ralph Waldo Emerson

The Pointlessness of Unplugging
Article by Casey N. Cep

The Raven
Poem by Edgar Allan Poe

The Feather Pillow
Short Story by Horacio Quiroga

Pastoral
Poem by Jennifer Chang

LONG READS

Recommendations

Fahrenheit 451
Novel
by Ray Bradbury

X: A Novel
Novel
by Ilyasah Shabazz and Kekla Magoon

A Paradise Built in Hell
Nonfiction
by Rebecca Solnit

UNIT 3 TASKS

WRITING

Ed

Go online for

- Unit and Selection Videos
- Interactive Annotation and Text Analysis
- Selection Audio Recordings
- SAT® Exam / ACT® Test Prep
- Collaborative Writing — Writable

UNIT 4

The Quest for Freedom

Page 378

ESSENTIAL QUESTIONS

When is self-determination possible?
What causes divisions between people?
How do we respond to defeat?
What is the price of progress?

KEY LEARNING OBJECTIVES

- Analyze and evaluate arguments
- Evaluate sources
- Analyze plot
- Analyze rhetoric
- Compare arguments
- Analyze speaker
- Compare structure

READER'S CHOICE

SHORT READS

Available online

Ed

LONG READS

Recommendations

UNIT 4 TASKS

Ed

Go online for	
Unit and Selection Videos	
Interactive Annotation and Text Analysis	
Selection Audio Recordings	
SAT® Exam / ACT® Test Prep	
Collaborative Writing	Writable

UNIT 5

America Transformed

Page 516

ESSENTIAL QUESTIONS

How much do we control our lives?
Why do humans cause harm?
What are the consequences of change?
What makes a place unique?

KEY LEARNING OBJECTIVES

- Analyze setting
- Analyze tone
- Analyze counterarguments
- Analyze point of view
- Analyze irony
- Analyze author's purpose
- Compare genres

READER'S CHOICE

SHORT READS

Available online Ed

LONG READS

Recommendations

UNIT 5 TASKS

Ed

Go online for	
Unit and Selection Videos	
Interactive Annotation and Text Analysis	
Selection Audio Recordings	
SAT® Exam / ACT® Test Prep	
Collaborative Writing	Writable

UNIT 6

Modern and Contemporary Voices

Page 640

ESSENTIAL QUESTIONS

How do we deal with rejection or isolation?
Can anyone achieve the American Dream?
When should personal integrity come before civic duty?
What would we do if there were no limits?

KEY LEARNING OBJECTIVES

- Analyze characters
- Evaluate interpretations of a drama
- Analyze structure
- Analyze literary devices
- Analyze development of ideas
- Analyze perspective
- Compare ideas across genres

COLLABORATE & COMPARE

Compare Ideas Across Genres

READER'S CHOICE

SHORT READS

Available online

Ed

Poems of the Harlem Renaissance
- **The Weary Blues** by Langston Hughes
- **Song of the Son** by Jean Toomer
- **From the Dark Tower** by Countee Cullen
- **A Black Man Talks of Reaping** by Arna Bontemps

Martin Luther King Jr.: He Showed Us the Way
Essay by César Chávez

Ten Kliks South
Short Story by Phil Klay

Poetry
Poem by Marianne Moore

YouTube Stars Stress Out, Just Like the Rest of Us
Article by Neda Ulaby

LONG READS

Recommendations

One Hundred Years of Solitude
Novel
by Gabriel García Márquez

They Called Us Enemy
Graphic Memoir
by George Takei, Justin Eisinger, Steven Scott, and Harmony Becker

The Things They Carried
Fiction
by Tim O'Brien

UNIT 6 TASKS

WRITING

Ed

Go online for
- Unit and Selection Videos
- Interactive Annotation and Text Analysis
- Selection Audio Recordings
- SAT® Exam / ACT® Test Prep
- Collaborative Writing — Writable

Selections by Genre

Informational Text

Letter/Aphorism

Narrative Nonfiction

DRAMA

MEDIA STUDY

into Literature™ Online

Experience the Power of *HMH Into Literature*

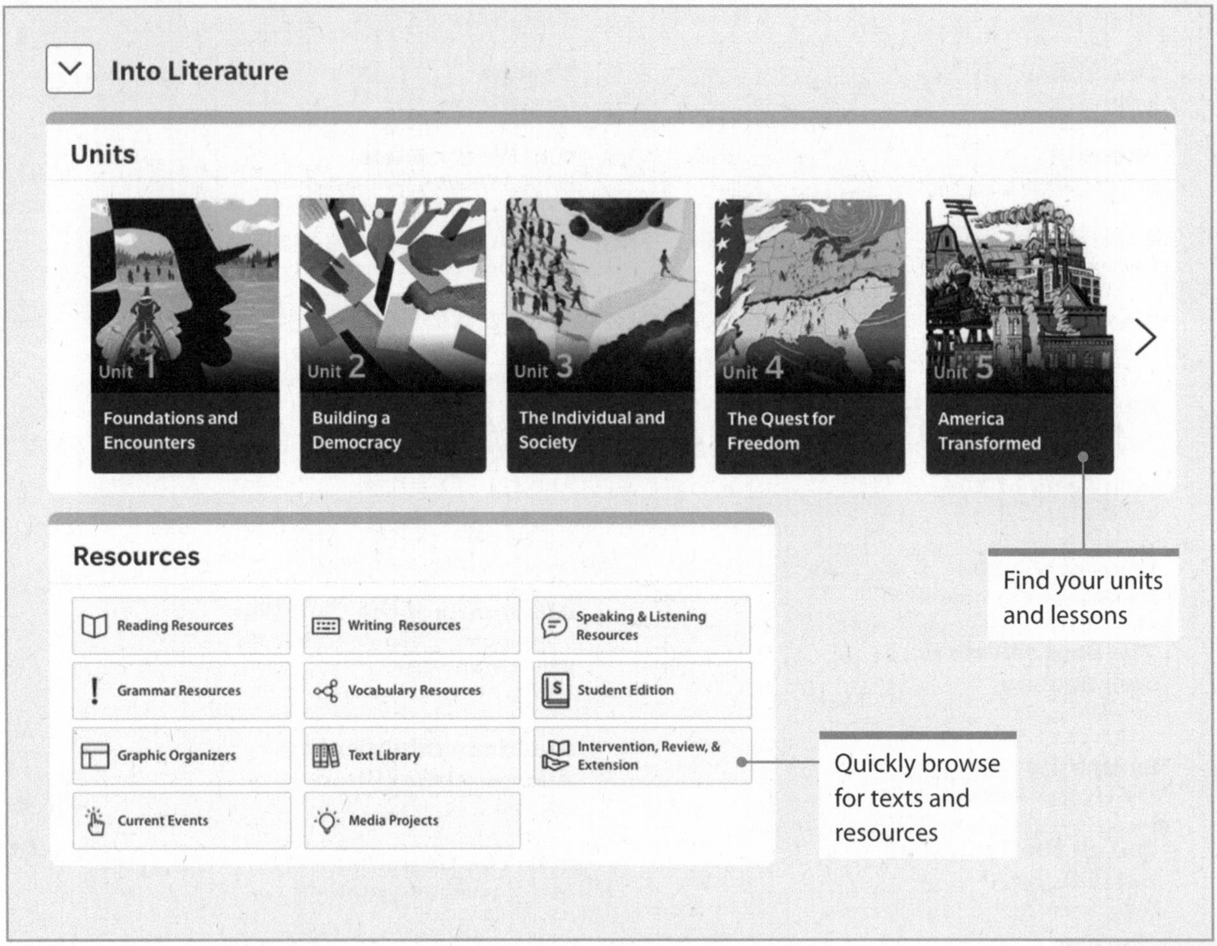

Into Literature

Units

- Unit 1 — Foundations and Encounters
- Unit 2 — Building a Democracy
- Unit 3 — The Individual and Society
- Unit 4 — The Quest for Freedom
- Unit 5 — America Transformed

Find your units and lessons

Resources

Reading Resources	Writing Resources	Speaking & Listening Resources
Grammar Resources	Vocabulary Resources	Student Edition
Graphic Organizers	Text Library	Intervention, Review, & Extension
Current Events	Media Projects	

Quickly browse for texts and resources

Tools for Today—All in One Place

Whether you're working alone or collaborating with others, it takes effort to analyze the complex texts and competing ideas that bombard us in this fast-paced world. What will help you succeed? Staying engaged and organized. The digital tools in this program will help you take charge of your learning.

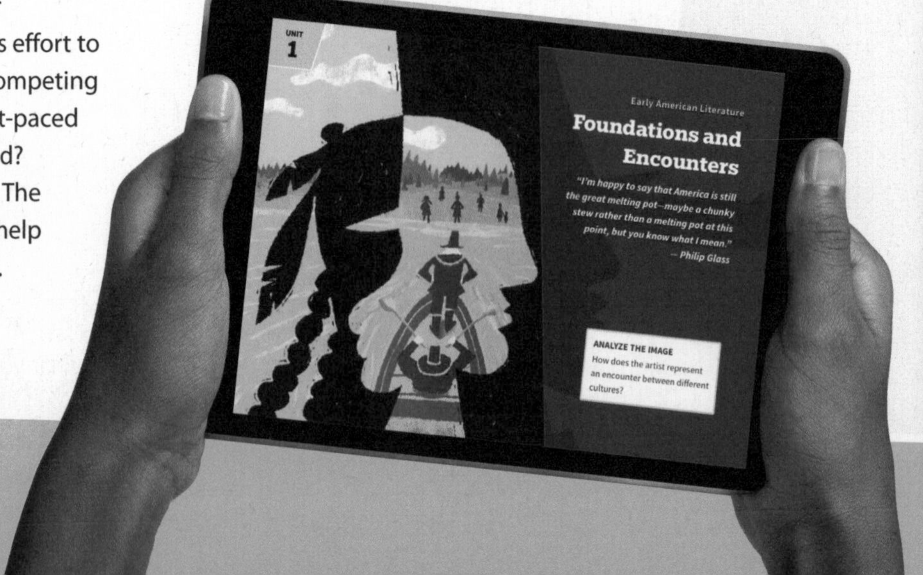

UNIT 1
Early American Literature
Foundations and Encounters
"I'm happy to say that America is still the great melting pot—maybe a chunky stew rather than a melting pot at this point, but you know what I mean."
— Philip Glass
ANALYZE THE IMAGE
How does the artist represent an encounter between different cultures?

Engage!

Spark Your Learning

These activities kick-start the unit and help get you thinking about the unit theme.

Engage Your Brain

Before you read, take some time to do a fun activity designed to rev up your brain and connect to the text.

Interact with the Texts

- As you read, highlight and take notes to mark the text in your own customized way.
- Use interactive graphic organizers to process, summarize, and track your thinking as you read.
- Play the audio to listen to the text read aloud. You can also turn on read-along highlighting.

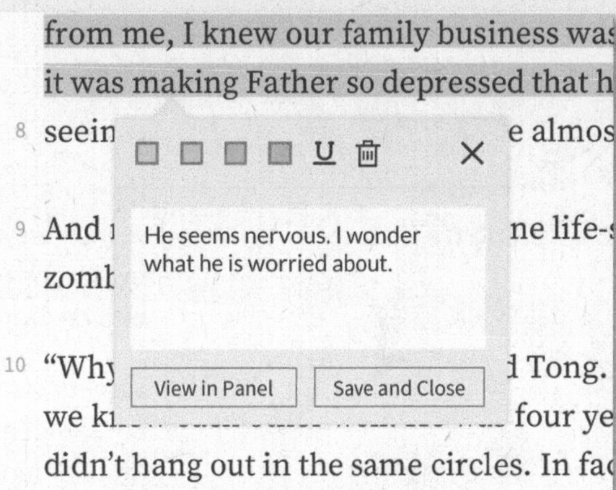

Choices

Choose from engaging activities, such as writing an advice column, creating a podcast, or participating in a debate, to demonstrate what you've learned.

Stay Involved!

Collaborate with and Learn from Your Peers

- Watch brief **Peer Coach Videos** to learn more about a particular skill.
- Flex your creative muscles by digging into **Media Projects** tied to each unit theme.
- Bring your writing online with **Writable,** where you can share your work and give and receive valuable feedback.

Writable

Read On!

Find helpful **Reader's Choice** suggestions with each unit, and access hundreds of texts online.

No Wi-Fi? No Problem!

With HMH *Into Literature,* you always have access; download when you're online and access what you need when you're offline.

NOTICE & NOTE

The Positive Disrupter

Dr. Kylene Beers

Dr. Robert E. Probst

Reading is Change: Thoughts by Two Teachers

by **Dr. Kylene Beers** and **Dr. Robert E. Probst**

Here you are, in the last years of high school, and for more of your school years than you might care to remember you've probably been told not to be disruptive. Sit still. Listen. Keep quiet. But now we're going to tell you to be a disrupter.

Sometimes, of course, you should be still and listen, learn, ponder. But sometimes you should speak up to make a change, to influence those around you, to cause a disruption. We're not encouraging you to misbehave. We're encouraging something much bigger than that.

Disruptions That Bring Change and Growth

Throughout our nation's history, we've grown due to technological disruptions: the horse and buggy eventually became the electric car, the telegram evolved into the text, and the rabbit-eared, three-channel TV became a three-hundred-channel smart device. We've also grown due to social and political disruptions. Women demanded the right to vote; African Americans fought for their freedom; and at one point reading and writing were things reserved for the privileged—ordinary people had to fight to upset that imbalance of power.

Disruptions are a part of life. Some will be positive: new and faster ways to communicate, better ways to grow food, easier ways to clean water. And some will be negative. One of the greatest disruptions we've faced as a nation and world was the COVID-19 pandemic of 2020. The "stay home, stay safe" order disrupted everyone's life. The questions we must ask are, "What did we learn" and "What will we carry forward?"

Other disruptions will affect only you, or you and your family or friend community. You may decide that your religious or political views differ from those of your friends or family. You may choose to be a musician though your parents wanted you to be a pharmacist, or a soldier though your parents wanted you to be a farmer. And there will be other personal choices that you will have to make.

Or others will make them for you. You are going to have to deal with those disruptions and the changes they will bring. You, and others your age, will make the decisions. It's important that you decide what you think. If you don't read and learn, the decisions will be made for you by those who do, or by those who are simply louder.

Some groups of people have always withheld power from others by making sure they know less. One of the most powerful ways of doing that is to ensure groups can't read or write. In some countries today, girls are denied schooling. And, too many who do learn to read and write fail to realize that the more they read, the more able they will be to use reason and evidence to question the world around them and influence their own futures. Too many choose not to read.

The Path to Positive Disruption

The texts you will read this year take on some of the issues every human must face: love, greed, hope, death, injustice, equity, and our relationship with nature, to name a few. Read these selections carefully. Though the story might have taken place in another time with a different group of people, the human emotions and issues remain relevant. Decide what matters to you. Wonder what the issues mean in your life today. And as you decide, think of the world that you will help to shape. You are tomorrow's builders, scientists, politicians, artists, teachers, and nurses. You are our brave soldiers who will defend this country, and our curious thinkers who will change it. And you will change it only by disrupting, slightly or significantly, what it is now.

Shape the world in which you live.

To do that you need to read well—attentively and thoughtfully. We'll help you do that with some tools we call the **Notice & Note Signposts**, explained throughout this program (see the chart on the next two pages). Recognizing signposts will help you better understand what you're reading and thus, what you're thinking.

Reading—smart reading—gives you the opportunity to weigh a thought, a value, a belief, and decide whether to hold onto it, change it, or dispose of it. If you don't decide for yourself, then someone else will. And if you allow that, then you no longer have much influence over the shape of the world in which you live. Don't be that person. Be a person with power, a positive disrupter.

COLLABORATIVE DISCUSSION

What is something you'd like to disrupt? How might reading help you do that?

Notice & Note Handbook
Peer Coach Videos

NOTICE & NOTE
Signposts

When you notice a signpost in your reading, mark the text with its initials.

LITERARY TEXTS

CONTRASTS AND CONTRADICTIONS — CC

A sharp contrast between what we would expect and what we observe the character doing; behavior that contradicts previous behavior or well-established patterns

When you notice this signpost, ask:

Why would the character act (feel) this way?

AHA MOMENT — AM

A sudden realization of something that shifts a character's actions or understanding of self, others, or the world

When you notice this signpost, ask:

How might this change things?

TOUGH QUESTIONS — TQ

Questions characters raise that reveal their inner struggles

When you notice this signpost, ask:

What does this question make me wonder about?

WORDS OF THE WISER — WW

The advice or insight about life that a wiser character, who is usually older, offers to the main character

When you notice this signpost, ask:

What is the life lesson, and how might this affect the character?

AGAIN AND AGAIN — AA

Events, images, or particular words that recur over a portion of the story

When you notice this signpost, ask:

Why might the author bring this up again and again?

MEMORY MOMENT — MM

A recollection by a character that interrupts the forward progress of the story

When you notice this signpost, ask:

Why might this memory moment be important?

Ed
Peer Coach Videos

INFORMATIONAL TEXTS

BIG QUESTIONS BQ

It's important to take a **Questioning Stance** or attitude when you read nonfiction.

- *What surprised me?*
- *What did the author think I already knew?*
- *What changed, challenged, or confirmed what I already knew?*

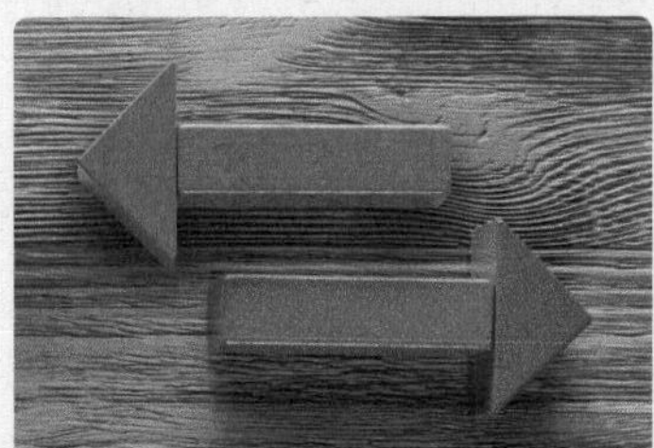

CONTRASTS AND CONTRADICTIONS CC

A sharp contrast between what we would expect and what we observe happening; a difference between two or more elements in the text

When you notice this signpost, ask:

What is the difference, and why does it matter?

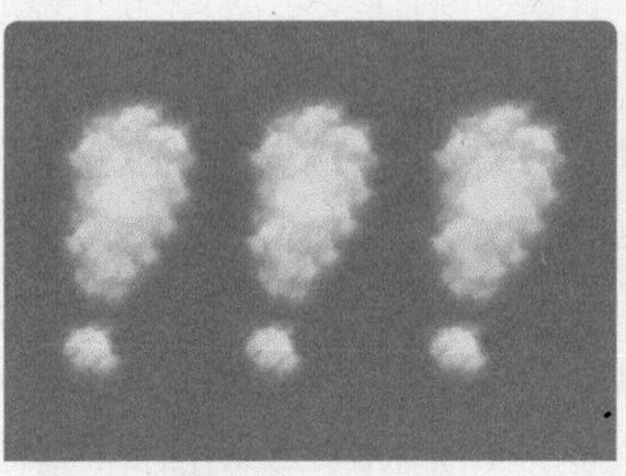

EXTREME OR ABSOLUTE LANGUAGE XL

Language that leaves no doubt about a situation or an event, allows no compromise, or seems to exaggerate or overstate a case

When you notice this signpost, ask:

Why did the author use this language?

NUMBERS AND STATS NS

Specific quantities or comparisons to depict the amount, size, or scale; or the writer is vague and imprecise about numbers when we would expect more precision

When you notice this signpost, ask:

Why did the author use these numbers or amounts?

QUOTED WORDS QW

Opinions or conclusions of someone who is an expert on the subject or someone who might be a participant in or a witness to an event; or the author might cite other people to provide support for a point

When you notice this signpost, ask:

Why was this person quoted or cited, and what did this add?

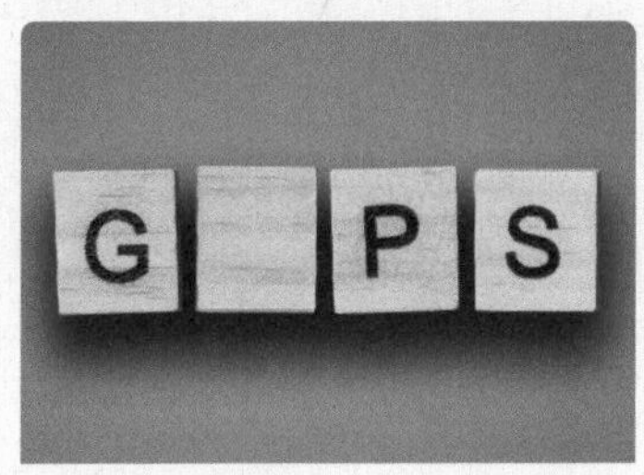

WORD GAPS WG

Vocabulary that is unfamiliar to the reader—for example, a word with multiple meanings, a rare or technical word, a discipline-specific word, or one with a far-removed antecedent

When you notice this signpost, ask:

Do I know this word from someplace else? Does this seem like technical talk for experts on this topic? Can I find clues in the text to help me understand the word?

Social & Emotional Learning

The Most Important Subject Is You!

by **Carol Jago**

You have essays to turn in. You have quizzes to take. You have group projects to complete. Your success in those areas depends on more than your understanding of the academic skills they cover. It also depends on how well you understand yourself, and how well you're able to extend that understanding to others. This might seem obvious, but there's an actual term for that type of learning—it's called **Social and Emotional Learning.**

Why It Matters

But doing well in school is not the only benefit to understanding yourself and others. When it comes to Social and Emotional Learning, the answer to the question, "When will I actually use this in my life?" is clear: every single day, forever. Whether you are with your family, your community, your friends, at a workplace, or by yourself on a deserted island, you will have a better chance of achieving satisfaction and making positive contributions if you're able to do things like the following:

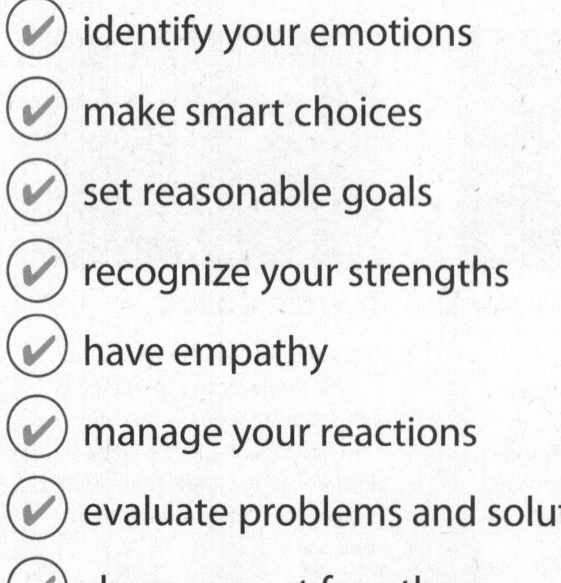

identify your emotions
make smart choices
set reasonable goals
recognize your strengths
have empathy
manage your reactions
evaluate problems and solutions
show respect for others

Where Literature Comes In

English Language Arts classes can provide some of the best opportunities to develop these skills. That's because reading literature allows you to imagine yourself in different worlds and to understand what it's like to be in a wide range of situations. You can think through your own feelings and values as you read about various characters, conflicts, historical figures, and ideas, and you can become more aware of why others might act and feel as they do.

Throughout this book, you will find opportunities for Social and Emotional Learning in the Choices section of many lessons. But you don't need to wait for a special activity to practice and learn. Reading widely and discussing thoughtfully is a natural way to gain empathy and self-knowledge. The chart below shows the five main areas of Social and Emotional Learning and tells how reading can help you strengthen them.

Areas of Social and Emotional Learning	How Reading Can Help
If you have **self-awareness,** you're conscious of your own emotions, thoughts, and values, and you understand how they affect your behavior.	Understanding why characters act the way they do can increase your understanding of your own responses and motivations.
If you're good at **self-management,** you are able to control your emotions, thoughts, and behaviors in different situations.	Paying attention to why characters explode in tumultuous ways or how they keep calm under pressure can help you recognize what to do and not to do when faced with stressful situations in your own life.
If you have **social awareness,** you can empathize with others, including people who are different from you.	Reading about people with different life experiences can help you understand the perspectives of others.
If you have well-developed **relationship skills,** you can get along with different kinds of people and function well in groups.	Reflecting on the conflicts between characters can help you gain insight into what causes the conflicts in your life and how to reach mutual satisfaction.
If you are good at **responsible decision-making,** you make good choices that keep you and others safe and keep you moving toward your goals.	Evaluating the choices characters make and thinking about what you would do in their place can help you understand the consequences of your decisions.

Having the Hard Conversations

The more widely and deeply you read, the more you'll strengthen your social and emotional skills, and the more likely you are to encounter ideas that are different from your own. Some texts might bring up strong reactions from you, and you'll need to take a step back to understand how you're feeling. Or, your classmates might have responses that are dramatically different from yours, and you'll need to take a breath and decide how to engage with them. Remember: it's okay to disagree with a text or with a peer. In fact, discussing a difference of opinion can be one of the most powerful ways to learn.

Tips for Talking About Controversial Issues

So what I hear you saying is . . .
Did I get that right?

Listen actively.
Try your best to understand what the other person is saying, and why they might think or feel that way. If you don't understand, ask questions or rephrase what you thought you heard and ask them if you're getting it right.

The reason I think so is because I've noticed that I . . .

Communicate clearly.
Speak honestly and carefully, rather than for dramatic effect. Notice if the person listening seems confused and give them room to ask questions.

When you use that word I have a negative reaction because it sounds like you are saying you think that person isn't smart.

I'm sorry. That's not what I meant.

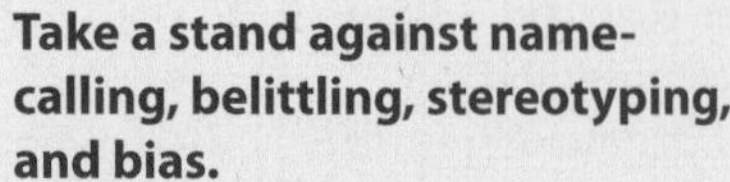

Take a stand against name-calling, belittling, stereotyping, and bias.
Always try exploring ideas further rather than making personal attacks. If someone feels hurt by something you said, listen to them with an open mind. Perhaps you expressed bias without realizing it. Apologize sincerely if that happens. And if you are hurt by a comment or hear something that could be interpreted as hurtful, calmly let the person who said it know why you feel that way.

I need to take a break from this conversation now.

Pay attention to your feelings.
Recognize the topics or situations that make it hard for you to stay calm. Try to separate your strong feelings from what the person is saying. If you need to, excuse yourself from the conversation and find a place where you can help yourself relax.

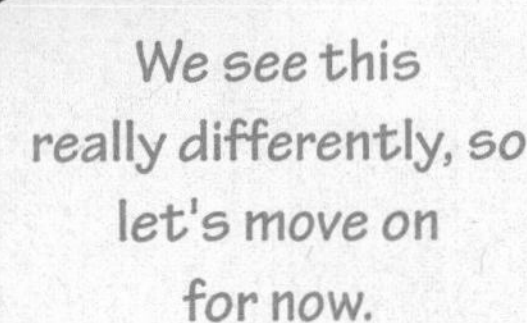

We see this really differently, so let's move on for now.

Consider the relationship.
It's likely that the people you're in class with are people you will be seeing regularly for years. You don't have to be friends with them or agree with their point of view, but you do have to get an education alongside each other. Speaking respectfully even if you're on opposite sides of an issue will make it easier to work together if you ever have to collaborate. Try to assume the best about them rather than the worst. Acknowledge that our experiences affect our points of view.

Agree to disagree.
Even after listening carefully and being listened to, you still might not agree. That's okay. You can acknowledge your differences, remain respectful, and exit the conversation.

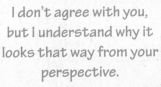

I don't agree with you, but I understand why it looks that way from your perspective.

Learning, growing, and working with others isn't always easy. If you read widely and deeply and try your best to speak honestly, you're likely to gain the understanding and compassion that can help you manage the stresses, challenges, and opportunities that life brings your way.

"My father was a slave and my people died to build this country, and I'm going to stay here and have a part of it."

—Paul Robeson

The Civil War and Its Aftermath

The Quest for Freedom

? As you read the texts in this unit, think about how they explore these **Essential Questions.**

When is self-determination possible?

Self-determination is the ability to act freely. At this time in America, enslaved people were forced to do what they were told, and women were often not permitted to make decisions.

What causes divisions between people?

In the first half of the 19th century, slavery was one of many issues that divided America. Race, nationality, ethnicity, language, and religion are issues that can be divisive today.

How do we respond to defeat?

After the war, parts of the South were in ruins, and the reunited country faced a long, difficult period of healing and rebuilding.

What is the price of progress?

During the 19th century, Americans were creating inventions that pushed the boundaries of farming and industry. But, as with advancements today, these innovations created unintended consequences.

ANALYZE THE IMAGE

What details in the image clearly reflect what happened in the Civil War? What details make you wonder about those events?

Explore unit themes and build background.

Stream to Start Video

Spark Your Learning

As you read, you can use the **Response Log** (page R4) to track your thinking about the Essential Questions.

Here are some opportunities to think about issues related to **Unit 4: The Quest for Freedom**.

Think About the **Essential Questions**

Review the Essential Questions on page 379. Which question is most intriguing to you? Perhaps it reminds you of a text you have read or a personal experience. Write down your thoughts.

Make the Connection

Sometimes myths about important events can overshadow what really happened. List three facts you know about the Civil War. Then, do some research to make sure that the facts you listed are actually true. Share your findings with the class.

Build Academic Vocabulary

You can use these Academic Vocabulary words to write and talk about the topics and themes in the unit. Which of these words do you already feel comfortable using when speaking or writing?

	I can use it!	I understand it.	I'll look it up.
confirm	☐	☐	☐
definitely	☐	☐	☐
deny	☐	☐	☐
format	☐	☐	☐
unify	☐	☐	☐

Prove It!

Use one of the academic vocabulary words in a sentence about whether we ought to prioritize progress over all else or proceed with caution.

Preview the Texts

Review the images, titles, and descriptions of the texts in the unit. Mark the title of the text that interests you most.

Second Inaugural Address

Speech by **Abraham Lincoln**

President Lincoln seeks unity as the Civil War nears its end.

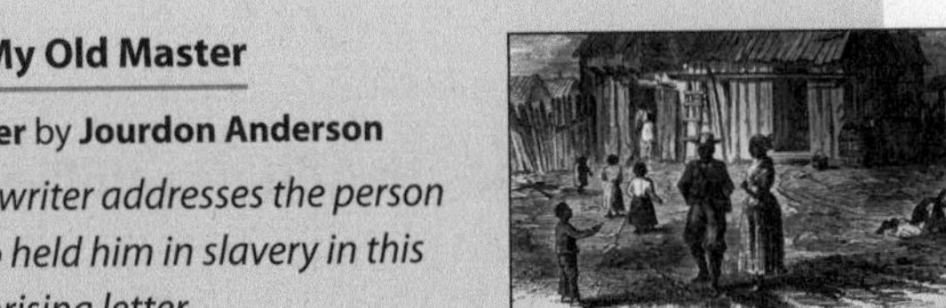

To My Old Master

Letter by **Jourdon Anderson**

The writer addresses the person who held him in slavery in this surprising letter.

The Aftermath of the Civil War

Diary and Media

A diary entry, infographic, and photograph show what life was like as the war drew to a close.

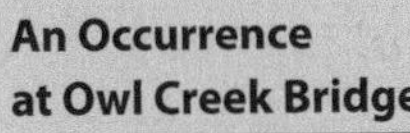

An Occurrence at Owl Creek Bridge

Short Story by **Ambrose Bierce**

This classic story begins at the moment when Peyton Farquhar is about to be hanged.

Building the Transcontinental Railroad

History Writing by **Iris Chang**

Learn about the vital contributions made by Chinese workers.

Declaration of Sentiments

Argument by **Elizabeth Cady Stanton**

This document inspired women to fight for the right to vote.

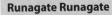

Speech to the American Equal Rights Association

Argument by **Sojourner Truth**

Truth demands that women be paid equally (a problem that persists to this day).

Runagate Runagate

Poem by **Robert Hayden**

Follow a runaway as he makes a break for freedom.

from **Incidents in the Life of a Slave Girl**

Autobiography by **Harriet Jacobs**

The main character of this text has escaped enslavement, but she is still in danger.

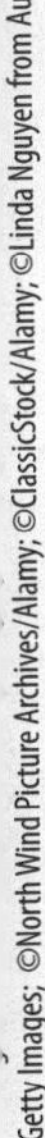

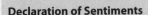

The Civil War and Its Aftermath

The Quest for Freedom

What brought America to the point of civil war? Since colonial times, the industrial North and the agricultural South had developed sharp regional differences. The South's economy and whole way of life had come to depend on a workforce of nearly 4 million enslaved Black people, while increasing numbers of northerners had come to view slavery as a monstrous violation of basic human rights.

The Fight to Abolish Slavery

Abolitionists—Black and white, male and female—led the fight by forming organizations, holding conventions, publishing newspapers, and swamping Congress with petitions for the sole purpose of ending what many considered an evil institution—slavery. Narratives by abolitionists,

1850
Fugitive Slave Act forces northern officials to return to captivity people who escaped enslavement.

1850

1857
Supreme Court delivers *Dred Scott* decision that people of African ancestry could not become citizens.

1860
Lincoln becomes president; southern states secede.

1861
Civil War begins with Confederates firing on Fort Sumter in Charleston, South Carolina.

Harriet Tubman (far left), a formerly enslaved person, abolitionist leader, and founder of the Underground Railroad.

such as Harriet Beecher Stowe and Frederick Douglass, a formerly enslaved person, helped bring the evils of slavery to life for many readers. In fact, Stowe's 1852 novel, *Uncle Tom's Cabin,* is cited as a contributing cause of the Civil War. Abolitionists also participated in the Underground Railroad, a network of people who helped enslaved people escape to freedom.

Although women were active in the abolition movement, they too faced social, economic, and political inequality. Working for abolition made women more aware of the rights they had been denied. Elizabeth Cady Stanton, Lucretia Mott, Sojourner Truth, and other reformers fought for women's rights, including the right to vote.

A Cataclysm Divides the Country

By 1850 the country was equally divided into free and slave states. In Congress, the debate over slavery raged on, with some arguing that states should have the right to choose on the issue of slavery. Addressing the Illinois Republican Convention in 1858, Abraham Lincoln warned, "A house divided against itself cannot stand." Although Lincoln promised not to abolish slavery, he vowed to stop its spread.

EXTEND

Think of a question you have about a topic, an event, or a person from the historical period. Then, research the answer and add it as an entry to the timeline.

1863
Lincoln issues the Emancipation Proclamation.

1865
Civil War ends; Lincoln is assassinated; 13th Amendment abolishes slavery.

1869
Transcontinental Railroad is completed at Promontory, Utah.

1877
Compromise allows Hayes to become president; Reconstruction ends.

1880

The Battle of Pea Ridge, Arkansas

When Lincoln was elected president in 1860, the southern states seceded and formed the Confederate States of America. In 1861, Confederates fired on Fort Sumter in South Carolina, and the Civil War began. Both sides expected a quick victory, but romantic ideals of heroism soon gave way to a harsher reality. By the end of the war in April 1865, approximately 620,000 soldiers had died, nearly as many as have died in all other wars that the United States has ever fought.

Healing a Broken Nation

With the end of the Civil War came the reunification of the United States. This period of rebuilding came to be known as Reconstruction. During the war, Lincoln had issued the Emancipation Proclamation (1863), freeing all enslaved people in the South. After the war in 1865, the Thirteenth Amendment to the Constitution outlawed slavery everywhere in the United States. Lincoln felt the South should not be punished for seceding. He wanted to bring the country back together peacefully and as quickly as possible. Unfortunately, Lincoln's plans for Reconstruction were cut short by his assassination within days of the war's end.

Some Republicans in Congress opposed Lincoln's views on Reconstruction. After his death, they imposed military rule on the South. During Reconstruction, the United States also resumed its westward expansion. In 1869 a golden spike was driven into the railroad track at Promontory, Utah, marking the completion of the country's first transcontinental railroad.

As Reconstruction dragged on, white southerners gradually retook control of state governments in the South, passing laws to undermine the rights of African Americans. In 1877 a compromise allowed Republican Rutherford B. Hayes to become president in exchange for the end of federal control over the South. This event marked the end of Reconstruction.

The Rise of Realism

The Civil War changed not only American society, but its literature as well. Northern and southern writers—Black and white, male and female, high-ranking officers and lowly foot soldiers and the women who stayed behind—all expressed different perspectives on their wartime experiences through diaries and letters. In contrast to these personal accounts were the public pronouncements of President Lincoln, whose inspiring Gettysburg Address proved to be one of the most enduring works of the Civil War. After the war, writers rejected Romanticism and began writing honest, unsentimental, and ironic fiction. Called realists, writers such as Ambrose Bierce and Stephen Crane focused on the human tragedy of the war. These writers would have a notable impact on the writing that followed after the turn of the century.

COLLABORATIVE DISCUSSION

Based on what you have learned, what would you expect to be the major themes of literature from this period?

Assessment Practice

Choose the best answer to each question.

1. What was the Underground Railroad?

- (A) the nation's first subway system
- (B) the nation's first transcontinental railroad
- (C) a railroad that ran from the southern United States to Canada
- (D) a network of abolitionists who helped enslaved people escape

2. Which of the following freed all enslaved people in the South?

- (A) Lincoln's Gettysburg Address
- (B) Lincoln's Emancipation Proclamation
- (C) the Transcontinental Railroad
- (D) the end of Reconstruction

3. What was Reconstruction?

- (A) the period of rebuilding after the Civil War
- (B) the harsh new restrictions on African Americans
- (C) the compromise to allow Rutherford B. Hayes to become president
- (D) the process for constructing the Transcontinental Railroad

Test-Taking Strategies

Get Ready

Second Inaugural Address

Speech by **Abraham Lincoln**

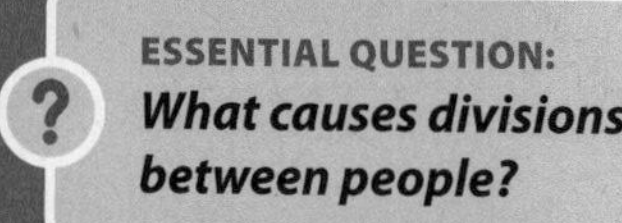

ESSENTIAL QUESTION:
What causes divisions between people?

Engage Your Brain

Choose one or more of these activities to start connecting with the speech you're about to read.

Second Inaugural Fun Facts

Form teams and go on an internet scavenger hunt to find information about Lincoln's second inauguration. Find the answers to the following questions, plus two more fun facts.

- By what percentage of the popular vote did Lincoln win the election?
- Approximately how many African Americans were in attendance?
- What natural event happened as Lincoln began his speech?
- Why did Mary Todd Lincoln miss her husband's speech?
- What famous or notable people were in the audience?

"A Sacred Effort"

After giving the Second Inaugural Address, Abraham Lincoln asked Frederick Douglass what he thought of the speech. Douglass replied: "Mr. Lincoln, that was a sacred effort." With a partner, discuss what you think he meant. What would make someone characterize a speech as "sacred"?

OMG, You're POTUS!

You've just been elected President of the United States! Now that you've finished your victory dance, what do you say to a nation longing to hear your plans for the future? As you write your speech, think about:

- policies and laws you want to enact
- problems you want to tackle
- principles you want the United States to stand for

Analyze Argument

Abraham Lincoln delivered his Second Inaugural Address as the American Civil War continued to rage. In this seminal text, Lincoln expresses the **premise,** or statement generally regarded as true, that the Union was close to winning the war. Lincoln then makes an argument to his fellow Americans for the best way forward for the country.

To analyze an argument, first identify, and then analyze its elements. As you read, use the chart to add examples of the structural elements of Lincoln's argument.

Focus on Genre
↳ **Speech**

- includes a clear claim
- supports ideas with reasons and evidence
- makes a call to action

Element	Definition	Example
Claim	the writer's position on an issue	
Reasons	declarations that support a claim	
Evidence	specific information, such as facts, quotations, and examples, that supports the thesis	
Premise	a general principle most people agree with; links the reasons and evidence to the claim	
Call to Action	an attempt to convince the audience to do something based on the argument	

Analyze Persuasive Techniques

Lincoln makes an argument to convince an audience to take action. To make his argument effective, he uses **persuasive techniques**, or methods to convince others to adopt opinions or beliefs or to act in a certain way. Note the following persuasive techniques in Lincoln's speech:

- **Parallelism:** the use of similar grammatical constructions to express ideas that are related
- **Allusion:** quotations or references to a familiar person, place, event, or literary work that resonate with the audience
- **Ethical appeal:** a kind of appeal where the writer links the claim to a widely accepted value

Annotation in Action

Here is an example of notes a student made about parallelism in Lincoln's speech. As you read, highlight examples of parallelism and other persuasive techniques that Lincoln uses to make his argument.

> Both parties deprecated war; but one of them would make war rather than let the nation survive; and the other would accept war rather than let it perish.
>
> *Parallelism shows differences between the two parties.*

Expand Your Vocabulary

Put a check mark next to the vocabulary words that you feel comfortable using when speaking or writing.

engross	☐
venture	☐
deprecate	☐
wring	☐

Then, turn to a partner and talk about a value or belief that you think most people share. Use as many vocabulary words as you can in your discussion. As you read Lincoln's Second Inaugural Address, use the definitions in the side-column to learn the vocabulary words you don't already know.

Background

Abraham Lincoln (1809–1865), elected president in 1860, told the South in his First Inaugural Address, "In your hands, my dissatisfied fellow countrymen, and not in mine, is the momentous issue of civil war." The southern states feared he would abolish slavery, and they eventually seceded. This led to the start of the Civil War. Four years later, the Union forces had gained the upper hand in the conflict, Lincoln had issued the Emancipation Proclamation and had been reelected, and the Union was about to be restored. But Lincoln would not see it, as he was assassinated less than six weeks after giving this speech.

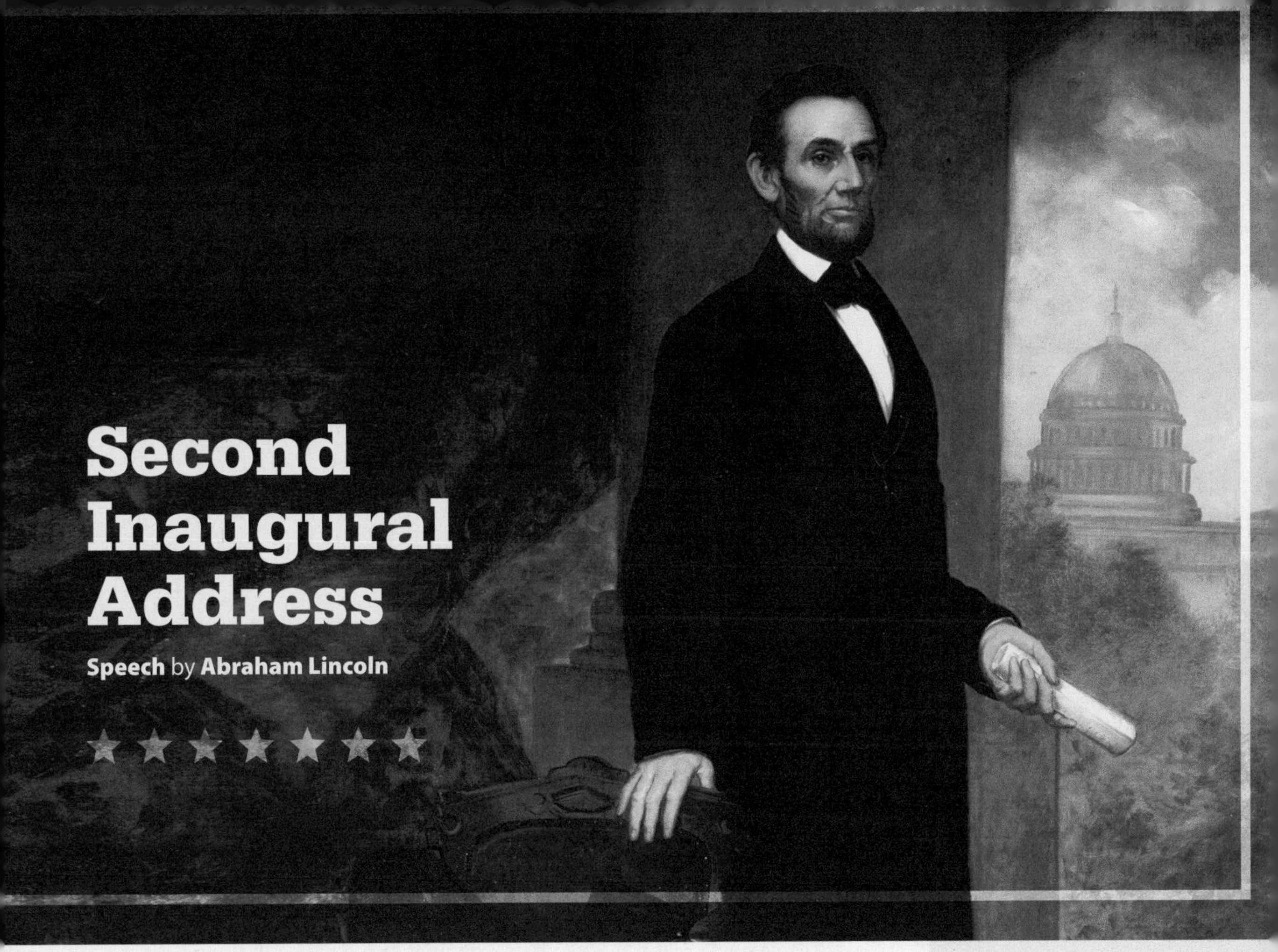

Second Inaugural Address

Speech by **Abraham Lincoln**

In the nation's darkest hour, President Lincoln makes the case to restore the Union.

NOTICE & NOTE
As you read, use the side margins to make notes about the text.

Fellow Countrymen:

1 At this second appearing to take the oath of the presidential office, there is less occasion for an extended address than there was at the first. Then a statement, somewhat in detail, of course to be pursued, seemed fitting and proper. Now, at the expiration of four years, during which public declarations have been constantly called forth on every point and phase of the great contest which still absorbs the attention and **engrosses** the energies of the nation, little that is new could be presented. The progress of our arms, upon which all else chiefly depends, is as well known to the public as to myself; and it is, I trust, reasonably satisfactory and encouraging to all. With high hope for the future, no prediction in regard to it is **ventured**.

engross
(ĕn-grōs´) *v.* to completely engage attention or interest.

venture
(vĕn´chər) *v.* to risk or dare.

ANALYZE ARGUMENT

Annotate: Mark the words in paragraph 2 that tell what Lincoln spoke about during his First Inaugural Address.

Infer: What do these words tell the reader about Lincoln's view of the Union?

deprecate
(dĕp´rĭ-kāt) *v.* to express disapproval.

2 On the occasion corresponding to this four years ago, all thoughts were anxiously directed to an impending civil war. All dreaded it—all sought to avert it. While the inaugural address was being delivered from this place, devoted altogether to saving the Union without war, insurgent agents were in the city seeking to destroy it without war—seeking to dissolve the Union, and divide effects, by negotiation. Both parties **deprecated** war; but one of them would make war rather than let the nation survive; and the other would accept war rather than let it perish. And the war came.

3 One-eighth of the whole population were colored slaves, not distributed generally over the Union, but localized in the Southern part of it. These slaves constituted a peculiar and powerful interest. All knew that this interest was, somehow, the cause of the war. To strengthen, perpetuate, and extend this interest was the object for which the insurgents would rend the Union, even by war; while the

Don't forget to **Notice & Note** as you read the text. 

government claimed no right to do more than to restrict the territorial enlargement of it.

4 Neither party expected for the war the magnitude or the duration which it has already attained. Neither anticipated that the cause of the conflict might cease with, or even before, the conflict itself should cease. Each looked for an easier triumph, and a result less fundamental and astounding. Both read the same Bible, and pray to the same God; and each invokes his aid against the other. It may seem strange that any men should dare to ask a just God's assistance in **wringing** their bread from the sweat of other men's faces; but let us judge not, that we be not judged. The prayers of both could not be answered—that of neither has been answered fully.

5 The Almighty has his own purposes. "Woe unto the world because of offences! for it must needs be that offences come; but woe to that man by whom the offence cometh." If we shall suppose that

ANALYZE PERSUASIVE TECHNIQUES

Annotate: Mark the examples of parallelism at the beginning of sentences in paragraph 4.

Evaluate: What is the effect of the use of parallelism in this paragraph?

wring
(rĭng) *v.* to obtain through force or pressure.

Close Read Screencast

Listen to a modeled close read of this text.

NOTICE & NOTE
QUOTED WORDS

When you notice the author citing other people to provide support for a point, you've found a **Quoted Words** signpost.

Notice & Note: Mark the biblical quote in paragraph 5.

Analyze: How do these quoted words relate to Lincoln's argument? Explain.

American slavery is one of those offences which, in the providence of God, must needs come, but which, having continued through his appointed time, he now wills to remove, and that he gives to both North and South this terrible war, as the woe due to those by whom the offence came, shall we discern therein any departure from those divine attributes[1] which the believers in a living God always ascribe to him? Fondly do we hope—fervently do we pray—that this mighty scourge of war may speedily pass away. Yet, if God wills that it continue until all the wealth piled by the bondman's two hundred and fifty years of unrequited toil shall be sunk, and until every drop of blood drawn with the lash shall be paid by another drawn with the sword, as was said three thousand years ago, so still it must be said, "The judgments of the Lord are true and righteous altogether."

6 With malice toward none; with charity for all: with firmness in the right, as God gives us to see the right, let us strive on to finish the work we are in; to bind up the nation's wounds; to care for him who shall have borne the battle, and for his widow, and his orphan—to do all which may achieve and cherish a just and lasting peace among ourselves, and with all nations.

[1] **attributes:** qualities or characteristics.

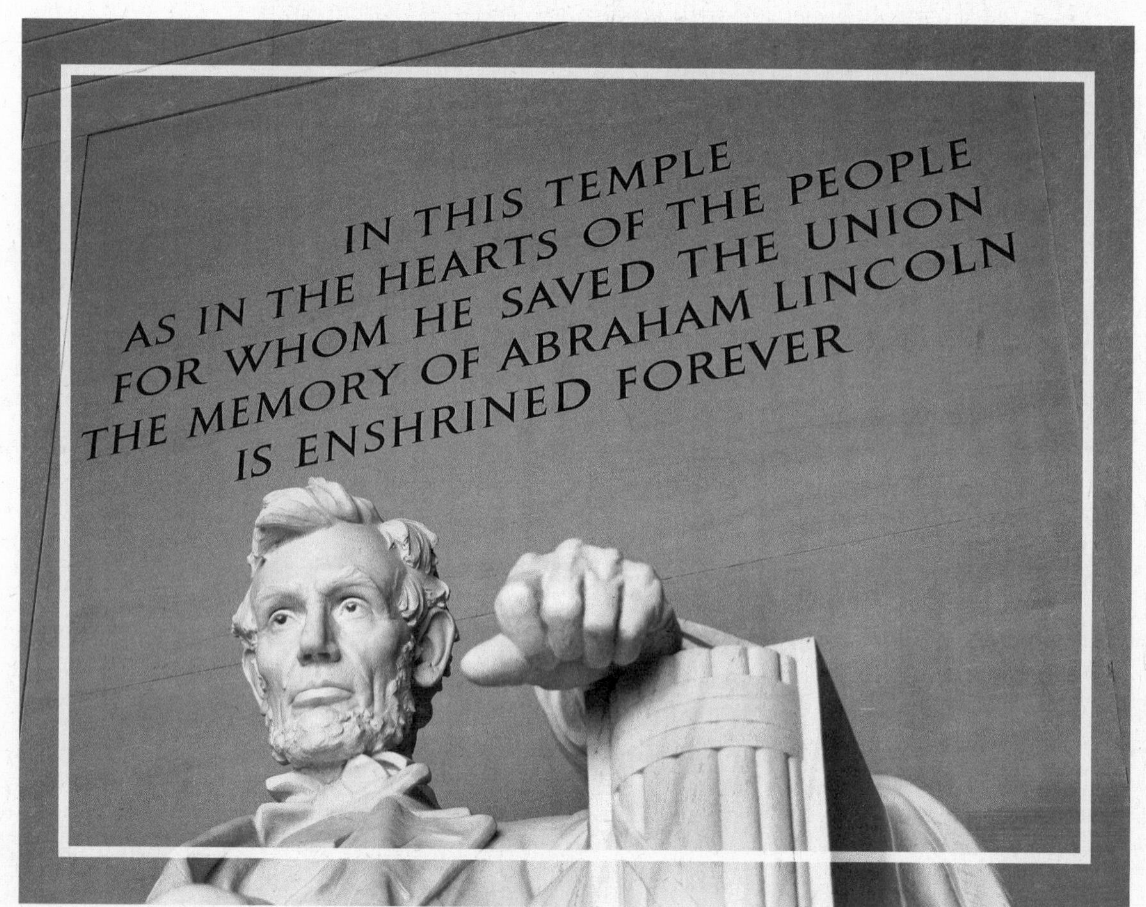

IN THIS TEMPLE
AS IN THE HEARTS OF THE PEOPLE
FOR WHOM HE SAVED THE UNION
THE MEMORY OF ABRAHAM LINCOLN
IS ENSHRINED FOREVER

COLLABORATIVE DISCUSSION

With a partner, discuss whether Lincoln showed that the country could be unified going forward.

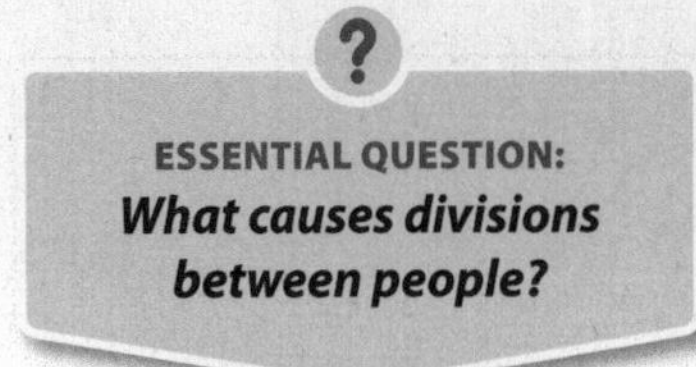
ESSENTIAL QUESTION:
What causes divisions between people?

Review your notes and add your thoughts to your **Response Log.**

Assessment Practice

Answer these questions before moving on to the **Analyze the Text** section on the following page.

1. What did Lincoln view as the primary reason for the war?

- (A) to punish the South
- (B) to preserve the Union
- (C) to divide the nation
- (D) to protect slavery

2. What does Lincoln say the North and South have in common?

- (A) Both expected the war to go on for a long time.
- (B) Both were determined to unite the country.
- (C) Both were looking to restrict slavery.
- (D) Both shared some of the same values.

3. What did Lincoln hope would happen when the war ended?

- (A) He hoped for healing and long-lasting peace.
- (B) He hoped the South would form its own nation.
- (C) He hoped that more territories would join the Union.
- (D) He hoped that more states would secede.

Ed

Test-Taking Strategies

Analyze the Text

Support your responses with evidence from the text.

NOTICE & NOTE

Review what you **noticed and noted** as you read the text. Your annotations can help you answer these questions.

1. **ANALYZE** Complete the chart with examples from Lincoln's speech.

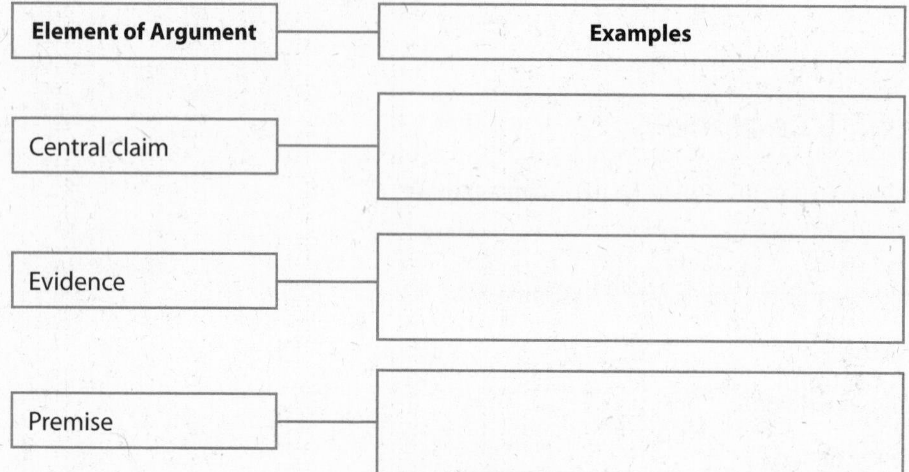

Element of Argument
Examples
Central claim
Evidence
Premise

2. **COMPARE** What similarities between northerners and southerners does Lincoln outline in the speech? What are their differences? How does highlighting these similarities and differences support Lincoln's purpose?

3. **INFER** How does the statement "The Almighty has his own purposes" (paragraph 5) support Lincoln's effort to convince his audience?

4. **EVALUATE** How does Lincoln use ethical appeals to build his argument? Cite text evidence in your response.

5. **ANALYZE** What persuasive technique does Lincoln use in the last paragraph of his speech? How does this technique relate to his argument?

6. **EVALUATE** What is Lincoln's call to action in paragraph 6? Is the call to action a logical response to the reasons he outlines?

7. **ANALYZE** How does Lincoln's use of **Quoted Words** from the Bible support his call to action?

Choices

Here are some other ways to demonstrate your understanding of the ideas in this lesson.

Writing

↳ Explanatory Essay

One of Lincoln's primary goals for his second term as president was to unify the nation after the Civil War. Write an essay explaining how his Second Inaugural Address supports that goal. Include the following:

- What interests and concerns does he address for people living in the North?
- What interests and concerns does he address for people living in the South?
- What are his plans for formerly enslaved people?
- What did he leave out that he should have included?

As you write and discuss, be sure to use the **Academic Vocabulary** words.

- confirm
- definitely
- deny
- format
- unify

Media

↳ Live Coverage of the Inaugural Address

In groups of four, imagine your news team goes back in time to March 4, 1865. "Film" Lincoln's Second Inauguration, reporting on the events as they unfold. After Lincoln reads his address, have your political pundits give their opinions.

Before you role-play, plan your storyboard:

- Which people will you interview?
- How will you balance coverage and commentary?
- What will your focus be: the political, the social, the cultural, or all of the above?

As you film:

- Give everyone a chance to write the script and play a role.
- Use social media and technology to bring the past to life.
- Post your news report online.

Research

↳ Lincoln's Post-War Vision

President Lincoln planned to reunite and heal the nation, but he was assassinated before he could put policies in place. Research Reconstruction and find two events that give evidence of a nation healing. Then find two events that show the nation was still divided.

Answer the following questions:

- What were some of Lincoln's plans or policies?
- What did his successor, Andrew Johnson, do in Lincoln's place?
- What long-term effects or consequences did these plans and policies have?

Keep in mind that sources on this topic may be biased, so be careful of strongly positive or negative viewpoints, loaded language, or sources that avoid addressing evidence that supports an opposing viewpoint.

Expand Your Vocabulary

PRACTICE AND APPLY

Choose the letter of the best answer to each question. Then, explain your response.

engrossed	deprecate	ventured	wring

1. If you are **engrossed** in a book, you find the book ______________.

- ○ tedious
- ○ fascinating

2. If you hear someone **deprecate** a new computer app, you know they ______________.

- ○ dislike the app
- ○ like the app

3. If a classmate **ventured** to take on a difficult task, he or she ______________.

- ○ risked failure
- ○ was certain of success

4. If you were watching a movie in which the villain was trying to **wring** information out of the hero, you'd know the villain was ______________.

- ○ patiently waiting for an answer
- ○ forcing the hero to answer questions

Vocabulary Strategy

↳ Pronunciation

Interactive Vocabulary Lesson: Using Reference Sources

In all English words that begin with *wr*, such as *write* and the vocabulary word *wring,* the *w* is silent. The correct word in Lincoln's speech (*wring*, not *ring*) is determined from context rather than the sound of the word.

Other words do not have consistent spelling and pronunciation rules. For example, in *trough* (a long, narrow container), the *gh* sounds like *f* and the word rhymes with *off*, but in *through*, the *gh* is silent and the vowel combination *ou* is also pronounced like *threw*.

PRACTICE AND APPLY

Use a dictionary to confirm the pronunciation and meaning of the words below. Practice the pronunciations and use each word in a sentence.

1. aisle
2. circuit
3. cliché
4. colonel
5. epitome
6. indict
7. respite
8. segue
9. silhouette
10. subtle

Watch Your Language!

Balanced Sentences

Lincoln wrote balanced sentences, both short and long, that help emphasize key ideas in his speeches. Consider this complex sentence in paragraph 5:

> **Yet, if God wills that it continue until all the wealth piled by the bondsman's two hundred and fifty years of unrequited toil shall be sunk, and until every drop of blood drawn with the lash shall be paid by another drawn with the sword, as was said three thousand years ago, so still it must be said, "The judgments of the Lord are true and righteous altogether."**

In this sentence, Lincoln balances the evils of war against the evils of slavery. The two ideas are connected through the syntax that Lincoln employs, creating balance between "blood drawn with the lash" and "drawn with the sword." He then concludes with another balanced statement about the enduring truth of God's judgments: "as was said three thousand years ago, so still it must be said." Lincoln constructs this extended, complex sentence to help make his meaning clear and strongly support his message.

Lincoln also creates balance in his shorter sentences. For example, in paragraph 2, Lincoln writes:

> **All dreaded it—all sought to avert it.**

These stylistic choices support Lincoln's message that the war was just and necessary, but in order to preserve the Union, it was time for the North and the South to come together and heal the nation's wounds.

Ed

Interactive Grammar Lesson: Sentence Structure

PRACTICE AND APPLY

Write a one-paragraph summary of how Lincoln wanted to unite the North and the South. Then revise your paragraph to make sure your sentences are balanced. Use Lincoln's speech as a model.

Get Ready

To My Old Master

Letter by Jourdon Anderson

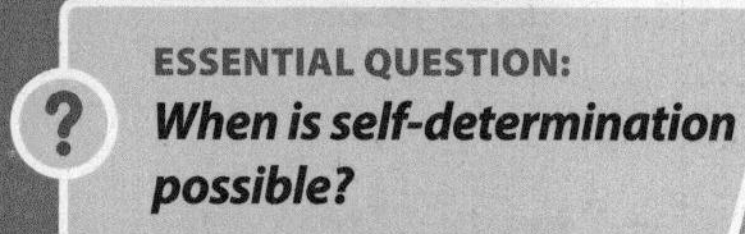
ESSENTIAL QUESTION:
When is self-determination possible?

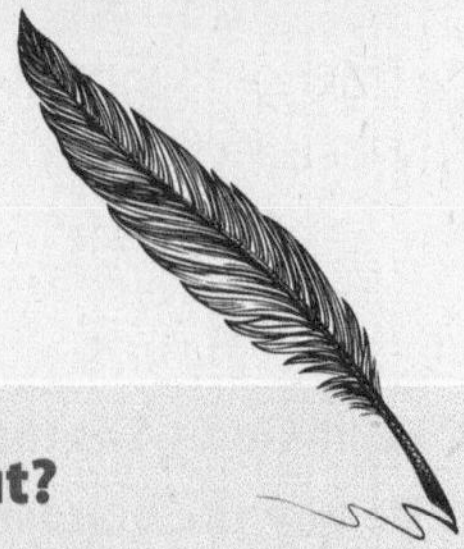

Engage Your Brain

Choose one or more of these activities to start connecting with the letter you're about to read.

What Is This About?

Here are three quotations from the letter you're about to read. Based on the quotations, what do you think it's about?

- "Sir: I got your letter and was glad to find that you had not forgotten Jourdon, and that you wanted me to come back and live with you again, promising to do better for me than anybody else can."
- "This will make us forget and forgive old scores, and rely on your justice and friendship in the future."
- "Surely there will be a day of reckoning for those who defraud the laborer of his hire."

Not Feelin' It

Someone you don't particularly know or like is asking you to do something you don't really want to do. With a partner, discuss how you can turn down the request without offending the person making it.

Say What You Think

The expression "speak truth to power" means to tell difficult facts to people in positions of power or authority who might not want to hear them. For example, younger people are speaking out about the need for immediate action on climate change. In a small group, discuss when you have seen an example of someone speaking truth to power. Together write a description of the situation and what, if anything, resulted from the situation. When you've finished, share your examples with the rest of the class.

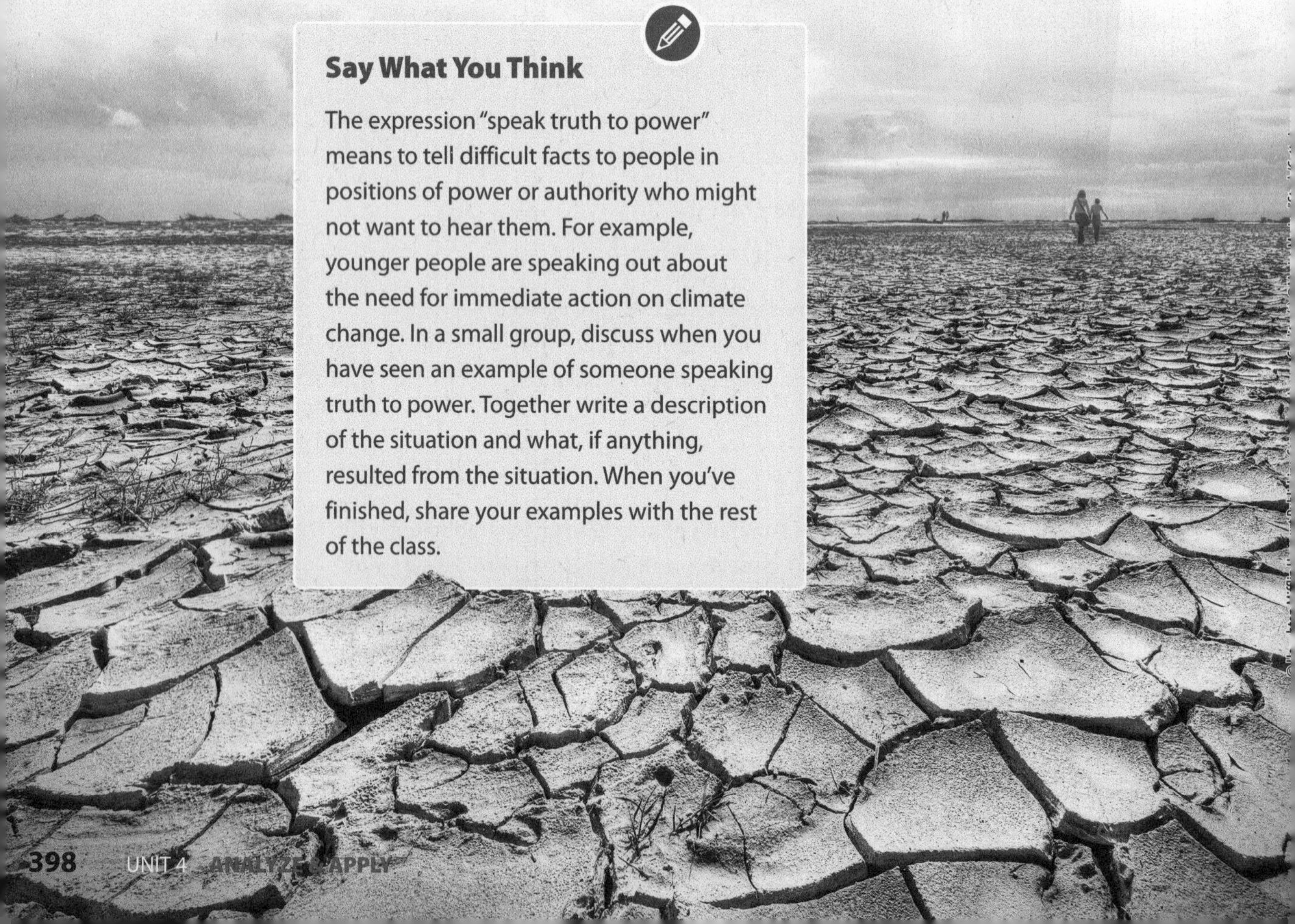

Analyze Tone

Tone is a writer's attitude. A writer may use literary devices to convey tone on a particular subject.

- direct statements: a clear statement of the writer's thoughts and feelings
- verbal irony: a contrast between what is stated and what is meant
- understatement: saying less than what is actually true
- sarcasm: saying the opposite of what is meant

A writer may use understatement to convey humor, but may use sarcasm to express anger about an issue. As you read, notice how the writer uses these devices to convey tone.

Focus on Genre
Letter

- **written by an individual to another person or to a group**
- **may be formal or informal**
- **a literary letter may be read by a wider audience because the author is famous or gives information about a time or place**
- **an open letter is addressed to a specific person but published for a broad readership**

Make Inferences

Letters are usually private, informal communications that convey information to an individual or a group. As someone who was formerly enslaved, Jourdon Anderson presents a definitive point of view about slavery in his letter. Sometimes he expresses his feelings directly. However, sometimes you will have to go beyond his words to understand his meaning. In these cases, you will have to make **inferences**, or educated guesses, about the text based on the information in the text as well as your prior knowledge.

Keep what you already know about slavery at this time in mind as you read Anderson's letter. Use a chart to infer what Anderson means.

Anderson's words	Prior knowledge	My inference
"was glad to find . . . you wanted me to come back and live with you again"	Why would someone want to return to horrible conditions?	Anderson may not mean what he says or is just being polite.

Annotation in Action

Here is an example of notes a student made about a passage in "To My Old Master." As you read, mark details that suggest Anderson's tone.

> It would do me good to go back to the dear old home again, and see Miss Mary and Miss Martha and Allen, Esther, Green, and Lee. Give my love to them all, and tell them I hope we will meet in the better world, if not in this. I would have gone back to see you all when I was working in the Nashville Hospital, but one of the neighbors told me that Henry intended to shoot me if he ever got a chance.

Why is his tone affectionate if someone is threatening to shoot him?

Expand Your Vocabulary

Put a check mark next to the vocabulary words that you feel comfortable using when writing or speaking.

- **disposed** ☐
- **recompense** ☐
- **reckoning** ☐
- **virtuous** ☐

Then, turn to a partner and use as many of the words as you can to explain what you know about the conditions African Americans faced at the time of the Civil War. As you read "To My Old Master," use the definitions in the side column to learn the vocabulary words you don't already know.

Background

Jourdon Anderson (1826–1907) was enslaved for the first 38 years of his life working on a plantation in Tennessee. He and his wife were freed during the Civil War when Union troops came to the plantation where they worked. They took their children to Ohio, where Anderson found work and they lived in freedom. A year later, after the war ended, the man who had held them in slavery wrote Anderson and asked him to come back to work, as the plantation was in dire straits. Anderson dictated this letter, which was sent in response. Later, it was published in a newspaper.

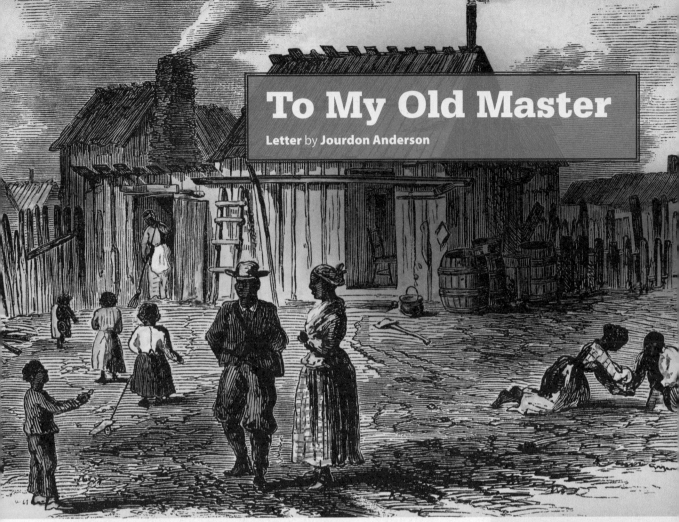

To My Old Master

Letter by **Jourdon Anderson**

An emancipated man considers a job offer from the person who once held him in slavery.

NOTICE & NOTE 

As you read, use the side margin to make notes about the text.

Dayton, Ohio

August 7, 1865

To My Old Master, Colonel P.H. Anderson, Big Spring, Tennessee

1 Sir: I got your letter, and was glad to find that you had not forgotten Jourdon, and that you wanted me to come back and live with you again, promising to do better for me than anybody else can. I have often felt uneasy about you. I thought the Yankees would have hung you long before this, for harboring Rebs they found at your house. I suppose they never heard about your going to Colonel Martin's to kill the Union soldier that was left by his company in their stable. Although you shot at me twice before I left you, I did not want to hear of your being hurt, and am glad you are still living. It would do me good to go back to the dear old home again, and see Miss Mary and Miss Martha and Allen, Esther, Green, and Lee. Give

ANALYZE TONE

Annotate: Mark the sentence in paragraph 1 that describes Jourdon Anderson's surprising response to Colonel Anderson's action.

Draw Conclusions: What does the writer convey by describing his response to this incident?

my love to them all, and tell them I hope we will meet in the better world, if not in this. I would have gone back to see you all when I was working in the Nashville Hospital, but one of the neighbors told me that Henry intended to shoot me if he ever got a chance.

2 I want to know particularly what the good chance is you propose to give me. I am doing tolerably well here. I get twenty-five dollars a month, with victuals[1] and clothing; have a comfortable home for Mandy,—the folks call her Mrs. Anderson,—and the children—Milly, Jane, and Grundy—go to school and are learning well. The teacher says Grundy has a head for a preacher. They go to Sunday school, and Mandy and me attend church regularly. We are kindly treated. Sometimes we overhear others saying, "Them colored people were slaves" down in Tennessee. The children feel hurt when they hear such remarks; but I tell them it was no disgrace in Tennessee to belong to Colonel Anderson. Many darkeys would have been proud, as I used to be, to call you master. Now if you will write and say what wages you will give me, I will be better able to decide whether it would be to my advantage to move back again.

ANALYZE TONE

Annotate: In paragraph 3, mark Jourdon Anderson's response to the Colonel's offer of freedom.

Analyze: What contrast is there between Anderson and the Colonel's understanding of Anderson's situation?

3 As to my freedom, which you say I can have, there is nothing to be gained on that score, as I got my free papers in 1864 from the Provost-Marshal-General of the Department of Nashville. Mandy says she would be afraid to go back without some proof that you were **disposed** to treat us justly and kindly; and we have concluded to test your sincerity by asking you to send us our wages for the time we served you. This will make us forget and forgive old scores, and rely on your justice and friendship in the future. I served you faithfully for thirty-two years, and Mandy twenty years. At twenty-five dollars a month for me, and two dollars a week for Mandy, our earnings would amount to eleven thousand six hundred and eighty dollars. Add to this the interest for the time our wages have been kept back, and deduct what you paid for our clothing, and three doctor's visits to me, and pulling a tooth for Mandy, and the balance will show what we are in justice entitled to. Please send the money by Adams's Express, in care of V. Winters, Esq., Dayton, Ohio. If you fail to pay us for faithful labors in the past, we can have little faith in your promises in the future. We trust the good Maker[2] has opened your eyes to the wrongs which you and your fathers have done to me and my fathers, in making us toil for you for generations without **recompense**. Here I draw my wages every Saturday night; but in Tennessee there was never any pay-day for the negroes any more than for the horses and cows. Surely there will be a day of **reckoning** for those who defraud the laborer of his hire.

disposed
(dĭ-spōzd´) *adj.* having a preference, disposition, or tendency.

recompense
(rĕk´əm-pĕns) *n.* payment in return for something, such as a service.

reckoning
(rĕk´ə-nĭng) *n.* a settlement of accounts.

4 In answering this letter, please state if there would be any safety for my Milly and Jane, who are now grown up, and both good-looking girls. You know how it was with poor Matilda and Catherine. I would rather stay here and starve—and die, if it come to that—than

[1] **victuals** (vĭt´lz): food fit for human consumption.
[2] **good Maker:** God.

have my girls brought to shame by the violence and wickedness of their young masters. You will also please state if there has been any schools opened for the colored children in your neighborhood. The great desire of my life now is to give my children an education, and have them form **virtuous** habits.

5 Say howdy to George Carter, and thank him for taking the pistol from you when you were shooting at me.

From your old servant,
Jourdon Anderson.

MAKE INFERENCES

Annotate: Mark Anderson's fears for his daughters in paragraph 4.

Analyze: Why does he have these specific fears?

virtuous
(vûr´cho͞o-əs) *adj.* having or showing virtue, especially moral excellence.

COLLABORATIVE DISCUSSION

With a partner, discuss why Anderson decided to send this letter.

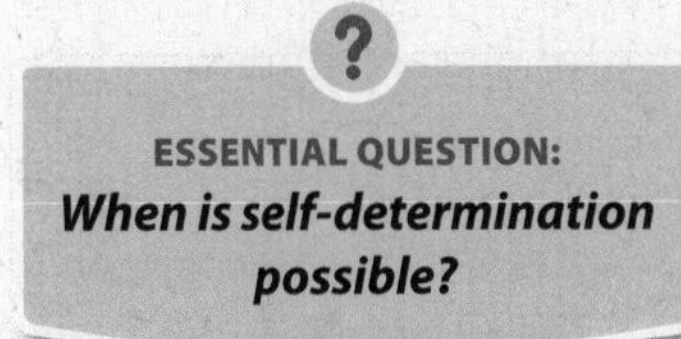
?
ESSENTIAL QUESTION:
When is self-determination possible?

Review your notes and add your thoughts to your **Response Log.**

Assessment Practice

Answer these questions before moving on to the **Analyze the Text** section.

1. What message does Anderson send in paragraph 1 when explaining his worries for the Colonel's safety?

- (A) The former master is fortunate not to have been punished.
- (B) The former master is a hothead who always gets into trouble.
- (C) Anderson wants to have nothing to do with the former master.
- (D) Anderson will return only if the former master apologizes for shooting at him.

2. What does Anderson ask for to test the Colonel's sincerity?

- (A) freedom for himself and his family
- (B) wages earned while they were enslaved
- (C) a role in the Nashville Hospital
- (D) greetings to his old friends

3. What does Anderson wish for his daughters?

- (A) a return to their childhood home
- (B) good marriages and jobs
- (C) safety and an education
- (D) good relations with the former master

Ed
Test-Taking Strategies

Analyze the Text

Support your responses with evidence from the text.

NOTICE & NOTE

Review what you **noticed and noted** as you read the text. Your annotations can help you answer these questions.

1. **INFER** What details about his current situation does Anderson include in paragraph 2? Why does he include this information?

2. **ANALYZE** What is ironic about the Colonel's willingness to grant Anderson his freedom? How does Anderson respond?

3. **ANALYZE** In paragraph 3, what does Anderson mean when he asks for "what we are in justice entitled to"? Why did he choose these words to express this idea?

4. **INFER** Consider the details the writer includes about his life serving Colonel Anderson. How are these examples pertinent to the Colonel's request? What do they suggest about the writer's life at that time and his feeling toward Colonel Anderson's request?

5. **SYNTHESIZE** Complete the chart with examples from the text of direct statements, verbal irony, sarcasm, and understatement.

Literary Element	Example
Direct Statement	
Verbal Irony	
Sarcasm	
Understatement	

6. **ANALYZE** How would you describe Anderson's overall tone in the text? Cite evidence in your response.

Choices

Here are some other ways to demonstrate your understanding of the ideas in this lesson.

Writing

↳ What the Constitution Means to Jourdon Anderson

At the time Jourdon Anderson sent his letter to Colonel Anderson, the Thirteenth Amendment had passed Congress, but had not yet been ratified by all states. Using evidence from the letter, write an explanatory essay describing how laws banning slavery had already changed Jourdon Anderson's life and would continue to do so. Make sure to correctly format and cite any quotations you use.

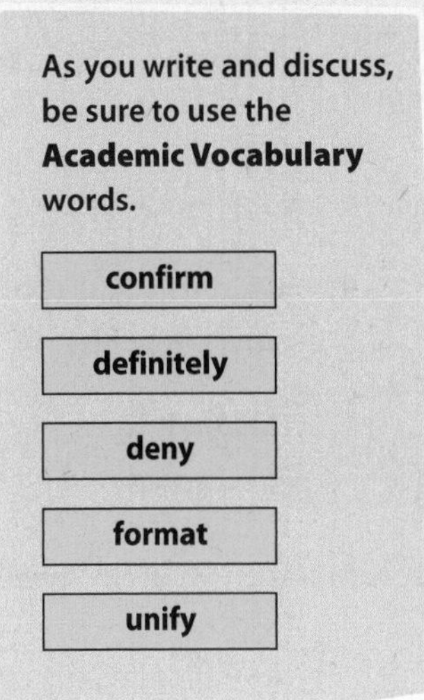
As you write and discuss, be sure to use the **Academic Vocabulary** words.
confirm
definitely
deny
format
unify

Social & Emotional Learning

↳ Group Discussion

Jourdon Anderson's letter shows a man very aware of who he is and what he wants. With two or three classmates, discuss the emotions, thoughts, and values that Anderson expresses in the letter, and how these self-perceptions reinforce his decision to stay where he is and continue his new life. Discuss examples from the letter that show Anderson's confidence and his ability to behave in a way that lets him accomplish his personal goals.

Research

↳ Amending the Constitution

In 1863, President Abraham Lincoln issued the Emancipation Proclamation and freed "all persons held as slaves." Why then did Congress pass the Thirteenth Amendment to the Constitution in 1865? Take notes to keep track of your findings.

Investigate the following:

- similarities and differences in the language of the Emancipation Proclamation and the Thirteenth Amendment
- what events were happening in society when this legislation was released to the public
- counter movements or negative reactions to the legislation

Expand Your Vocabulary

PRACTICE AND APPLY

Choose the correct word to complete each sentence.

disposed	recompense	reckoning	virtuous

1. "We will ______________ you fairly for your efforts on our behalf," the business owner told her lawyer.
2. Millions of fans were ______________ to embrace the newest entry in the popular movie franchise.
3. The final ______________ of the proceeds showed that the charity auction was a great success.
4. The children's education aimed to ensure that they would be ______________ and not immoral.

VOCABULARY STRATEGY

↳ Use Word Function to Determine Meaning

Many words in English can function as more than one part of speech. *Promising*, for instance, can be

- a gerund used to indicate the act of making a promise
- an adjective meaning something likely to succeed

With words that have multiple meanings, you can use a dictionary to verify meaning and determine parts of speech.

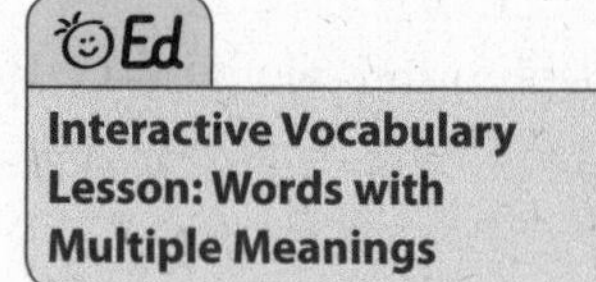

Ed
Interactive Vocabulary Lesson: Words with Multiple Meanings

PRACTICE AND APPLY

Read the following sentences. Write the part of speech and the correct meaning in context for each boldface word. Use a print or digital dictionary to validate your choices.

1. They **disposed** of the leftover supplies by dumping them in the trash.
2. The family was well **disposed** toward anyone who liked dogs.
3. The Tomlinsons offered **recompense** for the return of their cat.
4. How will we **recompense** the employees who exceeded expectations?
5. If you give me the **reckoning,** I will settle the bill.
6. The producers were **reckoning** that more people would attend the show.

Watch Your Language!

Noun Clauses

Noun clauses are subordinate clauses used as nouns. They are introduced either by pronouns, such as *that, what, who, whoever, which,* and *whose,* or by subordinating conjunctions, such as *how, when, where, why,* and *whether.*

However, these same words may introduce adjective clauses as well. For that reason, you need to consider how a clause functions within its sentence to determine which type of clause it is. One way of checking is to try substituting *something* or *someone* for the clause. If you do that and the sentence still makes sense, it is probably a noun clause.

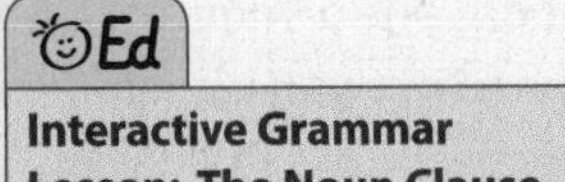

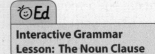

Interactive Grammar Lesson: The Noun Clause

This example is a noun clause serving as a direct object because you can say "I know *something*."

I know whose woods these are.

This example is an adjective clause because you cannot say "The book *something* has clearly been read many times."

The book that is tattered has clearly been read many times.

PRACTICE AND APPLY

Look at the following sentences from "To My Old Master." Determine whether the boldface phrases are noun clauses and, if so, what function they serve in the sentence. Are they a subject, a direct object, an indirect object, a predicate nominative, or the object of a preposition?

1. I got your letter, and was glad to find **that you had not forgotten Jourdon. . . .**

2. I would have gone back to see you all **when I was working in the Nashville Hospital,** . . . .

3. I want to know particularly **what the good chance is you propose to give me.**

4. I will be better able to decide **whether it would be to my advantage to move back again.**

5. . . . please state if there would be any safety for my Milly and Jane, **who are now grown up,** . . .

Get Ready

Aftermath of the Civil War

ESSENTIAL QUESTION: ***What causes divisions between people?***

Diary by **Mary Boykin Chesnut, Infographics** by **the Gilder Lehrman Institute of American History, Photography** by **Andrew J. Russell**

Engage Your Brain

Choose one or more of these activities to start connecting with the infographic you're about to study.

A Picture Is Worth a Thousand Words

You might have heard the expression, "A picture is worth a thousand words." Have you ever seen a picture that captures this saying, perhaps a photograph similar to the one below? See if you can find a photograph online that you find compelling. Share it with your group and explain how the picture conveys more than words can say.

Info-graph Your Class!

Use four different corners of the room to represent the following:

1. students who have read a book about the Civil War
2. students who have seen a movie/show about the Civil War
3. students who have done both
4. students who haven't done either

Record the number of students in each corner and create a fun infographic to represent this data. Be sure to include the number of students, the categories for each and a few titles of the works your peers have seen or read.

Evaluate Sources

When historians and writers research periods of history, they rely on primary and secondary sources relevant to the time period.

- **Primary sources** are materials created by people who were present at or experienced the immediate effects of an event. Diaries and photographs are examples of primary sources. Primary sources can evoke strong feelings, but be aware these feelings may reflect the author's **bias,** or strongly held viewpoint toward a particular side of a topic.
- **Secondary sources** are created by people who did not experience an event. Such sources can enhance your understanding of primary sources and reflect a perspective that may not have been known at the time. An infographic is an example of a secondary source because it reflects data that is gathered after time has passed.

Focus on Genre

↳ Diary and Media

- **A diary is a personal record of events, thoughts, and feelings.**
- **An infographic is a visual that combines text, numbers, pictures, or diagrams to present data in an effective way.**
- **Journalistic photography captures still images of people and events that convey a message through subject and composition.**

Synthesize Information

After you read and evaluate sources, you can use the information you learn to study a problem or question related to the topic. To explore what the end of the Civil War meant for people on both sides of the conflict, you can **synthesize information** from different types of sources. For example, you may write an essay where you use a quotation from a firsthand account as well as a diagram from a secondary source to support your ideas. To begin to synthesize information, gather the main ideas and perspectives from each source in your chart. Then, think about these guiding questions:

- What information is consistent across sources?
- Why might information be presented differently in different sources?
- How does the presentation of data and visual elements support an idea?
- Does information conflict with your own understanding? How can this be addressed?

Source	Main Ideas	Credibility/Bias
Diary		
Infographic		
Photograph		

Annotation in Action

Here is an example of notes a student made about a passage in "Diary from Dixie." As you read, mark details that evoke strong feelings.

"I hear horrid reports about Richmond. It is said that all below Ninth Street to the Rocketts has been burned by the rabble, who mobbed the town. The Yankee performances have not been chronicled. May God take our cause into His own hands."

Whoever wrote this is upset.

Expand Your Vocabulary

Put a check mark next to the vocabulary words that you feel comfortable using when speaking or writing.

capitulate	☐
improvise	☐
remnant	☐
penury	☐

Then see if you can use them to talk about a day in your life. As you read the diary entry from Mary Chesnut, use the definitions in the side column to learn the vocabulary words you don't already know.

Background

In this lesson you will read an excerpt from the diary of **Mary Boykin Chesnut,** (1823–1886) the influential wife of an aide to the Confederate president. Her first-hand account of life in the South during the Civil War is an invaluable source of information to historians. You will also analyze an infographic about the Civil War. Lastly, you will examine a photograph taken by **Andrew J. Russell,** (1829–1902) a renowned Civil War photographer whose camera captured the reality of war and brought it to people who lived far from the battlefields.

Aftermath of the Civil War

Diary by **Mary Boykin Chesnut, Infographics** by **the Gilder Lehrman Institute of American History, Photography** by **Andrew J. Russell**

Chesnut's views and accounts of conversations from other people reflect her fears about the future.

NOTICE & NOTE
As you read, use the side margins to make notes about the text.

from A Diary from Dixie

By **Mary Boykin Chesnut**

1 **April 7th**. Richmond has fallen and I have no heart to write about it. Grant broke through our lines and Sherman cut through them. Stoneman is this side of Danville. They are too many for us. Everything is lost in Richmond, even our archives. Blue black is our horizon. Hood says we shall all be obliged to go West—to Texas, I mean, for our own part of the country will be overrun.

2 Yes, a solitude and a wild waste it may become, but, as to that, we can rough it in the bush at home.

3 De Fontaine, in his newspaper, continues the old cry. "Now Richmond is given up," he says, "it was too heavy a load to carry, and we are stronger than ever." "Stronger than ever?" Nine-tenths of our army are under ground and where is another army to come from? Will they wait until we grow one?...

EVALUATE SOURCES

Annotate: Mark the quotation marks and the speaker in paragraph 3.

Draw Conclusions: Why does Chesnut quote this material? What do her own questions suggest about the speaker's views?

4 **April 17th**. A letter from Mrs. Davis, who writes: "Do come to me, and see how we get on. I shall have a spare room by the time you arrive, indifferently furnished, but, oh, so affectionately placed at your service. You will receive such a loving welcome....

5 "I hear horrid reports about Richmond. It is said that all below Ninth Street to the Rocketts has been burned by the rabble, who mobbed the town. The Yankee performances have not been chronicled. May God take our cause into His own hands."

6 **April 19th.** Just now, when Mr. Clay dashed up-stairs, pale as a sheet, saying, "General Lee has **capitulated**," I saw it reflected in Mary Darby's face before I heard him speak. She staggered to the table, sat down, and wept aloud. Mr. Clay's eyes were not dry. Quite beside herself Mary shrieked, "Now we belong to negroes and Yankees!" Buck said, "I do not believe it."

capitulate
(kə-pĭch´ə-lāt´) *intr. v.* to surrender under specified conditions.

7 How different from ours of them is their estimate of us. How contradictory is their attitude toward us. To keep the despised and

iniquitous[1] South within their borders, as part of their country, they are willing to enlist millions of men at home and abroad, and to spend billions, and we know they do not love fighting *per se*,[2] nor spending money. They are perfectly willing to have three killed for our one. We hear they have all grown rich, through "shoddy," whatever that is. Genuine Yankees can make a fortune trading jack-knives.

Don't forget to **Notice & Note** as you read the text. 

8 "Somehow it is borne in on me that we will have to pay the piper," was remarked to-day. "No; blood can not be squeezed from a turnip. You can not pour anything out of an empty cup. We have no money even for taxes or to be confiscated."

9 While the Preston girls are here, my dining-room is given up to them, and we camp on the landing, with our one table and six chairs. Beds are made on the dining-room floor. Otherwise there is no furniture, except buckets of water and bath-tubs in their **improvised** chamber. Night and day this landing and these steps are crowded with the *élite*[3] of the Confederacy, going and coming, and when night comes, or rather, bedtime, more beds are made on the floor of the landing-place for the war-worn soldiers to rest upon. The whole house is a bivouac.[4] As Pickens said of South Carolina in 1861, we are "an armed camp."

improvise
(ĭm´prə-vīz´) *v.* to make, compose, or perform with little or no preparation.

10 My husband is rarely at home. I sleep with the girls, and my room is given up to soldiers. General Lee's few, but undismayed, his **remnant** of an army, or the part from the South and West, sad and crestfallen, pass through Chester. Many discomfited[5] heroes find their way up these stairs. They say Johnston will not be caught as Lee was. He can retreat; that is his trade. If he would not fight Sherman in the hill country of Georgia, what will he do but retreat in the plains of North Carolina with Grant, Sherman, and Thomas all to the fore?

remnant
(rĕm´nənt) *n.* a surviving trace or vestige; a surviving group of people.

11 We are to stay here. Running is useless now; so we mean to bide a Yankee raid, which they say is imminent. Why fly? They are everywhere, these Yankees, like red ants, like the locusts and frogs which were the plagues of Egypt.

12 The plucky way in which our men keep up is beyond praise. There is no howling, and our poverty is made a matter of laughing. We deride our own **penury.** Of the country we try not to speak at all.

penury
(pĕn´yə-rē) *n.* extreme want or poverty; destitution.

SYNTHESIZE INFORMATION

Annotate: Mark details in paragraph 12 that show how the war has affected southerners financially.

Infer: Will the end of the war ease or worsen the southerners' poverty? Explain.

[1] **iniquitous:** wicked.
[2] **per se:** of, in, or by itself or oneself; intrinsically.
[3] **élite:** a group or class of persons considered to be superior to others because of their intelligence, social standing, or wealth.
[4] **bivouac:** a temporary encampment often in an unsheltered area.
[5] **discomfited:** made uneasy or perplexed; disconcerted.

As you examine these infographics, think about how both sides were affected by the war and how the aftermath also would have affected them.

Casualties and Costs of the Civil War

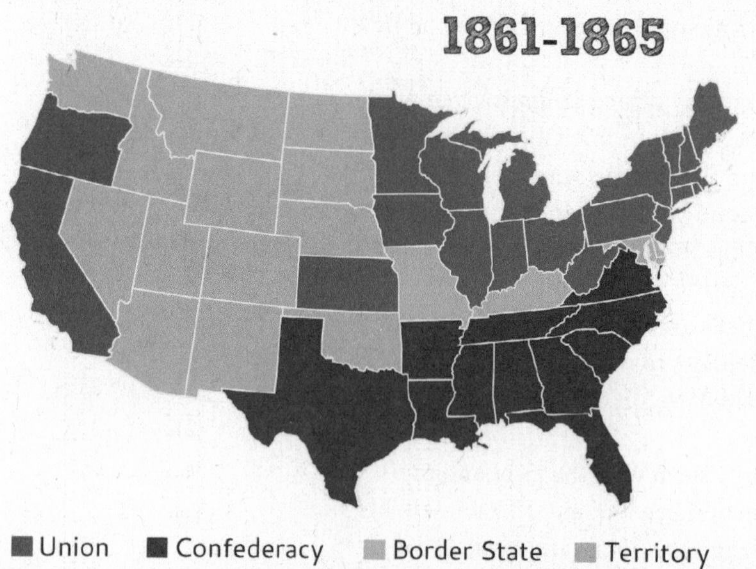

Did you know?

Not all states in the Union were free.

Four border states allowed slavery, but did not secede from the Union as the Confederate states did.

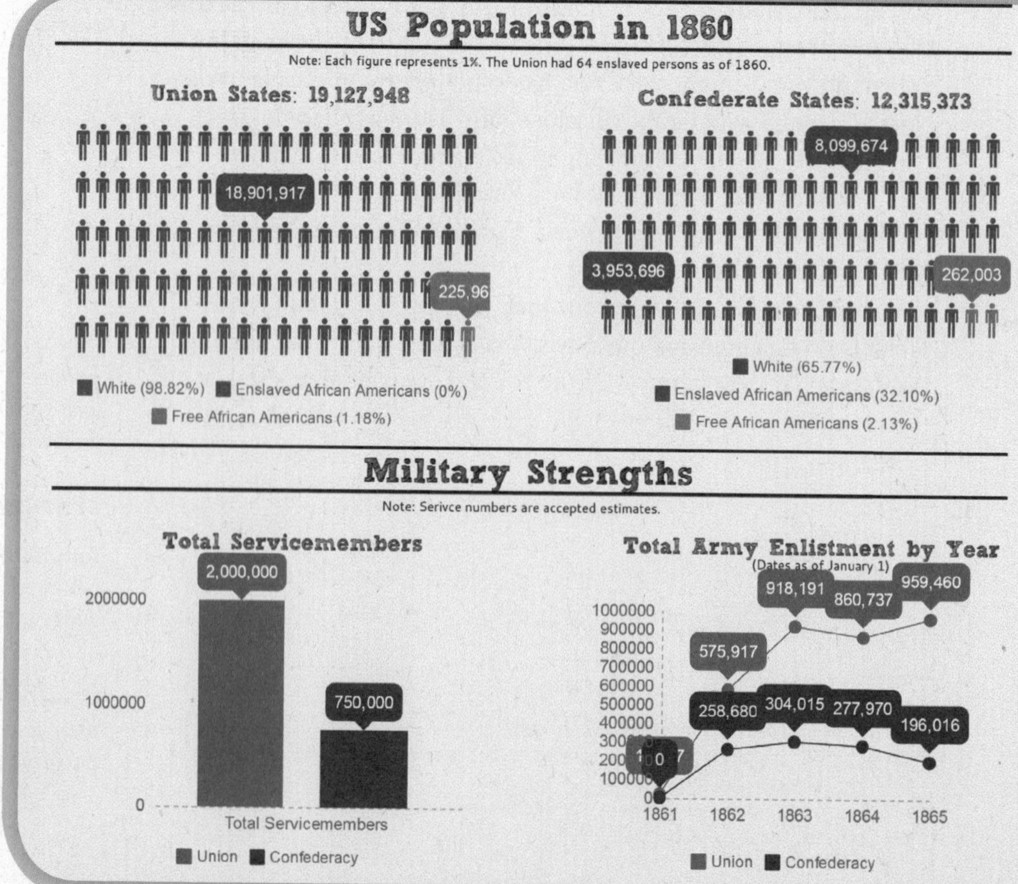

SYNTHESIZE INFORMATION

Annotate: Mark the number of soldiers for the Confederacy and the number for the Union.

Evaluate: How do these numbers support or disprove Chesnut's claim that the Yankees "are everywhere"? Explain.

Don't forget to **Notice & Note** as you read the text.

Note: Death totals are accepted estimates. Confederate numbers are estimated due to incomplete returns. Little is known about Confederate POWs.

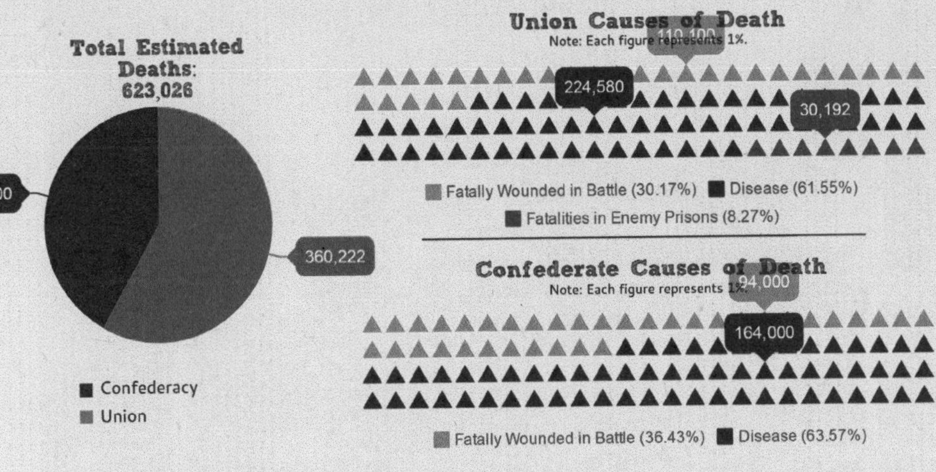

American Wars: Side by Side

Note: "Battle deaths" do not include death by disease, capture, or other deaths.

Total American Deaths in Battle

Revolutionary War	4,435
War of 1812	2,260
Indian Wars	1,000
Mexican War	1,733
Civil War	623,026
Spanish-American War	385
World War I	53,402
World War II	291,557
Korean War	33,739
Vietnam War	47,434
Persian Gulf War	148

Total War Costs (Period Value)

Revolutionary War	101 million
War of 1812	90 million
Indian Wars	260 million
Mexican War	71 million
Civil War	4,183 million
Spanish-American War	283 million
World War I	20 billion
World War II	296 billion
Korean War	30 billion
Vietnam War	111 billion
Persian Gulf War	61 billion

EVALUATE SOURCES

Annotate: Mark the number of deaths for Confederate and Union soldiers.

Draw Conclusions: What do these numbers show about the losses for each side? How might these losses affect each side after the war is over?

Andrew Russell wanted to tell a story through this photograph. Is it a story that ends well?

The Ruins of Richmond, Virginia

By **Andrew J. Russell**

The ruins of Richmond, Virginia, capital of the Confederacy, after the city surrendered on April 3, 1865. Andrew J. Russell, photographer

EVALUATE SOURCES

Annotate: What details in the photograph show the fate of the Confederate capital in the last months of the war?

Draw Conclusions: Richmond residents believed that General Robert E. Lee would never abandon the capital. What message would the photographer have wanted to convey? How do you think southerners reacted to this photo? How would northerners have reacted?

COLLABORATIVE DISCUSSION

Which detail from these sources left the strongest impression on you? Discuss your ideas with a partner.

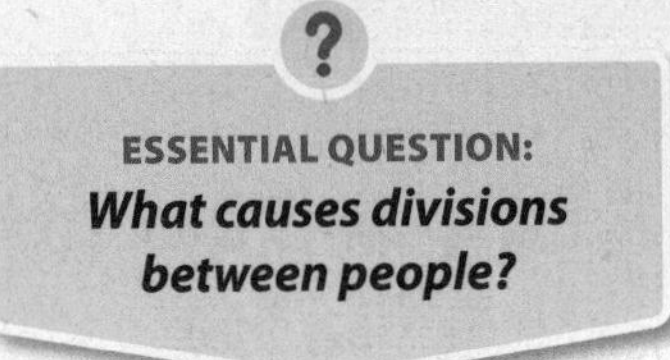
?
ESSENTIAL QUESTION:
What causes divisions between people?

Review your notes and add your thoughts to your **Response Log.**

Assessment Practice

Answer these questions before moving on to the **Analyze Text and Media** section on the following page.

1. Why does Mary Boykin Chesnut describe the North's effort to preserve the United States as "contradictory"?

(A) The North is willing to pillage and devastate the South in order to win the war.

(B) The North is willing to invest large amounts of money and troops to achieve victory.

(C) The North is eager to bring about peace as soon as possible to heal the nation.

(D) The North loves to fight and spend billions on warfare, whatever the cause.

2. In terms of the number of American deaths in battle, how does the Civil War compare to other wars?

(A) first

(B) second

(C) fifth

(D) last

3. What information about the fate of Richmond does the photograph convey?

(A) Richmond was damaged, but the city was still habitable and largely intact.

(B) Richmond was spared by the North because it was the Confederate capital.

(C) Richmond surrendered before the shelling started.

(D) Richmond was practically destroyed by the fighting.

Ed

Test-Taking Strategies

Analyze Text and Media

Support your responses with evidence from the text.

NOTICE & NOTE

Review what you **noticed and noted** as you read the text. Your annotations can help you answer these questions.

1. **INFER** What does Mr. De Fontaine imply when he writes that Richmond was a burden to the Confederacy? How could Richmond's fall make the South "stronger than ever"?

2. **COMPARE** Chesnut says she has "no heart" to write about the fall of Richmond. How does her entry of April 7 compare to the photograph in conveying what has happened to Richmond? Explain.

3. **CITE EVIDENCE** Chesnut writes that they might have to go to Texas. What motivated her to consider leaving Virginia? What information do the infographics give that support her view of Texas as a safe place?

4. **EVALUATE** Civil War photographer Alexander Gardner said that "verbal representations" of war "may or may not have the merit of accuracy; but photographic presentments of them will be accepted by posterity with an undoubting faith." Explain whether Russell's photo is a faithful presentation of war. What does a photograph of a city in wartime portray?

5. **CRITIQUE** The diary and photograph are primary sources and the infographics are secondary sources. Which source helped you understand the impact of the war most effectively? Consider the following in your response:
   - information each source emphasized
   - details that changed how you understood the past
   - features that may suggest bias

6. **ANALYZE** Using this group of sources, what can you synthesize about the Fall of Richmond and the subsequent end of the Civil War? Use the graphic organizer and cite evidence from the texts in your response.

Information from Chesnut's Diary	Information from Infographics	Information from Photo

Synthesized Information from All Sources

Choices

Here are some other ways to demonstrate your understanding of the ideas in this lesson.

Writing

↳ Diary Entry

The news that the Civil War has ended just reached the town where you live. Pick one of the persons listed below and write a diary entry from that person's point of view.

- a soldier in a hospital recovering from injury or illness, who can't return home yet
- a soldier who returns home after four years at war to find everything radically altered
- a mother whose son will not be returning home
- a formerly enslaved person who is trying to locate relatives
- an army commander whose post-war duties include contacting families to tell them their loved ones were killed in action
- a public figure who wants to influence the nation's recovery

Include details from additional resources, if necessary.

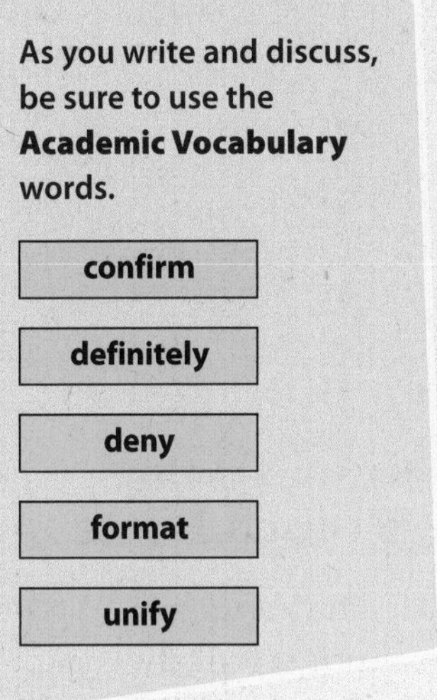
As you write and discuss, be sure to use the **Academic Vocabulary** words.
confirm
definitely
deny
format
unify

Research

↳ Report

In 1873, Mark Twain wrote that the Civil War "uprooted institutions that were centuries old, changed the politics of a people, and wrought so profoundly upon the entire national character that the influence cannot be measured short of two or three generations."

Six generations out, can we now measure its influence? With a classmate, pick a topic below. Research the subject and report your findings.

- Lack of universal health care
- Prison reform
- Voter suppression, gerrymandering
- Electoral College
- Consumer protection laws

Media

↳ Media Timeline

Create a timeline with embedded media that highlights events leading up to, during, and after the Civil War.

1. Decide the time period you want your timeline to cover.
2. Decide which perspective(s) you want to include. Will you represent a multitude of groups or keep your focus narrow?
3. Find or create the images, texts, and music that you want to use. If you use copyrighted material, credit it correctly.
4. Share your timeline with others, explaining the choices you made and why. Listen and respond as they share their timelines.

Expand Your Vocabulary

PRACTICE AND APPLY

Answer each question with a sentence that shows you understand the vocabulary words.

1. If a musician **improvises** a piece, what has she done?
2. In what situations will parents **capitulate** to their children's demands?
3. If a house is described as "showing **remnants** of its former glory," is it move-in ready?
4. What is life like for someone living in **penury**?

Vocabulary Strategy

↳ French Roots

This *American Heritage Dictionary of the English Language* entry for *improvise* shows how English words derive from other languages.

Interactive Vocabulary Lesson: Understanding Word Origins

im·pro·vise (ĭm prə-vīz´) *v.* im·pro·vised, im·pro·vis·ing, im·pro·vis·es

v.tr.

1. To make, compose, or perform with little or no preparation: improvise a solution to the problem; improvise variations on a melody.
2. To make or provide from available materials: improvised a dinner from what I found in the refrigerator.

v.intr.

3. To make, compose, or perform something extemporaneously.
4. To make do with whatever materials are at hand: There isn't much in the cabin. We'll just have to improvise.

[French *improviser*, from Italian *improvvisare*, from *improvviso*, unforeseen, from Latin *imprōvīsus* : in-, not; see IN-[1] + *prōvīsus*, past participle of prōvidēre, to foresee; see PROVIDE.]

Consider what the etymology shown for *improvise* tells you:

- The word's derivation is shown in brackets. It comes primarily from the French word *improviser*, which means "not to foresee."
- Notice how the origin comes from a Latin root that means "to foresee."
- The prefix *in* makes the meaning "unforeseen."
- *Improvise* has evolved to mean more than *unforeseen*, but knowing the origin can help you remember the definition.

PRACTICE AND APPLY

Consult a dictionary to find information about these vocabulary words: *capitulate, remnant*. Then, discuss with a partner how this knowledge might help you remember and use these words.

Watch Your Language!

Quotation Marks

Quotation marks are used by writers to indicate another person's exact words, or a direct quote. In Mary Boykin Chesnut's diary, she also uses quotation marks to indicate slang or an expression she doesn't know, as in the example below.

> **We hear they have all grown rich, through "shoddy," whatever that is. Genuine Yankees can make a fortune trading jackknives.**

She is also careful to use quotation marks to give credit to someone else for an expression that may be new or interesting to her:

> **As Pickens said of South Carolina in 1861, we are "an armed camp."**

This simple diary entry helps Chesnut to remember who used the phrase "an armed camp." The quoted phrase may also remind her of the context in which Pickens used it. Readers of her diary may not know who Pickens is, but her quotation marks help them know that the expression was not original to Chesnut.

Ed

Interactive Grammar Lesson: Quotation Marks

When doing research, be careful to use quotation marks around direct words that you integrate into your writing. Like Chesnut, choose only colorful or powerful sentences or phrases to quote directly, and your writing will be more effective.

PRACTICE AND APPLY

Write your own diary entry, using Mary Boykin Chesnut's entry as a model. Include quoted words and phrases to make your writing more interesting. Be careful not to plagiarize if you are quoting what another person said.

Get Ready

An Occurrence at Owl Creek Bridge

Short Story by **Ambrose Bierce**

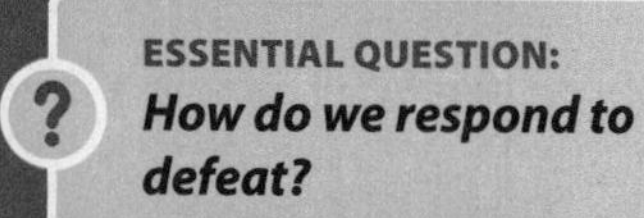

ESSENTIAL QUESTION:
How do we respond to defeat?

Engage Your Brain

Choose one or more of these activities to start connecting with the story you're about to read.

Wanted, Spy

You're the head of a spy agency, recruiting job applicants for a top-secret mission. Write a want ad that lists the job requirements and skills you think a qualified candidate should exhibit.

Lying and Subterfuge, Oh My!

Both the Union and the Confederacy used spies to further their respective causes. Do some research on Civil War spies to answer the following questions:

- Who are some well-known spies and which side did they fight for?
- What did these spies do to help the war effort?
- Were the spies effective?
- Did any of them get caught? If so, what happened to them?

If I Could Have Just One Thing...

With a partner, make a list of all the spy movies or TV shows you've seen or books you've read with spies as characters. What cool devices or gadgets did they have to help them get out of tight situations? Decide which one you'd want to have in your ultimate spy survival kit. Haven't seen a spy movie? No worries, invent your own gadget!

Analyze Point of View

One important element authors use to structure a story is **point of view,** the perspective from which the story is told. The **narrator** is the voice that tells the story; as a result, the reader knows only what the narrator is able to tell. Types of point of view include:

- **first-person:** told by a character in the work whose knowledge is limited by his or her own experiences
- **third-person omniscient:** told by a voice outside the story who knows the thoughts and feelings of all the characters
- **third-person limited:** told by a voice outside the story who focuses on one character's thoughts and feelings

As you read, look for clues that indicate a particular point of view and note how that perspective affects what and when you learn about events and characters in the story.

Focus on Genre
↳ Short Story

- **is a brief fictional work, usually written in prose**
- **is told from a point of view, which may shift depending on the structure of the story**
- **uses the relationship of literary elements to convey a theme**

Analyze Plot

To analyze a literary work, examine the relationship between its structure and the events in the plot. This story is divided into three numbered sections, each of which occurs at a different point in time. After you read each section, summarize the events that occur and note when they take place.

Section	What Happens	When
I		
II		
III		

Annotation in Action

Here are one student's notes about point of view in "An Occurrence at Owl Creek Bridge." As you read, notice clues that help identify the point of view of the story.

A man stood upon a railroad bridge in northern Alabama, looking down into the swift water twenty feet below. The man's hands were behind his back, the wrists bound with a cord. A rope closely encircled his neck. It was attached to a stout cross-timber above his head and the slack fell to the level of his knees.

The details suggest third-person point of view, although it's hard to tell if the perspective is omniscient or limited. It does reveal a character in trouble.

Expand Your Vocabulary

Put a check mark next to the vocabulary words that you feel comfortable using when speaking or writing.

summarily	☐
poignant	☐
effaced	☐
undulations	☐
presaging	☐
interminable	☐
malign	☐
ineffable	☐

Then, use the words to talk about a time you had a bad feeling about something. As you read "An Occurrence at Owl Creek Bridge," use the definitions in the side-column to learn the vocabulary words you don't already know.

Background

Ambrose Bierce (1842–1914) Born into a poor family, Bierce spent his early years on an Indiana farm until he left home at 15 to work at a newspaper. Three years later, he joined the Union army to fight in the Civil War. After the war, he moved to San Francisco and started publishing short stories in the 1870s. The contrast between soldiers' dreams of glory and the senselessness of warfare became a recurring theme in his work, as is seen in "An Occurrence at Owl Creek Bridge."

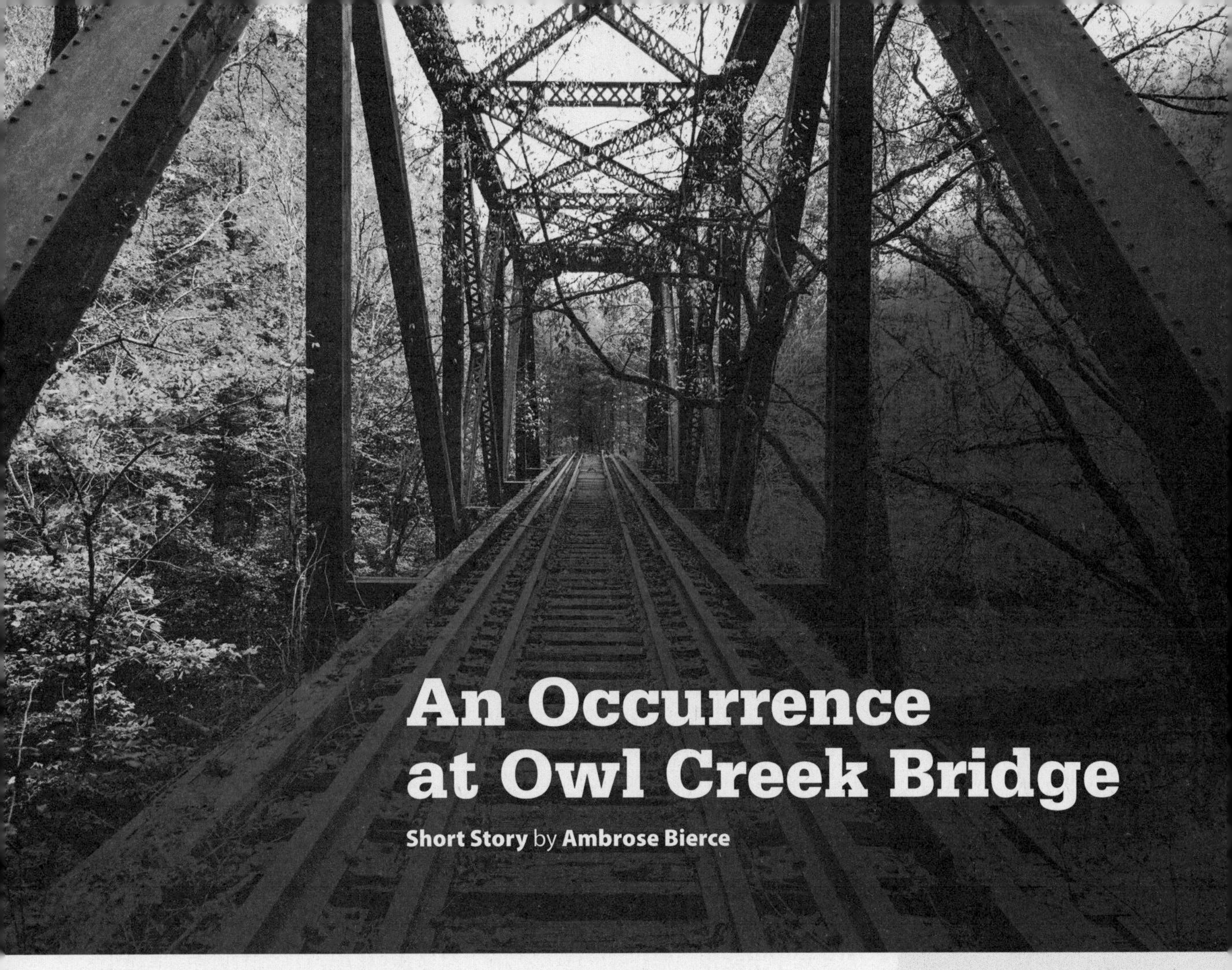

An Occurrence at Owl Creek Bridge

Short Story by **Ambrose Bierce**

Think about how the story is structured. How does its organization build suspense and keep your interest?

NOTICE & NOTE 
As you read, use the side margins to make notes about the text.

I

1 A man stood upon a railroad bridge in northern Alabama, looking down into the swift water twenty feet below. The man's hands were behind his back, the wrists bound with a cord. A rope closely encircled his neck. It was attached to a stout cross-timber above his head and the slack fell to the level of his knees. Some loose boards laid upon the sleepers[1] supporting the metals of the railway supplied a footing for him and his executioners—two private soldiers of the Federal army, directed by a sergeant who in civil life may have been a deputy sheriff. At a short remove upon the same temporary platform was an officer in the uniform of his rank, armed. He was a captain. A sentinel at each end of the bridge stood with his rifle in the position

ANALYZE PLOT

Annotate: Mark details in paragraph 1 that tell where and when the story takes place.

Predict: What is going to happen to the man?

[1] **sleepers:** railroad ties.

known as "support," that is to say, vertical in front of the left shoulder, the hammer resting on the forearm thrown straight across the chest—a formal and unnatural position, enforcing an erect carriage of the body. It did not appear to be the duty of these two men to know what was occurring at the center of the bridge; they merely blockaded the two ends of the foot planking that traversed it.

2 Beyond one of the sentinels nobody was in sight; the railroad ran straight away into a forest for a hundred yards, then, curving, was lost to view. Doubtless there was an outpost farther along. The other bank of the stream was open ground—a gentle acclivity[2] topped with a stockade of vertical tree trunks, loopholed for rifles, with a single embrasure[3] through which protruded the muzzle of a brass cannon commanding the bridge. Midway of the slope between bridge and fort were the spectators—a single company of infantry in line, at "parade rest," the butts of the rifles on the ground, the barrels inclining slightly backward against the right shoulder, the hands crossed upon the stock.[4] A lieutenant stood at the right of the line, the point of his sword upon the ground, his left hand resting upon his right. Excepting the group of four at the center of the bridge, not a man moved. The company faced the bridge, staring stonily, motionless. The sentinels, facing the banks of the stream, might have been statues to adorn the bridge. The captain stood with folded arms, silent, observing the work of his subordinates, but making no sign. Death is a dignitary who when he comes announced is to be received with formal manifestations of respect, even by those most familiar with him. In the code of military etiquette silence and fixity are forms of deference.

ANALYZE POINT OF VIEW

Annotate: Mark the phrases that indicate point of view in paragraph 3.

Evaluate: What point of view is used in paragraph 3? How does the point of view affect the perception of events?

3 The man who was engaged in being hanged was apparently about thirty-five years of age. He was a civilian, if one might judge from his habit, which was that of a planter. His features were good—a straight nose, firm mouth, broad forehead, from which his long, dark hair was combed straight back, falling behind his ears to the collar of his well-fitting frock-coat. He wore a mustache and pointed beard, but no whiskers; his eyes were large and dark gray, and had a kindly expression which one would hardly have expected in one whose neck was in the hemp. Evidently this was no vulgar assassin. The liberal military code makes provision for hanging many kinds of persons, and gentlemen are not excluded.

4 The preparations being complete, the two private soldiers stepped aside and each drew away the plank upon which he had been standing. The sergeant turned to the captain, saluted and

[2] **acclivity:** an upward slope.

[3] **embrasure:** a flared opening in a wall for a gun, with sides angled so that the inside opening is larger than that on the outside.

[4] **stock:** the wooden part of the rifle that serves as a handle.

placed himself immediately behind that officer, who in turn moved apart one pace. These movements left the condemned man and the sergeant standing on the two ends of the same plank, which spanned three of the cross-ties of the bridge. The end upon which the civilian stood almost, but not quite, reached a fourth. This plank had been held in place by the weight of the captain; it was now held by that of the sergeant. At a signal from the former the latter would step aside, the plank would tilt and the condemned man go down between two ties. The arrangement commended itself to his judgment as simple and effective. His face had not been covered nor his eyes bandaged. He looked a moment at his "unsteadfast footing," then let his gaze wander to the swirling water of the stream racing madly beneath his feet. A piece of dancing driftwood caught his attention and his eyes followed it down the current. How slowly it appeared to move! What a sluggish stream!

Don't forget to **Notice & Note** as you read the text.

5 He closed his eyes in order to fix his last thoughts upon his wife and children. The water, touched to gold by the early sun, the brooding mists under the banks at some distance down the stream, the fort, the soldiers, the piece of drift—all had distracted him. And now he became conscious of a new disturbance. Striking through the thought of his dear ones was a sound which he could neither ignore nor understand, a sharp, distinct, metallic percussion like the stroke of a blacksmith's hammer upon the anvil; it had the same ringing quality. He wondered what it was, and whether immeasurably distant or near by—it seemed both. Its recurrence was regular, but as slow as the tolling of a death knell.[5] He awaited each stroke with impatience and—he knew not why—apprehension. The intervals of silence grew progressively longer; the delays became maddening. With their greater infrequency the sounds increased in strength and sharpness. They hurt his ear like the thrust of a knife; he feared he would shriek. What he heard was the ticking of his watch.

ANALYZE POINT OF VIEW

Annotate: Mark details in paragraph 5 that tell you the narrator's thoughts.

Evaluate: How do these details portray a shift in point of view?

6 He unclosed his eyes and saw again the water below him. "If I could free my hands," he thought, "I might throw off the noose and spring into the stream. By diving I could evade the bullets and, swimming vigorously, reach the bank, take to the woods and get away home. My home, thank God, is as yet outside their lines; my wife and little ones are still beyond the invader's farthest advance."

7 As these thoughts, which have here to be set down in words, were flashed into the doomed man's brain rather than evolved from it the captain nodded to the sergeant. The sergeant stepped aside.

[5] **the tolling of a death knell:** the slow, steady ringing of a bell at a funeral or to indicate death.

II

8 Peyton Farquhar was a well-to-do planter, of an old and highly respected Alabama family. Being a slave owner and like other slave owners a politician he was naturally an original secessionist and ardently devoted to the Southern cause. Circumstances of an imperious nature, which it is unnecessary to relate here, had prevented him from taking service with the gallant army that had fought the disastrous campaigns ending with the fall of Corinth,[6] and he chafed under the inglorious restraint, longing for the release of his energies, the larger life of the soldier, the opportunity for distinction. That opportunity, he felt, would come, as it comes to all in war time. Meanwhile he did what he could. No service was too humble for him to perform in aid of the South, no adventure too perilous for him to undertake if consistent with the character of a civilian who was at heart a soldier, and who in good faith and without too much qualification assented to at least a part of the frankly villainous dictum that all is fair in love and war.

9 One evening while Farquhar and his wife were sitting on a rustic bench near the entrance to his grounds, a gray-clad soldier rode up to the gate and asked for a drink of water. Mrs. Farquhar was only too happy to serve him with her own white hands. While she was fetching the water her husband approached the dusty horseman and inquired eagerly for news from the front.

10 "The Yanks are repairing the railroads," said the man, "and are getting ready for another advance. They have reached the Owl Creek bridge, put it in order and built a stockade on the north bank. The commandant has issued an order, which is posted everywhere, declaring that any civilian caught interfering with the railroad, its bridges, tunnels or trains will be **summarily** hanged. I saw the order."

11 "How far is it to the Owl Creek bridge?" Farquhar asked.

12 "About thirty miles."

13 "Is there no force on this side the creek?"

14 "Only a picket post[7] half a mile out, on the railroad, and a single sentinel at this end of the bridge."

15 "Suppose a man—a civilian and student of hanging—should elude the picket post and perhaps get the better of the sentinel," said Farquhar, smiling, "what could he accomplish?"

16 The soldier reflected. "I was there a month ago," he replied. "I observed that the flood of last winter had lodged a great quantity of driftwood against the wooden pier at this end of the bridge. It is now dry and would burn like tow."[8]

17 The lady had now brought the water, which the soldier drank. He thanked her ceremoniously, bowed to her husband and rode away. An hour later, after nightfall, he repassed the plantation, going northward in the direction from which he had come. He was a Federal scout.

NOTICE & NOTE
MEMORY MOMENT

When you notice the narrator has interrupted the progress of a story by bringing up something from the past, you've found a **Memory Moment** signpost.

Notice & Note: When in time does Section II of the story actually take place?

Analyze: What information about the characters do you learn in this section?

summarily
(sə-mĕr´ə-lē) *adv.* quickly and without ceremony.

ANALYZE PLOT

Annotate: Compare paragraph 10 with the description in paragraphs 1 and 2. Mark details that connect the two sections.

Evaluate: What is the effect of including similar details in the two sections?

[6] **Corinth:** a town in Mississippi that was the site of a Civil War battle in 1862.
[7] **picket post:** the camp of soldiers who are assigned to guard against a surprise attack.
[8] **tow** (tō): coarse, dry fiber.

III

Don't forget to **Notice & Note** as you read the text.

18 As Peyton Farquhar fell straight downward through the bridge he lost consciousness and was as one already dead. From this state he was awakened—ages later, it seemed to him—by the pain of a sharp pressure upon his throat, followed by a sense of suffocation. Keen, **poignant** agonies seemed to shoot from his neck downward through every fiber of his body and limbs. These pains appeared to flash along well-defined lines of ramification[9] and to beat with an inconceivably rapid periodicity. They seemed like streams of pulsating fire heating him to an intolerable temperature. As to his head, he was conscious of nothing but a feeling of fullness—of congestion. These sensations were unaccompanied by thought. The intellectual part of his nature was already **effaced**; he had power only to feel, and feeling was torment. He was conscious of motion. Encompassed in a luminous cloud, of which he was now merely the fiery heart, without material substance, he swung through unthinkable arcs of oscillation,[10] like a vast pendulum. Then all at once, with terrible suddenness, the light about him shot upward with the noise of a loud plash; a frightful roaring was in his ears, and all was cold and dark. The power of thought was restored; he knew that the rope had broken and he had fallen into the stream. There was no additional strangulation; the noose about his neck was already suffocating him and kept the water from his lungs. To die of hanging at the bottom of a river!—the idea seemed to him ludicrous. He opened his eyes in the darkness and saw above him a gleam of light, but how distant, how inaccessible! He was still sinking, for the light became fainter and fainter until it was a mere glimmer. Then it began to grow and brighten, and he knew that he was rising toward the surface—knew it with reluctance, for he was now very comfortable. "To be hanged and drowned," he thought, "that is not so bad; but I do not wish to be shot. No; I will not be shot; that is not fair."

poignant
(poin′yənt) *adj.* physically or mentally painful.

efface
(ĭ-fās′) *v.tr.* to rub or wipe out; erase.

VOCABULARY

Etymology: Knowing where a word comes from can help you know what it means. "Pendulum" is a noun derived from the Latin verb *pendere*, "to hang or to cause to hang."

Analyze: Using the etymology and the context, what is a pendulum? Why would Bierce use it here?

[9] **flash . . . ramification:** spread out rapidly along branches from a central point.
[10] **oscillation:** the action of swinging back and forth.

19 He was not conscious of an effort, but a sharp pain in his wrist apprised him that he was trying to free his hands. He gave the struggle his attention, as an idler might observe the feat of a juggler, without interest in the outcome. What splendid effort!—what magnificent, what superhuman strength! Ah, that was a fine endeavor! Bravo! The cord fell away; his arms parted and floated upward, the hands dimly seen on each side in the growing light. He watched them with a new interest as first one and then the other pounced upon the noose at his neck. They tore it away and thrust it fiercely aside, its **undulations** resembling those of a water-snake. "Put it back, put it back!" He thought he shouted these words to his hands, for the undoing of the noose had been succeeded by the direst pang that he had yet experienced. His neck ached horribly; his brain was on fire; his heart, which had been fluttering faintly, gave a great leap, trying to force itself out at his mouth. His whole body was racked and wrenched with an insupportable anguish![11] But his disobedient hands gave no heed to the command. They beat the water vigorously with quick, downward strokes, forcing him to the surface. He felt

undulation
(ŭn-jə-lā´shən) *n.* a regular rising and falling or movement to alternating sides; movement in waves.

[11] **racked . . . anguish:** stretched and twisted with unendurable physical pain.

his head emerge; his eyes were blinded by the sunlight; his chest expanded convulsively, and with a supreme and crowning agony his lungs engulfed a great draught of air, which instantly he expelled in a shriek!

Don't forget to **Notice & Note** as you read the text.

20 He was now in full possession of his physical senses. They were, indeed, preternaturally keen and alert. Something in the awful disturbance of his organic system had so exalted and refined them that they made record of things never before perceived. He felt the ripples upon his face and heard their separate sounds as they struck. He looked at the forest on the bank of the stream, saw the individual trees, the leaves and the veining of each leaf—saw the very insects upon them: the locusts, the brilliant-bodied flies, the gray spiders stretching their webs from twig to twig. He noted the prismatic colors in all the dewdrops upon a million blades of grass. The humming of the gnats that danced above the eddies of the stream, the beating of the dragon-flies' wings, the strokes of the water-spiders' legs, like oars which had lifted their boat—all these made audible music. A fish slid along beneath his eyes and he heard the rush of its body parting the water.

21 He had come to the surface facing down the stream; in a moment the visible world seemed to wheel slowly round, himself the pivotal point, and he saw the bridge, the fort, the soldiers upon the bridge, the captain, the sergeant, the two privates, his executioners. They were in silhouette against the blue sky. They shouted and gesticulated, pointing at him. The captain had drawn his pistol, but did not fire; the others were unarmed. Their movements were grotesque and horrible, their forms gigantic.

22 Suddenly he heard a sharp report and something struck the water smartly within a few inches of his head, spattering his face with spray. He heard a second report, and saw one of the sentinels with his rifle at his shoulder, a light cloud of blue smoke rising from the muzzle. The man in the water saw the eye of the man on the bridge gazing into his own through the sights of the rifle. He observed that it was a gray eye and remembered having read that gray eyes were keenest, and that all famous marksmen had them. Nevertheless, this one had missed.

ANALYZE PLOT

Annotate: Mark details in paragraphs 21 and 22 that describe the soldiers' reaction to Farquhar's escape.

Synthesize: Explain whether the details in this description are realistic. Cite text evidence in your response.

23 A counter-swirl had caught Farquhar and turned him half round; he was again looking into the forest on the bank opposite the fort. The sound of a clear, high voice in a monotonous singsong now rang out behind him and came across the water with a distinctness that pierced and subdued all other sounds, even the beating of the ripples in his ears. Although no soldier, he had frequented camps enough to know the dread significance of that deliberate, drawling, aspirated chant; the lieutenant on shore was taking a part in the morning's work. How coldly and pitilessly—with what an even, calm intonation, **presaging,** and enforcing tranquility in the men—with what accurately measured intervals fell those cruel words:

24 "Attention, company! . . . Shoulder arms! . . . Ready! . . . Aim! . . . Fire!"

presaging
(prĕs´ĭj-ĭng) *adj.* predicting.

ANALYZE POINT OF VIEW

Annotate: Mark details in paragraphs 25–27 that reveal Farquhar's perspective.

Evaluate: How does learning about these events from Farquhar's perspective build suspense?

25 Farquhar dived—dived as deeply as he could. The water roared in his ears like the voice of Niagara, yet he heard the dulled thunder of the volley and, rising again toward the surface, met shining bits of metal, singularly flattened, oscillating slowly downward. Some of them touched him on the face and hands, then fell away, continuing their descent. One lodged between his collar and neck; it was uncomfortably warm and he snatched it out.

26 As he rose to the surface, gasping for breath, he saw that he had been a long time under water; he was perceptibly farther down stream—nearer to safety. The soldiers had almost finished reloading; the metal ramrods flashed all at once in the sunshine as they were drawn from the barrels, turned in the air, and thrust into their sockets. The two sentinels fired again, independently and ineffectually.

27 The hunted man saw all this over his shoulder; he was now swimming vigorously with the current. His brain was as energetic as his arms and legs; he thought with the rapidity of lightning.

28 "The officer," he reasoned, "will not make that martinet's[12] error a second time. It is as easy to dodge a volley as a single shot. He has probably already given the command to fire at will. God help me, I cannot dodge them all!"

29 An appalling plash within two yards of him was followed by a loud, rushing sound, *diminuendo*,[13] which seemed to travel back through the air to the fort and died in an explosion which stirred the very river to its deeps! A rising sheet of water curved over him, fell down upon him, blinded him, strangled him! The cannon had taken a hand in the game. As he shook his head free from the commotion of the smitten water he heard the deflected shot humming through the air ahead, and in an instant it was cracking and smashing the branches in the forest beyond.

30 "They will not do that again," he thought; "the next time they will use a charge of grape.[14] I must keep my eye upon the gun; the smoke will apprise me—the report arrives too late; it lags behind the missile. That is a good gun."

ANALYZE POINT OF VIEW

Annotate: Mark details in paragraph 31 that describe Farquhar's movement.

Analyze: How does Farquhar feel while he is moving? How does he feel when he stops? From what point of view is the scene described?

31 Suddenly he felt himself whirled round and round—spinning like a top. The water, the banks, the forests, the now distant bridge, fort and men—all were commingled and blurred. Objects were represented by their colors only; circular horizontal streaks of color—that was all he saw. He had been caught in a vortex and was being whirled on with a velocity of advance and gyration that made him giddy and sick. In a few moments he was flung upon the gravel at the foot of the left bank of the stream—the southern bank—and behind a projecting point which concealed him from his enemies. The sudden arrest of his motion, the abrasion of one of his hands on

[12] **martinet's:** alluding to a strict disciplinarian or person who demands that regulations be followed exactly.

[13] ***diminuendo*** (dĭ-mĭn-yo͞o-ĕn´dō) *Italian:* gradually decreasing in loudness.

[14] **grape:** short for *grapeshot,* a cluster of several small iron balls fired in one shot from a cannon.

Don't forget to **Notice & Note** as you read the text.

the gravel, restored him, and he wept with delight. He dug his fingers into the sand, threw it over himself in handfuls and audibly blessed it. It looked like diamonds, rubies, emeralds; he could think of nothing beautiful which it did not resemble. The trees upon the bank were giant garden plants; he noted a definite order in their arrangement, inhaled the fragrance of their blooms. A strange, roseate light shone through the spaces among their trunks and the wind made in their branches the music of æolian harps.[15] He had no wish to perfect his escape—was content to remain in that enchanting spot until retaken.

32 A whiz and rattle of grapeshot among the branches high above his head roused him from his dream. The baffled cannoneer had fired him a random farewell. He sprang to his feet, rushed up the sloping bank, and plunged into the forest.

33 All that day he traveled, laying his course by the rounding sun. The forest seemed **interminable;** nowhere did he discover a break in it, not even a woodman's road. He had not known that he lived in so wild a region. There was something uncanny in the revelation.

interminable
(ĭn-tûr´mə-nə-bəl) *adj.* endless.

34 By night fall he was fatigued, footsore, famishing. The thought of his wife and children urged him on. At last he found a road which led him in what he knew to be the right direction. It was as wide and straight as a city street, yet it seemed untraveled. No fields bordered it, no dwelling anywhere. Not so much as the barking of a dog suggested human habitation. The black bodies of the trees formed a straight wall on both sides, terminating on the horizon in a point, like a diagram in a lesson in perspective. Overhead, as he looked up through this rift in the wood, shone great golden stars looking unfamiliar and grouped in strange constellations. He was sure they were arranged in some order which had a secret and **malign** significance. The wood on either side was full of singular noises, among which—once, twice, and again, he distinctly heard whispers in an unknown tongue.

malign
(mə-līn´) *adj.* evil in disposition, nature, or intent.

35 His neck was in pain and lifting his hand to it he found it horribly swollen. He knew that it had a circle of black where the rope had bruised it. His eyes felt congested; he could no longer close them. His tongue was swollen with thirst; he relieved its fever by thrusting it forward from between his teeth into the cold air. How softly the turf had carpeted the untraveled avenue—he could no longer feel the roadway beneath his feet!

36 Doubtless, despite his suffering, he had fallen asleep while walking, for now he sees another scene—perhaps he has merely recovered from a delirium. He stands at the gate of his own home. All is as he left it, and all bright and beautiful in the morning sunshine. He must have traveled the entire night. As he pushes open the gate and passes up the wide white walk, he sees a flutter of

[15] **music of æolian**(ē-ō´lē-ən) **harps:** heavenly, or unearthly, music.

ineffable
(ĭn-ĕf´ə-bəl) *adj.* beyond description; inexpressible.

ANALYZE PLOT

Annotate: Reread paragraphs 34–36. Mark details that suggest Peyton Farquhar is going to escape his situation.

Infer: What can you infer about how he is going to escape? Does this support or contradict what happens at the end of the story?

female garments; his wife, looking fresh and cool and sweet, steps down from the veranda to meet him. At the bottom of the steps she stands waiting, with a smile of **ineffable** joy, an attitude of matchless grace and dignity. Ah, how beautiful she is! He springs forward with extended arms. As he is about to clasp her he feels a stunning blow upon the back of the neck; a blinding white light blazes all about him with a sound like the shock of a cannon—then all is darkness and silence!

37 Peyton Farquhar was dead; his body, with a broken neck, swung gently from side to side beneath the timbers of the Owl Creek bridge.

ESSENTIAL QUESTION:
How do we respond to defeat?

Review your notes and add your thoughts to your **Response Log.**

COLLABORATIVE DISCUSSION

Pair up with a classmate and discuss your reaction to the story's ending. How did the point of view affect your understanding of what happens? Would you have used a different perspective?

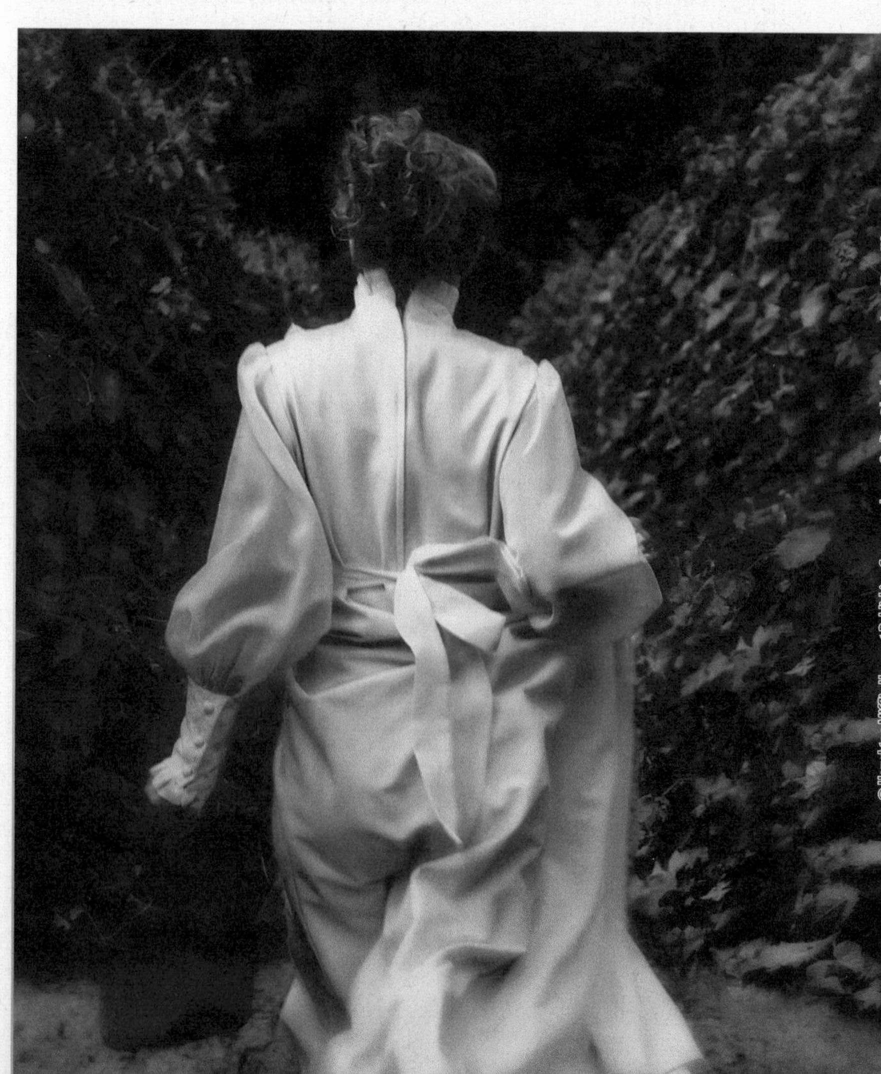

Assessment Practice

Answer these questions before moving on to the **Analyze the Text** section on the following page.

1. Why does the soldier who visited Farquhar give him such detailed information about the bridge?
   - (A) He wants to help Farquhar become a war hero.
   - (B) He made a plan to take action against the Union.
   - (C) He was trying to trick Farquhar into committing a crime.
   - (D) He only appears in Farquhar's imagination.

2. Which of the following details is an example of the use of third-person limited point of view?
   - (A) *He wore a mustache and pointed beard.*
   - (B) *The preparations being complete, the two private soldiers stepped aside.*
   - (C) *Peyton Farquhar was a well-to-do planter.*
   - (D) *By night fall he was fatigued, footsore, famishing.*

3. What is the significance of the ticking watch in the story?
   - (A) It reminds the man of his family.
   - (B) It represents hope and a desire to escape.
   - (C) It tells the reader how much time has passed.
   - (D) It conveys fear and anxiety in the situation.

Test-Taking Strategies

Analyze the Text

Support your responses with evidence from the text.

NOTICE & NOTE

Review what you **noticed and noted** as you read the text. Your annotations can help you answer these questions.

1. **ANALYZE** Review the chart you filled out as you read. How would the story be different if it were told in chronological order? Why did the writer structure the story the way he did? Explain.

2. **INFER** What is the Union soldiers' reason for hanging Farquhar? Cite text evidence in your response.

3. **ANALYZE** Find examples in the story where the perspective shifts from third-person limited to third-person omniscient point of view. Use the chart to track the clues in the text that alert you to the shift. What information is revealed to you, or hidden from you, as the perspective shifts? What is the effect on your understanding as the narration shifts?

Third-Person Limited	**Text Clues**	**Information Revealed/Hidden**
Third-Person Omniscient	**Text Clues**	**Information Revealed/Hidden**

4. **EVALUATE** Citing at least two examples from the story, explain how the shifts in point of view impact the plot and build suspense. What would be different about the story if it were told entirely from the third-person omniscient point of view?

5. **EVALUATE** Explain whether the author intended Farquhar's escape to be believable. Cite text evidence in your response.

6. **DRAW CONCLUSIONS** In Section II, Peyton Farquhar's **Memory Moment** reveals his desire for "the larger life of the soldier, the opportunity for distinction." Based on his dreams of glory and his ultimate fate, what theme does Bierce express about heroism and the realities of war?

Choices

Here are some other ways to demonstrate your understanding of the ideas in this lesson.

Writing

↳ An OAOCB Reboot

Ambrose Bierce published this short story in 1890, and it's due for an overhaul. Write a modern-day version of the story.

1. Create a storyboard or graphic organizer to plot your retelling.
2. Decide on a setting: You might choose virtual reality, sci-fi/ fantasy landscape, underworld, corporate espionage. . . .
3. Choose the character traits you want to highlight, based on what you think their motivations are.
4. Structure your story to build suspense or to keep readers guessing.
5. Publish your story on a school or class website.

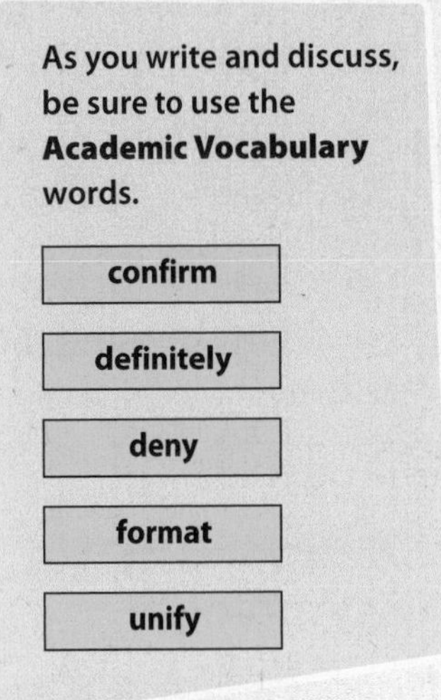
As you write and discuss, be sure to use the **Academic Vocabulary** words.
confirm
definitely
deny
format
unify

Speaking & Listening

↳ Do-over

In a small group, discuss this hypothetical situation: Peyton Farquhar has a chance to hit the reset button. Knowing how it all ends, does he make the same choice to be a spy, or does he do things differently?

Ideas to consider:

- the consequences of his actions
- his well-being and that of his family
- what it means to be loyal
- religious, moral, and/or ethical beliefs that can drive decisions

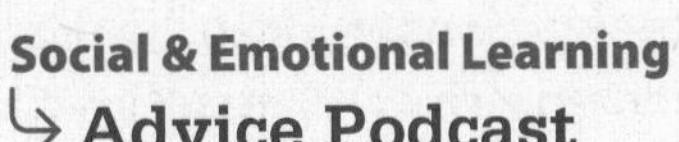

Social & Emotional Learning

↳ Advice Podcast

You are the host of a weekly podcast, known for your honest, but compassionate, advice. You get the following question from a listener:

. . . I want very much to serve my country but am not able to do so in a military capacity. I recently was given some intelligence that could help a military operation, but I might have to break some laws to do it. Should I attempt it? #TemptedbutCautious

Give advice to your listener, making sure to consider the issue from several perspectives, with the goal of reaching an ethical decision. Let your classmates comment on your answer, saying whether they agree with your advice or not, and why.

Expand Your Vocabulary

PRACTICE AND APPLY

Mark the vocabulary words that are used incorrectly in the sentences.

1. Carlito was asked to put up paintings on the newly **effaced**, white walls, which he did **summarily**—it took him the entire day.
2. As the waves' **undulations** became more rapid, heavy clouds formed, **presaging** rain; this caused Troy to make a **poignant** journey from the door to the car.
3. To punish her brother for his **malign** behaviors, Niko sent him to an **interminable** cabin. When he arrived, the confusion on his face was **ineffable**.

Vocabulary Strategy

↳ Etymology

Ed

Interactive Vocabulary Lesson: Understanding Word Origins

Etymology is the study of the origin of words and how the meaning of words has evolved over time. The word *etymology*, for example, derives from the Greek word *etumos*, meaning "true." Etumologia was the study of words' true meanings. This evolved into *etymology,* from the Old French word *ethimologie*.

Knowing the etymology of a word can help you use it effectively. You can identify subtle differences with similar or related words. You also begin to see patterns and relationships between languages, which enriches your ability to communicate with others and understand what you are reading. When reading texts that were written a long time ago, understanding the etymology of words can help clarify meanings that might otherwise become lost or misconstrued.

PRACTICE AND APPLY

The etymologies of the words below have been provided. Explain the connection between the definition of the word and its etymology, using the clues provided.

1. **confirm** – Latin: *con* – together; *firmare* – strengthen
2. **definitely** – Latin: *definitus* – bounded, limited
3. **deny** – Latin: *denagare* – refuse, reject
4. **format** – Latin: *formare* – shape
5. **unify** – Latin: *unificare* – make one

Watch Your Language!

Commas

Commas are punctuation marks that separate or set off words, phrases, or clauses within a sentence. They may be used to separate:

- parts of a compound sentence
- items in a series
- adjectives of equal rank that modify the same noun
- words to avoid confusion

Commas may also be used to set off:

- an introductory word, phrase, or dependent clause
- a parenthetical expression
- a nonessential phrase
- "not" phrases or negation
- terms of address
- parts of dates and addresses

Authors like Ambrose Bierce use commas not only to create long, complex sentences but also to add interest to their work by varying their syntax. Read this sentence from "An Occurrence at Owl Creek Bridge":

> **Encompassed in a luminous cloud, of which he was now merely the fiery heart, without material substance, he swung through unthinkable arcs of oscillation, like a vast pendulum.**

The author employs many different uses of the comma in this single sentence, creating a syntax unlike any other in the story.

- The first pair of commas set off a parenthetical phrase ("of which he was now merely the fiery heart").
- The next comma sets off an introductory adjective phrase modifying "he" ("Encompassed in a luminous cloud . . . without material substance,").
- The final comma sets off a nonessential phrase ("like a vast pendulum").

PRACTICE AND APPLY

Using the examples above as models, write your own sentences and use commas to correctly punctuate them. Your sentences should include: 1) a list of three or more items 2) a term of address 3) two adjectives that modify a noun 4) a parenthetical expression.

Get Ready

Building the Transcontinental Railroad

History Writing by **Iris Chang**

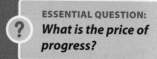

ESSENTIAL QUESTION:
What is the price of progress?

Engage Your Brain

Choose one or more of these activities to start connecting with the text you're about to read.

They Just Up and Left

In the mid-1800s, people left Guangdong, China, and emigrated all over the world. Research events and circumstances in China at that time. Which events were significant enough to induce thousands of people to leave their homeland?

Best. Invention. Ever!

Bona fide genius and world-famous inventor (your name here)______________________ just revealed an invention to solve the problem of:

______________________________.

With a partner, take turns describing your invention. Imagine trying it out in the real world. Can you foresee problems or unintended consequences?

All Aboard!

"Tell your fellow Americans that you plan to cross the United States by train, and their reactions will range from amusement at your spellbinding eccentricity to naked horror that they, through some fatal social miscalculation, have become acquainted with a person who would plan to cross the United States by train."

This quote is from New York Times travel reporter Caity Weaver, who made a cross-country trip by train. (Most Americans, incidentally, have never ridden one.) With a partner, discuss why you think Americans don't travel by train. If you have taken a train somewhere, describe your experience and your impressions of people who choose to travel long distances by train.

Analyze Ideas and Events

"Building the Transcontinental Railroad" is a **historical narrative,** an account of real events that happened in the past. Writers of historical narratives try to accurately depict events as they happened. As you read, notice the inclusion of details such as economic or cultural factors that tell you about what life was like at the time.

Writers of historical narratives usually present events in **chronological order,** or the order in which they occurred. This organizational design allows Chang to develop the sequence of events over the course of the text. Dates and time-order signal words, such as *finally, later,* and *then,* help show the connections between events. As you read, use the chart to record important events and dates.

Focus on Genre

History Writing

- is written in the third person
- usually presents events in chronological order
- places events in their historical, social, or economic context
- is based on facts from primary and secondary sources

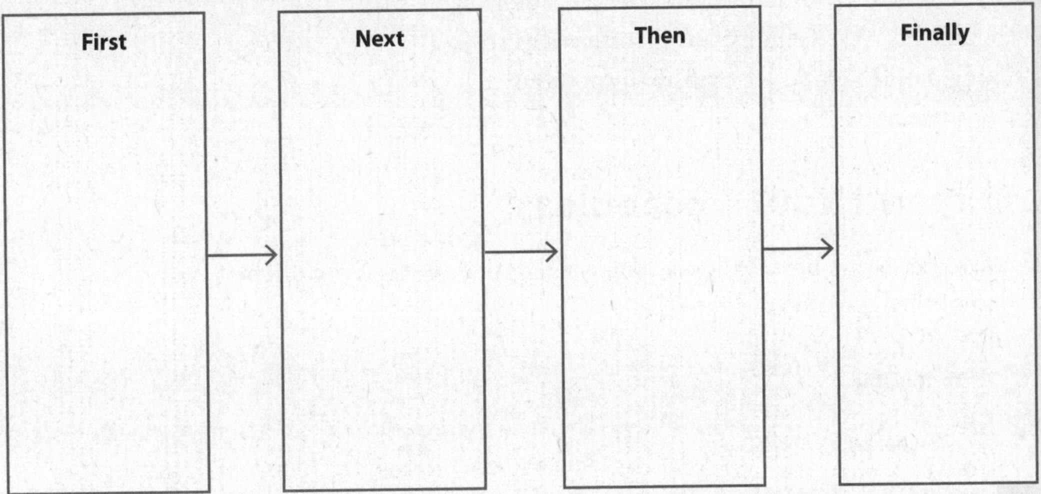

Analyze Tone

Authors write for all kinds of reasons, and it may not be clear to the reader why an author chooses to write about a topic. An author's purpose may be suggested by her diction and the way she describes events. For example, phrases that reveal Iris Chang's **tone**, or attitude toward her topic, might suggest her purpose for telling the story of Chinese laborers. An author might also include particular information from primary or secondary sources that reflect this attitude.

Ask yourself these questions to analyze Iris Chang's tone:

- What is Chang's attitude toward the treatment of Chinese laborers?
- What details and events does Chang emphasize in the account?
- How do certain descriptions and quotations from other sources reflect Chang's attitude and strengthen her message?

Annotation in Action

Here are some notes a student made about Chang's tone. As you read, mark details that suggest Chang's attitude toward her subject.

Making the vision real, however, was dangerous and frustrating. The territory between the coasts was unsettled and there was no reliable transport or route. Crossing the continent meant braving death by disease, brigands, Native Americans, starvation, thirst, heat, or freezing. This was true especially for those headed straight to the gold hills of California, but the gold rushers weren't the only ones frustrated by the lack of a safe passage between the settled East and the new state of California in the sparsely populated West. Californians themselves were impatient at waiting months to receive mail and provisions.

Chang's description of the dangers and challenges that people faced when crossing the continent suggests a serious attitude toward the subject.

Expand Your Vocabulary

Put a check mark next to the vocabulary words that you feel comfortable using when speaking or writing.

formidable	☐
expedience	☐
diligence	☐
systematize	☐

Then use the words to talk about effective teamwork. As you read "Building the Transcontinental Railroad" use the definitions in the side column to learn the vocabulary words you don't already know.

Background

Iris Chang (1968–2004) was a historian who sought to shed light on acts of injustice. Her international bestseller, *The Rape of Nanking*, documents previously unpublished accounts of brutal violence by the Japanese military during their occupation of China prior to World War II. In *The Chinese in America,* Chang traces her ethnic group's immigration experiences and achievements from the mid-19th century to the present day. This chapter from her book details the role of Chinese laborers in building a vital transportation link that fueled westward expansion in the United States.

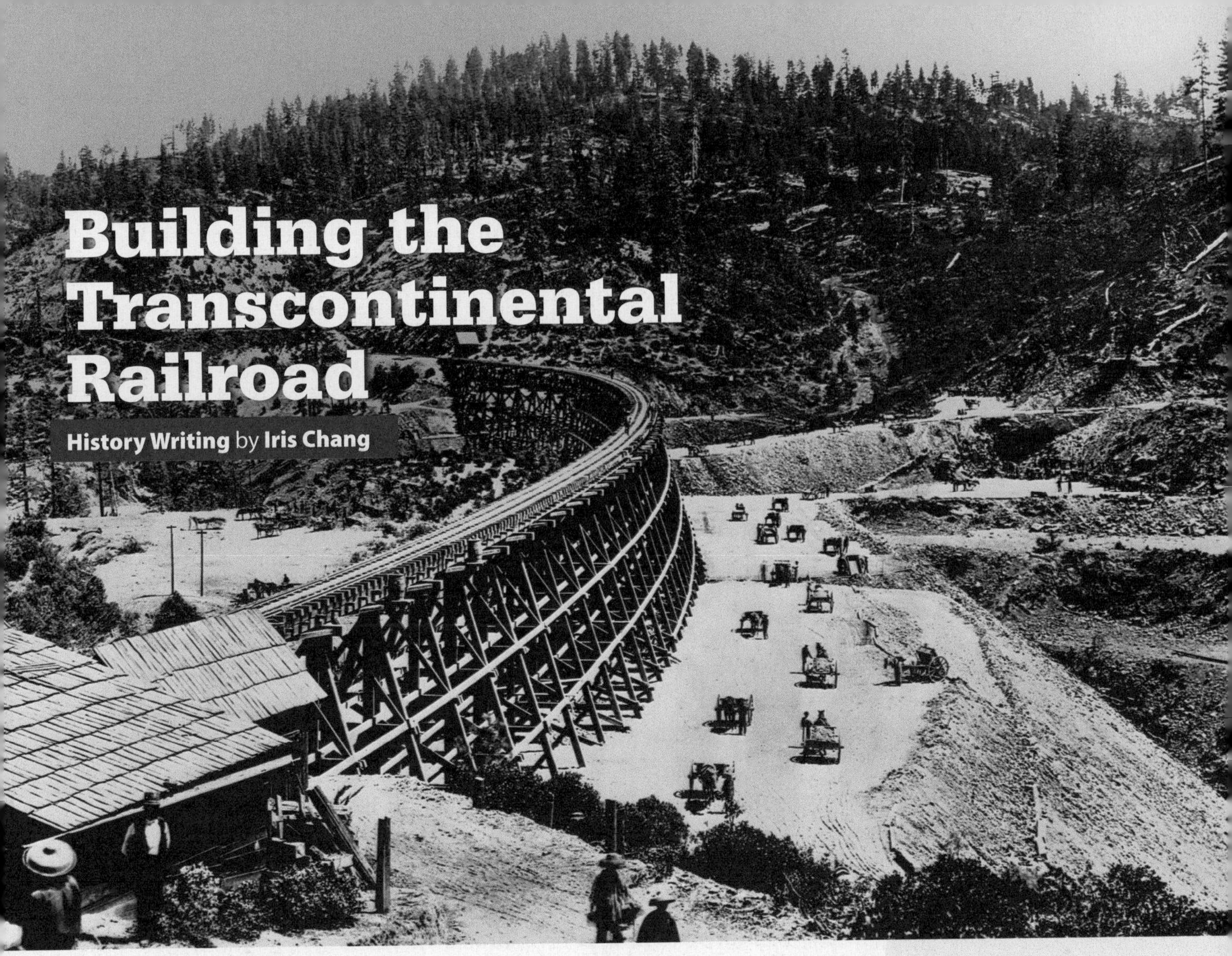

Building the Transcontinental Railroad

History Writing by **Iris Chang**

Note details that reveal Chang's attitude toward her subject and her purpose for writing.

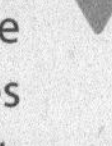

NOTICE & NOTE
As you read, use the side margins to make notes about the text.

1 *From sea to shining sea.* In the decade of the 1840s, Americans were consumed by this vision, articulated in the doctrine of Manifest Destiny, which proclaimed it the right and duty of the United States to expand its democratic way of life across the entire continent, from the Atlantic to the Pacific, from the Rio Grande in the south to the 54th parallel in the north. The country was feeling confident (during this decade, it acquired the territories of Texas, California, and Oregon), its population was increasing, and many wanted to push west, especially to California, made famous by gold and Richard Henry Dana's recounting of his adventures there, in *Two Years Before the Mast.*

2 Making the vision real, however, was dangerous and frustrating. The territory between the coasts was unsettled and there was no reliable transport or route. Crossing the continent meant braving death by disease, brigands,[1] Native Americans, starvation, thirst,

ANALYZE IDEAS AND EVENTS

Annotate: Mark two statements of time in paragraph 1 that indicate chronological order is the organization of the text.

Predict: What other details provide clues about when the events took place?

[1] **brigands:** bandits.

heat, or freezing. This was true especially for those headed straight to the gold hills of California, but the gold rushers weren't the only ones frustrated by the lack of a safe passage between the settled East and the new state of California in the sparsely populated West. Californians themselves were impatient at waiting months to receive mail and provisions. Washington, too, recognized the economic as well as political benefits of linking the country's two coasts. In the West lay rich farmland waiting for settlement, gold and silver to be mined and taxed. What was needed was a transcontinental railroad to move more people west and natural resources safely and profitably to major markets back east.

3 There were only two overland routes west—over the Rockies or along the southern route through Apache and Comanche territory—both hazardous. It took longer, but was almost always safer, to get to California from anywhere east of the Missouri by sea. This meant heading east to the Atlantic Ocean or south to the Gulf of Mexico, boarding a ship that would sail almost to the southern tip of South America, passing through the Strait of Magellan, and heading back north to California. The sea voyage could be shortened considerably by disembarking on the eastern coast of Central America, traveling by wagon across the isthmus,[2] and then hitching a ride on the first steamer headed north.[3]

ANALYZE TONE

Annotate: In paragraph 4, mark the role of the Chinese in building the transcontinental railroad.

Draw Conclusions: Why do you think Chang includes this information? What does including this information suggest about her purpose and tone?

4 The need for a transcontinental railroad was so strongly argued that Congress, with the support of President Lincoln, passed legislation to finance the railroad with government bonds, even though the country was already at war. Two companies divided the task of actual construction. In 1862, the Central Pacific Railroad Corporation, headed by the "Big Four"—Leland Stanford, Collis P. Huntington, Charles Crocker, and Mark Hopkins—was awarded the contract to lay tracks eastward from Sacramento, while its rival, the Union Pacific, was awarded the path westward from Omaha, Nebraska, which was already connected to the East through existing rail lines. The goal was to meet in the middle, connecting the nation with a continuous stretch of railroad tracks from the Atlantic to the Pacific. The Union Pacific's job—laying track over plains—was much easier, while the Central Pacific had to go over steep mountains. The Central Pacific engineers promised that the **formidable** physical obstacles could be overcome, and to a great extent, it was Chinese labor, and even, here and there, Chinese ingenuity, that helped make the transcontinental railroad a reality.

formidable
(fôr´mĭ-də-bəl) *adj.* difficult and intimidating.

5 The first and largest challenge was figuring out how to cut a path through California's and Nevada's rugged Sierra Nevada, which stood as a final barrier to the West. The workers of the Central Pacific had the dangerous task of ramming tunnels through these mountains, and then laying tracks across the parched Nevada and Utah deserts. Some

[2] **isthmus** (ĭs´məs): a thin strip of land between two bodies of water.

[3] Eventually, U.S. engineers would build the Panama Canal in the early twentieth century. [Author's note]

engineers, watching the project from afar, said this was impossible. In a major recruitment drive for five thousand workers, the Central Pacific sent advertisements to every post office in the state of California, offering high wages to any white man willing to work. But the appeal secured only eight hundred. Why toil for wages when an instant fortune was possible in the mines? Many men who did sign on were, in the words of company superintendent James Strobridge, "unsteady men, unreliable. Some of them would stay a few days, and some would not go to work at all. Some would stay until payday, get a little money, get drunk, and clear out." The company thought of asking the War Department for five thousand Confederate prisoners to put to work, but Lee's surrender at the Appomattox Court House ended the war and this plan.

Don't forget to **Notice & Note** as you read the text.

6 Fortunately for the Central Pacific, Chinese immigrants provided a vast pool of cheap, plentiful, and easily exploitable labor. By 1865, the number of Chinese in California reached close to fifty thousand, at least 90 percent of them young men. In the spring of that year, when white laborers demanded higher pay and threatened to strike, Charles Crocker, the Central Pacific's chief contractor, ordered Superintendent Strobridge to recruit Chinese workers. The tactic worked, and the white workers agreed to return, as long as no Chinese were hired, but by then the Central Pacific had the upper hand and hired fifty Chinese anyway—former miners, laundry men, domestic servants, and market gardeners—to do the hard labor of preparing the route and laying track. Many claimed the railroad did this as a reminder to the white workers that others were ready to replace them. Needless to say, this did not contribute to harmony between the whites and the Chinese.

7 Of course prejudice against the Chinese railroad workers did not start with the white laborers. Initially, Superintendent Strobridge was unhappy with their being hired. "I will not boss Chinese!" he roared, suggesting that the Chinese were too delicate for the job. (The Chinese averaged four feet ten inches in height and weighed 120 pounds.) Crocker, however, pointed out that a race of people who had built the Great Wall of China could build a railroad. Grudgingly, Strobridge put the Chinese to work, giving them light jobs, like filling dump carts.

8 To the surprise of many—but apparently not the Chinese themselves—the first fifty hired excelled at their work, becoming such disciplined, fast learners that the railroad soon gave them other responsibilities, such as rock cuts. In time, the Central Pacific hired another fifty Chinese, and then another fifty, until eventually the company employed thousands of Chinese laborers—the overwhelming majority of the railroad workforce. E. B. Crocker, brother of Charles, wrote to Senator Cornelius Cole (R-Calif.) that the Chinese were nearly equal to white men in the amount of work they could do and far more reliable. Leland Stanford, the railroad's president, and later the founder of Stanford University, praised the

ANALYZE IDEAS AND EVENTS

Annotate: Mark the phrases in paragraph 8 that signal chronological order.

Analyze: How do these phrases help you understand the sequence of events?

expedience
(ĭk-spē´dē-əns) *n.* a self-interested means to an end.

Chinese as "quiet, peaceable, patient, industrious and economical." (Stanford's position on the Chinese was governed by **expedience.** In 1862, to please the racist sentiments of the state, he called the Chinese in California the "dregs" of Asia, a "degraded" people. A few years later, he was praising the Chinese to President Andrew Johnson and others in order to justify the Central Pacific's mass hiring of Chinese. Later still—notably in 1884, when he ran for the U.S. Senate—he would ally himself with those who favored a ban on Chinese immigration.)

9 Delighted by the productivity of the Chinese, railroad executives became fervent[4] advocates of Chinese immigration to California. "I like the idea of your getting over more Chinamen," Collis Huntington, one of the "Big Four" executives at the Central Pacific, wrote to Charlie Crocker in 1867. "It would be all the better for us and the State if there should a half million come over in 1868."

10 The Central Pacific printed handbills and dispatched recruiters to China, especially the Guangdong province, to find new workers. It negotiated with a steamship company to lower their rates for travel. And, fortuitously[5] for the Central Pacific, Sino-American diplomacy would create more favorable conditions for Chinese immigration to the United States. In 1868, China and the U.S. government signed the Burlingame Treaty. In exchange for "most favored nation" status in trade, China agreed to recognize the "inherent and inalienable right of man to change his home and allegiance and also the mutual advantage of free migration and emigration of their citizens and subjects respectively from one country to the other for purposes of curiosity or trade or as permanent residents."

11 The new Chinese recruits docked at San Francisco and were immediately transported by riverboat to Sacramento, and then by the Central Pacific's own train to the end of the laid tracks, which was a moving construction site. There they were organized into teams of about a dozen or so, with each team assigned its own cook and headman, who communicated with the Central Pacific foreman. The Chinese paid for their own food and cooked it themselves—they were even able to procure special ingredients like cuttlefish, bamboo shoots, and abalone. At night they slept in tents provided by the railroad, or in dugouts in the earth. At the peak of construction, Central Pacific would employ more than ten thousand Chinese men.

NOTICE & NOTE
QUOTED WORDS

When you notice the author citing other people to provide support for a point, you've found a **Quoted Words** signpost.

Notice & Note: Mark the quotations in paragraph 12 that describe the work ethic of the various groups laboring on the railroad.

Compare: What point is the author reinforcing by including these quotations?

12 The large number of Chinese made white workers uncomfortable. As Lee Chew, a railroad laborer, later recalled in a spasm of national pride, the Chinese were "persecuted not for their vices but for their virtues. No one would hire an Irishman, German, Englishman or Italian when he could get a Chinese, because our countrymen are so much more honest, industrious, steady, sober and painstaking." Crocker explicitly acknowledged this work ethic. After recruiting

[4] **fervent:** avid, enthusiastic.
[5] **fortuitously:** luckily; by favorable chance.

Don't forget to **Notice & Note** as you read the text.

some Cornish miners from Virginia City, Nevada, to excavate one end of a tunnel and the Chinese the other, he commented, "The Chinese, without fail, always outmeasured the Cornish miners. That is to say, they would cut more rock in a week than the Cornish miners did. And here it was hard work, steady pounding on the rock, bone-labor." The Cornish eventually walked off the job, vowing that "they would not work with Chinamen anyhow," and soon, Crocker recalled, "the Chinamen had possession of the whole work."

13 White laborers began to feel that Chinese **diligence** forced everyone to work harder for less reward. Crocker recalled that one white laborer near Auburn was questioned by a gentleman about his wages. "I think we were paying $35 a month and board to white laborers, and $30 a month to Chinamen and they boarded themselves," Crocker said. "The gentleman remarked, 'That is pretty good wages.' 'Yes,' says he, 'but begad if it wasn't for them damned nagurs we would get $50 and not do half the work.' "

diligence
(dĭl´ə-jəns) *n.* consistent, thorough effort and dedication.

14 Some white laborers on the Central Pacific whispered among themselves about driving the Chinese off the job, but when Charles Crocker got wind of this, he threatened to replace all the whites with Chinese. Eventually the white workers gave up, placated[6] perhaps by being told that they alone could be promoted to the position of foreman. The more Chinese workers, the fewer whites in the labor force and the less competition for foreman positions among the whites. And foremen were paid several times the wages of a Chinese laborer.

[6] **placated:** made peaceful or less angry.

15 In the process of laying the track across northern California, Nevada, and Utah, hundreds of men—Chinese, Irish, German, and others—cleared a path through some of the world's largest trees, some with stumps so deeply rooted that ten barrels of gunpowder were often needed to unearth them. It was dangerous work—work that loosened boulders, started landslides, and filled the air with flying debris. Even more dangerous was the work that began upon reaching the Sierra Nevada.

16 Ideally, the roadbed[7] through the mountains would be tunneled through by heavy machinery. This machinery was unavailable, however, because it was expensive and difficult to transport (entire bridges would have had to be rebuilt for such machinery to reach the current site). Thus the Chinese were forced to chisel tunnels through the granite using only handheld drills, explosives, and shovels. In some places they encountered a form of porphyritic[8] rock so hard it was impervious[9] to frontal attack, even with gunpowder. Work proceeded, on average, seven inches a day, at a cost of as much as a million dollars for one mile of tunnel.

ANALYZE TONE

Annotate: Mark in paragraphs 17 and 18 what Chinese workers did and what happened to some of them.

Analyze: What tone is suggested by the diction in these paragraphs?

17 In the summer of 1866, to move farther faster, the railroad kept several shifts of men going day and night. Shoulder to shoulder, hour after hour, the Chinese railroad workers chipped away at the rock, breathing granite dust, sweating and panting by the dim flickering glow of candlelight, until even the strongest of them fainted from exhaustion.

18 Finally, to speed up the process, the Central Pacific brought in nitroglycerin. Only the Chinese—a people experienced with fireworks—were willing to handle this unpredictable explosive, pouring it into the tunnel through holes drilled in the granite. Countless workers perished in accidental blasts, but the Central Pacific did not keep track of the numbers.

19 Still the workers struggled on. One terrifying challenge lay at Cape Horn, the nickname for a three-mile stretch of gorge above the American River three miles east of Colfax, California, and fifty-seven miles east of Sacramento. Through much of the way, a flat roadbed had to be carved along a steep cliff, and a Chinese headman suggested to Strobridge that they employ an ancient method used to create fortresses along the Yangtze River gorges: they could dangle supplies down to the work site in reed baskets, attached to ropes secured over the tops of mountains.

20 Reeds were shipped out immediately from San Francisco to Cape Horn. At night the Chinese workers wove them into wicker baskets and fastened them to sturdy ropes. When everything was ready, workers were lowered in the baskets to drill holes and tamp in dynamite, literally sculpting the rail bed out of the face of sheer rock. The lucky ones were hauled up in time to escape the explosions;

[7] **roadbed:** the path or foundation on which railroad tracks are laid.
[8] **porphyritic** (pôr´fə-rĭt´ĭk): rock containing relatively large, visible crystals.
[9] **impervious:** immune or resistant.

others, peppered with shards of granite and shale, fell to their deaths in the valley below.

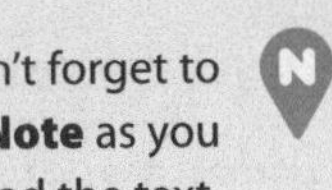

Don't forget to **Notice & Note** as you read the text.

21 Disease swept through the ranks of the exhausted railroad workers, but the Chinese fared better than whites. Caucasian laborers, subsisting largely on salt beef, potatoes, bread, coffee, and rancid butter, lacked vegetables in their diet, while the Chinese employed their own cooks and ate better-balanced meals. White workers succumbed to dysentery after sharing communal dippers from greasy pails, but the Chinese drank fresh boiled tea, which they kept in whiskey barrels or powder kegs suspended from each end of a bamboo pole. They also avoided alcohol and, "not having acquired the taste of whiskey," as one contemporary observed, "they have fewer fights and no blue Mondays." Most important, they kept themselves clean, which helped prevent the spread of germs. The white men had "a sort of hydrophobia," one writer observed, whereas the Chinese bathed every night before dinner, in powder kegs filled with heated water.

ANALYZE TONE

Annotate: Mark the direct quotations from a primary source in paragraph 21.

Infer: What is the purpose of including this account in the narrative?

22 In the Sierras, the railroad workers endured two of the worst winters in American history. In 1865, they faced thirty-foot drifts and spent weeks just shoveling snow. The following year brought the "Homeric winter" of 1866–67, one of the most brutal ever recorded, which dropped forty feet of snow on the crews and whipped up drifts more than eighty feet high. Power snowplows, driven forward by twelve locomotives linked together, could scarcely budge the densest of these drifts. Sheds built to protect the uncompleted tracks collapsed under the weight of the snow, which snapped even the best timber. On the harshest days, travel was almost impossible; as horses broke the icy crust, sharp edges slashed their legs to the bone. They received mail from a Norwegian postal worker on cross-country skis.

23 Making the best of the situation, the Chinese carved a working city under the snow. Operating beneath the crust by lantern light, they trudged through a labyrinth of snow tunnels, with snow chimneys and snow stairs leading up to the surface. Meanwhile, they continued to shape the rail bed out of rock, using materials lowered down to them through airshafts in the snow.

24 The cost in human life was enormous. Snow slides and avalanches swept away entire teams of Chinese workers. On Christmas Day 1866, the *Dutch Flat Enquirer* announced that "a gang of Chinamen employed by the railroad . . . were covered up by a snow slide and four or five died before they could be exhumed. Then snow fell to such a depth that one whole camp of Chinamen was covered up during the night and parties were digging them out when our informant left." When the snow melted in the spring, the company found corpses still standing erect, their frozen hands gripping picks and shovels.

ANALYZE TONE

Annotate: Mark in paragraph 25 obstacles the laborers faced.

Draw Conclusions: Why does the writer include such vivid details? What tone, or attitude, does the inclusion of these details suggest?

25 Winter was only one obstacle. Other conditions also affected the workers. Landslides rolled tons of soil across the completed track, blocking its access and often smothering workers. Melting snow mired wagons, carts, and stagecoaches in a sea of mud. Once through the mountains, the crews faced terrible extremes of weather in the Nevada and Utah deserts. There the temperature could plummet to 50 degrees below zero—freezing the ground so hard it required blasting, as if it were bedrock—or soar above 120, causing heat stroke and dehydration.

systematize
(sĭs´tə-mə-tīz) *v.* to form something into an organized plan or scheme.

26 The Chinese labored from sunrise to sunset six days a week, in twelve-hour shifts. Only on Sundays did they have time to rest, mend their clothes, talk, smoke, and, of course, gamble.[10] The tedium of their lives was aggravated by the **systematized** abuse and contempt heaped on them by the railroad executives. The Chinese worked longer and harder than whites, but received less pay: because the Chinese had to pay for their own board, their wages were two-thirds those of white workers and a fourth those of the white foremen. (Even the allocation for feed for horses—fifty dollars a month for each—was twenty dollars more than the average Chinese worker earned.) Worst of all, they endured whippings from their overseers, who treated them like slaves.

[10] Gambling was as addictive for Chinese railroad workers as whiskey among their white counterparts. Chinese gamblers left their mark on Nevada, where casinos credit the nineteenth-century Chinese railroad workers with introducing the game of keno, based on the Chinese lottery game of *pak kop piu*. [Author's note]

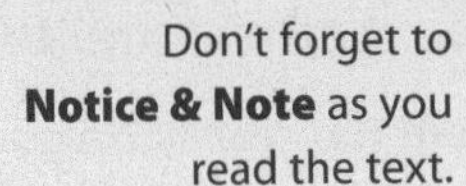

27 Finally, the Chinese rebelled. In June 1867, as the Central Pacific tottered[11] on the brink of bankruptcy (Leland Stanford later described a two-week period when there was not a dollar of cash in the treasury), some two thousand Chinese in the Sierras walked off the job. As was their way in a strange land, they conducted the strike politely, appointing headmen to present James Strobridge a list of demands that included more pay and fewer hours in the tunnels. They also circulated among themselves a placard written in Chinese, explaining their rights. In retrospect, it is surprising that they managed to organize a strike at all, for there are also reports of frequent feuds erupting between groups of Chinese workers, fought with spades, crowbars, and spikes. But organize they did.

ANALYZE IDEAS AND EVENTS

Annotate: Mark words in paragraph 27 that suggest chronological order.

Summarize: Restate the sequence of events in the paragraph.

28 The Central Pacific reacted swiftly and ruthlessly. An enraged Charles Crocker contacted employment agencies in an attempt to recruit ten thousand recently freed American blacks to replace the Chinese. He stopped payments to the Chinese and cut off the food supply, effectively starving them back to work. Because most of them could not speak English, could not find work elsewhere, and lacked transportation back to California, the strike lasted only a week. However, it did achieve a small victory, securing the Chinese a raise of two dollars a month. More important, by staging the largest Chinese strike of the nineteenth century, they demonstrated to their current and future employers that while they were willing and easily managed workers, if pushed hard enough they were able to organize to protect themselves, even in the face of daunting odds.

29 Later, the railroad management expressed admiration at the orderliness of the strike. "If there had been that number of whites in a strike, there would have been murder and drunkenness and disorder," Crocker marveled. "But with the Chinese it was just like Sunday. These men stayed in their camps. They would come out and walk around, but not a word was said; nothing was done. No violence was perpetuated[12] along the whole line."

30 The Chinese were certainly capable, however, of violence. As the railroad neared completion, the Chinese encountered the Irish workers of the Union Pacific for the first time. When the two companies came within a hundred feet of each other, the Union Pacific Irish taunted the Chinese with catcalls and threw clods of dirt. When the Chinese ignored them, the Irish swung their picks at them, and to the astonishment of the whites, the Chinese fought back. The level of antagonism continued to rise. Several Chinese were wounded by blasting powder the whites had secretly planted near their side. Several days later, a mysterious explosion killed several Irish workers. The presumption was that the Chinese had retaliated in kind. At that point, the behavior of white workers toward the Chinese immediately improved.

[11] **tottered:** wobbled unsteadily.
[12] **perpetuated:** sustained.

ANALYZE IDEAS AND EVENTS

Annotate: Mark the date and time in paragraph 31.

Evaluate: How does the use of dates and times help you understand the bet and how Crocker felt about the Chinese laborers?

31 If relations were often tense between the Chinese and the Irish, there were also moments of camaraderie.[13] In April 1869, the Central Pacific and Union Pacific competed to see who could throw down track the fastest. The competition arose after Charlie Crocker bragged that the Chinese could construct ten miles of track a day. (In some regions, the Union Pacific had averaged only one mile a week.) So confident was Crocker in his employees that he was willing to wager $10,000 against Thomas Durant, the vice president of Union Pacific. On the day of the contest, the Central Pacific had eight Irish workers unload materials while the Chinese spiked, gauged, and bolted the track, laying it down as fast as a man could walk. They broke the Union Pacific record by completing more than ten miles of track within twelve hours and forty-five minutes.

32 On May 10, 1869, when the railways from the east and west were finally joined at Promontory Point, Utah, the Central Pacific had built 690 miles of track and the Union Pacific 1,086 miles. The two coasts were now welded together. Before the transcontinental railroad, trekking across the country took four to six months. On the railroad, it would take six days. This accomplishment created fortunes for the moguls of the Gilded Age, but it also exacted a monumental sacrifice in blood and human life. On average, three laborers perished for every two miles of track laid, and eventually more than one thousand Chinese railroad workers died, with twenty thousand pounds of their bones shipped to China.[14] Without Chinese labor and know-how, the railroad would not have been completed. Nonetheless, the Central Pacific Railroad cheated the Chinese railway workers of everything they could. They tried to write the Chinese out of history altogether. The Chinese workers were not only excluded from the ceremonies, but from the famous photograph of white American laborers celebrating as the last spike, the golden spike, was driven into the ground. Of more immediate concern, the Central Pacific immediately laid off most of the Chinese workers, refusing to give them even their promised return passage to California. The company retained only a few hundred of them for maintenance work, some of whom spent their remaining days in isolated small towns along the way, a few living in converted boxcars.

33 The rest of the Chinese former railway workers were now homeless as well as jobless, in a harsh and hostile environment. Left to fend for themselves, some straggled by foot through the hinterlands[15] of America, looking for work that would allow them to survive, a journey that would disperse them throughout the nation.

---

[13] **camaraderie:** friendly companionship.

[14] Years later, some of the Chinese railroad workers would journey back to the Sierra Nevada to search for the remains of their colleagues. On these expeditions, known as *jup seen you* ("retrieving deceased friends"), they would hunt for old grave sites, usually a heap of stones near the tracks marked by a wooden stake. Digging underneath the stones, they would find a skeleton next to a wax-sealed bottle, holding a strip of cloth inscribed with the worker's name, birth date, and district of origin. [Author's note]

[15] **hinterlands:** remote areas.

COLLABORATIVE DISCUSSION

Pair up with a classmate and discuss how prejudice and racism complicated the Chinese workers' efforts to build the railroad. Cite text evidence to support your ideas.

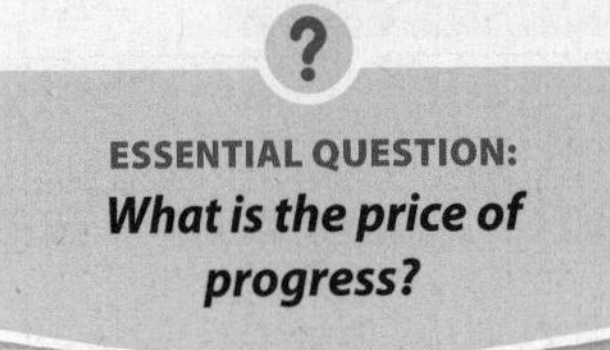
?
ESSENTIAL QUESTION:
What is the price of progress?

Review your notes and add your thoughts to your **Response Log.**

Assessment Practice

Answer these questions before moving on to the **Analyze the Text** section on the following page.

1. Why did the Central Pacific hire so many Chinese workers?

- (A) Americans generally preferred Chinese workers.
- (B) The Chinese had experience building railroads.
- (C) The Chinese were diligent and effective workers.
- (D) The government required hiring Chinese workers.

2. Why did Crocker remind Strobridge that the Chinese had built the Great Wall of China?

- (A) to show that the Chinese could do demanding work
- (B) to demonstrate knowledge about Chinese history
- (C) to bring harmony between Chinese and white workers
- (D) to suggest that the Chinese build a wall as well as the railroad

3. When white workers plotted to drive off the Chinese workers, Charles Crocker —

- (A) offered the white workers more money to stay on the job
- (B) threatened to replace all the whites with Chinese workers
- (C) encouraged them to follow through with their plans
- (D) fired all the white workers for having a bad attitude

Ed

Test-Taking Strategies

Analyze the Text

Support your responses with evidence from the text.

NOTICE & NOTE

Review what you **noticed and noted** as you read the text. Your annotations can help you answer these questions.

1. **INFER** What is Iris Chang's purpose for writing "Building the Transcontinental Railroad"? Cite evidence from the text that helps you infer her purpose.

2. **ANALYZE** Provide examples of word choice and details that reflect her tone. Based on your evidence, what tone does Chang convey on the topic of Chinese workers?

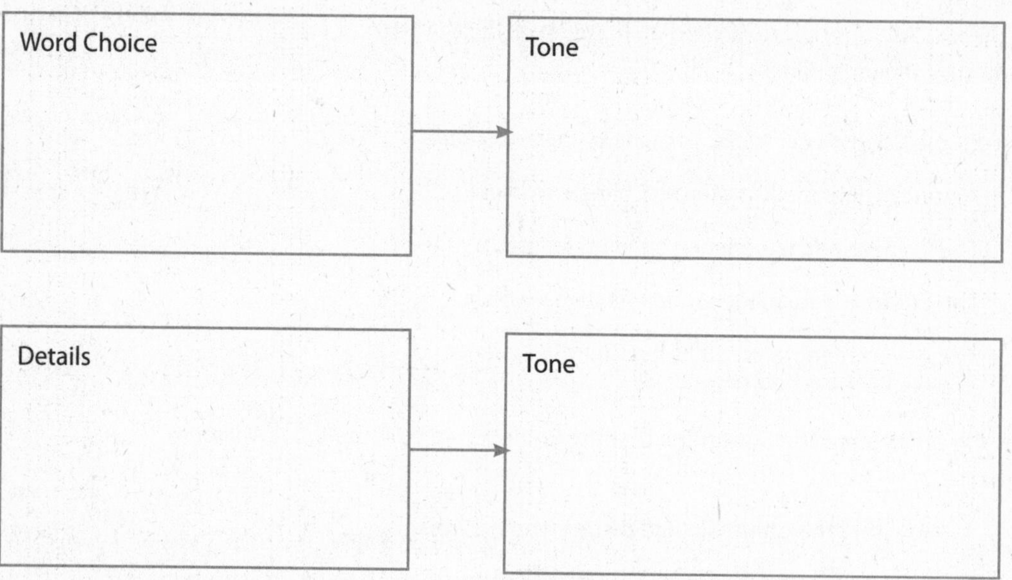

3. **CAUSE AND EFFECT** According to Chang, what economic, social, and political forces caused the United States to decide that building the railroad was important?

4. **EVALUATE** Chang includes quotations from primary sources in the text. How does Chang's use of these **Quoted Words** contribute to the effectiveness of her message? Cite specific examples in your response.

5. **ANALYZE** Why does the author present examples of how the Chinese usually acted as well as instances when they were assertive or aggressive? What does this contrast add to your understanding of these workers?

6. **SUMMARIZE** Look back at the chart on page 441 that you filled in as you read. In your own words, summarize the events that led to the completion of the Transcontinental Railroad. Does your summary follow the events Chang laid out? Did Chang follow a strict chronological order?

Choices

Here are some other ways to demonstrate your understanding of the ideas in this lesson.

Writing

↳ Explanation

Iris Chang recounts that Chinese railroad workers returned to the Sierra Nevada and retrieved the remains of the workers who died so their bones could be returned to China. Research traditional Chinese funeral rites, then write a paragraph that explains why the railway workers would have tried to find their fallen colleagues.

As you write and discuss, be sure to use the **Academic Vocabulary** words.

- confirm
- definitely
- deny
- format
- unify

Media

↳ The Golden Spike

As a class, find photographs related to the Golden Spike monument. Post them to a photo-sharing site and create a response thread.

1. Everyone in the class should contribute at least one photo and one comment.
2. Provide a credit if the photograph is not in the public domain.
3. If you respond to someone else's post, be respectful, even if you dislike the photo or disagree with the comment.
4. When everyone has commented, summarize the responses. What was the class reaction to this historical event?

Speaking & Listening

↳ Class Discussion

In a speech that marked the 150th anniversary of the completion of the Transcontinental Railroad, Connie Young Yu, a descendant of a Chinese railroad worker, recounted the story of Chinese and Irish workers who laid 10 miles of track in a day. She then made this claim:

"This record-setting feat on the road to Promontory is unequaled in history. The trust and cooperation between workers with a common purpose was a zenith of the human spirit."

As a class, discuss whether the building of the Transcontinental Railroad as described in Chang's account did in fact require effort and teamwork that is uparallelled in human history. Before the discussion, research other examples of outstanding human achievements that could rival the Transcontinental Railroad as representing the "zenith of the human spirit."

Expand Your Vocabulary

PRACTICE AND APPLY

Use your knowledge of the vocabulary words in your written responses.

formidable	expedience	diligence	systematize

1. Describe something you did with **diligence**.
2. Identify an action that someone took that was driven by **expedience**.
3. Tell about a **formidable** task that you have studied in history.
4. Explain how to **systematize** the college application process.

Vocabulary Strategy
Context Clues

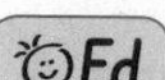

Interactive Vocabulary Lesson: Using Context Clues

Context clues—the words and ideas in the surrounding phrases and sentences—can help you determine the meaning of an unknown word. For example, the writer might include an example, an explanation, a definition, or suggest a similarity or contrast. Notice how the highlighted context clues in the examples from "Building the Transcontinental Railroad" can help you determine the meaning of the boldfaced words.

Context Clue	Example
Suggest a similarity: diligence is hard work	. . . Chinese **diligence** forced everyone to work harder for less reward.
Suggest a contrast: something formidable is difficult to overcome	The Central Pacific engineers promised that the **formidable** physical obstacles could be overcome, . . .

PRACTICE AND APPLY

Use context clues in "Building the Transcontinental Railroad" to determine the meaning of the following words and terms. Confirm the meaning of each word in a dictionary and then use it in a new sentence.

1. doctrine of Manifest Destiny (paragraph 1)
2. parched (paragraph 5)
3. succumb (paragraph 21)
4. exhume (paragraph 24)

Watch Your Language!

Misplaced Modifiers

Modifiers are words or groups of words that change or limit the meaning of other words. For example, adjectives and adjectival phrases modify nouns by telling which one, what kind, how many, or how much. Adverbs and adverbial phrases modify verbs, adjectives, and other adverbs by telling where, when, how, or to what extent. Chang's careful placement of modifiers contributes to the clarity and readability of her text.

In less professional writing, a modifier is sometimes placed in the wrong place or so far away from the word it modifies that the intended meaning of the sentence is unclear. To correct a sentence with a misplaced modifier, you must first find the word being modified. Then, place the modifying word or phrase as close as possible to the word it modifies.

Interactive Grammar Lesson: Misplaced Modifiers

Read the following sentence with a misplaced modifier:

The railroad workers gathered the necessary supplies to finish the tunnel before starting.

The placement of the prepositional phrase *before starting* creates confusion, because it seems to modify "to finish the tunnel." Finishing the tunnel before starting would be impossible.

Here the sentence has been revised for clarity so that the prepositional phrase properly functions as the adverb modifying the verb *gathered*.

Before starting, the railroad workers gathered the necessary supplies to finish the tunnel.

PRACTICE AND APPLY

Find the misplaced modifiers in each sentence and briefly explain why they are confusing. Then, revise each sentence to correct the misplaced modifiers. Refer to the text if you are unsure about the intended meaning of a sentence.

1. Disembarking the ship and crossing the Isthmus of Panama on the sea voyage by wagon could shorten the trip to the West Coast considerably.
2. The Union Pacific Railroad was contracted to build westward from Omaha, Nebraska, across the plains already connected to other railways in the East.
3. Unpredictable and dangerous, many workers were killed by the explosives.
4. Everyone praised the railroad workers' accomplishments at the ceremony.

Collaborate & Compare

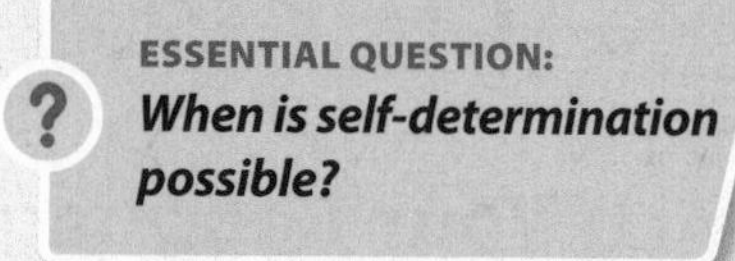

Compare Arguments

Trace the development of each argument by identifying its claim and the reasons and evidence that support the claim. Consider how the arguments are similar and how they are different.

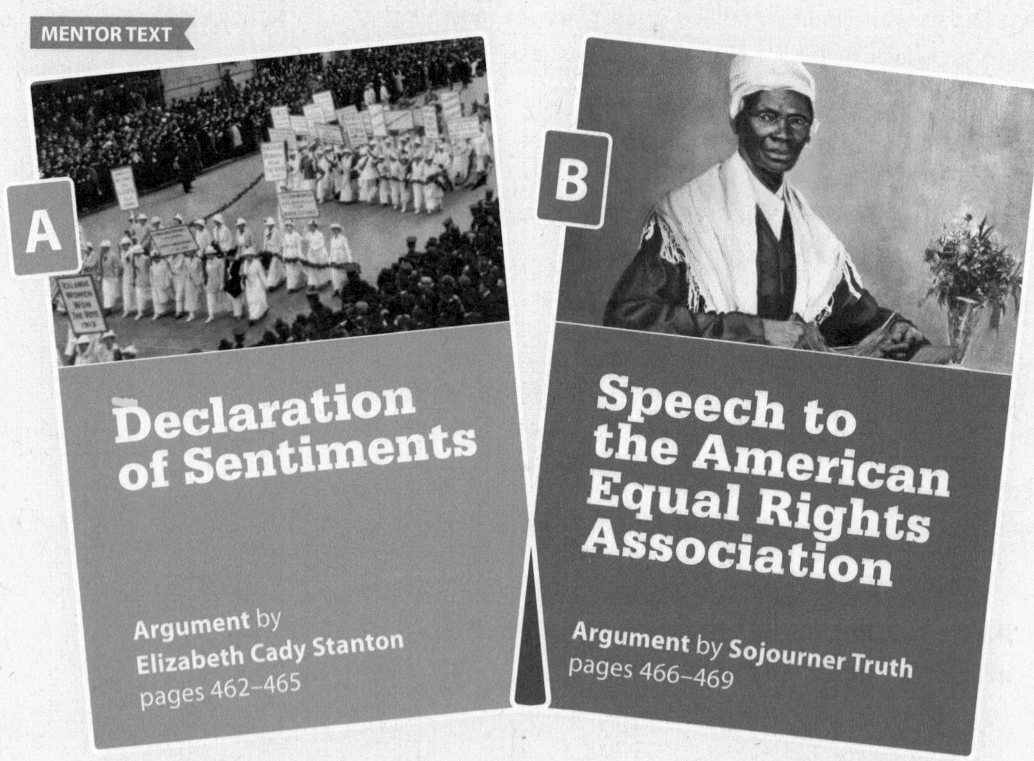

After you have read the arguments, you will evaluate the effectiveness and validity of each claim and the reasoning that supports the claims. You will follow these steps:

- Evaluate both arguments
- Choose and organize details to support your evaluation
- Present your ideas in a group discussion

Declaration of Sentiments

Argument by **Elizabeth Cady Stanton**

Speech to the American Equal Rights Association

Argument by **Sojourner Truth**

Engage Your Brain

Choose one or more of these activities to start connecting with the arguments you're about to read.

Convince Me

Your friend wants to watch *Avengers: End Game* for the bazillionth time. Which of these arguments works best to convince you?

- "Seriously, it's the best movie ever. The plot is gripping, the characters are engaging—it's the ultimate battle of good v. evil! Awesome acting, fabulous special effects… it's easily the best of the Marvel movies."
- "You're my best friend. I concede that I might be obsessed with this movie. But best friends are morally obligated to support their friends and loved ones as they work through their obsessions."
- "You LOVE that part where Iron Man steals the Stones and destroys Thanos. You've told me over and over that it's your favorite scene—makes you cry every time. C'mon, you know you wanna see it again. You know you do!"

Then, get with a partner and try using similar arguments to convince your classmate to read a book, see a movie, or attend an event. Which approach works best?

Your Vote, Your Voice

"The vote is the emblem of your equality, women of America, the guarantee of your liberty. That vote of yours has cost millions of dollars and the lives of thousands of women. …Women have suffered agony of soul which you can never comprehend, that you and your daughters might inherit political freedom. That vote has been costly. Prize it! The vote is a power, a weapon of offense and defense, a prayer. Understand what it means and what it can do for your country. Use it intelligently, conscientiously, prayerfully."

Carrie Chapman Catt, founder of The League of Women Voters, wrote that in 1920, shortly after the Nineteenth Amendment was ratified. Are her views still relevant today? If so, for whom? Discuss with a partner.

Bring Back the American Equal Rights Association

The American Equal Rights Association was founded in 1866, shortly after the Civil War ended. It lasted until 1869 and promoted causes like a woman's right to vote. If an organization by this name were around today, what issues and problems do you think it would tackle?

Analyze Rhetoric

Writers of arguments use **rhetorical appeals** to sway readers to adopt a position or take an action. The forms of appeal used in the strongest arguments are defined in the chart.

Appeal	Definition
Logical appeal (Logos)	use of reason and evidence to persuade
Emotional appeal (Pathos)	an appeal to the audience's humor, compassion, sense of beauty, or other emotions to reinforce the logical argument
Ethical appeal (Ethos)	an appeal to the audience's sense of fairness and morality
Appeal to time and place (Kairos)	an appeal with the appropriate tone and structure for the audience at the time

Be aware that not all appeals are effective. For example, emotional appeals that misrepresent an opponent's argument or logical appeals that include errors in reasoning are ineffective. As you read, evaluate the effectiveness of the appeals Stanton and Truth use to persuade their audiences.

Evaluate Arguments

The purpose of an argument is to convince the audience to agree with a position or to take a certain action. Authors may use these **persuasive techniques** to make their arguments more compelling.

- **repetition**—repeated words and phrases. Writers may use repetition to emphasize ideas. If a writer repeats a word or phrase at the beginning of consecutive lines or sentences, then that repetition is called **anaphora.**
- **parallelism**—the use of components in a sentence that are grammatically similar. It may be used to tell readers that ideas are equally important.
- **allusion**—a reference to another familiar person, place, or event. Writers may use allusion to make a connection.

Stanton's text alludes to the Declaration of Independence written by Thomas Jefferson. Stanton went beyond simple adaptation by incorporating the style and content, as well as the format of Jefferson's text. As you read, think about why Stanton uses Jefferson's structure and rhetoric for her own argument.

Focus on Genre
Argument

- contains a clearly stated claim or opinion
- includes reasons and evidence that support the claim
- uses appeals to reason, emotion, and ethics to persuade the reader

Annotation in Action

Here are one student's comments on Stanton's use of appeals to strengthen her argument. As you read, notice how the writers support their arguments.

We hold these truths to be self-evident; that all men and women are created equal; that they are endowed by their Creator with certain inalienable rights; that among these are life, liberty, and the pursuit of happiness

This is from the Declaration of Independence. Does her argument have something in common with it?

Expand Your Vocabulary

Put a check mark next to the vocabulary words that you feel comfortable using when speaking or writing.

transient	☐
supposition	☐
delinquency	☐
abject	☐
consolation	☐

Then write a synonym next to the words you are already familiar with. As you read the "Declaration of Sentiments" and the "Speech to the American Equal Rights Association," use the definitions in the side-column to learn the vocabulary words you don't already know.

Background

The 1848 "Declaration of Sentiments" was presented at the Seneca Falls Convention, the birthplace of the women's rights movement in the United States. **Elizabeth Cady Stanton** (1815–1902) and Lucretia Mott (1793–1880) had first discussed the idea for the conference at the World Anti-Slavery Convention in London in 1840. Active abolitionists, the women had been denied the right to participate in the convention because of their gender.

Sojourner Truth (c. 1797–1883) was born into slavery. She escaped in 1827 and lived the rest of her life as a free woman. A religious woman, she changed her name from Isabella Baumfree to Sojourner Truth in 1843. As an advocate for the rights of African Americans and women, Truth delivered this candid address to a progressive audience not long after the signing of the Emancipation Proclamation, which freed three million enslaved people.

Declaration of Sentiments

Argument by **Elizabeth Cady Stanton**

NOTICE & NOTE

As your read, use the side margins to make notes about the text.

Think about the problem Stanton identifies and how she crafts her argument to propose a solution for it.

Put forth at Seneca Falls, N.Y., July 19th *and* 20th, 1848.

EVALUATE ARGUMENTS

Annotate: Mark details in paragraphs 1 and 2 that recall the Declaration of Independence.

Infer: Why might this allusion be appealing to Stanton's audience?

1 When, in the course of human events, it becomes necessary for one portion of the family of man to assume among the people of the earth a position different from that which they have hitherto occupied, but one to which the laws of nature, and of nature's God entitle them, a decent respect to the opinions of mankind requires that they should declare the causes that impel them to such a course.

2 We hold these truths to be self-evident; that all men and women are created equal; that they are endowed by their Creator with certain inalienable rights; that among these are life, liberty, and the pursuit of happiness; that to secure these rights governments are instituted, deriving their just powers from the consent of the governed. Whenever any form of Government becomes destructive of those ends, it is the right of those who suffer from it, to refuse allegiance to it, and to insist upon the institution of a new government, laying its foundation on such principles, and organizing its powers in such

form as to them shall seem most likely to effect their safety and happiness. Prudence, indeed, will dictate, that governments long established should not be changed for light and **transient** causes; and accordingly, all experience hath shown that mankind are more disposed to suffer, while evils are sufferable, than to right themselves by abolishing the forms to which they are accustomed. But when a long train of abuses and usurpations, pursuing invariably the same object, evinces[1] a design to reduce them under absolute despotism, it is their duty to throw off such government, and provide new guards for their future security. Such has been the patient sufferance of the women under this government, and such is now the necessity which constrains them to demand the equal station, to which they are entitled.

transient
(trăn´zē-ənt) *adj.* temporary; short-term.

3 The history of mankind is a history of repeated injuries and usurpations on the part of man toward woman, having in direct object the establishment of an absolute tyranny over her. To prove this, let facts be submitted to a candid world.

EVALUATE ARGUMENTS

Annotate: Mark the statement in paragraph 3 that is supported by the evidence in paragraphs 4–10.

Analyze: How does the evidence strengthen Stanton's portrait of women as oppressed citizens?

4 He has never permitted her to exercise her inalienable right to the elective franchise.[2]

5 He has compelled her to submit to laws, in the formation of which she had no voice.

6 He has withheld from her rights which are given to the most ignorant and degraded men—both natives and foreigners.

7 Having deprived her of this first right of a citizen, the elective franchise, thereby leaving her without representation in the halls of legislation, he has oppressed her on all sides.

8 He has made her, if married, in the eye of the law, civilly dead.

9 He has taken from her all right in property, even to the wages she earns.

10 He has made her, morally, an irresponsible being, as she can commit many crimes with impunity, provided they be done in the presence of her husband. In the covenant[3] of marriage, she is compelled to promise obedience to her husband, he becoming, to all intents and purposes, her master—the law giving him power to deprive her of her liberty, and to administer chastisement.[4]

11 He has so framed the laws of divorce, as to what shall be the proper causes of divorce, in case of separation, to whom the guardianship of children shall be given; as to be wholly regardless of the happiness of women—the law, in all cases, going upon the false **supposition** of the supremacy of man, and giving all power into his hands.

supposition
(sŭp-ə-zĭsh´ən) *n.* the act of supposing; an assumption.

12 After depriving her of all rights as a woman, if single and the owner of property, he has taxed her to support a government, which recognizes her only when her property can be made profitable to it.

[1] **evince:** to reveal or give evidence of
[2] **inalienable right to the elective franchise:** unassailable right to vote.
[3] **covenant:** agreement or contract.
[4] **chastisement:** punishment.

13 He has monopolized nearly all the profitable employments; and from those she is permitted to follow, she receives but a scanty remuneration.[5]

14 He closes against her all avenues to wealth and distinction, which he considers most honorable to himself. As a teacher of Theology, Medicine or Law, she is not known.

15 He has denied her the facilities for obtaining a thorough education—all colleges being closed against her.

16 He allows her in Church as well as State, but a subordinate position, claiming Apostolic[6] authority for her exclusion from the ministry, and with some exceptions, from any public participation in the affairs of the Church.

17 He has created a false public sentiment, by giving to the world a different code of morals for man and woman, by which moral **delinquencies** which exclude women from society, are not only tolerated but deemed of little account when committed by man.

delinquency
(dĭ-lĭng´kwən-sē) *n.* shortcoming or misbehavior.

18 He has usurped the prerogative of Jehovah himself, claiming it as his right to assign for her a sphere of action, when that belongs to her conscience and her God.

19 He has endeavored in every way that he could, to destroy her confidence in her own powers, to lessen her self-respect, and to make her willing to lead a dependent and **abject** life.

abject
(ăb´jĕkt) *adj.* miserable and submissive.

20 Now, in view of this entire disfranchisement of one half the people of this country, their social and religious degradation—in view of the unjust laws above mentioned and because women do feel themselves aggrieved, oppressed and fraudulently deprived of their most sacred rights, we insist that they have immediate admission to all the rights and privileges, which belong to them as citizens of these United States.

ANALYZE RHETORIC

Annotate: In paragraph 20, mark what Stanton says she wants for women.

Analyze: What type of appeal does Stanton use in this paragraph? How do the claims in the previous paragraphs help you identify the appeal?

21 In entering upon the great work before us, we anticipate no small amount of misconception, misrepresentation and ridicule; but we shall use every instrumentality within our power to effect our object. We shall employ agents, circulate tracts, petition the State and National Legislatures, and endeavor to enlist the pulpit and the press in our behalf. We hope this Convention will be followed by a series of Conventions, embracing every part of the country.

22 Firmly relying upon the final triumph of the Right and the True, we do this day affix our signatures to this declaration.

[5] **scanty remuneration:** minimal payment.
[6] **Apostolic:** from the Apostles, the initial followers of Jesus.

?

ESSENTIAL QUESTION:
When is self-determination possible?

Review your notes and add your thoughts to your **Response Log.**

COLLABORATIVE DISCUSSION

With a partner, discuss how other women might have reacted to this argument. Then discuss how men might have reacted.

Assessment Practice

Answer these questions about "Declaration of Sentiments" before moving on to the next selection.

1. Which point does Stanton make about taxation?
   - (A) Women are not even allowed to pay taxes.
   - (B) Women pay more taxes when divorced than they do married.
   - (C) Women pay more taxes than men do, even though they earn less money.
   - (D) Women pay taxes but are not recognized or represented in government.

2. Which point does Stanton make about women's employment?
   - (A) Women are not allowed to be employed.
   - (B) Women are hired only for jobs that men don't want.
   - (C) Women are not allowed the education needed for higher paying jobs.
   - (D) Women have few ways to save money so they can accumulate real wealth.

3. What lines from the text serve as Stanton's call to action?
   - (A) *We hold these truths to be self-evident. . . .*
   - (B) *The history of mankind is a history of repeated injuries. . . .*
   - (C) *He has endeavored in every way that he could. . . .*
   - (D) *We insist that they have immediate admission to all the rights and privileges. . . .*

Test-Taking Strategies

Speech to the American Equal Rights Association

Argument by **Sojourner Truth**

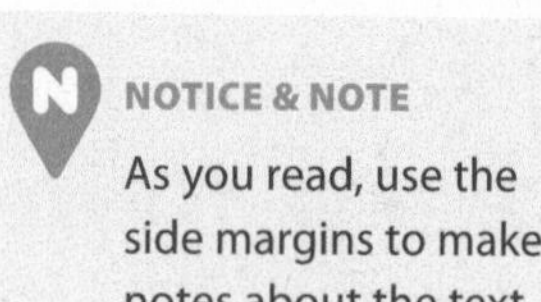
NOTICE & NOTE
As you read, use the side margins to make notes about the text.

Consider how Sojourner Truth's claim and reasoning are similar to and different from Stanton's.

May 9, 1867

1 My friends, I am rejoiced that you are glad, but I don't know how you will feel when I get through. I come from another field—the country of the slave. They have got their liberty—so much good luck to have slavery partly destroyed; not entirely. I want it root and branch destroyed. Then we will all be free indeed. I feel that if I have to answer for the deeds done in my body just as much as a man, I have a right to have just as much as a man. There is a great stir about colored men getting their rights, but not a word about the colored women; and if colored men get their rights, and not colored women theirs, you see the colored men will be masters over the women, and

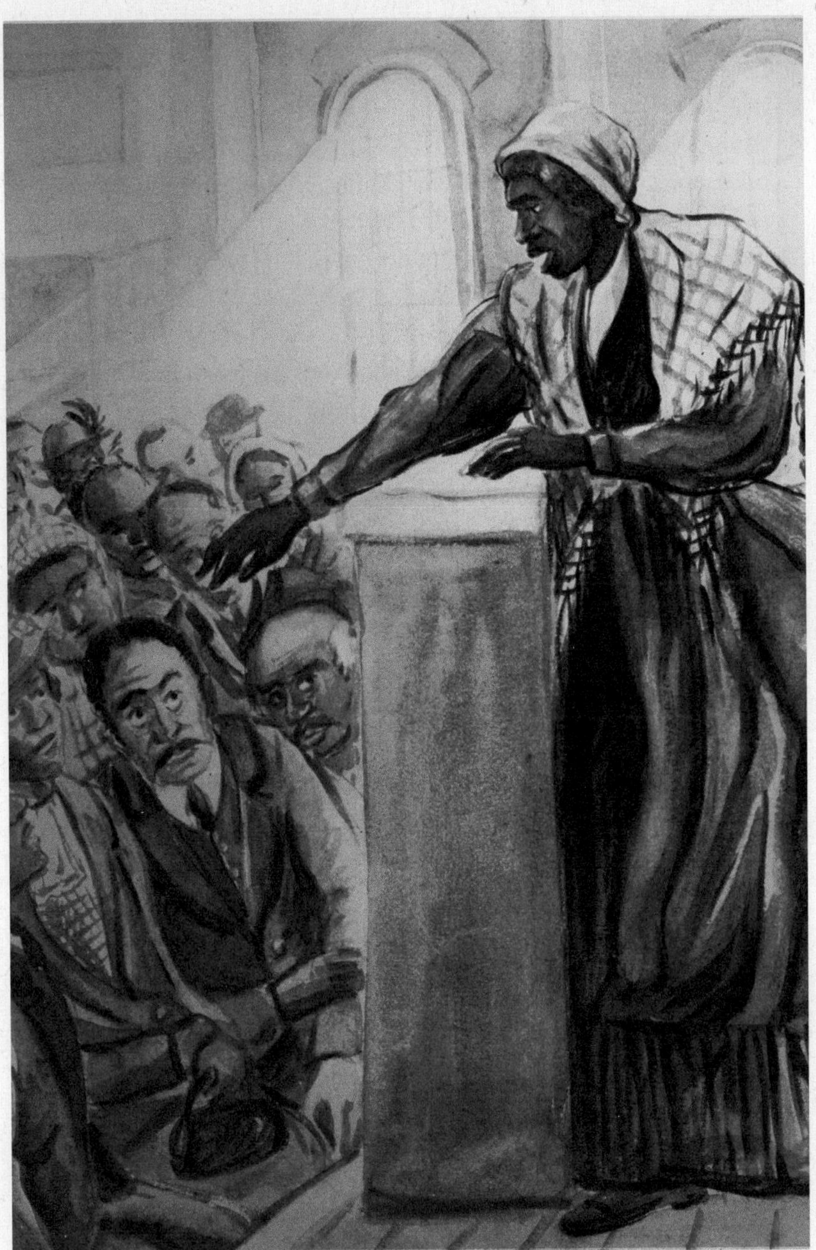

Don't forget to **Notice & Note** as you read the text.

it will be just as bad as it was before. So I am for keeping the thing going while things are stirring; because if we wait till it is still, it will take a great while to get it going again. . . . I want women to have their rights. In the courts women have no right, no voice; nobody speaks for them. I wish woman to have her voice there among the pettifoggers.[1] If it is not a fit place for women, it is unfit for men to be there.

2 I am above eighty years old; it is about time for me to be going. I have been forty years a slave and forty years free, and would be

EVALUATE ARGUMENTS

Annotate: Mark the reasons Truth says women ought to "have their rights."

Analyze: What is Sojourner Truth's main claim? How do these reasons support her argument?

[1] **pettifoggers:** legal practitioners known for dealing with petty cases and using sometimes questionable methods.

here forty years more to have equal rights for all. I suppose I am kept here because something remains for me to do; I suppose I am yet to help to break the chain. I have done a great deal of work; as much as a man, but did not get so much pay. I used to work in the field and bind grain, keeping up with the cradler;[2] but men doing no more, got twice as much pay; so with the German women. They work in the field and do as much work, but do not get the pay. We do as much, we eat as much, we want as much. I suppose I am about the only colored woman that goes about to speak for the rights of the colored women. I want to keep the thing stirring, now that the ice is cracked. What we want is a little money. You men know that you get as much again as women when you write, or for what you do. When we get our rights we shall not have to come to you for money, for then we shall have money enough in our own pockets; and may be you will ask us for money. But help us now until we get it. It is a good **consolation** to know that when we have got this battle fought we shall not be coming to you any more. You have been having our rights so long, that you think, like a slaveholder, that you own us. I know that it is hard for one who has held the reins for so long to give up; it cuts like a knife. It will feel all the better when it closes up again. I have been in Washington about three years, seeing about these colored people. Now colored men have the right to vote. There ought to be equal rights now more than ever, since colored people have got their freedom.

consolation
(kŏn-sə-lā´shən) *n.* act of giving comfort.

ANALYZE RHETORIC

Annotate: In paragraph 2, mark the reason why Truth believes women should have equal rights "now more than ever."

Interpret: How does Truth use an appeal to the time and place to support her argument?

[2] **cradler:** worker who uses a scythe-like tool for reaping grain in a crop field.

COLLABORATIVE DISCUSSION

Sojourner Truth delivered this speech to a progressive audience shortly after the Thirteenth Amendment abolished slavery in the United States. With a partner, discuss the following question: Given the political and social context, how effective do you think her audience would have found her reasoning in advocating for women's rights?

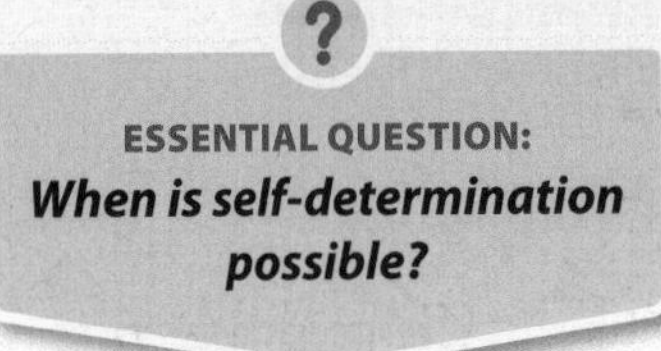
?
ESSENTIAL QUESTION:
When is self-determination possible?

Review your notes and add your thoughts to your **Response Log.**

Assessment Practice

Answer these questions before moving on to the **Analyze the Texts** section on the following page.

1. What doubt does Sojourner Truth express at the beginning of her speech?

- (A) She is unsure about how the audience will react.
- (B) She doubts that women can achieve as much as men.
- (C) She is unsure about the value of speaking out for equal rights.
- (D) She doubts that someone her age can be effective.

2. Why does Sojourner Truth think she is still alive at her advanced age?

- (A) because long life runs in her family
- (B) because she stopped working so hard
- (C) because she has had good health all her life
- (D) because there is still something for her to do

3. Which of the following supports the idea of full civil rights for women?

- (A) *I come from another field—the country of the slave.*
- (B) *There is a great stir about colored men getting their rights. . . .*
- (C) *They work in the field and do as much work, but do not get the pay.*
- (D) *I know that it is hard for one who has held the reins for so long to give up. . . .*

Ed

Test-Taking Strategies

Analyze the Texts

Support your responses with evidence from the texts.

NOTICE & NOTE

Review what you **noticed and noted** as you read the text. Your annotations can help you answer these questions.

1. **ANALYZE** In an argument, a **claim** is an author's position on an issue. What claim does Stanton make in paragraph 1, and how does she say she will support the claim elsewhere in the document?

2. **DRAW CONCLUSIONS** In paragraph 2, Stanton adds the phrase "and women" to the language used in the Declaration of Independence. How does using this sentence—and the addition of this phrase—contribute to the persuasiveness of her argument?

3. **INTERPRET** In paragraph 2, Stanton writes, "Such has been the patient sufferance of the women under this government, and such is now the necessity which constrains them to demand the equal station, to which they are entitled." Given the context, is this a valid premise? How well does this statement set up the support for her argument?

4. **INTERPRET** Sojourner Truth begins her speech "My friends, I am rejoiced that you are glad, but I don't know how you will feel when I get through." What does she mean by this, and does it strengthen or undermine her argument? Explain your answer.

5. **ANALYZE** Which persuasive techniques does Truth use in her speech to the American Equal Rights Association? How does her use of these techniques contribute to the power and persuasiveness of the speech?

6. **COMPARE** Complete the chart with examples of the appeals that each author makes to persuade her audience. Is there a type of appeal one author prefers to use? Is it the most effective appeal for the argument? Why or why not?

	Logos	Pathos	Ethos	Kairos
Elizabeth Cady Stanton				
Sojourner Truth				

Choices

Here are some other ways to demonstrate your understanding of the ideas in this lesson.

Writing

Speech! Speech!

Choose an issue you're passionate about and write a brief speech that will persuade an audience to support your cause.

1. Stake your claim! Clearly state what your stance on the issue is.
2. Back up your stance with solid reasoning and good supporting evidence.
3. Consider the tone of your argument. Will you include more logical appeals like Stanton or more emotional appeals in the style of Truth?
4. Add visuals or other media if it will help you make a compelling case.

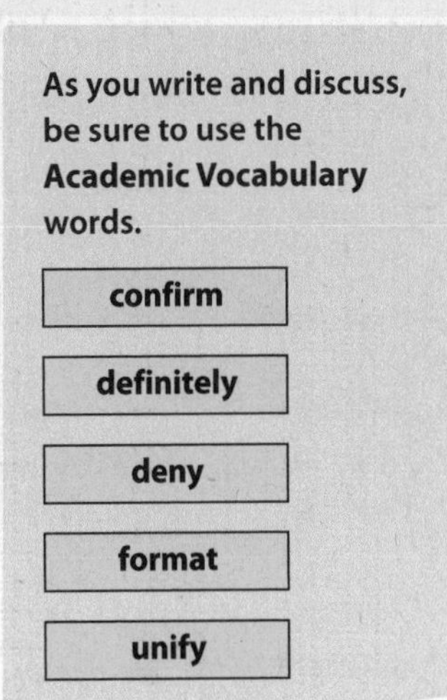
As you write and discuss, be sure to use the **Academic Vocabulary** words.
confirm
definitely
deny
format
unify

Research

Timeline

Laws guaranteeing equal rights for women have been passed over a long period of time. Research the following legislation and create a timeline that includes when they passed and what rights they granted.

- 19th Amendment to the Constitution
- Equal Pay
- Civil Rights Act
- Title IX
- Military Service

Are there any laws that still need to be passed for women to obtain equal rights? Add them, along with the date when you predict that will happen.

Social & Emotional Learning

Building a Team

To advance the cause of equal rights for women, Elizabeth Cady Stanton and Sojourner Truth had to work with people who weren't sympathetic to their cause. What skills did they need to make this possible? Look at their arguments to find evidence of how they might have negotiated conflict and recruited supporters.

Think about:

- how they approach the problem they want to solve
- how they communicate the goals or outcomes they want to achieve
- what difficulties they believe they will face
- how they look to other people for help

Once you've gathered information, make a list of the people skills they would have needed to work effectively with others.

Expand Your Vocabulary

PRACTICE AND APPLY

Use your knowledge of the vocabulary words to answer each question in a complete sentence.

1. If people live in **abject** poverty, what are their lives like?
2. What **consolation** does Sojourner Truth hope for?
3. When Stanton refers to moral **delinquencies**, is she more likely referring to major crimes or social misconduct?
4. Why does Stanton claim that the denial of women's rights has not been a **transient** situation?
5. What **supposition** does Stanton make about women's rights?

Vocabulary Strategy

↳ Suffixes

The word *consolation,* from Speech to the American Equal Rights Association, is formed by adding the noun suffix *-tion* (meaning "state of being") to the verb *console*. When a different suffix is added to a word, the meaning of the word changes. For example, adding the suffix *-able* (meaning "capable of being") to the verb *console* forms the adjective *consolable,* which means "capable of being consoled."

Interactive Vocabulary Lesson: Common Roots, Prefixes and Suffixes

PRACTICE AND APPLY

The words in the chart are found in this lesson's selections. For each, write a related verb and, if one exists, a related adjective.

Verb	Noun	Adjective
	education	
	declaration	
	participation	
	association	

Watch Your Language!

Vary Syntax

"WHEN I SAY 'RUNNED', YOU KNOW I MEAN 'RAN'. LET'S NOT QUIBBLE."

Writers **vary syntax,** or use a variety of sentence types, to hold the reader's attention, demonstrate style, and support meaning in the text. There are four types of sentences: simple, compound, complex, and compound-complex. All sentences are made up of clauses, which contain a subject and a verb. **Independent clauses** can stand alone, while **subordinate clauses** cannot.

- A **simple sentence** is an **independent clause.**
- A **compound sentence** is made up of two or more independent clauses joined by a semicolon or a comma and a conjunction *(and, but, or, for, nor, so,* and *yet).*
- A **complex sentence** consists of one independent clause and one or more **subordinate clauses.**
- A **compound-complex sentence** contains two or more independent clauses and one or more subordinate clauses.

The chart below defines types of subordinate clauses and provides an example of each from Stanton's argument.

Definition	Example
A **relative clause** gives information to help identify a person or thing. They typically begin with *who, whom, whose, which,* or *that.*	**He closes against her all avenues to wealth and distinction, which he considers most honorable to himself.**
An **adverb clause** gives information about a verb, an adjective, or an adverb and usually occurs at the beginning or end of a sentence.	**He has usurped the prerogative of Jehovah himself, claiming it as his right to assign for her a sphere of action, when that belongs to her conscience and her God.**

PRACTICE AND APPLY

Review an example of your own writing and consider how varying your syntax would make your speech more engaging. Underline at least three sentences. Revise them to vary your syntax.

Compare Arguments

Both Declaration of Sentiments and Speech to the American Equal Rights Association argue for an expansion of rights and freedoms. Even though the arguments feature different styles and levels of formality, they contain some of the same characteristics. Fill in the chart with examples of the following:

- a **claim,** or the writer's position on an issue
- **evidence,** or the information that supports the claim. Types of evidence include facts, statistics, quotations, and personal experiences.
- **appeals,** or messages to the audience. Two common appeals are **logical appeals,** which rely on reasoning and intellect, and **emotional appeals,** which evoke strong feelings such as fear or pity in the reader.
- a **call to action,** or an attempt to get the audience to do something in response to the argument.

	A Declaration of Sentiments	B Speech to the American Equal Rights Association
Claim		
Evidence		
Appeals		
Call to Action		

Analyze the Texts

Discuss these questions in your group.

1. **COMPARE** With your group, review the claims you cited in your chart. In what ways are the claims similar? In what ways are they different?
2. **EVALUATE** Does each writer include enough evidence to support her claim? Are there other types of evidence they could have included? Explain.
3. **INTERPRET** Explain whether each argument appeals to logic, to emotion, or to ethics. Cite evidence from the text in your response.
4. **ANALYZE** How does each writer strike a balance between arguing *against* something and arguing *for* something? How does including a positive call to action affect the argument?

Collaborate and Discuss

Continue exploring the ideas in these texts by having a group discussion in which you evaluate the strengths and weaknesses of each argument. Follow these steps:

1. **EVALUATE THE ARGUMENTS** With your group, review your notes and determine the criteria you will use to assess the arguments. You might consider:
   - whether the authors convince you that their claims are valid
   - what is the strongest or weakest evidence the authors included
   - whether the authors use appeals convincingly
2. **CHOOSE AND ORGANIZE DETAILS** In the chart, add passages from each text that demonstrate the strengths and weaknesses of each argument.

	A Declaration of Sentiments	B Speech to the American Equal Rights Association
Strengths		
Weaknesses		

3. **HAVE A GROUP DISCUSSION** Share your views on whether each argument was convincing. Cite evidence from the text in your discussion. Invite your audience to ask questions and address their concerns respectfully.

Collaborate & Compare

ESSENTIAL QUESTION:
What causes divisions between people?

Compare Structures

In this lesson, you'll read two texts that express ideas about slavery in America. One is a poem written in the twentieth century, and the other is an excerpt from the autobiography of a formerly enslaved woman. After you read the selections, you'll work with some classmates to examine the structural elements of each text and identify similarities and differences.

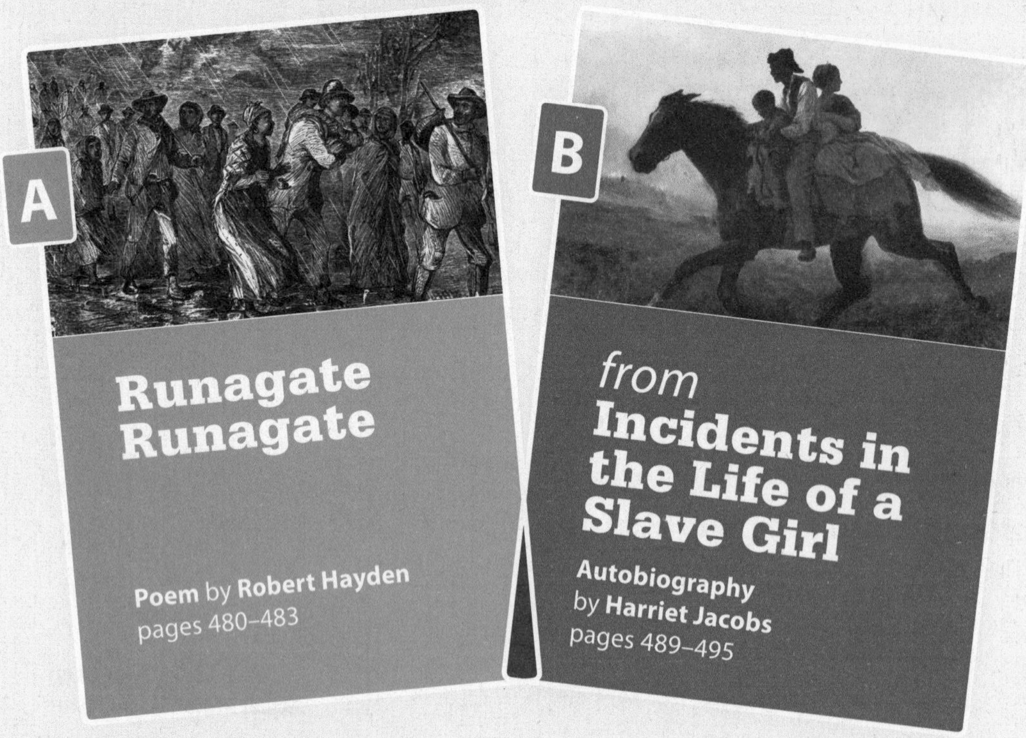

A
Runagate Runagate
Poem by Robert Hayden
pages 480–483
B
from
Incidents in the Life of a Slave Girl
Autobiography
by Harriet Jacobs
pages 489–495

After you have read the poem and the autobiography, you will explore the ideas of both by collaborating with a small group to develop a group presentation on how the structure of each text helped the authors develop their ideas about slavery. You will follow these steps:

- Trace both authors' development of ideas
- Evaluate the effectiveness of each structure
- Present your preferred structure

Runagate Runagate

Poem by **Robert Hayden** - pages 480–483

Engage Your Brain

Choose one or more of these activities to start connecting with the poem you're about to read.

I Wonder If It's . . .

Here are the first two lines of the poem, "Runagate Runagate." Based on these two lines, what do you think the poem is about? Share your predictions with a partner.

Runs falls rises stumbles on from darkness into darkness
And the darkness thicketed with shapes of terror

Three Truths and a Lie

One of these statements is false. Can you tell which one it is?

- Harriet Tubman's birth name was Araminta Ross.
- Harriet Tubman was eventually caught in Harper's Ferry, VA, as she assisted runaway slaves.
- In Maryland, you can still travel the Harriet Tubman Underground Railroad Byway.
- Among other survival skills, Harriet Tubman could catch muskrats with her bare hands.

There's a Map for That!

Fact: The Underground Railroad is neither underground nor a railroad. Research the routes taken by the "conductors" of the Underground Railroad. Then draw the routes in the map. Where did they start and stop?

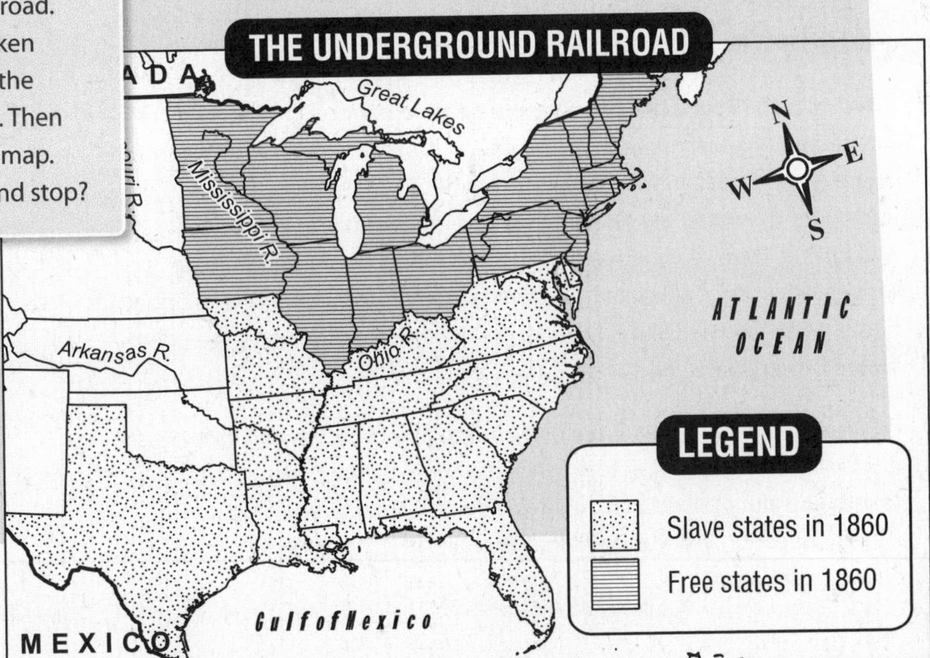

Analyze Speaker

In poetry, a **speaker** is a persona, or character, who talks to the reader, similar to a narrator in fiction. In a longer poem, the poet may use more than one speaker to bring the verses to life. To tell the speakers apart, use the following steps:

- Look at how the poet structures the verses. Are the lines set in a particular pattern? Do the patterns change from stanza to stanza?
- Read the poem aloud to find places where the tone or the rhythm of the verses change. Whenever you see or hear a change, it could be a clue to a change in speaker.

As you read, make notes in the chart about the speakers in the poem and how they impact the poem's structure and meaning.

Focus on Genre
Poetry

- uses rhythm and may use rhyme
- may contain more than one speaker
- is often arranged in stanzas
- may include allusions to deepen the meaning of the work

Speaker	Lines	Structure/Meaning

Analyze Rhythm

Rhythm is the sound produced by the arrangement of stressed and unstressed syllables, along with the intervals of time that fall between them. A good poet creates a relationship between rhythm, structure, and content by carefully selecting words and controlling line lengths and format. Even the title Hayden chooses for his poem—"Runagate Runagate"—uses rhythm to heighten its meaning. Imagine that the poet had chosen "Escaped Slave" instead; the experience of reading the poem would be very different.

Poets, like musicians, manipulate rhythm to express ideas and emotions. As you read, pay attention to when, how, and why the poem's rhythm rushes you along, slows you down, or suddenly makes you stop and change direction. Ask yourself what changes in structure are signaled by a change in rhythm.

Analyze Allusions

An **allusion** is a reference to a well-known historical or literary figure, event, or composition. Writers choose allusions that their readers will understand, such as references to the Bible. Hayden employs several, including a reference to Ezekiel (line 59). For an allusion to succeed, the reader must recognize it. Use the chart to track the allusions you find in the poem.

Allusion	Meaning
John Brown	well-known abolitionist
Ezekiel	

Annotation in Action

Here are one student's notes on the rhythm in "Runagate Runagate." As you read, notice how rhythm and meaning relate.

Runs falls rises stumbles on from darkness into darkness
and the darkness thicketed with shapes of terror
and the hunters pursuing and the hounds pursuing
and the night cold and the night long and the river

The run-on line and repetition create a rushed rhythm and a threatening atmosphere.

Background

Robert Hayden (1913–1980) endured a childhood marred by poverty, a broken family, and a dysfunctional foster home. Plagued by depression, vision problems, and bullying peers, the Detroit native withdrew into a world of books. He researched African American folklore for the Federal Writers' Project in 1936, published his first book of poems in 1940, and earned a master's degree in English. Hayden then began his own lengthy career as a teacher while continuing to produce volumes of poetry. Much of his award-winning work explores the history and legacy of racial injustice in America.

Runagate Runagate

Poem by **Robert Hayden**

NOTICE & NOTE

As you read, use the side margins to make notes about the text.

Note the references to slavery described in the poem. This information will help you compare the poem with *Incidents in the Life of a Slave Girl,* which follows it.

I.

ANALYZE RHYTHM

Annotate: Mark the point where the rhythm changes in this stanza.

Interpret: What effect does this change have on the poem?

Runs falls rises stumbles on from darkness into darkness
and the darkness thicketed with shapes of terror
and the hunters pursuing and the hounds pursuing
and the night cold and the night long and the river
to cross and the jack-muh-lanterns[1] beckoning beckoning
and blackness ahead and when shall I reach that somewhere
morning and keep on going and never turn back and keep on going
Runagate[2]
Runagate
Runagate
Many thousands rise and go
many thousands crossing over

O mythic North
O star-shaped yonder Bible city

[1] **jack-muh-lanterns:** a mythical goblin, popular in African American folklore.
[2] **Runagate:** a fugitive slave.

Some go weeping and some rejoicing
some in coffins and some in carriages
some in silks and some in shackles
        Rise and go or fare you well

No more auction block for me
no more driver's lash for me

        If you see my Pompey, 30 yrs of age,
        new breeches, plain stockings, negro shoes;
        if you see my Anna, likely young mulatto[3]
        branded E on the right cheek, R on the left,
        catch them if you can and notify subscriber.[4]
        Catch them if you can, but it won't be easy.
        They'll dart underground when you try to catch them,
        plunge into quicksand, whirlpools, mazes,
        turn into scorpions when you try to catch them.

And before I'll be a slave
I'll be buried in my grave

        North star and bonanza gold
        I'm bound for the freedom, freedom-bound
        and oh Susyanna don't you cry for me[5]

                Runagate

                        Runagate

ANALYZE SPEAKER

Annotate: Circle the individual stanzas in lines 19–31.

Interpret: How can you tell that there are different speakers in these lines?

II.

Rises from their anguish and their power,

                Harriet Tubman,

                woman of earth, whipscarred,
                a summoning, a shining

                Mean to be free

        And this was the way of it, brethren brethren,
        way we journeyed from Can't to Can.
        Moon so bright and no place to hide,
        the cry up and the patterollers[6] riding,
        hound dogs belling[7] in bladed air.
        And fear starts a-murbling, Never make it,
        we'll never make it. *Hush that now,*
        and she's turned upon us, levelled pistol

ANALYZE ALLUSIONS

Annotate: Mark the reference to a well-known person in lines 37–41.

Interpret: How does this allusion connect to the topic of the poem?

[3] **mulatto:** of mixed white and Black ancestry.

[4] **subscriber:** a person placing a notice for a fugitive slave.

[5] **oh Susyanna don't you cry for me:** an allusion to the chorus of "Oh! Susanna" by Stephen Foster.

[6] **patterollers:** people who watched and restricted the movement of black slaves at night.

[7] **belling:** barking.

ANALYZE RHYTHM

Annotate: Pauses between some syllables or words contribute to the rhythm of the lines. Reread lines 51–58 silently and mark any visual cues you see for pauses.

Compare: Contrast the rhythms and meanings in lines 51–52 and lines 53–58.

glinting in the moonlight:
Dead folks can't jaybird-talk,[8] she says;
you keep on going now or die, she says.

Wanted   Harriet Tubman   alias The General
Alias Moses   Stealer of Slaves

In league with Garrison   Alcott   Emerson
Garrett   Douglass   Thoreau   John Brown

Armed and known to be Dangerous

Wanted   Reward   Dead or Alive

Tell me, Ezekiel, oh tell me do you see
mailed[9] Jehovah coming to deliver me?

Hoot-owl calling in the ghosted air,
five times calling to the hants[10] in the air.
Shadow of a face in the scary leaves,
shadow of a voice in the talking leaves:

Come ride-a my train

Oh that train, ghost-story train
through swamp and savanna movering movering,
over trestles of dew, through caves of the wish,
Midnight Special on a sabre track movering movering,
first stop Mercy and the last Hallelujah.

Come ride-a my train

Mean mean mean to be free.

[8] **jaybird-talk:** talk like fools.
[9] **mailed:** covered with a flexible armor made of rings or plates.
[10] **hants:** ghosts.

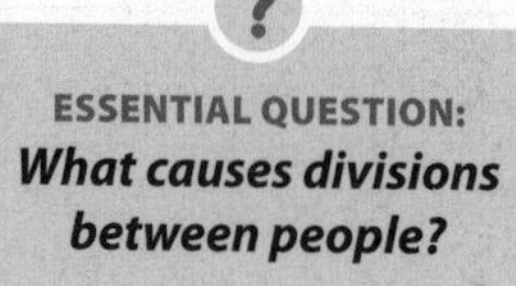
?
ESSENTIAL QUESTION:
What causes divisions between people?

Review your notes and add your thoughts to your **Response Log.**

COLLABORATIVE DISCUSSION

With a partner, discuss the voices and the images in the poem. Which ones stuck with you after you finished reading?

Assessment Practice

Answer these questions before moving on to the **Analyze the Text** section.

1. Which of the following words best describes the speakers in the poem?

(A) frightened

(B) sarcastic

(C) determined

(D) hesitant

2. Which of the following lines features a rushing rhythm?

(A) *No more auction block for me / no more driver's lash for me*

(B) *And fear starts a-murbling, Never make it, / we'll never make it.*

(C) *I'm bound for the freedom, freedom-bound / and oh Susyanna don't you cry for me*

(D) *Runagate / Runagate*

3. Which of the following items is an example of an allusion?

(A) *O star-shaped yonder Bible city*

(B) *my Pompey, 30 yrs of age*

(C) *Dead folks can't jaybird-talk, she says*

(D) *Hoot-owl calling in the ghosted air*

Test-Taking Strategies

Analyze the Text

Support your responses with evidence from the text.

NOTICE & NOTE

Review what you **noticed and noted** as you read the text. Your annotations can help you answer these questions.

1. **ANALYZE** The opening stanza portrays a frightened narrator fleeing through darkness. How does the rhythm reflect and enhance the speaker's experience?

2. **IDENTIFY** What allusions to religion or the Bible can you find in the poem? Why might religious imagery and biblical allusions be appropriate for this topic?

3. **INTERPRET** Consider the stanza that begins "And this was the way of it" (lines 42–52). Who are the two speakers in the stanza, and how do the rhythms of their speech reflect the differences in their attitudes?

4. **SYNTHESIZE** Read the two stanzas in lines 59–64, starting with the one that begins "Tell me, Ezekiel." How do the rhythms in these stanzas differ from most other parts of the poem? How do the rhythms and the meanings of the verses combine to convey a certain feeling?

5. **ANALYZE** How would you describe the structure in "Runagate Runagate"? What beliefs does Hayden reveal through details in the poem?

6. **INFER** Many people escaped from slavery by following the Underground Railroad. In the poem, what words and phrases does Hayden use to allude to the Underground Railroad? Which references were familiar and which ones did you guess? Use the chart to record your thoughts.

Allusions I Knew	How I Knew Them
Allusions I Inferred	How I Guessed Them

Choices

Here are some other ways to demonstrate your understanding of the ideas in this lesson.

Writing

↳ That's a Reference to...

You've seen how Robert Hayden used allusions to give deeper meaning to his poem. Write your own poem and include at least two allusions.

Take into consideration:

- Allusions can be references to many things, including books, movies, music, TV shows, or famous people and events.
- Your allusions will be more effective if your audience can identify them.

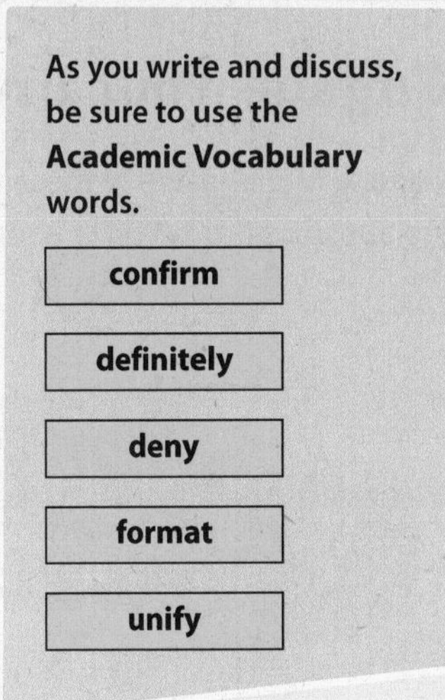
As you write and discuss, be sure to use the **Academic Vocabulary** words.
confirm
definitely
deny
format
unify

Speaking & Listening

↳ Understanding the Large Hearts of Heroes

In groups of four, compare "Runagate Runagate" with lines 17–24 of "I Understand the Large Hearts of Heroes," by Walt Whitman (pp. 262–263). Both Hayden and Whitman imagine the plight of fugitives from slavery. Discuss the following aspects of each poem:

- how each poet's background is reflected in the poems
- how the poets use figurative language, allusions, and imagery
- how rhythm contributes to the structure of the poems
- what the purpose of each poet was in writing the poems
- the themes of each poem and whether they have any themes in common

Media

↳ Poetry Slam

Pick a poem you like and recite it to a rhythm. You can create the rhythm yourself, use a drum app with pre-recorded rhythms, or have classmates provide the beat as you recite. Record your presentation and share it with your classmates.

from Incidents in the Life of a Slave Girl

Autobiography by **Harriet Jacobs**
pages 489–495

Engage Your Brain

Choose one or more of these activities to start connecting with the autobiography you're about to read.

It's in the Cloud

What words do you associate with the institution of slavery in America?

- Have each person in class submit the first three words that occur to them.
- Run them through a word cloud app to see which words were most used.
- Print the word cloud and display it in your classroom.
- Discuss any words you find surprising.

Decisions, Decisions

Often it takes a major event to motivate people to change. How do you know when it is time to make a change in your life? How do you determine what to change immediately and what to push farther down the road? Write your ideas in a paragraph.

To Be Me or Not to Be Me

You want to write your life story. Do you fictionalize it by using a different name or creating a character? Or do you tell it in your own voice using your own name? Discuss your decision and reasons why with a partner.

Analyze Character

Characters develop over the course of a story as the narrator reveals details about them through direct and indirect characterization.

- With **direct characterization,** the narrator states what a character is like, such as "He is a friendly neighbor."
- With **indirect characterization,** the narrator uses certain details to reveal a character. These details may include physical descriptions; a character's thoughts, words, or actions; and how other characters react to a character.

As you read, note the details that "Linda" (Harriet Jacobs) uses to characterize Dr. and Mrs. Flint, Sally, and her grandmother. Does she use direct or indirect characterization? What information about the characters does she reveal as the story progresses?

Focus on Genre
Autobiography

- **is told from the first-person point of view**
- **utilizes direct and indirect characterization to develop character**

Character	Details
Dr. Flint	
Mrs. Flint	
Sally	
Linda's grandmother	

Analyze Plot

While *Incidents in the Life of a Slave Girl* is an autobiography, Jacobs uses many narrative techniques typically found in fiction to structure her account. She tells her story in an engaging way, describing events and her reactions to them in vivid detail. The events and emotions she describes create internal and external conflict.

- An **internal conflict** is a struggle within a character.
- An **external conflict** is a struggle between a character and an outside force.

These conflicts result in suspense, or excitement and tension, as the reader wonders what will happen next. As you read, analyze how Jacobs builds suspense by presenting both internal and external conflicts. What events and emotions create these conflicts?

Annotation in Action

Here are one student's notes on the characters in *Incidents in the Life of a Slave Girl.* As you read, mark details that tell you what characters are like and note whether they are examples of direct or indirect characterization.

Mr. Flint was hard pushed for house servants, and rather than lose me he had restrained his malice. I did my work faithfully, though not, of course, with a willing mind. They were evidently afraid I should leave them. Mr. Flint wished that I should sleep in the great house instead of the servants' quarters. His wife agreed to the proposition, but said I mustn't bring my bed into the house, because it would scatter feathers on her carpet.

Jacobs describes the characters' wishes, fears, words, and actions. This is indirect characterization.

Expand Your Vocabulary

Put a check mark next to the vocabulary words that you feel comfortable using when speaking or writing.

proposition	☐
induced	☐
provocation	☐
tidings	☐
compelled	☐
reckless	☐

Then use these words to talk about a situation in which you or someone you know had to make a really tough decision. As you read the excerpt from *Incidents in the Life of a Slave Girl,* use the definitions in the side column to learn the vocabulary words you don't already know.

Background

Harriet Jacobs (1813–1897) was born into slavery in North Carolina. At age 12, she was given to the daughter of Dr. James Norcom. Norcom made inappropriate advances toward Jacobs, and to avoid him she started a relationship with Samuel Sawyer ("Mr. Sands"), with whom she had two children. Norcom then sent Jacobs and her children to work elsewhere, and she made the painful decision to flee and leave her children. Sawyer bought the children to save them from plantation life, while Jacobs hid in an attic for seven years before escaping to New York. In 1861, she published her account under the name Linda Brent.

from Incidents in the Life of a Slave Girl

Autobiography by **Harriet Jacobs**

NOTICE & NOTE
As you read, use the side margins to make notes about the text.

Note the characterization of the people in the narrator's life and details that reveal internal and external conflicts.

The Flight

1 MR. FLINT was hard pushed for house servants, and rather than lose me he had restrained his malice. I did my work faithfully, though not, of course, with a willing mind. They were evidently afraid I should leave them. Mr. Flint wished that I should sleep in the great house instead of the servants' quarters. His wife agreed to the **proposition**, but said I mustn't bring my bed into the house, because it would scatter feathers on her carpet. I knew when I went there that they would never think of such a thing as furnishing a bed of any kind for me and my little one. I therefore carried my own bed, and now I was forbidden to use it. I did as I was ordered. But now that I was certain my children were to be put in their power, in order to give them a stronger hold on me, I resolved to leave them that night. I remembered the grief this step would bring upon my dear old grandmother; and nothing less than the freedom of my children

proposition
(prŏp-ə-zĭsh´ən) *n.* a plan suggested for acceptance; a proposal.

induced
(ĭn-do͞ost´) *v.* led or moved, as to a course of action, by influence or persuasion.

would have **induced** me to disregard her advice. I went about my evening work with trembling steps. Mr. Flint twice called from his chamber door to inquire why the house was not locked up. I replied that I had not done my work. "You have had time enough to do it," said he. "Take care how you answer me!"

2 I shut all the windows, locked all the doors, and went up to the third story, to wait till midnight. How long those hours seemed, and how fervently I prayed that God would not forsake me in this hour of utmost need! I was about to risk everything on the throw of a die; and if I failed, O what would become of me and my poor children? They would be made to suffer for my fault.

ANALYZE CHARACTER

Annotate: Mark the sentence in paragraph 3 that gives Linda's characterization of Sally.

Interpret: How does Linda characterize her?

3 At half past twelve I stole softly down stairs. I stopped on the second floor, thinking I heard a noise. I felt my way down into the parlor, and looked out of the window. The night was so intensely dark that I could see nothing. I raised the window very softly and jumped out. Large drops of rain were falling, and the darkness bewildered me. I dropped on my knees, and breathed a short prayer to God for guidance and protection. I groped my way to the road, and rushed towards the town with almost lightning speed. I arrived at my grandmother's house, but dared not see her. She would say, "Linda, you are killing me;" and I knew that would unnerve me. I tapped softly at the window of a room, occupied by a woman, who had lived in the house several years. I knew she was a faithful friend, and could be trusted with my secret. I tapped several times before she heard me. At last she raised the window, and I whispered, "Sally, I have run away. Let me in, quick." She opened the door softly, and said in low tones, "For God's sake, don't. Your grandmother is trying to buy you and de chillern. Mr. Sands was here last week. He tole her he was going away on business, but he wanted her to go ahead about buying you and de chillern, and he would help her all he could. Don't run away, Linda. Your grandmother is all bowed down wid trouble now."

4 I replied, "Sally, they are going to carry my children to the plantation tomorrow; and they will never sell them to any body so long as they have me in their power. Now, would you advise me to go back?"

5 "No, chile, no," answered she. "When dey finds you is gone, dey won't want de plague[1] ob de chillern; but where is you going to hide? Dey knows ebery inch ob dis house."

6 I told her I had a hiding-place, and that was all it was best for her to know. I asked her to go into my room as soon as it was light, and take all my clothes out of my trunk, and pack them in hers; for I knew Mr. Flint and the constable would be there early to search my room. I feared the sight of my children would be too much for my full heart; but I could not go out into the uncertain future without one last look. I bent over the bed where lay my little Benny and baby Ellen.

[1] **plague:** nuisance.

Poor little ones! fatherless and motherless! Memories of their father came over me. He wanted to be kind to them; but they were not all to him, as they were to my womanly heart. I knelt and prayed for the innocent little sleepers. I kissed them lightly, and turned away.

7 As I was about to open the street door, Sally laid her hand on my shoulder, and said, "Linda, is you gwine all alone? Let me call your uncle."

8 "No, Sally," I replied, "I want no one to be brought into trouble on my account."

9 I went forth into the darkness and rain. I ran on till I came to the house of the friend who was to conceal me.

10 Early the next morning Mr. Flint was at my grandmother's inquiring for me. She told him she had not seen me, and supposed I was at the plantation. He watched her face narrowly, and said, "Don't you know any thing about her running off?" She assured him that she did not. He went on to say, "Last night she ran off without the least **provocation**. We had treated her very kindly. My wife liked her. She will soon be found and brought back. Are her children with you?" When told that they were, he said, "I am very glad to hear that. If they are here, she cannot be far off. If I find out that any of my niggers have had any thing to do with this damned business, I'll give 'em five hundred lashes." As he started to go to his father's, he turned round and added, persuasively, "Let her be brought back, and she shall have her children to live with her."

Don't forget to **Notice & Note** as you read the text.

ANALYZE CHARACTER

Annotate: Mark the phrases Linda uses in paragraph 10 to characterize Mr. Flint when he talks to her grandmother.

Evaluate: What type of characterization is this, and what do the phrases show about Mr. Flint?

provocation
(prŏv-ə-kā´shən) *n.* the act of provoking or inciting.

tidings
(tī´dĭngs) *pl.n.* information or news.

ANALYZE PLOT

Annotate: Mark the sentences in paragraph 11 that reveal Linda's internal conflict.

Interpret: How does the conflict build suspense?

11 The **tidings** made the old doctor rave and storm at a furious rate. It was a busy day for them. My grandmother's house was searched from top to bottom. As my trunk was empty, they concluded I had taken my clothes with me. Before ten o'clock every vessel northward bound was thoroughly examined, and the law against harboring[2] fugitives was read to all on board. At night a watch was set over the town. Knowing how distressed my grandmother would be, I wanted to send her a message; but it could not be done. Every one who went in or out of her house was closely watched. The doctor said he would take my children, unless she became responsible for them; which of course she willingly did. The next day was spent in searching. Before night, the following advertisement was posted at every corner, and in every public place for miles round:—

12 *$300 REWARD! Ran away from the subscriber,[3] an intelligent, bright, mulatto[4] girl, named Linda, 21 years of age. Five feet four inches high. Dark eyes, and black hair inclined to curl; but it can be made straight. Has a decayed spot on a front tooth. She can read and write, and in all probability will try to get to the Free States. All persons are forbidden, under penalty of the law, to harbor or employ said slave. $150 will be given to whoever takes her in the state, and $300 if taken out of the state and delivered to me, or lodged in jail. DR. FLINT.*

For a week, Linda hides in the house of an unnamed friend. Her pursuers come so close to finding her that she rushes from the house into the bushes, where she is bitten by a poisonous snake or lizard. She suffers greatly until an old woman treats her with a folk remedy. Vowing "give me liberty or death," she refuses to return to the Flints. Then a sympathetic white woman, an old friend of her grandmother's, offers to conceal Linda in a small storage room in her house. The woman sends her cook, Linda's friend Betty, to meet Linda and take her to the house. The woman makes them promise never to tell, as she is the wife of a prominent slaveholder.

[2] **harboring:** sheltering or protecting.
[3] **the subscriber:** the person placing the notice, Dr. Flint.
[4] **mulatto:** of mixed Black and white ancestry.

Don't forget to **Notice & Note** as you read the text.

NOTICE & NOTE
TOUGH QUESTIONS

When you notice characters asking questions that reveal their internal struggles, you've found a **Tough Questions** signpost.

Notice & Note: Mark details in paragraph 14 that tell you what happened to Linda's family.

Analyze: What inner struggle does Linda face at this point in the story?

Months of Peril

13 I went to sleep that night with the feeling that I was for the present the most fortunate slave in town. Morning came and filled my little cell with light. I thanked the heavenly Father for this safe retreat. Opposite my window was a pile of feather beds. On the top of these I could lie perfectly concealed, and command a view of the street through which Dr. Flint passed to his office. Anxious as I was, I felt a gleam of satisfaction when I saw him. Thus far I had outwitted him, and I triumphed over it. Who can blame slaves for being cunning? They are constantly **compelled** to resort to it. It is the only weapon of the weak and oppressed against the strength of their tyrants.

compelled
(kəm-pĕld´) *v.* forced (a person) to do something; drove or constrained.

14 I was daily hoping to hear that my master had sold my children; for I knew who was on the watch to buy them. But Dr. Flint cared even more for revenge than he did for money. My brother William, and the good aunt who had served in his family twenty years, and my little Benny, and Ellen, who was a little over two years old, were thrust into jail, as a means of compelling my relatives to give some information about me. He swore my grandmother should never see one of them again till I was brought back. They kept these facts from me for several days. When I heard that my little ones were in a loathsome jail, my first impulse was to go to them. I was encountering dangers for the sake of freeing them, and must I be the cause of their death? The thought was agonizing. My benefactress[5]

[5] **benefactress:** a woman who gives aid.

reckless
(rĕk´lĭs) *adj.* heedless or careless, rash.

tried to soothe me by telling me that my aunt would take good care of the children while they remained in jail. But it added to my pain to think that the good old aunt, who had always been so kind to her sister's orphan children, should be shut up in prison for no other crime than loving them. I suppose my friends feared a **reckless** movement on my part, knowing, as they did, that my life was bound up in my children. I received a note from my brother William. It was scarcely legible, and ran thus: "Wherever you are, dear sister, I beg of you not to come here. We are all much better off than you are. If you come, you will ruin us all. They would force you to tell where you had been, or they would kill you. Take the advice of your friends; if not for the sake of me and your children, at least for the sake of those you would ruin."

Poor William! He also must suffer for being my brother. I took his advice and kept quiet. My aunt was taken out of jail at the end of a month, because Mrs. Flint could not spare her any longer. She was tired of being her own housekeeper. It was quite too fatiguing to order her dinner and eat it too. My children remained in jail, where brother William did all he could for their comfort. Betty went to see them sometimes, and brought me tidings. She was not permitted to enter the jail; but William would hold them up to the grated window while she chatted with them. When she repeated their prattle, and told me how they wanted to see their ma, my tears would flow. Old Betty would exclaim, "Lors, chile! what's you crying 'bout? Dem young uns vil kill you dead. Don't be so chick'n hearted! If you does, you vil nebber git thro' dis world."

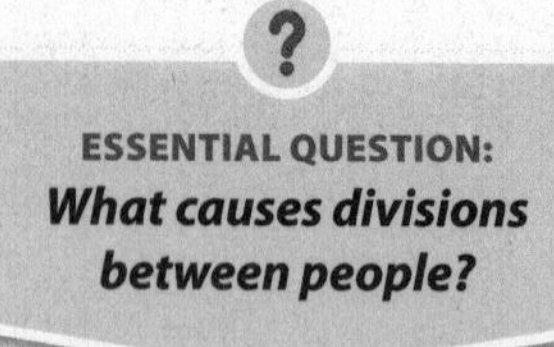
?
ESSENTIAL QUESTION:
What causes divisions between people?

Review your notes and add your thoughts to your **Response Log.**

COLLABORATIVE DISCUSSION

With a classmate, discuss how Linda's perspective affected the way you perceived characters and events. How would your perception change if the narrator were different?

Assessment Practice

Answer these questions before moving on to the **Analyze the Text** section on the following page.

1. What prompts Linda to make the decision to escape?

   (A) She learns that her grandmother is going to be moving away.

   (B) She is told by Mrs. Flint she cannot move her bed into the family's house.

   (C) She learns the Flints are going to take her children in order to control her.

   (D) She overhears the Flints deciding that they are going to sell her.

2. Which of the following actions do the Flints *not* take after they find out Linda has left?

   (A) They search her grandmother's house and northbound ships.

   (B) They send people north to find out where she is.

   (C) They offer a reward for her capture.

   (D) They jail her relatives.

3. Why does Linda want the Flints to sell her children?

   (A) She wants Mr. Sands to buy them so they can be with their father.

   (B) She thinks another owner will treat them with more kindness.

   (C) She wants them to learn other skills at another household.

   (D) She believes other owners will allow them to have freedom.

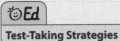

Ed
Test-Taking Strategies

Analyze the Text

Support your responses with evidence from the text.

NOTICE & NOTE

Review what you **noticed and noted** as you read the text. Your annotations can help you answer these questions.

1. **ANALYZE** How does the writer present herself? Discuss what you learn about her character and values from her attitude toward work (paragraph 1), her thoughts as she visits her children (paragraph 6), and her insistence upon escaping alone (paragraph 8).

2. **SUMMARIZE** Contrast the writer's portrayal of herself with her portrayal of the Flints. What does she reveal about the Flints' character and values?

3. **ANALYZE** Even though this is an autobiography, readers can clearly see that Jacobs uses the narrative techniques of fiction to tell her story. Using the diagram, plot out the events in this excerpt and label where the conflicts force a plot development.

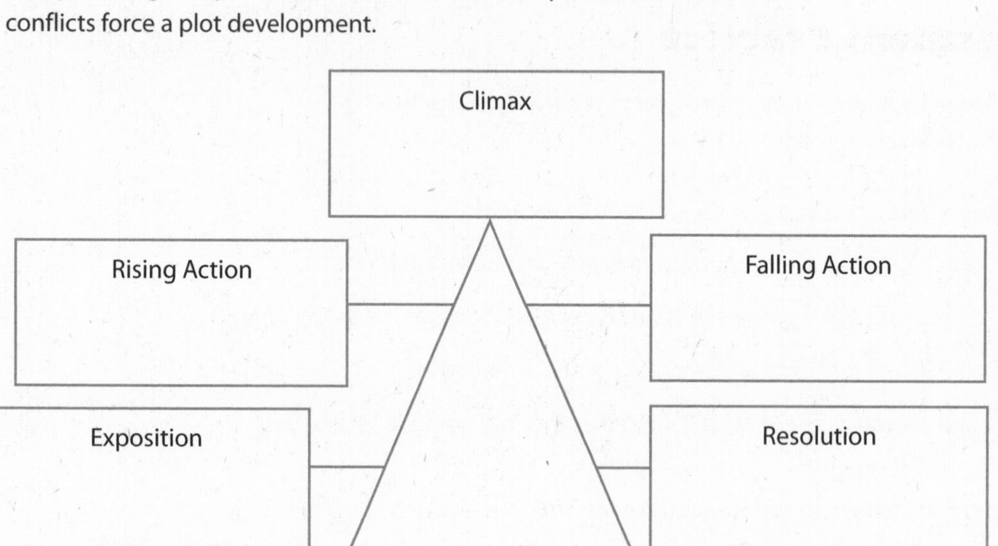

4. **INTERPRET** In paragraph 15, Jacobs writes, "When she repeated their prattle and told me how they wanted to see their ma, my tears would flow." What does that statement tell you about Linda's internal conflict?

5. **EVALUATE** When writers create a work for a particular audience, it can influence which details they include. How might the knowledge that she was writing for a primarily northern, white audience have influenced Jacobs's characterizations?

6. **ANALYZE** Describe the different conflicts that Linda faces in this excerpt. In those moments where she has to ask herself **Tough Questions,** what do the internal and external conflicts reveal about the institution of slavery and the sacrifices it forces people to make?

Choices

Here are some other ways to demonstrate your understanding of the ideas in this lesson.

Writing

↳ Character Sketch

A character sketch is a written description of a character. Write a three- to four-paragraph character sketch of Linda's grandmother, her friend Sally, or her brother William. Briefly describe how this character would have perceived and experienced the events Jacobs tells in her autobiography. Use any details from the excerpt that you can, then fill in the gaps using your imagination. Include:

- a physical description
- personality traits
- motivations
- conflicts

As you write and discuss, be sure to use the Academic Vocabulary words.

- **confirm**
- **definitely**
- **deny**
- **format**
- **unify**

Media

↳ Graphic Novel

Retell a scene from Harriet Jacobs's life story in a graphic novel format. Review the events she recounts and select the one that is best represented visually. As you plan, think about this advice from graphic novel creators:

- The more characters and locations you have, the more you have to draw. It may help to keep it simple.
- First create the manuscript in script format, complete with scene headings, transitions, dialogue, and descriptions of the actions and settings to be drawn.
- Use the script to create page roughs with thumbnail images. You want to get the visual story arc and panel placement correct. Keep in mind that one page in a graphic novel will usually have 3–5 panels. You may have to tweak the script once the roughs are complete.
- Refine the art and add the text (lettering). (Some artists recommend adding the text first, then drawing the images around it. This is useful advice if you have a lot of dialogue or text.) When done, color it in.

Speaking & Listening

↳ Group Discussion

In small groups, pick one of the moments when Linda has to make a decision. Discuss how the events would have played out and how the outcome of those events might have changed if Linda had made a different decision at that time.

Expand Your Vocabulary

PRACTICE AND APPLY

For each of the following words, list the vocabulary word that is the most opposite in meaning. Discuss your answers with a partner.

proposition	induced	provocation
tidings	compelled	reckless

1. discouraged ____________
2. cautious ____________
3. refusal ____________
4. blocked ____________
5. silence ____________
6. compliment ____________

Vocabulary Strategy

↳ Synonyms

Synonyms are words that have the same or almost the same meaning. There can be shades of meanings between synonyms. Many words have two kinds of meaning. There's the **denotative meaning,** or dictionary definition, and the **connotative meaning,** which is a feeling or tone associated with it. For example, *giggle* and *snicker* both mean "to laugh," but *snicker* has the connotation of a mean type of laughter.

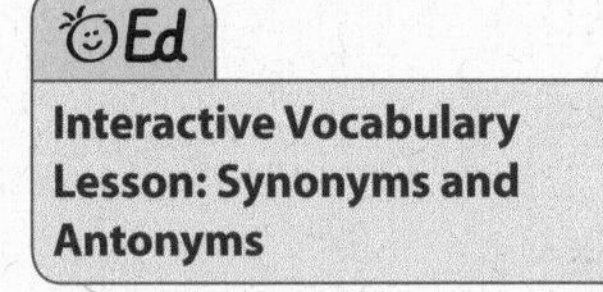

PRACTICE AND APPLY

To learn more about the vocabulary words, fill out the following chart with a synonym for each word and its connotation. Check your work with a dictionary or thesaurus and write the definition in the chart.

Word	Synonym	Connotation and Confirmed Meaning
proposition		
induced		
provocation		
tidings		
compelled		
reckless		

Watch Your Language!

Dialect and Idioms

Dialect is a way of speaking that is particular to a specific area or group of people. At times, dialect may include unconventional usage. However, Jacobs's use of dialect allows her to portray her characters with authenticity. Her autobiography provides a glimpse into her community in North Carolina during the early years of the 19th century. Writers often spell dialect the way it would be pronounced and use nonstandard English to capture characters and make them appear authentic.

- **Dialect:** "Lors, chile! what's you crying 'bout. Dem young uns vil kill you dead. Don't be so chick'n hearted."
- **Standard English:** "Lord, child! What are you crying about? Those kids will get you killed. Don't be so scared!"

Idioms are common expressions in which the literal meanings of the words are not the same as the actual meanings. For example, the idiom "it's raining cats and dogs" means that it is raining heavily; cats and dogs aren't actually falling from the sky. Take a look at the following example from the text and think about what the words actually mean compared to their literal definition.

- **Idiom:** I was about to risk everything on the throw of a die.
- **Actual Meaning:** I was about to do something really risky, gambling with my life in a game of chance.

PRACTICE AND APPLY

Answer the following questions about idioms and dialect.

1. Linda imagines her grandmother saying, "Linda, you are killing me." What does she mean by this idiom?
2. In the following chart, write the dialogue as it would be said in standard English.

Dialect	Standard English
"Your grandmother is all bowed down wid trouble now."	
"When dey finds you is gone, dey won't want de plague ob de chillern."	
"Dey knows ebery inch ob dis house."	
"Linda, is you gwine all alone?"	
"If you does, you vil nebber git thro' dis world."	

Compare Structure

When you compare how structural elements convey meaning in multiple texts on the same topic, you identify key ideas and make connections between them. It's easier to do this when the texts you're comparing are the same genre, such as two poems. But you can get a thorough understanding of the topic by comparing texts from different genres, such as a poem and an autobiography.

In a small group, complete the Venn diagram with similarities and differences between the structural elements in the two texts you read. One example is completed for you.

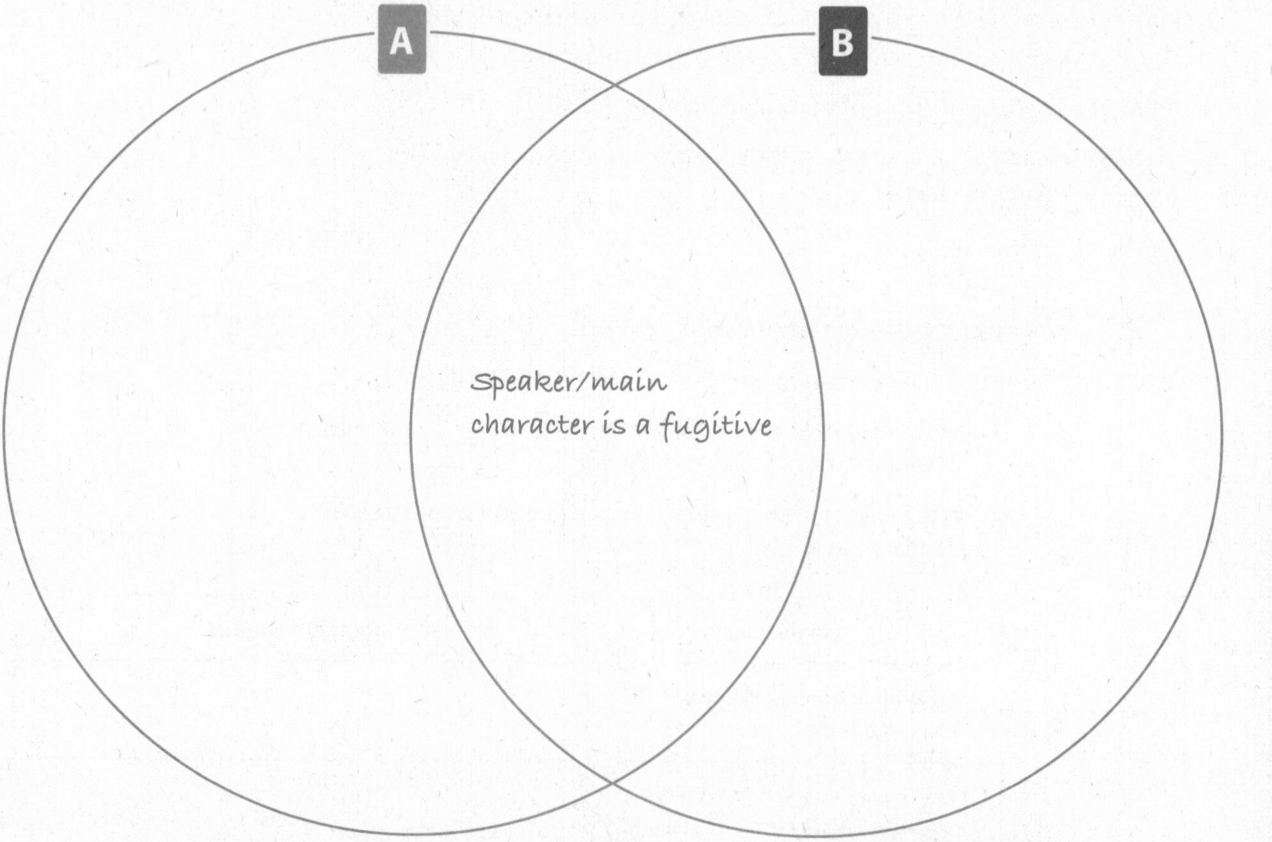

A | B

Both: *Speaker/main character is a fugitive*

"Runagate Runagate" | Both | *from* Incidents in the Life of a Slave Girl

Analyze the Texts

Discuss these questions in your group.

1. **ANALYZE** How does each author use word choice to portray the speakers or characters in their works?
2. **CONTRAST** What differences are there between the structure of the two works?
3. **EVALUATE** Why do you think each author chose their particular genre to convey their message about slavery?
4. **CITE EVIDENCE** Both writers strongly condemn slavery. Find an example from each work that shows their feelings.

Collaborate and Share

Now, your group can continue exploring what you've been learning about structure through a group presentation. The focus will be to answer this question: How does the structure of each text help the authors develop their ideas about slavery?

1. **TRACE DEVELOPMENT OF IDEAS** Although the texts you read are from different genres, each contains a strong message against slavery. Scan the texts for ideas about slavery that the poet or writer introduces. Look for ideas stated directly and ideas that can be inferred from details in the texts. Note the ideas and details that elaborate on them.

	A "Runagate Runagate"	B *from* Incidents in the Life of a Slave Girl
Ideas Introduced	**1.** **2.** **3.**	**1.** **2.** **3.**
Elaboration of Ideas	**1.** **2.** **3.**	**1.** **2.** **3.**

2. **EVALUATE** Now that you have noted the ideas about slavery in the texts, think about how the writers reveal their attitudes toward slavery. For example, do they include details that affect readers emotionally or do they try to appeal to the readers' sense of right and wrong? If so, are they effective? Which text did you prefer and why?

3. **SHARE WHAT YOU LEARN** In a small group, discuss which structure you preferred and why, supporting your preference with evidence from the text. Listen carefully to any questions and respond thoughtfully. Then, ask questions to help others clarify their ideas.

Reader's Choice

Continue your exploration of the Essential Questions for this unit by doing some independent reading. Read the titles and descriptions shown. Then mark the texts that interest you.

ESSENTIAL QUESTION:
Review the four Essential Questions for this unit on page 379.

Short Reads

Available on 

These texts are available in your ebook. Choose one to read and rate. Then defend your rating to the class.

Letter to Sarah Ballou

Letter by **Sullivan Ballou**

What does a Civil War officer write to his wife when he is not sure he will survive an upcoming battle?

Rate It 

from The Fortunes

Novel by **Peter Ho Davies**

Find out what happens when the railroad baron Charles Crocker asks his valet, Ah Ling, to help resolve a labor dispute on the Transcontinental Railroad.

Rate It 

What to the Slave Is the Fourth of July?

Speech by **Frederick Douglass**

How should someone who was once held in slavery respond to the celebration of freedom while many are still enslaved?

Rate It ☆☆☆☆☆

Go Down, Moses; Follow the Drinking Gourd; Swing Low, Sweet Chariot

Spirituals

Experience the longing and hopefulness of enslaved people through the words of three traditional spirituals.

Rate It 

Imagine the Angels of Bread

Poem by **Martín Espada**

Can injustice and suffering lead people to hope and inspire them to action?

Rate It ☆☆☆☆☆

Long Reads

Here are three recommended books that connect to this unit topic. For additional options, ask your teacher, school librarian, or peers. Which titles spark your interest?

Their Eyes Were Watching God

Novel by **Zora Neale Hurston**

Janie retells her search for love through three marriages. She has a mind of her own, but rigid gender expectations get in her way.

Born a Crime

Autobiography by **Trevor Noah**

Comedian Trevor Noah describes his childhood in South Africa under Apartheid..

Homegoing

Novel by **Yaa Gyasi**

One sister marries into a life of comfort, while the other is sold into slavery. These events affect their descendants through eight generations.

Extension

↳ Connect & Create

WITH FREEDOM COMES... The four Essential Questions imply that freedom requires sacrifice or has restrictions. Is this true for the text you chose? If so, what sacrifices were made or how was freedom limited? Discuss your ideas with others who read the same text you did, or create a web page or podcast to share your thoughts.

DIVIDE AND CONQUER Division between people is a theme that runs through many of the texts in this unit. In the texts you read independently, what divides the characters from their family, their community, or the larger society? Can they control what divides them in any way? If you were in their shoes, what would you do to bridge the divide?

NOTICE & NOTE

- **Pick one of the texts and annotate the Notice & Note signposts you find.**
- **Then use the Notice & Note Writing Frames to help you write about the significance of the signposts.**
- **Compare your findings with those of other students who read the same text.**

Notice & Note Writing Frames

Write an Argument

Writing Prompt

Write an argument for publication on your school website. Identify a current barrier to self-determination. Then, specify a solution to the problem so that self-determination is possible for more members of society.

Manage your time carefully so that you can

- review the texts in the unit;
- plan your argument;
- write your argument; and
- revise and edit your argument.

Be sure to

- state your claim;
- cite evidence from multiple sources;
- address an opposing claim; and
- maintain a formal and objective tone.

Review the Mentor Text

For an example of a well-written text that you can use as a mentor text and source for your argument, review

- **"Declaration of Sentiments"** (pages 462–464)

Consult your notes and annotations about this text. Think about how the author makes her arguments convincing.

Consider Your Sources

Review the list of texts in the unit and choose at least three that you may want to use as support for your argument.

As you review potential sources, consult the notes you made on your **Response Log** and make additional notes about ideas that might be useful as you write. Include titles and page numbers so that you can easily find the information later.

UNIT 4 SOURCES

- [ ] **Second Inaugural Address**
- [ ] **To My Old Master**
- [ ] **Aftermath of the Civil War** MEDIA
- [ ] **An Occurrence at Owl Creek Bridge**
- [ ] **Building the Transcontinental Railroad**
- [ ] **Declaration of Sentiments**
- [ ] **Speech to the American Equal Rights Association**
- [ ] **Runagate Runagate**
- [ ] *from* **Incidents in the Life of a Slave Girl**

Analyze the Prompt

Review the prompt to make sure you understand the assignment.

Circle the sentence in the prompt that identifies the topic. Rephrase the topic in your own words.

Then, look for words that indicate the purpose and audience of your argument. Write a sentence describing each.

Find a Purpose

Two common purposes of an argument are

- to convince others to agree with your position
- to motivate others to take action

What is my topic? What is my writing task?

What is my purpose for writing the argument?

Who is my audience?

Review the Rubric

Your argument will be scored using a rubric. As you write, focus on the characteristics of a high-scoring essay as described in the chart. You will learn more about these characteristics as you work through the lesson.

Purpose, Focus, and Organization	Evidence and Elaboration	Conventions of Standard English
The response includes • a strongly maintained claim • effective responses to opposing claims • use of transitions to connect ideas • logical progression of ideas • appropriate style and tone	The response includes • integrated thorough and relevant evidence • precise references to sources • effective use of elaboration • varied sentence structure	The response may include • some minor errors in usage but no pattern of errors • correct punctuation, capitalization, sentence formation, and spelling • command of basic conventions

1 PLAN YOUR ARGUMENT

Develop a Claim

In an argument, the **claim** is the writer's position on an issue. A good claim is clear, direct, and focused on a single idea. Use the questions in the chart to develop your claim.

What are some barriers to self-determination today?	
When is self-determination possible?	
How can people or society work to overcome these barriers?	
What is your position, or claim?	

Identify Support

To build a strong argument, you must have solid support for your claim. Support consists of reasons and evidence.

- **Reasons** explain why you have taken your position on an issue.
- **Evidence**—facts, statistics, examples, or expert opinions—support your reasons.

Use the chart to outline your support for your argument.

Record Your Sources

Be sure to write down the title, author, and page numbers for any source you use as evidence for your argument.

Reason:	Evidence:	Source:
Reason:	Evidence:	Source:
Reason:	Evidence:	Source:
Reason:	Evidence:	Source:

Address Opposing Claims

Some readers may disagree with your position. They may believe that other circumstances are necessary to create self-determination. Your argument should include:

- An **opposing claim** in which you restate at least one differing view;
- A **counterclaim**, or refutation, in which you explain why your position is more valid.

Use the following chart to plan how you will refute an opposing claim.

Opposing Claim:
Counterclaim:

Help with Planning

Consult **Interactive Writing Lesson: Writing Arguments**

Organize Your Ideas

As you write your argument, make sure readers can follow your line of reasoning. Use the table below to help you organize your ideas.

INTRODUCTION	• Clearly introduce your claim. • Include an interesting anecdote, quotation, or statistic to grab your reader's attention.
BODY PARAGRAPHS	• Support your thesis with reasons and evidence. • Include an opposing claim and your counterclaim. • Link your ideas with transitional words and phrases. • Clarify relationships among your claim, reasons, evidence, opposing claims, and counterclaims.
CONCLUSION	• Restate the claim in a new way. • Emphasize the significance of the issue or include a call to action.

Put It in Order

Consider presenting your ideas in order of importance. Try one of these options:

- **Begin with your strongest reason and end with the second-strongest reason.**
- **Begin with the second-strongest reason and end with the strongest one.**

2 DEVELOP A DRAFT

Now it is time to draft your essay. You can improve your writing by analyzing what the experts do. Take a look at the techniques professional writers use to craft their arguments.

Refer to Sources

EXAMINE THE MENTOR TEXT

Notice how the author of "Declaration of Sentiments" imitates the language of the Declaration of Independence. By doing so, her words resonate with patriotic Americans and establish the metaphor that men act toward women just like King George acted toward the colonists.

The author **refers to** language in the Declaration of Independence.

> The history of mankind is a history of repeated injuries and usurpations on the part of man toward woman, having in direct object the establishment of an absolute tyranny over her. To prove this, let facts be submitted to a candid world.

Here she **quotes** Jefferson's words directly.

APPLY TO YOUR DRAFT

As you develop your reasons, you will need to cite some information from sources directly. Use signal phrases to identify the source. Then, paraphrase or quote from the source. Finally, elaborate on how ideas in the source support your reason.

Elaborative Techniques

You can use the following techniques to elaborate on your evidence and support your ideas on self-determination.

- **Examples:** provide specific information to illustrate the detail.
- **Description:** use vivid details to create a picture for the reader.
- **Definition:** provide the meaning of a concept that might be unfamiliar.

Signal Phrase	Paraphrase or Quotation	Elaborate
As [author] states in [title], . . .		
According to [author], . . .		
[Author] clearly asserts that . . .		

Address Opposing Claims

Drafting Online

Check your assignment list for a writing task from your teacher.

EXAMINE THE MENTOR TEXT

Addressing opposing claims can strengthen your argument. Notice how Elizabeth Cady Stanton addresses an opposing claim on page 463 of "Declaration of Sentiments."

The author includes an **opposing claim** that **challenges** her view.

> Prudence, indeed, will dictate, that governments long established should not be changed for light and transient causes; and accordingly, all experience hath shown that mankind are more disposed to suffer, while evils are sufferable, than to right themselves by abolishing the forms to which they are accustomed. But when a long train of abuses and usurpations, pursuing invariably the same object, evinces a design to reduce them under absolute despotism, it is their duty to throw off such government, and provide new guards for their future security.

Here she uses a **counterclaim** to **refute** the opposing claim.

APPLY TO YOUR DRAFT

In your argument, refute at least one opposing claim and explain the importance of your counterclaim. Use the chart as a guide as you refute and crush opposing claims.

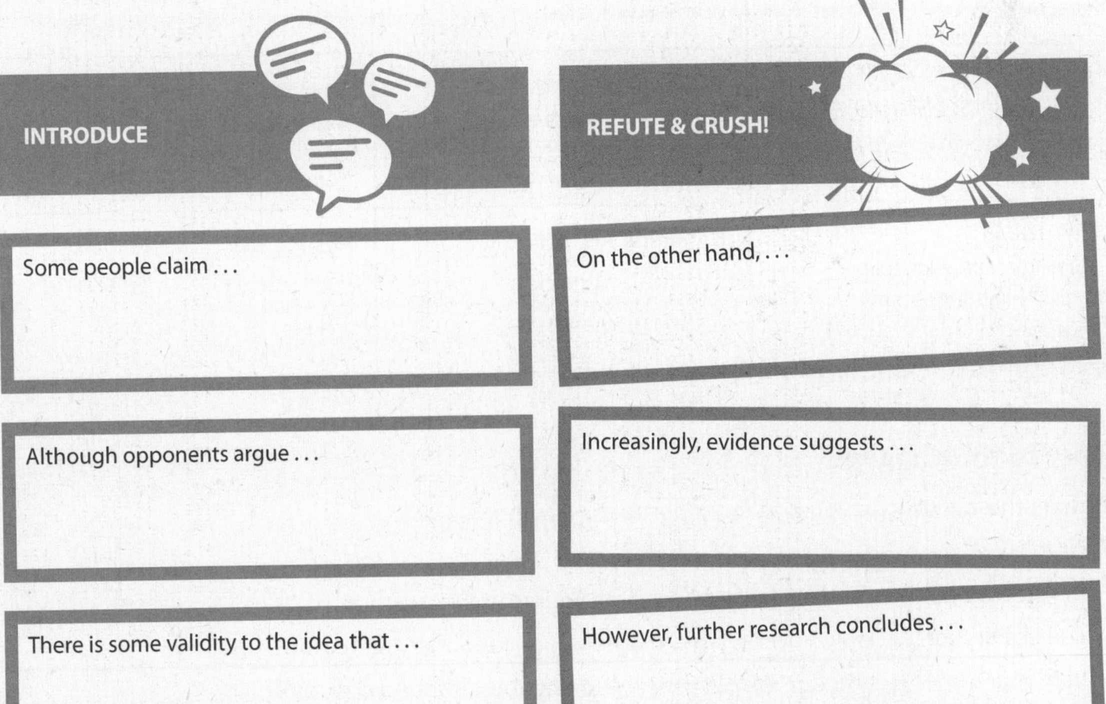

INTRODUCE
REFUTE & CRUSH!
Some people claim . . .
On the other hand, . . .
Although opponents argue . . .
Increasingly, evidence suggests . . .
There is some validity to the idea that . . .
However, further research concludes . . .

REVISE YOUR ARGUMENT

Experienced writers rethink their ideas and rework their prose to be sure their arguments are strong and clear. Use the guide to help you revise your argument.

Help with Revision

Find a **Peer Review Guide** and **Student Models** online.

REVISION GUIDE		
Ask Yourself	**Prove It**	**Revise It**
Introduction Does my introduction establish my claim and its significance?	**Circle** your claim. **Set a star** (★) beside your statement of significance.	**Reword** your introduction so that it clearly states your claim and communicates its significance.
Support Do I support my claim with strong reasons? Is my evidence strong and relevant?	**Highlight** each reason. **Underline** evidence that supports each reason.	**Add** one reason per paragraph. **Revise** weak or unexplained evidence.
Citing Sources Do I cite my sources?	**Set a star** (★) beside each citation.	**State** the title or author's name where citations are missing.
Opposing Claims Have I addressed and refuted an opposing claim.	**Highlight** the opposing claim. **Underline** the counterclaim.	**Add** the opposing claim and counterclaim.
Organization Is my essay logically organized with transitions linking ideas and evidence?	**Bracket** [ ] major sections that reflect your organizational structure. **Circle** transitions.	**Reorder** paragraphs as needed. **Add** transitions to clarify relationships between ideas.
Style Do I use formal, precise language and maintain an objective tone?	**Cross out** (✗) slang or informal language. **Put a check** (✓) beside biased perspectives.	**Reword** to increase formality. **Replace** sentences that express an attitude or opinion.
Conclusion Does my conclusion follow logically and support my reasoning?	**Underline** your conclusion.	**Restate** your claim in different words and clarify its significance.

APPLY TO YOUR DRAFT

Consider the following as you look for opportunities to improve your writing:

- In your introduction, add a detail that will grab your reader's attention.
- Use elaboration to clarify how each piece of evidence supports your reasons.
- Vary your sentence structure so that your argument doesn't sound choppy or dense.

Peer Review in Action

ANALYZE A STUDENT MODEL

Now that you have revised your argument, exchange papers with a partner for a **peer review.** During your peer review, give suggestions for how to improve each other's drafts.

Read a developing paragraph from a student's draft and examine her peer reviewer's comments.

First Draft

"Finding a Voice for Self-Determination"
By Priscilla Washington, Southmost High School

For most of us, self-determination means making our own choices with hope and confidence that we will have a good future. Some, such as people with intellectual disabilities, have traditionally been excluded. However, in today's society, self-determination is possible when barriers to self-determination are overcome through political action and public speaking.

Try to make your first sentence more dramatic.

Your claim is clear, but maybe you could reword to build interest.

Now read the revised introduction below. Notice how the writer has improved her draft by making revisions based on her peer reviewer's comments.

Revision

"Finding a Voice for Self-Determination"
By Priscilla Washington, Southmost High School

My brother Simon has Down syndrome. When he was younger, he spent many hours working with a speech therapist and an occupational therapist. Today, Simon has surmounted a huge barrier to his self-determination: He has a job. He has a sense of independence. He can make some choices based on hope and confidence that he will have a good life. Although Simon has some barriers to self-determination, because of political action and speeches to Congress about the importance of people such as Simon, he is one of thousands who, thanks to those who cared truly about the principle of self-determination for all, has found his voice.

Much better! This story brings the issue to life and hooks the reader.

This phrase shows there are people like Simon who deserve self-determination.

APPLY TO YOUR DRAFT

As you review your partner's work, give specific suggestions to support claims and reasons more effectively. Use your revision guide to help you.

When facing feedback from a partner, listen attentively and ask questions to make sure that you fully understand your reviewer's suggestions.

4 EDIT YOUR ARGUMENT

Apply the finishing touches to your draft. Edit your draft to check for proper use of standard English conventions and to correct any misspellings or grammatical errors.

Interactive Grammar Lesson: Verb Tense

Watch Your Language!

USE THE CORRECT VERB TENSE

The tense of a verb indicates the time of action or a state of being. Time of action can be past, present, future, ongoing action in the past, or a continuing action or state.

Read the following sentences from "Declaration of Sentiments." Then use the information in the "What Time Is It?" box to help identify the verb tenses.

He **has compelled** her to submit to laws, in the formation of which she **had** no voice.

Whenever any form of Government **becomes** destructive of those ends, it **is** the right of those who **suffer** from it . . .

We **shall employ** agents, **circulate** tracts, **petition** the State and National Legislatures, and **endeavor** to enlist the pulpit and the press in our behalf.

What Time Is It?

Use the correct verb tense to clarify when actions occur.

The **simple present** describes facts that are always true or actions that happen habitually.

The **simple past** describes an action or a state that has been completed.

The **present perfect** describes an action or a state that began in the past and continues.

The **future tense** describes an action or a state that will occur in the future.

APPLY TO YOUR DRAFT

Now apply what you have learned to your own work.

1. **Read your paper aloud.** Listen to your word choices and the rhythm of your sentences.
2. **Check your verb choices.** Make sure you have used the correct verb tense for the ideas you wish to convey.
3. **Exchange drafts** with a peer and review your writing, checking the conventions and grammar, including verb tenses.

5 PUBLISH YOUR ARGUMENT

Share It!

Finalize your argument for your class website. You may also use your report as inspiration for other projects.

Ways to Share

- **Stage an interview in which you use a question-and-answer format to argue your points in front of your class.**
- **Post your argument to a blog and invite your classmates to comment on your ideas.**
- **Argue your ideas in a class debate in which your classmates challenge you with opposing claims. See the next task for tips.**

Speaking & Listening

Prepare a Debate

Now that you have supported your claim with strong reasons and evidence, it's time to persuade others to agree with you. Adapt your argument for a **debate**.

Plan Your Debate Presentation

In a group, assign a moderator and decide on a debate format. Then divide the group into teams. One team will argue the pro side of your argument on self-determination; the other team will argue the opposing side.

As you work with your team, be sure to assign

- each reason to a different team member
- one or two team members to refute opposing claims
- a team member to develop and present your digital media

Use these questions as you plan with your team.

Be Prepared

Every member of your team must participate actively during your planning sessions.
Use the following steps to get ready for the debate:

- Always come prepared.
- Give and accept constructive feedback.
- Set clear goals and deadlines.
- Accept tasks.
- Meet your deadlines.

Questions	Answers	Notes
What claim are you making about barriers to self-determination?		
What reasons and evidence will you present to support your claim?		
What opposing claims do you anticipate? How will you refute them?		
How can you adapt language to simplify ideas and create a more persuasive effect?		
What statistics and visuals will be effective for your arguments?		
How can you conclude compellingly so that the audience will take your side?		

Practice Your Debate

Work collaboratively with your team to build confidence in one another and to ensure that the debate will go smoothly. Practice as often as necessary so that you are ready for an audience.

Now it's time to practice with your team. Listen and take notes as your team members present their reasons and evidence. Make sure your suggestions are courteous and respectful.

Use these questions to take notes and provide specific suggestions for improvement.

Respect Your Opponents and Your Audience

- **Listen thoughtfully to your opponents' line of reasoning.**
- **Respectfully acknowledge and refute opposing claims.**
- **Address all sides of the issue.**
- **Recognize your audience's prior knowledge.**

Questions	Yes	No	Suggestions
Are the main points and the speaker's stance on the issue clear?			
Are the relationships among claims, reasons, and evidence clear to the listener?			
Does the speaker effectively use rhetorical devices such as questions, repetition, and humor?			
Does the speaker convey confidence and speak clearly?			
Do the speaker's visuals clarify ideas without distracting from the presentation?			

Record Your Debate

After your group has practiced, work with your teacher to plan a method for recording your debate. Ask yourself:

- Was our argument clear?
- Was our tone and pace appropriate?
- Did the use of media enhance our argument?

Interactive Speaking & Listening Lesson: Giving a Presentation

Share It!

- **Present the video to your class.** Discuss debate etiquette and how speakers showed respect for their opponents.
- **Send the video** to an organization that fights barriers to self-determination in society.
- **Take a class poll** to determine which team's arguments were most convincing.

Reflect & Extend

Here are some other ways to show your understanding of the ideas in Unit 4.

Reflect on the Essential Questions

Think about the Essential Question you identified as most intriguing on page 380. Has your answer to the question changed after reading the texts in the unit? Discuss your ideas.

You can use these sentence starters to help you reflect on your learning:

- **One change that occurred from the Civil War was . . .**
- **I was surprised by . . .**
- **One question I still have is . . .**

Project-Based Learning

Create a Documentary

You've read about the Civil War and its aftermath. Now, explore one of the events, issues, or people discussed in this unit as the subject of a documentary. Research a range of views from historic writings of the era as well as the insights of historians today. Consider performing a reenactment of an event, or conduct interviews with Civil War historians.

Use your research to plan a script. Develop an objective view with your narration, presenting various points of view. Then, answer these questions:

- How do the views of Civil War contemporaries compare with those of historians looking back at the time?
- Does your choice of visuals, reenactments, interviews, or sound effects accurately reflect the multiple viewpoints surrounding the era?
- What biases did you uncover during your research? What do those biases reveal about the era and its importance in American history?

Media Project

To find help with this task online, access **Create a Documentary.**

Writing

Write an Informative Essay

Examine one or two groups in society who faced barriers to self-determination and write about how these people gained more control over their lives.

As you plan and write your informative essay, be sure to

- state a central idea in your introduction;
- use evidence from reliable primary and secondary sources;
- develop a clear and coherent structure; and
- conclude with a reminder of your central idea and an interesting thought.

"Reality is that which, when you stop believing it, doesn't go away."

—Philip K. Dick

An Age of Realism

America Transformed

As you read the texts in this unit, think about how they explore these Essential Questions.

How much do we control our lives?
After the Civil War, it seemed that life was unfair for immigrants, laborers, and other oppressed groups. Despite their efforts, their circumstances did not improve.

Why do humans cause harm?
Powerful people showed cruelty toward those who could not defend themselves in the decades after the Civil War. In this unit, you will consider the impact harmful acts can have on others.

What are the consequences of change?
For some people, such as industrialists and oligarchs, their lives and fortunes improved as a result of the Civil War. But others suffered because of the changes that took place.

What makes a place unique?
In the late 19th century, people in the United States were proud of their regional identities. However, holding on to distinctive traits proved difficult in an era of rapid change.

ANALYZE THE IMAGE
How does the image reflect transition and transformation?

Explore unit themes and build background.

Stream to Start Video

Spark Your Learning

As you read, you can use the **Response Log** (page R5) to track your thinking about the Essential Questions.

Here are some opportunities to think about issues related to **Unit 5: America Transformed.**

Think About the **Essential Questions**

Review the Essential Questions on page 517. Which question is most intriguing to you? Perhaps it relates to something you have read or reminds you of a personal experience. Write down your thoughts.

Make the Connection

A transformation is a meaningful, thorough change. When we talk about the transformation of a person, we might refer to a change in their physical appearance or way of thinking. What does it mean for a country to transform? Discuss your ideas with a classmate.

Build Academic Vocabulary

You can use these Academic Vocabulary words to write and talk about the topics and themes in the unit. Which of these words do you already feel comfortable using when speaking or writing?

	I can use it!	I understand it.	I'll look it up.
ambiguous			
clarify			
implicit			
revise			
somewhat			

Prove It!
Use one of the Academic Vocabulary words in a sentence about a place you have been that you thought was unique.

Preview the Texts

Review the images, titles, and descriptions of the texts in the unit. Mark the title of the text that interests you most.

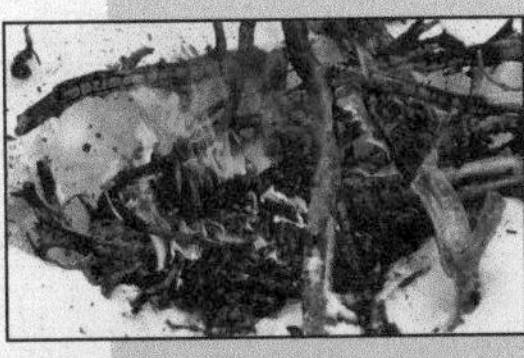

To Build a Fire

Short Story by **Jack London**

A man traverses the freezing Yukon territory with only a dog to help him.

The Lowest Animal

Essay by **Mark Twain**

Humans may not feel proud of themselves after reading this scathing essay.

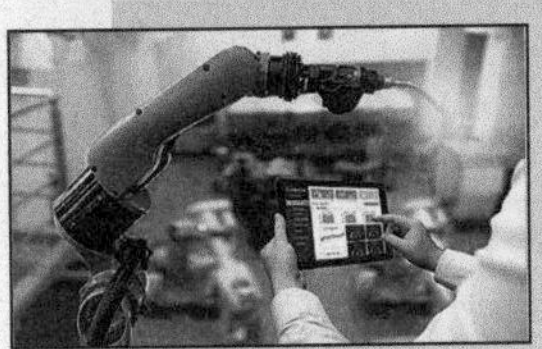

The Fourth Industrial Revolution Is Here. Are You Ready?

Article by **Bernard Marr**

Learn about the way work will change and how it will affect you.

The Story of an Hour

Short Story by **Kate Chopin**

A masterful writer shows us how many twists and turns can happen in a short time.

Chicago

Poem by **Carl Sandburg**

An iconic American city is celebrated in this classic poem.

from **The Jungle**

Novel by **Upton Sinclair**

Follow Jurgis Rudkus as he learns more about his job in the meatpacking industry.

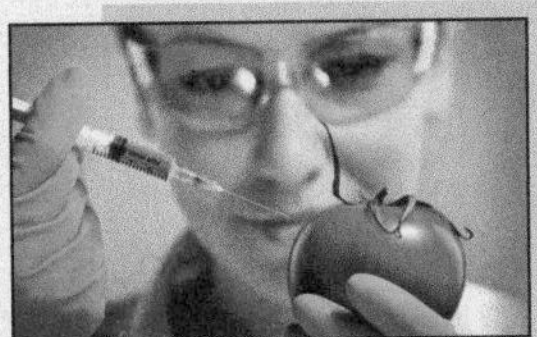

Food Product Design
from **Fast Food Nation**

Investigative Journalism by **Eric Schlosser**

There may be more to your lunch than meets the eye.

An Age of Realism

America Transformed

After the Civil War, America underwent radical change. The Transcontinental Railroad carried thousands of settlers to the West. The huge herds of bison that had roamed the plains were decimated, and Native Americans were driven off their land to make way for settlers. By the 1880s, most Native Americans were confined to reservations, usually on land deemed worthless by white settlers. The West would never be the same.

New Wealth on Display

A very small group of men controlled the vast share of the country's growing industry, including the enormously profitable steel, railroad, oil, and meatpacking sectors. This era became known as the "Gilded Age." It was a time of sparkle and glitter, luxury and excess, and it was dominated by "robber barons" like railroad mogul Cornelius Vanderbilt, oil tycoon John D. Rockefeller, and steel magnate Andrew Carnegie.

Many ordinary people had more money, too, and all sorts of new things to spend it on. The rising middle class could take the train to the amusement parks and shop in new department stores. Even some blue-collar workers could afford inventions such as automobiles, telephones, and electricity.

1880

1880 John D. Rockefeller's Standard Oil Company of Ohio controls U.S. oil refining.

1884 Mark Twain publishes *The Adventures of Huckleberry Finn.*

1892 New York's Ellis Island becomes the busiest entry point for European immigrants.

Women continued to chafe under social and economic restrictions imposed on them. An increasing number of those from the middle class achieved the goal of a university education as a step toward a broader role in society. Women's rights activist Susan B. Anthony credited the bicycle with doing "more to emancipate women than anything else in the world." The movement to secure their right to vote was reinvigorated as women sought a larger voice in public life.

The Have-Nots

The railroad industry fueled industrial growth, and new manufacturing centers grew rapidly around railroad hubs in Pittsburgh, Cleveland, Detroit, and Chicago. People from the country streamed into urban areas in search of work, and immigrants came to America looking for a better life. Unfortunately, many new city dwellers found themselves working 16-hour days in airless, dangerous sweatshops for low wages.

Farmers and African Americans also faced hard times. Farmers borrowed money from banks, but high interest rates meant many of them lost their land. The failures of Reconstruction left many African Americans powerless and poor. People knew they were missing out on the prosperity, and it made them angry. Workers began to form labor unions, and many farmers, white and Black, joined the Populist Party, hoping to make the government more responsive to their needs.

EXTEND

Think of a question you have about a topic, event, or person from the historical period. Then, research the answer and add it as an entry to the timeline.

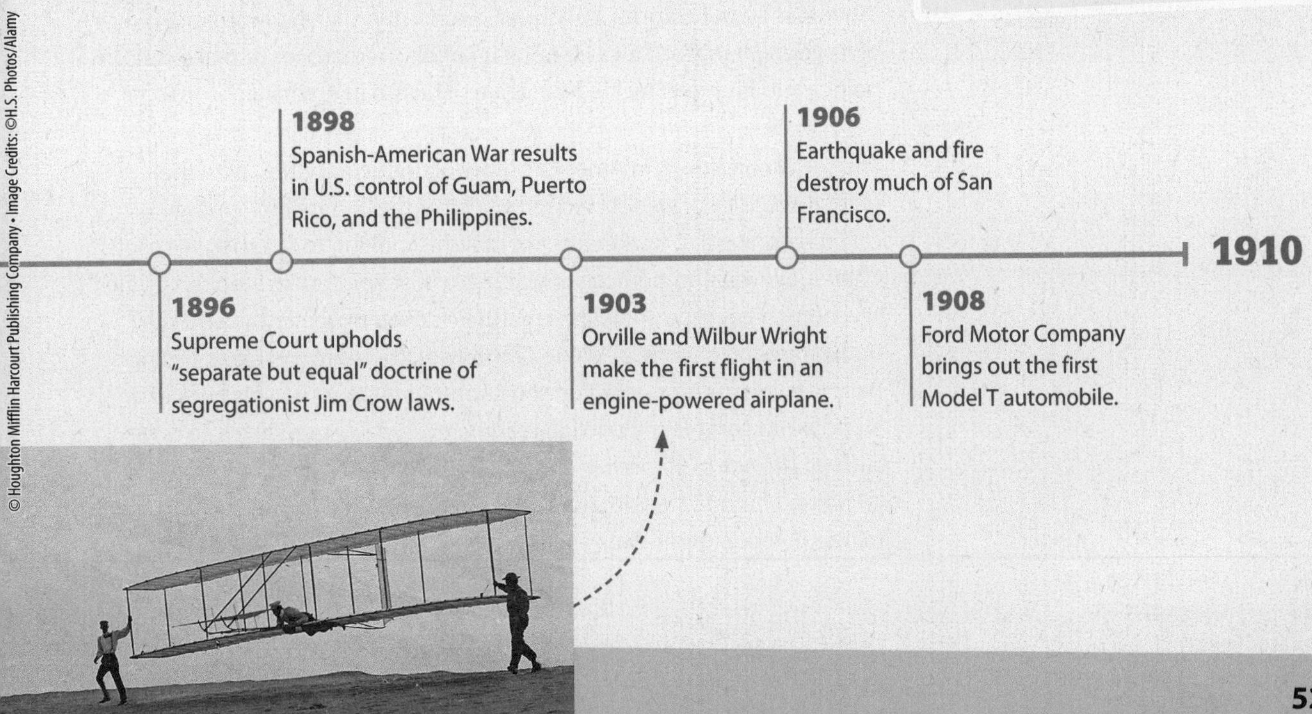

1896
Supreme Court upholds "separate but equal" doctrine of segregationist Jim Crow laws.
1898
Spanish-American War results in U.S. control of Guam, Puerto Rico, and the Philippines.
1903
Orville and Wilbur Wright make the first flight in an engine-powered airplane.
1906
Earthquake and fire destroy much of San Francisco.
1908
Ford Motor Company brings out the first Model T automobile.
1910

Realism Takes Root

The changing world was reflected in the work of realist writers who portrayed ordinary lives as they were, without romance or sentimentality, through a variety of genres and forms. Some writers began to capture the customs, characters, and landscapes of the nation's distinct regions—a type of writing called regionalism. Mark Twain, Kate Chopin, and Willa Cather celebrated America's diversity in settings ranging from Mississippi River towns and the city of New Orleans to the plains of Nebraska. The publication in 1884 of Twain's *The Adventures of Huckleberry Finn* marked the high point of regionalism. It was the first novel written entirely in "American"—the colorful, colloquial, and frequently ungrammatical voice of its young narrator, Huck Finn. Twain often used humor to make serious points, and his novel tackled the issue of racism in America.

The social conditions in America's growing industrial cities, with their great disparities of wealth, led to the rise of the literary movement called naturalism, a starker form of realism. Looking to the theories of Charles Darwin and other scientists, naturalist writers like Stephen Crane saw human beings as helpless creatures moved by forces beyond their understanding or control. While Crane and others gave voice to ordinary people living in cities, Jack London captured readers with his tales of an arctic world completely outside readers' everyday experiences. In novels such as *The Age of Innocence* and *The House of Mirth,* Edith Wharton combined naturalism with her own experiences to decry the stifling small-mindedness of upper-class society.

Reform-minded journalists influenced by naturalism were part of a progressive movement that aimed to restore economic opportunities and correct injustices in American life. One group, known as "muckrakers," sought to expose the political and economic corruption that resulted from the excessive power of large corporations. Among this group was Upton Sinclair, whose novel *The Jungle* tells the story of a Lithuanian immigrant who works in the Chicago meatpacking industry. The novel's descriptions of the appalling conditions in packing plants and the contaminated meat they produced helped lead to the passage of new laws regulating the food industry.

COLLABORATIVE DISCUSSION

In a small group, review the essay and the timeline. Discuss the literary or other kinds of events that had the most impact on this era in America.

Assessment Practice

Choose the best answer to each question.

1. Why was this period referred to as the "Gilded Age"?

- (A) It was a time of luxury and excess for some.
- (B) Many people discovered gold in the West.
- (C) Industry was run by philanthropists.
- (D) The majority of Americans belonged to the middle class.

2. *The Adventures of Huckleberry Finn* was the first novel to —

- (A) tackle the issue of racism
- (B) be written entirely in "American"
- (C) expose corruption in large corporations
- (D) be written by an African American

3. Who were "muckrakers"?

- (A) white settlers who drove the Native Americans from their land
- (B) immigrants who lived in crowded tenements and worked for low wages
- (C) writers who sought to expose corruption
- (D) leaders of industry who exploited their workers

Test-Taking Strategies

Get Ready

To Build a Fire

Short Story by **Jack London**

ESSENTIAL QUESTION:
How much do we control our lives?

Engage Your Brain

Choose one or more of these activities to start connecting with the story you're about to read.

Into the Wild

Spending time in the wilderness can be exciting and fun. But it is really important that you are prepared before you go. Imagine you're going on an expedition in the wilderness alone. What will you include in your backpack? Think about

- clothes
- food
- personal necessities
- tools

Remember, you have just one backpack, so you have to make some difficult decisions.

How's the Weather Up There?

"To Build a Fire" takes place in the Yukon, a territory in northwestern Canada. Do some research to learn what life is like there.

- Find three notable facts about the climate in the Yukon.
- Pick a date and find out what the weather would be like on that day.
- Create a weather report for that day and share it with the class.

Animal Instinct

Some people believe that animals have a "sixth sense" that helps them identify danger or perceive their environment in a way that humans can't. Have you ever seen or read about an animal that made you believe it had a "sixth sense"? Share your ideas with the class.

Analyze Character

When you read a story, you may ask yourself *why* a character behaved a certain way. The answer to this question is the character's **motivation**—the reason behind the actions. Sometimes a character's motivation is uncertain or may change depending on the situation. It is up to you to infer the motivation based on details in the text.

A character's behavior can lead to conflicts and may determine how they are resolved. As you read, note how the writer shows the character changing as the plot develops. Use the chart to record notable behaviors and infer the underlying motivations.

Character	Behavior	Motivation
Man		
Dog		

Focus on Genre
Short Story

- features a conflict that affects a main character
- features a theme, or message about life that the author wants to share
- may have a setting that reflects the historical and cultural context of a certain time period

Analyze Setting

Setting is the time and place in which a story takes place. When writers depict the setting, they may describe details about the environment. They also may add details that reflect the historical and cultural context of the time, like descriptions of architecture or social expectations. The setting in "To Build a Fire" reflects two literary movements that were popular when Jack London wrote this story: realism and naturalism.

Movement	Characteristics
Realism	• presents life objectively and without sentimentality • focuses on how progress impacts people in the middle and lower classes • depicts the cultural and political realities of the time
Naturalism	• influenced by scientific ideas such as Charles Darwin's theory of natural selection • shows that one's environment and instincts determine behavior • portrays human destiny as out of an individual's control

As you read, look for details about setting. Notice how London uses characteristics of realism and naturalism in his setting.

Annotation in Action

Here are notes a student made about the opening paragraph from "To Build a Fire." As you read, highlight details that describe the setting and reflect the influence of realism and naturalism.

Day had broken cold and gray, exceedingly cold and gray, when the man turned aside from the main Yukon trail and climbed the high earth bank, where a dim and little-traveled trail led eastward through the fat spruce timberland. It was a steep bank, and he paused for breath at the top, excusing the act to himself by looking at his watch.

Lots of details about the weather and the place. The setting will be important.

Expand Your Vocabulary

Put a check mark next to the vocabulary words that you feel comfortable using when writing or speaking.

intangible	☐
apprehension	☐
panic	☐
imperative	☐
extremity	☐

Then, write a short description of being lost in the wilderness, using as many of the words as you can. As you read "To Build a Fire," use the definitions in the side column to learn the vocabulary words you don't already know.

Background

Jack London (1876–1916) not only wrote adventure stories, he lived them. London traveled as a hobo across the United States, tried his luck in the Klondike Gold Rush, escaped a typhoon on a seal-hunting ship, and sailed the South Seas in his own boat, the *Snark*. London's formal education was limited, but he read widely using public libraries. Many of his works, including the story "To Build a Fire," have themes involving survival and humans versus nature. His novel *The Call of the Wild* (1903) brought London fame and is still one of his best-known works. London died in California at age 40.

To Build a Fire

Short Story by **Jack London**

A man and a dog face extreme weather conditions in very different ways.

NOTICE & NOTE
As you read, use the side margins to make notes about the text.

1 Day had broken cold and gray, exceedingly cold and gray, when the man turned aside from the main Yukon trail and climbed the high earth bank, where a dim and little-traveled trail led eastward through the fat spruce timberland. It was a steep bank, and he paused for breath at the top, excusing the act to himself by looking at his watch. It was nine o'clock. There was no sun or hint of sun, though there was not a cloud in the sky. It was a clear day, and yet there seemed an **intangible** pall[1] over the face of things, a subtle gloom that made the day dark, and that was due to the absence of sun. This fact did not worry the man. He was used to the lack of sun. It had been days since he had seen the sun, and he knew that a few more days must pass before that cheerful orb, due south, would just peep above the skyline and dip immediately from view.

intangible
(ĭn-tăn´jə-bəl) *adj.* unable to be defined or understood.

[1] **pall:** overspreading atmosphere of gloom and depression.

2 The man flung a look back along the way he had come. The Yukon lay a mile wide and hidden under three feet of ice. On top of this ice were as many feet of snow. It was all pure white, rolling in gentle undulations where the ice jams of the freeze-up had formed. North and south, as far as his eye could see, it was unbroken white, save for a dark hairline that curved and twisted from around the spruce-covered island to the south, and that curved and twisted away into the north, where it disappeared behind another spruce-covered island. This dark hairline was the trail—the main trail—that led south five hundred miles to the Chilkoot Pass, Dyea, and salt water; and that led north seventy miles to Dawson, and still on to the north a thousand miles to Nulato, and finally to St. Michael on the Bering Sea, a thousand miles and half a thousand more.

ANALYZE CHARACTER

Annotate: Mark words or phrases in paragraph 3 that describe the man.

Infer: What does this description of the man suggest about how he will fare during his journey?

3 But all this—the mysterious, far-reaching hairline trail, the absence of sun from the sky, the tremendous cold, and the strangeness and weirdness of it all—made no impression on the man. It was not because he was long used to it. He was a newcomer in the land, a cheechako,[2] and this was his first winter. The trouble with him was that he was without imagination. He was quick and alert in the things of life, but only in the things, and not in the significances. Fifty degrees below zero meant eighty-odd degrees of frost. Such fact impressed him as being cold and uncomfortable, and that was all. It did not lead him to meditate upon his frailty as a creature of temperature, and upon man's frailty in general, able only to live within certain narrow limits of heat and cold, and from there on it did not lead him to the conjectural[3] field of immortality and man's place in the universe. Fifty degrees below zero stood for a bite of frost that hurt and that must be guarded against by the use of mittens, earflaps, warm moccasins, and thick socks. Fifty degrees below zero was to him just precisely fifty degrees below zero. That there should be anything more to it than that was a thought that never entered his head.

ANALYZE SETTING

Annotate: In paragraphs 4–5, mark words that describe the weather conditions.

Predict: How will the weather affect the events of the story?

4 As he turned to go on, he spat speculatively. There was a sharp, explosive crackle that startled him. He spat again. And again, in the air, before it could fall to the snow, the spittle crackled. He knew that at fifty below, spittle crackled on the snow, but this spittle had crackled in the air. Undoubtedly it was colder than fifty below—how much colder he did not know. But the temperature did not matter. He was bound for the old claim[4] on the left fork of Henderson Creek, where the boys were already. They had come over across the divide from the Indian Creek country, while he had come the roundabout way to take a look at the possibilities of getting out

Close Read Screencast

Listen to a modeled close read of this text.

[2] **cheechako:** Chinook jargon for "newcomer" or "tenderfoot."

[3] **conjectural:** based on guesswork or uncertain evidence.

[4] **claim:** piece of land staked out by a miner.

logs in the spring from the islands in the Yukon. He would be into camp by six o'clock; a bit after dark, it was true, but the boys would be there, a fire would be going, and a hot supper would be ready. As for lunch, he pressed his hand against the protruding bundle under his jacket. It was also under his shirt, wrapped up in a handkerchief and lying against the naked skin. It was the only way to keep the biscuits from freezing. He smiled agreeably to himself as he thought of those biscuits, each cut open and sopped in bacon grease, and each enclosing a generous slice of fried bacon.

5 He plunged in among the big spruce trees. The trail was faint. A foot of snow had fallen since the last sled had passed over, and he was glad he was without a sled, traveling light. In fact, he carried nothing but the lunch wrapped in the handkerchief. He was surprised, however, at the cold. It certainly was cold, he concluded, as he rubbed his numb nose and cheekbones with his mittened hand. He was a warm-whiskered man, but the hair on his face did not protect the high cheekbones and the eager nose that thrust itself aggressively into the frosty air.

6 At the man's heels trotted a dog, a big native husky, the proper wolf dog, gray coated and without any visible or temperamental difference from its brother, the wild wolf. The animal was depressed by the tremendous cold. It knew that it was no time for traveling. Its instinct told it a truer tale than was told to the man by the man's judgment. In reality, it was not merely colder than fifty below zero; it was colder than sixty below, than seventy below. It was seventy-five below zero. Since the freezing point is thirty-two above zero, it meant that one hundred and seven degrees of frost obtained. The dog did not know anything about thermometers. Possibly in its brain there was no sharp consciousness of a condition of very cold such as was in the man's brain. But the brute had its instinct. It experienced a vague but menacing **apprehension** that subdued it and made it slink along at the man's heels, and that made it question eagerly every unwonted[5] movement of the man, as if expecting him to go into camp or to seek shelter somewhere and build a fire. The dog had learned fire, and it wanted fire, or else to burrow under the snow and cuddle its warmth away from the air.

7 The frozen moisture of its breathing had settled on its fur in a fine powder of frost, and especially were its jowls, muzzle, and eyelashes whitened by its crystaled breath. The man's red beard and moustache were likewise frosted, but more solidly, the deposit taking the form of ice and increasing with every warm, moist breath he exhaled. Also, the man was chewing tobacco, and the muzzle of ice held his lips so rigidly that he was unable to clear his chin when he expelled the juice. The result was that a crystal beard of the color and

Don't forget to **Notice & Note** as you read the selection.

ANALYZE CHARACTER

Annotate: Mark details in paragraph 6 that describe the dog's behavior.

Analyze: How does the dog's behavior differ from the man's?

apprehension (ăp-rĭ-hĕn´shən) *n.* fear or anxiety; dread.

[5] **unwonted:** unusual.

solidity of amber was increasing its length on his chin. If he fell down it would shatter itself, like glass, into brittle fragments. But he did not mind the appendage.[6] It was the penalty all tobacco chewers paid in that country, and he had been out before in two cold snaps. They had not been so cold as this, he knew, but by the spirit thermometer[7] at Sixty Mile he knew they had been registered at fifty below and at fifty-five.

8 He held on through the level stretch of woods for several miles, crossed a wide flat, and dropped down a bank to the frozen bed of a small stream. This was Henderson Creek, and he knew he was ten miles from the forks. He looked at his watch. It was ten o'clock. He was making four miles an hour, and he calculated that he would arrive at the forks at half past twelve. He decided to celebrate that event by eating his lunch there.

9 The dog dropped in again at his heels, with a tail drooping discouragement, as the man swung along the creek bed. The furrow of the old sled trail was plainly visible, but a dozen inches of snow covered the marks of the last runners. In a month no man had come up or down that silent creek. The man held steadily on. He was not much given to thinking, and just then particularly, he had nothing to think about save that he would eat lunch at the forks and that at six o'clock he would be in camp with the boys. There was nobody to talk to; and, had there been, speech would have been impossible because of the ice muzzle on his mouth. So he continued monotonously to chew tobacco and to increase the length of his amber beard.

10 Once in a while the thought reiterated[8] itself that it was very cold and that he had never experienced such cold. As he walked along he rubbed his cheekbones and nose with the back of his mittened hand. He did this automatically, now and again changing hands. But rub as he would, the instant he stopped his cheekbones went numb, and the following instant the end of his nose went numb. He was sure to frost his cheeks; he knew that, and experienced a pang of regret that he had not devised a nose strap of the sort Bud wore in the cold snaps. Such a strap passed across the cheeks, as well, and saved them. But it didn't matter much, after all. What were frosted cheeks? A bit painful, that was all; they were never serious.

11 Empty as the man's mind was of thought, he was keenly observant, and he noticed the changes in the creek, the curves and bends and timber jams, and always he sharply noted where he placed his feet. Once, coming around a bend, he shied abruptly, like a startled horse, curved away from the place where he had been walking, and retreated several paces back along the trail. The creek, he knew, was frozen clear to the bottom—no creek could contain water in that arctic winter—but he knew also that there were springs

ANALYZE SETTING

Annotate: In paragraph 11, mark the clues that convey how dangerous the trail is.

Predict: What do you think will happen, based on the details about the springs?

[6] **appendage:** something attached to another object.

[7] **spirit thermometer:** alcohol thermometer. In places where the temperature often drops below the freezing point of mercury, alcohol is used in thermometers.

[8] **reiterated:** repeated.

Don't forget to **Notice & Note** as you read the selection.

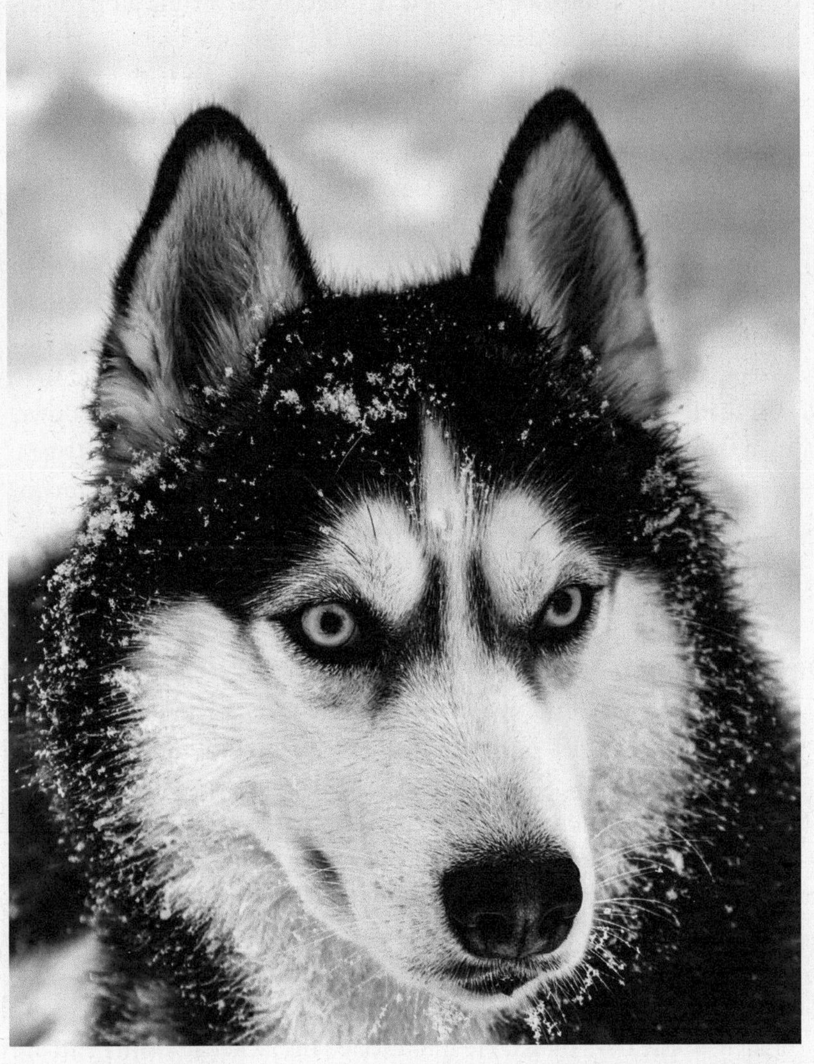

that bubbled out from the hillsides and ran along under the snow and on top of the ice of the creek. He knew that the coldest snaps never froze these springs, and he knew likewise their danger. They were traps. They hid pools of water under the snow that might be three inches deep, or three feet. Sometimes a skin of ice half an inch thick covered them, and in turn was covered by the snow. Sometimes there were alternate layers of water and ice skin, so that when one broke through he kept on breaking through for a while, sometimes wetting himself to the waist.

12 That was why he had shied in such **panic.** He had felt the give under his feet and heard the crackle of a snow-hidden ice skin. And to get his feet wet in such a temperature meant trouble and danger. At the very least it meant delay, for he would be forced to stop and build a fire, and under its protection to bare his feet while he dried his socks and moccasins. He stood and studied the creek bed and its banks, and decided that the flow of water came from the right. He reflected awhile, rubbing his nose and cheeks, then skirted to the left, stepping gingerly and testing the footing for each step. Once clear of

panic
(păn′ĭk) *n.* sudden, overpowering feeling of fear.

the danger, he took a fresh chew of tobacco and swung along at his four-mile gait.

13 In the course of the next two hours he came upon several similar traps. Usually the snow above the hidden pools had a sunken, candied appearance that advertised the danger. Once again, however, he had a close call; and once, suspecting danger, he compelled the dog to go on in front. The dog did not want to go. It hung back until the man shoved it forward, and then it went quickly across the white, unbroken surface. Suddenly it broke through, floundered to one side, and got away to firmer footing. It had wet its forefeet and legs, and almost immediately the water that clung to it turned to ice. It made quick efforts to lick the ice off its legs, then dropped down in the snow and began to bite out the ice that had formed between the toes. This was a matter of instinct. To permit the ice to remain would mean sore feet. It did not know this. It merely obeyed the mysterious prompting that arose from the deep crypts[9] of its being. But the man knew, having achieved a judgment on the subject, and he removed the mitten from his right hand and helped tear out the ice particles. He did not expose his fingers more than a minute, and was astonished at the swift numbness that smote[10] them. It certainly was cold. He pulled on the mitten hastily, and beat the hand savagely across his chest.

ANALYZE CHARACTER

Annotate: In paragraph 14, mark what the man forgets to do and how he feels.

Infer: What does this action tell you about the man and how nature might be affecting him? What effect will these actions have on him?

14 At twelve o'clock the day was at its brightest. Yet the sun was too far south on its winter journey to clear the horizon. The bulge of the earth intervened between it and Henderson Creek, where the man walked under a clear sky at noon and cast no shadow. At half past twelve, to the minute, he arrived at the forks of the creek. He was pleased at the speed he had made. If he kept it up, he would certainly be with the boys by six. He unbuttoned his jacket and shirt and drew forth his lunch. The action consumed no more than a quarter of a minute, yet in that brief moment the numbness laid hold of the exposed fingers. He did not put the mitten on, but instead struck the fingers a dozen sharp smashes against his leg. Then he sat down on a snow-covered log to eat. The sting that followed upon the striking of his fingers against his leg ceased so quickly that he was startled. He had had no chance to take a bite of biscuit. He struck the fingers repeatedly and returned them to the mitten, baring the other hand for the purpose of eating. He tried to take a mouthful, but the ice muzzle prevented. He had forgotten to build a fire and thaw out. He chuckled at his foolishness, and as he chuckled he noted the numbness creeping into the exposed fingers. Also, he noted that the stinging which had first come to his toes when he sat down was already passing away. He wondered whether the toes were warm or numb. He moved them inside the moccasins and decided that they were numb.

15 He pulled the mitten on hurriedly and stood up. He was a bit frightened. He stamped up and down until the stinging returned

[9] **crypts:** hidden recesses.

[10] **smote:** powerfully struck.

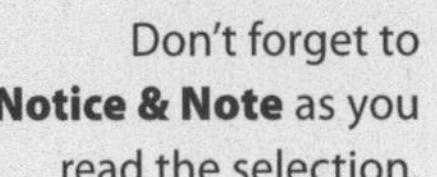

Don't forget to **Notice & Note** as you read the selection.

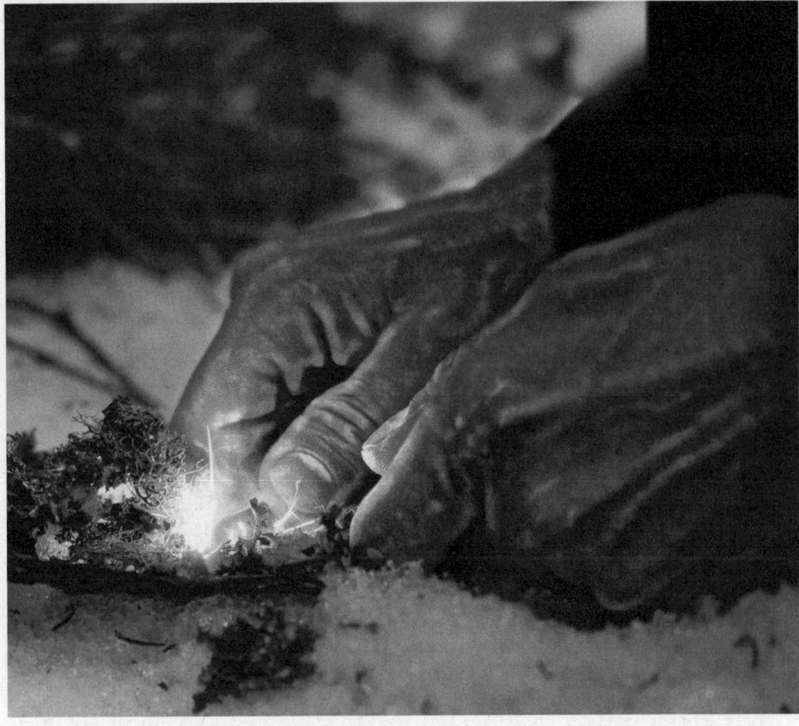

into the feet. It certainly *was* cold, was his thought. That man from Sulphur Creek had spoken the truth when telling how cold it sometimes got in the country. And he had laughed at him at the time! That showed one must not be too sure of things. There was no mistake about it, it was cold. He strode up and down, stamping his feet and threshing his arms, until reassured by the returning warmth. Then he got out matches and proceeded to make a fire. From the undergrowth, where high water of the previous spring had lodged a supply of seasoned twigs, he got his firewood. Working carefully from a small beginning, he soon had a roaring fire, over which he thawed the ice from his face and in the protection of which he ate his biscuits. For the moment the cold of space was outwitted. The dog took satisfaction in the fire, stretching out close enough for warmth and far enough away to escape being singed.

16 When the man had finished, he filled his pipe and took his comfortable time over a smoke. Then he pulled on his mittens, settled the earflaps of his cap firmly about his ears, and took the creek trail up the left fork. The dog was disappointed and yearned back toward the fire. This man did not know cold. Possibly all the generations of his ancestry had been ignorant of cold, of real cold, of cold one hundred and seven degrees below freezing point. But the dog knew; all its ancestry knew, and it had inherited the knowledge. And it knew that it was not good to walk abroad in such fearful cold. It was the time to lie snug in a hole in the snow and wait for a curtain of cloud to be drawn across the face of outer space whence this cold came. On the other hand, there was no keen intimacy between the dog and the man. The one was the toil slave of the other, and the only caresses it

ANALYZE SETTING

Annotate: In paragraph 16, mark the words that contrast what the dog and the man understand about the cold.

Summarize: How does this paragraph reflect the ideas of naturalism?

had ever received were the caresses of the whiplash and of harsh and menacing throat sounds that threatened the whiplash. So the dog made no effort to communicate its apprehension to the man. It was not concerned in the welfare of the man; it was for its own sake that it yearned back toward the fire. But the man whistled, and spoke to it with the sound of whiplashes, and the dog swung in at the man's heels and followed after.

17 The man took a chew of tobacco and proceeded to start a new amber beard. Also, his moist breath quickly powdered with white his mustache, eyebrows, and lashes. There did not seem to be so many springs on the left fork of the Henderson, and for half an hour the man saw no signs of any. And then it happened. At a place where there were no signs, where the soft, unbroken snow seemed to advertise solidity beneath, the man broke through. It was not deep. He wet himself halfway to the knees before he floundered out to the firm crust.

18 He was angry, and cursed his luck aloud. He had hoped to get into camp with the boys at six o'clock, and this would delay him an hour, for he would have to build a fire and dry out his footgear. This was **imperative** at that low temperature—he knew that much; and he turned aside to the bank, which he climbed. On top, tangled in the underbrush about the trunks of several small spruce trees, was a high-water deposit of dry firewood—sticks and twigs, principally, but also larger portions of seasoned branches and fine, dry, last year's grasses. He threw down several large pieces on top of the snow. This served for a foundation and prevented the young flame from drowning itself in the snow it otherwise would melt. The flame he got by touching a match to a small shred of birch bark that he took from his pocket. This burned even more readily than paper. Placing it on the foundation, he fed the young flame with wisps of dry grass and with the tiniest dry twigs.

imperative
(ĭm-pĕr´ə-tĭv) *adj.* of great importance; essential.

19 He worked slowly and carefully, keenly aware of his danger. Gradually, as the flame grew stronger, he increased the size of the twigs with which he fed it. He squatted in the snow, pulling the twigs out from their entanglement in the brush and feeding directly to the flame. He knew there must be no failure. When it is seventy-five below zero, a man must not fail in his first attempt to build a fire—that is, if his feet are wet. If his feet are dry, and he fails, he can run along the trail for a half a mile and restore his circulation. But the circulation of wet and freezing feet cannot be restored by running when it is seventy-five below. No matter how fast he runs, the wet feet will freeze the harder.

20 All this the man knew. The old-timer on Sulphur Creek had told him about it the previous fall, and now he was appreciating the advice. Already all sensation had gone out of his feet. To build the fire, he had been forced to remove his mittens, and the fingers had

quickly gone numb. His pace of four miles an hour had kept his heart pumping blood to the surface of his body and to all the **extremities.** But the instant he stopped, the action of the pump eased down. The cold of space smote the unprotected tip of the planet, and he, being on that unprotected tip, received the full force of the blow. The blood of his body recoiled before it. The blood was alive, like the dog, and like the dog it wanted to hide away and cover itself up from the fearful cold. So long as he walked four miles an hour, he pumped that blood, willy-nilly,[11] to the surface; but now it ebbed away and sank down into the recesses of his body. The extremities were the first to feel its absence. His wet feet froze the faster, and his exposed fingers numbed the faster, though they had not yet begun to freeze. Nose and cheeks were already freezing, while the skin of all his body chilled as it lost its blood.

extremity
(ĭk-strĕm´ĭ-tē) *n.* the outermost or farthest point or portion; the hand or foot.

21 But he was safe. Toes and nose and cheeks would be only touched by the frost, for the fire was beginning to burn with strength. He was feeding it twigs the size of his finger. In another minute he would be able to feed it with branches the size of his wrist, and then he could remove his wet footgear, and, while it dried, he could keep his naked feet warm by the fire, rubbing them at first, of course, with snow. The fire was a success. He was safe. He remembered the advice of the old-timer on Sulphur Creek, and smiled. The old-timer had been very serious in laying down the law that no man must travel alone in the Klondike after fifty below. Well, here he was; he had had the accident; he was alone; and he had saved himself. Those old-timers were rather womanish, some of them, he thought. All a man had to do was to keep his head and he was all right. Any man who was a man could travel alone. But it was surprising, the rapidity with which his cheeks and nose were freezing. And he had not thought his fingers could go lifeless in so short a time. Lifeless they were, for he could scarcely make them move together to grip a twig, and they seemed remote from his body and from him. When he touched a twig, he had to look and see whether or not he had hold of it. The wires were pretty well down between him and his finger ends.

ANALYZE CHARACTER

Annotate: In paragraph 21, mark what the old-timer said and how the man reacts to it.

Evaluate: Were the old-timer's words wiser than the man first believed? Cite text evidence to explain your answer.

22 All of which counted for little. There was the fire, snapping and crackling and promising life with every dancing flame. He started to untie his moccasins. They were coated with ice; the thick German socks were like sheaths of iron halfway to the knees; and the moccasin strings were like rods of steel all twisted and knotted as by some conflagration.[12] For a moment he tugged with his numb fingers, then, realizing the folly of it, he drew his sheath knife.

23 But before he could cut the strings it happened. It was his own fault, or, rather, his mistake. He should not have built the fire under the spruce tree. He should have built it in the open. But it had been easier to pull the twigs from the bush and drop them directly on the fire. Now the tree under which he had done this carried a

[11] **willy-nilly:** without choice.
[12] **conflagration:** large fire.

weight of snow on its boughs. No wind had blown for weeks, and each bough was fully freighted. Each time he had pulled a twig he had communicated a slight agitation to the tree—an imperceptible agitation, so far as he was concerned, but an agitation sufficient to bring about the disaster. High up in the tree one bough capsized its load of snow. This fell on the boughs beneath, capsizing them. This process continued, spreading out and involving the whole tree. It grew like an avalanche, and it descended without warning upon the man and the fire, and the fire was blotted out! Where it had burned was a mantle of fresh and disordered snow.

24 The man was shocked. It was as though he had just heard his own sentence of death. For a moment he sat and stared at the spot where the fire had been. Then he grew very calm. Perhaps the old-timer on Sulphur Creek was right. If he had only had a trail mate, he would have been in no danger now. The trail mate could have built the fire. Well, it was up to him to build the fire over again, and this second time there must be no failure. Even if he succeeded, he would most likely lose some toes. His feet must be badly frozen by now, and there would be some time before the second fire was ready.

25 Such were his thoughts, but he did not sit and think them. He was busy all the time they were passing through his mind. He made a new foundation for a fire, this time in the open, where no treacherous tree could blot it out. Next he gathered dry grasses and tiny twigs from the high-water flotsam.[13] He could not bring his fingers together to pull them out, but he was able to gather them by the handful. In this way he got many rotten twigs and bits of green moss that were undesirable, but it was the best he could do. He worked methodically, even collecting an armful of the larger branches to be used later when the fire gathered strength. And all the while the dog sat and watched him, a certain yearning wistfulness in its eyes, for it looked upon him as the fire provider, and the fire was slow in coming.

26 When all was ready, the man reached in his pocket for a second piece of birch bark. He knew the bark was there, and, though he could not feel it with his fingers, he could hear its crisp rustling as he fumbled for it. Try as he would, he could not clutch hold of it. And all the time, in his consciousness, was the knowledge that each instant his feet were freezing. This thought tended to put him in a panic, but he fought against it and kept calm. He pulled on his mittens with his teeth, and threshed his arms back and forth, beating his hands with all his might against his sides. He did this sitting down, and he stood up to do it; and all the while the dog sat in the snow, its wolf brush of a tail curled around warmly over its forefeet, its sharp wolf ears pricked forward intently as it watched the man. And the man, as he beat and threshed with his arms and hands, felt a great surge of envy

[13] **high-water flotsam:** branches and debris washed ashore by a stream or river during the warm months, when the water is high.

as he regarded the creature that was warm and secure in its natural covering.

27 After a time he was aware of the first faraway signals of sensation in his beaten fingers. The faint tingling grew stronger till it evolved into a stinging ache that was excruciating, but which the man hailed with satisfaction. He stripped the mitten from his right hand and fetched forth the birch bark. The exposed fingers were quickly going numb again. Next he brought out his bunch of sulphur matches. But the tremendous cold had already driven the life out of his fingers. In his effort to separate one match from the others, the whole bunch fell in the snow. He tried to pick it out of the snow, but failed. The dead fingers could neither touch nor clutch. He was very careful. He drove the thought of his freezing feet, and nose, and cheeks, out of his mind, devoting his whole soul to the matches. He watched, using the sense of vision in place of that of touch, and when he saw his fingers on each side of the bunch, he closed them—that is, he willed to close them, for the wires were down, and the fingers did not obey. He pulled the mitten on the right hand, and beat it fiercely against his knee. Then, with both mittened hands, he scooped the bunch of matches, along with much snow, into his lap. Yet he was no better off.

28 After some manipulation he managed to get the bunch between the heels of his mittened hands. In this fashion he carried it to his mouth. The ice crackled and snapped when by a violent effort he opened his mouth. He drew the lower jaw in, curled the upper lip out of the way, and scraped the bunch with his upper teeth in order to separate a match. He succeeded in getting one, which he dropped on his lap. He was no better off. He could not pick it up. Then he devised a way. He picked it up in his teeth and scratched it on his leg. Twenty times he scratched before he succeeded in lighting it. As it flamed he held it with his teeth to the birch bark. But the burning brimstone went up his nostrils and into his lungs, causing him to cough spasmodically.[14] The match fell into the snow and went out.

29 The old-timer on Sulphur Creek was right, he thought in the moment of controlled despair that ensued: After fifty below, a man should travel with a partner. He beat his hands, but failed in exciting any sensation. Suddenly he bared both hands, removing the mittens with his teeth. He caught the whole bunch between the heels of his hands. His arm muscles, not being frozen, enabled him to press the hand heels tightly against the matches. Then he scratched the bunch along his leg. It flared into flame, seventy sulphur matches at once! There was no wind to blow them out. He kept his head to one side to escape the strangling fumes, and held the blazing bunch to the birch bark. As he so held it, he became aware of sensation in his hand. His flesh was burning. He could smell it. Deep down below the surface he could feel it. The sensation developed into pain that grew acute. And

[14] **spasmodically:** in a sudden, violent manner; fitfully.

Don't forget to **Notice & Note** as you read the selection.

ANALYZE SETTING

Annotate: Mark the sentences in paragraph 27 that depict the man's struggle with nature.

Draw Conclusions: How do these details represent naturalist ideas?

NOTICE & NOTE

WORDS OF THE WISER

When you notice a wiser character giving advice about life to the main character, you've found a **Words of the Wiser** signpost.

Notice & Note: In paragraph 29, mark the advice the "old-timer on Sulphur Creek" had offered to the man.

Analyze: How has this advice affected the main character up to this point?

still he endured it, holding the flame of matches clumsily to the bark that would not light readily because his own burning hands were in the way, absorbing most of the flame.

30 At last, when he could endure no more, he jerked his hands apart. The blazing matches fell sizzling into the snow, but the birch bark was alight. He began laying dry grass and the tiniest twigs on the flame. He could not pick and choose, for he had to lift the fuel between the heels of his hands. Small pieces of rotten wood and green moss clung to the twigs, and he bit them off as well as he could with his teeth. He cherished the flame carefully and awkwardly. It meant life, and it must not perish. The withdrawal of blood from the surface of his body now made him begin to shiver, and he grew more awkward. A large piece of green moss fell squarely on the little fire. He tried to poke it out with his fingers, but his shivering frame made him poke too far, and he disrupted the nucleus of the little fire, the burning grasses and tiny twigs separating and scattering. He tried to poke them together again, but in spite of the tenseness of the effort, his shivering got away with him, and the twigs were hopelessly scattered. Each twig gushed a puff of smoke and went out. The fire provider had failed. As he looked apathetically[15] about him, his eyes chanced on the dog, sitting across the ruins of the fire from him, in the snow, making restless, hunching movements, slightly lifting one forefoot and then the other, shifting its weight back and forth on them with wistful eagerness.

ANALYZE SETTING

Annotate: Mark the point in paragraph 31 where the narrative shifts from the man's perspective to the dog's perspective.

Compare: One naturalist idea is that humans are simply animals. How do the thoughts of the man and the instincts of the dog suggest that London views them both as animals trying to survive?

31 The sight of the dog put a wild idea into his head. He remembered the tale of the man, caught in a blizzard, who killed a steer and crawled inside the carcass, and so was saved. He would kill the dog and bury his hands in the warm body until the numbness went out of them. Then he could build another fire. He spoke to the dog, calling it to him; but in his voice was a strange note of fear that frightened the animal, who had never known the man to speak in such a way before. Something was the matter, and its suspicious nature sensed danger—it knew not what danger, but somewhere, somehow, in its brain arose an apprehension of the man. It flattened its ears down at the sound of the man's voice, and its restless, hunching movements and the liftings and shiftings of its forefeet became more pronounced; but it would not come to the man. He got on his hands and knees and crawled toward the dog. This unusual posture again excited suspicion, and the animal sidled mincingly[16] away.

32 The man sat up in the snow for a moment and struggled for calmness. Then he pulled on his mittens, by means of his teeth, and got up on his feet. He glanced down at first in order to assure himself

[15] **apathetically:** with little interest or concern; indifferently.

[16] **sidled mincingly:** moved sideways with small steps.

that he was really standing up, for the absence of sensation in his feet left him unrelated to the earth. His erect position in itself started to drive the webs of suspicion from the dog's mind; and when he spoke peremptorily,[17] with the sound of whiplashes in his voice, the dog rendered its customary allegiance and came to him. As it came within reaching distance, the man lost his control. His arms flashed out to the dog, and he experienced genuine surprise when he discovered that his hands could not clutch, that there was neither bend nor feeling in the fingers. He had forgotten for the moment that they were frozen and that they were freezing more and more. All this happened quickly, and before the animal could get away, he encircled its body with his arms. He sat down in the snow, and in this fashion held the dog, while it snarled and whined and struggled.

33 But it was all he could do, hold its body encircled in his arms and sit there. He realized that he could not kill the dog. There was no way to do it. With his helpless hands he could neither draw nor hold his sheath knife nor throttle the animal. He released it, and it plunged wildly away, its tail between its legs and still snarling. It halted forty feet away and surveyed him curiously, with ears sharply pricked forward. The man looked down at his hands in order to locate them, and found them hanging on the ends of his arms. It struck him as curious that one should have to use his eyes in order to find out where his hands were. He began threshing his arms back and forth, beating the mittened hands against his sides. He did this for five minutes, violently, and his heart pumped enough blood up to the surface to put a stop to his shivering. But no sensation was aroused in his hands. He had an impression that they hung like weights on the ends of his arms, but when he tried to run the impression down, he could not find it.

34 A certain fear of death, dull and oppressive, came to him. This fear quickly became poignant[18] as he realized that it was no longer a mere matter of freezing his fingers and toes, or of losing his hands and feet, but that it was a matter of life and death, with the chances against him. This threw him into a panic, and he turned and ran up the creek bed along the old, dim trail. The dog joined in behind and kept up with him. He ran blindly, without intention, in fear such as he had never known in his life. Slowly, as he plowed and floundered through the snow, he began to see things again—the banks of the creek, the old timber jams, the leafless aspens, and the sky. The running made him feel better. He did not shiver. Maybe, if he ran on, his feet would thaw out; and, anyway, if he ran far enough, he would reach the camp and the boys. Without doubt he would lose some fingers and toes and some of his face; but the boys would take care

Don't forget to **Notice & Note** as you read the selection.

ANALYZE CHARACTER

Annotate: Mark the words in paragraph 34 that show a shift in the man's attitude.

Evaluate: What underlying motivations drive his choices and actions now?

[17] **peremptorily:** in a commanding way.
[18] **poignant:** painfully affecting feelings; touching.

of him, and save the rest of him when he got there. And, at the same time, there was another thought in his mind that said he would never get to the camp and the boys; that it was too many miles away, that the freezing had too great a start on him, and that he would soon be stiff and dead. This thought he kept in the background and refused to consider. Sometimes it pushed itself forward and demanded to be heard, but he thrust it back and strove to think of other things.

It struck him as curious that he could run at all on feet so frozen that he could not feel them when they struck the earth and took the weight of his body. He seemed to himself to skim along above the surface, and to have no connection with the earth. Somewhere he had once seen a winged Mercury,[19] and he wondered if Mercury felt as he felt when skimming over the earth.

[19] **Mercury:** in Roman mythology, messenger of the gods, who is depicted wearing winged sandals and a winged hat.

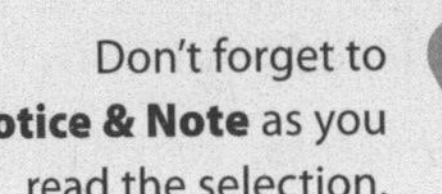

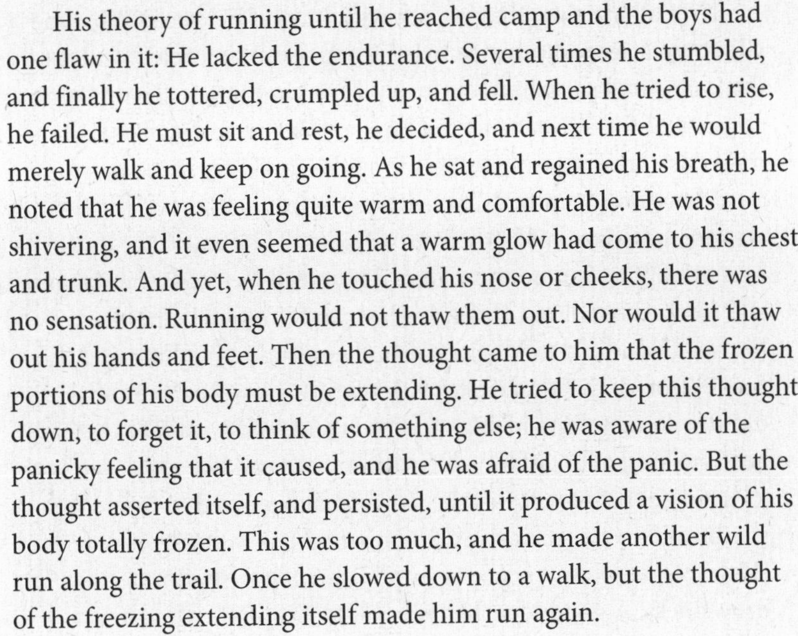

36 His theory of running until he reached camp and the boys had one flaw in it: He lacked the endurance. Several times he stumbled, and finally he tottered, crumpled up, and fell. When he tried to rise, he failed. He must sit and rest, he decided, and next time he would merely walk and keep on going. As he sat and regained his breath, he noted that he was feeling quite warm and comfortable. He was not shivering, and it even seemed that a warm glow had come to his chest and trunk. And yet, when he touched his nose or cheeks, there was no sensation. Running would not thaw them out. Nor would it thaw out his hands and feet. Then the thought came to him that the frozen portions of his body must be extending. He tried to keep this thought down, to forget it, to think of something else; he was aware of the panicky feeling that it caused, and he was afraid of the panic. But the thought asserted itself, and persisted, until it produced a vision of his body totally frozen. This was too much, and he made another wild run along the trail. Once he slowed down to a walk, but the thought of the freezing extending itself made him run again.

ANALYZE SETTING

Annotate: Mark details in paragraph 37 that indicate the man's fate is sealed.

Analyze: In what ways has the setting led the man to this moment?

37 And all the time the dog ran with him, at his heels. When he fell down a second time, it curled its tail over its forefeet and sat in front of him, facing him, curiously eager and intent. The warmth and security of the animal angered him, and he cursed it till it flattened down its ears appeasingly. This time the shivering came more quickly upon the man. He was losing in this battle with the frost. It was creeping into his body from all sides. The thought of it drove him on, but he ran no more than a hundred feet when he staggered and pitched headlong. It was his last panic. When he had recovered his breath and control, he sat up and entertained in his mind the conception of meeting death with dignity. However, the conception did not come to him in such terms. His idea of it was that he had been making a fool of himself, running around like a chicken with its head cut off—such was the simile that occurred to him. Well, he was bound to freeze anyway, and he might as well take it decently. With this newfound peace of mind came the first glimmerings of drowsiness. A good idea, he thought, to sleep off to death. It was like taking an anesthetic.[20] Freezing was not so bad as people thought. There were lots worse ways to die.

ANALYZE CHARACTER

Annotate: Mark details in paragraph 38 that show the man is dying.

Draw Conclusions: How do his thoughts signal the resolution of the story? What is the man's final realization?

38 He pictured the boys finding his body next day. Suddenly he found himself with them, coming along the trail and looking for himself. And, still with them, he came around a turn in the trail and found himself lying in the snow. He did not belong with himself anymore, for even then he was out of himself, standing with the boys and looking at himself in the snow. It certainly was cold, was his thought. When he got back to the States, he could tell the folks what real cold was. He drifted on from this to a vision of the old-timer on Sulphur Creek. He could see him quite clearly, warm and comfortable, and smoking a pipe.

39 "You were right, old hoss; you were right," the man mumbled to the old-timer of Sulphur Creek.

40 Then the man drowsed off into what seemed to him the most comfortable and satisfying sleep he had ever known. The dog sat facing him and waiting. The brief day drew to a close in a long, slow twilight. There were no signs of a fire to be made, and, besides, never in the dog's experience had it known a man to sit like that in the snow and make no fire. As the twilight drew on, its eager yearning for the fire mastered it, and with a great lifting and shifting of forefeet, it whined softly, then flattened its ears down in anticipation of being chidden[21] by the man. But the man remained silent. Later, the dog whined loudly. And still later it crept close to the man and caught the scent of death. This made the animal bristle and back away. A little longer it delayed, howling under the stars that leaped and danced and shone brightly in the cold sky. Then it turned and trotted up the trail in the direction of the camp it knew, where were the other food providers and fire providers.

---

[20] **anesthetic:** medication that causes loss of the sensation of pain.
[21] **chidden:** scolded.

COLLABORATIVE DISCUSSION

With a partner, discuss what the man could have done differently to improve his outcome.

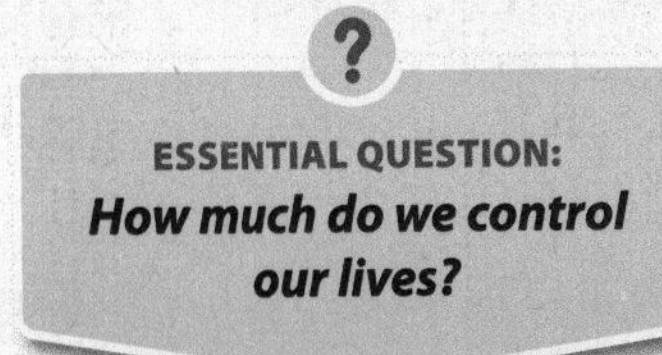
ESSENTIAL QUESTION:
How much do we control our lives?

Review your notes and add your thoughts to your **Response Log.**

Assessment Practice

Answer these questions before moving on to the **Analyze the Text** section on the following page.

1. How does the man's attitude change toward the old-timer on Sulphur Creek?

- (A) He begins to distrust him.
- (B) He begins to respect him.
- (C) He intends to ignore him.
- (D) He hopes not to meet him.

2. Why did the man watch the terrain so carefully as he walked?

- (A) He was looking for rabbit holes under the snow.
- (B) He thought he would lose the trail if he didn't watch.
- (C) He feared breaking through to water under the snow.
- (D) He was looking for the matches he had dropped.

3. Why did the man think he would make it to the camp?

- (A) He thought he knew and understood the cold.
- (B) The camp was close and the path was well traveled.
- (C) The men he would be meeting had marked the route.
- (D) The old-timer on Sulphur Creek had told him he would.

Ed

Test-Taking Strategies

Analyze the Text

Support your responses with evidence from the text.

NOTICE & NOTE

Review what you **noticed and noted** as you read the text. Your annotations can help you answer these questions.

1. **CITE EVIDENCE** What details from the first two paragraphs of the story reflect what you know about realism? How do these details impact your understanding of what follows?

2. **EVALUATE** At the beginning of the story, what motivates the man to travel? How do his motivations change over the course of his journey?

3. **COMPARE** Reread paragraph 3 and paragraph 6. How do the dog and the man differ in their understanding of the cold? Which of them seems better adapted to the setting? Cite text evidence in the chart.

Character	Evidence
Man	
Dog	

4. **DRAW CONCLUSIONS** What purpose does the dog serve in the story? How do London's descriptions of the dog reveal its function in the story?

5. **ANALYZE** As the man tries a second time to start a fire, he remembers the **Words of the Wiser** from the old-timer. How has the man's opinion of the old-timer's words changed? What message do you think London intends to convey by describing this change?

6. **ANALYZE** Works of naturalism often address the theme of survival of the fittest. Give examples that show how London's story develops this theme. What message does the story convey about the survival of the fittest?

7. **EVALUATE** Naturalism also considers larger forces that control human lives, such as nature or fate. Does London think that the man ever had a chance in this harsh climate, or was he doomed from the start? Explain.

Choices

Here are some other ways to demonstrate your understanding of the ideas in this lesson.

Writing

↳ Analyze the Themes

Write a literary analysis in which you analyze the naturalist themes in "To Build a Fire."

1. Review your answer to item 6 in Analyze the Text on page 544. Think about how London develops the theme of survival of the fittest.
2. Then, review your answer to item 7 to explore how London examines how larger forces control the man's life.
3. Consider how these two themes relate to one another.
4. Cite details and examples from the text to support your ideas about the story's themes and how they interact.

As you write and discuss, be sure to use the **Academic Vocabulary** words.

- ambiguous
- clarify
- implicit
- revise
- somewhat

Speaking & Listening

↳ How Do You Get Inspired?

In his lifetime, Jack London worked as an investigative journalist in London, was a war correspondent in Korea, and even tried to sail around the world. He once said, "Don't loaf and invite inspiration; light out after it with a club, and if you don't get it you will nonetheless get something that looks remarkably like it."

Think about whether travel is essential for inspiration, or you can find inspiration in your everyday surroundings. Share your thoughts with the class.

Social & Emotional Learning

↳ Evaluate the Ending

London's original version of "To Build a Fire" tells a similar story, but the man survives and becomes a wiser person from his experience. Do you prefer the ending in this version or in the version that you just read? Express your view in a class poll. Then, form teams based on the results and give reasons to justify your opinion.

Expand Your Vocabulary

PRACTICE AND APPLY

Answer the questions to demonstrate your knowledge of the vocabulary words.

intangible	apprehension	panic	imperative	extremity

1. What are some **intangible** characteristics that make athletes successful?
2. Why might you feel **apprehension** right before an important exam?
3. Under what circumstances might someone feel **panic**?
4. Why is it **imperative** that you wear a seat belt when riding in a car?
5. Why is it hard for a country to defend the **extremity** of a border?

Vocabulary Strategy

Allusions and Word Origins

Interactive Vocabulary Lesson: Understanding Word Origins

Many English words are derived from Greek and Roman mythology. For example, the word *panic* alludes to the Greek god Pan, who was said to instill fear in people. *Panic* literally means "of or relating to Pan," but it more commonly refers to fear-induced agitation. You may also know the word *mercurial*. It is an **allusion,** or indirect reference, to the Roman god Mercury, who was a messenger to the other gods. *Mercurial* means having the characteristics of eloquence, shrewdness, swiftness, and thievishness attributed to Mercury. It can also mean "quick" or "changeable."

PRACTICE AND APPLY

Use reference materials to determine which allusions the following words derive from. Note the English meaning and how the allusion clarifies the meaning of each word.

1. cereal
2. martial
3. echo
4. nemesis
5. music

Watch Your Language!

Syntax

Syntax is the sentence structure the writer uses. Syntax includes the use of different sentence types (simple, complex, compound, compound-complex) or sentence fragments. It can also describe the writer's sentence length. In the passage below, London's syntax involves the use of short sentences for effect.

> **But before he could cut the strings it happened. It was his own fault, or, rather, his mistake. He should not have built the fire under the spruce tree. He should have built it in the open. But it had been easier to pull the twigs from the bush and drop them directly on the fire.**

The short sentences in this passage fit the simple, blunt truth they reveal: the man has made a mistake and may die because of it. Additionally, the short sentences help create the detached tone of the passage, which states the truth of what is happening in realistic detail but without emotion.

In this earlier passage, however, London uses longer sentences:

> **The frozen moisture of [the dog's] breathing had settled on its fur in a fine powder of frost, and especially were its jowls, muzzle, and eyelashes whitened by its crystaled breath. The man's red beard and moustache were likewise frosted, but more solidly, the deposit taking the form of ice and increasing with every warm, moist breath he exhaled.**

Interactive Grammar Lesson: Sentence Structure

These longer sentences create a different effect as they describe the ways in which the extreme cold affects the dog and the man. The details build up through the long sentences to illustrate the dangerous level of cold.

PRACTICE AND APPLY

Using varied syntax, write your own paragraph to describe a memorable event. Think carefully about when and why you would use sentences of different lengths. Also, consider what effect your syntax will create.

Get Ready

The Lowest Animal

Essay by **Mark Twain**

ESSENTIAL QUESTION:
Why do humans cause harm?

Engage Your Brain

Choose one or more of these activities to start connecting with the essay you're about to read.

It. Was. The. Most. Awesome. Thing. EVER.

Everybody likes to exaggerate now and then, making objects or events bigger and better (or smaller and worse) than they really are.

- Jot down a couple of things that happened to you and your friends this week.
- Now describe one of them but add details that make it seem more interesting or more important than it really was.
- Share your description with a few classmates. Then discuss how you tried to make your stories more entertaining.

LOL!

Think of a time when a comic made you laugh by pointing out a funny or odd human behavior.

- What behavior was the comic making fun of?
- Did you think it was funny? Why or why not?
- What one word would you use to describe the comic's tone?

Analyze Satire

Satire is a literary form that ridicules the shortcomings of people or institutions in an attempt to change or improve something in society. Techniques you may find in satire include the following:

- **humor:** describing something in a way that causes laughter or amusement
- **exaggeration:** overstating something to draw attention to it and make a point
- **absurdity:** describing extreme situations that are impossible to take seriously
- **irony:** stating the opposite of what is really meant

As you read, note Twain's use of these techniques and whether they are effective. What does Twain hope to change by writing this satire?

Focus on Genre
↳ **Satire**

- exposes the vices and folly of humans and society
- uses humor, irony, exaggeration, absurdity, and other techniques
- is often intended to bring about social or political change

Analyze Tone

The **tone** of a work is the writer's attitude toward his or her subject. A writer reveals tone through word choice, details, and sometimes direct statements of his or her position.

Twain's subject is a comparison of humans to other animals. As you read, notice the difference in Twain's tone when he discusses humans as opposed to animals. You can use the chart to note details that reveal Twain's tone.

Attitude Toward Humans	Attitude Toward Animals

Annotation in Action

Here is an example of notes a student made about Twain's tone in "The Lowest Animal." As you read, notice other details that reveal Twain's tone.

I have been studying the traits and dispositions of the "lower animals" (so-called) and contrasting them with the traits and dispositions of man. I find the result humiliating to me. For it obliges me to renounce my allegiance to the Darwinian theory of the Ascent of Man from the Lower Animals, since it now seems plain to me that that theory ought to be vacated in favor of a new and truer one, this new and truer one to be named the Descent of Man from the Higher Animals.

Twain likes "lower animals" better than humans.

Expand Your Vocabulary

Put a check mark next to the vocabulary words that you feel comfortable using when writing or speaking.

disposition	☐
caliber	☐
transition	☐
atrocious	☐

Then, write a description of a time you saw an animal behave in a memorable way. Use as many vocabulary words as you can in your description. As you read "The Lowest Animal," use the definitions in the side-column to learn the vocabulary words you don't already know.

Background

Mark Twain (1835–1910) was the pen name of Samuel Langhorne Clemens, the American author best known for his novel *The Adventures of Huckleberry Finn*, based on his own boyhood in Missouri. As a journalist, moralist, and lecturer, he frequently used humor to communicate his ideas. In his later years, Twain wrote many satirical essays commenting on the human species. This essay, first published in 1962, was probably written in 1896. In it, Twain refers to Charles Darwin's theory of evolution, first published in *On the Origin of Species* in 1859.

The Lowest Animal

Essay by **Mark Twain**

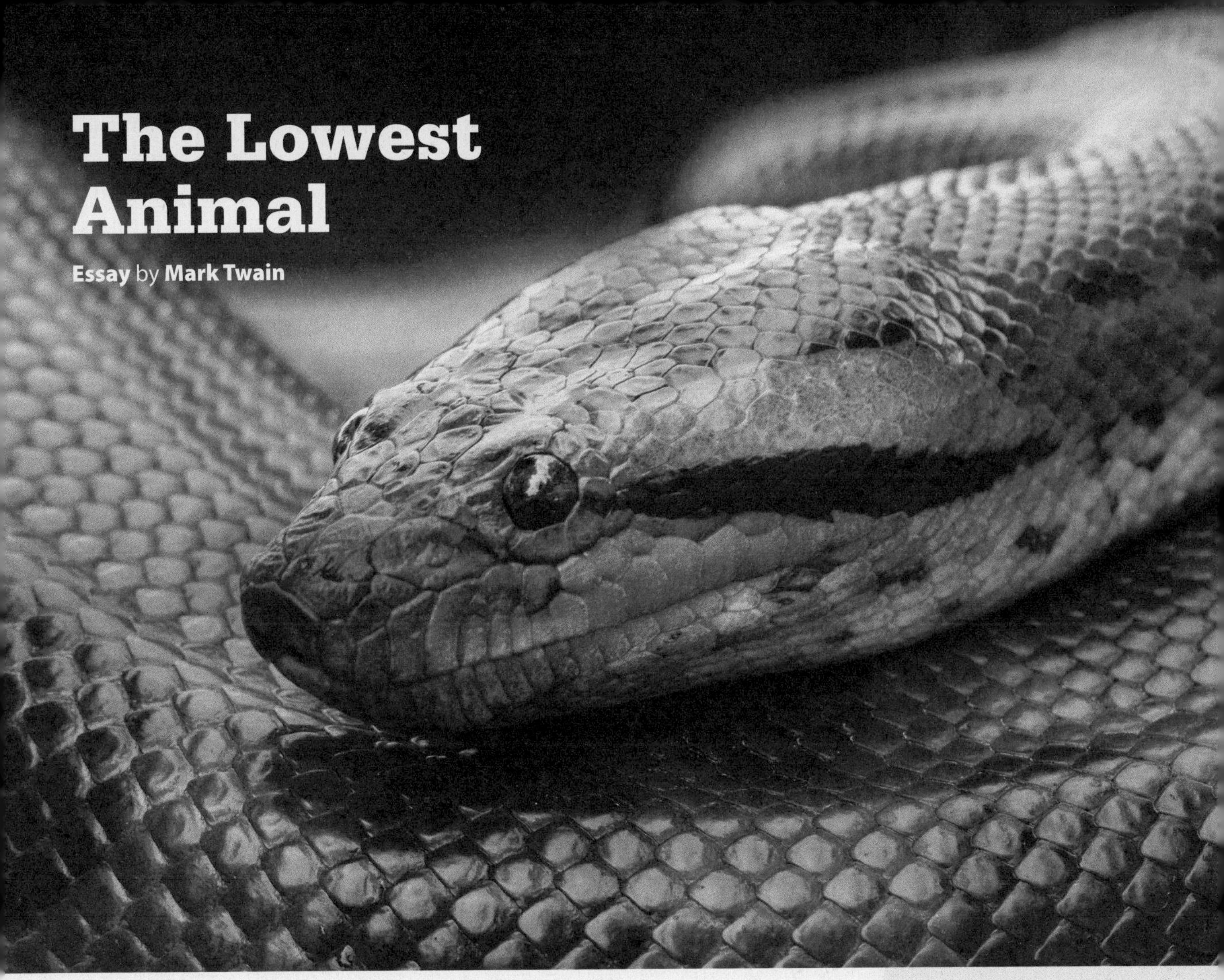

NOTICE & NOTE
As you read, use the side margins to make notes about the text.

Note how Twain describes the various "painstaking" experiments he performed.

1 I have been studying the traits and **dispositions** of the "lower animals" (so-called) and contrasting them with the traits and dispositions of man. I find the result humiliating to me. For it obliges me to renounce[1] my allegiance to the Darwinian theory of the Ascent of Man from the Lower Animals, since it now seems plain to me that that theory ought to be vacated in favor of a new and truer one, this new and truer one to be named the Descent of Man from the Higher Animals.

2 In proceeding toward this unpleasant conclusion, I have not guessed or speculated or conjectured, but have used what is commonly called the scientific method.[2] That is to say, I have subjected every postulate[3] that presented itself to the crucial test of actual experiment and have adopted it or rejected it according

disposition

(dĭs-pə-zĭsh´ən) *n.* character or temperament.

ANALYZE TONE

Annotate: Mark the words that suggest Twain's tone in paragraph 1.

Analyze: How would you describe Twain's attitude toward humans and animals? Explain.

[1] **renounce:** give up; reject.
[2] **scientific method:** research method in which a hypothesis is tested by careful, documented experiments.
[3] **postulate:** assumption.

to the result. Thus, I verified and established each step of my course in its turn before advancing to the next. These experiments were made in the London Zoological Gardens and covered many months of painstaking and fatiguing work.

3 Before particularizing any of the experiments, I wish to state one or two things which seem to more properly belong in this place than further along. This in the interest of clearness. The massed experiments established to my satisfaction certain generalizations, to wit:

4 1. That the human race is of one distinct species. It exhibits slight variations—in color, stature, mental **caliber,** and so on—due to climate, environment, and so forth; but it is a species by itself and not to be confounded with any other.

caliber
(kăl´ə-bər) *n.* level of ability.

5 2. That the quadrupeds[4] are a distinct family, also. This family exhibits variations—in color, size, food preferences, and so on; but it is a family by itself.

6 3. That the other families—the birds, the fishes, the insects, the reptiles, etc.—are more or less distinct, also. They are in the procession. They are links in the chain which stretches down from the higher animals to man at the bottom.

ANALYZE SATIRE

Annotate: Mark the repeated phrase at the beginning of paragraphs 4, 5, and 6.

Analyze: How does Twain's use of repetition add to the humor in this section?

7 Some of my experiments were quite curious. In the course of my reading, I had come across a case where, many years ago, some hunters on our Great Plains organized a buffalo hunt for the entertainment of an English earl—that, and to provide some fresh meat for his larder.[5] They had charming sport. They killed seventy-two of those great animals and ate part of one of them and left the seventy-one to rot. In order to determine the difference between an anaconda[6] and an earl—if any—I caused seven young calves to be turned into the anaconda's cage. The grateful reptile immediately crushed one of them and swallowed it, then lay back satisfied. It showed no further interest in the calves and no disposition to harm them. I tried this experiment with other anacondas, always with the same result. The fact stood proven that the difference between an earl and an anaconda is that the earl is cruel and the anaconda isn't; and that the earl wantonly destroys what he has no use for, but the anaconda doesn't. This seemed to suggest that the anaconda was not descended from the earl. It also seemed to suggest that the earl was descended from the anaconda, and had lost a good deal in the **transition.**

transition
(trăn-zĭsh´ən) *n.* process of change.

8 I was aware that many men who have accumulated more millions of money than they can ever use have shown a rabid hunger for more, and have not scrupled[7] to cheat the ignorant and the helpless

[4] **quadrupeds:** four-footed animals.
[5] **larder:** supply of food or place where food supplies are kept.
[6] **anaconda:** long, heavy snake that crushes its prey.
[7] **scrupled:** hesitated because of feelings of guilt.

out of their poor servings in order to partially appease[8] that appetite. I furnished a hundred different kinds of wild and tame animals the opportunity to accumulate vast stores of food, but none of them would do it. The squirrels and bees and certain birds made accumulations, but stopped when they had gathered a winter's supply and could not be persuaded to add to it either honestly or by chicane.[9] In order to bolster up a tottering reputation, the ant pretended to store up supplies, but I was not deceived. I know the ant. These experiments convinced me that there is this difference between man and the higher animals: He is avaricious and miserly, they are not.

9 In the course of my experiments, I convinced myself that among the animals man is the only one that harbors[10] insults and injuries, broods over them, waits till a chance offers, then takes revenge. The passion of revenge is unknown to the higher animals.

10 Roosters keep harems,[11] but it is by consent of their concubines;[12] therefore no wrong is done. Men keep harems, but it is by brute force, privileged by **atrocious** laws which the other sex was allowed no hand in making. In this matter man occupies a far lower place than the rooster.

Don't forget to **Notice & Note** as you read the selection.

ANALYZE SATIRE

Annotate: Mark assertions in paragraph 8 that should not be taken literally.

Analyze: How are Twain's "experiments" an example of absurdity?

atrocious
(ə-trō´shəs) *adj.* evil or brutal.

[8] **appease:** satisfy; pacify.
[9] **chicane** (shĭ-kān´)**:** clever deception; trickery.
[10] **harbors:** clings to.
[11] **harems:** groups of females who mate and live with one male.
[12] **concubines:** secondary wives.

ANALYZE TONE

Annotate: Mark words in paragraph 12 that reveal Twain's attitude toward humans. Then mark words that describe his feelings about animals.

Cite Evidence: How does Twain's word choice help you discern his attitude toward "higher animals" and toward humans?

VOCABULARY

Nuances in Word Meaning: Mark the title Twain gives to "man" in paragraph 13.

Analyze: How would your perception of humans be different if Twain had used the word *harmful* to describe humanity in place of *cruel*? Which word has a stronger impact?

11 Cats are loose in their morals, but not consciously so. Man, in his descent from the cat, has brought the cat's looseness with him but has left the unconsciousness behind—the saving grace which excuses the cat. The cat is innocent, man is not.

12 Indecency, vulgarity, obscenity—these are strictly confined to man; he invented them. Among the higher animals there is no trace of them. They hide nothing; they are not ashamed. Man, with his soiled mind, covers himself. He will not even enter a drawing room with his breast and back naked, so alive are he and his mates to indecent suggestion. Man is the Animal that Laughs. But so does the monkey, as Mr. Darwin pointed out, and so does the Australian bird that is called the laughing jackass. No—Man is the Animal that Blushes. He is the only one that does it—or has occasion to.

13 At the head of this article we see how "three monks were burnt to death" a few days ago and a prior was "put to death with atrocious cruelty." Do we inquire into the details? No; or we should find out that the prior was subjected to unprintable mutilations. Man—when he is a North American Indian—gouges out his prisoner's eyes; when he is King John,[13] with a nephew to render untroublesome, he uses a red-hot iron; when he is a religious zealot[14] dealing with heretics[15] in the Middle Ages, he skins his captive alive and scatters salt on his back; in the first Richard's[16] time, he shuts up a multitude of Jewish families in a tower and sets fire to it; in Columbus's time he captures a family of Spanish Jews and—but that is not printable; in our day in England, a man is fined ten shillings for beating his mother nearly to death with a chair, and another man is fined forty shillings for having four pheasant eggs in his possession without being able to satisfactorily explain how he got them. Of all the animals, man is the only one that is cruel. He is the only one that inflicts pain for the pleasure of doing it. It is a trait that is not known to the higher animals. The cat plays with the frightened mouse; but she has this excuse, that she does not know that the mouse is suffering. The cat is moderate—unhumanly moderate: She only scares the mouse, she does not hurt it; she doesn't dig out its eyes, or tear off its skin, or drive splinters under its nails—man fashion; when she is done playing with it, she makes a sudden meal of it and puts it out of its trouble. Man is the Cruel Animal. He is alone in that distinction.

---

[13] **King John:** king of England from 1199 to 1216, known for seizing the throne from his nephew Arthur.

[14] **zealot** (zĕl′ət)**:** overly enthusiastic person; fanatic.

[15] **heretics:** people who hold beliefs opposed to those of the church.

[16] **first Richard's:** refers to Richard I (1157–1199), also called Richard the Lion-Hearted, king of England from 1189 to 1199.

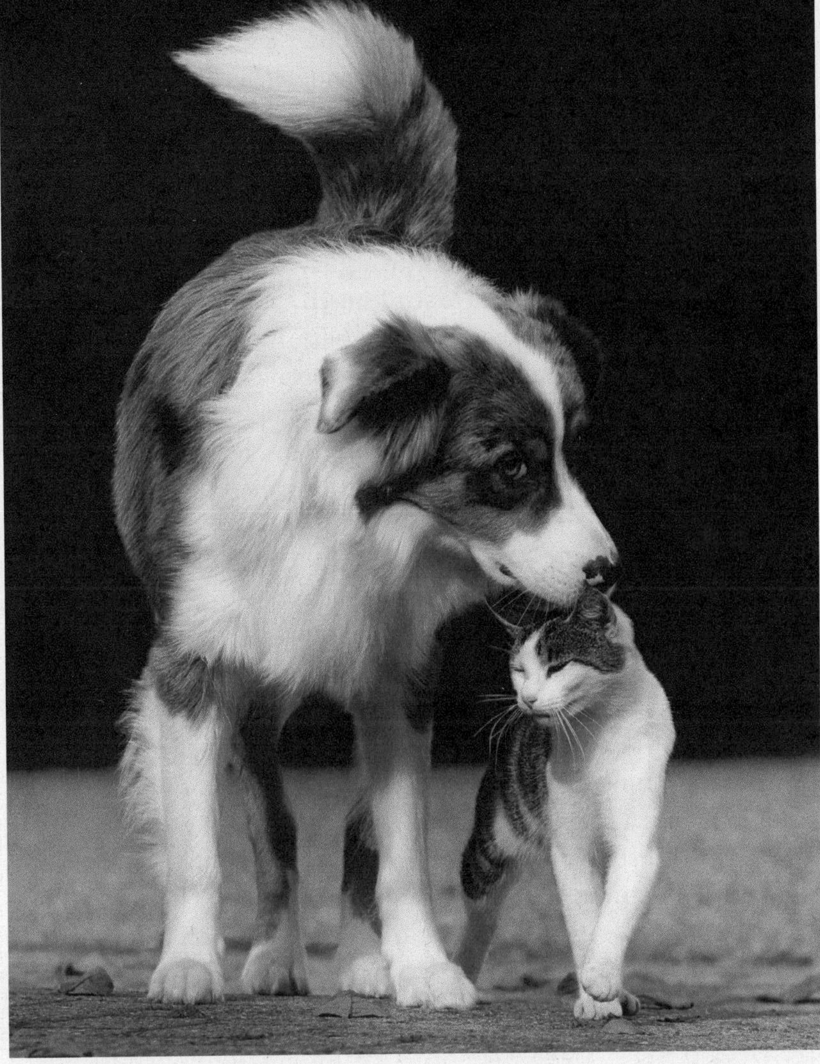

Don't forget to **Notice & Note** as you read the selection.

14 The higher animals engage in individual fights, but never in organized masses. Man is the only animal that deals in that atrocity of atrocities, war. He is the only one that gathers his brethren about him and goes forth in cold blood and with calm pulse to exterminate his kind. He is the only animal that for sordid wages will march out, as the Hessians[17] did in our Revolution, and as the boyish Prince Napoleon did in the Zulu war,[18] and help to slaughter strangers of his own species who have done him no harm and with whom he has no quarrel.

15 Man is the only animal that robs his helpless fellow of his country—takes possession of it and drives him out of it or destroys him. Man has done this in all the ages. There is not an acre of ground on the globe that is in possession of its rightful owner, or that has not been taken away from owner after owner, cycle after cycle, by force and bloodshed.

ANALYZE SATIRE

Annotate: Mark the contrast Twain describes at the beginning of paragraph 14.

Analyze: Is Twain using the techniques of satire? If so, which ones and to what effect?

---

[17] **Hessians** (hĕsh′ənz): German soldiers who served for pay in the British army during the American Revolution.

[18] **Prince Napoleon . . . Zulu war:** In search of adventure, Prince Napoleon, son of Napoleon III, joined the British campaign against Zululand (part of South Africa) in 1879.

16 Man is the only Slave. And he is the only animal who enslaves. He has always been a slave in one form or another, and has always held other slaves in bondage under him in one way or another. In our day he is always some man's slave for wages and does that man's work; and this slave has other slaves under him for minor wages, and they do *his* work. The higher animals are the only ones who exclusively do their own work and provide their own living.

17 Man is the only Patriot. He sets himself apart in his own country, under his own flag, and sneers at the other nations, and keeps multitudinous uniformed assassins on hand at heavy expense to grab slices of other people's countries and keep *them* from grabbing slices of *his*. And in the intervals between campaigns, he washes the blood off his hands and works for "the universal brotherhood of man"—with his mouth.

ANALYZE TONE

Annotate: In paragraph 18, mark the ways Twain says that humanity is unique.

Draw Conclusions: Does Twain regard humanity's uniqueness as a positive trait? What about his tone helps you determine this?

18 Man is the Religious Animal. He is the only Religious Animal. He is the only animal that has the True Religion—several of them. He is the only animal that loves his neighbor as himself, and cuts his throat if his theology isn't straight. He has made a graveyard of the globe in trying his honest best to smooth his brother's path to happiness and heaven. He was at it in the time of the Caesars, he was at it in Mahomet's[19] time, he was at it in the time of the Inquisition, he was at it in France a couple of centuries, he was at it in England in Mary's day,[20] he has been at it ever since he first saw the light, he is at it today in Crete—he will be at it somewhere else tomorrow. The higher animals have no religion. And we are told that they are going to be left out, in the hereafter. I wonder why. It seems questionable taste.

19 Man is the Reasoning Animal. Such is the claim. I think it is open to dispute. Indeed, my experiments have proven to me that he is the Unreasoning Animal. Note his history, as sketched above. It seems plain to me that whatever he is, he is *not* a reasoning animal. His record is the fantastic record of a maniac. I consider that the strongest count against his intelligence is the fact that with that record back of him, he blandly sets himself up as the head animal of the lot; whereas by his own standards, he is the bottom one.

20 In truth, man is incurably foolish. Simple things which the other animals easily learn he is incapable of learning. Among my experiments was this. In an hour I taught a cat and a dog to be friends. I put them in a cage. In another hour I taught them to be friends with a rabbit. In the course of two days I was able to add a fox, a goose, a squirrel, and some doves. Finally a monkey. They lived together in peace, even affectionately.

21 Next, in another cage I confined an Irish Catholic from Tipperary, and as soon as he seemed tame, I added a Scottish Presbyterian from Aberdeen. Next a Turk from Constantinople, a Greek Christian from Crete, an Armenian, a Methodist from the

[19] **Mahomet's:** Muhammad (c. A.D. 570–632) was an Arab prophet and founder of Islam.

[20] **in Mary's day:** during the reign of Queen Mary (1553–1558), who was given the nickname "Bloody Mary" when she ordered the deaths of many Protestants.

wilds of Arkansas, a Buddhist from China, a Brahman from Benares. Finally, a Salvation Army colonel from Wapping. Then I stayed away two whole days. When I came back to note results, the cage of Higher Animals was all right, but in the other there was but a chaos of gory odds and ends of turbans and fezzes and plaids and bones and flesh—not a specimen left alive. These Reasoning Animals had disagreed on a theological detail and carried the matter to a higher court.

COLLABORATIVE DISCUSSION

How realistic were the experiments described by Twain? Discuss whether they added to your enjoyment of the essay.

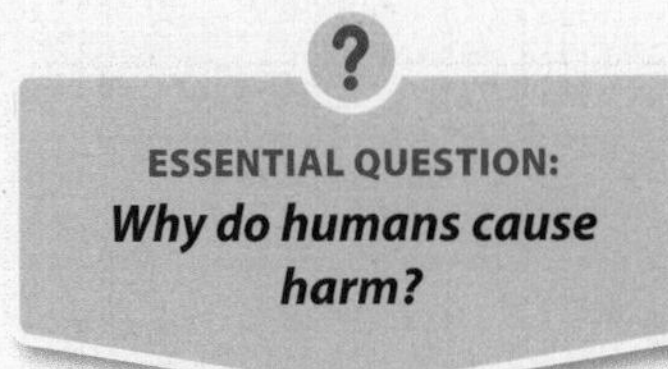
?
ESSENTIAL QUESTION:
Why do humans cause harm?

Review your notes and add your thoughts to your **Response Log.**

Assessment Practice

Answer these questions before moving on to the **Analyze the Text** section on the following page.

1. Twain's admiration of Darwin is undermined by what?

- (A) Reading the work of other scientists
- (B) Studying the behavior of animals
- (C) Studying the behavior of humans
- (D) Rereading Darwin's books and ideas

2. Why does Twain consider the behavior of cats superior to that of humans?

- (A) Cats are always moral.
- (B) Cats aren't conscious of morals.
- (C) Humans don't think about morals.
- (D) Humans don't understand cats.

3. Which of the following is an example of exaggeration?

- (A) *He has made a graveyard of the globe. . . .*
- (B) *Man has done this in all the ages.*
- (C) *He is the only Religious Animal.*
- (D) *They lived together in peace, even affectionately.*

Ed

Test-Taking Strategies

Analyze the Text

Support your responses with evidence from the text.

NOTICE & NOTE

Review what you **noticed and noted** as you read the text. Your annotations can help you answer these questions.

1 **CITE EVIDENCE** In the chart, cite examples of Twain's use of each satirical technique. Review the techniques on page 549 if you need help.

Technique	Example
Humor	
Exaggeration	
Absurdity	
Irony	

2 **EVALUATE** In paragraph 2, Twain says that he reached his conclusions by following the scientific method. Explain whether this claim is intended to be taken seriously.

3 **INFER** When describing a buffalo hunt, Twain writes, "They had charming sport" (paragraph 7). How does the rest of the passage reveal the irony of this statement?

4 **INFER** What does Twain mean when he writes that "Man is the Animal that Blushes. He is the only one that does it—or has occasion to" (paragraph 12)?

5 **EVALUATE** What is Twain's overall purpose in writing this essay? How effective is his use of satire in achieving that purpose?

6 **ANALYZE** How does Twain's **tone,** or attitude, change over the course of the piece? Cite text evidence in your response.

Choices

Here are some other ways to demonstrate your understanding of the ideas in this lesson.

Writing

↳ Satire

Use the same techniques as Twain to create a satire in which you mock some part of everyday life.

1. Choose an aspect of life as the subject of your satire.
2. What format do you want to use to make your satire? You could write an essay like Twain, but consider writing a song, newspaper article, or other form that interests you.
3. Write your satire. Include elements such as humor, irony, and exaggeration in your work.
4. Share your work. Make your satire something to celebrate.

As you write and discuss, be sure to use the **Academic Vocabulary** words.

- ambiguous
- clarify
- implicit
- revise
- somewhat

Research

↳ The Mark Twain Prize

There is a prestigious award given by the Kennedy Center called the Mark Twain Prize. Conduct some research to answer these questions.

- Why is the award named for Mark Twain?
- Why is someone chosen to receive the Mark Twain Prize?
- Who are three people who have received the award?

As a bonus, think about someone you think would be a worthy recipient of the Mark Twain Prize. Write a paragraph in which you introduce the person you have chosen to receive the award.

Social & Emotional Learning

↳ Evaluate the Effectiveness of Satire

Satire can be an effective tool for critiquing an aspect of society. But is it possible that some readers may find the use of satire off-putting? Think about "The Lowest Animal" and consider the following in a group discussion:

- whether Twain communicates his ideas clearly and effectively
- if some readers would be less receptive to Twain's ideas because of his tone
- other ways in which Twain could have conveyed his ideas

Cite specific examples from "The Lowest Animal" in your discussion.

Expand Your Vocabulary

PRACTICE AND APPLY

Write the word that best completes each statement.

disposition	caliber	transition	atrocious

1. The boss of a company wants to hire someone with skills that are of a high __________ for the job.
2. Many people agree that the effects of war can be __________.
3. Leaving home to go to college can be a challenging __________.
4. A salesperson needs to have a very outgoing __________ if he or she is going to be successful.

Vocabulary Strategy

↳ Nuances in Word Meaning

Ed

Interactive Vocabulary Lesson: Denotations and Connotations

In "The Lowest Animal," Twain used the word *atrocious* to describe laws that allow men in some nations to keep harems. Twain chose a word with the right **nuance,** or shade of meaning. He wanted to emphasize how evil or brutal he thought the laws were. Adjectives that have similar meanings but different nuances might be arranged on a continuum, as shown below, with the word representing the least degree on the left and the word representing the greatest degree on the right.

BAD	HARMFUL	WICKED	CRUEL	ATROCIOUS

PRACTICE AND APPLY

For each word in the chart below, create a continuum of four other words that have similar meanings but show different nuances. Words should move from the least degree on the left to the greatest degree on the right.

1. cold				
2. happy				
3. smell				
4. pretty				

Watch Your Language!

Anaphora and Parallelism

In "The Lowest Animal," Mark Twain uses a particular type of repetition known as **anaphora,** the repetition of a word or words at the beginning of successive lines, clauses, sentences, or paragraphs. This literary device is particularly effective in poetry, but it also has a place in argumentative prose. Consider this example from two sentences in paragraph 12.

Man is the Animal that Laughs. . . . No—Man is the Animal that Blushes.

These sentences also share a **parallel construction,** meaning that they use similar grammatical structures to express ideas that are related or equal in value. By using these literary devices, Twain emphasizes his central ideas and creates a rhythm that strengthens the rhetorical effect.

Here are other examples of anaphora from this essay. These appear at the beginning of successive paragraphs, beginning with paragraph 15.

Man is the only animal that robs his helpless fellow of his country. . . .
Man is the only Slave.
Man is the only Patriot.
Man is the Religious Animal.
Man is the Reasoning Animal.

Twain uses these devices to build a cumulative list of the aspects of human conduct that he wants to satirize. Clearly, Twain's use of anaphora is deliberate. In his hands, it has an artistic effect, and he successfully uses it to hammer home the point he wants to make, which is that humans are not the highest animals (though they may believe otherwise).

PRACTICE AND APPLY

Review a piece of your own writing. Revise it to include the use of anaphora and parallelism.

Get Ready

The Fourth Industrial Revolution Is Here. Are You Ready?

Article by **Bernard Marr**

ESSENTIAL QUESTION:
What are the consequences of change?

Engage Your Brain

Choose one or more of these activities to start connecting with the article you're about to read.

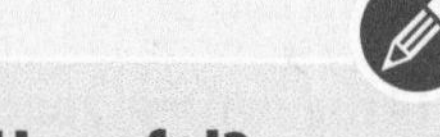

Helpful or Harmful?

Every piece of technology has pros and cons. Think about a calculator: It helps us do complicated math quickly, but we aren't as good at math problems on our own because of it. Think of an example of technology you can't live without, like a personal computer or smartphone. Then list two benefits and two drawbacks of the example you chose.

Wait, What Do You Mean "Fourth"?

When you read the title of the article, you may not have realized that there have been four industrial revolutions. Form a group of three and have each member research one of the previous industrial revolutions.

- Describe where and when they happened.
- Sum up the advancements that took place.
- Describe the effects of the changes on everyday life.

A Little Help from a Friend

New technology is often supposed to make life easier for people. And what would make life easier than a robot partner who obeys your commands? Imagine you were allowed to have a robot assistant for the day. What would you ask it to do? Discuss your ideas with a partner.

Analyze Structure

Writers may structure their essays by combining elements of different types of writing, depending on their reason for writing. In this article, Marr combines elements of argumentative and informative writing.

- **Argumentative writing** tries to persuade a reader by stating a claim and backing it up with reasons and supporting evidence.
- **Informative writing** explains a particular topic and includes several central ideas that are supported by facts and examples.

Marr's article presents a complex set of ideas and develops them over the course of the text. As you read, use a chart to note details that reflect each kind of writing. Though writers may mix styles, their goal is the same: to structure an essay that is clear and engaging.

Focus on Genre
Article

- may combine structural elements of more than one type of writing, such as argumentative and informative
- may have graphic features to express or clarify ideas
- may include counterarguments to address opposing views

Argumentative	Informative
"It's well on its way and will change most of our jobs."	

Analyze Counterarguments

Authors not only build their arguments using supporting evidence—facts, examples, quotations, expert opinions, and statistics—but also consider opposing points and address them through counterarguments. If the writer's argument does not hold up against opposing points, the writer's claim might be weak and the argument ineffective.

Rebuttals and concessions are two elements of counterarguments. A **rebuttal** is a statement that proves an opposing claim is false or invalid. A **concession** is an acknowledgment that an aspect of an opposing claim has merit. To effectively make a concession, an author must explain why the claim is still true despite the merits of the opposing viewpoint. Rebuttals and concessions add to the text's power because they anticipate and address opposing views.

When evaluating counterarguments, ask yourself these questions:

- Does the counterargument address the opposing view?
- Is the opposing view effectively rebutted, or disproved? If so, how?
- Does the writer make a concession?
- Has the writer effectively defended why his or her claim still holds true despite the concession?

Annotation in Action

Here is an example of notes a student made about a counterargument in "The Fourth Industrial Revolution Is Here. Are You Ready?" As you read, note the writer's use of counterarguments against opposing claims.

Many experts suggest that the fourth industrial revolution will benefit the rich much more than the poor, especially as low-skill, low-wage jobs disappear in favor of automation.

But this isn't new. Historically, industrial revolutions have always begun with greater inequality followed by periods of political and institutional change.

He is pushing back against the opposing claim.

Expand Your Vocabulary

Put a check mark next to the vocabulary words that you feel comfortable using when writing or speaking.

augmented	☐
regenerate	☐
postulate	☐
automation	☐

Then, write a sentence about a job that may be performed by technology in the future. As you read the article, use the definitions in the side column to learn the vocabulary words you don't already know.

"The future is happening around us."

—Bernard Marr

Background

Bernard Marr lives near London, England, and is a best-selling author of many business books, such as *Big Data* and *The Intelligent Company.* Marr also contributes weekly columns to *Forbes* and *LinkedIn,* and his advice is sought out by publications like the *Wall Street Journal*, the *Guardian*, and the *Financial Times*. He has also worked as an advisor for many organizations around the world, including the United Nations, Microsoft, and T-Mobile.

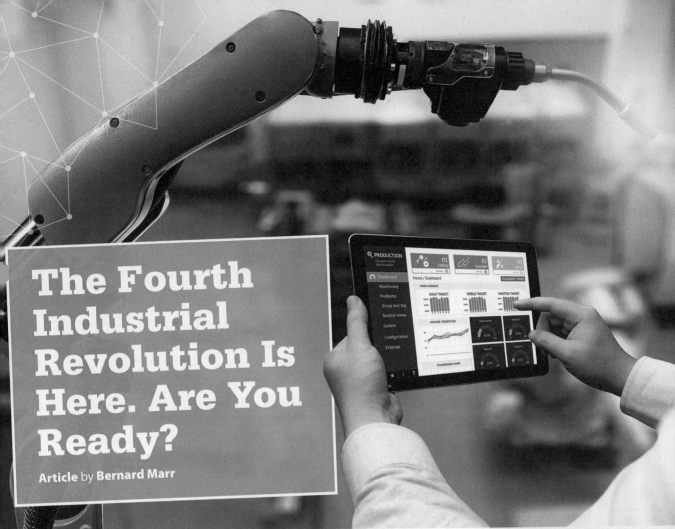

The Fourth Industrial Revolution Is Here. Are You Ready?

Article by **Bernard Marr**

The author says a change is coming that may have consequences for lots of people.

NOTICE & NOTE
As you read, use the side margins to make notes about the text.

1 First came steam and water power; then electricity and assembly lines; then computerization . . . So what comes next?

2 Some call it the fourth industrial revolution, or industry 4.0, but whatever you call it, it represents the combination of cyber-physical systems,[1] the Internet of Things, and the Internet of Systems.[2]

3 In short, it is the idea of smart factories in which machines are **augmented** with web connectivity and connected to a system that can visualize the entire production chain and make decisions on its own.

4 And it's well on its way and will change most of our jobs.

augment
(ôg-mĕnt´) *v.* to make (something already developed or well underway) greater, as in size, extent, or quantity.

ANALYZE STRUCTURE

Annotate: Underline details in paragraphs 3–4 that describe the fourth industrial revolution.

Analyze: Which details are informative and which are argumentative? Explain.

[1] **cyber-physical systems:** systems composed of physical elements (such as robotics) and computer algorithms.

[2] **Internet of Things, and the Internet of Systems:** respectively, tangible things and systems connected to the Internet, such as smartphones or ATMs.

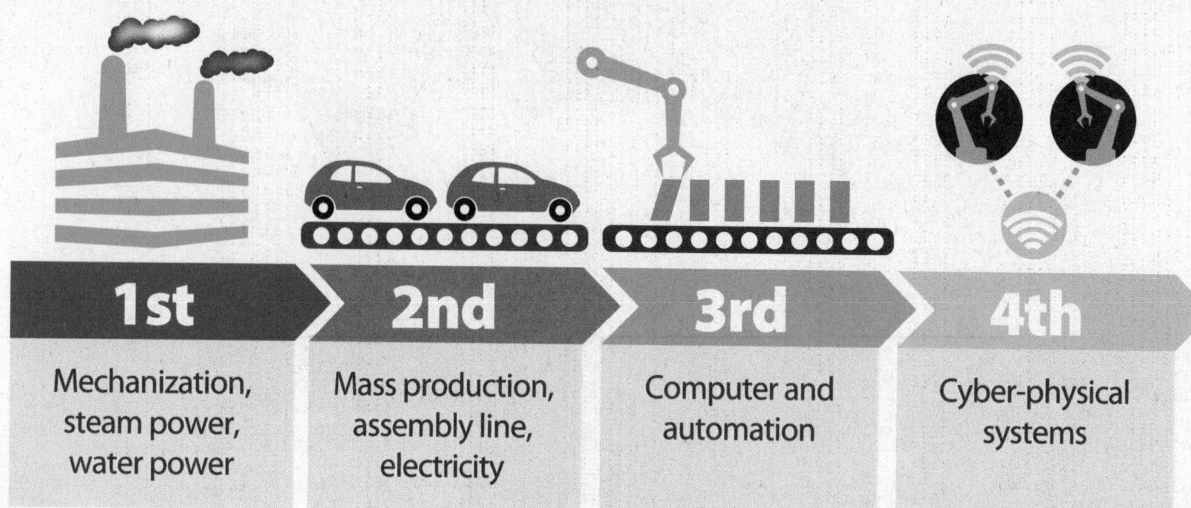

Source: *The 4 Industrial Revolutions* (by Christoph Roser at AllAboutLean.com)

5 Professor Klaus Schwab, Founder and Executive Chairman of the World Economic Forum, has published a book entitled *The Fourth Industrial Revolution* in which he describes how this fourth revolution is fundamentally different from the previous three, which were characterized mainly by advances in technology.

6 In this fourth revolution, we are facing a range of new technologies that combine the physical, digital and biological worlds. These new technologies will impact all disciplines, economies and industries, and even challenge our ideas about what it means to be human.

7 These technologies have great potential to continue to connect billions more people to the web, drastically improve the efficiency of business and organizations and help **regenerate** the natural environment through better asset management, potentially even undoing all the damage previous industrial revolutions have caused.

regenerate (rĭ-jĕn´ə-rāt) *v.* to form, construct, or create anew.

ANALYZE STRUCTURE

Annotate: Mark the graphic feature from *The 4 Industrial Revolutions* that is used on the page.

Analyze: What does the graphic explain? How does the information in paragraphs 6–7 add to your understanding of the graphic?

8 But there are also grave potential risks. Schwab outlines his concerns that organizations could be unable or unwilling to adapt to these new technologies and that governments could fail to employ or regulate these technologies properly. In the book he **postulates** that shifting power will create important new security concerns, and that inequalities could grow rather than shrink if things are not managed properly.

9 For example, as **automation** increases, computers and machines will replace workers across a vast spectrum of industries, from drivers to accountants and estate agents to insurance agents. By one estimate, as many as 47 percent of U.S. jobs are at risk from automation.

10 Many experts suggest that the fourth industrial revolution will benefit the rich much more than the poor, especially as low-skill, low-wage jobs disappear in favor of automation.

11 But this isn't new. Historically, industrial revolutions have always begun with greater inequality followed by periods of political and institutional change. The industrial revolution that began at the beginning of the 19th century originally led to a huge polarization of wealth and power, before being followed by nearly 100 years of change including the spread of democracy, trade unions, progressive taxation and the development of social safety nets.

ANALYZE COUNTERARGUMENTS

Annotate: In paragraph 8, mark the details that suggest risks.

Analyze: How do these risks form the basis of an opposing view against the writer's claim?

postulate
(pŏs´chə-lāt) *v.* to assume or assert the truth, reality, or necessity of, especially as a basis of an argument.

automation
(ô-tə-mā´shən) *n.* the automatic operation or control of equipment, a process, or a system.

ANALYZE COUNTERARGUMENTS

Annotate: Mark the words in paragraph 11 that signal the author is examining an opposing claim.

Evaluate: How does the author's counterargument effectively respond to this opposing view?

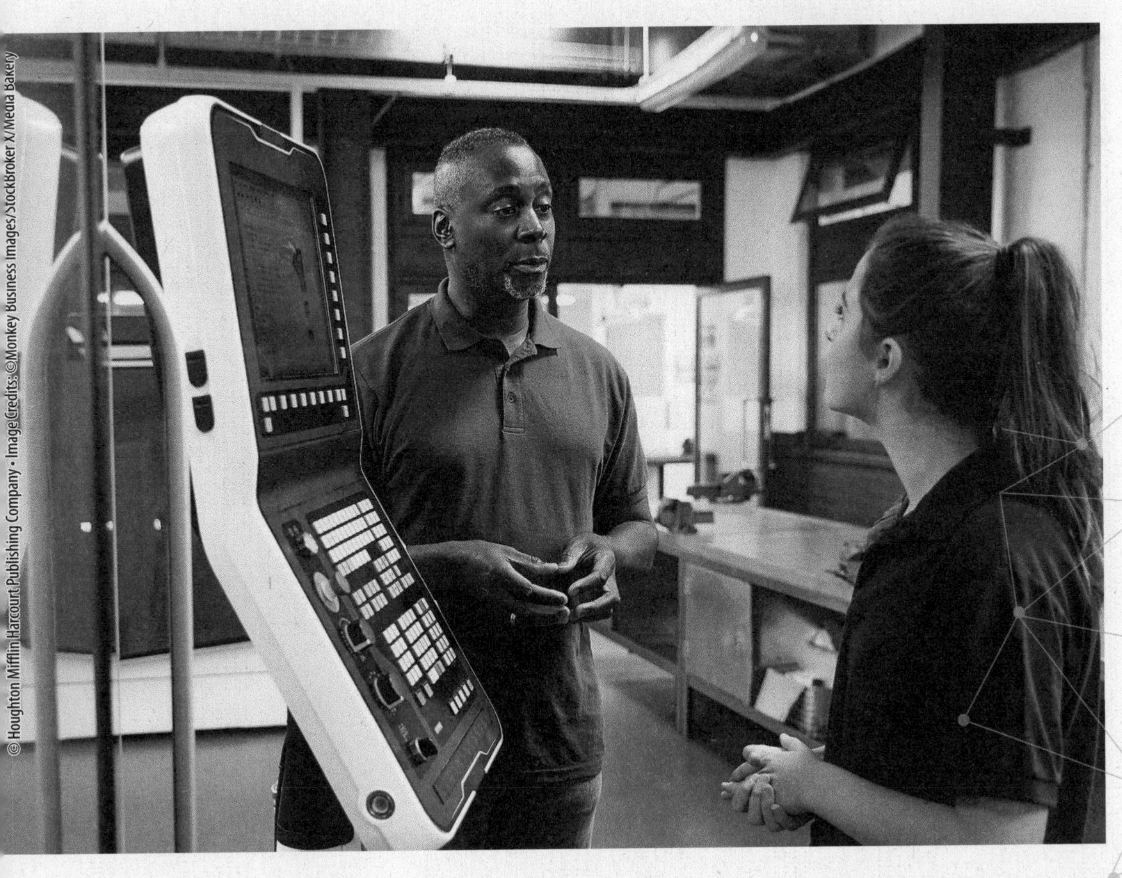

12 It seems a safe bet to say, then, that our current political, business, and social structures may not be ready or capable of absorbing all the changes a fourth industrial revolution would bring, and that major changes to the very structure of our society may be inevitable.

NOTICE & NOTE
QUOTED WORDS

When you notice the author has quoted the opinions or conclusions of an expert to provide support for a point, you've found a **Quoted Words** signpost.

Notice & Note: Mark the expert's words in paragraph 13.

Evaluate: Why was this expert cited, and is his opinion relevant to the argument?

13 Schwab said, "The changes are so profound that, from the perspective of human history, there has never been a time of greater promise or potential peril. My concern, however, is that decision makers are too often caught in traditional, linear (and non-disruptive) thinking or too absorbed by immediate concerns to think strategically about the forces of disruption and innovation shaping our future."

14 The future is happening around us. And we must rise to the challenge to meet it and thrive in the new industrial revolution.

COLLABORATIVE DISCUSSION

What is the biggest challenge people will face as part of the fourth industrial revolution? Discuss your ideas with a partner.

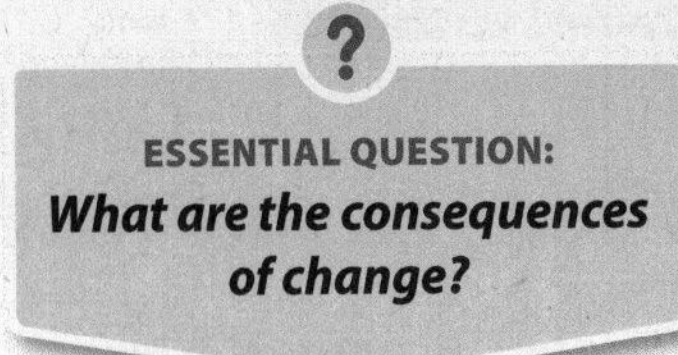

Review your notes and add your thoughts to your **Response Log.**

Assessment Practice

Answer these questions before moving on to the **Analyze the Text** section on the following page.

1. According to the author, what is the fourth industrial revolution?

Ⓐ Computers and automation

Ⓑ Mass production, assembly line, electricity

Ⓒ Cyber-physical systems

Ⓓ Mechanization, water power, steam power

2. According to the author, how will the fourth revolution be different from the previous three?

Ⓐ It will combine a range of technologies that impact all disciplines.

Ⓑ It will result in people making a lot of money.

Ⓒ It will involve great risks for some people and very little risk for others.

Ⓓ It will improve efficiencies of businesses.

3. The graphic feature included in this text could best be described as a —

Ⓐ map

Ⓑ chart

Ⓒ graph

Ⓓ diagram

Test-Taking Strategies

Analyze the Text

Support your responses with evidence from the text.

NOTICE & NOTE

Review what you **noticed and noted** as you read the text. Your annotations can help you answer these questions.

1. **EVALUATE** What evidence does the author provide to support his claim? Is the evidence sufficient and reliable? Explain.

2. **ANALYZE** In paragraph 7, what does the author argue are benefits of the fourth industrial revolution? Why does the author include this information?

3. **EVALUATE** Does the graphic feature contribute to the effectiveness of the writer's argument? Explain.

4. **EVALUATE** Use the chart to identify one of the opposing claims the writer includes in the article and explain whether the writer uses a counterargument to effectively address it. Note any rebuttals and concessions.

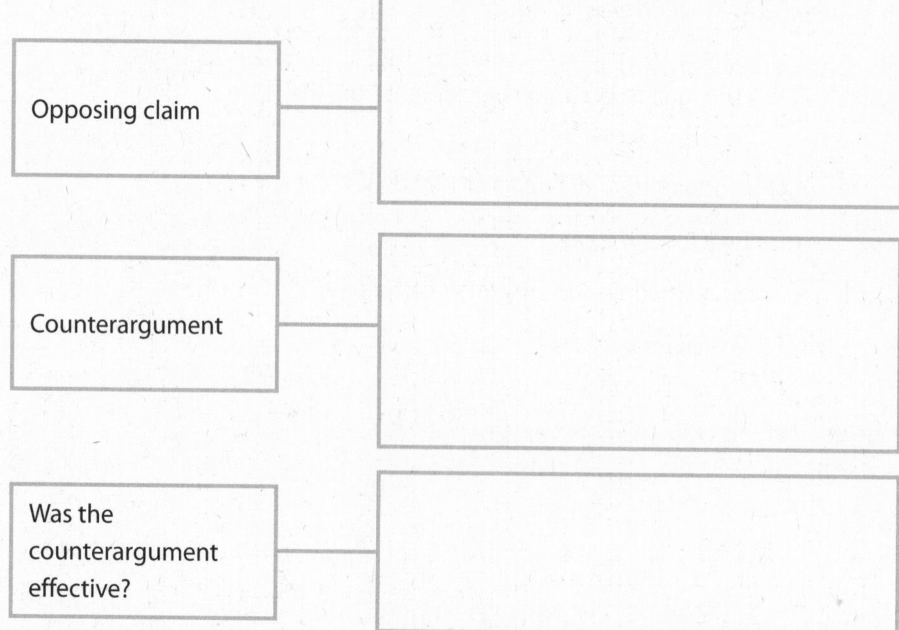

5. **EVALUATE** This essay uses a blend of argumentative and informative structures. How effective is this mixture of structures for explaining the author's ideas?

6. **ANALYZE** What was the purpose of the **Quoted Words** you saw in the article?

Choices

Here are some other ways to demonstrate your understanding of the ideas in this lesson.

Writing

↳ Personal Essay

Write a personal essay in which you tell about a time when using technology didn't work out the way you planned. Maybe you failed to save a big assignment or entered information on your phone that suddenly disappeared. Describe the consequences of what happened and how you might have handled it differently.

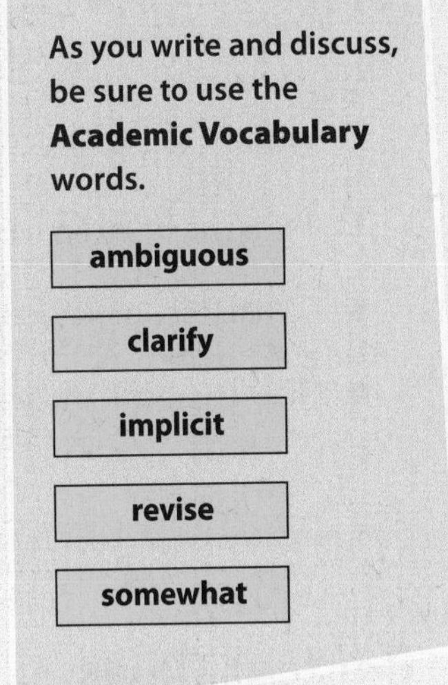
As you write and discuss, be sure to use the **Academic Vocabulary** words.
ambiguous
clarify
implicit
revise
somewhat

Social & Emotional Learning

↳ Reflect on Your Reading

As the author describes it, the fourth industrial revolution can improve our lives, but some of us will face risks as a result. Think about how certain details in the text made you feel, and share your ideas with a partner. Use these sentence starters to help you.

- Thinking about the fourth industrial revolution makes me feel ____ because . . .
- I feel ready for the fourth industrial revolution because . . .
- I may be affected by the fourth industrial revolution because . . .

Speaking & Listening

↳ Respond to the Article

Give a presentation to your classmates in which you take a stand on whether the fourth industrial revolution will take place and have the impact the writer suggests.

1. Write a paragraph or some bullet points stating your claim and key evidence.
2. Consider creating a graphic to convey key information or clarify your ideas.
3. Remember to speak slowly and use eye contact to connect with your audience.
4. Allow time for your audience to ask questions. Be prepared to defend your argument.

Expand Your Vocabulary

PRACTICE AND APPLY

Answer each question with a sentence that shows your understanding of the vocabulary words.

augment	regenerate	postulate	automation

1. What has a scientist done if he or she **postulates** a theory?
2. Why might an architect decide that her plans need to be **augmented**?
3. What does a medical researcher mean when he says he can **regenerate** injured cells?
4. If a school put **automation** in the lunchroom, what might you expect?

Vocabulary Strategy
↳ Context Clues

Interactive Vocabulary Lesson: Using Context Clues

As you read, you can look at **context clues**—such as examples, definitions, restatements, synonyms, or antonyms—to help you determine the meaning of unfamiliar words. For example, the author uses *regenerate* in the sentence "These technologies have great potential to . . . help regenerate the natural environment through better asset management, potentially even undoing all the damage previous industrial revolutions have caused." Marr helps define *regenerate* with the imagery suggested by "natural environment" and "undoing all the damage previous industrial revolutions have caused." Using these context clues, the reader can determine that *regenerate* means "to form, construct, or create anew."

PRACTICE AND APPLY

State the meaning of each boldfaced word in these sentences from the article. Then, mark the context clues that helped you determine the meaning of each word.

1. But there are also **grave** potential risks.
2. For example, as automation increases, computers and machines will replace workers across a vast **spectrum** of industries, from drivers to accountants and estate agents to insurance agents.
3. The industrial revolution that began at the beginning of the 19th century originally led to a huge **polarization** of wealth and power, before being followed by nearly 100 years of change including the spread of democracy, trade unions, progressive taxation and the development of social safety nets.

Watch Your Language!

Capitalization

"As you can see, boys and girls, the alphabet comes in caps lock on, and caps lock off ."

When writing, it is important to use capitalization appropriately. The following list includes examples of words that should be capitalized.

- Names of people, titles before names, and ethnic and national groups

  Jack London, Professor Wilson, African Americans

- First word in a sentence or quotation

  She stopped suddenly. He said, "What's wrong?"

- Adjectives formed from proper nouns

  Chinese cooking, Pacific coast

- Geographical names, such as cities, states, and countries

  Austin, Virginia, United States

- Names of organizations, government bodies, and historical periods and events

  Girl Scouts, House of Representatives, World War II

- Titles of works, such as books, newspapers, songs, and artwork, except for internal articles *(a, an, the)*, coordinating conjunctions, the *to* in infinitives, and prepositions

  Life on the Mississippi*, the *New York Times
  "The Star-Spangled Banner"

Interactive Grammar Lesson: Capital Letters

PRACTICE AND APPLY

Rewrite the following sentences with proper capitalization.

1. My father is a member of the atlanta city council.

2. I'd like to go to the yucatán peninsula and see cancún someday.

3. She said, "the director starts each day by reading *usa today*."

4. The playwright tennessee williams, known for writing groundbreaking plays, was inducted into the american theater hall of fame.

Get Ready

MENTOR TEXT

The Story of an Hour

Short Story by **Kate Chopin**

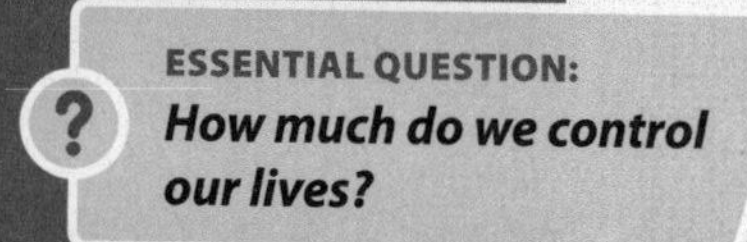
ESSENTIAL QUESTION:
How much do we control our lives?

Engage Your Brain

Choose one or more of these activities to start connecting with the story you're about to read.

Isn't It Ironic?

Alanis Morissette had a hit song, "Ironic," that outlined multiple situations, followed by the line: "Isn't it ironic?" She was widely criticized for not knowing what *ironic* meant.

- Look up the word in a dictionary.
- Find a video or recording of the song and listen to the lyrics.
- Use the definition you found to see if you can pick the "ironic" situations that weren't so ironic after all.
- What word should she have used instead? Explain your ideas in a paragraph.

Two Truths and a Lie

You may recall the complaints Elizabeth Cady Stanton made in the Declaration of Sentiments about the rights women had or didn't have in 1848. "The Story of an Hour" was published about 50 years later, in 1895. Which of the following statements is false? (You may have to do some research to come up with the right answer.)

1. In 1895, women could not own their own property.
2. In 1895, women were able to trade stocks.
3. By 1895, women had earned the right to a university education.

That Did NOT Just Happen!

Some people like predictability, while others like the unexpected.

- Think of a movie you've seen or a book you've read that has a surprise ending.
- What did you think was going to happen?
- How was the ending different from what you expected?
- Find a classmate who saw the same movie or read the same book. Talk about whether the surprise ending was as awesome as your endings would have been.

Analyze Point of View

Point of view refers to the perspective from which a story is told. "The Story of an Hour" is told from a **third-person point of view.** The narrator is not a character, but observes the action from the outside looking in. Point of view may also be characterized by what the narrator knows or shares. If the narrator tells readers what only one character thinks and feels, the point of view is **limited.** An **omniscient** narrator describes the thoughts and feelings of all the characters. Authors choose point of view carefully because it impacts how readers perceive the plot and conflict.

Focus on Genre
Short Story

- follows a sequence of events
- centers around one main conflict and resolution
- is written from a specific point of view

From what point of view is "The Story of an Hour" told?	How can you tell?	How does using this point of view affect how you understand the plot?
3rd-person limited ☐ 3rd-person omniscient ☐		

Analyze Irony

When analyzing a story, note that a narrator helps readers see contrasts, such as

- what a character feels versus how he or she behaves
- what characters believe versus what is true
- what readers might expect to happen versus what does happen

All of these are examples of irony, a contrast between appearance and reality. This chart describes the three basic types of irony.

Verbal Irony: What is said is the opposite of what is meant. Can include • sarcasm (criticism meant to mock) • understatement (emphasis by way of saying less than is actually true) • hyperbole (exaggeration for effect)	Your friend says: "I'm having a great day!" She then tells you she woke up late, didn't eat breakfast, and left her homework on the bus. This context lets you know her statement is ironic.
Situational Irony: A character or reader expects one thing to happen, but something else happens instead.	Your friend expects to get a zero for forgetting her homework, but a famous author finds it on the bus, brings it to the school, and gives a talk to the class. Your friend gets an A.
Dramatic Irony: The audience or reader knows something that the characters do not know.	In the novel based on your friend's experience, readers know the woman on the bus is a famous author, while your friend is ignorant of that fact.

Annotation in Action

Here are some notes a student made about point of view in "The Story of an Hour." As you read, note details that indicate the type of narration the author has chosen to tell the story.

Knowing that Mrs. Mallard was afflicted with a heart trouble, great care was taken to break to her as gently as possible the news of her husband's death.

It was her sister Josephine who told her, in broken sentences; veiled hints that revealed in half concealing.

third-person point of view

Expand Your Vocabulary

Put a check mark next to the vocabulary words that you feel comfortable using when speaking or writing.

abandonment	☐
vacant	☐
illumination	☐
composed	☐

Then, use the words to talk about a time you felt really happy. As you read "The Story of an Hour," use the definitions in the side-column to learn the vocabulary words you don't already know.

Background

Kate Chopin (1851–1904) wrote more than one hundred short stories and two novels. Her work features intelligent and sensitive female characters and is often set in Louisiana, where she spent her married life. Her first novel, *At Fault* (1890), received little attention when it was published. Her second, *The Awakening* (1899), told the story of a woman who leaves her family and eventually commits suicide. It was widely condemned by critics as shocking and morbid. However, since its rediscovery in the 1950s, it has been hailed as an insightful work that foreshadowed the feminist movement in literature.

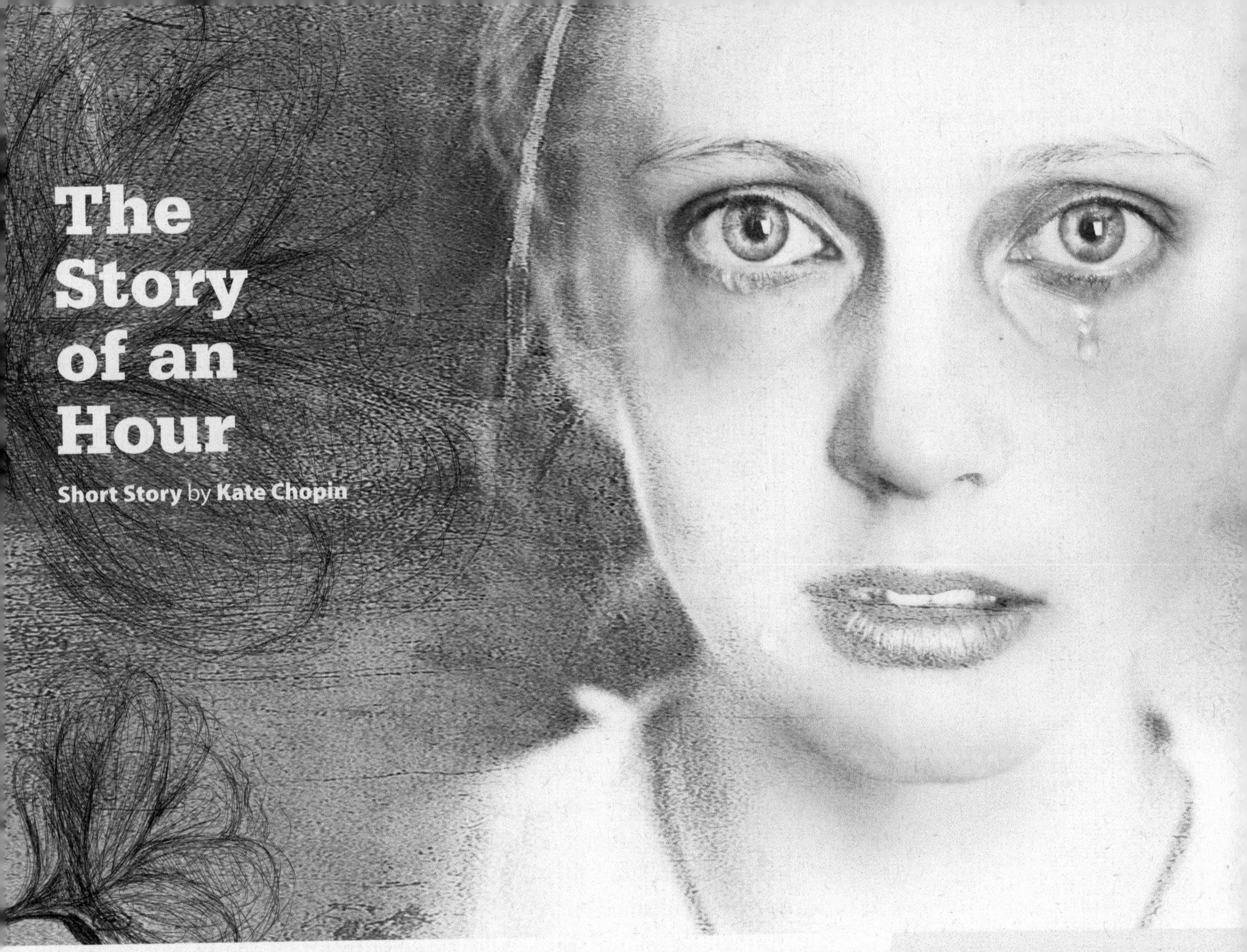

The Story of an Hour

Short Story by **Kate Chopin**

Note details that tell you how Mrs. Mallard feels about her life.

NOTICE & NOTE 
As you read, use the side margins to make notes about the text.

1 Knowing that Mrs. Mallard was afflicted with a heart trouble, great care was taken to break to her as gently as possible the news of her husband's death.

2 It was her sister Josephine who told her, in broken sentences; veiled hints that revealed in half concealing. Her husband's friend Richards was there, too, near her. It was he who had been in the newspaper office when intelligence of the railroad disaster was received, with Brently Mallard's name leading the list of "killed." He had only taken the time to assure himself of its truth by a second telegram, and had hastened to forestall any less careful, less tender friend in bearing the sad message.

3 She did not hear the story as many women have heard the same, with a paralyzed inability to accept its significance. She wept at once, with sudden, wild **abandonment,** in her sister's arms. When the storm of grief had spent itself she went away to her room alone. She would have no one follow her.

ANALYZE POINT OF VIEW

Annotate: Mark the clues in paragraphs 1–3 that indicate the point of view.

Evaluate: Which type of narrator is Chopin using? What is the effect of this point of view?

abandonment
(ə-băn´dən-mĕnt) *n.* a lack of restraint or inhibition.

ANALYZE POINT OF VIEW

Annotate: Mark text in paragraphs 4–6 that show what Mrs. Mallard is seeing.

Interpret: How does the point of view give you clues to Mrs. Mallard's state of mind?

4 There stood, facing the open window, a comfortable, roomy armchair. Into this she sank, pressed down by a physical exhaustion that haunted her body and seemed to reach into her soul.

5 She could see in the open square before her house the tops of trees that were all aquiver with the new spring life. The delicious breath of rain was in the air. In the street below a peddler was crying his wares. The notes of a distant song which someone was singing reached her faintly, and countless sparrows were twittering in the eaves.

6 There were patches of blue sky showing here and there through the clouds that had met and piled one above the other in the west facing her window.

7 She sat with her head thrown back upon the cushion of the chair, quite motionless, except when a sob came up into her throat and shook her, as a child who has cried itself to sleep continues to sob in its dreams.

8 She was young, with a fair, calm face, whose lines bespoke repression and even a certain strength. But now there was a dull stare in her eyes, whose gaze was fixed away off yonder on one of those patches of blue sky. It was not a glance of reflection, but rather indicated a suspension of intelligent thought.

9 There was something coming to her and she was waiting for it, fearfully. What was it? She did not know; it was too subtle and elusive to name. But she felt it, creeping out of the sky, reaching toward her through the sounds, the scents, the color that filled the air.

10 Now her bosom rose and fell tumultuously. She was beginning to recognize this thing that was approaching to possess her, and she was

striving to beat it back with her will—as powerless as her two white slender hands would have been.

11 When she abandoned herself a little whispered word escaped her slightly parted lips. She said it over and over under her breath: "free, free, free!" The **vacant** stare and the look of terror that had followed it went from her eyes. They stayed keen and bright. Her pulses beat fast, and the coursing blood warmed and relaxed every inch of her body.

vacant
(vā´kənt) *adj.* blank, expressionless.

12 She did not stop to ask if it were or were not a monstrous joy that held her. A clear and exalted perception enabled her to dismiss the suggestion as trivial.

13 She knew that she would weep again when she saw the kind, tender hands folded in death; the face that had never looked save with love upon her, fixed and gray and dead. But she saw beyond that bitter moment a long procession of years to come that would belong to her absolutely. And she opened and spread her arms out to them in welcome.

14 There would be no one to live for her during those coming years; she would live for herself. There would be no powerful will bending hers in that blind persistence with which men and women believe they have a right to impose a private will upon a fellow creature. A kind intention or a cruel intention made the act seem no less a crime as she looked upon it in that brief moment of **illumination.**

illumination
(ĭ-lo͞o-mə-nā´shən) *n.* awareness or enlightenment.

15 And yet she had loved him—sometimes. Often she had not. What did it matter! What could love, the unsolved mystery, count for in face of this possession of self-assertion which she suddenly recognized as the strongest impulse of her being!

16 "Free! Body and soul free!" she kept whispering.

NOTICE & NOTE
AHA MOMENT

When you notice a sudden realization that shifts a character's actions or understanding, you've found an **Aha Moment** signpost.

Notice & Note: Mark the signs in paragraphs 11–12 that describe Mrs. Mallard's reaction to the news she's received.

Cite Evidence: How do you know she has realized something that will change her life?

17 Josephine was kneeling before the closed door with her lips to the keyhole, imploring for admission. "Louise, open the door! I beg; open the door—you will make yourself ill. What are you doing, Louise? For heaven's sake open the door."

18 "Go away. I am not making myself ill." No; she was drinking in a very elixir of life[1] through that open window.

19 Her fancy was running riot along those days ahead of her. Spring days, and summer days, and all sorts of days that would be her own. She breathed a quick prayer that life might be long. It was only yesterday she had thought with a shudder that life might be long.

20 She arose at length and opened the door to her sister's importunities. There was a feverish triumph in her eyes, and she carried herself unwittingly like a goddess of Victory. She clasped her sister's waist, and together they descended the stairs. Richards stood waiting for them at the bottom.

21 Someone was opening the front door with a latchkey. It was Brently Mallard who entered, a little travel-stained, **composedly** carrying his grip-sack[2] and umbrella. He had been far from the scene of accident, and did not even know there had been one. He stood amazed at Josephine's piercing cry; at Richards' quick motion to screen him from the view of his wife.

22 But Richards was too late.

23 When the doctors came they said she had died of heart disease—of joy that kills.

[1] **elixir of life:** a medicine that restores vigor or the essence of life.
[2] **grip-sack:** a small traveling bag or satchel.

ANALYZE IRONY

Annotate: Mark Josephine's words to Mrs. Mallard in paragraph 17.

Analyze: What do readers know about this situation that Josephine does not? What kind of irony is formed by this difference in knowledge?

composed
(kəm-pōzd´) *adj.* self-possessed; calm.

ANALYZE POINT OF VIEW

Annotate: Mark words and phrases in paragraph 21 that show how each character feels or what they know.

Evaluate: How does the author's use of point of view contribute to the irony of the story's resolution?

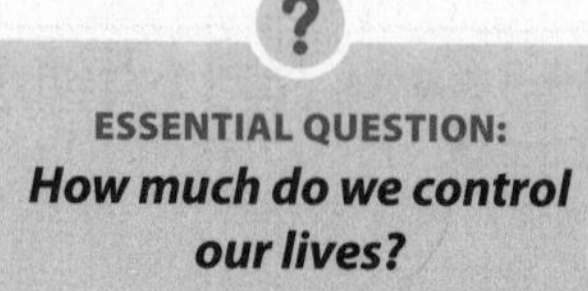
?
ESSENTIAL QUESTION:
How much do we control our lives?

Review your notes and add your thoughts to your **Response Log.**

COLLABORATIVE DISCUSSION

Pair up with a classmate and discuss your reaction to the story's ending. What point do you think the author was trying to make?

Assessment Practice

Answer these questions before moving on to the **Analyze the Text** section on the following page.

1. Why do you think the short story is titled "The Story of an Hour"?
   - (A) The accident happened over an hour-long period.
   - (B) The story takes place in an hour.
   - (C) It is all the time Mrs. Mallard needed to grieve.
   - (D) It is the amount of time it takes before she accepts the death.

2. Who informs Mrs. Mallard about her husband's death?
   - (A) A servant
   - (B) Richards
   - (C) The doctors
   - (D) Josephine

3. What causes Mrs. Mallard's death, according to the doctors?
   - (A) The fright at seeing a ghost
   - (B) Pneumonia
   - (C) Heart disease
   - (D) A broken heart

Test-Taking Strategies

Analyze the Text

Support your responses with evidence from the text.

NOTICE & NOTE

Review what you **noticed and noted** as you read the text. Your annotations can help you answer these questions.

1. **ANALYZE** Part of a narrator's role is to help readers see contrasts in the characters' perceptions, beliefs, and behaviors. What contrasts does this narrator point out to readers?

2. **CITE EVIDENCE** Is the narrator of the story limited or omniscient? At what point in the story do readers learn whose thoughts and feelings the narrator can describe?

3. **ANALYZE** In paragraph 11, Mrs. Mallard has an **Aha Moment**. What does this realization suggest about Mrs. Mallard's life prior to this point? In what ways will her life change?

4. **INFER** In paragraph 14, the narrator begins to reveal Mrs. Mallard's true feelings about being a widow. What does this point of view suggest about the story's theme?

5. **ANALYZE** The doctors say that Mrs. Mallard dies of "joy that kills." Explain whether this is an example of dramatic irony or not, and why.

6. **ANALYZE** Use the chart to list examples of irony you found in the story. Choose the one you think best suggests the theme of the story.

Verbal Irony	Situational Irony	Dramatic Irony
Theme:		

Choices

Here are some other ways to demonstrate your understanding of the ideas in this lesson.

Writing

↳ Diary Entry

Imagine that Louise Mallard's husband *does* die in a tragic train wreck and she is left a wealthy widow. Write her diary entry in which you detail what she plans to do and what hurdles she will face.

Take into consideration

- her desires and plans for life as a single woman in 1895
- her relatives' concern for her health
- how her family and society at large might react to her plans
- her response to their reaction

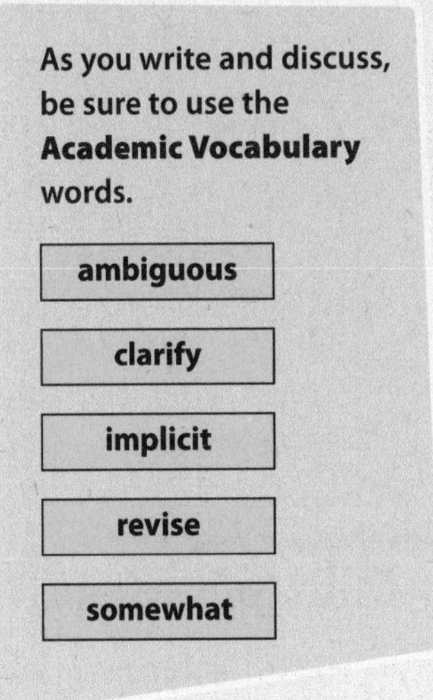
As you write and discuss, be sure to use the **Academic Vocabulary** words.
ambiguous
clarify
implicit
revise
somewhat

Speaking & Listening

↳ Roundtable

In her book *Unveiling Kate Chopin,* critic Emily Toth describes the ending of "The Story of an Hour": "She had to have her heroine die. A story in which an unhappy wife is suddenly widowed, becomes rich, and lives happily ever after . . . would have been much too radical, far too threatening in the 1890s."

In a small group, answer the following question: At what point in history have attitudes changed enough that Louise Mallard doesn't have to die?

Before you discuss, make some notes:

- Would the ending be different or not, depending on the year of publication?
- If so, how would it differ?
- If not, why would it stay the same?
- How do attitudes about a topic change?

Media

↳ The Story of a Minute

Flash drama is a short form of theater that has one to three characters, a minimalist set, and a single, very simple plot. The script is around 1,000 words, and the performance usually lasts less than 10 minutes. In a small group, write and film an alternate ending to "The Story of an Hour" that conforms to the flash drama format.

- Choose one to three characters from the story.
- Keep the action simple.
- Give everyone a role in front of, or behind, the camera.
- Post your video to a class or school website.
- Invite other groups to comment on your performance.
- Give others feedback on their videos.

Expand Your Vocabulary

PRACTICE AND APPLY

Write a short answer for each of the following questions. Explain your responses.

1. What outdoor activity is likely to inspire wild **abandonment**?
2. What might cause a person to have a **vacant** stare?
3. How might a scientist experience a moment of **illumination**?
4. When is it helpful to maintain a **composed** demeanor?

Vocabulary Strategy

↳ Multiple-Meaning Words

Interactive Vocabulary Lesson: Words with Multiple Meanings

In the English language, many words have more than one meaning. The meaning of a word often changes according to its part of speech. For example, the vocabulary word *composed* means "self-possessed" and "calm" when used as an adjective to describe someone. *Compose* is also a verb. The past-tense verb *composed* can mean "created a literary or musical piece" or "arranged something aesthetically or artistically."

When you come across a multiple-meaning word, first think about how it is used in the sentence. For example, is it an adjective or a verb? Then use context clues—examples, synonyms, or antonyms—to help you determine what it means in the sentence. It is useful to refer to an online or print dictionary to find all of the word's meanings and see which one best fits the sentence.

PRACTICE AND APPLY

Find two meanings for each of the words below. Use a dictionary to check your work. Then write sentences for both meanings.

1. time
2. patches
3. spread
4. fancy

Watch Your Language!

Effective Sentences

Chopin's distinct writing style comes from effectively varying the pattern of words and phrases in her sentences. By varying syntax, writers can adjust the rhythm of their sentences to convey mood and ideas effectively. They can also improve fluency and clarity. Punctuation, word choice, and well-chosen details all contribute to a writer's syntax and overall style. Authors also use a variety of sentence structures and sentence beginnings to craft effective sentences. The chart shows some of the techniques Chopin used.

Writing Tool	Purpose	Example
Exclamation	to convey excitement or emphasis	**What did it matter!** (paragraph 15)
Dash	to call attention to ideas by setting them off	**When the doctors came they said she had died of heart disease—of joy that kills.** (paragraph 23)
Sensory details	to create a full, vivid picture for the reader; to enhance characterization	**But now there was a dull stare in her eyes, whose gaze was fixed away off yonder on one of those patches of blue sky.** (paragraph 8)
Precise words and phrases	to communicate ideas effectively	**The notes of a distant song which someone was singing reached her faintly, and countless sparrows were twittering in the eaves.** (paragraph 5)
Repetition	to create rhythm and mood; to emphasize a particular point or idea	**When she abandoned herself a little whispered word escaped her slightly parted lips. She said it over and over under her breath: "free, free, free!"** (paragraph 11)

PRACTICE AND APPLY

Write a paragraph about someone's response to shocking news. Craft effective sentences by using some of the techniques above. When you have finished, share your paragraph with a partner and discuss the techniques you used to vary your sentences. Then, revise your paragraph based on your discussion.

Chicago

Poem by **Carl Sandburg**

ESSENTIAL QUESTION:
What makes a place unique?

Engage Your Brain

Choose one or more of these activities to start connecting with the poem you're about to read.

My Kind of Town

Jot down some vivid phrases or images that describe your hometown. To come up with ideas, ask yourself the following questions:

- What do you like about living there?
- What is your town known for?
- How has the town changed in your lifetime?

Remember, images are especially effective when they appeal to the five senses—sight, touch, taste, smell, and hearing. Create images that make your town come to life.

Create a Trivia Game

Chicago is a vibrant American city with a rich history. Learn more about it and then create a Chicago trivia game with your class.

- What do you want to know about Chicago? It may be related to history, the arts, sports, or any other area of interest.
- Use your newfound knowledge to create three trivia questions about the city.
- Try to stump your friends!

Write a Caption

The image here shows modern-day Chicago. What stands out to you? Write a creative and memorable two-line caption that describes what you see in the picture.

Analyze Free Verse

"Chicago" is a free verse poem. A free verse poem does not have regular patterns of rhythm and rhyme. Additionally, its stanzas and lines can be any length. However, that does not mean the stanzas and line breaks are random or that the poem has no structure. Rather, these elements support the ideas and feelings the poet is trying to express, and they create a unique voice for the speaker of the poem.

Free Verse Poem Elements	Possible Effects
Line length	Shorter lines may create an energetic, fast-paced feeling, while longer lines may create a slower, thoughtful effect.
Stanza length	Shorter stanzas can add urgency to a poem; stanza breaks may signal a change in time or space, a change in speaker, or a change in the speaker's tone.
Line breaks	Line breaks in the middle of sentences create tension, while ending lines with punctuation often creates a sense of resolution or stability. By breaking lines where readers do not expect them to do so, poets create a sense of suspense.
Natural rhythm	The rhythm of free verse poems echoes the cadences of natural speech or song.

Focus on Genre

Free Verse Poem

- does not contain formal meter or rhyme scheme
- uses line length and stanza breaks to convey meaning
- contains rhythm that mirrors everyday speech

Analyze Imagery

Free verse poems often use literary devices, such as imagery, to communicate meaning. **Imagery** is the use of words and phrases that appeal to the five senses, so that readers experience the text in a vivid way. For example, Carl Sandburg once wrote, "The fog comes on little cat feet," so that the reader pictures the fog as a cat creeping forward as it stalks its prey. In "Chicago," Sandburg uses imagery to describe the city he called home.

While reading "Chicago," analyze the writer's use of imagery. Fill in the chart with words or phrases from the poem that help you form mental pictures. Which senses does Sandburg appeal to most?

Images	Senses

Analyze Tone

Tone is the attitude or feeling the poem's speaker has toward the subject of the poem. Poets convey tone by precisely choosing their words and arranging them to create maximum impact. Sometimes the tone of a poem can be difficult to perceive and describe. Other times the tone is very obvious. In "Chicago," Carl Sandburg lists action after action, creating a fast-paced rhythm that suggests he sees the city as hardworking.

Fierce as a dog with tongue lapping for action, cunning
as a savage pitted against the wilderness,
Bareheaded,
Shoveling,
Wrecking,
Planning,
Building, breaking, rebuilding,

Annotation in Action

Here are one student's notes about the tone at the beginning of "Chicago." As you read, highlight images that help set the tone of the poem.

Hog Butcher for the World,
Tool Maker, Stacker of Wheat,
Player with Railroads and the Nation's Freight
Handler;
Stormy, husky, brawling,
City of the Big Shoulders:

Sandburg admires the city's strength.

Background

Carl Sandburg (1878–1967) grew up in America's heartland in Galesburg, Illinois. Given to wanderlust from an early age, he traveled throughout the country, soaking up America's sights and sounds. When he ran out of money, he returned to the Midwest, writing for journals in Chicago. Sandburg became a reporter, editorial writer, and columnist for the *Chicago Daily News* and began publishing his verse in *Poetry*, a prominent literary magazine. His first collection of poems, *Chicago Poems*, was published in 1916.

Chicago

Poem by **Carl Sandburg**

A poet sees his beloved city in bold and beautiful ways that others don't.

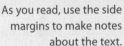

NOTICE & NOTE
As you read, use the side margins to make notes about the text.

Hog Butcher for the World,
Tool Maker, Stacker of Wheat,
Player with Railroads and the Nation's Freight Handler;
Stormy, husky, brawling,
City of the Big Shoulders:

They tell me you are wicked and I believe them, for I have seen your painted women under the gas lamps luring the farm boys.
And they tell me you are crooked and I answer: Yes, it is true I have seen the gunman kill and go free to kill again.
And they tell me you are brutal and my reply is: On the faces of women and children I have seen the marks of wanton[1] hunger.

ANALYZE TONE

Annotate: Mark the harsh words in lines 6–9. Mark the language in line 10 that contrasts with this harshness.

Analyze: What do these contrasts reveal about Sandburg's feelings toward the city as well as its critics?

[1] **wanton:** without limitation.

ANALYZE FREE VERSE

Annotate: Mark the word that begins an important shift in line length in lines 12–17.

Analyze: How does this shift reflect the content and meaning of these lines?

ANALYZE IMAGERY

Annotate: Mark words and phrases that appeal to the senses in lines 18–22.

Analyze: How do these images help share the writer's ideas about his city?

And having answered so I turn once more to those who
  sneer at this my city, and I give them back the sneer
  and say to them:
Come and show me another city with lifted head singing
  so proud to be alive and coarse and strong and cunning.
Flinging magnetic curses amid the toil of piling job on
  job, here is a tall bold slugger set vivid against the
  little soft cities;
Fierce as a dog with tongue lapping for action, cunning
  as a savage pitted against the wilderness,
    Bareheaded,
    Shoveling,
    Wrecking,
    Planning,
    Building, breaking, rebuilding,
Under the smoke, dust all over his mouth, laughing with
  white teeth,
Under the terrible burden of destiny laughing as a young
  man laughs,
Laughing even as an ignorant fighter laughs who has
  never lost a battle,
Bragging and laughing that under his wrist is the pulse, and
  under his ribs the heart of the people,
      Laughing!
Laughing the stormy, husky, brawling laughter of
  Youth, half-naked, sweating, proud to be Hog
  Butcher, Tool Maker, Stacker of Wheat, Player with
  Railroads and Freight Handler to the Nation.

COLLABORATIVE DISCUSSION

With a partner, take turns describing the image of Chicago in the poem that you thought was the strongest. What do you think the poet's attitude toward Chicago is?

ESSENTIAL QUESTION:
What makes a place unique?

Review your notes and add your thoughts to your **Response Log.**

Assessment Practice

Answer these questions before moving on to the **Analyze the Text** section on the following page.

1. How is stanza 1 different from stanza 2?

- (A) Stanza 1 has a rhyme scheme and stanza 2 does not.
- (B) Stanza 1 is about Chicago and stanza 2 is not.
- (C) Stanza 2 contains vivid images and stanza 1 does not.
- (D) Stanza 2 contains long lines and stanza 1 does not.

2. What proof of Chicago's reputation as brutal does the poem's speaker give?

- (A) The speaker thinks the people who live in Chicago are insensitive.
- (B) The speaker has seen dogs fighting in the streets.
- (C) The speaker thinks the people who live in Chicago grab all the wealth.
- (D) The speaker has seen hungry women and children.

3. According to the poem, how does Chicago feel about its reputation?

- (A) Sad
- (B) Angry
- (C) Proud
- (D) Sorrowful

Test-Taking Strategies

Analyze the Text

Support your responses with evidence from the text.

Review what you **noticed and noted** as you read the text. Your annotations can help you answer these questions.

1. **INTERPRET** How does the structure of the poem as a whole reflect its subject matter? Consider the stanzas and line breaks in your response.

2. **ANALYZE** What is the tone of the poem? Cite examples of words and phrases from the poem that help create the tone.

Words and Phrases	Tone

3. **ANALYZE** Look back at the chart on page 587 that you filled in as you read. Does Sandburg's language appeal more to one sense than to others? How does this language help develop his tone?

4. **EVALUATE** Explain whether the person described beginning in line 18 is an appropriate symbol for a great American city. Cite examples of particular images in your response.

5. **CONNECT** Although Carl Sandburg has been an extremely popular American poet for almost a century, some readers consider his work sentimental. Does Sandburg portray the city sentimentally or realistically—or both?

6. **SYNTHESIZE** Think about the **litany,** or list, of images and ideas in "Chicago." Based on this detailed list, what statement does the poem make about the people who live and work in the city?

Choices

Here are some other ways to demonstrate your understanding of the ideas in this lesson.

Writing

↳ Tag-Team Poetry

Take a few moments to come up with words and phrases people use to describe where you live. In a small group, pool your answers into a single word bank. Then create a tag-team poem. One person should write the first line, then hand it off to the next. That person writes a line, hands it off, and so on. When everyone has contributed a line, work together to revise and publish it.

- Before you start, decide whether to use a certain rhythm or rhyme scheme.
- Rearrange lines to create stanzas that cohere around a single theme or image.
- Use strong imagery to represent your hometown.
- Read your poem out loud as you edit to help get the right rhythm and flow.

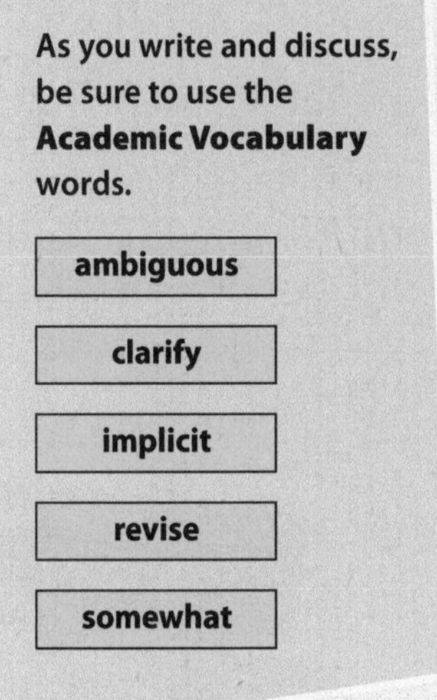
As you write and discuss, be sure to use the **Academic Vocabulary** words.
ambiguous
clarify
implicit
revise
somewhat

Research

↳ They Said That?

William Carlos Williams (1883–1963), a contemporary of Carl Sandburg, said that Sandburg's poetry was a "formless mass." Research what others have said about Sandburg's *Chicago Poems*. Keep in mind that the best sources for this research are literary journals. If you need keywords for your search, try

- *Chicago Poems*, criticism at publication
- Robert Frost, *Chicago Poems*
- Amy Lowell, *Chicago Poems*
- *The Dial, Chicago Poems*

Speaking & Listening

↳ Share Impressions

Think about the images you've seen and what you've learned about Chicago. How did reading the poem add to or change your impression of the city? Synthesize what you know and share your impressions about Chicago with a partner. You may want to include

- observations about the city's past
- observations about present-day Chicago
- what places you'd be interested in visiting
- how it might be similar to or different from where you live

Collaborate & Compare

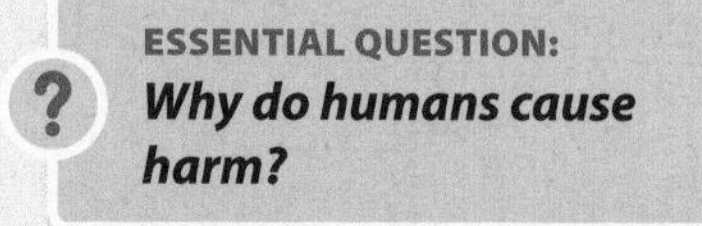

Compare Genres

In this lesson, you'll read texts from two different genres about how food is processed. One is a work of fiction based on undercover reporting; the other is an excerpt from a lengthy investigative report. After you read, consider how the genre contributes to the effectiveness of each author's message.

A
from
The Jungle
Novel by Upton Sinclair
pages 598–603
B
Food
Product
Design
Investigative Journalism by
Eric Schlosser
pages 611–621

After you read both texts, you will work in a group to

- Analyze genre characteristics
- Synthesize information
- Present your ideas

from The Jungle

Novel by **Upton Sinclair**

Engage Your Brain

Choose one or more of these activities to start connecting with the text you're about to read.

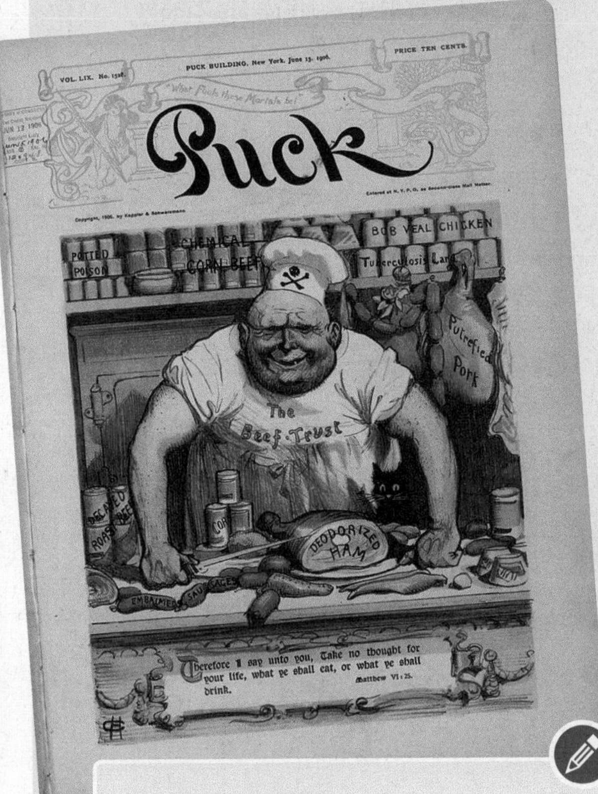

Back in the Day...

The Jungle created a stir when it was published. Take a look at this comic that came out shortly after Sinclair's book was released. Write a brief response to these questions:

- What does the comic suggest about what you might find in the novel?
- Based on the comic, do you think that Upton Sinclair painted a positive or a negative picture about the meatpacking industry? Why?

Do You Know Where Your Food Comes From?

No, the answer is not "a grocery store"! If you don't know where and how food is grown, raised, or produced for the U.S. consumer, there are plenty of documentaries and books to help you learn more.

- Research the names of books or films that talk about food production.
- Watch a trailer or read a review about two of the titles you found.
- Share your findings with a partner. Which one(s) would you be interested in exploring further?

You Muckraker, You!

Upton Sinclair was referred to as a "muckraker." It sounds like an insult, but being a muckraker isn't so bad.

- Write down what you think the word means.
- Look it up. What are one or two facts about muckrakers you were surprised to learn?

Determine Themes

Most authors start with a **topic**, or subject, they want to explore. As they write, they develop the **theme**, or insight, they want readers to understand about the topic. **Recurring themes** are themes that appear in multiple works in which different authors tackle the same or related topics. To determine a theme, readers may

- examine key events in the plot and statements from characters
- analyze words that convey the writer's attitude toward the topic
- note contradictions between what characters say and do

As you read, note details about the workers' jobs to see if you can determine the themes Sinclair is developing.

Focus on Genre
↳ Novel

- is an extended work of fiction
- has one or more complex plots and/or characters
- has a purpose that can be determined through examination of key details
- conveys a strong message about a topic

Analyze Author's Purpose

An author's **purpose**, or reason, for writing may be to inform, to entertain, or to persuade. Some authors may want to move readers to take action. Usually, readers must infer the writer's purpose based on a work's content and style. Upton Sinclair was a journalist for a socialist newspaper when he went to Chicago to investigate working conditions in the stockyards. However, he ended up writing *The Jungle,* a novel that shows the lives of a family of Lithuanian immigrants who work in the stockyards. As you read, use the chart to analyze Sinclair's purpose in writing this novel.

Questions	Answers
What topics does Sinclair write about in this excerpt?	
What messages or themes do you see in his work?	
What action might Sinclair have wanted readers to take after reading *The Jungle*?	

Annotation in Action

Here are one student's notes about the excerpt from *The Jungle*. As you read, note the words and phrases that could be clues to the text's theme.

Jurgis heard of these things little by little, in the gossip of those who were obliged to perpetrate them. It seemed as if every time you met a person from a new department, you heard of new swindles and new crimes. There was, for instance, a Lithuanian who was a cattle butcher for the plant where Marija had worked, which killed meat for canning only; and to hear this man describe the animals which came to his place would have been worthwhile for a Dante or a Zola.

This sounds sinister— "obliged" suggests coercion; "perpetrate" and "new swindles and new crimes" make me think of criminal behavior.

Expand Your Vocabulary

Put a check mark next to the vocabulary words that you feel comfortable using when speaking or writing.

oblige	☐
ingenious	☐
ostensibly	☐
sceptical	☐

Then, use these words to talk about a scheme to make money. As you read the excerpt from *The Jungle*, use the definitions in the side column to learn the vocabulary words you don't already know.

Background

Upton Sinclair (1878–1968) was sent by a newspaper to Chicago to investigate working conditions in the stockyards, where animals were processed into meat. His research led not only to an investigative report but to his most famous novel, *The Jungle* (1906), which he was forced to self-publish after several publishers turned down the manuscript. The novel exposed unsanitary conditions in the meatpacking industry and led to reforms. Jurgis Rudkus, the main character, is a Lithuanian immigrant who works in the stockyards.

NOTICE & NOTE

As you read, use the side margins to make notes about the text.

from

The Jungle

Novel by **Upton Sinclair**

Note details that suggest the author's purpose. You will compare this text with the investigative journalism article "Food Product Design" that follows.

oblige
(ə-blīj´) *v.* to compel or require (someone) to do something.

1 Jurgis heard of these things little by little, in the gossip of those who were **obliged** to perpetrate them. It seemed as if every time you met a person from a new department, you heard of new swindles and new crimes. There was, for instance, a Lithuanian who was a cattle butcher for the plant where Marija had worked, which killed meat for canning only; and to hear this man describe the animals which came to his place would have been worthwhile for a Dante or a Zola.[1] It seemed that they must have agencies all over the country, to hunt out old and crippled and diseased cattle to be canned. There were cattle which had been fed on "whiskey malt," the refuse of the breweries, and had become what the men called "steerly"—which

[1] **a Dante or a Zola:** Dante Alighieri (1265–1321), Florentine poet who wrote the *Inferno*, about a journey through Hell; Emile Zola (1840–1902), French novelist and playwright who focused on social and political ills.

means covered with boils. It was a nasty job killing these, for when you plunged your knife into them they would burst and splash foul-smelling stuff into your face; and when a man's sleeves were smeared with blood, and his hands steeped in it, how was he ever to wipe his face, or to clear his eyes so that he could see? It was stuff such as this that made the "embalmed beef" that had killed several times as many United States soldiers as all the bullets of the Spaniards; only the army beef, besides, was not fresh canned, it was old stuff that had been lying for years in the cellars.

Don't forget to **Notice & Note** as you read the text. 

2 Then one Sunday evening, Jurgis sat puffing his pipe by the kitchen stove, and talking with an old fellow whom Jonas had introduced, and who worked in the canning-rooms at Durham's; and so Jurgis learned a few things about the great and only Durham canned goods, which had become a national institution. They were regular alchemists at Durham's; they advertised a mushroom-catsup, and the men who made it did not know what a mushroom looked like. They advertised "potted chicken"—and it was like the boarding-house soup of the comic papers, through which a chicken had walked with rubbers on. Perhaps they had a secret process for making chickens chemically—who knows? said Jurgis's friend; the things that went into the mixture were tripe,[2] and the fat of pork, and beef suet, and hearts of beef, and finally the waste ends of veal, when they had any. They put these up in several grades, and sold them at several prices; but the contents of the cans all came out of the same hopper. And then there was "potted game" and "potted grouse," "potted ham," and "deviled ham"—de-vyled, as the men called it. "De-vyled" ham was made out of the waste ends of smoked beef that were too small to be sliced by the machines; and also tripe, dyed with chemicals so that it would not show white, and trimmings of hams and corned

DETERMINE THEMES

Annotate: Mark the details in paragraph 2 that reveal a difference between what an ingredient should be and what it is.

Infer: What do these differences suggest Sinclair's message might be?

[2] **tripe:** the rubbery lining of the stomach of cattle or other ruminants, used as food.

ingenious
(ĭn-jēn´yəs) *adj.* having great inventive skill and imagination.

ostensibly
(ŏ-stĕn´sə-blē) *adv.* apparently

beef, and potatoes, skins and all, and finally the hard cartilaginous gullets of beef, after the tongues had been cut out. All this **ingenious** mixture was ground up and flavored with spices to make it taste like something. Anybody who could invent a new imitation had been sure of a fortune from old Durham, said Jurgis's informant, but it was hard to think of anything new in a place where so many sharp wits had been at work for so long; where men welcomed tuberculosis[3] in the cattle they were feeding, because it made them fatten more quickly; and where they bought up all the old rancid butter left over in the grocery stores of a continent, and "oxidized" it by a forced-air process, to take away the odor, rechurned it with skim milk, and sold it in bricks in the cities! Up to a year or two ago it had been the custom to kill horses in the yards—**ostensibly** for fertilizer; but after long agitation the newspapers had been able to make the public realize that the horses were being canned. Now it was against the law to kill horses in Packingtown, and the law was really complied with—for the present, at any rate. Any day, however, one might see sharp-horned and shaggy-haired creatures running with the sheep—and yet what a job you would have to get the public to believe that a good part of what it buys for lamb and mutton is really goat's flesh!

[3] **tuberculosis:** an infectious disease that causes the growth of nodules on lung tissue.

Don't forget to **Notice & Note** as you read the text.

3 There was another interesting set of statistics that a person might have gathered in Packingtown—those of the various afflictions of the workers. When Jurgis had first inspected the packing plants with Szedvilas, he had marveled while he listened to the tale of all the things that were made out of the carcasses of animals, and of all the lesser industries that were maintained there; now he found that each one of these lesser industries was a separate little inferno, in its way as horrible as the killing-beds, the source and fountain of them all. The workers in each of them had their own peculiar diseases. And the wandering visitor might be **sceptical** about all the swindles, but he could not be sceptical about these, for the worker bore the evidence of them about on his own person—generally he had only to hold out his hand.

4 There were the men in the pickle rooms, for instance, where old Antanas had gotten his death; scarce a one of these that had not some spot of horror on his person. Let a man so much as scrape his finger pushing a truck in the pickle rooms, and he might have a sore that would put him out of the world; all the joints in his fingers might be eaten by the acid, one by one. Of the butchers and floorsmen, the beef boners and trimmers, and all those who used knives, you could scarcely find a person who had the use of his thumb; time and time again the base of it had been slashed, till it was a mere lump of flesh against which the man pressed the knife to hold it. The hands of these men would be criss-crossed with cuts, until you could no longer pretend to count them or to trace them. They would have no nails,—they had worn them off pulling hides; their knuckles were swollen so that their fingers spread out like a fan. There were men who worked in the cooking rooms, in the midst of steam and sickening odors, by artificial light; in these rooms the germs of tuberculosis might live for two years, but the supply was renewed every hour. There were the beef luggers, who carried two-hundred-pound quarters into the refrigerator cars, a fearful kind of work, that began at four o'clock in the morning, and that wore out the most powerful men in a few years. There were those who worked in the

VOCABULARY

Word Families: The word *afflictions* in paragraph 3 has other forms derived from the same root. You can build your vocabulary by using all the words in a family.

Analyze: To *afflict* is to cause an injury. How does knowing the meaning of the verb help you understand what *affliction* means?

sceptical
(skĕp´tĭ-kəl) *adj.* marked by or given to doubt; questioning.

NOTICE & NOTE
AGAIN AND AGAIN

When you notice certain words recurring over a portion of the story, you've found an **Again and Again** signpost.

Notice & Note: Mark the repetition of the phrase "There were . . ." in paragraph 4.

Analyze: Why might the author repeat this wording throughout this paragraph?

chilling rooms, and whose special disease was rheumatism;[4] the time limit that a man could work in the chilling rooms was said to be five years. There were the wool pluckers, whose hands went to pieces even sooner than the hands of the pickle men; for the pelts of the sheep had to be painted with acid to loosen the wool, and then the pluckers had to pull out this wool with their bare hands, till the acid had eaten their fingers off. There were those who made the tins for the canned meat, and their hands, too, were a maze of cuts, and each cut represented a chance for blood poisoning. Some worked at the stamping machines, and it was very seldom that one could work long there at the pace that was set, and not give out and forget himself, and have a part of his hand chopped off. There were the "hoisters," as they were called, whose task it was to press the lever which lifted the dead cattle off the floor. They ran along upon a rafter, peering down through the damp and the steam, and as old Durham's architects had not built the killing room for the convenience of the hoisters, at every few feet they would have to stoop under a beam, say four feet above the one they ran on, which got them into the habit of stooping, so that in a few years they would be walking like chimpanzees. Worst of any, however, were the fertilizer men, and those who served in the cooking rooms. These people could not be shown to the visitor—for the odor of a fertilizer man would scare any ordinary visitor at a hundred yards, and as for the other men, who worked in tank rooms full of steam, and in some of which there were open vats near the level of the floor, their peculiar trouble was that they fell into the vats; and when they were fished out, there was never enough of them left to be worth exhibiting—sometimes they would be overlooked for days, till all but the bones of them had gone out to the world as Durham's Pure Leaf Lard!

ANALYZE AUTHOR'S PURPOSE

Annotate: Mark the final clause of the last sentence in paragraph 4.

Analyze: Why does Sinclair build the sentence so that it concludes with this disturbing detail?

[4] **rheumatism** (ro͞o´mə-tĭz´əm): a disease that causes inflammation and pain in muscles and joints.

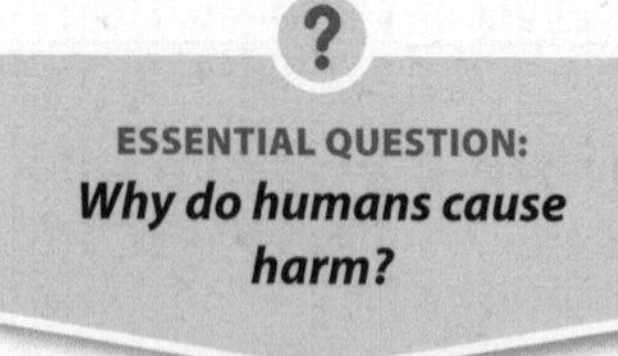
?
ESSENTIAL QUESTION:
Why do humans cause harm?

Review your notes and add your thoughts to your **Response Log.**

COLLABORATIVE DISCUSSION

With a partner, discuss how Sinclair's descriptions affected you. Was there one in particular that made you react strongly?

Assessment Practice

Answer these questions before moving on to the **Analyze the Text** section on the following page.

1. How does Jurgis learn about what happened in the canning department at Durham?
   - (A) By working in the department for several months
   - (B) By reading accounts in the newspapers
   - (C) By talking to workers in that department
   - (D) By hearing stories from his wife, Marija

2. According to the company, what was the advantage of cattle that had tuberculosis?
   - (A) They were easier to kill.
   - (B) They fattened more quickly.
   - (C) They had better flavor.
   - (D) They could be sold as veal.

3. Why was the time men were able to work in the chilling rooms limited to five years?
   - (A) Their hands were disfigured by acid.
   - (B) They lost fingers from butchering the cold beef.
   - (C) They sickened from tuberculosis.
   - (D) They tended to get rheumatism.

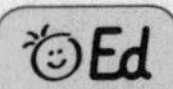

Test-Taking Strategies

Analyze the Text

Support your responses with evidence from the text.

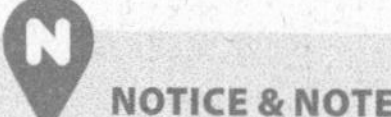

Review what you **noticed and noted** as you read the text. Your annotations can help you answer these questions.

1. **ANALYZE** What is Sinclair's implicit idea in the first two sentences of the selection about workers in the stockyards? How do these sentences reflect his purpose?

2. **INFER** What does Sinclair mean when he writes, "They were regular alchemists at Durham's" (paragraph 2)?

3. **DRAW CONCLUSIONS** What is Sinclair's topic in the third and fourth paragraphs? What message does he communicate about the topic?

4. **SYNTHESIZE** Describe the imagery Sinclair uses **Again and Again.** What is the effect of this imagery on his message?

5. **ANALYZE** In this excerpt, Sinclair uses third-person point of view. A narrator outside of the action tells the story, focusing mainly on the thoughts, actions, and observations of Jurgis, the main character. How does choosing this point of view help Sinclair achieve his purpose?

6. **DRAW CONCLUSIONS** Readers in Sinclair's time were more concerned about his revelations in the first two paragraphs than about the revelations in the rest of the selection. Why might this have been, and how does this relate to Sinclair's purpose?

7. **DRAW CONCLUSIONS** How did Sinclair's choice to use elements of fiction help him achieve a purpose that readers might expect to find in writing by a journalist? Use the chart to gather details.

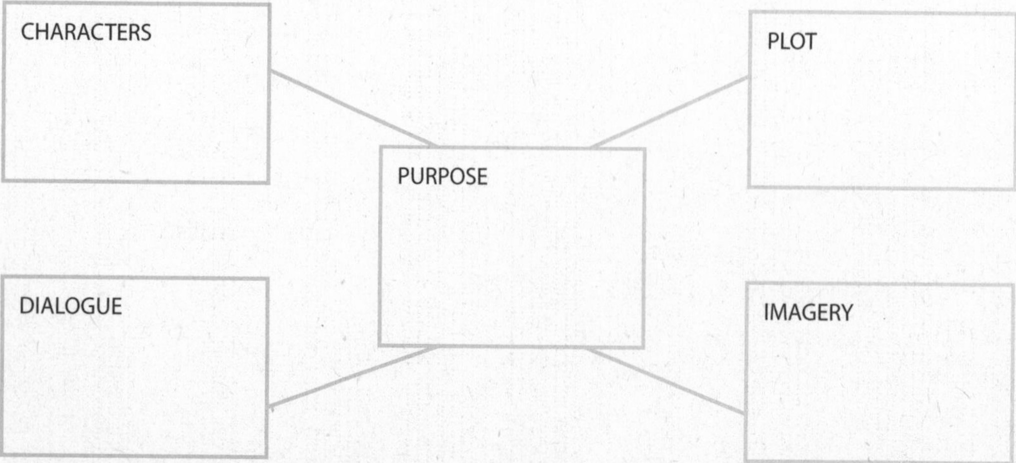

Choices

Here are some other ways to demonstrate your understanding of the ideas in this lesson.

Writing

↳ Taking a Stand

Imagine there is a meatpackers union in the factory where Jurgis Rudkus works and that you are the president. You've asked the company owners and managers for better pay and working conditions but haven't gotten a response. Now you're taking your protest public. Write a speech detailing your demands. Structure it to be persuasive and to drive people to action.

Take into consideration

- what a fair wage should be, given the difficulty of the work
- safety and health concerns
- what should happen in the case of injury
- your audience and what you want their response to be

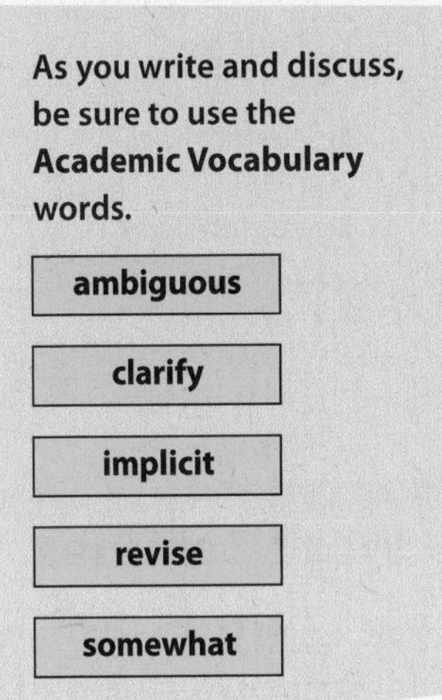
As you write and discuss, be sure to use the **Academic Vocabulary** words.
ambiguous
clarify
implicit
revise
somewhat

Media

↳ Is Meat Made of Slime?

In the early 2000s, media attention turned to a beef filler known as "pink slime," which was used to make hamburger patties and other products for fast food outlets. With a partner, find a news report or documentary online that investigates the use of pink slime. Then write an analysis about the accuracy of the reporting. Address the following:

- What sources did the report use to make and support the claims?
- How credible and reliable are those sources?
- Is the reasoning in the report free of logical fallacies?
- Is the report as a whole accurate and compelling?

Share your findings with your classmates. If they read or viewed a different report, then compare your analyses.

Social & Emotional Learning

↳ Who Is Responsible?

The publication of *The Jungle* led to the passage of laws and regulations to reform the meatpacking industry. Should it be up to an outside observer like Sinclair to effect change? Who ought to ensure that companies are behaving responsibly and not putting people at risk? Discuss the following possibilities:

- industry leaders
- individual employees
- lawmakers
- investigative journalists

Expand Your Vocabulary

PRACTICE AND APPLY

Find examples of the vocabulary words in advertisements, articles, or books. Write a definition of each word based on your examples. Note that the preferred spelling of *sceptical* in American dictionaries is now *skeptical*.

1. **oblige**
2. **ingenious**
3. **ostensibly**
4. **sceptical**

Vocabulary Strategy

Word Families

Oblige is part of the word family with the Latin root *ligare*, meaning "to bind." *Oblige* is formed by adding the prefix *ob-* (meaning "to") to the root so that the word means "to require (someone) to do something." Words may have prefixes or suffixes and act as different parts of speech. Knowing a root's meaning will help you find the meaning of words in a word family.

Interactive Vocabulary Lesson: Common Roots, Prefixes, and Suffixes

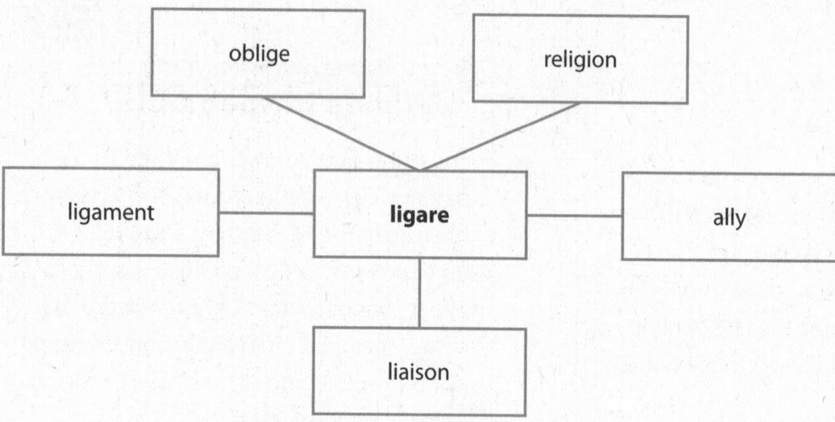

PRACTICE AND APPLY

Work with a partner to create a list of four words related to each root below. Write the part of speech and definition next to each word. Consult a dictionary to confirm the meaning and etymology of the words.

1. Greek root *path-*, meaning "to feel or suffer"
2. Latin root *spec-*, meaning "to see or look at"
3. Latin root *medi-*, meaning "middle"
4. Greek root *chron-*, meaning "time"

Watch Your Language!

Prepositions and Prepositional Phrases

A **preposition** shows the relationship between a noun or a pronoun and another word in a sentence. Common prepositions include *in, of, for, by, above, below, before,* and *after*. A preposition is always followed by a word or group of words that serves as its object. The preposition, its object, and modifiers of the object form a **prepositional phrase**. Prepositional phrases can be as short as two words: *at home*. They can be longer if the object is modified: *in his comfortable, welcoming home*.

A prepositional phrase can function in a sentence as either an adjective or an adverb.

As an adjective modifying *man*: The man *near the door* looks suspicious.

As an adverb modifying *rose*: The jet rose *into the sky*.

Prepositional phrases must be as near as possible to the words they modify.

Incorrect: The waves *against the rocks* crashed noisily.

Correct: The waves crashed *against the rocks* noisily.

You can use prepositional phrases to improve the fluency and clarity of sentences.

Interactive Grammar Lessons: Prepositions; Prepositional Phrases

PRACTICE AND APPLY

Use prepositional phrases to revise each group of sentences into one sentence that has greater clarity and fluency.

1. There was a podium. The speaker stood there. She gave a spellbinding speech. She told her life story.

2. The chef cooked a meal. It took an hour to make it. It was hard work. He served the meal. His customers ate it.

3. The runner struggled. He felt disheartened. The finish line seemed far off. Then he felt an adrenaline rush. He ran faster.

4. The couple signed the mortgage. They used a pen. Now they owned the country house.

Food Product Design *from* Fast Food Nation

Investigative Journalism by **Eric Schlosser**

ESSENTIAL QUESTION:
Why do humans cause harm?

Engage Your Brain

Choose one or more of these activities to start connecting with the investigative report you're about to read.

Survey Says...!

As a class, take a poll to find out the answers to the following questions.

- How often do you eat fast food?
- When was the last time you ate a fast food meal?
- What did you order?
- What fast food is the absolute best, iyho?
- What fast food is the absolute worst?

Mmmmmmm, Fast Food

For some, fast food is a tasty thrill. For others, not so much. What's your take on it?

- Write at least one reason why you like or dislike fast food.
- Look at this photo of a fast food meal. Does it make you change your mind?

Keepin' It Real

Sometimes we think that food is more healthful than it actually is. To keep us honest, we turn to the humble calorie counter.

1. Think of a meal you've eaten in the last few days. Write down all the ingredients in it that you can think of. Guess the total number of calories in the meal.
2. Go online to find a calorie counter. Enter in each ingredient to see how many calories it has. Total up the individual calorie counts.
3. Compare your guess with the actual calorie count. Were you over or under? By how much?

Determine Central Idea

To talk knowledgeably about his subject, Eric Schlosser uses specialized vocabulary and writes complex paragraphs filled with details. If you have trouble identifying the central idea, try to **paraphrase** his statements—or put them in your own words—to make the text more clear. To paraphrase, follow these steps.

- Reread the part of the text you're paraphrasing until you think you understand it. Look up words you don't know to ensure you know what they mean.
- Write your own version of the text. It may help to pretend you're explaining it to a friend.
- Compare what you wrote to the author's text. Check to see if you've accurately rewritten the author's ideas in your own words, or if you've rearranged the author's words to sound "different enough."

As you read "Food Product Design," use the margins to paraphrase any sections you don't understand.

Focus on Genre
↳ **Investigative Journalism**

- **uses facts and quotations to support ideas**
- **exposes actions or events hidden from public view**
- **appears in newspapers, in magazines, or on websites**

Analyze Author's Purpose

Eric Schlosser's general **purpose** for writing is to inform or to persuade—or some combination of the two. As an investigative journalist, he may also want to encourage people to take a particular action based on the information he presents. Analyzing the details in the text will allow you to infer Schlosser's specific purpose for writing this text.

Use the chart to help you analyze Schlosser's purpose.

What topics does Schlosser write about?	
What messages and themes do you see in this excerpt?	
What actions do you think Schlosser wants readers to take?	

Annotation in Action

Here are one student's notes about "Food Product Design." As you read, note how the author uses language to suggest his purpose.

Open your refrigerator, your freezer, your kitchen cupboards, and look at the labels on your food. You'll find "natural flavor" or "artificial flavor" in just about every list of ingredients. The similarities between these two broad categories of flavor are far more significant than their differences.

Why is the writer noting similarities between food flavorings?

Expand Your Vocabulary

Put a check mark next to the vocabulary words that you feel comfortable using when speaking or writing.

stem	☐
volatile	☐
infinitesimal	☐
catalyst	☐
conjure	☐

Then, see if you can use them to talk about your science class. As you read the excerpt from *Fast Food Nation,* use the definitions in the side column to learn the vocabulary words you don't already know.

Background

Eric Schlosser (b. 1959) became a journalist after studying history in college. In 1998, the magazine *Rolling Stone* published his two-part investigative series on the fast food industry. Schlosser then expanded the articles into a best-selling book, *Fast Food Nation: The Dark Side of the All-American Meal* (2001), which examines the effects of the fast food industry on workers, consumers, and the landscape. Later that same year, the book was made into a movie, with Schlosser cowriting the screenplay.

B

Food Product Design

from Fast Food Nation

Investigative Journalism by **Eric Schlosser**

NOTICE & NOTE
As you read, use the side margins to make notes about the text.

Two authors writing on a similar subject may not have the same purpose. As you read, note where Schlosser's purpose seems similar to, or different from, Sinclair's.

1 The taste of McDonald's french fries has long been praised by customers, competitors, and even food critics. James Beard loved McDonald's fries. Their distinctive taste does not **stem** from the type of potatoes that McDonald's buys, the technology that processes them, or the restaurant equipment that fries them. Other chains buy their french fries from the same large processing companies, use Russet Burbanks, and have similar fryers in their restaurant kitchens. The taste of a fast food fry is largely determined by the cooking oil. For decades, McDonald's cooked its french fries in a mixture of about 7 percent cottonseed oil and 93 percent beef tallow. The mix gave the fries their unique flavor—and more saturated beef fat per ounce than a McDonald's hamburger.

stem
(stĕm) *v.* to have or take origin or descent.

2 Amid a barrage of criticism over the amount of cholesterol in their fries, McDonald's switched to pure vegetable oil in 1990. The switch presented the company with an enormous challenge: how to

make fries that subtly taste like beef without cooking them in tallow. A look at the ingredients now used in the preparation of McDonald's french fries suggests how the problem was solved. At the end of the list is a seemingly innocuous, yet oddly mysterious phrase: "natural flavor." That ingredient helps to explain not only why the fries taste so good, but also why most fast food—indeed, most of the food Americans eat today—tastes the way it does.

ANALYZE AUTHOR'S PURPOSE

Annotate: Mark the words and phrases in paragraph 3 that suggest a widespread use of natural flavors in the United States.

Analyze: How do these details suggest that the topic is important? Explain.

3 Open your refrigerator, your freezer, your kitchen cupboards, and look at the labels on your food. You'll find "natural flavor" or "artificial flavor" in just about every list of ingredients. The similarities between these two broad categories of flavor are far more significant than their differences. Both are man-made additives that give most processed food its taste. The initial purchase of a food item may be driven by its packaging or appearance, but subsequent purchases are determined mainly by its taste. About 90 percent of the money that Americans spend on food is used to buy processed food. But the canning, freezing, and dehydrating techniques used to process food destroy most of its flavor. Since the end of World War II, a vast industry has arisen in the United States to make processed food palatable. Without this flavor industry, today's fast food industry could not exist. The names of the leading American fast food chains and their best-selling menu items have become famous worldwide, embedded in our popular culture. Few people, however, can name the companies that manufacture fast food's taste.

4 The flavor industry is highly secretive. Its leading companies will not divulge[1] the precise formulas of flavor compounds or the identities of clients. The secrecy is deemed essential for protecting the reputation of beloved brands. The fast food chains, understandably, would like the public to believe that the flavors of their food somehow originate in their restaurant kitchens, not in distant factories run by other firms.

5 The New Jersey Turnpike runs through the heart of the flavor industry, an industrial corridor dotted with refineries and chemical plants. International Flavors & Fragrances (IFF), the world's largest flavor company, has a manufacturing facility off Exit 8A in Dayton, New Jersey; Givaudan, the world's second-largest flavor company, has a plant in East Hanover. Haarmann & Reimer, the largest German flavor company, has a plant in Teterboro, as does Takasago, the largest Japanese flavor company. Flavor Dynamics has a plant in South Plainfield; Frutarom is in North Bergen; Elan Chemical is in Newark. Dozens of companies manufacture flavors in New Jersey industrial parks between Teaneck and South Brunswick. Indeed, the area produces about two-thirds of the flavor additives sold in the United States.

6 The IFF plant in Dayton is a huge pale blue building with a modern office complex attached to the front. It sits in an industrial

[1] **divulge:** to make known (something private or secret).

park, not far from a BASF plastics factory, a Jolly French Toast factory, and a plant that manufactures Liz Claiborne cosmetics. Dozens of tractor-trailers were parked at the IFF loading dock the afternoon I visited, and a thin cloud of steam floated from the chimney. Before entering the plant, I signed a nondisclosure form, promising not to reveal the brand names of products that contain IFF flavors. The place reminded me of Willy Wonka's chocolate factory. Wonderful smells drifted through the hallways, men and women in neat white lab coats cheerfully went about their work, and hundreds of little glass bottles sat on laboratory tables and shelves. The bottles contained powerful but fragile flavor chemicals, shielded from light by the brown glass and the round plastic caps shut tight. The long chemical names on the little white labels were as mystifying to me as medieval Latin. They were the odd-sounding names of things that would be mixed and poured and turned into new substances, like magic potions.

Don't forget to **Notice & Note** as you read the text.

7 I was not invited to see the manufacturing areas of the IFF plant, where it was thought I might discover trade secrets. Instead, I toured various laboratories and pilot kitchens, where the flavors of well-established brands are tested or adjusted, and where whole new flavors are created. IFF's snack and savory lab is responsible for the flavor of potato chips, corn chips, breads, crackers, breakfast cereals, and pet food. The confectionery lab devises the flavor for ice cream, cookies, candies, toothpastes, mouthwashes, and antacids. Everywhere I looked, I saw famous, widely advertised products sitting on laboratory desks and tables. The beverage lab is full of brightly colored liquids in clear bottles. It comes up with the flavor for popular soft drinks, sport drinks, bottled teas, and wine coolers, for all-natural juice drinks, organic soy drinks, beers, and malt liquors. In one pilot kitchen I saw a dapper chemist, a middle-aged man with an elegant tie beneath his lab coat, carefully preparing a batch of cookies with white frosting and pink-and-white sprinkles. In another pilot kitchen I saw a pizza oven, a grill, a milk-shake machine, and a french fryer identical to those I'd seen behind the counter at countless fast food restaurants.

DETERMINE CENTRAL IDEA

Annotate: Mark the lists Schlosser makes in paragraph 7.

Synthesize: How can the lists be categorized so that the text of the paragraph can be easily summed up or paraphrased in one sentence?

8 In addition to being the world's largest flavor company, IFF manufactures the smell of six of the ten best-selling fine perfumes in the United States. It makes the smell of Estée Lauder's Beautiful, Clinique's Happy, Ralph Lauren's Polo, and Calvin Klein's Eternity. It also makes the smell of household products such as deodorant, dishwashing detergent, bath soap, shampoo, furniture polish, and floor wax. All of these aromas are made through the same basic process: the manipulation of **volatile** chemicals to create a particular smell. The basic science behind the scent of your shaving cream is the same as that governing the flavor of your TV dinner.

volatile
(vŏl´ə-tl) *adj.* evaporating readily at normal temperatures and pressures.

9 The aroma of a food can be responsible for as much as 90 percent of its flavor. Scientists now believe that human beings acquired the sense of taste as a way to avoid being poisoned. Edible plants generally taste sweet; deadly ones, bitter. Taste is supposed to help

us differentiate food that's good for us from food that's not. The taste buds on our tongues can detect the presence of half a dozen or so basic tastes, including: sweet, sour, bitter, salty, astringent,[2] and umami (a taste discovered by Japanese researchers, a rich and full sense of deliciousness triggered by amino acids in foods such as shellfish, mushrooms, potatoes, and seaweed). Taste buds offer a relatively limited means of detection, however, compared to the human olfactory system, which can perceive thousands of different chemical aromas. Indeed "flavor" is primarily the smell of gases being released by the chemicals you've just put in your mouth.

DETERMINE CENTRAL IDEA

Annotate: Mark an example of technical language in paragraph 10.

Infer: Does Schlosser assume the reader will grasp the meaning of this technical language? Explain. How would you define that same word?

10 The act of drinking, sucking, or chewing a substance releases its volatile gases. They flow out of the mouth and up the nostrils, or up the passageway in the back of the mouth, to a thin layer of nerve cells called the olfactory epithelium, located at the base of the nose, right between the eyes. The brain combines the complex smell signals from the epithelium with the simple taste signals from the tongue, assigns a flavor to what's in your mouth, and decides if it's something you want to eat.

11 Babies like sweet tastes and reject bitter ones; we know this because scientists have rubbed various flavors inside the mouths

[2] **astringent:** sharp and penetrating; pungent or severe.

of infants and then recorded their facial reactions. A person's food preferences, like his or her personality, are formed during the first few years of life, through a process of socialization. Toddlers can learn to enjoy hot and spicy food, bland health food, or fast food, depending upon what the people around them eat. The human sense of smell is still not fully understood and can be greatly affected by psychological factors and expectations. The color of a food can determine the perception of its taste. The mind filters out the overwhelming majority of chemical aromas that surround us, focusing intently on some, ignoring others. People can grow accustomed to bad smells or good smells; they stop noticing what once seemed overpowering. Aroma and memory are somehow inextricably linked. A smell can suddenly evoke a long-forgotten moment. The flavors of childhood foods seem to leave an indelible mark, and adults often return to them, without always knowing why. These "comfort foods" become a source of pleasure and reassurance, a fact that fast food chains work hard to promote. Childhood memories of Happy Meals can translate into frequent adult visits to McDonald's, like those of the chain's "heavy users," the customers who eat there four or five times a week.

12 The human craving for flavor has been a largely unacknowledged and unexamined force in history. Royal empires have been built, unexplored lands have been traversed, great religions and

Don't forget to **Notice & Note** as you read the text.

VOCABULARY

Patterns of Word Change: *Socialization* (paragraph 11) is a noun formed by adding the suffix *-ation* to *socialize,* to indicate the process of getting together with others.

Analyze: The definition Schlosser is using for *socialization* comes from *sociology,* the study of human behavior. How does this help you better understand the meaning of the word?

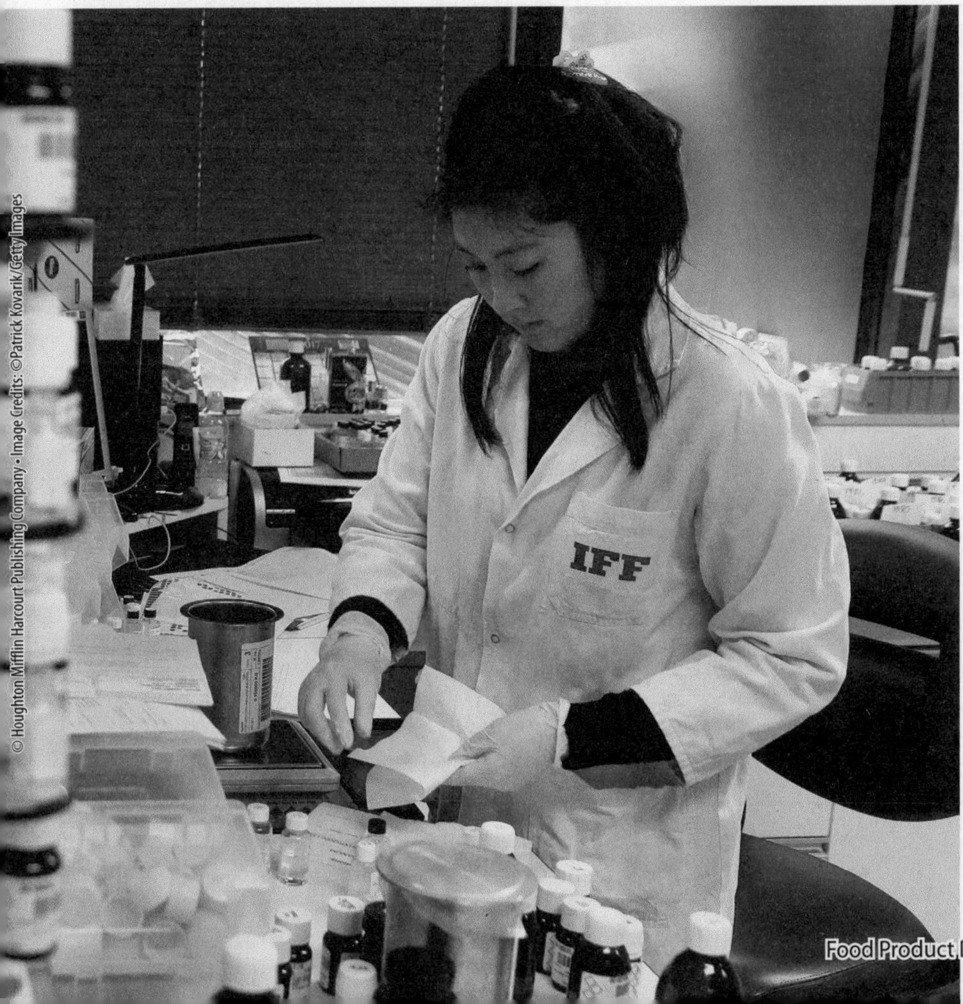

philosophies have been forever changed by the spice trade. In 1492 Christopher Columbus set sail to find seasoning. Today the influence of flavor in the world marketplace is no less decisive. The rise and fall of corporate empires—of soft drink companies, snack food companies, and fast food chains—is frequently determined by how their products taste.

NOTICE & NOTE
WORD GAPS

When you notice vocabulary that is unfamiliar—for example, a rare or technical word, or a discipline-specific word—you've found a **Word Gaps** signpost.

Notice & Note: Mark the science-related words in paragraph 13.

Infer: You can probably guess the meaning of *chromatographs* and *spectrometers* from the context Schlosser provides. Using all of paragraph 13 as context, can you guess the meaning of *synthesized*?

13 The flavor industry emerged in the mid-nineteenth century, as processed foods began to be manufactured on a large scale. Recognizing the need for flavor additives, the early food processors turned to perfume companies that had years of experience working with essential oils and volatile aromas. The great perfume houses of England, France, and the Netherlands produced many of the first flavor compounds. In the early part of the twentieth century, Germany's powerful chemical industry assumed the technological lead in flavor production. Legend has it that a German scientist discovered methyl anthranilate, one of the first artificial flavors, by accident while mixing chemicals in his laboratory. Suddenly the lab was filled with the sweet smell of grapes. Methyl anthranilate later became the chief flavoring compound of grape Kool-Aid. After World War II, much of the perfume industry shifted from Europe to the United States, settling in New York City near the garment district and the fashion houses. The flavor industry came with it, subsequently moving to New Jersey to gain more plant capacity. Man-made flavor additives were used mainly in baked goods, candies, and sodas until the 1950s, when sales of processed food began to soar. The invention of gas chromatographs and mass spectrometers—machines capable of detecting volatile gases at low levels—vastly increased the number of flavors that could be synthesized. By the mid-1960s the American flavor industry was churning out compounds to supply the taste of Pop Tarts, Bac-Os, Tab, Tang, Filet-O-Fish sandwiches, and literally thousands of other new foods.

14 The American flavor industry now has annual revenues of about $1.4 billion. Approximately ten thousand new processed food products are introduced every year in the United States. Almost all of them require flavor additives. And about nine out of every ten of these new food products fail. The latest flavor innovations and corporate realignments are heralded in publications such as *Food Chemical News, Food Engineering, Chemical Market Reporter,* and *Food Product Design*. The growth of IFF has mirrored that of the flavor industry as a whole. IFF was formed in 1958, through the merger of two small companies. Its annual revenues have grown almost fifteenfold since the early 1970s, and it now has manufacturing facilities in twenty countries.

15 The quality that people seek most of all in a food, its flavor, is usually present in a quantity too **infinitesimal** to be measured by any traditional culinary terms such as ounces or teaspoons. Today's sophisticated spectrometers, gas chromatographs, and headspace vapor analyzers provide a detailed map of a food's flavor components, detecting chemical aromas in amounts as low as one part per billion.

infinitesimal
(ĭn-fĭn-ĭ-tĕs´ə-məl) *adj.* immeasurably or incalculably minute.

The human nose, however, is still more sensitive than any machine yet invented. A nose can detect aromas present in quantities of a few parts per trillion—an amount equivalent to 0.000000000003 percent. Complex aromas, like those of coffee or roasted meat, may be composed of volatile gases from nearly a thousand different chemicals. The smell of a strawberry arises from the interaction of at least 350 different chemicals that are present in minute amounts. The chemical that provides the dominant flavor of bell pepper can be tasted in amounts as low as .02 parts per billion; one drop is sufficient to add flavor to five average size swimming pools. The flavor additive usually comes last, or second to last, in a processed food's list of ingredients (chemicals that add color are frequently used in even smaller amounts). As a result, the flavor of a processed food often costs less than its packaging. Soft drinks contain a larger proportion of flavor additives than most products. The flavor in a twelve-ounce can of Coke costs about half a cent.

Don't forget to **Notice & Note** as you read the text.

NOTICE & NOTE
NUMBERS AND STATS

When you notice the use of specific quantities or comparisons to show amounts, size, or scale, you've found a **Numbers and Stats** signpost.

Notice & Note: Mark the numbers the author includes in paragraph 15.

Summarize: What point does Schlosser support by including these statistics?

16 The Food and Drug Administration does not require flavor companies to disclose the ingredients of their additives, so long as all the chemicals are considered by the agency to be GRAS (Generally Regarded As Safe). This lack of public disclosure enables the companies to maintain the secrecy of their formulas. It also hides the fact that flavor compounds sometimes contain more ingredients than the foods being given their taste. The ubiquitous phrase "artificial strawberry flavor" gives little hint of the chemical wizardry and manufacturing skill that can make a highly processed food taste like a strawberry.

17 A typical artificial strawberry flavor, like the kind found in a Burger King strawberry milk shake, contains the following ingredients: amyl acetate, amyl butyrate, amyl valerate, anethol, anisyl formate, benzyl acetate, benzyl isobutyrate, butyric acid, cinnamyl isobutyrate, cinnamyl valerate, cognac essential oil, diacetyl, dipropyl ketone, ethyl acetate, ethyl amylketone, ethyl butyrate, ethyl cinnamate, ethyl heptanoate, ethyl heptylate, ethyl lactate, ethyl methylphenylglycidate, ethyl nitrate, ethyl propionate, ethyl valerate, heliotropin, hydroxyphrenyl-2-butanone (10 percent solution in alcohol), α-ionone, isobutyl anthranilate, isobutyl butyrate, lemon essential oil, maltol, 4-methylacetophenone, methyl anthranilate, methyl benzoate, methyl cinnamate, methyl heptine carbonate, methyl naphthyl ketone, methyl salicylate, mint essential oil, neroli essential oil, nerolin, neryl isobutyrate, orris butter, phenethyl alcohol, rose, rum ether, γ-undecalactone, vanillin, and solvent.

18 Although flavors usually arise from a mixture of many different volatile chemicals, a single compound often supplies the dominant aroma. Smelled alone, that chemical provides an unmistakable sense of the food. Ethyl-2-methyl butyrate, for example, smells just like an apple. Today's highly processed foods offer a blank palette: whatever chemicals you add to them will give them specific tastes. Adding methyl-2-peridylketone makes something taste like popcorn. Adding ethyl-3-hydroxybutanoate makes it taste like marshmallow. The

DETERMINE CENTRAL IDEA

Annotate: Mark the details in paragraph 18 about the chemicals and what they do.

Infer: What idea is the author supporting by including the names of the chemicals?

possibilities are now almost limitless. Without affecting the appearance or nutritional value, processed foods could even be made with aroma chemicals such as hexanal (the smell of freshly cut grass) or 3-methyl butanoic acid (the smell of body odor).

ANALYZE AUTHOR'S PURPOSE

Annotate: Mark the sentence in paragraph 19 about consumer preferences.

Analyze: What is the author's purpose for including this information?

19 The 1960s were the heyday of artificial flavors. The synthetic versions of flavor compounds were not subtle, but they did not need to be, given the nature of most processed food. For the past twenty years food processors have tried hard to use only "natural flavors" in their products. According to the FDA, these must be derived entirely from natural sources—from herbs, spices, fruits, vegetables, beef, chicken, yeast, bark, roots, etc. Consumers prefer to see natural flavors on a label, out of a belief that they are healthier. The distinction between artificial and natural flavors can be somewhat arbitrary and absurd, based more on how the flavor has been made than on what it actually contains. "A natural flavor," says Terry Acree, a professor of food science technology at Cornell University, "is a flavor that's been derived with an out-of-date technology." Natural flavors and artificial flavors sometimes contain exactly the same chemicals, produced through different methods. Amyl acetate, for example, provides the dominant note of banana flavor. When you distill it from bananas with a solvent, amyl acetate is a natural flavor. When you produce it by mixing vinegar with amyl alcohol, adding sulfuric acid as a **catalyst**, amyl acetate is an artificial flavor. Either way it smells and tastes the same. The phrase "natural flavor" is now listed among the ingredients of everything from Stonyfield Farm Organic Strawberry Yogurt to Taco Bell Hot Taco Sauce.

catalyst
(kăt′l-ĭst) *n.* a substance, usually used in small amounts relative to the reactants, that modifies and increases the rate of a reaction without being consumed in the process.

20 A natural flavor is not necessarily healthier or purer than an artificial one. When almond flavor (benzaldehyde) is derived from natural sources, such as peach and apricot pits, it contains traces of hydrogen cyanide, a deadly poison. Benzaldehyde derived through a different process—by mixing oil of clove and the banana flavor, amyl acetate—does not contain any cyanide. Nevertheless, it is legally considered an artificial flavor and sells at a much lower price. Natural and artificial flavors are now manufactured at the same chemical plants, places that few people would associate with Mother Nature. Calling any of these flavors "natural" requires a flexible attitude toward the English language and a fair amount of irony.

Don't forget to **Notice & Note** as you read the text.

21 The small and elite group of scientists who create most of the flavor in most of the food now consumed in the United States are called "flavorists." They draw upon a number of disciplines in their work: biology, psychology, physiology, and organic chemistry. A flavorist is a chemist with a trained nose and a poetic sensibility. Flavors are created by blending scores of different chemicals in tiny amounts, a process governed by scientific principles but demanding a fair amount of art. In an age when delicate aromas, subtle flavors, and microwave ovens do not easily coexist, the job of the flavorist is to **conjure** illusions about processed food and, in the words of one flavor company's literature, to ensure "consumer likeability." The flavorists with whom I spoke were charming, cosmopolitan, and ironic. They were also discreet, in keeping with the dictates of their trade. They were the sort of scientist who not only enjoyed fine wine, but could also tell you the chemicals that gave each vintage its unique aroma. One flavorist compared his work to composing music. A well-made flavor compound will have a "top note," followed by a "dry-down," and a "leveling-off," with different chemicals responsible for each stage. The taste of a food can be radically altered by minute changes in the flavoring mix. "A little odor goes a long way," one flavorist said.

conjure
(kŏn´jər) *v.* to influence or effect by or as if by magic.

22 In order to give a processed food the proper taste, a flavorist must always consider the food's "mouthfeel"— the unique combination of textures and chemical interactions that affects how the flavor is perceived. The mouthfeel can be adjusted through the use of various fats, gums, starches, emulsifiers, and stabilizers. The aroma chemicals of a food can be precisely analyzed, but mouthfeel is much harder to measure. How does one quantify a french fry's crispness? Food technologists are now conducting basic research in rheology, a branch of physics that examines the flow and deformation of materials. A number of companies sell sophisticated devices that attempt to measure mouthfeel. The Universal TA-XT2 Texture Analyzer, produced by the Texture Technologies Corporation, performs calculations based on data derived from twenty-five separate probes. It is essentially a mechanical mouth. It gauges the most important rheological properties of a food—the bounce, creep, breaking point, density, crunchiness, chewiness, gumminess, lumpiness, rubberiness, springiness, slipperiness, smoothness, softness, wetness, juiciness, spreadability, spring-back, and tackiness.

DETERMINE CENTRAL IDEA

Annotate: Mark details that help you understand what *rheology* means in paragraph 22.

Analyze: Why do companies employ specialists from scientific branches such as rheology?

23 Some of the most important advances in flavor manufacturing are now occurring in the field of biotechnology. Complex flavors are being made through fermentation, enzyme reactions, fungal cultures, and tissue cultures. All of the flavors being created through these methods—including the ones being synthesized by funguses—are considered natural flavors by the FDA. The new enzyme-based processes are responsible for extremely lifelike dairy flavors. One company now offers not just butter flavor, but also fresh creamy butter, cheesy butter, milky butter, savory melted butter, and super-concentrated butter flavor, in liquid or powder form. The development of new fermentation techniques, as well as new techniques for heating mixtures of sugar and amino acids, have led to the creation of much more realistic meat flavors. The McDonald's Corporation will not reveal the exact origin of the natural flavor added to its french fries. In response to inquiries from *Vegetarian Journal*, however, McDonald's did acknowledge that its fries derive some of their characteristic flavor from "animal products."

24 Other popular fast foods derive their flavor from unexpected sources. Wendy's Grilled Chicken Sandwich, for example, contains beef extracts. Burger King's BK Broiler Chicken Breast Patty contains "natural smoke flavor." A firm called Red Arrow Products Company specializes in smoke flavor, which is added to barbecue sauces and processed meats. Red Arrow manufactures natural smoke flavor by charring sawdust and capturing the aroma chemicals released into the air. The smoke is captured in water and then bottled, so that other companies can sell food which seems to have been cooked over a fire.

25 In a meeting room at IFF, Brian Grainger let me sample some of the company's flavors. It was an unusual taste test; there wasn't any food to taste. Grainger is a senior flavorist at IFF, a soft-spoken chemist with graying hair, an English accent, and a fondness for understatement. He could easily be mistaken for a British diplomat or the owner of a West End brasserie with two Michelin stars. Like many in the flavor industry, he has an Old World, old-fashioned sensibility which seems out of step with our brand-conscious, egocentric age. When I suggested that IFF should put its own logo on the products that contain its flavors—instead of allowing other brands to enjoy the consumer loyalty and affection inspired by those flavors—Grainger politely disagreed, assuring me such a thing would never be done. In the absence of public credit or acclaim, the small and secretive fraternity of flavor chemists praises one another's work. Grainger can often tell, by analyzing the flavor formula of a product, which of his counterparts at a rival firm devised it. And he enjoys walking down supermarket aisles, looking at the many products that contain his flavors, even if no one else knows it.

ANALYZE AUTHOR'S PURPOSE

Annotate: Mark the source of the smells the author experiences in paragraph 26.

Analyze: Why does the author present the information this way?

26 Grainger had brought a dozen small glass bottles from the lab. After he opened each bottle, I dipped a fragrance testing filter into it. The filters were long white strips of paper designed to absorb aroma chemicals without producing off-notes. Before placing the strips of paper before my nose, I closed my eyes. Then I inhaled deeply, and

one food after another was conjured from the glass bottles. I smelled fresh cherries, black olives, sautéed onions, and shrimp. Grainger's most remarkable creation took me by surprise. After closing my eyes, I suddenly smelled a grilled hamburger. The aroma was uncanny, almost miraculous. It smelled like someone in the room was flipping burgers on a hot grill. But when I opened my eyes, there was just a narrow strip of white paper and a smiling flavorist.

COLLABORATIVE DISCUSSION

With a partner, discuss how this report made you feel about natural and artificial flavors. Are you likely to read food labels to see if what you're eating has them?

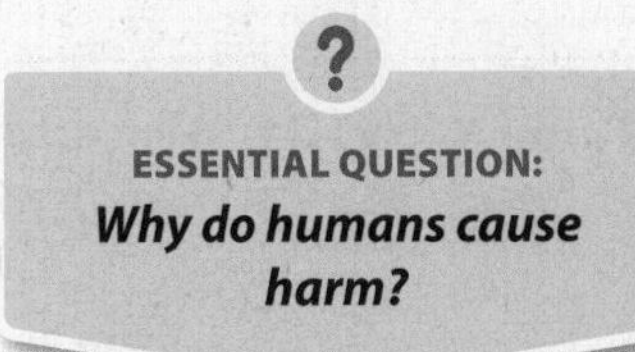
?
ESSENTIAL QUESTION:
Why do humans cause harm?

Review your notes and add your thoughts to your **Response Log.**

Assessment Practice

Answer these questions before moving on to the **Analyze the Text** section on the following page.

1. What caused the growth of the flavor industry after World War II?

- (A) The rise of fast-food chains
- (B) The shift toward healthier eating
- (C) The spread of processed foods
- (D) The arrival of German chemists in the United States

2. How much of food's flavor is probably a function of smell?

- (A) 30 percent
- (B) 50 percent
- (C) 75 percent
- (D) 90 percent

3. Which industry spearheaded the development of food flavors?

- (A) Chemical
- (B) Agriculture
- (C) Medical
- (D) Dairy

Ed

Test-Taking Strategies

Analyze the Text

Support your responses with evidence from the text.

NOTICE & NOTE

Review what you **noticed and noted** as you read the text. Your annotations can help you answer these questions.

1. **INFER** What is the central idea of this text? Use your margin notes and cite text evidence to support your answer.

2. **SYNTHESIZE** What do the first two paragraphs suggest about the author's purpose? Cite text evidence in your response.

3. **DRAW CONCLUSIONS** Why does Schlosser include so much detail, including **Numbers and Stats**, about his visit to the IFF plant in New Jersey?

4. **COMPARE** What are the similarities and differences between "artificial flavors" and "natural flavors"? Why does Schlosser explain the terms in such detail? Fill in the chart to organize your answer.

Natural *v.* Artificial Flavors
Similarities
Differences

5. **DRAW CONCLUSIONS** What might Schlosser want his audience to do after reading this selection?

6. **ANALYZE** Many readers are likely to notice **Word Gaps** in paragraph 17, where Schlosser lists all the chemical ingredients in "a typical artificial strawberry flavor, like the kind found in a Burger King strawberry milk shake." Why might Schlosser include so many unfamiliar words?

7. **EVALUATE** What is Schlosser's overall purpose in writing this text? How effective is his style for achieving that purpose?

Choices

Here are some other ways to demonstrate your understanding of the ideas in this lesson.

Writing

↳ Evaluate the Text

In 2009, Eric Schlosser described struggling with how to write about fast food: "I didn't want to write something that was snobby and elitist, you know, a put-down of Americans and of their plastic fast-food culture. . . . I really like hamburgers and French fries. . . . So I knew what I didn't want the article to be, but I wasn't really sure what it should or could be." Do you think Schlosser succeeded in not writing a "snobby and elitist" piece? Consider in your response

- why Schlosser chose this aspect of the food industry to research
- what larger problem or issue he is tackling
- how well his writing makes or breaks the case for eating fast food
- what call to action, if any, he proposes
- his language and tone

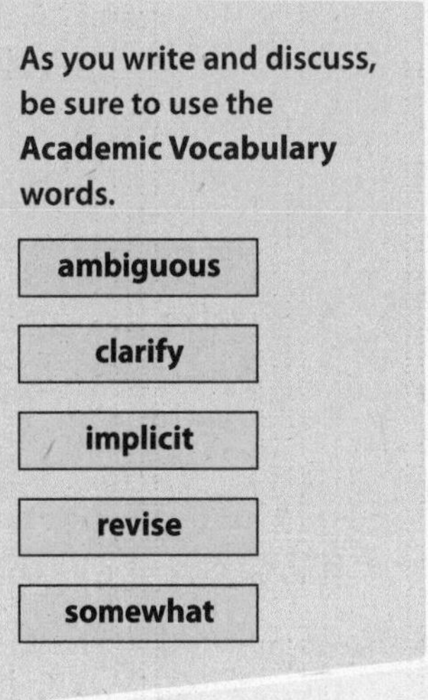

As you write and discuss, be sure to use the **Academic Vocabulary** words.

ambiguous

clarify

implicit

revise

somewhat

Media

↳ Create an Infographic

In a small group, create an infographic that combines data and graphics on fast food consumption in the United States. Divide the research between group members and explore two or three of the following data points:

- who eats fast food and why
- how much money is spent on fast food, by both consumers and producers
- the "hidden" costs of fast food, such as damage to the environment
- the effects of fast food on health and well-being (both consumers and workers)
- food deserts and the fast food divide

Work together to create the final graphic. Decide which information is best conveyed by text and which by graphics.

Speaking & Listening

↳ Debate

Fast food outlets can be found around the globe, but not everyone loves the way of life they represent. As a class, research the Slow Food movement to get an idea of what it stands for and how it fights fast food practices. Then, divide into two groups, one arguing that fast food has its place, and the other that slow food is the better alternative. As you debate:

- pay attention to the other side's arguments, especially the reasoning behind them
- challenge claims you believe are weak or not supported
- follow the rules of debate and remain civil
- in the end, summarize each argument and resolve differences of opinion

Expand Your Vocabulary

PRACTICE AND APPLY

Complete each sentence to show your knowledge of the meaning of each vocabulary word.

1. Producing artificial flavors requires a **catalyst** like sulfuric acid because —
2. The taste of fast food french fries **stems** now from —
3. Everyday measuring spoons cannot be used to measure the **infinitesimal** amounts of chemicals in a particular flavor because —
4. Some chemists seem to **conjure** foods because —
5. **Volatile** chemicals have to be kept in closed containers because —

Vocabulary Strategy

↳ Patterns of Word Change

Suffixes are word parts added to the end of a word that can change the word's form or meaning. Adding a suffix to the vocabulary word *volatility* can change its form:

Ed
Interactive Vocabulary Lesson: Prefixes and Suffixes

volatile + ity = volatility

Volatility is a noun meaning "the state of rapidly changing." Although the form of the word has changed, the meaning is still similar. This is not always true. The vocabulary word *infinitesimal* means "very, very small," but the base word, *infinite,* means the opposite—"endless or boundless."

This chart shows some common suffixes and their meanings.

Suffix:	-ity	-ful	-tion, -ation	-less	-able, -ible	-ly	-ment
Meaning:	state or quality of	full of	process or action	without	possible	similar to	action or result

PRACTICE AND APPLY

Work with a partner to brainstorm a list of potential new words based on the base words below. Add suffixes to each base to change its meaning or part of speech. Use the chart to find possible suffixes, or think of your own. Consult a dictionary to confirm correct spellings and meanings.

1. color **2.** act **3.** public **4.** flavor **5.** enjoy

Watch Your Language!

Dashes

Sometimes a writer wants to interrupt the main thought of a sentence with a word, expression, phrase, or sentence called a **parenthetical element.** Usually such parenthetical elements are set off with parentheses or with commas. However, writers sometimes use dashes to set off elements in a sentence. If the break in thought is abrupt, the parenthetical element is set off with dashes.

> **That ingredient helps to explain not only why the fries taste so good, but also why most fast food—indeed, most of the food Americans eat today—tastes the way it does.**

Interactive Grammar Lesson: Dashes, Parentheses, and Brackets

Sometimes dashes are used to create pauses, often for ironic, satirical, or dramatic effect.

> **The mix gave the fries their unique flavor—and more saturated beef fat per ounce than a McDonald's hamburger.**

PRACTICE AND APPLY

Add the italicized parenthetical elements to the following sentences, setting them off with dashes.

1. Flavors made from natural ingredients are sometimes considered healthier. *herbs, fruits, vegetables, chicken, yeast, and bark*
2. The french fries are delicious. *and very fattening*
3. Flavorists create the flavor in most of the food we eat. *scientists with trained noses and poetic sensibilities*
4. One remarkable creation took Schlosser by surprise. *a strip of paper that smelled just like a grilled hamburger*

Compare Genres

As you've read the excerpts from *The Jungle* and *Fast Food Nation,* you've thought about their ideas and purpose. Despite the fact that Sinclair and Schlosser used different genres and wrote in distinct eras, they convey similar ideas about food processing. Is one message clearer, more memorable, or more effective because of the genre the writer chose? Use the graphic below to evaluate the effectiveness of each genre to deliver an author's message.

Novel • Imagined account that may be based on real people or events • Detailed descriptions help convey a strong message or theme • Characters are well developed and plot is complex • Longest form of fiction writing	Allows author to . . .	Keeps author from . . .
Investigative Journalism • Reveals actions or events hidden from the public • Combines information and analysis • Uses facts and quotes to support claims • May include a call to action for the reader • Length of text varies, based on the published format	Allows author to . . .	Keeps author from . . .

Analyze the Texts

Discuss these questions in your group.

1. **ANALYZE** What are the settings described in each selection? What is your sense of the general working conditions in the food industry?

2. **COMPARE** How does the tone of each selection reflect the different genres and the different authors' purposes?

3. **EVALUATE** Assuming you are a contemporary reader for each excerpt, which text most makes you want to take action? Why? Cite details from the text in your answer.

4. **SYNTHESIZE** What similar topics do these selections address? What are similarities and differences in the approaches that the writers use to present these topics?

Collaborate and Present

Now your group can continue exploring how an author's choice of genre affects how readers perceive the message. Follow these steps:

1. **ANALYZE GENRE CHARACTERISTICS** Work with each other to answer the following questions. Record each person's answers and don't worry about reaching a consensus.

	A *from* The Jungle	B "Food Product Design"
What genre characteristics helped you determine the theme or central idea? Was the main message of each text easy to find?		
How did you determine the author's purpose? What genre characteristics helped you figure it out?		
How effective is the message of each text? What about the genre makes it compelling or convincing? Were any details or features ineffective?		

2. **SYNTHESIZE INFORMATION** Review your responses and draw conclusions about each text's effectiveness. Give examples of details that contribute to each text's effectiveness. Would a text be more or less effective if the genre were different? Summarize your conclusions and note whether your group reaches a consensus or not.

3. **PRESENT TO THE CLASS** Work together to present your ideas about the two types of texts. Your presentation should include

- definitions and characteristics of novels and investigative journalism
- a comparison of the authors' purposes and a claim about how effectively each text met its author's purpose
- a statement about the benefits and drawbacks of each type of text
- evidence from the texts to support your ideas
- relevant images and text to clarify your points and add interest

Reader's Choice

Continue your exploration of the Essential Questions for this unit by doing some independent reading. Read the titles and descriptions shown. Then mark the texts that interest you.

?
ESSENTIAL QUESTIONS:
Review the four Essential Questions for this unit on page 517.

Short Reads

Available on 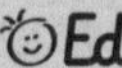

These texts are available in your ebook. Choose one to read and rate. Then defend your rating to the class.

Ode to Cheese Fries

Poem by **José Olivarez**

Sometimes food is so much more than a means to stave off hunger.

Rate It ☆☆☆☆☆

The Men in the Storm

Short Story by **Stephen Crane**

Wait outside in a blizzard with a group of homeless men as they anxiously line up to be let into a charity house.

Rate It ☆☆☆☆☆

A Journey

Short Story by **Edith Wharton**

Find out how a woman, accompanied by her gravely ill husband, copes with a cross-country train journey.

Rate It ☆☆☆☆☆

Glass-Lung

Short Story by **Anjali Sachdeva**

A young woman's life is forever changed when her father suffers an accident in a factory.

Rate It ☆☆☆☆☆

Healthy Eaters, Strong Minds: What School Gardens Teach Kids

Article by **Paige Pfleger**

Why are teenagers across the country digging in dirt, and what do they get from it?

Rate It ☆☆☆☆☆

Long Reads

Here are three recommended books that connect to this unit. For additional options, ask your teacher, school librarian, or peers. Which titles spark your interest?

The Great Gatsby

Novel by **F. Scott Fitzgerald**

A 1920s tale of fortune, fame, and recklessness. What drives Nick, Gatsby, and Daisy as they each pursue their own dreams?

Escape to Gold Mountain: A Graphic History of the Chinese in North America

Graphic Novel by **David H. T. Wong**

The Chinese immigrant experience is often overlooked or misunderstood. See the challenges and triumphs the Wong family has faced over the past 150 years.

How the García Girls Lost Their Accents

Novel by **Julia Álvarez**

In New York, the García sisters begin to abandon their Dominican roots to become more American. Caught between two worlds, they feel both free and lost.

Extension

↳ Connect & Create

CHANGE, CHANGE, CHANGE A major theme running through this unit is how people react to unexpected change. How does this theme apply to the text you chose? Discuss your ideas with others who read the same text you did, or create a social media post that outlines your observations.

SUCH A PHILOSOPHER If you chose a text with a strong central character, how would he or she respond to one of the four Essential Questions? Write an interview in which you ask the character which question is most relevant to the text and how he or she would answer it.

NOTICE & NOTE

- Pick one of the texts and annotate the Notice & Note signposts you find.
- Then use the **Notice & Note Writing Frames** to help you write about the significance of the signposts.
- Compare your findings with those of other students who read the same text.

Notice & Note Writing Frames

Write a Short Story

Writing Prompt

Using ideas, information, and examples from multiple texts in this unit, write a short story for a website of teen fiction. Explore how much individuals have control over their lives.

Manage your time carefully so that you can

- review the short stories in the unit;
- plan your short story;
- write your short story; and
- revise and edit your short story.

Be sure to

- introduce complex characters;
- build an interesting conflict;
- establish a coherent sequence of events;
- use strong narrative techniques; and
- use figurative language and sensory details.

Review the Mentor Text

For an example of a well-written short story that you can use as a mentor text and source for your short story, review

- **"The Story of an Hour"** (pages 577–580)

Consult your notes and annotations about this text. Think about how the author makes her story engaging.

Consider Your Sources

Review the list of texts in the unit and choose at least three that you may want to use as inspiration for your short story.

As you review selections, consult the notes you made on your **Response Log** and make additional notes about ideas that might be useful as you write. Especially consider how the writer structured plot events, used figurative language, and employed other narrative techniques.

UNIT 5 SOURCES

- [ ] **To Build a Fire**
- [ ] **The Lowest Animal**
- [ ] **The Fourth Industrial Revolution Is Here. Are You Ready?**
- [ ] **The Story of an Hour**
- [ ] **Chicago**
- [ ] *from* **The Jungle**
- [ ] **Food Product Design** *from* **Fast Food Nation**

Analyze the Prompt

Review the prompt to make sure you understand the assignment.

Then, look for words that indicate the purpose and audience of your short story. Write a sentence describing each.

Find Your Purpose

Short stories generally have two purposes:

- to entertain readers
- to communicate a **theme,** or message

What is my writing task?

____

What is my purpose for writing this short story?

____

Who is my audience?

____

Review the Rubric

Your short story will be scored using a rubric. As you write, focus on the characteristics of a high-scoring essay as described in the chart. You will learn more about these characteristics as you work through the lesson.

Purpose, Focus, and Organization	Narrative Technique	Conventions of Standard English
The response includes • an engaging introduction • a well-developed plot structure • use of transitions to convey sequence and connect ideas • logical sequence of events • a conclusion that resolves the story's main conflict	The response includes • use of descriptive details and sensory language • effective use of narrative techniques • varied sentence structure	The response may include • some minor errors in usage but no pattern of errors • correct punctuation, capitalization, sentence formation, and spelling • command of basic conventions

1 PLAN YOUR SHORT STORY

Develop Your Ideas

A well-written short story contains complex characters, an interesting conflict, and a clearly described setting. In the chart, decide on a topic you want to write about. Then, brainstorm ideas for your short story.

Topic:		
Characters	**Conflict**	**Setting**
• how they look	• with other characters	• vivid details
• how they behave	• internal struggles	• details that set mood
• what they think and say	• struggles against society	• details that relate to conflict

What's Your Perspective?

The narration of your short story can take various forms. Consider telling the story from

- **a first-person point of view, using the pronouns *I, me,* and *my* to share just one person's thoughts and feelings**
- **a third-person point of view, as if you are watching the action and describing what your characters (*he* or *she*) are doing**
- **an omniscient point of view, so you can describe what all your characters are doing and thinking**

Develop a Sequence of Events

Once you have a good plan for your characters, conflict, and setting, consider how you will build your plot.

Use the chart to outline plot elements for your short story.

Elements of Plot	
Main conflict	
Rising action: 1st complication	
2nd complication	
Climax: Crisis of the conflict	
Falling action: Resolution of the conflict	

Use Narrative Techniques

Help with Planning

Consult **Interactive Writing Lesson: Writing Narratives.**

Authors use **narrative techniques** to make their writing come to life for their readers. Narrative techniques include

- natural **dialogue** that reveals characters' personalities
- **descriptive details** that help readers visualize the story's events
- **sensory details** that allow readers to experience the scenes through description of sights, sounds, smells, tastes, and textures
- **figurative language** that describes story elements in surprising ways

Use the chart to help you plan which narrative techniques you will use in your story.

Dialogue	
Descriptive details	
Sensory details	
Figurative language	

Organize Your Short Story

Organize your ideas in a way that will help you draft your short story. Make sure your ideas flow smoothly so that your readers can follow your sequence of events.

Use the table below to organize your ideas.

INTRODUCTION	• Introduce your characters. • Set up your conflict. • Establish your setting.
BODY PARAGRAPHS	• Describe events as they happen. • Include foreshadowing or flashbacks to add suspense. • Vary the pacing of your events to create tension and develop the mood or tone of your story. • Build to an exciting climax, or high point in your story. • Use transitional words and phrases to clarify the order of events.
CONCLUSION	• Resolve the conflict in an interesting or unexpected way.

Construct Your Narrative

The **narrative structure** of a short story is usually **chronological.** Events follow one another, building to a particular outcome or resolution. However, think about how you might experiment with these elements:

- Add **foreshadowing** to hint at future events in the story.
- Add **flashbacks** to reveal experiences from the characters' past.

2 DEVELOP A DRAFT

Now it is time to draft your story. Take time to notice how professional authors craft short stories. You can use similar techniques in your own writing.

Use Figurative Language

EXAMINE THE MENTOR TEXT

Figurative language helps readers visualize the characters, setting, or plot events. **Metaphors** and **similes** compare unlike things in surprising, nonliteral ways. Notice how the author of "The Story of an Hour" uses figurative language to draw her readers into her story.

The author uses a **metaphor** to describe the sudden onslaught of grief as if it were a storm.

When the storm of grief had spent itself she went away to her room alone. She would have no one follow her. . . .

She sat with her head thrown back upon the cushion of the chair, quite motionless, except when a sob came up into her throat and shook her, as a child who has cried itself to sleep continues to sob in its dreams.

Here she uses a **simile** to compare her character's emotions to those of a child.

APPLY TO YOUR DRAFT

Use this chart to practice using figurative language in your writing. Then, apply this narrative technique as you describe elements of your short story.

Try These Suggestions

- Use a **metaphor** to imply comparisons. For example, "The delicious breath of rain was in the air."
- Use a **simile** to state a comparison directly, using *like* or *as*. For example, "She carried herself unwittingly like a goddess of Victory."

Use a metaphor to describe . . .	Use a simile to describe . . .
an element of the setting:	an element of the setting:
a character's emotions or actions:	a character's emotions or actions:

Draft a Surprising Ending

Drafting Online

Check your assignment list for a writing task from your teacher.

EXAMINE THE MENTOR TEXT

Some writers lead readers to draw one conclusion about characters or events only to surprise them with a twist later in the story. Notice how Kate Chopin surprises her readers repeatedly in "The Story of an Hour."

The **author's first surprise** is the widow's happiness after her husband has died in a train accident.

She arose at length and opened the door to her sister's importunities. There was a feverish triumph in her eyes, and she carried herself unwittingly like a goddess of Victory. She clasped her sister's waist, and together they descended the stairs. . . .

Someone was opening the front door with a latchkey. It was Brently Mallard who entered. . . . He stood amazed at Josephine's piercing cry. . . .

When the doctors came they said she had died of heart disease—of joy that kills.

The **shocking second surprise** is that her husband is alive.

The **last surprise** is her death, ironically, not of joy at her husband's survival, but of sorrow for her lost freedom.

APPLY TO YOUR DRAFT

As you develop your plot, consider adding a surprise ending. For your ending to be plausible, be sure to include clues that foreshadow what happens. Some clues may be deliberately misleading, but all clues should inform the reader of the meaning of your ending. Record ideas in the chart.

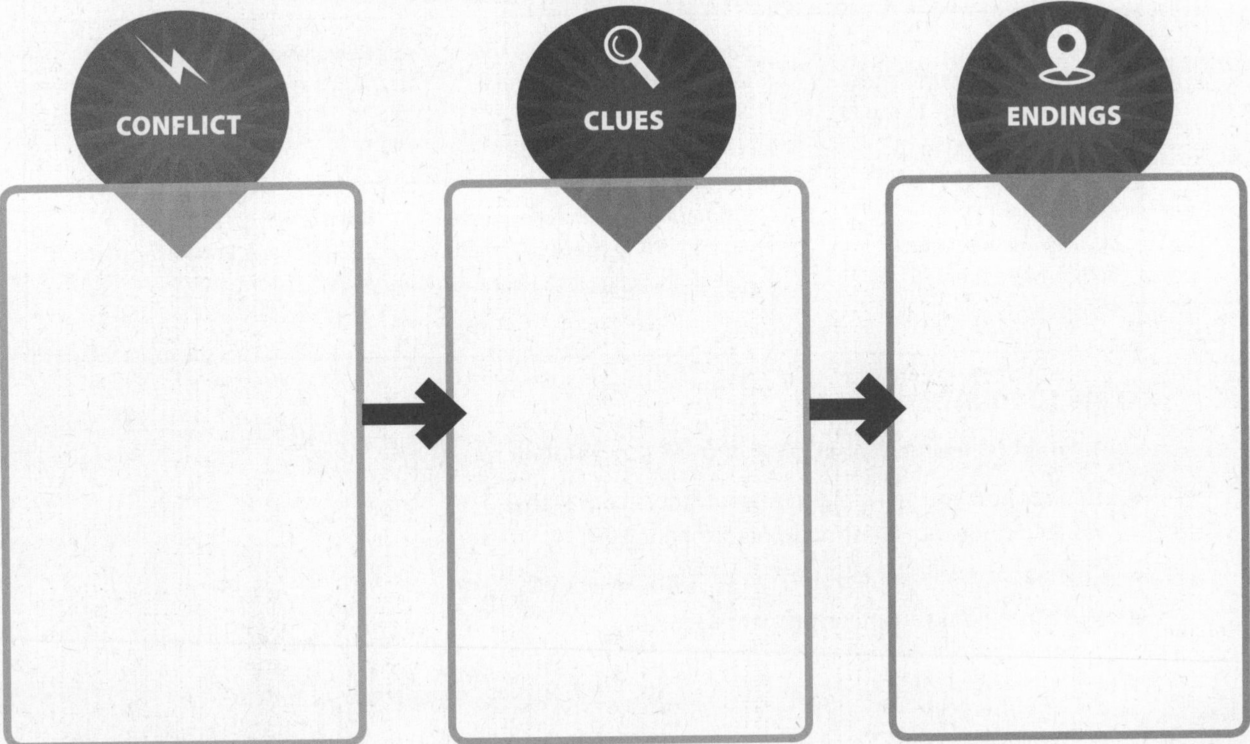

3 REVISE YOUR SHORT STORY

Professional writers rework their description and details to engage their readers and make their stories easy to follow. Use the guide to help you revise your short story.

Ed Help with Revision

Find a **Peer Review Guide** and **Student Models** online.

REVISION GUIDE		
Ask Yourself	**Prove It**	**Revise It**
Introduction Do I introduce my characters and conflict early on in the story?	**Set a star** (★) beside the introduction of each character. **Circle** your conflict.	**Reword** your introduction so that it introduces characters and hints at the conflict.
Organization Do I present an engaging narrative structure, using transitions to show the sequence of events?	**Highlight** transitions used to show sequence.	**Add** transitions where your sequence of events is unclear.
Narrative Techniques Do I use dialogue, descriptive details, and imagery to develop my plot and characters?	**Circle** dialogue. **Highlight** descriptive details and imagery.	**Revise** to add dialogue for character development. **Add** descriptive and sensory details.
Plot Elements Does my short story contain rising action and a climax?	**Bracket** [ ] paragraphs that show rising action. **Circle** the climax.	**Revise** to add suspense through rising action and a clear turning point in the story.
Style Do I use precise words and figurative language to engage my readers?	**Cross out** (X) flat words and ideas. **Circle** metaphors and similes.	**Reword** to use more concrete words and figurative details.
Conclusion Do I resolve the conflict and convey a theme in my conclusion?	**Underline** the resolution of the conflict. **Put a check** (✓) beside details that suggest a theme.	**Revise** your conclusion to strengthen its impact for your story.

APPLY TO YOUR DRAFT

Consider the following as you look to improve your writing:

- Think of how you can reorganize your story in a way that would include more flashbacks or foreshadowing.
- Change the pacing as the story progresses to build suspense.
- Make the ending an interesting surprise.

Peer Review in Action

ANALYZE A STUDENT MODEL

Once you finish revising your short story, exchange papers with a partner in a **peer review.** During your peer review, give suggestions for how to improve each other's draft.

Read the closing paragraph from a student's short story and examine his peer reviewer's comments.

First Draft

"Becoming K.D."

By JoJohn DuPuy, Okalunka High School

At last, Coach Blistic sent me in, and immediately I was fouled. Then I stepped up to the free throw line and missed my first shot. I tried again. This time I made it. The crowd went wild. Then I woke up. It had all been a dream.

Try adding a more dramatic ending, maybe with a message.

These short sentences add excitement.

Now read the revised conclusion below. Notice how the writer has improved his draft by making revisions based on his peer reviewer's comments.

Revision

"Becoming K.D."

By JoJohn DuPuy, Okalunka High School

Coach Blistic grimaced and signaled for me to go in as a decoy. Me, the five-foot-five-inch Hot Shot. Raymond tossed me the ball, and immediately I was fouled. Stepping up to the free throw line, I pushed too hard, and the ball rimmed the net and bounced off. The crowd moaned their disappointment. I sighed to myself, "What would K.D. do?" One more time I toed the free throw line. Bouncing the ball five times, shimmying my shoulders as I went into a crouch, I looked up, and in one fluid motion, I arced the basketball toward the net. Swish! We had won the game by ONE point! The crowd went wild. Someone in the cheer band was blaring his horn over and over and over again. "*Blah*! *Blah*! *Blah*!" That horn would not shut up. Then my eyes popped open, as I heard my alarm for school. No more the hero, I was still just a five-foot-five-inch Not-So-Hot-Shot, but a great dreamer.

Much better at explaining the importance of the moment for the character.

I love the vivid language. It makes this much more exciting.

Good job with this ending. It's fun and adds meaning.

Nice contrast between long and short sentences.

APPLY TO YOUR DRAFT

As you review your partner's work, give specific suggestions for how to make the short story more engaging. Use the revision guide to help you.

When listening to feedback from a partner, listen attentively and ask questions to make sure that you fully understand your reviewer's suggestions.

4 EDIT YOUR SHORT STORY

Apply the finishing touches to your draft. Edit your draft to check for proper use of standard English conventions and to correct any misspellings or grammatical errors.

Watch Your Language!

USE COORDINATING CONJUNCTIONS

Coordinating conjunctions—*and, but, or, nor, for,* and sometimes *so* and *yet*—link two independent clauses in a compound sentence. Sometimes authors begin sentences with a coordinating conjunction so that the idea of the preceding sentence carries over to the next sentence, giving each equal importance.

Read the following sentences from "The Story of an Hour."

> There was something coming to her **and** she was waiting for it, fearfully.

> **But** she saw beyond that bitter moment a long procession of years to come that would belong to her absolutely. **And** she opened and spread her arms out to them in welcome.

Using coordinating conjunctions and compound sentences adds variety to sentence patterns and slows down the rhythm of prose.

Use Semicolons

- A **semicolon** separates **two independent clauses.**
- A **semicolon** separates **two independent clauses linked by a conjunction** if the clauses already contain internal commas.

APPLY TO YOUR DRAFT

Now apply what you have learned to your own work.

1. **Read your story aloud.** Make sure your descriptions are clear.
2. **Check your sentence variety.** Consider combining two short sentences with a coordinating conjunction. Pay attention to how your sentence structure and variety affect the tone or mood of your story.
3. **Exchange drafts** with a peer, and check for grammatical errors.

5 PUBLISH YOUR SHORT STORY

Share It!

Finalize your short story for a website of teen fiction. You may also use your short story as inspiration for other projects.

Ways to Share

- **Create a dramatic presentation** of you reading your story. Have your peers read the dialogue of your different characters.
- **Record your story for a podcast** and invite your classmates to comment.
- **Make a video** of yourself reading your short story, and upload it to a video-sharing website for comments.

Reflect & Extend

Here are some other ways to show your understanding of the ideas in Unit 5.

Reflect on the Essential Questions

Think about the Essential Question you identified as most intriguing on page 518. Has your answer to the question changed after reading the texts in the unit? Discuss your ideas.

You can use these sentence starters to help you reflect on your learning:

- **This text affected my thinking because . . .**
- **I still don't understand . . .**
- **I want to learn more about . . .**

Project-Based Learning

↳ Create a Movie Trailer

This unit deals with hard realities and unsettling changes. Create a movie trailer that will inspire viewers' interest in one of the selections in this unit. For example, think about how the scene and sound effects could introduce the conflict in "To Build a Fire."

Develop your script to include clips from the story that will reveal the theme. Then, answer these questions:

- How much of the story can be conveyed through dialogue, and how much will need voice-over narration?
- How can music convey the story's mood?
- How can you close the movie trailer in a way that will create excitement and interest in the full story?

Ed

Media Project

To find more help with this task online, access **Create a Movie Trailer.**

Writing

↳ Write a Literary Analysis

Write a literary analysis in which you analyze the literary techniques and evaluate the meaning of one of the texts in this unit. To prepare to write, ask yourself these questions:

- What text will I write about?
- What claim will I make about the text?
- What literary elements will I focus on?
- What reasons and evidence will I include?

"Everything is connected in the end."
—Don DeLillo

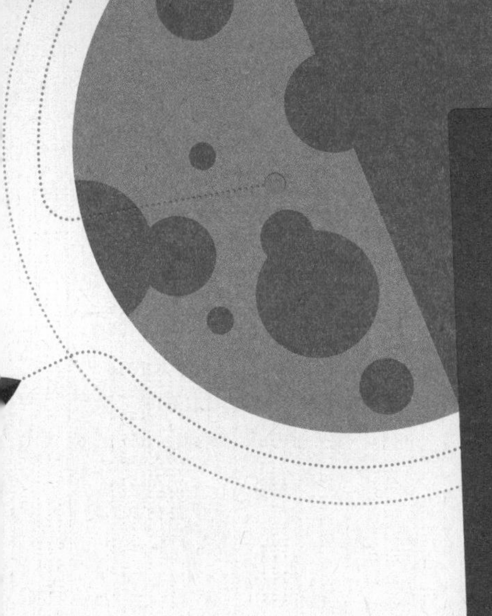

UNIT 6

The Modern Period to the Present Day

Modern and Contemporary Voices

As you read the texts in this unit, think about how they explore these **Essential Questions.**

How do we deal with rejection or isolation?

Exclusion based on characteristics such as race or ethnicity has been devastating to people as well as to society as a whole. However, people still strive to overcome it.

Can anyone achieve the American Dream?

For some, the American Dream has meant political and religious freedom, economic opportunity, and a chance for a better life. But history shows us that it has not been accessible to everyone.

When should personal integrity come before civic duty?

In the years after World War II, playwright Arthur Miller refused to reveal to the U.S. Congress the names of people with Communist leanings. Think about ideals that are worth standing up for today.

What would we do if there were no limits?

Some people tell themselves that there is no point in trying to do something difficult because they won't succeed. But others have accomplished the seemingly impossible.

ANALYZE THE IMAGE

Explain how the artist suggests that "everything is connected."

Explore unit themes and build background.

Stream to Start Video

Spark Your Learning

Here are some opportunities to think about issues related to **Unit 6: Modern and Contemporary Voices.**

As you read, you can use your **Response Log** (page R6) to track your thinking about the Essential Questions.

Make the Connection

Think about the quote by Don DeLillo on page 640. What are the ways in which "everything is connected"? What gets in the way of things being connected? Discuss your ideas with a partner.

Think About the Essential Questions

Review the Essential Questions on page 641. Which question is most intriguing to you? Perhaps it relates to something you have read or reminds you of a personal experience. Write down your thoughts.

Build Academic Vocabulary

You can use these Academic Vocabulary words to write and talk about the topics and themes in the unit. Which of these words do you already feel comfortable using when speaking or writing?

	I can use it!	I understand it.	I'll look it up.
contemporary	☐	☐	☐
global	☐	☐	☐
infinite	☐	☐	☐
simulated	☐	☐	☐
virtual	☐	☐	☐

Prove It!
Use one of the Academic Vocabulary words in a sentence in which you discuss what the American Dream means to you.

Preview the Texts

Review the images, titles, and descriptions of the texts in the unit. Mark the title of the text that interests you most.

A Rose for Emily

Short Story by **William Faulkner**

The people in town spread rumors about Emily; the truth is even more shocking.

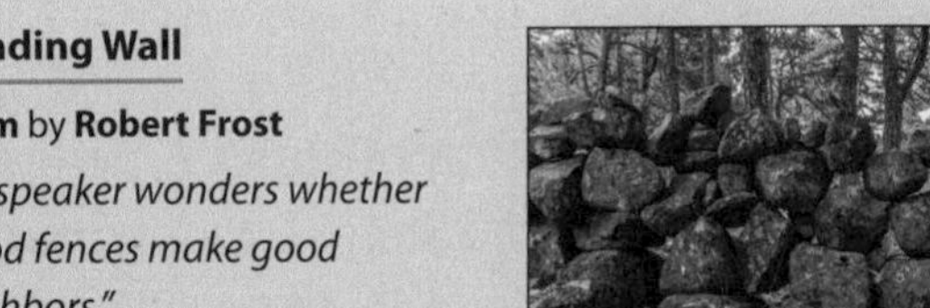

Mending Wall

Poem by **Robert Frost**

The speaker wonders whether "good fences make good neighbors."

from **They Called Us Enemy**

Graphic Memoir by **George Takei**

The Star Trek actor tells about his experience in an internment camp during World War II.

The Crucible

Drama by **Arthur Miller**

In 1692, a witch-hunt changes life in the small town of Salem, Massachusetts.

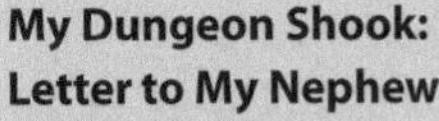

from **The Crucible**

Audio Excerpt and Production Images

See and hear performances of Arthur Miller's masterpiece.

My Dungeon Shook: Letter to My Nephew

Open Letter by **James Baldwin**

The writer offers advice to help his nephew navigate an often hostile world.

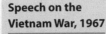

The Latin Deli: An Ars Poetica

Poem by **Judith Ortiz Cofer**

Customers come to the deli and find reminders of homes far away.

Speech on the Vietnam War, 1967

Speech by **Martin Luther King, Jr.**

The civil rights activist voices opposition to the war that was destroying the soul of our nation.

Ambush

Short Story by **Tim O'Brien**

A soldier's actions continue to haunt him long after the war's end.

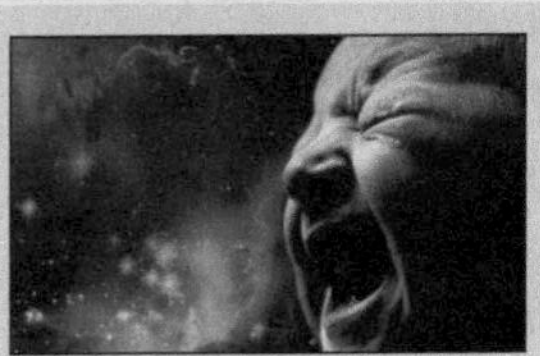

The Universe as Primal Scream

Poem by **Tracy K. Smith**

This poem begins with a baby's cry and expands to the infinite.

First Verse

Poem by **Tim Seibles**

The speaker ponders humanity's impact on the world.

How It Feels to Be Colored Me

Essay by **Zora Neale Hurston**

The writer's view of the world is changed when she discovers she is a "colored girl."

from **The Warmth of Other Suns**

History Writing by **Isabel Wilkerson**

The author compares how whites and African Americans lived during the late 1800s and early 1900s.

Modern and Contemporary Voices

In the 20th century, America exploded with challenges and changes. The United States experienced world wars, the economic collapse of the Great Depression, the proliferation of nuclear weapons, and new technologies that launched the Space Age. Changes in our social fabric caused attitudes about women's place in society to shift, and a neighborhood in Manhattan called Harlem became the cultural center of African American life after a Great Migration from the South brought millions of Black farmers and sharecroppers northward seeking freedom from racial oppression.

America's Century of War

World War I (1914–1918) was perhaps the most influential force on American writers of the early 20th century. Modernist writers responded to the social and political upheaval of the so-called Great War by experimenting with innovative styles and forms, focusing on the

Unemployed workers outside a soup kitchen during the Great Depression.

1910

1917 The United States enters World War I.

1920 The Nineteenth Amendment gives women the right to vote.

1929 Wall Street stock market crashes and the Great Depression begins.

1945 The United States drops two atomic bombs on Japan, ending World War II in the Pacific.

1954 In *Brown v. Board of Education*, the Supreme Court declares segregated schools unconstitutional.

alienation of the individual in modern society, and struggling to make sense of the brutality and moral complexities of war. During the Roaring Twenties, young people rebelled against the values of the past. Women shortened their skirts and cut their hair as they entered the workplace in large numbers. Industrial workers formed unions and demanded reforms. As the Great Depression took hold in the 1930s, many artists and writers were interested in, and influenced by, Communism or Communist ideas.

World War II propaganda poster advertising bonds to help the war effort

Only 21 years after the Great War ended, the world was plunged into another catastrophe. World War II (1939–1945) was the first war in history in which more civilians died than soldiers, including more than six million Jews and other persecuted groups in the Holocaust. When it ended, the United States and the Soviet Union emerged as rival superpowers and engaged in a decades-long Cold War, competing in a deadly arms race that threatened the world with a nuclear apocalypse. To contain the spread of Communism, the United States became involved in civil wars in Korea and Vietnam. Americans were deeply divided over their country's involvement in these conflicts. Students, pacifists, and even some returning veterans protested the American role in the Vietnam War and called for the U.S. to withdraw.

The Cold War ended with the breakup of the Soviet Union in 1991, but American warfare continued. That same year, U.S. troops were sent to protect Kuwait from an Iraqi invasion. In 2001, the September 11 attacks on the World Trade Center and the Pentagon led to U.S. invasions of Afghanistan and Iraq. In recent years, international terrorism, cyber attacks, and the spread of nuclear weapons have created a heightened feeling of insecurity.

EXTEND

Think of a question you have about a topic, an event, or a person from the historical period. Then, research the answer and add it as an entry to the timeline.

1965
First U.S. combat forces land in Vietnam.

1977
First practical home computer, Apple II, hits the market.

2001
Hijackers fly commercial planes into the World Trade Center and the Pentagon, killing thousands.

2012
The number of smartphone users worldwide tops 1 billion.

2020
Outbreak of COVID-19 coronavirus causes global pandemic.

The Fight for Rights and Recognition

The civil rights movement of the 1950s and 1960s was perhaps the most important catalyst for social change in modern times. In 1954, the Supreme Court struck down school segregation as unconstitutional. Dr. Martin Luther King, Jr., advocated nonviolent civil disobedience, eventually leading Congress to pass the 1964 Civil Rights Act, which outlawed segregation in public places and guaranteed legal equality to African Americans. In the years that followed, other groups drew on the ideals and tactics of the civil rights movement in the struggle to end discrimination based on gender, ethnicity, and sexual orientation.

As the civil rights movement gathered momentum, African American and other writers from diverse global backgrounds gained wider recognition. In a variety of genres, authors made powerful statements about the harmful effects of racism and the need for change. While earlier writers of color often focused on the experience of discrimination, contemporary authors would also explore the individual, culture, and a sense of place, forming a unique mosaic of American voices.

The Promise and Peril of Technology

Imagine the world in 1910, when cars, telephones, and electricity were not commonly available to most people. Fast forward to today, when robotics has transformed manufacturing and medicine, and advances in communications technology—especially the Internet and smartphones—give people around the globe instant access to information. A big question of our time is how to make the best use of this technology in a way that enhances the quality of life for all.

Advances in technology have come with costs, especially to the environment. Cars, trucks, and planes, as well as electric power plants, have largely relied on nonrenewable fossil fuels such as oil, coal, and natural gas. Our supply of natural resources once seemed infinite, but we now know it is not. In addition, our use of fossil fuels has contributed to global climate change. Contemporary writers continue to explore and express the implications of these challenges for life today and for the future of the human race.

COLLABORATIVE DISCUSSION

In a small group, discuss events from the historical essay that you believe have had a lasting effect on American life and literature. Why do you think this is so?

Assessment Practice

Choose the best answer to each question.

1. What was a result of the Great Migration?

- (A) Harlem became a major cultural center of African American life.
- (B) Modernist writers spent time living and working in Europe.
- (C) Young people rebelled against the values of the past.
- (D) Fossil fuels polluted the air and water and led to global warming.

2. What was one effect the Cold War had on the United States?

- (A) Many American artists and writers turned to Communism.
- (B) The United States became involved in other countries' civil wars.
- (C) Congress struck down school segregation and passed civil rights legislation.
- (D) Millions of African Americans moved north in search of a better life.

3. How did the civil rights movement affect the United States?

- (A) It led many people to protest against the war in Vietnam.
- (B) People used its tactics to fight other types of discrimination.
- (C) The Civil Rights Act changed the way people communicated.
- (D) It influenced writers to reject conventional values.

Test-Taking Strategies

A Rose for Emily

Short Story by **William Faulkner**

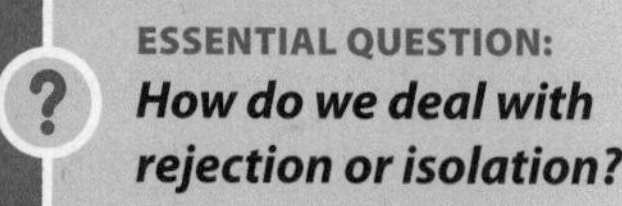
ESSENTIAL QUESTION:
How do we deal with rejection or isolation?

Engage Your Brain

Choose one or more of these activities to connect with the story you're about to read.

But How Will I Know?

When it comes to having a relationship with someone else, the first step is usually the hardest. How do you or people you know let someone know that you like them? Write or sketch your ideas.

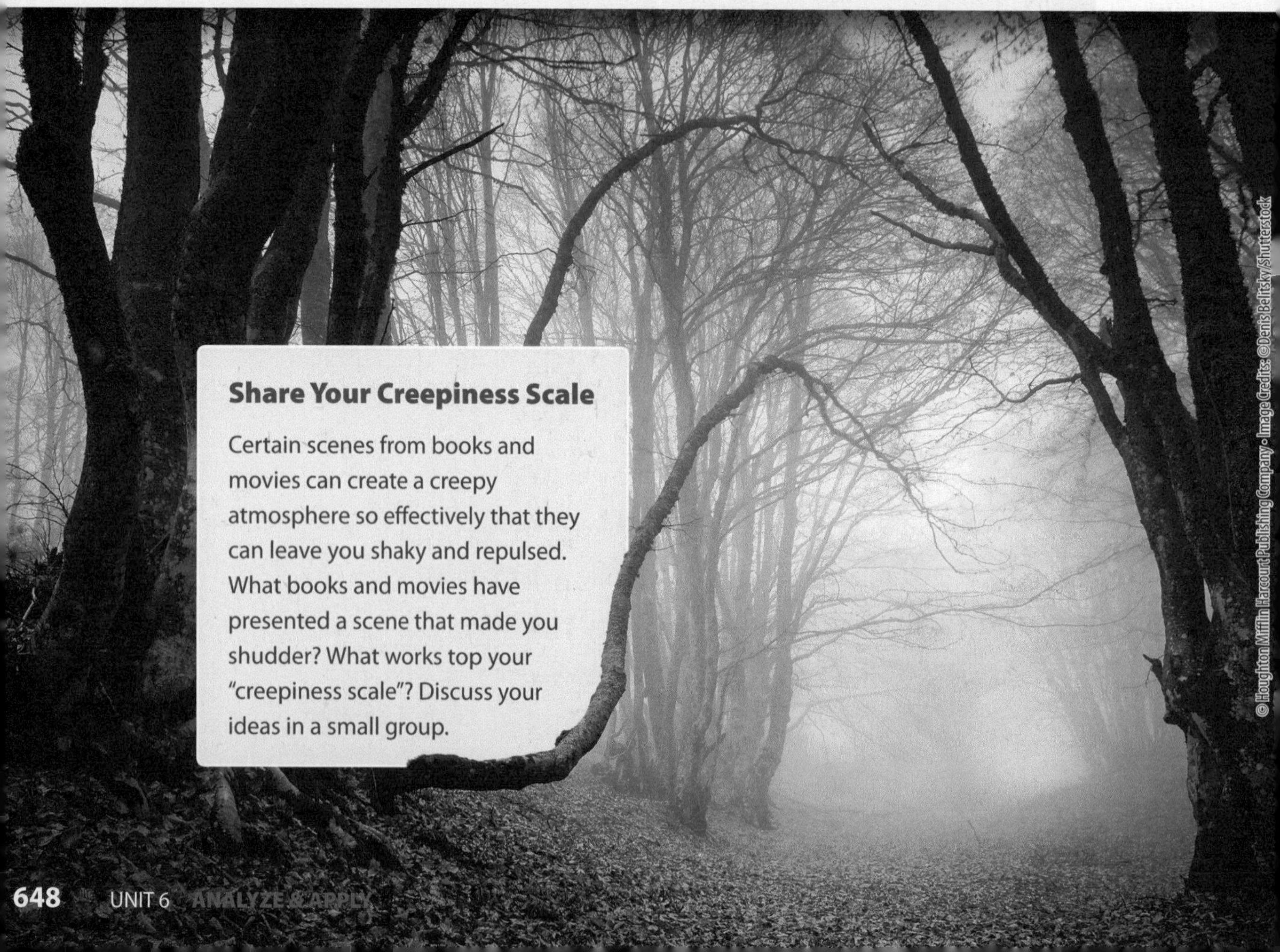

Rumors Running Amok

It can be tempting to join in when people are spreading rumors. But gossiping about others can be hurtful. In a small group, discuss the following questions:

- Why do people choose to participate in spreading rumors?
- What are the effects when people spread rumors about others?
- How can you tell when spreading a rumor becomes hurtful?

Share Your Creepiness Scale

Certain scenes from books and movies can create a creepy atmosphere so effectively that they can leave you shaky and repulsed. What books and movies have presented a scene that made you shudder? What works top your "creepiness scale"? Discuss your ideas in a small group.

Make Inferences

An **inference** is an educated guess about ideas not directly stated in a text. To make an inference, you combine the information in a text with your prior knowledge to arrive at a logical conclusion. As you read, you may find sections where the text can be interpreted in more than one way. For example, you may suspect the characters are presenting their own interpretation of events or choosing not to reveal important information. In these cases, you may infer that the writer intentionally left matters uncertain. Use the chart to help you make inferences as you read.

Text Evidence	Prior Knowledge	Inference

Focus on Genre
Short Story

- adds context to setting with historical, economic, and social details
- typically includes details that hint at how the main conflict will be resolved
- may leave some matters uncertain or unresolved

Analyze Setting

The **setting** of a story is the time and place in which the action occurs. The time may be the past, present, future, or a combination, and the place may be realistic or imaginary. In addition, a writer may use historical, economic, and social details to add context and deeper meaning to the events that take place.

"A Rose for Emily" is set in a small town in the deep South at the turn of the 20th century. In the description, Faulkner uses details about Miss Emily's house to bring the setting to life while also telling you about the social norms in the community at the time.

> **It was a big, squarish frame house that had once been white, decorated with cupolas and spires and scrolled balconies in the heavily lightsome style of the seventies, set on what had once been our most select street. But garages and cotton gins had encroached and obliterated even the august names of that neighborhood; only Miss Emily's house was left, lifting its stubborn and coquettish decay above the cotton wagons and the gasoline pumps—an eyesore among eyesores.**

As you read, notice how Faulkner develops the setting by using details about the historical, economic, and social conditions of the town.

Annotation in Action

Here is an example of notes a student made about the opening lines of "A Rose for Emily." As you read, note details that help you make inferences about what is happening.

> When Miss Emily Grierson died, our whole town went to her funeral: the men through a sort of respectful affection for a fallen monument, the women mostly out of curiosity to see the inside of her house, which no one save an old manservant—a combined gardener and cook—had seen in at least ten years.

These are odd reasons to go to a funeral.

Expand Your Vocabulary

Put a check mark next to the vocabulary words that you feel comfortable using when speaking or writing.

archaic	☐
tableau	☐
vindicate	☐
noblesse oblige	☐
cabal	☐
circumvent	☐
virulent	☐
acrid	☐

Then, turn to a partner and talk about a movie or television show that features a scary or creepy setting. Use as many vocabulary words as you can in your conversation. As you read the story, use the definitions in the side-column to learn the vocabulary words you don't already know.

Background

William Faulkner (1897–1962) struggled to find his ideal subject matter. When he finally decided to focus on his home state of Mississippi, he turned out masterpieces such as *The Sound and the Fury* (1929) and *As I Lay Dying* (1930). Many of his short stories and novels take place in his imaginary world of Yoknapatawpha County and are populated with memorable characters. His first readers found Faulkner's world too hard to understand. Today, Faulkner's works are revered for their strong themes and narrative technique.

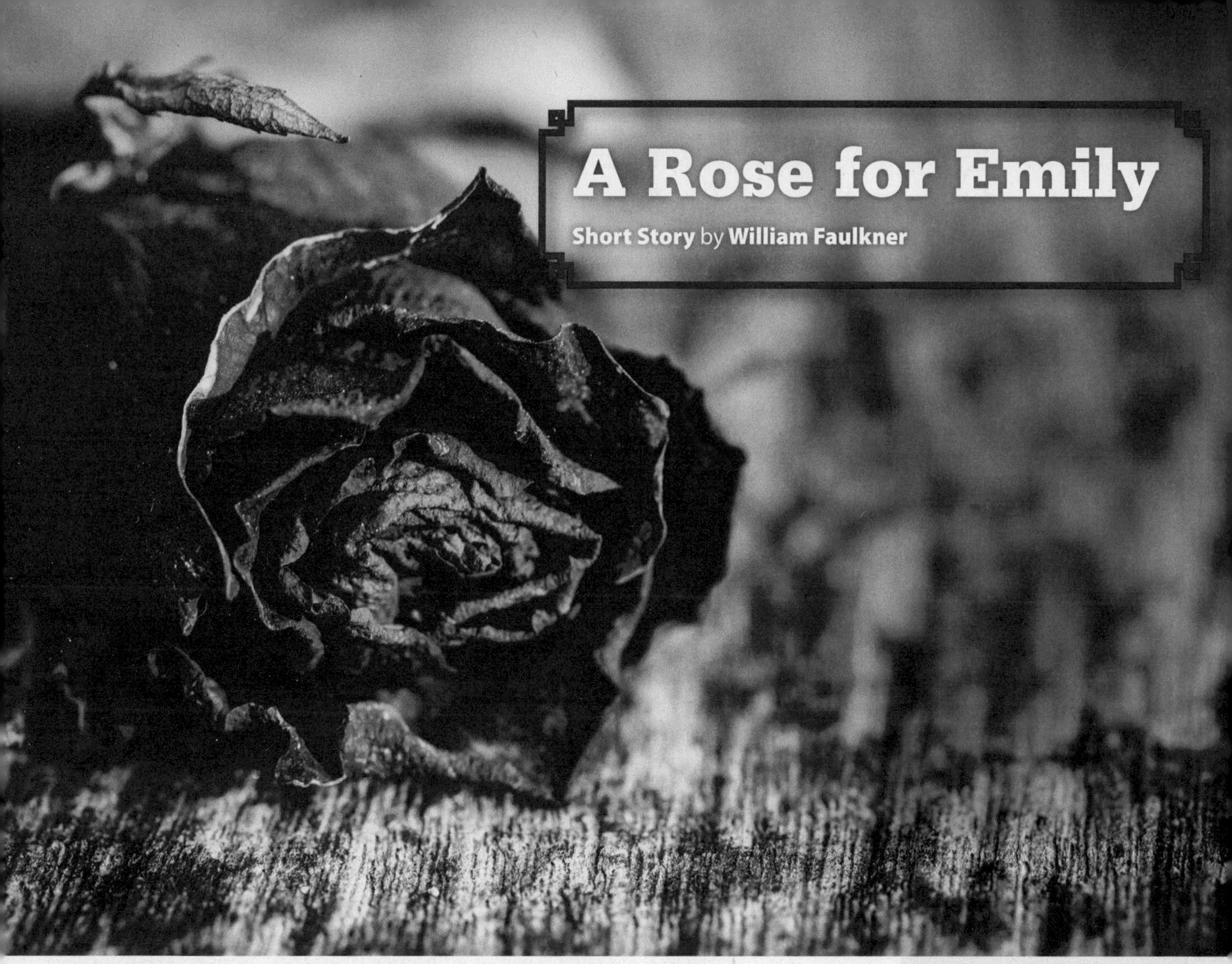

A Rose for Emily

Short Story by **William Faulkner**

Think about how the townspeople influence your understanding of events.

NOTICE & NOTE 
As you read, use the side margin to make notes about the text.

I

1 When Miss Emily Grierson died, our whole town went to her funeral: the men through a sort of respectful affection for a fallen monument, the women mostly out of curiosity to see the inside of her house, which no one save an old manservant—a combined gardener and cook—had seen in at least ten years.

2 It was a big, squarish frame house that had once been white, decorated with cupolas and spires and scrolled balconies in the heavily lightsome style of the seventies,[1] set on what had once been our most select street. But garages and cotton gins had encroached and obliterated even the august names of that neighborhood; only Miss Emily's house was left, lifting its stubborn and coquettish decay above the cotton wagons and the gasoline pumps—an eyesore among

ANALYZE SETTING

Annotate: Mark the details in paragraph 2 that describe the setting.

Analyze: What do these details tell you about the social and economic conditions of the time? How do they shape your perceptions about Emily?

[1] **the seventies:** the 1870s.

eyesores. And now Miss Emily had gone to join the representatives of those august names where they lay in the cedar-bemused[2] cemetery among the ranked and anonymous graves of Union and Confederate soldiers who fell at the battle of Jefferson.

ANALYZE SETTING

Annotate: Mark the details in paragraph 3 that indicate the time in which Miss Emily was exempted from paying taxes.

Interpret: What do these details tell you about the setting?

3 Alive, Miss Emily had been a tradition, a duty, and a care; a sort of hereditary obligation upon the town, dating from that day in 1894 when Colonel Sartoris, the mayor—he who fathered the edict that no Negro woman should appear on the streets without an apron—remitted her taxes, the dispensation dating from the death of her father on into perpetuity.[3] Not that Miss Emily would have accepted charity. Colonel Sartoris invented an involved tale to the effect that Miss Emily's father had loaned money to the town, which the town, as a matter of business, preferred this way of repaying. Only a man of Colonel Sartoris' generation and thought could have invented it, and only a woman could have believed it.

4 When the next generation, with its more modern ideas, became mayors and aldermen, this arrangement created some little dissatisfaction. On the first of the year they mailed her a tax notice. February came, and there was no reply. They wrote her a formal letter, asking her to call at the sheriff's office at her convenience. A week later the mayor wrote her himself, offering to call or to send

[2] **cedar-bemused:** almost lost in cedar trees.

[3] **remitted . . . perpetuity:** released her from paying taxes forever from the time of her father's death.

his car for her, and received in reply a note on paper of an **archaic** shape, in a thin, flowing calligraphy in faded ink, to the effect that she no longer went out at all. The tax notice was also enclosed, without comment.

5 They called a special meeting of the Board of Aldermen. A deputation waited upon her, knocked at the door through which no visitor had passed since she ceased giving china-painting lessons eight or ten years earlier. They were admitted by the old Negro into a dim hall from which a stairway mounted into still more shadow. It smelled of dust and disuse—a close, dank smell. The Negro led them into the parlor. It was furnished in heavy, leather-covered furniture. When the Negro opened the blinds of one window, they could see that the leather was cracked; and when they sat down, a faint dust rose sluggishly about their thighs, spinning with slow motes in the single sun-ray. On a tarnished gilt easel before the fireplace stood a crayon portrait of Miss Emily's father.

6 They rose when she entered—a small, fat woman in black, with a thin gold chain descending to her waist and vanishing into her belt, leaning on an ebony cane with a tarnished gold head. Her skeleton was small and spare; perhaps that was why what would have been merely plumpness in another was obesity in her. She looked bloated, like a body long submerged in motionless water, and of that pallid hue. Her eyes, lost in the fatty ridges of her face, looked like two small pieces of coal pressed into a lump of dough as they moved from one face to another while the visitors stated their errand.

7 She did not ask them to sit. She just stood in the door and listened quietly until the spokesman came to a stumbling halt. Then they could hear the invisible watch ticking at the end of the gold chain.

8 Her voice was dry and cold. "I have no taxes in Jefferson. Colonel Sartoris explained it to me. Perhaps one of you can gain access to the city records and satisfy yourselves."

9 "But we have. We are the city authorities, Miss Emily. Didn't you get a notice from the sheriff, signed by him?"

10 "I received a paper, yes," Miss Emily said. "Perhaps he considers himself the sheriff . . . I have no taxes in Jefferson."

11 "But there is nothing on the books to show that, you see. We must go by the—"

12 "See Colonel Sartoris. I have no taxes in Jefferson."

13 "But, Miss Emily—"

14 "See Colonel Sartoris." (Colonel Sartoris had been dead almost ten years.) "I have no taxes in Jefferson. Tobe!" The Negro appeared. "Show these gentlemen out."

Don't forget to **Notice & Note** as you read the text.

archaic
(är-kā´ĭk) *adj.* relating to, being, or characteristic of a much earlier period.

MAKE INFERENCES

Annotate: In paragraph 5, mark the words and phrases that describe the room.

Infer: What do the details of the room suggest about Miss Emily's situation?

II

15 So she vanquished them, horse and foot, just as she had vanquished their fathers thirty years before about the smell. That was two years after her father's death and a short time after her sweetheart—the one we believed would marry her—had deserted her. After her father's death she went out very little; after her sweetheart went away, people hardly saw her at all. A few of the ladies had the temerity[4] to call, but were not received, and the only sign of life about the place was the Negro man—a young man then—going in and out with a market basket.

16 "Just as if a man—any man—could keep a kitchen properly," the ladies said; so they were not surprised when the smell developed. It was another link between the gross, teeming world and the high and mighty Griersons.

17 A neighbor, a woman, complained to the mayor, Judge Stevens, eighty years old.

18 "But what will you have me do about it, madam?" he said.

19 "Why, send her word to stop it," the woman said. "Isn't there a law?"

20 "I'm sure that won't be necessary," Judge Stevens said. "It's probably just a snake or a rat that nigger of hers killed in the yard. I'll speak to him about it."

21 The next day he received two more complaints, one from a man who came in diffident deprecation.[5] "We really must do something about it, Judge. I'd be the last one in the world to bother Miss Emily, but we've got to do something." That night the Board of Aldermen met—three graybeards and one younger man, a member of the rising generation.

22 "It's simple enough," he said. "Send her word to have her place cleaned up. Give her a certain time to do it in, and if she don't . . ."

23 "Dammit, sir," Judge Stevens said, "will you accuse a lady to her face of smelling bad?"

24 So the next night, after midnight, four men crossed Miss Emily's lawn and slunk about the house like burglars, sniffing along the base of the brickwork and at the cellar openings while one of them performed a regular sowing motion with his hand out of a sack slung from his shoulder. They broke open the cellar door and sprinkled lime there, and in all the outbuildings. As they recrossed the lawn, a window that had been dark was lighted and Miss Emily sat in it, the light behind her, and her upright torso motionless as that of an idol. They crept quietly across the lawn and into the shadow of the locusts that lined the street. After a week or two the smell went away.

[4] **temerity** (tə-mĕr´ĭ-tē): foolish boldness.

[5] **diffident deprecation:** timid disapproval.

25 That was when people had begun to feel really sorry for her. People in our town, remembering how old lady Wyatt, her great-aunt, had gone completely crazy at last, believed that the Griersons held themselves a little too high for what they really were. None of the young men were quite good enough for Miss Emily and such. We had long thought of them as a **tableau**, Miss Emily a slender figure in white in the background, her father a spraddled silhouette in the foreground, his back to her and clutching a horsewhip, the two of them framed by the backflung front door. So when she got to be thirty and was still single, we were not pleased exactly, but **vindicated**; even with insanity in the family she wouldn't have turned down all of her chances if they had really materialized.

26 When her father died, it got about that the house was all that was left to her; and in a way, people were glad. At last they could pity Miss Emily. Being left alone, and a pauper, she had become humanized. Now she too would know the old thrill and the old despair of a penny more or less.

27 The day after his death all the ladies prepared to call at the house and offer condolence and aid, as is our custom. Miss Emily met them at the door, dressed as usual and with no trace of grief on her face. She told them that her father was not dead. She did that for three days, with the ministers calling on her, and the doctors, trying to persuade her to let them dispose of the body. Just as they were about to resort to law and force, she broke down, and they buried her father quickly.

28 We did not say she was crazy then. We believed she had to do that. We remembered all the young men her father had driven away, and we knew that with nothing left, she would have to cling to that which had robbed her, as people will.

III

29 She was sick for a long time. When we saw her again, her hair was cut short, making her look like a girl, with a vague resemblance to those angels in colored church windows—sort of tragic and serene.

30 The town had just let the contracts for paving the sidewalks, and in the summer after her father's death they began the work. The construction company came with niggers and mules and machinery, and a foreman named Homer Barron, a Yankee—a big, dark, ready man, with a big voice and eyes lighter than his face. The little boys would follow in groups to hear him cuss the niggers, and the niggers singing in time to the rise and fall of picks. Pretty soon he knew everybody in town. Whenever you heard a lot of laughing anywhere about the square, Homer Barron would be in the center of the group. Presently we began to see him and Miss Emily on Sunday afternoons driving in the yellow-wheeled buggy and the matched team of bays from the livery stable.

Don't forget to **Notice & Note** as you read the text.

tableau
(tăb´lō) *n.* a dramatic scene or picture.

vindicate
(vĭn´dĭ-kāt) *v.* to demonstrate or prove the validity of; justify.

MAKE INFERENCES

Annotate: Mark the words in paragraph 26 that describe the townspeople's reaction to Miss Emily's inheritance.

Infer: What does their reaction suggest they thought or felt about Miss Emily before her father died?

noblesse oblige
(nō-blĕs´ ō-blēzh´) *n.* the responsibility of people in a high social position to behave in a noble fashion.

31 At first we were glad that Miss Emily would have an interest, because the ladies all said, "Of course a Grierson would not think seriously of a Northerner, a day laborer." But there were still others, older people, who said that even grief could not cause a real lady to forget ***noblesse oblige***—without calling it *noblesse oblige*. They just said, "Poor Emily. Her kinsfolk should come to her." She had some kin in Alabama; but years ago her father had fallen out with them over the estate of old lady Wyatt, the crazy woman, and there was no communication between the two families. They had not even been represented at the funeral.

32 And as soon as the old people said, "Poor Emily," the whispering began. "Do you suppose it's really so?" they said to one another. "Of course it is. What else could . . ." This behind their hands; rustling of craned silk and satin behind jalousies[6] closed upon the sun of Sunday afternoon as the thin, swift clop-clop-clop of the matched team passed: "Poor Emily."

MAKE INFERENCES

Annotate: In paragraph 33, mark phrases that indicate Miss Emily's dignity was important to her. In paragraph 34, mark the purchase Miss Emily makes.

Infer: Why do you think Miss Emily bought the poison?

33 She carried her head high enough—even when we believed that she was fallen. It was as if she demanded more than ever the recognition of her dignity as the last Grierson; as if it had wanted that touch of earthiness to reaffirm her imperviousness.[7] Like when she bought the rat poison, the arsenic. That was over a year after they had begun to say "Poor Emily," and while the two female cousins were visiting her.

34 "I want some poison," she said to the druggist. She was over thirty then, still a slight woman, though thinner than usual, with cold, haughty black eyes in a face the flesh of which was strained across the temples and about the eye-sockets as you imagine a lighthouse-keeper's face ought to look. "I want some poison," she said.

35 "Yes, Miss Emily. What kind? For rats and such? I'd recom—"

36 "I want the best you have. I don't care what kind."

37 The druggist named several. "They'll kill anything up to an elephant. But what you want is—"

38 "Arsenic," Miss Emily said. "Is that a good one?"

39 "Is . . . arsenic? Yes, ma'am. But what you want—"

40 "I want arsenic."

41 The druggist looked down at her. She looked back at him, erect, her face like a strained flag. "Why, of course," the druggist said. "If that's what you want. But the law requires you to tell what you are going to use it for."

42 Miss Emily just stared at him, her head tilted back in order to look him eye for eye, until he looked away and went and got the arsenic and wrapped it up. The Negro delivery boy brought her the package; the druggist didn't come back. When she opened the package at home there was written on the box, under the skull and bones: "For rats."

[6] **jalousies** (jăl´ə-sēz): blinds or shutters containing overlapping slats that can be opened or closed.

[7] **imperviousness** (ĭm-pûr´vē-əs-nəs): an inability to be affected or disturbed.

IV

43 So the next day we all said, "She will kill herself"; and we said it would be the best thing. When she had first begun to be seen with Homer Barron, we had said, "She will marry him." Then we said, "She will persuade him yet," because Homer himself had remarked—he liked men, and it was known that he drank with the younger men in the Elks' Club—that he was not a marrying man. Later we said, "Poor Emily" behind the jalousies as they passed on Sunday afternoon in the glittering buggy, Miss Emily with her head high and Homer Barron with his hat cocked and a cigar in his teeth, reins and whip in a yellow glove.

44 Then some of the ladies began to say that it was a disgrace to the town and a bad example to the young people. The men did not want to interfere, but at last the ladies forced the Baptist minister—Miss Emily's people were Episcopal—to call upon her. He would never

divulge what happened during that interview, but he refused to go back again. The next Sunday they again drove about the streets, and the following day the minister's wife wrote to Miss Emily's relations in Alabama.

45 So she had blood-kin under her roof again and we sat back to watch developments. At first nothing happened. Then we were sure that they were to be married. We learned that Miss Emily had been to the jeweler's and ordered a man's toilet set in silver, with the letters H. B. on each piece. Two days later we learned that she had bought a complete outfit of men's clothing, including a nightshirt, and we said, "They are married." We were really glad. We were glad because the two female cousins were even more Grierson than Miss Emily had ever been.

46 So we were not surprised when Homer Barron—the streets had been finished some time since—was gone. We were a little disappointed that there was not a public blowing-off,[8] but we believed that he had gone on to prepare for Miss Emily's coming, or to give her a chance to get rid of the cousins. (By that time it was a **cabal**, and we were all Miss Emily's allies to help **circumvent** the cousins.) Sure enough, after another week they departed. And, as we had expected all along, within three days Homer Barron was back in town. A neighbor saw the Negro man admit him at the kitchen door at dusk one evening.

cabal
(kə-bäl´) *n.* a group united in a secret plot.

circumvent
(sûr-kəm-vĕnt´) *v.* to avoid or get around by artful maneuvering.

MAKE INFERENCES

Annotate: Mark the sentence in paragraph 47 that mentions Homer Barron.

Infer: What connection does the disappearance of Homer Barron have to the night that the men sprinkled lime in Miss Emily's yard?

47 And that was the last we saw of Homer Barron. And of Miss Emily for some time. The Negro man went in and out with the market basket, but the front door remained closed. Now and then we would see her at a window for a moment, as the men did that night when they sprinkled the lime, but for almost six months she did not appear on the streets. Then we knew that this was to be expected too; as if that quality of her father which had thwarted her woman's life so many times had been too **virulent** and too furious to die.

virulent
(vîr´yə-lənt) *adj.* extremely hostile or malicious.

48 When we next saw Miss Emily, she had grown fat and her hair was turning gray. During the next few years it grew grayer and grayer until it attained an even pepper-and-salt iron-gray, when it ceased turning. Up to the day of her death at seventy-four it was still that vigorous iron-gray, like the hair of an active man.

49 From that time on her front door remained closed, save for a period of six or seven years, when she was about forty, during which she gave lessons in china-painting. She fitted up a studio in one of the downstairs rooms, where the daughters and granddaughters of Colonel Sartoris' contemporaries were sent to her with the same regularity and in the same spirit that they were sent to church on Sundays with a twenty-five-cent piece for the collection plate. Meanwhile her taxes had been remitted.

[8] **blowing-off:** here, a celebration.

50 Then the newer generation became the backbone and the spirit of the town, and the painting pupils grew up and fell away and did not send their children to her with boxes of color and tedious brushes and pictures cut from the ladies' magazines. The front door closed upon the last one and remained closed for good. When the town got free postal delivery, Miss Emily alone refused to let them fasten the metal numbers above her door and attach a mailbox to it. She would not listen to them.

51 Daily, monthly, yearly we watched the Negro grow grayer and more stooped, going in and out with the market basket. Each December we sent her a tax notice, which would be returned by the post office a week later, unclaimed. Now and then we would see her in one of the downstairs windows—she had evidently shut up the top floor of the house—like the carven torso of an idol in a niche, looking or not looking at us, we could never tell which. Thus she passed from generation to generation—dear, inescapable, impervious, tranquil, and perverse.

52 And so she died. Fell ill in the house filled with dust and shadows, with only a doddering Negro man to wait on her. We did not even know she was sick; we had long since given up trying to get any information from the Negro. He talked to no one, probably not even to her, for his voice had grown harsh and rusty, as if from disuse.

53 She died in one of the downstairs rooms, in a heavy walnut bed with a curtain, her gray head propped on a pillow yellow and moldy with age and lack of sunlight.

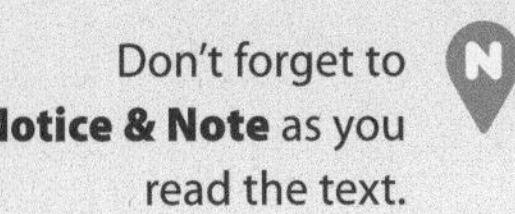

ANALYZE SETTING

Annotate: In paragraphs 48–52, mark words that indicate the passing of time.

Draw Conclusions: What contrast between Miss Emily and the townspeople is illustrated by the passing of time?

V

54 The Negro met the first of the ladies at the front door and let them in, with their hushed, sibilant[9] voices and their quick, curious glances, and then he disappeared. He walked right through the house and out the back and was not seen again.

55 The two female cousins came at once. They held the funeral on the second day, with the town coming to look at Miss Emily beneath a mass of bought flowers, with the crayon face of her father musing profoundly above the bier[10] and the ladies sibilant and macabre; and the very old men—some in their brushed Confederate uniforms—on the porch and the lawn, talking of Miss Emily as if she had been a contemporary of theirs, believing that they had danced with her and courted her perhaps, confusing time with its mathematical progression, as the old do, to whom all the past is not a diminishing road but, instead, a huge meadow which no winter ever quite touches, divided from them now by the narrow bottleneck of the most recent decade of years.

[9] **sibilant:** characterized by a hissing sound.

[10] **bier:** coffin along with its stand

56 Already we knew that there was one room in that region above stairs which no one had seen in forty years, and which would have to be forced. They waited until Miss Emily was decently in the ground before they opened it.

57 The violence of breaking down the door seemed to fill this room with pervading dust. A thin, **acrid** pall[11] as of the tomb seemed to lie everywhere upon this room decked and furnished as for a bridal: upon the valance curtains of faded rose color, upon the rose-shaded lights, upon the dressing table, upon the delicate array of crystal and the man's toilet things backed with tarnished silver, silver so tarnished that the monogram was obscured. Among them lay a collar and tie, as if they had just been removed, which, lifted, left upon the surface a pale crescent in the dust. Upon a chair hung the suit, carefully folded; beneath it the two mute shoes and the discarded socks.

acrid
(ăk´rĭd) *adj.* unpleasantly sharp, pungent, or bitter to the taste or smell.

58 The man himself lay in the bed.

59 For a long while we just stood there, looking down at the profound and fleshless grin. The body had apparently once lain in the attitude of an embrace, but now the long sleep that outlasts love, that conquers even the grimace of love, had cuckolded him.[12] What was left of him, rotted beneath what was left of the nightshirt, had become inextricable from the bed in which he lay; and upon him and upon the pillow beside him lay that even coating of the patient and biding dust.

60 Then we noticed that in the second pillow was the indentation of a head. One of us lifted something from it, and leaning forward, that faint and invisible dust dry and acrid in the nostrils, we saw a long strand of iron-gray hair.

NOTICE & NOTE
AHA MOMENT

When you notice a sudden realization that shifts a character's actions or understandings, you've found an **Aha Moment** signpost.

Notice & Note: Reread paragraphs 56–58. In paragraph 56, mark what the townspeople knew.

Infer: Explain whether the townspeople experienced an **Aha Moment** when they entered the room. Cite text evidence in your response.

[11] **acrid pall:** bitter-smelling gloom.
[12] **cuckolded him:** made his wife or lover unfaithful to him.

?
ESSENTIAL QUESTION:
How do we deal with rejection or isolation?

Review your notes and add your thoughts to your **Response Log.**

COLLABORATIVE DISCUSSION

What is your reaction to the end of the story? Discuss your ideas with a partner.

Assessment Practice

Answer these questions before moving on to the **Analyze the Text** section on the following page.

1. How did Emily react to her father's death?

- (A) She wept and could not be comforted.
- (B) For days, she denied that he was dead.
- (C) She sent for her relatives from Alabama.
- (D) For days, she celebrated his being gone.

2. Why did Emily buy the rat poison?

- (A) to kill herself
- (B) to kill the rats
- (C) to kill Homer
- (D) to kill her father

3. How did people's attitudes toward Emily change when the cousins arrived?

- (A) They became Emily's allies.
- (B) They became suspicious of Emily.
- (C) They became friends with the cousins.
- (D) They became more distant than before.

Test-Taking Strategies

Analyze the Text

Support your responses with evidence from the text.

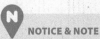

NOTICE & NOTE

Review what you **noticed and noted** as you read the text. Your annotations can help you answer these questions.

1. **SYNTHESIZE** Look back through your annotations about the setting. What do the details help you understand about the town?

2. **INFER** Why do the townspeople notify Miss Emily's relatives when she begins her courtship with Homer Barron? Why does the town's oversight change?

3. **ANALYZE** What contradictions are revealed in the town's attitude toward Emily? Explain what you think Faulkner is saying about small-town life in the South with this story.

4. **SYNTHESIZE** Drawing from Faulkner's description of the town and events, what was the larger historical, social, and economic context in the South when this story takes place?

5. **ANALYZE** What hints or clues throughout the story foreshadow the gruesome ending? Did these hints prepare you for the **Aha Moment**, or were you surprised by it? Explain.

6. **DRAW CONCLUSIONS** Why does Emily murder Homer? Can you draw a definitive conclusion or does the text leave the matter uncertain? Consider the following details in your response:
   - Homer's intentions
   - Emily's father's reaction to her suitors
   - the opinions of the townspeople

Choices

Here are some other ways to demonstrate your understanding of the ideas in this lesson.

Writing

↳ Miss Emily Up Close

Write a character analysis of Miss Emily. Review the notes you took and inferences you made as you read. In your analysis, consider including the following details:

- Miss Emily's actions and behavior
- what other people thought of Miss Emily
- how the setting affected her character

You must include your view of Emily's motivation for her crime and draw a conclusion about her character.

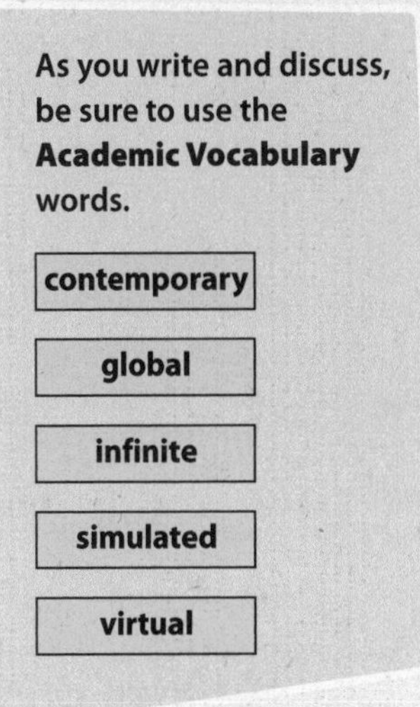

As you write and discuss, be sure to use the **Academic Vocabulary** words.

- contemporary
- global
- infinite
- simulated
- virtual

Media

↳ Re-create a Scene

Miss Emily's house and life are rooted in the 1870s, with details about customs, transportation, and social behavior that reflect the period throughout the story. What would a scene from the story look like if it took place today?

1. Choose a scene from the story to retell in a modern setting.
2. With a partner or group, discuss the details that would change if this story were to take place today.
3. Make your own version of the scene. You may choose to rewrite the scene, create an illustration, or present it with a group for your class.

Social & Emotional Learning

↳ Group Discussion

In a small group, discuss whether the townspeople bear any responsibility for what becomes of Miss Emily. Do their actions contribute to Emily's feelings and actions? Review the text for details and evidence that you can cite in your discussion.

Expand Your Vocabulary

PRACTICE AND APPLY

Fill in the word that best completes each sentence.

archaic	tableau	vindicate	noblesse oblige
cabal	circumvent	virulent	acrid

1. Out of ________________, the princess treated her subjects quite well.
2. The museum's visitors were impressed with the splendid ________________ in the main gallery.
3. Some people put a lot of effort into trying to ________________ the rules.
4. The people who wanted to overthrow the government formed a(n) ________________.
5. A(n) ________________ smell told us we'd left the plastic bowl near the fire.
6. She knows that further scientific inquiry will ________________ her theory.
7. The ________________ emotions of the crowd spilled over into violence.
8. Compared to modern cellphones, old dial phones seem ________________.

Vocabulary Strategy

↳ Foreign Words and Phrases

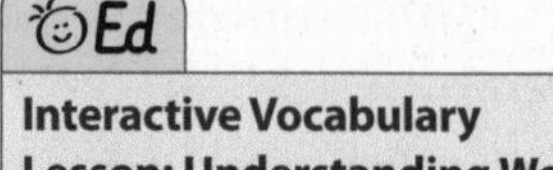

Interactive Vocabulary Lesson: Understanding Word Origins

English borrows many words from other languages. In "A Rose for Emily," *tableau* and *noblesse oblige* are two examples of words that were borrowed from French. Some foreign words change pronunciation in the English language, but their spellings and general meanings remain the same.

PRACTICE AND APPLY

Look up each of the following words or phrases in a print or digital dictionary. State its meaning and the language it comes from. Digital resources may also offer an audio function that provides a pronunciation of the word or phrase in addition to a definition.

1. faux pas
2. non sequitur
3. en masse
4. fait accompli
5. carte blanche
6. modus operandi
7. bona fide
8. ad hoc
9. prima donna
10. status quo

Watch Your Language!

Interactive Grammar Lesson: Semicolons and Colons

Colons and Semicolons

Faulkner's style is known for long, intricate sentences. This syntax choice allows him to build detail upon detail to create deep characters. He uses semicolons and colons as punctuation aids to help the reader navigate through compound, complex, and compound-complex sentences. Notice, for example, the way he uses a semicolon to set off a long appositive that expands on what the narrator means about Miss Emily becoming a tradition.

> **Alive, Miss Emily had been a tradition, a duty, and a care; a sort of hereditary obligation upon the town, dating from that day in 1894 when Colonel Sartoris, the mayor—he who fathered the edict that no Negro woman should appear on the streets without an apron—remitted her taxes, the dispensation dating from the death of her father . . . .**

"Yes, a winky face is correct... But in ancient times, the semicolon was actually used to separate archaic written devices known as 'complete sentences.'"

Semicolons are often used to link two simple sentences that are closely related in thought. Faulkner, however, uses semicolons to join two complex sentences, suggesting a closer relationship between the cracked leather and the dust rising when they sat down.

> **When the Negro opened the blinds of one window, they could see that the leather was cracked; and when they sat down, a faint dust rose sluggishly about their thighs, spinning with slow motes in the single sun-ray.**

Colons are used to link two independent clauses when the second one tells you more about the first. Faulkner uses this construction in two ways: to show the relationship between two ideas and to communicate a simpler idea that summarizes and characterizes the meaning of the preceding clause. Notice Faulkner's use of the colon in the following two sentences:

> **When Miss Emily Grierson died, our whole town went to her funeral: the men through a sort of respectful affection for a fallen monument, the women mostly out of curiosity to see the inside of her house, which no one save an old manservant—a combined gardener and cook—had seen in at least ten years.**

> **This behind their hands; rustling of craned silk and satin behind jalousies closed upon the sun of Sunday afternoon as the thin, swift clop-clop-clop of the matched team passed: "Poor Emily."**

PRACTICE AND APPLY

Try writing several sentences with a semicolon linking closely related ideas. Then, write sentences with colons linking one idea to a second idea that tells more about the first.

Get Ready

Mending Wall

Poem by **Robert Frost**

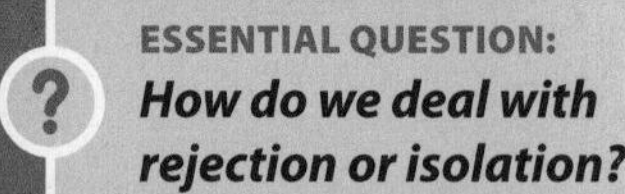
ESSENTIAL QUESTION:
How do we deal with rejection or isolation?

Engage Your Brain

Choose one or more of these activities to connect with the poem you're about to read.

Thoughts About Walls

You may not give walls much thought, but they are a part of where you live, where you go to school, and other aspects of everyday life. Write your answers to the following questions:

- What are some purposes that a wall can serve?
- Do you feel positively or negatively about walls? Explain.
- If you were to build a wall, how would you use it?

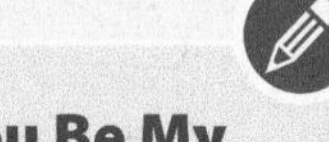

Won't You Be My Neighbor?

What does it mean to be a good neighbor? Freewrite or draw your ideas.

Better Alone or Better Together?

Think about activities you like to do alone and those you like to do with someone else. For instance, some people prefer to study alone, while others would rather study with a friend or in a group. Share your ideas in a group discussion.

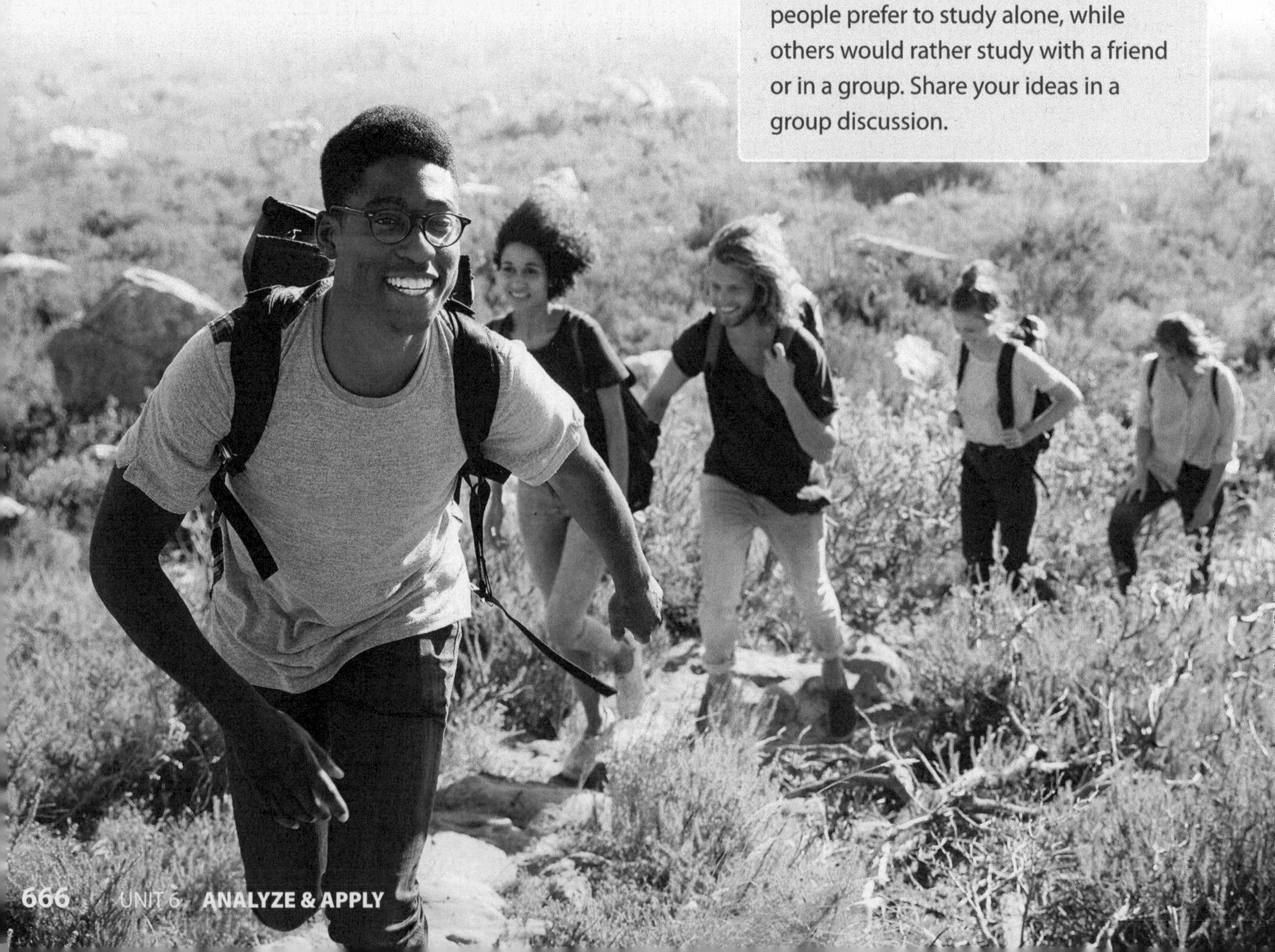

Analyze Blank Verse

"Mending Wall" is written in **blank verse,** a poetic structure of unrhymed lines of iambic pentameter. In other words, each line has five pairs of syllables. In most pairs, an unstressed syllable is followed by a stressed syllable. Note the stressed (in italics) and unstressed syllables in "Mending Wall."

And *on* a *day* we *meet* to *walk* the *line*
And *set* the *wall* be*tween* us *once* a*gain*.

The stressed and unstressed syllables imitate the rhythms of English speech. So do the line breaks, which emphasize natural pauses or stops in speech. This rhythm appealed to Frost because he loved his neighbors' speech patterns. As you read, note the way elements of poetry, such as rhythm and repetition, affect the poem's meaning.

Try writing a sentence or two about your day or your week using blank verse and iambic pentameter. Use the two lines above from "Mending Wall" as a guide.

Focus on Genre
↳ Blank Verse

- **imitates the cadence of English speech**
- **uses iambic pentameter**
- **has lines that do not rhyme**

Analyze Language

Diction, or the words a poet chooses, can affect other literary elements of a poem, including the following:

- **Tone,** or the attitude toward the subject: Is Frost's language simple and direct, or complex? What attitude does this convey?
- **Mood,** or the atmosphere in a work of literature: Think about the words Frost uses in the poem and how they create a distinct mood.
- **Voice,** or the personality that emerges from a work: How does the language convey this personality?

As you read, notice the way diction contributes to the tone, mood, and voice of the poem.

Make Inferences

The **theme** of a poem is its central idea about life. Readers must use details to determine the theme. In this poem, the speaker asks his neighbor about the wall, which signals that his message will be about separations people create.

> **He only says, "Good fences make good neighbors."**
> **Spring is the mischief in me, and I wonder**
> **If I could put a notion in his head:**
> **"*Why* do they make good neighbors? . . ."**

The phrase "good fences make good neighbors" is an ambiguous statement, meaning it can be interpreted in more than one way. The reader's task is to make inferences about Frost's meaning and support that inference with evidence. As you read, note details that help you infer Frost's theme.

Annotation in Action

Here is one student's inference about the meaning of the opening lines of "Mending Wall." As you read, continue to make inferences based on details in the text, including when matters are ambiguous or uncertain.

Something there is that doesn't love a wall,
That sends the frozen-ground-swell under it,
And spills the upper boulders in the sun;
And makes gaps even two can pass abreast.
The work of hunters is another thing:
I have come after them and made repair
Where they have left not one stone on a stone,

The images show how a wall that seems solid really isn't—it can be broken.

Background

Robert Frost (1874–1963) was born in San Francisco, but his family moved to New England when Frost's father died. Frost worked as a teacher but later became a farmer while trying to establish himself as a poet. At age 38, Frost uprooted the family and moved to England. There he was able to publish his first book of poetry, *A Boy's Will.* During World War I, in 1915, Frost and his family returned to the United States. He was greeted as a leading American poet and was celebrated for his skill at capturing American colloquial speech. However, a series of personal tragedies affected his later poems, which conveyed a bleak outlook on life.

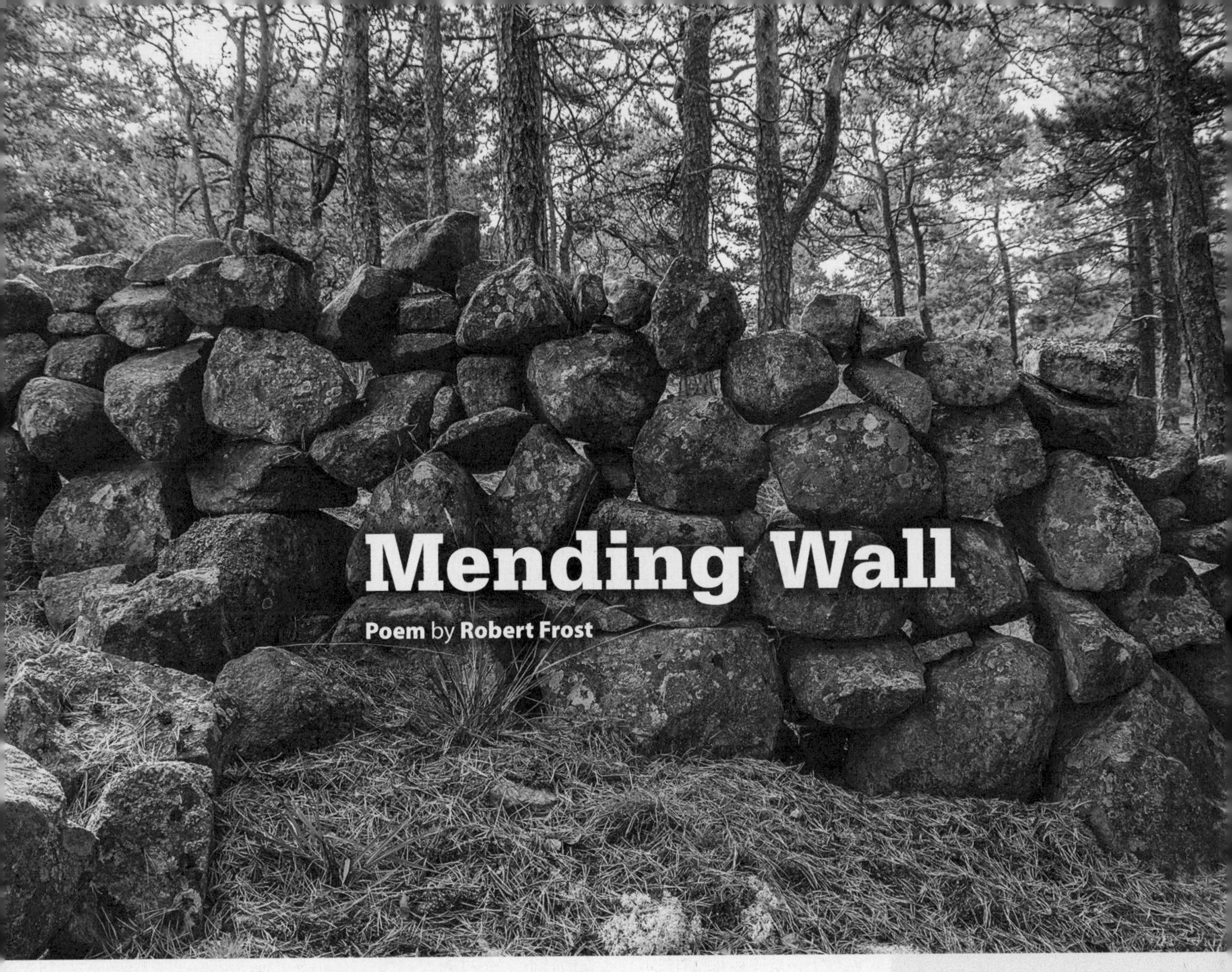

Mending Wall

Poem by **Robert Frost**

Pay attention to the details that tell you what each person thinks of the wall.

NOTICE & NOTE

As you read, use the side margins to make notes about the text.

Something there is that doesn't love a wall,
That sends the frozen-ground-swell under it,
And spills the upper boulders in the sun;
And makes gaps even two can pass abreast.
The work of hunters is another thing:
I have come after them and made repair
Where they have left not one stone on a stone,
But they would have the rabbit out of hiding,
To please the yelping dogs. The gaps I mean,
No one has seen them made or heard them made,
But at spring mending-time we find them there.
I let my neighbor know beyond the hill;
And on a day we meet to walk the line
And set the wall between us once again.
We keep the wall between us as we go.
To each the boulders that have fallen to each.
And some are loaves and some so nearly balls
We have to use a spell to make them balance:

ANALYZE LANGUAGE

Annotate: Mark the phrases in lines 1–5 that appeal to your senses.

Compare: How does this imagery help create a particular mood?

ANALYZE BLANK VERSE

Annotate: Mark the stressed syllables in lines 14–15.

Interpret: What is the significance of the repeated phrase in these lines?

MAKE INFERENCES

Annotate: In lines 32–34, mark what the speaker would want to know before building a wall.

Analyze: What message about walls is expressed in these lines?

"Stay where you are until our backs are turned!"
We wear our fingers rough with handling them.
Oh, just another kind of out-door game,
One on a side. It comes to little more:
There where it is we do not need the wall:
He is all pine and I am apple orchard.
My apple trees will never get across
And eat the cones under his pines, I tell him.
He only says, "Good fences make good neighbors."
Spring is the mischief in me, and I wonder
If I could put a notion in his head:
"*Why* do they make good neighbors? Isn't it
Where there are cows? But here there are no cows.
Before I built a wall I'd ask to know
What I was walling in or walling out,
And to whom I was like to give offence.
Something there is that doesn't love a wall,
That wants it down." I could say "Elves" to him,
But it's not elves exactly, and I'd rather
He said it for himself. I see him there
Bringing a stone grasped firmly by the top
In each hand, like an old-stone savage armed.
He moves in darkness as it seems to me,
Not of woods only and the shade of trees.
He will not go behind his father's saying,
And he likes having thought of it so well
He says again, "Good fences make good neighbors."

NOTICE & NOTE

AGAIN AND AGAIN

When you notice certain words recurring over a portion of the poem, you've found an **Again and Again** signpost.

Notice & Note: Mark the phrase the neighbor repeats throughout the poem.

Draw Conclusions: Why does the neighbor repeat this phrase?

?

ESSENTIAL QUESTION:

How do we deal with rejection or isolation?

Review your notes and add your thoughts to your **Response Log.**

COLLABORATIVE DISCUSSION

How would you describe the speaker's relationship with his neighbor? Share your ideas with a partner.

Assessment Practice

Answer these questions before moving on to the **Analyze the Text** section on the following page.

1. Why do the hunters damage the wall?

(A) They want to force a rabbit out of hiding.

(B) They believe in the value of walls.

(C) They need a gap they can pass through.

(D) They don't understand why the wall is there.

2. What notion does the speaker want to put in his neighbor's head?

(A) to hire someone else to repair the wall

(B) to combine their resources to buy cattle

(C) to ask himself why walls make good neighbors

(D) to wait until autumn to repair the wall

3. Why does the speaker think the wall is unnecessary?

(A) There are cows in the neighborhood.

(B) There are not enough stones available.

(C) There is nothing to keep out or keep in.

(D) The hunters are annoyed by the wall.

Test-Taking Strategies

Analyze the Text

Support your responses with evidence from the text.

NOTICE & NOTE

Review what you **noticed and noted** as you read the text. Your annotations can help you answer these questions.

1. **INFER** Why do you think Frost repeats the line "Something there is that doesn't love a wall" **Again and Again**?

2. **INTERPRET** How does Frost use ambiguity to present the message about walls and neighbors? What evidence supports the idea that the speaker believes "Good fences make good neighbors"? What details suggest otherwise?

Speaker Believes	Speaker Does Not Believe

3. **ANALYZE** What tone does the speaker convey when he thinks of their activity as an "out-door game" and says his apple trees will never eat his neighbor's pine cones?

4. **ANALYZE** How do lines 39–42 characterize the neighbor? How does this relate to the theme of the poem? Cite specific details in your response.

5. **INTERPRET** What ideas does the use of repetition in the poem emphasize? Cite at least two examples in your response.

6. **DRAW CONCLUSIONS** Recall that blank verse reflects the cadence of everyday speech. Why do you think Frost chose to use blank verse to convey the events in the poem?

7. **INTERPRET** What might the wall symbolize? Cite text evidence in your response.

Choices

Here are some other ways to demonstrate your understanding of the ideas in this lesson.

Writing

↳ Examine a Detail from the Poem

How do you explain the fact that the man who doesn't see the need for a wall is the one who, every spring, is the first to call upon his neighbor and so make sure the wall is rebuilt? Might he want something more from his neighbor than merely a hand with repair work? Write your thoughts in a paragraph.

As you write and discuss, be sure to use the **Academic Vocabulary** words.

- contemporary
- global
- infinite
- simulated
- virtual

Speaking & Listening

↳ Three Words About Life

Robert Frost once said: "In three words I can sum up everything I've learned about life: it goes on." Come up with your own three-word statement about life. Then get together with a small group and compare your statements.

Media

↳ Get Visual

Do you believe that "Good fences make good neighbors"? What are your thoughts about this statement? Represent your ideas visually in a presentation. You may choose to:

- draw an illustration
- make a collage
- create a media slideshow
- use any other form—be creative

Get Ready

from They Called Us Enemy

ESSENTIAL QUESTION:
Can anyone achieve the American Dream?

Graphic Memoir by **George Takei, Justin Eisinger, Steven Scott,** and **Harmony Becker**

Engage Your Brain

Choose one or more of these activities to connect with the graphic novel you're about to read.

Relatable Role Model

George Takei is a famous actor and Internet influencer. In his role as Mr. Sulu on *Star Trek*, he provided a positive role model for Asian American viewers. How do you identify particular figures as your role models? Is it important for you to see positive role models on television shows or in movies? Write your ideas in a paragraph.

Executive Order 9066

In the excerpt, George Takei depicts the impact Executive Order 9066 had on him and his family. Do some research to answer the following questions:

- Who was the president that signed Executive Order 9066?
- What did Executive Order 9066 state?
- When did Executive Order 9066 go into effect?
- Where did the people affected by Executive Order 9066 live?
- Why is Executive Order 9066 so significant?

Create a Graphic Novel Guide

You are about to read an excerpt from a graphic novel, a genre that is popular with readers of all ages. With a group, discuss the following questions:

- What do you like about graphic novels in general?
- What are the best graphic novels you've read?
- Have you ever read an illustrated version of true events? How did the images affect your understanding of what happened?

Then, create a reading list of graphic novel recommendations. Share your suggestions with the class.

Analyze Graphic Novel

A **graphic novel** is a story told through images and text. It is laid out like the pages of a comic book but is longer and more complex.

- Segments containing images and text are called **panels**. A full-page panel is called a **splash panel**.
- The illustrations depict events, settings, and the actions and reactions of characters. The text conveys narration, dialogue, and characters' internal thoughts.
- Dialogue and internal thoughts appear in **speech and thought bubbles**, and narration appears in **captions**.
- The lines and borders around the panels are called **frames**, and the **gutter** is the space that separates frames. Sometimes the contents of a panel will go beyond the frame.
- The visual elements of a graphic novel add depth, movement, drama, emotion, and meaning to the reader's experience.

Focus on Genre
↳ Graphic Novel

- **tells a story through images and text**
- **contains panels, frames, captions, and speech and thought bubbles**
- **makes use of dialogue and visual elements to affect the reader's experience**

As you read, use the chart to record how the following elements in the excerpt from *They Called Us Enemy* affect your understanding of events.

Graphic Novel Element	Effect
Panel lengths vary.	
Images include closeups of action and characters.	
Speech bubbles appear for characters shown and not shown in the panel.	
The narration is broken up into several captions.	

Analyze Author's Purpose

An author's **purpose**, or reason, for writing may be to inform, to entertain, or to persuade the reader.

- To understand the writer's purpose, look at the content and style of the work. Takei was writing about a personal experience caused by a government order during wartime. How does he present this experience?
- The choices an author makes to include certain details, and what the author chooses to emphasize, can suggest the author's purpose.
- Some authors may have more than one purpose in mind. For example, they may want to help readers understand an event in a new, entertaining way while also persuading them to think about it from a different perspective.

As you read this excerpt from *They Called Us Enemy*, think about the purpose, or purposes, Takei wants to achieve by telling his story.

Background

George Takei started acting and providing voiceovers in the late 1950s, but he did not become known to the public until his role as Hikaru Sulu, helmsman on the classic television series *Star Trek* (1966–1969). He went on to act in other television shows, in feature films (including six *Star Trek* films), and on stage as well. He wrote a science fiction novel and an autobiography. When Takei joined social media in 2011, he quickly gained followers for his frequent humorous posts, topping 10 million followers by 2018. He uses his platform to engage in activism to support causes he believes in, such as human rights.

In 2017, the federal government's new immigration policies led Takei to write *They Called Us Enemy*, co-written with Justin Eisinger and Steven Scott, and illustrated by Harmony Becker, creator of her own acclaimed comics, such as *Himawari Share*. The graphic memoir was published in 2019 to much critical acclaim and chronicles Takei's experience in the Japanese American internment camps during World War II.

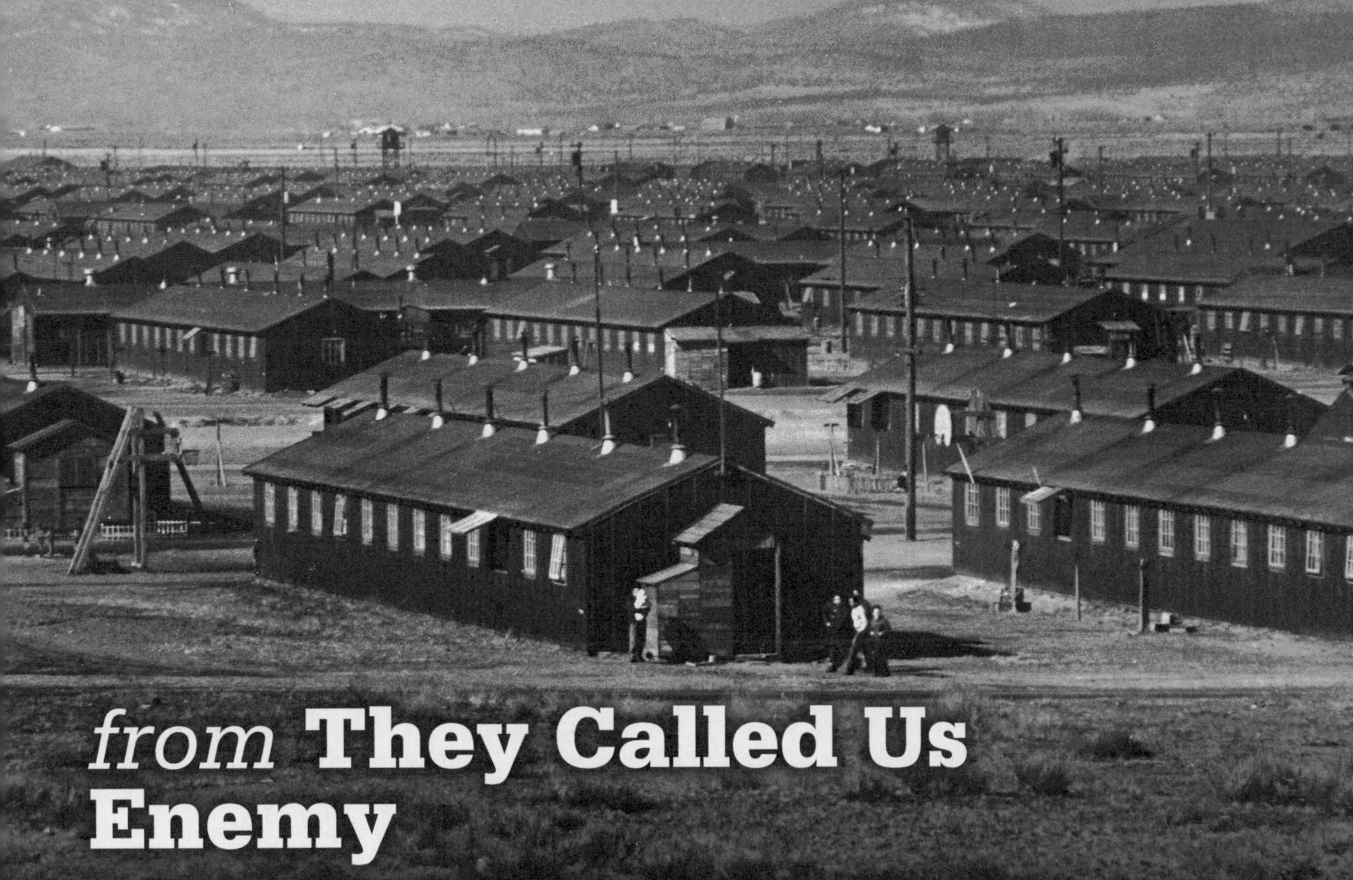

from They Called Us Enemy

Graphic Memoir by **George Takei, Justin Eisinger, Steven Scott,** and **Harmony Becker**

George Takei describes his family's imprisonment in an internment camp during World War II.

NOTICE & NOTE
As you read, use the side margins to make notes about the text.

After Japan bombed Pearl Harbor in 1941, the United States entered World War II and life for Japanese Americans changed radically. Ten weeks later, on February 19, 1942, President Franklin D. Roosevelt signed Executive Order 9066, which led to the imprisonment of 120,000 Japanese Americans. The order gave the military the authorization to name groups of people who could no longer freely live in certain areas, transport those people from those areas, and provide accommodations elsewhere. Though the order did not mention "Japanese" and "camps" specifically, within ten days the entire West Coast was off limits for people of Japanese descent, even if they were American citizens. The policy lasted from 1942 to 1945.

George Takei and his mother and father were among the U.S. citizens who were stripped of their rights and property and forced to live in internment camps. They were sent from Los Angeles to Camp Rohwer, Arkansas, where they lived for about five months before George's parents were asked to swear complete loyalty to the U.S. government. In the excerpt that follows, Takei describes the difficult choices his parents had to make between keeping their family together and trying to regain their legal status.

ANALYZE GRAPHIC NOVEL

Annotate: Mark the words that tell you the actions Japanese Americans took and the response they received.

Analyze: How do the images in these frames affect your understanding of the experiences of Japanese Americans at this time?

Don't forget to **Notice & Note** as you read the text.

ANALYZE AUTHOR'S PURPOSE

Annotate: Mark the details on this page that show a difference between how Japanese Americans perceived themselves and how they were perceived by others.

Analyze: What is Takei's purpose for showing this difference?

ANALYZE GRAPHIC NOVEL

Annotate: Mark the images of President Roosevelt on this page.

Analyze: How does showing the setting of the president announcing a change in policy, followed by a closeup of him, affect the reader?

Don't forget to **Notice & Note** as you read the text.

ANALYZE GRAPHIC NOVEL

Annotate: Recall that the space that separates frames in graphic novels is called the **gutter**. Mark the gutter on this page that seems to have a special purpose.

Analyze: Why did the authors and artist treat this gutter differently?

ANALYZE AUTHOR'S PURPOSE

Annotate: Mark the image that repeats and reinforces the text in a caption for that panel.

Analyze: What are the purpose and effect of the repetition of this text?

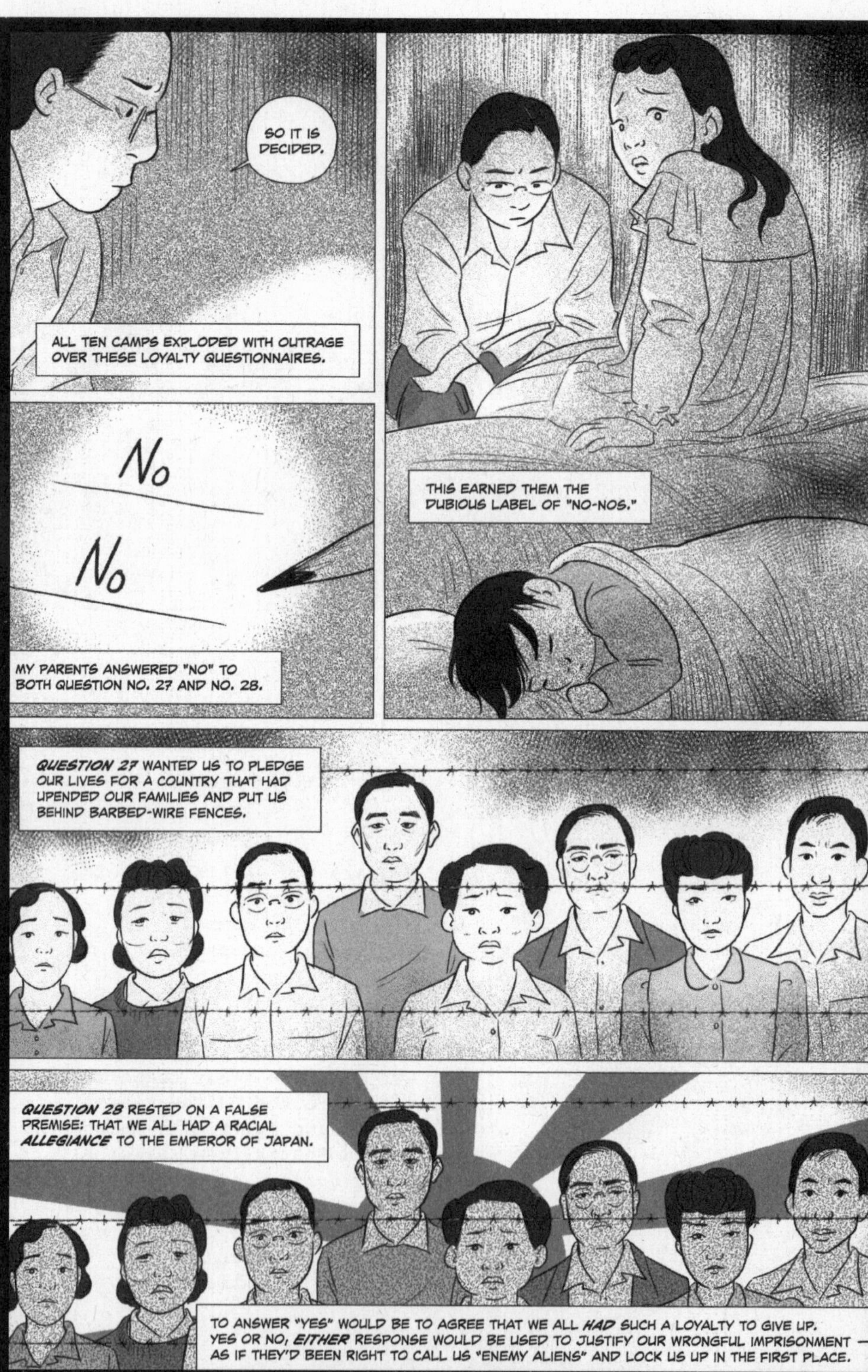

Don't forget to **Notice & Note** as you read the text.

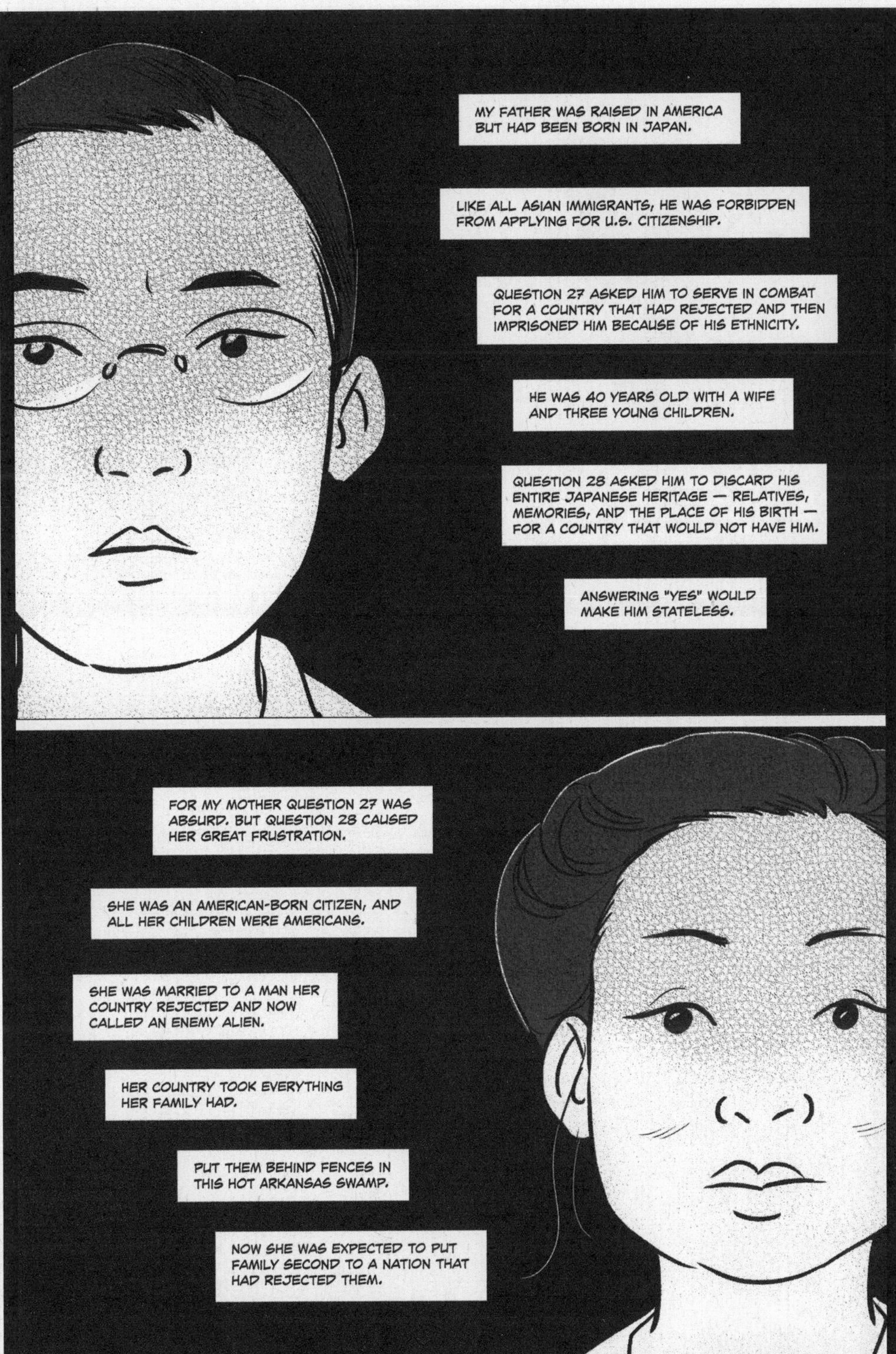

ANALYZE AUTHOR'S PURPOSE

Annotate: Mark the captions that show how Takei's parents felt about questions 27 and 28.

Analyze: Why do you think the creators broke out the captions in this way?

ANALYZE AUTHOR'S PURPOSE

Annotate: Mark the direction of the characters' gaze.

Analyze: How does presenting the characters in this way affect the reader?

ESSENTIAL QUESTION:
Can anyone achieve the American Dream?

Review your notes and add your thoughts to your **Response Log.**

COLLABORATIVE DISCUSSION

Get together with a partner and talk about whether it was equally honorable to answer No-No or Yes-Yes to questions 27 and 28.

Assessment Practice

Answer these questions before moving on to the **Analyze the Text** section on the following page.

1. Which of the following is an element unique to graphic novels and comic books?

- (A) dialogue
- (B) speech bubbles
- (C) narrative
- (D) text

2. What can you infer from the tombstones on page 680?

- (A) The tombstones were expensive.
- (B) The war was expensive.
- (C) Many soldiers were dying.
- (D) Many cemeteries were full.

3. Why did the author include the reasons some Japanese Americans answered yes to questions 27 and 28?

- (A) to contradict the rationale of the NO-NOS
- (B) to confuse the reader about the right way to respond
- (C) to suggest that the government was right to ask the questions
- (D) to show there were other ways of thinking about the questions

Test-Taking Strategies

Analyze the Text

Support your responses with evidence from the text.

NOTICE & NOTE

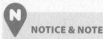

Review what you **noticed and noted** as you read the text. Your annotations can help you answer these questions.

1. **ANALYZE** Why do you think Takei chose to tell his story in a graphic novel format?

2. **ANALYZE** Review the use of dialogue in the excerpt. Why do you think the creators chose to have most of the dialogue spoken by people in positions of authority rather than Japanese Americans?

3. **EVALUATE** How effective is the artist's use of closeups? Cite examples in your response.

4. **EVALUATE** Was it surprising to read the panel about the Japanese Americans answering yes to questions 27 and 28? Explain.

5. **INTERPRET** On page 682, the final two panels show the same people with the same expressions but with different backgrounds and different shading on their faces. What do these changes in the images suggest?

6. **INFER** To understand panels in a graphic novel, the reader may need to make inferences based on the text and image. Fill in the chart below to explain some inferences in the excerpt from *They Called Us Enemy*.

Image	Text	Inference
Japanese American soldiers surrendering their weapons on page 679	". . . were required to surrender their weapons."	
An American flag being laid on a coffin on page 680	"America needed new soldiers."	
George's parents looking at him sleeping on page 682	"This earned them the dubious label of 'No-Nos.'"	

Choices

Here are some other ways to demonstrate your understanding of the ideas in this lesson.

Writing

↳ A Letter to the Past

We recognize the injustice of Executive Order 9066 today, but you can see that many people in power at the time felt that this action was defensible. Imagine you could write a letter to the politicians who supported Executive Order 9066 and send it to them in 1942. What would you say to show them that their view is wrong? You can include details from the excerpt you have read as well as any historical information you have learned or researched on your own.

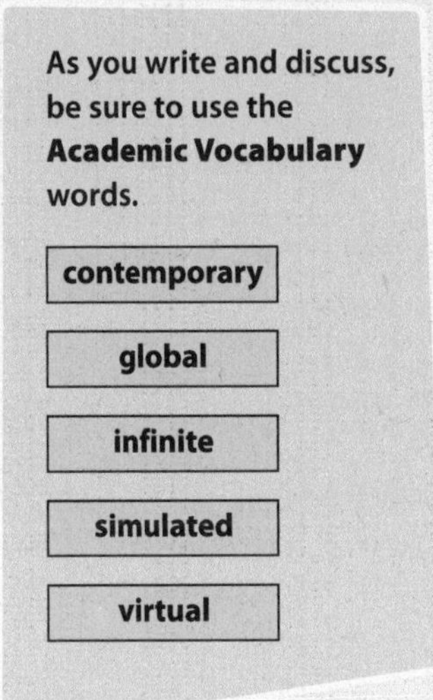
As you write and discuss, be sure to use the **Academic Vocabulary** words.
contemporary
global
infinite
simulated
virtual

Social & Emotional Learning

↳ Can We Make Wrongs Right?

As part of the Civil Liberties Act in 1988, President Ronald Reagan formally apologized on behalf of the U.S. government to Japanese Americans and granted every surviving internee $20,000. George Takei was active in getting this action passed as law. Are actions such as these effective in demonstrating respect for others and regret for injustices of the past? Write a paragraph sharing your thoughts.

Speaking & Listening

↳ What Made Star Trek Special

George Takei portrayed Mr. Sulu in the first *Star Trek* series. Gene Roddenberry, creator of *Star Trek,* once said of the show:

> "*Star Trek* was an attempt to say that humanity will reach maturity and wisdom on the day that it begins not just to tolerate, but take a special delight in differences in ideas and differences in life forms."

Based on this quote and what you have learned about Takei, why do you think the role of Mr. Sulu would appeal to Takei? Discuss with a small group and cite evidence from the text to support your answer.

Modern American Drama

The Rise of American Drama

Though drama is one of the oldest forms of literature, it was one of the last of the literary genres to develop in the United States. The Puritans in New England regarded theatrical performances as frivolous, so few plays were staged in the 1600s. During the 18th and 19th centuries, drama gradually became an accepted form of entertainment.

The 19th century in particular was a very active period in American theater. Most productions consisted of wildly theatrical spectacles such as simulated chariot races and burning cities, all staged by means of dazzling special effects. Every town of any size had its own theater or "opera house." In spite of all this theatrical activity, not one truly significant American drama was staged during the 1800s, a period that produced Herman Melville, Ralph Waldo Emerson, Walt Whitman, Emily Dickinson, and Mark Twain. Most of the plays performed in the United States were imported from Europe or adapted from novels.

The Black Crook is a work of musical theatre first produced, with great success, in New York in 1866.

Eugene O'Neill

The Trend Toward Realism

By the early 20th century, however, American playwrights began to reject the extravagant approach of the commercial theater. Instead, these writers favored realistic settings, characters, actions, and emotions that mirrored ordinary life. As with many artistic revolutions, this movement toward realism began outside the mainstream. By 1916, however, big New York audiences were flocking to small, obscure, off-Broadway theaters to see the works of writers such as Eugene O'Neill (1888–1953). His play *Beyond the Horizon* marked a turning point in presenting true-to-life characters who were struggling to understand their lives. Eventually, mainstream theaters began to showcase realistic plays, too, and realism became established as the dominant mode of American drama.

Building on O'Neill's achievement, American playwrights Thornton Wilder and Lillian Hellman created dramas in the 1930s and 1940s that met with critical and popular success. The post-World War II years also introduced Edward Albee and Lorraine Hansberry, who made significant contributions to the theater. Two notable figures of this time were Tennessee Williams (1911–1983) and Arthur Miller (1915–2005), playwrights who experimented with stagecraft while exploring modern themes and creating works of social relevance.

Lillian Hellman

Edward Albee

Lorraine Hansberry

Tennessee Williams

Death of a Salesman

The Glass Menagerie

A Raisin in the Sun

Themes in Modern American Drama

One of the most common themes explored by these playwrights was that of the American Dream. Willy Loman, the main character in Arthur Miller's *Death of a Salesman*, became the trademark figure of postwar American theater. A lowly salesman who has been discarded by the system to which he has mistakenly devoted his life, Willy Loman proved how the American Dream could become twisted and broken. In *The Glass Menagerie* and *A Streetcar Named Desire*, southerner Tennessee Williams portrayed characters who, unsuited to modern life, retreat into the fantasy world of an earlier era. In *A Raisin in the Sun*, Lorraine Hansberry (1930–1965) looked at the American Dream from the perspective of those who had been excluded. The first major Broadway play by an African American writer, *A Raisin in the Sun* was hailed by critics as "universal," while also capturing unique aspects of the African American experience. Politics, too, influenced playwrights. In the 1950s the U.S. government, suspicious of Communist activity in society, held hearings to root out Communist sympathizers. Senator Joseph McCarthy led the effort to identify people with ties to Communism and to pressure them into revealing the names of others who were also supporters of the cause. Miller's personal experiences with the House Un-American Activities Committee were the creative fodder for his most acclaimed play, *The Crucible*, in which he compared this "Red Scare" to the Salem witch trials.

The Crucible

In contemporary theater, there has been a shift back toward spectacular productions as commercial theater once again relies upon special effects, imaginative settings, and imaginary worlds. Musical theater has become very popular, and many musicals now have touring companies that take productions from Broadway to theaters all over the country. Like any art form, drama undergoes infinite adaptations to reflect the spirit of the times.

Conventions of Drama

The two main types of drama are tragedy and comedy. A **tragedy** recounts the downfall of a central character, while a **comedy** is light and humorous in tone and usually ends happily. **Farces** and **melodramas** are exaggerations of these two forms that feature absurd plots, stereotypical characters, humorous dialogue, and over-the-top emotional displays. Most dramas employ many of the narrative techniques seen in fiction, but there are a few elements unique to the genre.

Dramatic Elements	
Script	the text of the play, similar to a book, structured and organized by acts and scenes
Act	a major unit of action, similar to a chapter in a book. Some plays have as many as five acts
Scene	a subdivision of an act that often signals a change in time or place
Dialogue	the conversations characters have with each other. Critical moments in the dialogue can reveal key ideas and themes, character motivations, and conflict
Actions	movements that correspond to the dialogue, which can help move the plot along or offer insight into emotions and motivations
Stage Directions	italicized instructions that describe details about characters, such as when they enter and exit, and how they look, speak, and react to plot events and other characters. The stage directions also present details about the setting, props, costumes, lighting, and mood of a play
Exposition	background information that helps the audience understand events happening offstage or prior to other events, or explains the broader cultural, social, and historical context of a play. In Arthur Miller's *The Crucible,* the script relies heavily on exposition to explain the playwright's views on McCarthyism and the parallels he saw between the 1692 Salem witch trials and the 1954 Senate and House hearings on Communist activities

Get Ready

The Crucible

Drama by **Arthur Miller**

ESSENTIAL QUESTION:
When should personal integrity come before civic duty?

Engage Your Brain

Choose one or more of these activities to start connecting with the drama you're about to read.

Between a Rock and a Hard Place

Have you been in (or can you imagine) a situation where you had to make a choice and none of your options were good? Write a paragraph about the situation.

Mob Mentality

The phrase *mob mentality* refers to how people can by influenced to act emotionally rather than rationally. When you see a large group of people clamoring to purchase a popular gift, you are seeing mob mentality in action. With a group, create a list of examples of mob mentality that you have seen in books, shows, movies, or news stories. Then, discuss the effects of mob mentality in these examples.

What Was the House Un-American Activities Committee?

In 1956, Arthur Miller was subpoenaed to testify before the House Un-American Activities Committee. Conduct some research and answer the following questions.

- Why was the House Un-American Activities Committee formed?
- Why did they want to speak to Arthur Miller?
- What happened as a result of the committee's work?

Analyze Plot

The **plot** is the series of related events that make up a story or drama. To understand how Miller structures his plot, look for these elements:

- The **conflict** is a struggle between opposing forces. In Act One, local and personal conflicts escalate into a major, widespread conflict.
- **Complications** are additional problems that make the conflict more difficult to resolve. In Act Two, several events occur that add intensity.
- The **climax** is the point of highest tension or excitement. In Act Three, an event occurs that could change the outcome of the conflict.
- The **resolution** is the part of the play where conflicts are brought to a close. In Act Four, plot threads are tied up and questions are answered.

As you read, notice how dramatic elements, such as dialogue, stage directions, and exposition, advance the plot and develop the theme.

Focus on Genre
↳ **Drama**

- **is meant to be performed in front of an audience**
- **uses stage directions to describe characters, actions, setting, and mood**
- **uses dialogue to move the plot forward and convey the concerns of characters**

Analyze Characters

Miller reveals his characters' traits, relationships, and **motivations**—or reasons for behavior—through direct and indirect characterization. In **direct characterization,** specific details about a character are stated explicitly—often in the stage directions. **Indirect characterization** occurs when readers infer what a character is like based on clues in the text. Stage directions may provide these clues, but you should also look closely at what characters say (their **dialogue**) and how they behave (their **actions**).

In *The Crucible,* Miller incorporates three types of characters. As you read, note which characters fulfill these roles and how their interactions impact events.

- The **protagonist** is the central character of the play. This character is at the center of the conflict and often undergoes radical changes during the course of the play.
- The **antagonist** often opposes the protagonist, giving rise to the central conflict of the play.
- A **foil** is a minor character who provides a striking contrast to another character, thus emphasizing the other character's traits.

Throughout the play, the characters face **moral dilemmas—**situations in which there is a difficult choice between two courses of action. As you read, think about how motivations influence a character's choices when he or she is faced with a moral dilemma. What impact do these choices have on the plot and theme of the play?

Analyze Literary Devices

An **allegory** is a work with a literal and a symbolic meaning. In such a work, the characters and events represent broader ideas and concepts. The purpose of an allegory may be to convey a general truth about life, to teach a moral lesson, or to criticize a social institution.

At a glance, *The Crucible* is about the Salem witch trials, in which 200 individuals were accused of witchcraft between 1692 and 1693. However, Arthur Miller wrote *The Crucible* in the 1950s at the height of the Red Scare. Knowing this, the play can be read as an allegory on McCarthyism.

In addition to allegory, Miller employs other literary devices in the play.

As you read, use a chart like this one to keep track of literary devices and how they help advance the plot, set a mood, or suggest a theme.

Paradox	Dramatic Irony	Figurative Language
Statement that seems to contradict itself but suggests an important truth. Example from text: "It was . . . an autocracy by consent. . . ." Autocracies are usually dictatorships—no consent is given; rulers just seize power from the people.	Contrast between appearance and reality in which the reader knows more about a situation than the characters do. Example from text: "Let either of you breathe a word . . . and I will bring a pointy reckoning. . . ." The reader knows what Abigail and the girls did in the woods, but other characters don't.	Descriptive language that is not literally true, such as similes, metaphors, and symbols. Example from text: "The road past my house is a pilgrimage to Salem all morning." Proctor's metaphor compares the road to Salem with the religious practice of journeying to holy shrines.

Annotation in Action

Here are one student's notes on characters and their motives in *The Crucible.* As you read, focus on details that help you see why characters act the way they do.

Susanna. Aye, sir, he have been searchin' his books since he left you, sir. But he bid me tell you, that you might look to unnatural things for the cause of it.

Parris (*his eyes going wide*). No—no. There be no unnatural cause here. Tell him I have sent for Reverend Hale of Beverly, and Mr. Hale will surely confirm that. Let him look to medicine and put out all thought of unnatural causes here. There be none.

The reaction of Parris to the idea his daughter is sick by "unnatural causes" shows he is very worried that this was even said. Fear may influence his future actions.

The Crucible

Drama by **Arthur Miller**

Arthur Miller (1915–2005)

Arthur Miller was born in New York City into an upper-middle-class family. His comfortable early life changed when the Great Depression eroded his family's economic circumstances. Miller was unable to go to college until he earned the tuition money by working in a warehouse. Eventually, he attended the University of Michigan. Miller won several awards for his plays during college and chose to pursue a career in the theater. *All My Sons* and *Death of a Salesman*, a play that won a Pulitzer Prize in 1949, made Miller a star.

Around the same time, hearings were being conducted by Congress to identify suspected Communists. Miller was called to testify before the committee about his association with the American Communist Party. Although he admitted to having attended a few meetings years earlier, he refused to "name names" of other people involved in the meetings. As a result, he was cited for contempt of Congress; this conviction was later overturned. The events of this time period inspired him to write *The Crucible*, set during the Salem, Massachusetts, witch trials of 1692. He wrote the play to warn against mass hysteria and to plead for freedom and tolerance. In general, Miller's writing explores issues relevant to contemporary readers, such as the complexities of family relationships, personal responsibility, and morality. Many consider him to be the 20th century's greatest American playwright.

"I don't see how you can write anything decent without using as your basis the question of right or wrong."

—Arthur Miller

NOTICE & NOTE

As you read, use the side margins to make notes about the text.

There is something afoot in Salem, Massachusetts. Is the devil walking among the residents or is the mischief something more human in nature?

Cast of Characters

(In Order of Appearance)

Reverend Samuel Parris
Betty Parris
Tituba
Abigail Williams
Susanna Walcott
Mrs. Ann Putnam
Thomas Putnam
Mercy Lewis
Mary Warren
John Proctor
Rebecca Nurse
Giles Corey
Reverend John Hale
Elizabeth Proctor
Francis Nurse
Ezekiel Cheever
Marshal Herrick
Judge Hathorne
Martha Corey
Deputy Governor Danforth
Girls of Salem
Sarah Good

ACT ONE

An Overture

1 *(A small upper bedroom in the home of Reverend Samuel Parris, Salem, Massachusetts, in the spring of the year 1692.*

2 *There is a narrow window at the left. Through its leaded panes the morning sunlight streams. A candle still burns near the bed, which is at the right. A chest, a chair, and a small table are the other furnishings. At the back a door opens on the landing of the stairway to the ground floor. The room gives off an air of clean spareness. The roof rafters are exposed, and the wood colors are raw and unmellowed.*

3 *As the curtain rises,* Reverend Parris *is discovered kneeling beside the bed, evidently in prayer. His daughter,* Betty Parris, *aged ten, is lying on the bed, inert.)*

ANALYZE CHARACTERS

Annotate: Mark words and phrases in paragraph 4 that describe Parris.

Infer: What impression do you get about Parris from these details? Are these details an example of direct characterization or indirect characterization? Explain.

4 At the time of these events Parris was in his middle forties. In history he cut a villainous path, and there is very little good to be said for him. He believed he was being persecuted wherever he went, despite his best efforts to win people and God to his side. In meeting, he felt insulted if someone rose to shut the door without first asking his permission. He was a widower with no interest in children, or talent with them. He regarded them as young adults, and until this strange crisis he, like the rest of Salem, never conceived that the children were anything but thankful for being permitted to walk straight, eyes slightly lowered, arms at the sides, and mouths shut until bidden to speak.

Don't forget to **Notice & Note** as you read the text.

5 His house stood in the "town"—but we today would hardly call it a village. The meeting house[1] was nearby, and from this point outward—toward the bay or inland—there were a few small-windowed, dark houses snuggling against the raw Massachusetts winter. Salem had been established hardly forty years before. To the European world the whole province was a barbaric frontier inhabited by a sect of fanatics who, nevertheless, were shipping out products of slowly increasing quantity and value.

6 No one can really know what their lives were like. They had no novelists—and would not have permitted anyone to read a novel if one were handy. Their creed forbade anything resembling a theater or "vain enjoyment." They did not celebrate Christmas, and a holiday from work meant only that they must concentrate even more upon prayer.

7 Which is not to say that nothing broke into this strict and somber way of life. When a new farmhouse was built, friends assembled to "raise the roof," and there would be special foods cooked and probably some potent cider passed around. There was a good supply of ne'er-do-wells in Salem, who dallied at the shovelboard[2] in Bridget Bishop's tavern. Probably more than the creed, hard work kept the morals of the place from spoiling, for the people were forced to fight the land like heroes for every grain of corn, and no man had very much time for fooling around.

8 That there were some jokers, however, is indicated by the practice of appointing a two-man patrol whose duty was to "walk forth in the time of God's worship to take notice of such as either lye about the meeting house, without attending to the word and ordinances, or that lye at home or in the fields without giving good account thereof, and to take the names of such persons, and to present them to the magistrates, whereby they may be accordingly proceeded against." This predilection for minding other people's business was time-honored among the people of Salem, and it undoubtedly created many of the suspicions which were to feed the coming madness. It was also, in my opinion, one of the things that a John Proctor would rebel against, for the time of the armed camp had almost passed, and since the country was reasonably—although not wholly—safe, the old disciplines were beginning to rankle. But, as in all such matters, the issue was not clear-cut, for danger was still a possibility, and in unity still lay the best promise of safety.

9 The edge of the wilderness was close by. The American continent stretched endlessly west, and it was full of mystery for them. It stood, dark and threatening, over their shoulders night and day, for out of it Indian tribes marauded from time to time, and Reverend Parris had parishioners who had lost relatives to these heathen.

[1] **meeting house:** the most important building in the Puritan community, used both for worship and for meetings.

[2] **shovelboard:** a game in which a coin or disc is shoved across a board by hand.

10 The parochial snobbery of these people was partly responsible for their failure to convert the Indians. Probably they also preferred to take land from heathens rather than from fellow Christians. At any rate, very few Indians were converted, and the Salem folk believed that the virgin forest was the Devil's last preserve, his home base and the citadel of his final stand. To the best of their knowledge the American forest was the last place on earth that was not paying homage to God.

11 For these reasons, among others, they carried about an air of innate resistance, even of persecution. Their fathers had, of course, been persecuted in England. So now they and their church found it necessary to deny any other sect its freedom, lest their New Jerusalem[3] be defiled and corrupted by wrong ways and deceitful ideas.

12 They believed, in short, that they held in their steady hands the candle that would light the world. We have inherited this belief, and it has helped and hurt us. It helped them with the discipline it gave them. They were a dedicated folk, by and large, and they had to be to survive the life they had chosen or been born into in this country.

13 The proof of their belief 's value to them may be taken from the opposite character of the first Jamestown settlement, farther south, in Virginia. The Englishmen who landed there were motivated mainly by a hunt for profit. They had thought to pick off the wealth of the new country and then return rich to England. They were a band of individualists, and a much more ingratiating group than the Massachusetts men. But Virginia destroyed them. Massachusetts tried to kill off the Puritans, but they combined; they set up a communal society which, in the beginning, was little more than an armed camp with an autocratic and very devoted leadership. It was, however, an autocracy by consent, for they were united from top to bottom by a commonly held ideology whose perpetuation was the reason and justification for all their sufferings. So their self-denial, their purposefulness, their suspicion of all vain pursuits, their hard-handed justice, were altogether perfect instruments for the conquest of this space so antagonistic to man.

14 But the people of Salem in 1692 were not quite the dedicated folk that arrived on the *Mayflower*. A vast differentiation had taken place, and in their own time a revolution had unseated the royal government and substituted a junta which was at this moment in power.[4] The times, to their eyes, must have been out of joint, and to the common folk must have seemed as insoluble and complicated as do ours today. It is not hard to see how easily many could have been led to believe that the time of confusion had been brought upon them by deep and darkling forces. No hint of such speculation appears on the court

[3] **New Jerusalem:** in Christianity, a heavenly city and the last resting place of the souls saved by Jesus. It was considered the ideal city, and Puritans modeled their communities after it.

[4] **a junta** (ho͝on´tə) **. . . power:** Junta is a Spanish term meaning "a small, elite ruling council." The reference here is to the group that led England's Glorious Revolution of 1688–1689.

record, but social disorder in any age breeds such mystical suspicions, and when, as in Salem, wonders are brought forth from below the social surface, it is too much to expect people to hold back very long from laying on the victims with all the force of their frustrations.

15 The Salem tragedy, which is about to begin in these pages, developed from a paradox. It is a paradox in whose grip we still live, and there is no prospect yet that we will discover its resolution. Simply, it was this: for good purposes, even high purposes, the people of Salem developed a theocracy, a combine of state and religious power whose function was to keep the community together, and to prevent any kind of disunity that might open it to destruction by material or ideological enemies. It was forged for a necessary purpose and accomplished that purpose. But all organization is and must be grounded on the idea of exclusion and prohibition, just as two objects cannot occupy the same space. Evidently the time came in New England when the repressions of order were heavier than seemed warranted by the dangers against which the order was organized. The witch-hunt was a perverse manifestation of the panic which set in among all classes when the balance began to turn toward greater individual freedom.

16 When one rises above the individual villainy displayed, one can only pity them all, just as we shall be pitied someday. It is still impossible for man to organize his social life without repressions, and the balance has yet to be struck between order and freedom.

17 The witch-hunt was not, however, a mere repression. It was also, and as importantly, a long overdue opportunity for everyone so inclined to express publicly his guilt and sins, under the cover of accusations against the victims. It suddenly became possible—and patriotic and holy—for a man to say that Martha Corey had come into his bedroom at night, and that, while his wife was sleeping at his side, Martha laid herself down on his chest and "nearly suffocated him." Of course it was her spirit only, but his satisfaction at confessing himself was no lighter than if it had been Martha herself. One could not ordinarily speak such things in public.

18 Long-held hatreds of neighbors could now be openly expressed, and vengeance taken, despite the Bible's charitable injunctions. Land-lust which had been expressed before by constant bickering over boundaries and deeds, could now be elevated to the arena of morality; one could cry witch against one's neighbor and feel perfectly justified in the bargain. Old scores could be settled on a plane of heavenly combat between Lucifer and the Lord; suspicions and the envy of the miserable toward the happy could and did burst out in the general revenge.

19 (Reverend Parris *is praying now, and, though we cannot hear his words, a sense of his confusion hangs about him. He mumbles, then seems about to weep; then he weeps, then prays again; but his daughter does not stir on the bed.*

Don't forget to **Notice & Note** as you read the text.

ANALYZE LITERARY DEVICES

Annotate: Mark the paradox that Miller refers to in the final section of the exposition.

Interpret: How does the paradox illuminate the playwright's perspective on his subject?

20 *The door opens, and his Negro slave enters.* Tituba *is in her forties.* Parris *brought her with him from Barbados, where he spent some years as a merchant before entering the ministry. She enters as one does who can no longer bear to be barred from the sight of her beloved, but she is also very frightened because her slave sense has warned her that, as always, trouble in this house eventually lands on her back.*)

21 **Tituba** (*already taking a step backward*). My Betty be hearty soon?

Ed

Close Read Screencast

Listen to a modeled close read of this text.

22 **Parris.** Out of here!

23 **Tituba** (*backing to the door*). My Betty not goin' die . . .

24 **Parris** (*scrambling to his feet in a fury*). Out of my sight! (*She is gone.*) Out of my—(*He is overcome with sobs. He clamps his teeth against them and closes the door and leans against it, exhausted.*) Oh, my God! God help me! (*Quaking with fear, mumbling to himself through his sobs, he goes to the bed and gently takes* Betty's *hand.*) Betty. Child. Dear child. Will you wake, will you open up your eyes! Betty, little one . . .

ANALYZE CHARACTERS

Annotate: Mark the description of Abigail's personality in paragraph 25.

Infer: What does this description suggest about whether Parris should believe what she says?

25 (*He is bending to kneel again when his niece,* Abigail Williams, *seventeen, enters—a strikingly beautiful girl, an orphan, with an endless capacity for dissembling. Now she is all worry and apprehension and propriety.*)

26 **Abigail.** Uncle? (*He looks to her.*) Susanna Walcott's here from Doctor Griggs.

27 **Parris.** Oh? Let her come, let her come.

28 **Abigail** (*leaning out the door to call to Susanna, who is down the hall a few steps*). Come in, Susanna. (Susanna Walcott, *a little younger than* Abigail, *a nervous, hurried girl, enters.*)

29 **Parris** (*eagerly*). What does the doctor say, child?

30 **Susanna** (*craning around* Parris *to get a look at* Betty). He bid me come and tell you, reverend sir, that he cannot discover no medicine for it in his books.

31 **Parris.** Then he must search on.

32 **Susanna.** Aye, sir, he have been searchin' his books since he left you, sir. But he bid me tell you, that you might look to unnatural things for the cause of it.

33 **Parris** (*his eyes going wide*). No—no. There be no unnatural cause here. Tell him I have sent for Reverend Hale of Beverly, and Mr. Hale will surely confirm that. Let him look to medicine and put out all thought of unnatural causes here. There be none.

34 **Susanna.** Aye, sir. He bid me tell you. (*She turns to go.*)

35 **Abigail.** Speak nothin' of it in the village, Susanna.

36 **Parris.** Go directly home and speak nothing of unnatural causes.

Don't forget to **Notice & Note** as you read the text.

37 **Susanna.** Aye, sir. I pray for her. (*She goes out.*)

38 **Abigail.** Uncle, the rumor of witchcraft is all about; I think you'd best go down and deny it yourself. The parlor's packed with people, sir. I'll sit with her.

39 **Parris** (*pressed, turns on her*). And what shall I say to them? That my daughter and my niece I discovered dancing like heathen in the forest?

40 **Abigail.** Uncle, we did dance; let you tell them I confessed it—and I'll be whipped if I must be. But they're speakin' of witchcraft. Betty's not witched.

41 **Parris.** Abigail, I cannot go before the congregation when I know you have not opened with me. What did you do with her in the forest?

42 **Abigail.** We did dance, uncle, and when you leaped out of the bush so suddenly, Betty was frightened and then she fainted. And there's the whole of it.

43 **Parris.** Child. Sit you down.

44 **Abigail** (*quavering, as she sits*). I would never hurt Betty. I love her dearly.

45 **Parris.** Now look you, child, your punishment will come in its time. But if you trafficked with[5] spirits in the forest I must know it now, for surely my enemies will, and they will ruin me with it.

46 **Abigail.** But we never conjured spirits.

47 **Parris.** Then why can she not move herself since midnight? This child is desperate! (Abigail *lowers her eyes.*) It must come out—my enemies will bring it out. Let me know what you done there. Abigail, do you understand that I have many enemies?

48 **Abigail.** I have heard of it, uncle.

49 **Parris.** There is a faction that is sworn to drive me from my pulpit. Do you understand that?

50 **Abigail.** I think so, sir.

51 **Parris.** Now then, in the midst of such disruption, my own household is discovered to be the very center of some obscene practice. Abominations are done in the forest—

52 **Abigail.** It were sport, uncle!

53 **Parris** (*pointing at* Betty). You call this sport? (*She lowers her eyes. He pleads.*) Abigail, if you know something that may help the doctor, for God's sake tell it to me. (*She is silent.*) I saw Tituba waving her arms over the fire when I came on you. Why was she doing that? And I heard a screeching and gibberish coming from her mouth. She were swaying like a dumb beast over that fire!

[5] **trafficked with:** met with.

54 **Abigail.** She always sings her Barbados songs, and we dance.

55 **Parris.** I cannot blink what I saw, Abigail, for my enemies will not blink it. I saw a dress lying on the grass.

56 **Abigail** (*innocently*). A dress?

57 **Parris** (*It is very hard to say*). Aye, a dress. And I thought I saw—someone naked running through the trees!

58 **Abigail** (*in terror*). No one was naked! You mistake yourself, uncle!

59 **Parris** (*with anger*). I saw it! (*He moves from her. Then, resolved*) Now tell me true, Abigail. And I pray you feel the weight of truth upon you, for now my ministry's at stake, my ministry and perhaps your cousin's life. Whatever abomination you have done, give me all of it now, for I dare not be taken unaware when I go before them down there.

60 **Abigail.** There is nothin' more. I swear it, uncle.

61 **Parris** (*studies her, then nods, half convinced*). Abigail, I have fought here three long years to bend these stiff-necked people to me, and now, just now when some good respect is rising for me in the parish, you compromise my very character. I have given you a home, child, I have put clothes upon your back—now give me upright answer. Your name in the town—it is entirely white, is it not?

62 **Abigail** (*with an edge of resentment*). Why, I am sure it is, sir. There be no blush about my name.[6]

63 **Parris** (*to the point*). Abigail, is there any other cause than you have told me, for your being discharged from Goody[7] Proctor's service? I have heard it said, and I tell you as I heard it, that she comes so rarely to the church this year for she will not sit so close to something soiled. What signified that remark?

64 **Abigail.** She hates me, uncle, she must, for I would not be her slave. It's a bitter woman, a lying, cold, sniveling woman, and I will not work for such a woman!

NOTICE & NOTE

CONTRASTS AND CONTRADICTIONS

When you notice behavior that contradicts previous behavior or well-established patterns, you've found a **Contrasts and Contradictions** signpost.

Notice & Note: Mark words in paragraphs 66–68 that show a new side of Abigail.

Cite Text Evidence: What contradictory behavior is revealed in Abigail's statements and the stage directions in these lines?

65 **Parris.** She may be. And yet it has troubled me that you are now seven month out of their house, and in all this time no other family has ever called for your service.

66 **Abigail.** They want slaves, not such as I. Let them send to Barbados for that. I will not black my face for any of them! (*with ill-concealed resentment at him*) Do you begrudge my bed, uncle?

67 **Parris.** No—no.

68 **Abigail** (*in a temper*). My name is good in the village! I will not have it said my name is soiled! Goody Proctor is a gossiping liar!

69 (*Enter* Mrs. Ann Putnam. *She is a twisted soul of forty-five, a death-ridden woman, haunted by dreams.*)

---

[6] **There be . . . my name:** There is nothing wrong with my reputation.
[7] **Goody:** short for *goodwife*, the Puritan equivalent of *Mrs.*

Don't forget to **Notice & Note** as you read the text.

70 **Parris** (*as soon as the door begins to open*). No—no, I cannot have anyone. (*He sees her, and a certain deference springs into him, although his worry remains.*) Why, Goody Putnam, come in.

71 **Mrs. Putnam** (*full of breath, shiny-eyed*). It is a marvel. It is surely a stroke of hell upon you.

72 **Parris.** No, Goody Putnam, it is—

73 **Mrs. Putnam** (*glancing at* Betty). How high did she fly, how high?

74 **Parris.** No, no, she never flew—

75 **Mrs. Putnam** (*very pleased with it*). Why, it's sure she did. Mr. Collins saw her goin' over Ingersoll's barn, and come down light as bird, he says!

76 **Parris.** Now, look you, Goody Putnam, she never— (*Enter* Thomas Putnam, *a well-to-do, hard-handed landowner, near fifty.*) Oh, good morning, Mr. Putnam.

77 **Putnam.** It is a providence the thing is out now! It is a providence. (*He goes directly to the bed.*)

78 **Parris.** What's out, sir, what's—?

79 (Mrs. Putnam *goes to the bed.*)

80 **Putnam** (*looking down at* Betty). Why, *her eyes* is closed! Look you, Ann.

81 **Mrs. Putnam.** Why, that's strange. (*to* Parris) Ours is open.

82 **Parris** (*shocked*). Your Ruth is sick?

83 **Mrs. Putnam** (*with vicious certainty*). I'd not call it sick; the Devil's touch is heavier than sick. It's death, y'know, it's death drivin' into them, forked and hoofed.

84 **Parris.** Oh, pray not! Why, how does Ruth ail?

85 **Mrs. Putnam.** She ails as she must—she never waked this morning, but her eyes open and she walks, and hears naught, sees naught, and cannot eat. Her soul is taken, surely.

86 (Parris *is struck.*)

87 **Putnam** (*as though for further details*). They say you've sent for Reverend Hale of Beverly?

88 **Parris** (*with dwindling conviction now*). A precaution only. He has much experience in all demonic arts, and I—

89 **Mrs. Putnam.** He has indeed; and found a witch in Beverly last year, and let you remember that.

90 **Parris.** Now, Goody Ann, they only thought that were a witch, and I am certain there be no element of witchcraft here.

91 **Putnam.** No witchcraft! Now look you, Mr. Parris—

92 **Parris.** Thomas, Thomas, I pray you, leap not to witchcraft. I know that you—you least of all, Thomas, would ever wish so disastrous a charge laid upon me. We cannot leap to witchcraft. They will howl me out of Salem for such corruption in my house.

93 A word about Thomas Putnam. He was a man with many grievances, at least one of which appears justified. Some time before, his wife's brother-in-law, James Bayley, had been turned down as minister of Salem. Bayley had all the qualifications, and a two-thirds vote into the bargain, but a faction stopped his acceptance, for reasons that are not clear.

94 Thomas Putnam was the eldest son of the richest man in the village. He had fought the Indians at Narragansett,[8] and was deeply interested in parish affairs. He undoubtedly felt it poor payment that the village should so blatantly disregard his candidate for one of its more important offices, especially since he regarded himself as the intellectual superior of most of the people around him.

95 His vindictive nature was demonstrated long before the witchcraft began. Another former Salem minister, George Burroughs, had had to borrow money to pay for his wife's funeral, and, since the parish was remiss in his salary, he was soon bankrupt. Thomas and his brother John had Burroughs jailed for debts the man did not owe. The incident is important only in that Burroughs succeeded in becoming minister where Bayley, Thomas Putnam's brother-in-law, had been rejected; the motif of resentment is clear here. Thomas

[8] **fought the Indians at Narragansett:** The Puritans fought a series of battles against the Narragansett Indians over territory that both groups had settled on.

Putnam felt that his own name and the honor of his family had been smirched by the village, and he meant to right matters however he could.

96 Another reason to believe him a deeply embittered man was his attempt to break his father's will, which left a disproportionate amount to a stepbrother. As with every other public cause in which he tried to force his way, he failed in this.

97 So it is not surprising to find that so many accusations against people are in the handwriting of Thomas Putnam, or that his name is so often found as a witness corroborating the supernatural testimony, or that his daughter led the crying-out at the most opportune junctures of the trials, especially when—But we'll speak of that when we come to it.

Don't forget to **Notice & Note** as you read the text.

98 **Putnam** (*At the moment he is intent upon getting* Parris, *for whom he has only contempt, to move toward the abyss*). Mr. Parris, I have taken your part in all contention here, and I would continue; but I cannot if you hold back in this. There are hurtful, vengeful spirits layin' hands on these children.

ANALYZE PLOT

Annotate: Mark details in paragraph 98 that suggest a threat from Mr. Putman against Parris.

Analyze: What conflict is evident in the exchange between Putnam and Parris?

99 **Parris.** But, Thomas, you cannot—

100 **Putnam.** Ann! Tell Mr. Parris what you have done.

101 **Mrs. Putnam.** Reverend Parris, I have laid seven babies unbaptized in the earth. Believe me, sir, you never saw more hearty babies born. And yet, each would wither in my arms the very night of their birth. I have spoke nothin', but my heart has clamored intimations.[9] And now, this year, my Ruth, my only—I see her turning strange. A secret child she has become this year, and shrivels like a sucking mouth were pullin' on her life too. And so I thought to send her to your Tituba—

102 **Parris.** To Tituba! What may Tituba—?

103 **Mrs. Putnam.** Tituba knows how to speak to the dead, Mr. Parris.

104 **Parris.** Goody Ann, it is a formidable sin to conjure up the dead!

105 **Mrs. Putnam.** I take it on my soul, but who else may surely tell us what person murdered my babies?

106 **Parris** (*horrified*). Woman!

107 **Mrs. Putnam.** They were murdered, Mr. Parris! And mark this proof! Mark it! Last night my Ruth were ever so close to their little spirits; I know it, sir. For how else is she struck dumb now except some power of darkness would stop her mouth? It is a marvelous sign, Mr. Parris!

108 **Putnam.** Don't you understand it, sir? There is a murdering witch among us, bound to keep herself in the dark. (Parris *turns to* Betty, *a frantic terror rising in him.*) Let your enemies make of it what they will, you cannot blink it more.

[9] **clamored intimations** (klăm´ərd ĭn´tə-mā´-shənz): nagging suspicions.

109 **Parris** (*to* Abigail). Then you were conjuring spirits last night.

110 **Abigail** (*whispering*). Not I, sir—Tituba and Ruth.

111 **Parris** (*turns now, with new fear, and goes to* Betty, *looks down at her, and then, gazing off*). Oh, Abigail, what proper payment for my charity! Now I am undone.

112 **Putnam.** You are not undone! Let you take hold here. Wait for no one to charge you—declare it yourself. You have discovered witchcraft—

113 **Parris.** In my house? In my house, Thomas? They will topple me with this! They will make of it a—

114 (*Enter* Mercy Lewis, *the Putnams' servant, a fat, sly, merciless girl of eighteen.*)

115 **Mercy.** Your pardons. I only thought to see how Betty is.

116 **Putnam.** Why aren't you home? Who's with Ruth?

117 **Mercy.** Her grandma come. She's improved a little, I think—she give a powerful sneeze before.

118 **Mrs. Putnam.** Ah, there's a sign of life!

119 **Mercy.** I'd fear no more, Goody Putnam. It were a grand sneeze; another like it will shake her wits together, I'm sure. (*She goes to the bed to look.*)

120 **Parris.** Will you leave me now, Thomas? I would pray a while alone.

121 **Abigail.** Uncle, you've prayed since midnight. Why do you not go down and—

122 **Parris.** No—no. (*to* Putnam) I have no answer for that crowd. I'll wait till Mr. Hale arrives. (*to get* Mrs. Putnam *to leave*) If you will, Goody Ann . . .

123 **Putnam.** Now look you, sir. Let you strike out against the Devil, and the village will bless you for it! Come down, speak to them—pray with them. They're thirsting for your word, Mister! Surely you'll pray with them.

124 **Parris** (*swayed*). I'll lead them in a psalm, but let you say nothing of witchcraft yet. I will not discuss it. The cause is yet unknown. I have had enough contention since I came; I want no more.

125 **Mrs. Putnam.** Mercy, you go home to Ruth, d'y'hear?

126 **Mercy.** Aye, mum.

127 (Mrs. Putnam *goes out.*)

128 **Parris** (*to* Abigail). If she starts for the window, cry for me at once.

129 **Abigail.** I will, uncle.

130 **Parris** (*to* Putnam). There is a terrible power in her arms today. (*He goes out with* Putnam.)

131 **Abigail** (*with hushed trepidation*). How is Ruth sick?

132 **Mercy.** It's weirdish, I know not—she seems to walk like a dead one since last night.

133 **Abigail** (*turns at once and goes to* Betty, *and now, with fear in her voice*). Betty? (Betty *doesn't move. She shakes her.*) Now stop this! Betty! Sit up now!

134 (Betty *doesn't stir.* Mercy *comes over.*)

135 **Mercy.** Have you tried beatin' her? I gave Ruth a good one and it waked her for a minute. Here, let me have her.

136 **Abigail** (*holding* Mercy *back*). No, he'll be comin' up. Listen, now; if they be questioning us, tell them we danced—I told him as much already.

137 **Mercy.** Aye. And what more?

138 **Abigail.** He knows Tituba conjured Ruth's sisters to come out of the grave.

139 **Mercy.** And what more?

140 **Abigail.** He saw you naked.

141 **Mercy** (*clapping her hands together with a frightened laugh*). Oh, Jesus!

142 (*Enter* Mary Warren, *breathless. She is seventeen, a subservient, naive, lonely girl.*)

143 **Mary Warren.** What'll we do? The village is out! I just come from the farm; the whole country's talkin' witchcraft! They'll be callin' us witches, Abby!

144 **Mercy** (*pointing and looking at* Mary Warren). She means to tell, I know it.

145 **Mary Warren.** Abby, we've got to tell. Witchery's a hangin' error, a hangin' like they done in Boston two year ago! We must tell the truth, Abby! You'll only be whipped for dancin', and the other things!

146 **Abigail.** Oh, *we'll* be whipped!

147 **Mary Warren.** I never done none of it, Abby. I only looked!

148 **Mercy** (*moving menacingly toward* Mary). Oh, you're a great one for lookin', aren't you, Mary Warren? What a grand peeping courage you have!

149 (Betty, *on the bed, whimpers.* Abigail *turns to her at once.*)

150 **Abigail.** Betty? (*She goes to* Betty.) Now, Betty, dear, wake up now. It's Abigail. (*She sits* Betty *up and furiously shakes her.*) I'll beat you, Betty! (Betty *whimpers.*) My, you seem improving. I talked to your papa and I told him everything. So there's nothing to—

151 **Betty** (*darts off the bed, frightened of* Abigail, *and flattens herself against the wall*). I want my mama!

Don't forget to **Notice & Note** as you read the text.

152 **Abigail** (*with alarm, as she cautiously approaches* Betty). What ails you, Betty? Your mama's dead and buried.

153 **Betty.** I'll fly to Mama. Let me fly! (*She raises her arms as though to fly, and streaks for the window, gets one leg out.*)

154 **Abigail** (*pulling her away from the window*). I told him everything; he knows now, he knows everything we—

155 **Betty.** You drank blood, Abby! You didn't tell him that!

156 **Abigail.** Betty, you never say that again! You will never—

157 **Betty.** You did, you did! You drank a charm to kill John Proctor's wife! You drank a charm to kill Goody Proctor!

ANALYZE CHARACTERS

Annotate: Mark details in paragraphs 158–160 that reveal Abigail's relationship to the other girls.

Analyze: What does Abigail's behavior in these lines reveal about her character and motivations?

158 **Abigail** (*smashes her across the face*). Shut it! Now shut it!

159 **Betty** (*collapsing on the bed*). Mama, Mama! (*She dissolves into sobs.*)

160 **Abigail.** Now look you. All of you. We danced. And Tituba conjured Ruth Putnam's dead sisters. And that is all. And mark this. Let either of you breathe a word, or the edge of a word, about the other things, and I will come to you in the black of some terrible night and I will bring a pointy reckoning that will shudder you.[10] And you know I can do it; I saw Indians smash my dear parents' heads on the pillow next to mine, and I have seen some reddish work done at night, and I can make you wish you had never seen the sun go down! (*She goes to* Betty *and roughly sits her up.*) Now, you—sit up and stop this!

161 (*But* Betty *collapses in her hands and lies inert on the bed.*)

162 **Mary Warren** (*with hysterical fright*). What's got her? (Abigail *stares in fright at* Betty.) Abby, she's going to die! It's a sin to conjure, and we—

163 **Abigail** (*starting for* Mary). I say shut it, Mary Warren! (*Enter* John Proctor. *On seeing him,* Mary Warren *leaps in fright.*)

164 Proctor was a farmer in his middle thirties. He need not have been a partisan of any faction in the town, but there is evidence to suggest that he had a sharp and biting way with hypocrites. He was the kind of man—powerful of body, even-tempered, and not easily led—who cannot refuse support to partisans without drawing their deepest resentment. In Proctor's presence a fool felt his foolishness instantly—and a Proctor is always marked for calumny[11] therefore.

165 But as we shall see, the steady manner he displays does not spring from an untroubled soul. He is a sinner, a sinner not only against the moral fashion of the time, but against his own vision of decent conduct. These people had no ritual for the washing away of sins. It is another trait we inherited from them, and it has helped to discipline us as well as to breed hypocrisy among us. Proctor, respected and even feared in Salem, has come to regard himself as a kind of fraud. But no hint of this has yet appeared on the surface, and as he enters

[10] **bring . . . shudder you:** inflict a terrifying punishment on you.

[11] **marked for calumny** (kăl´əm-nē)**:** singled out to have lies told about him.

from the crowded parlor below it is a man in his prime we see, with a quiet confidence and an unexpressed, hidden force. Mary Warren, his servant, can barely speak for embarrassment and fear.

Don't forget to **Notice & Note** as you read the text.

166 **Mary Warren.** Oh! I'm just going home, Mr. Proctor.

167 **Proctor.** Be you foolish, Mary Warren? Be you deaf? I forbid you leave the house, did I not? Why shall I pay you? I am looking for you more often than my cows!

168 **Mary Warren.** I only come to see the great doings in the world.

169 **Proctor.** I'll show you a great doin' on your arse one of these days. Now get you home; my wife is waitin' with your work! (*Trying to retain a shred of dignity, she goes slowly out.*)

170 **Mercy Lewis** (*both afraid of him and strangely titillated*). I'd best be off. I have my Ruth to watch. Good morning, Mr. Proctor.

171 (Mercy *sidles out. Since* Proctor*'s entrance,* Abigail *has stood as though on tiptoe, absorbing his presence, wide-eyed. He glances at her, then goes to* Betty *on the bed.*)

172 **Abigail.** Gah! I'd almost forgot how strong you are, John Proctor!

173 **Proctor** (*looking at* Abigail *now, the faintest suggestion of a knowing smile on his face*). What's this mischief here?

174 **Abigail** (*with a nervous laugh*). Oh, she's only gone silly somehow.

175 **Proctor.** The road past my house is a pilgrimage to Salem all morning. The town's mumbling witchcraft.

176 **Abigail.** Oh, posh! (*Winningly she comes a little closer, with a confidential, wicked air.*) We were dancin' in the woods last night, and my uncle leaped in on us. She took fright, is all.

177 **Proctor** (*his smile widening*). Ah, you're wicked yet, aren't y'! (*A trill of expectant laughter escapes her, and she dares come closer, feverishly looking into his eyes.*) You'll be clapped in the stocks before you're twenty.

178 (*He takes a step to go, and she springs into his path.*)

179 **Abigail.** Give me a word, John. A soft word. (*Her concentrated desire destroys his smile.*)

180 **Proctor.** No, no, Abby. That's done with.

181 **Abigail** (*tauntingly*). You come five mile to see a silly girl fly? I know you better.

182 **Proctor** (*setting her firmly out of his path*). I come to see what mischief your uncle's brewin' now. (*with final emphasis*) Put it out of mind, Abby.

183 **Abigail** (*grasping his hand before he can release her*). John—I am waitin' for you every night.

184 **Proctor.** Abby, I never give you hope to wait for me.

185 **Abigail** (*now beginning to anger—she can't believe it*). I have something better than hope, I think!

186 **Proctor.** Abby, you'll put it out of mind. I'll not be comin' for you more.

187 **Abigail.** You're surely sportin' with me.

188 **Proctor.** You know me better.

189 **Abigail.** I know how you clutched my back behind your house and sweated like a stallion whenever I come near! Or did I dream that? It's she put me out, you cannot pretend it were you. I saw your face when she put me out, and you loved me then and you do now!

190 **Proctor.** Abby, that's a wild thing to say—

191 **Abigail.** A wild thing may say wild things. But not so wild, I think. I have seen you since she put me out; I have seen you nights.

192 **Proctor.** I have hardly stepped off my farm this sevenmonth.

193 **Abigail.** I have a sense for heat, John, and yours has drawn me to my window, and I have seen you looking up, burning in your loneliness. Do you tell me you've never looked up at my window?

194 **Proctor.** I may have looked up.

ANALYZE PLOT

Annotate: Mark details in paragraph 195 that reveal how Abigail feels about Proctor.

Interpret: What conflict emerges between Abigail and Proctor?

195 **Abigail** (*now softening*). And you must. You are no wintry man. I *know* you, John. I know you. (*She is weeping.*) I cannot sleep for dreamin'; I cannot dream but I wake and walk about the house as though I'd find you comin' through some door. (*She clutches him desperately*).

196 **Proctor** (*gently pressing her from him, with great sympathy but firmly*). Child—

197 **Abigail** (*with a flash of anger*). How do you call me child!

198 **Proctor.** Abby, I may think of you softly from time to time. But I will cut off my hand before I'll ever reach for you again. Wipe it out of mind. We never touched, Abby.

199 **Abigail.** Aye, but we did.

200 **Proctor.** Aye, but we did not.

201 **Abigail** (*with a bitter anger*). Oh, I marvel how such a strong man may let such a sickly wife be—

202 **Proctor** (*angered—at himself as well*). You'll speak nothin' of Elizabeth!

203 **Abigail.** She is blackening my name in the village! She is telling lies about me! She is a cold, sniveling woman, and you bend to her! Let her turn you like a—

204 **Proctor** (*shaking her*). Do you look for whippin'?

205 (*A psalm is heard being sung below.*)

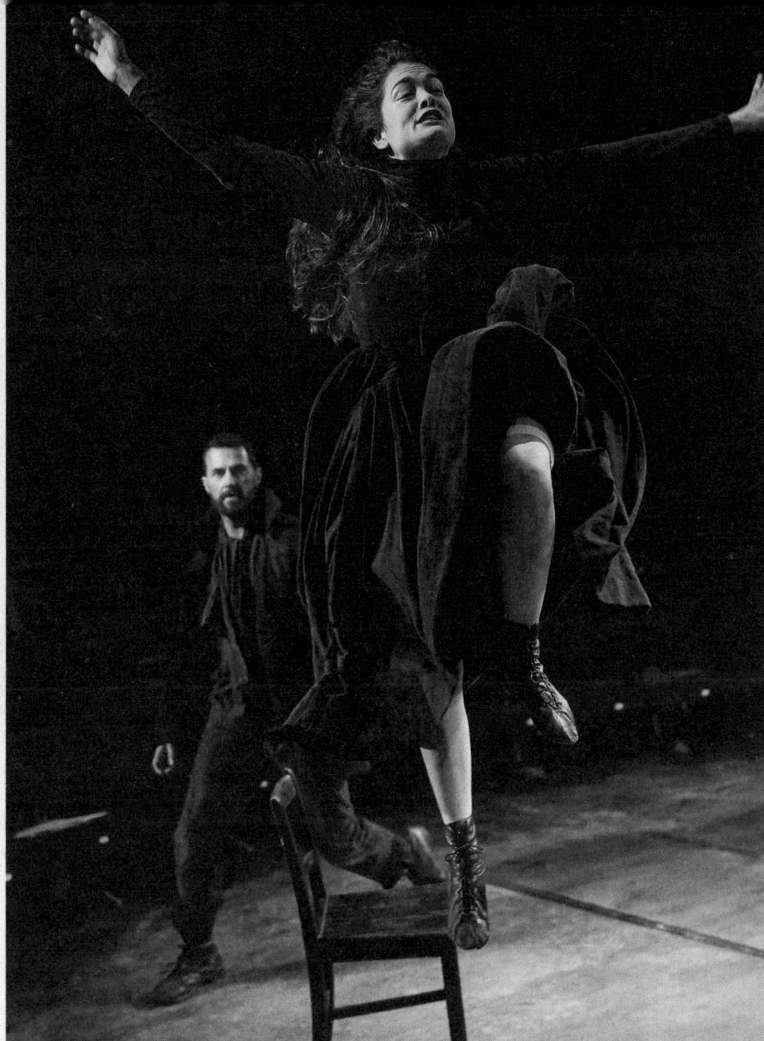

Don't forget to **Notice & Note** as you read the text.

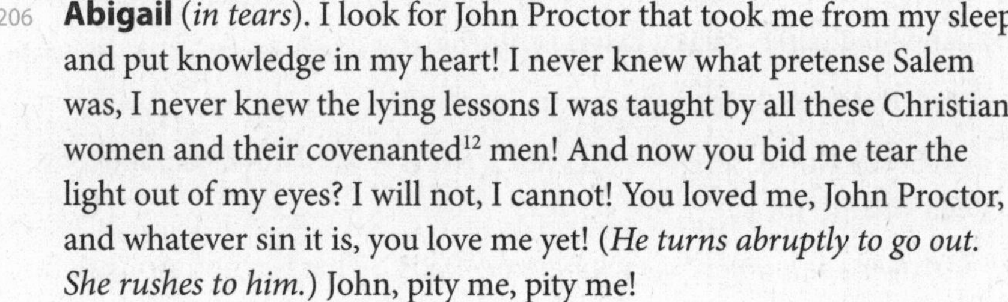

206 **Abigail** (*in tears*). I look for John Proctor that took me from my sleep and put knowledge in my heart! I never knew what pretense Salem was, I never knew the lying lessons I was taught by all these Christian women and their covenanted[12] men! And now you bid me tear the light out of my eyes? I will not, I cannot! You loved me, John Proctor, and whatever sin it is, you love me yet! (*He turns abruptly to go out. She rushes to him.*) John, pity me, pity me!

207 (*The words "going up to Jesus" are heard in the psalm, and* Betty *claps her ears suddenly and whines loudly.*)

208 **Abigail.** Betty? (*She hurries to* Betty, *who is now sitting up and screaming.* Proctor *goes to* Betty *as* Abigail *is trying to pull her hands down, calling* "Betty!")

209 **Proctor** (*growing unnerved*). What's she doing? Girl, what ails you? Stop that wailing!

210 (*The singing has stopped in the midst of this, and now* Parris *rushes in.*)

[12] **covenanted** (kŭv´ə-nən-tĭd): In Puritan religious practice, the men of a congregation would make an agreement, or covenant, to govern the community and abide by its beliefs and practices.

211 **Parris.** What happened? What are you doing to her? Betty! (*He rushes to the bed, crying,* "Betty, Betty!" Mrs. Putnam *enters, feverish with curiosity, and with her* Thomas Putnam *and* Mercy Lewis. Parris, *at the bed, keeps lightly slapping* Betty's *face, while she moans and tries to get up.*)

212 **Abigail.** She heard you singin' and suddenly she's up and screamin'.

213 **Mrs. Putnam.** The psalm! The psalm! She cannot bear to hear the Lord's name!

214 **Parris.** No. God forbid. Mercy, run to the doctor! Tell him what's happened here! (Mercy Lewis *rushes out.*)

215 **Mrs. Putnam.** Mark it for a sign, mark it!

216 (Rebecca Nurse, *seventy-two, enters. She is white-haired, leaning upon her walking-stick.*)

217 **Putnam** (*pointing at the whimpering* Betty). That is a notorious sign of witchcraft afoot, Goody Nurse, a prodigious sign!

218 **Mrs. Putnam.** My mother told me that! When they cannot bear to hear the name of—

219 **Parris** (*trembling*). Rebecca, Rebecca, go to her, we're lost. She suddenly cannot bear to hear the Lord's—

220 (Giles Corey, *eighty-three, enters. He is knotted with muscle, canny, inquisitive, and still powerful.*)

221 **Rebecca.** There is hard sickness here, Giles Corey, so please to keep the quiet.

222 **Giles.** I've not said a word. No one here can testify I've said a word. Is she going to fly again? I hear she flies.

223 **Putnam.** Man, be quiet now!

Don't forget to **Notice & Note** as you read the text.

224 (*Everything is quiet.* Rebecca *walks across the room to the bed. Gentleness exudes from her.* Betty *is quietly whimpering, eyes shut.* Rebecca *simply stands over the child, who gradually quiets.*)

225 And while they are so absorbed, we may put a word in for Rebecca. Rebecca was the wife of Francis Nurse, who, from all accounts, was one of those men for whom both sides of the argument had to have respect. He was called upon to arbitrate disputes as though he were an unofficial judge, and Rebecca also enjoyed the high opinion most people had for him. By the time of the delusion,[13] they had three hundred acres, and their children were settled in separate homesteads within the same estate. However, Francis had originally rented the land, and one theory has it that, as he gradually paid for it and raised his social status, there were those who resented his rise.

226 Another suggestion to explain the systematic campaign against Rebecca, and inferentially against Francis, is the land war he fought with his neighbors, one of whom was a Putnam. This squabble grew to the proportions of a battle in the woods between partisans of both sides, and it is said to have lasted for two days. As for Rebecca herself, the general opinion of her character was so high that to explain how anyone dared cry her out for a witch—and more, how adults could bring themselves to lay hands on her—we must look to the fields and boundaries of that time.

227 As we have seen, Thomas Putnam's man for the Salem ministry was Bayley. The Nurse clan had been in the faction that prevented Bayley's taking office. In addition, certain families allied to the Nurses by blood or friendship, and whose farms were contiguous with the Nurse farm or close to it, combined to break away from the Salem town authority and set up Topsfield, a new and independent entity whose existence was resented by old Salemites.

228 That the guiding hand behind the outcry was Putnam's is indicated by the fact that, as soon as it began, this Topsfield-Nurse faction absented themselves from church in protest and disbelief. It was Edward and Jonathan Putnam who signed the first complaint against Rebecca; and Thomas Putnam's little daughter was the one who fell into a fit at the hearing and pointed to Rebecca as her attacker. To top it all, Mrs. Putnam—who is now staring at the bewitched child on the bed—soon accused Rebecca's spirit of "tempting her to iniquity," a charge that had more truth in it than Mrs. Putnam could know.

229 **Mrs. Putnam** (*astonished*). What have you done?

230 (Rebecca, *in thought, now leaves the bedside and sits.*)

231 **Parris** (*wondrous and relieved*). What do you make of it, Rebecca?

[13] **the time of the delusion:** the era of the witchcraft accusations and trials.

232 **Putnam** (*eagerly*). Goody Nurse, will you go to my Ruth and see if you can wake her?

233 **Rebecca** (*sitting*). I think she'll wake in time. Pray calm yourselves. I have eleven children, and I am twenty-six times a grandma, and I have seen them all through their silly seasons, and when it come on them they will run the Devil bowlegged keeping up with their mischief. I think she'll wake when she tires of it. A child's spirit is like a child, you can never catch it by running after it; you must stand still, and, for love, it will soon itself come back.

234 **Proctor.** Aye, that's the truth of it, Rebecca.

235 **Mrs. Putnam.** This is no silly season, Rebecca. My Ruth is bewildered, Rebecca; she cannot eat.

236 **Rebecca.** Perhaps she is not hungered yet. (*to* Parris) I hope you are not decided to go in search of loose spirits, Mr. Parris. I've heard promise of that outside.

237 **Parris.** A wide opinion's running in the parish that the Devil may be among us, and I would satisfy them that they are wrong.

238 **Proctor.** Then let you come out and call them wrong. Did you consult the wardens[14] before you called this minister to look for devils?

239 **Parris.** He is not coming to look for devils!

240 **Proctor.** Then what's he coming for?

241 **Putnam.** There be children dyin' in the village, Mister!

242 **Proctor.** I seen none dyin'. This society will not be a bag to swing around your head, Mr. Putnam. (*to* Parris) Did you call a meeting before you—?

ANALYZE CHARACTERS

Annotate: Mark details in paragraph 245 that show Rebecca is religious.

Interpret: How does her faith in God differ from Mr. Putnam's?

243 **Putnam.** I am sick of meetings; cannot the man turn his head without he have a meeting?

244 **Proctor.** He may turn his head, but not to Hell!

245 **Rebecca.** Pray, John, be calm. (*Pause. He defers to her.*) Mr. Parris, I think you'd best send Reverend Hale back as soon as he come. This will set us all to arguin' again in the society, and we thought to have peace this year. I think we ought rely on the doctor now, and good prayer.

246 **Mrs. Putnam.** Rebecca, the doctor's baffled!

247 **Rebecca.** If so he is, then let us go to God for the cause of it. There is prodigious danger in the seeking of loose spirits. I fear it, I fear it. Let us rather blame ourselves and—

248 **Putnam.** How may we blame ourselves? I am one of nine sons; the Putnam seed have peopled this province. And yet I have but one child left of eight—and now she shrivels!

249 **Rebecca.** I cannot fathom that.

[14] **wardens:** officers appointed to keep order.

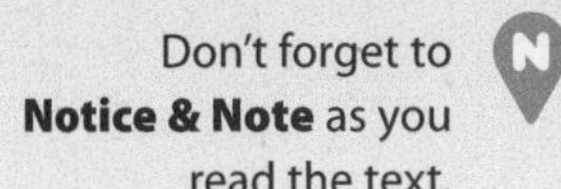

250 **Mrs. Putnam** (*with a growing edge of sarcasm*). But I must! You think it God's work you should never lose a child, nor grandchild either, and I bury all but one? There are wheels within wheels in this village, and fires within fires!

251 **Putnam** (*to* Parris). When Reverend Hale comes, you will proceed to look for signs of witchcraft here.

252 **Proctor** (*to* Putnam). You cannot command Mr. Parris. We vote by name in this society, not by acreage.

253 **Putnam.** I never heard you worried so on this society, Mr. Proctor. I do not think I saw you at Sabbath meeting since snow flew.

254 **Proctor.** I have trouble enough without I come five mile to hear him preach only hellfire and bloody damnation. Take it to heart, Mr. Parris. There are many others who stay away from church these days because you hardly ever mention God any more.

255 **Parris** (*now aroused*). Why, that's a drastic charge!

256 **Rebecca.** It's somewhat true; there are many that quail to bring their children—

257 **Parris.** I do not preach for children, Rebecca. It is not the children who are unmindful of their obligations toward this ministry.

258 **Rebecca.** Are there really those unmindful?

259 **Parris.** I should say the better half of Salem village—

260 **Putnam.** And more than that!

261 **Parris.** Where is my wood? My contract provides I be supplied with all my firewood. I am waiting since November for a stick, and even in November I had to show my frostbitten hands like some London beggar!

262 **Giles.** You are allowed six pound a year to buy your wood, Mr. Parris.

263 **Parris.** I regard that six pound as part of my salary. I am paid little enough without I spend six pound on firewood.

264 **Proctor.** Sixty, plus six for firewood—

265 **Parris.** The salary is sixty-six pound, Mr. Proctor! I am not some preaching farmer with a book under my arm; I am a graduate of Harvard College.

266 **Giles.** Aye, and well instructed in arithmetic!

267 **Parris.** Mr. Corey, you will look far for a man of my kind at sixty pound a year! I am not used to this poverty; I left a thrifty business in the Barbados to serve the Lord. I do not fathom it, why am I persecuted here? I cannot offer one proposition but there be a howling riot of argument. I have often wondered if the Devil be in it somewhere; I cannot understand you people otherwise.

268 **Proctor.** Mr. Parris, you are the first minister ever did demand the deed to this house—

269 **Parris.** Man! Don't a minister deserve a house to live in?

270 **Proctor.** To live in, yes. But to ask ownership is like you shall own the meeting house itself; the last meeting I were at you spoke so long on deeds and mortgages I thought it were an auction.

271 **Parris.** I want a mark of confidence, is all! I am your third preacher in seven years. I do not wish to be put out like the cat whenever some majority feels the whim. You people seem not to comprehend that a minister is the Lord's man in the parish; a minister is not to be so lightly crossed and contradicted—

272 **Putnam.** Aye!

273 **Parris.** There is either obedience or the church will burn like Hell is burning!

274 **Proctor.** Can you speak one minute without we land in Hell again? I am sick of Hell!

275 **Parris.** It is not for you to say what is good for you to hear!

276 **Proctor.** I may speak my heart, I think!

277 **Parris** (*in a fury*). What, are we Quakers?[15] We are not Quakers here yet, Mr. Proctor. And you may tell that to your followers!

278 **Proctor.** My followers!

279 **Parris** (*Now he's out with it*). There is a party in this church. I am not blind; there is a faction and a party.

280 **Proctor.** Against you?

281 **Putnam.** Against him and all authority!

282 **Proctor.** Why, then I must find it and join it.

283 (*There is shock among the others.*)

284 **Rebecca.** He does not mean that.

285 **Putnam.** He confessed it now!

286 **Proctor.** I mean it solemnly, Rebecca; I like not the smell of this "authority."

287 **Rebecca.** No, you cannot break charity[16] with your minister. You are another kind, John. Clasp his hand, make your peace.

288 **Proctor.** I have a crop to sow and lumber to drag home. (*He goes angrily to the door and turns to* Corey *with a smile.*) What say you, Giles, let's find the party. He says there's a party.

289 **Giles.** I've changed my opinion of this man, John. Mr. Parris, I beg your pardon. I never thought you had so much iron in you.

---

[15] **Quakers:** an English religious sect—much hated by the Puritans—who often "spoke their heart" during their religious meetings.

[16] **break charity:** break off; end the relationship.

Don't forget to **Notice & Note** as you read the text.

290 **Parris** (*surprised*). Why, thank you, Giles!

291 **Giles.** It suggests to the mind what the trouble be among us all these years. (*to all*) Think on it. Wherefore is everybody suing everybody else? Think on it now, it's a deep thing, and dark as a pit. I have been six time in court this year—

292 **Proctor** (*familiarly, with warmth, although he knows he is approaching the edge of* Giles' *tolerance with this*). Is it the Devil's fault that a man cannot say you good morning without you clap him for defamation?[17] You're old, Giles, and you're not hearin' so well as you did.

293 **Giles** (*He cannot be crossed*). John Proctor, I have only last month collected four pound damages for you publicly sayin' I burned the roof off your house, and I—

294 **Proctor** (*laughing*). I never said no such thing, but I've paid you for it, so I hope I can call you deaf without charge. Now come along, Giles, and help me drag my lumber home.

295 **Putnam.** A moment, Mr. Proctor. What lumber is that you're draggin', if I may ask you?

296 **Proctor.** My lumber. From out my forest by the riverside.

297 **Putnam.** Why, we are surely gone wild this year. What anarchy is this? That tract is in my bounds, it's in my bounds, Mr. Proctor.

298 **Proctor.** In your bounds! (*indicating* Rebecca) I bought that tract from Goody Nurse's husband five months ago.

299 **Putnam.** He had no right to sell it. It stands clear in my grandfather's will that all the land between the river and—

300 **Proctor.** Your grandfather had a habit of willing land that never belonged to him, if I may say it plain.

301 **Giles.** That's God's truth; he nearly willed away my north pasture but he knew I'd break his fingers before he'd set his name to it. Let's get your lumber home, John. I feel a sudden will to work coming on.

302 **Putnam.** You load one oak of mine and you'll fight to drag it home!

303 **Giles.** Aye, and we'll win too, Putnam—this fool and I. Come on! (*He turns to* Proctor *and starts out.*)

304 **Putnam.** I'll have my men on you, Corey! I'll clap a writ on you!

305 (*Enter* Reverend John Hale *of Beverly.*)

306 Mr. Hale is nearing forty, a tight-skinned, eager-eyed intellectual. This is a beloved errand for him; on being called here to ascertain witchcraft he felt the pride of the specialist whose unique knowledge has at last been publicly called for. Like almost all men of learning, he spent a good deal of his time pondering the invisible

[17] **clap . . . defamation** (dĕf-ə-mā´shən): imprison him for slander.

world, especially since he had himself encountered a witch in his parish not long before. That woman, however, turned into a mere pest under his searching scrutiny, and the child she had allegedly been afflicting recovered her normal behavior after Hale had given her his kindness and a few days of rest in his own house. However, that experience never raised a doubt in his mind as to the reality of the underworld or the existence of Lucifer's many-faced lieutenants. And his belief is not to his discredit. Better minds than Hale's were—and still are—convinced that there is a society of spirits beyond our ken. One cannot help noting that one of his lines has never yet raised a laugh in any audience that has seen this play; it is his assurance that "We cannot look to superstition in this. The Devil is precise." Evidently we are not quite certain even now whether diabolism is holy and not to be scoffed at. And it is no accident that we should be so bemused.

307 Like Reverend Hale and the others on this stage, we conceive the Devil as a necessary part of a respectable view of cosmology.[18] Ours is a divided empire in which certain ideas and emotions and actions are of God, and their opposites are of Lucifer. It is as impossible for most men to conceive of a morality without sin as of an earth without "sky." Since 1692 a great but superficial change has wiped out God's beard and the Devil's horns, but the world is still gripped between two diametrically opposed absolutes. The concept of unity, in which positive and negative are attributes of the same force, in which good and evil are relative, ever-changing, and always joined to the same phenomenon—such a concept is still reserved to the physical sciences and to the few who have grasped the history of ideas. When it is recalled that until the Christian era the underworld was never regarded as a hostile area, that all gods were useful and essentially friendly to man despite occasional lapses; when we see the steady and methodical inculcation into humanity of the idea of man's worthlessness—until redeemed—the necessity of the Devil may become evident as a weapon, a weapon designed and used time and time again in every age to whip men into a surrender to a particular church or church-state.

ANALYZE LITERARY DEVICES

Annotate: Miller interrupts the action of the play after Mr. Hale enters. Mark lines in this section of exposition that show how Miller compares the use of the Devil as a spiritual threat to the fight against Communism in America in the 1950s.

Evaluate: What similarities are there? What larger point is Miller making about "diabolism" in society?

308 Our difficulty in believing the—for want of a better word—political inspiration of the Devil is due in great part to the fact that he is called up and damned not only by our social antagonists but by our own side, whatever it may be. The Catholic Church, through its Inquisition,[19] is famous for cultivating Lucifer as the arch-fiend, but the Church's enemies relied no less upon the Old Boy to keep the human mind enthralled. Luther[20] was himself accused of alliance with Hell, and he in turn accused his enemies. To complicate matters further, he believed that he had had contact with the Devil and had

---

[18] **cosmology** (kŏz-mŏl′ə-jē): a branch of philosophy dealing with the structure of the universe.

[19] **Inquisition:** a former tribunal in the Roman Catholic Church dedicated to the discovery and punishment of heresy.

[20] **Luther:** Martin Luther (1483–1546), the German theologian who led the Protestant Reformation.

argued theology with him. I am not surprised at this, for at my own university a professor of history—a Lutheran, by the way—used to assemble his graduate students, draw the shades, and commune in the classroom with Erasmus.[21] He was never, to my knowledge, officially scoffed at for this, the reason being that the university officials, like most of us, are the children of a history which still sucks at the Devil's teats. At this writing, only England has held back before the temptations of contemporary diabolism. In the countries of the Communist ideology, all resistance of any import is linked to the totally malign capitalist succubi,[22] and in America any man who is not reactionary in his views is open to the charge of alliance with the Red hell. Political opposition, thereby, is given an inhumane overlay which then justifies the abrogation of all normally applied customs of civilized intercourse. A political policy is equated with moral right, and opposition to it with diabolical malevolence. Once such an equation is effectively made, society becomes a congerie of plots and counterplots, and the main role of government changes from that of the arbiter to that of the scourge of God.

Don't forget to **Notice & Note** as you read the text. 

309 The results of this process are no different now from what they ever were, except sometimes in the degree of cruelty inflicted, and not always even in that department. Normally the actions and deeds of a man were all that society felt comfortable in judging. The secret intent of an action was left to the ministers, priests, and rabbis to deal with. When diabolism rises, however, actions are the least important manifests of the true nature of a man. The Devil, as Reverend Hale said, is a wily one, and, until an hour before he fell, even God thought him beautiful in Heaven.[23]

310 The analogy, however, seems to falter when one considers that, while there were no witches then, there are Communists and capitalists now, and in each camp there is certain proof that spies of each side are at work undermining the other. But this is a snobbish objection and not at all warranted by the facts. I have no doubt that people *were* communing with, and even worshiping, the Devil in Salem, and if the whole truth could be known in this case, as it is in others, we should discover a regular and conventionalized propitiation of the dark spirit. One certain evidence of this is the confession of Tituba, the slave of Reverend Parris, and another is the behavior of the children who were known to have indulged in sorceries with her.

311 There are accounts of similar *klatches* in Europe, where the daughters of the towns would assemble at night and, sometimes with fetishes, sometimes with a selected young man, give themselves to love, with some bastardly results. The Church, sharp-eyed as it must be when gods long dead are brought to life, condemned these

[21] **Erasmus** (ĭ-răz´məs)**:** Desiderius Erasmus (1466?–1536), a Dutch scholar who sought to restore Christian faith by a study of the Scriptures and classical texts.

[22] **succubi** (sŭk´yə-bī)**:** demons that assume female form. Demons that assume male form are called incubi (ĭn´kyə-bī).

[23] **The Devil . . . beautiful in Heaven:** According to Christian belief, Lucifer was God's favorite angel until the angel rebelled and was cast out of Heaven.

orgies as witchcraft and interpreted them, rightly, as a resurgence of the Dionysiac forces[24] it had crushed long before. Sex, sin, and the Devil were early linked, and so they continued to be in Salem, and are today. From all accounts there are no more puritanical mores in the world than those enforced by the Communists in Russia, where women's fashions, for instance, are as prudent and all-covering as any American Baptist would desire. The divorce laws lay a tremendous responsibility on the father for the care of his children. Even the laxity of divorce regulations in the early years of the revolution was undoubtedly a revulsion from the nineteenth-century Victorian immobility of marriage and the consequent hypocrisy that developed from it. If for no other reasons, a state so powerful, so jealous of the uniformity of its citizens, cannot long tolerate the atomization of the family. And yet, in American eyes at least, there remains the conviction that the Russian attitude toward women is lascivious. It is the Devil working again, just as he is working within the Slav[25] who is shocked at the very idea of a woman's disrobing herself in a burlesque show. Our opposites are always robed in sexual sin, and it is from this unconscious conviction that demonology gains both its attractive sensuality and its capacity to infuriate and frighten.

ANALYZE CHARACTERS

Annotate: Mark details in paragraph 312 that tell you how Reverend Hale views himself.

Analyze: What is Hale's motivation for coming to Salem? Cite evidence from the text in your response.

312 Coming into Salem now, Reverend Hale conceives of himself much as a young doctor on his first call. His painfully acquired armory of symptoms, catchwords, and diagnostic procedures are now to be put to use at last. The road from Beverly is unusually busy this morning, and he has passed a hundred rumors that make him smile at the ignorance of the yeomanry in this most precise science. He feels himself allied with the best minds of Europe—kings, philosophers, scientists, and ecclesiasts of all churches. His goal is light, goodness and its preservation, and he knows the exaltation of the blessed whose intelligence, sharpened by minute examinations of enormous tracts, is finally called upon to face what may be a bloody fight with the Fiend himself.

313 *(He appears loaded down with half a dozen heavy books.)*

314 **Hale.** Pray you, someone take these!

315 **Parris** (*delighted*). Mr. Hale! Oh! It's good to see you again! (*taking some books*) My, they're heavy!

316 **Hale** (*setting down his books*). They must be; they are weighted with authority.

317 **Parris** (*a little scared*). Well, you do come prepared!

318 **Hale.** We shall need hard study if it comes to tracking down the Old Boy. (*noticing* Rebecca) You cannot be Rebecca Nurse?

---

[24] **Dionysiac** (dĭ-ə-nĭs´ē-ăk) **forces:** forces associated with Dionysus, the Greek god of wine and ecstasy.

[25] **Slav:** a generic reference to Russians and other Slavic-speaking peoples of Eastern Europe who were under the control of the Soviet Union.

319 **Rebecca.** I am, sir. Do you know me?

320 **Hale.** It's strange how I knew you, but I suppose you look as such a good soul should. We have all heard of your great charities in Beverly.

321 **Parris.** Do you know this gentleman? Mr. Thomas Putnam. And his good wife Ann.

322 **Hale.** Putnam! I had not expected such distinguished company, sir.

323 **Putnam** (*pleased*). It does not seem to help us today, Mr. Hale. We look to you to come to our house and save our child.

324 **Hale.** Your child ails too?

325 **Mrs. Putnam.** Her soul, her soul seems flown away. She sleeps and yet she walks . . .

326 **Putnam.** She cannot eat.

327 **Hale.** Cannot eat! (*Thinks on it. Then, to* Proctor *and* Giles Corey.) Do you men have afflicted children?

328 **Parris.** No, no, these are farmers. John Proctor—

329 **Giles Corey.** He don't believe in witches.

330 **Proctor** (*to* Hale). I never spoke on witches one way or the other. Will you come, Giles?

331 **Giles.** No—no, John, I think not. I have some few queer questions of my own to ask this fellow.

332 **Proctor.** I've heard you to be a sensible man, Mr. Hale. I hope you'll leave some of it in Salem.

333 (Proctor *goes.* Hale *stands embarrassed for an instant.*)

334 **Parris** (*quickly*). Will you look at my daughter, sir? (*leads* Hale *to the bed*) She has tried to leap out the window; we discovered her this morning on the highroad, waving her arms as though she'd fly.

335 **Hale** (*narrowing his eyes*). Tries to fly.

336 **Putnam.** She cannot bear to hear the Lord's name, Mr. Hale; that's a sure sign of witchcraft afloat.

337 **Hale** (*holding up his hands*). No, no. Now let me instruct you. We cannot look to superstition in this. The Devil is precise; the marks of his presence are definite as stone, and I must tell you all that I shall not proceed unless you are prepared to believe me if I should find no bruise of hell upon her.

338 **Parris.** It is agreed, sir—it is agreed—we will abide by your judgment.

339 **Hale.** Good then. (*He goes to the bed, looks down at* Betty. *To* Parris.) Now, sir, what were your first warning of this strangeness?

340 **Parris.** Why, sir—I discovered her—(*indicating* Abigail) and my niece and ten or twelve of the other girls, dancing in the forest last night.

341 **Hale** (*surprised*). You permit dancing?

342 **Parris.** No, no, it were secret—

343 **Mrs. Putnam** (*unable to wait*). Mr. Parris's slave has knowledge of conjurin', sir.

344 **Parris** (*to* Mrs. Putnam). We cannot be sure of that, Goody Ann—

345 **Mrs. Putnam** (*frightened, very softly*). I know it, sir. I sent my child—she should learn from Tituba who murdered her sisters.

346 **Rebecca** (*horrified*). Goody Ann! You sent a child to conjure up the dead?

347 **Mrs. Putnam.** Let God blame me, not you, not you, Rebecca! I'll not have you judging me any more! (*to* Hale) Is it a natural work to lose seven children before they live a day?

348 **Parris.** Sssh!

349 (Rebecca, *with great pain, turns her face away. There is a pause.*)

350 **Hale.** Seven dead in childbirth.

351 **Mrs. Putnam** (*softly*). Aye. (*Her voice breaks; she looks up at him. Silence.* Hale *is impressed.* Parris *looks to him. He goes to his books, opens one, turns pages, then reads. All wait, avidly.*)

352 **Parris** (*hushed*). What book is that?

353 **Mrs. Putnam.** What's there, sir?

354 **Hale** (*with a tasty love of intellectual pursuit*). Here is all the invisible world, caught, defined, and calculated. In these books the Devil stands stripped of all his brute disguises. Here are all your familiar spirits—your incubi and succubi; your witches that go by land, by air, and by sea; your wizards of the night and of the day. Have no fear now—we shall find him out if he has come among us, and I mean to crush him utterly if he has shown his face! (*He starts for the bed.*)

355 **Rebecca.** Will it hurt the child, sir?

356 **Hale.** I cannot tell. If she is truly in the Devil's grip we may have to rip and tear to get her free.

357 **Rebecca.** I think I'll go, then. I am too old for this. (*She rises.*)

358 **Parris** (*striving for conviction*). Why, Rebecca, we may open up the boil of all our troubles today!

359 **Rebecca.** Let us hope for that. I go to God for you, sir.

360 **Parris** (*with trepidation—and resentment*). I hope you do not mean we go to Satan here! (*slight pause*)

361 **Rebecca.** I wish I knew. (*She goes out; they feel resentful of her note of moral superiority.*)

362 **Putnam** (*abruptly*). Come, Mr. Hale, let's get on. Sit you here.

363 **Giles.** Mr. Hale, I have always wanted to ask a learned man—what signifies the readin' of strange books?

364 **Hale.** What books?

365 **Giles.** I cannot tell; she hides them.

366 **Hale.** Who does this?

367 **Giles.** Martha, my wife. I have waked at night many a time and found her in a corner, readin' of a book. Now what do you make of that?

368 **Hale.** Why, that's not necessarily—

369 **Giles.** It discomfits me! Last night—mark this—I tried and tried and could not say my prayers. And then she close her book and walks out of the house, and suddenly—mark this—I could pray again!

370 Old Giles must be spoken for, if only because his fate was to be so remarkable and so different from that of all the others. He was in his early eighties at this time, and was the most comical hero in the history. No man has ever been blamed for so much. If a cow was missed, the first thought was to look for her around Corey's house; a fire blazing up at night brought suspicion of arson to his door. He didn't give a hoot for public opinion, and only in his last years—after he had married Martha—did he bother much with the church. That she stopped his prayer is very probable, but he forgot to say that he'd only recently learned any prayers and it didn't take much to make him stumble over them. He was a crank and a nuisance, but withal a deeply innocent and brave man. In court once, he was asked if it were true that he had been frightened by the strange behavior of a hog and had then said he knew it to be the Devil in an animal's shape. "What frighted you?" he was asked. He forgot everything but the word "frighted," and instantly replied, "I do not know that I ever spoke that word in my life."

371 **Hale.** Ah! The stoppage of prayer—that is strange. I'll speak further on that with you.

372 **Giles.** I'm not sayin' she's touched the Devil, now, but I'd admire to know what books she reads and why she hides them. She'll not answer me, y' see.

373 **Hale.** Aye, we'll discuss it. (*to all*) Now mark me, if the Devil is in her you will witness some frightful wonders in this room, so please to keep your wits about you. Mr. Putnam, stand close in case she flies. Now, Betty, dear, will you sit up? (Putnam *comes in closer, ready-handed.* Hale *sits* Betty *up, but she hangs limp in his hands.*) Hmmm. (*He observes her carefully. The others watch breathlessly.*) Can you hear me? I am John Hale, minister of Beverly. I have come to help you, dear. Do you remember my two little girls in Beverly? (*She does not stir in his hands.*)

374 **Parris** (*in fright*). How can it be the Devil? Why would he choose my house to strike? We have all manner of licentious people in the village!

375 **Hale.** What victory would the Devil have to win a soul already bad? It is the best the Devil wants, and who is better than the minister?

ANALYZE PLOT

Annotate: Foreshadowing occurs when a writer provides hints that suggest future events. Mark where Giles' dialogue may foreshadow, or hint at, later events in the play.

Predict: What do you think will happen, based on Giles' story?

376 **Giles.** That's deep, Mr. Parris, deep, deep!

377 **Parris** (*with resolution now*). Betty! Answer Mr. Hale! Betty!

378 **Hale.** Does someone afflict you, child? It need not be a woman, mind you, or a man. Perhaps some bird invisible to others comes to you—perhaps a pig, a mouse, or any beast at all. Is there some figure bids you fly? (*The child remains limp in his hands. In silence he lays her back on the pillow. Now, holding out his hands toward her, he intones.*) In nomine Domini Sabaoth sui filiique ite ad infernos.[26] (*She does not stir. He turns to* Abigail, *his eyes narrowing.*) Abigail, what sort of dancing were you doing with her in the forest?

379 **Abigail.** Why—common dancing is all.

380 **Parris.** I think I ought to say that I—I saw a kettle in the grass where they were dancing.

381 **Abigail.** That were only soup.

382 **Hale.** What sort of soup were in this kettle, Abigail?

383 **Abigail.** Why, it were beans—and lentils, I think, and—

384 **Hale.** Mr. Parris, you did not notice, did you, any living thing in the kettle? A mouse, perhaps, a spider, a frog—?

385 **Parris** (*fearfully*). I—do believe there were some movement—in the soup.

386 **Abigail.** That jumped in, we never put it in!

387 **Hale** (*quickly*). What jumped in?

ANALYZE CHARACTERS

Annotate: Mark the person who Abigail says called the Devil.

Infer: Why does Abigail raise this person's name in her admission? Cite text evidence in your response.

388 **Abigail.** Why, a very little frog jumped—

389 **Parris.** A frog, Abby!

390 **Hale** (*grasping* Abigail). Abigail, it may be your cousin is dying. Did you call the Devil last night?

391 **Abigail.** I never called him! Tituba, Tituba . . .

392 **Parris** (*blanched*). She called the Devil?

393 **Hale.** I should like to speak with Tituba.

394 **Parris.** Goody Ann, will you bring her up? (Mrs. Putnam *exits.*)

395 **Hale.** How did she call him?

396 **Abigail.** I know not—she spoke Barbados.

397 **Hale.** Did you feel any strangeness when she called him? A sudden cold wind, perhaps? A trembling below the ground?

398 **Abigail.** I didn't see no Devil! (*shaking* Betty) Betty, wake up. Betty! Betty!

399 **Hale.** You cannot evade me, Abigail. Did your cousin drink any of the brew in that kettle?

[26] **In nomine . . . infernos (Latin):** "In the name of the Father and Son, get thee back to Hell."

Don't forget to **Notice & Note** as you read the text.

400 **Abigail.** She never drank it!

401 **Hale.** Did you drink it?

402 **Abigail.** No, sir!

403 **Hale.** Did Tituba ask you to drink it?

404 **Abigail.** She tried, but I refused.

405 **Hale.** Why are you concealing? Have you sold yourself to Lucifer?

406 **Abigail.** I never sold myself! I'm a good girl! I'm a proper girl!

407 (Mrs. Putnam *enters with* Tituba, *and instantly* Abigail *points at* Tituba.)

408 **Abigail.** She made me do it! She made Betty do it!

409 **Tituba** (*shocked and angry*). Abby!

410 **Abigail.** She makes me drink blood!

411 **Parris.** Blood!!

412 **Mrs. Putnam.** My baby's blood?

413 **Tituba.** No, no, chicken blood. I give she chicken blood!

414 **Hale.** Woman, have you enlisted these children for the Devil?

415 **Tituba.** No, no, sir, I don't truck with no Devil!

416 **Hale.** Why can she not wake? Are you silencing this child?

417 **Tituba.** I love me Betty!

418 **Hale.** You have sent your spirit out upon this child, have you not? Are you gathering souls for the Devil?

419 **Abigail.** She sends her spirit on me in church; she makes me laugh at prayer!

420 **Parris.** She have often laughed at prayer!

421 **Abigail.** She comes to me every night to go and drink blood!

422 **Tituba.** You beg *me* to conjure! She beg *me* make charm—

423 **Abigail.** Don't lie! (*to* Hale) She comes to me while I sleep; she's always making me dream corruptions!

424 **Tituba.** Why you say that, Abby?

425 **Abigail.** Sometimes I wake and find myself standing in the open doorway and not a stitch on my body! I always hear her laughing in my sleep. I hear her singing her Barbados songs and tempting me with—

426 **Tituba.** Mister Reverend, I never—

427 **Hale** (*resolved now*). Tituba, I want you to wake this child.

428 **Tituba.** I have no power on this child, sir.

429 **Hale.** You most certainly do, and you will free her from it now! When did you compact with the Devil?

430 **Tituba.** I don't compact with no Devil!

431 **Parris.** You will confess yourself or I will take you out and whip you to your death, Tituba!

432 **Putnam.** This woman must be hanged! She must be taken and hanged!

433 **Tituba** (*terrified, falls to her knees*). No, no, don't hang Tituba! I tell him I don't desire to work for him, sir.

434 **Parris.** The Devil?

435 **Hale.** Then you saw him! (Tituba *weeps.*) Now Tituba, I know that when we bind ourselves to Hell it is very hard to break with it. We are going to help you tear yourself free—

436 **Tituba** (*frightened by the coming process*). Mister Reverend, I do believe somebody else be witchin' these children.

437 **Hale.** Who?

438 **Tituba.** I don't know, sir, but the Devil got him numerous witches.

439 **Hale.** Does he! (*It is a clue.*) Tituba, look into my eyes. Come, look into me. (*She raises her eyes to his fearfully.*) You would be a good Christian woman, would you not, Tituba?

440 **Tituba.** Aye, sir, a good Christian woman.

441 **Hale.** And you love these little children?

442 **Tituba.** Oh, yes, sir, I don't desire to hurt little children.

443 **Hale.** And you love God, Tituba?

444 **Tituba.** I love God with all my bein'.

445 **Hale.** Now, in God's holy name—

446 **Tituba.** Bless Him. Bless Him. (*She is rocking on her knees, sobbing in terror.*)

447 **Hale.** And to His glory—

448 **Tituba.** Eternal glory. Bless Him—bless God . . .

449 **Hale.** Open yourself, Tituba—open yourself and let God's holy light shine on you.

450 **Tituba.** Oh, bless the Lord.

451 **Hale.** When the Devil comes to you does he ever come—with another person? (*She stares up into his face.*) Perhaps another person in the village? Someone you know.

452 **Parris.** Who came with him?

453 **Putnam.** Sarah Good? Did you ever see Sarah Good with him? Or Osburn?

454 **Parris.** Was it man or woman came with him?

455 **Tituba.** Man or woman. Was—was woman.

Don't forget to **Notice & Note** as you read the text.

456 **Parris.** What woman? A woman, you said. What woman?

457 **Tituba.** It was black dark, and I—

458 **Parris.** You could see him, why could you not see her?

459 **Tituba.** Well, they was always talking; they was always runnin' round and carryin' on—

460 **Parris.** You mean out of Salem? Salem witches?

461 **Tituba.** I believe so, yes, sir.

462 (*Now* Hale *takes her hand. She is surprised.*)

463 **Hale.** Tituba. You must have no fear to tell us who they are, do you understand? We will protect you. The Devil can never overcome a minister. You know that, do you not?

464 **Tituba** (*kisses* Hale's *hand*). Aye, sir, oh, I do.

465 **Hale.** You have confessed yourself to witchcraft, and that speaks a wish to come to Heaven's side. And we will bless you, Tituba.

466 **Tituba** (*deeply relieved*). Oh, God bless you, Mr. Hale!

467 **Hale** (*with rising exaltation*). You are God's instrument put in our hands to discover the Devil's agents among us. You are selected, Tituba, you are chosen to help us cleanse our village. So speak utterly, Tituba, turn your back on him and face God—face God, Tituba, and God will protect you.

468 **Tituba** (*joining with him*). Oh, God, protect Tituba!

469 **Hale** (*kindly*). Who came to you with the Devil? Two? Three? Four? How many?

470 (Tituba *pants, and begins rocking back and forth again, staring ahead.*)

471 **Tituba.** There was four. There was four.

472 **Parris** (*pressing in on her*). Who? Who? Their names, their names!

473 **Tituba** (*suddenly bursting out*). Oh, how many times he bid me kill you, Mr. Parris!

474 **Parris.** Kill me!

475 **Tituba** (*in a fury*). He say Mr. Parris must be kill! Mr. Parris no goodly man, Mr. Parris mean man and no gentle man, and he bid me rise out of my bed and cut your throat! (*They gasp.*) But I tell him "No! I don't hate that man. I don't want to kill that man." But he say, "You work for me, Tituba, and I make you free! I give you pretty dress to wear, and put you way high up in the air, and you gone fly back to Barbados!" And I say, "You lie, Devil, you lie!" And then he come one stormy night to me, and he say, "Look! I have *white* people belong to me." And I look—and there was Goody Good.

476 **Parris.** Sarah Good!

477 **Tituba** (*rocking and weeping*). Aye, sir, and Goody Osburn.

ANALYZE LITERARY DEVICES

Annotate: Dramatic irony occurs when the audience of a drama knows something that some or all of the characters do not know or expect. Find an example of dramatic irony in paragraphs 465–468.

Analyze: Why is this an example of dramatic irony? How does it affect the play?

478 **Mrs. Putnam.** I knew it! Goody Osburn were midwife to me three times. I begged you, Thomas, did I not? I begged him not to call Osburn because I feared her. My babies always shriveled in her hands!

479 **Hale.** Take courage, you must give us all their names. How can you bear to see this child suffering? Look at her, Tituba. (*He is indicating* Betty *on the bed.*) Look at her God-given innocence; her soul is so tender; we must protect her, Tituba; the Devil is out and preying on her like a beast upon the flesh of the pure lamb. God will bless you for your help.

480 (Abigail *rises, staring as though inspired, and cries out.*)

481 **Abigail.** I want to open myself! (*They turn to her, startled. She is enraptured, as though in a pearly light.*) I want the light of God, I want the sweet love of Jesus! I danced for the Devil; I saw him; I wrote in his book; I go back to Jesus; I kiss His hand. I saw Sarah Good with the Devil! I saw Goody Osburn with the Devil! I saw Bridget Bishop with the Devil!

482 (*As she is speaking,* Betty *is rising from the bed, a fever in her eyes, and picks up the chant.*)

483 **Betty** (*staring too*). I saw George Jacobs with the Devil! I saw Goody Howe with the Devil!

484 **Parris.** She speaks! (*He rushes to embrace* Betty.) She speaks!

485 **Hale.** Glory to God! It is broken, they are free!

486 **Betty** (*calling out hysterically and with great relief*). I saw Martha Bellows with the Devil!

487 **Abigail.** I saw Goody Sibber with the Devil! (*It is rising to a great glee.*)

488 **Putnam.** The marshal, I'll call the marshal!

489 (Parris *is shouting a prayer of thanksgiving.*)

490 **Betty.** I saw Alice Barrow with the Devil!

491 (*The curtain begins to fall.*)

492 **Hale** (*as* Putnam *goes out*). Let the marshal bring irons!

493 **Abigail.** I saw Goody Hawkins with the Devil!

494 **Betty.** I saw Goody Bibber with the Devil!

495 **Abigail.** I saw Goody Booth with the Devil!

496 (*On their ecstatic cries, the curtain falls.*)

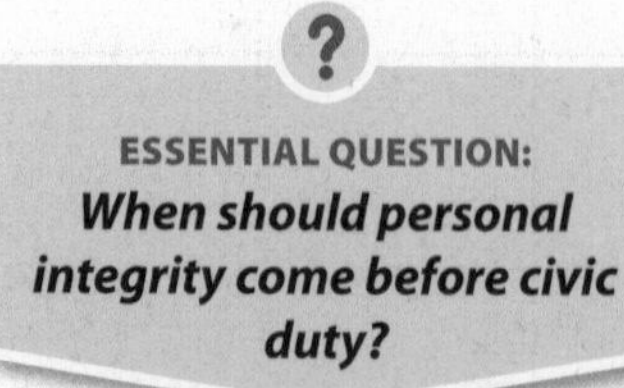
?
ESSENTIAL QUESTION:
When should personal integrity come before civic duty?

Review your notes and add your thoughts to your **Response Log.**

COLLABORATIVE DISCUSSION

With a classmate, discuss how Abigail's feelings toward John Proctor influence the events that take place in this act. Support your response with examples from the text.

Assessment Practice

Answer these questions before moving on to the **Analyze the Text** section on the following page.

1. What is the source of the main conflict in this act of the play?

(A) the cause of Betty's strange illness

(B) Tituba's presence in the woods

(C) Abigail's intimidation of other girls

(D) differences between Parris and Putnam

2. What is Reverend Hale's main qualification for the job of discerning witchcraft?

(A) He has already identified many witches.

(B) He is recognized everywhere as an expert on witchcraft.

(C) He identified a woman as a witch in his own church, and she was shown to be guilty.

(D) He identified a woman as a witch in his own church, and she was shown to be not guilty.

3. Why is Mrs. Putnam so passionate in her belief that there is witchcraft afoot?

(A) She is secretly in love with Reverend Hale.

(B) She witnessed a ritual where witchcraft was done.

(C) She has lost seven newborns and believes the cause was supernatural.

(D) She believes her opposition to witchcraft will insulate her from accusations.

Ed

Test-Taking Strategies

Analyze the Text

Support your responses with evidence from the text.

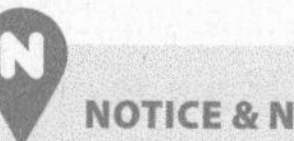

Review what you **noticed and noted** as you read the text. Your annotations can help you answer these questions.

1. **ANALYZE** What does the exposition in the beginning of Act One tell readers about the way they are to perceive the events that follow? Explain.

2. **ANALYZE** Reread paragraphs 107–127. In this part of the play readers learn information that the other characters do not have. This is called **dramatic irony.** How does this dramatic irony help readers to understand the real reasons behind the girls' symptoms and the events that result?

3. **CITE EVIDENCE** What do the stage directions reveal about Reverend Parris and Thomas Putnam's motives? Cite examples in your response.

4. **INFER** Miller describes John Proctor as a man who "has come to regard himself as a kind of fraud" (paragraph 165). Why does he say that?

5. **ANALYZE** John Proctor says he mistrusts the way Salem uses religion to control others. Then in paragraph 330, he says he "never spoke on witches one way or the other." What **Contrasts and Contradictions** does Proctor's statement reveal? What is his motivation for saying it? Explain.

Choices

Here are some other ways to demonstrate your understanding of Act One.

Writing

↳ Character Sketch

Pick a character from Act One and write a character sketch, following these guidelines.

1. Create a backstory: friends, family, daily life, etc.
2. List the character's mental and physical attributes, including motivations and stressors.
3. Define the character's function in the story, including how the character's actions affect the plot.

Social & Emotional Learning

↳ Group Discussion

In a small group, discuss why people shouldn't rush to judgment, using the events at the end of Act One of *The Crucible* as a case study. Address these questions:

- Who drives the accusations of witchcraft, and what motivates that person? Jealousy? Fear?
- Who controls the situation? What will happen if the situation gets out of hand?
- Is there a better way to handle the situation?

Don't forget to **Notice & Note** as you read the text.

Act Two

1 (*The common room of* Proctor's *house, eight days later.*

2 *At the right is a door opening on the fields outside. A fireplace is at the left, and behind it a stairway leading upstairs. It is the low, dark, and rather long living room of the time. As the curtain rises, the room is empty. From above,* Elizabeth *is heard softly singing to the children. Presently the door opens and* John Proctor *enters, carrying his gun. He glances about the room as he comes toward the fireplace, then halts for an instant as he hears her singing. He continues on to the fireplace, leans the gun against the wall as he swings a pot out of the fire and smells it. Then he lifts out the ladle and tastes. He is not quite pleased. He reaches to a cupboard, takes a pinch of salt, and drops it into the pot. As he is tasting again, her footsteps are heard on the stair. He swings the pot into the fireplace and goes to a basin and washes his hands and face.* Elizabeth *enters.*)

3 **Elizabeth.** What keeps you so late? It's almost dark.

4 **Proctor.** I were planting far out to the forest edge.

5 **Elizabeth.** Oh, you're done then.

6 **Proctor.** Aye, the farm is seeded. The boys asleep?

7 **Elizabeth.** They will be soon. (*And she goes to the fireplace, proceeds to ladle up stew in a dish.*)

8 **Proctor.** Pray now for a fair summer.

9 **Elizabeth.** Aye.

10 **Proctor.** Are you well today?

11 **Elizabeth.** I am. (*She brings the plate to the table, and, indicating the food.*) It is a rabbit.

12 **Proctor** (*going to the table*). Oh, is it! In Jonathan's trap?

13 **Elizabeth.** No, she walked into the house this afternoon; I found her sittin' in the corner like she come to visit.

14 **Proctor.** Oh, that's a good sign walkin' in.

15 **Elizabeth.** Pray God. It hurt my heart to strip her, poor rabbit. (*She sits and watches him taste it.*)

16 **Proctor.** It's well seasoned.

17 **Elizabeth** (*blushing with pleasure*). I took great care. She's tender?

18 **Proctor.** Aye. (*He eats. She watches him.*) I think we'll see green fields soon. It's warm as blood beneath the clods.

19 **Elizabeth.** That's well.

20 (Proctor *eats, then looks up.*)

21 **Proctor.** If the crop is good I'll buy George Jacobs' heifer. How would that please you?

22 **Elizabeth.** Aye, it would.

23 **Proctor** (*with a grin*). I mean to please you, Elizabeth.

24 **Elizabeth** (*It is hard to say*). I know it, John.

25 (*He gets up, goes to her, kisses her. She receives it. With a certain disappointment, he returns to the table.*)

26 **Proctor** (*as gently as he can*). Cider?

27 **Elizabeth** (*with a sense of reprimanding herself for having forgot*). Aye! (*She gets up and goes and pours a glass for him. He now arches his back.*)

28 **Proctor.** This farm's a continent when you go foot by foot droppin' seeds in it.

29 **Elizabeth** (*coming with the cider*). It must be.

30 **Proctor** (*drinks a long draught, then, putting the glass down*). You ought to bring some flowers in the house.

31 **Elizabeth.** Oh! I forgot! I will tomorrow.

32 **Proctor.** It's winter in here yet. On Sunday let you come with me, and we'll walk the farm together; I never see such a load of flowers on the earth. (*With good feeling he goes and looks up at the sky through the open doorway.*) Lilacs have a purple smell. Lilac is the smell of nightfall, I think. Massachusetts is a beauty in the spring!

33 **Elizabeth.** Aye, it is.

34 (*There is a pause. She is watching him from the table as he stands there absorbing the night. It is as though she would speak but cannot. Instead, now, she takes up his plate and glass and fork and goes with them to the basin. Her back is turned to him. He turns to her and watches her. A sense of their separation rises.*)

35 **Proctor.** I think you're sad again. Are you?

36 **Elizabeth** (*She doesn't want friction, and yet she must*). You come so late I thought you'd gone to Salem this afternoon.

37 **Proctor.** Why? I have no business in Salem.

38 **Elizabeth.** You did speak of going, earlier this week.

39 **Proctor** (*He knows what she means*). I thought better of it since.

40 **Elizabeth.** Mary Warren's there today.

41 **Proctor.** Why'd you let her? You heard me forbid her go to Salem any more!

42 **Elizabeth.** I couldn't stop her.

43 **Proctor** (*holding back a full condemnation of her*). It is a fault, it is a fault, Elizabeth—you're the mistress here, not Mary Warren.

44 **Elizabeth.** She frightened all my strength away.

45 **Proctor.** How may that mouse frighten you, Elizabeth? You—

Don't forget to **Notice & Note** as you read the text.

46 **Elizabeth.** It is a mouse no more. I forbid her go, and she raises up her chin like the daughter of a prince and says to me, "I must go to Salem, Goody Proctor; I am an official of the court!"

47 **Proctor.** Court! What court?

48 **Elizabeth.** Aye, it is a proper court they have now. They've sent four judges out of Boston, she says, weighty magistrates of the General Court, and at the head sits the Deputy Governor of the Province.

49 **Proctor** (*astonished*). Why, she's mad.

50 **Elizabeth.** I would to God she were. There be fourteen people in the jail now, she says. (*Proctor simply looks at her, unable to grasp it.*) And they'll be tried, and the court have power to hang them too, she says.

51 **Proctor** (*scoffing, but without conviction*). Ah, they'd never hang—

52 **Elizabeth.** The Deputy Governor promise hangin' if they'll not confess, John. The town's gone wild, I think. She speak of Abigail, and I thought she were a saint, to hear her. Abigail brings the other girls into the court, and where she walks the crowd will part like the sea for Israel. And folks are brought before them, and if they scream and howl and fall to the floor—the person's clapped in the jail for bewitchin' them.

53 **Proctor** (*wide-eyed*). Oh, it is a black mischief.

54 **Elizabeth.** I think you must go to Salem, John. (*He turns to her.*) I think so. You must tell them it is a fraud.

55 **Proctor** (*thinking beyond this*). Aye, it is, it is surely.

56 **Elizabeth.** Let you go to Ezekiel Cheever—he knows you well. And tell him what she said to you last week in her uncle's house. She said it had naught to do with witchcraft, did she not?

57 **Proctor** (*in thought*). Aye, she did, she did. (*now, a pause*)

58 **Elizabeth** (*quietly, fearing to anger him by prodding*). God forbid you keep that from the court, John. I think they must be told.

59 **Proctor** (*quietly, struggling with his thought*). Aye, they must, they must. It is a wonder they do believe her.

60 **Elizabeth.** I would go to Salem now, John—let you go tonight.

61 **Proctor.** I'll think on it.

62 **Elizabeth** (*with her courage now*). You cannot keep it, John.

63 **Proctor** (*angering*). I know I cannot keep it. I say I will think on it!

64 **Elizabeth** (*hurt, and very coldly*). Good, then, let you think on it. (*She stands and starts to walk out of the room.*)

65 **Proctor.** I am only wondering how I may prove what she told me, Elizabeth. If the girl's a saint now, I think it is not easy to prove she's fraud, and the town gone so silly. She told it to me in a room alone—I have no proof for it.

66 **Elizabeth.** You were alone with her?

ANALYZE PLOT

Annotate: Mark in paragraph 46 the surprising news Mary Warren shared with Elizabeth.

Analyze: How does this news function as a plot complication? What effect does it have on the play?

ANALYZE CHARACTERS

Annotate: Mark a repeated word in the stage directions in paragraphs 58–59.

Analyze: What do the stage directions tell you about the different motivations of the characters?

Close Read Screencast

Listen to a modeled close read of this text.

67 **Proctor** (*stubbornly*). For a moment alone, aye.

68 **Elizabeth.** Why, then, it is not as you told me.

69 **Proctor** (*his anger rising*). For a moment, I say. The others come in soon after.

70 **Elizabeth** (*quietly—she has suddenly lost all faith in him*). Do as you wish, then. (*She starts to turn.*)

71 **Proctor.** Woman. (*She turns to him.*) I'll not have your suspicion any more.

72 **Elizabeth** (*a little loftily*). I have no—

73 **Proctor.** I'll not have it!

74 **Elizabeth.** Then let you not earn it.

75 **Proctor** (*with a violent undertone*). You doubt me yet?

76 **Elizabeth** (*with a smile, to keep her dignity*). John, if it were not Abigail that you must go to hurt, would you falter now? I think not.

77 **Proctor.** Now look you—

78 **Elizabeth.** I see what I see, John.

79 **Proctor** (*with solemn warning*). You will not judge me more, Elizabeth. I have good reason to think before I charge fraud on

Abigail, and I will think on it. Let you look to your own improvement before you go to judge your husband any more. I have forgot Abigail, and—

Don't forget to **Notice & Note** as you read the text.

80 **Elizabeth.** And I.

81 **Proctor.** Spare me! You forget nothin' and forgive nothin'. Learn charity, woman. I have gone tiptoe in this house all seven month since she is gone. I have not moved from there to there without I think to please you, and still an everlasting funeral marches round your heart. I cannot speak but I am doubted, every moment judged for lies, as though I come into a court when I come into this house!

82 **Elizabeth.** John, you are not open with me. You saw her with a crowd, you said. Now you—

83 **Proctor.** I'll plead my honesty no more, Elizabeth.

84 **Elizabeth** (*now she would justify herself*). John, I am only—

85 **Proctor.** No more! I should have roared you down when first you told me your suspicion. But I wilted, and, like a Christian, I confessed. Confessed! Some dream I had must have mistaken you for God that day. But you're not, you're not, and let you remember it! Let you look sometimes for the goodness in me, and judge me not.

86 **Elizabeth.** I do not judge you. The magistrate sits in your heart that judges you. I never thought you but a good man, John—(*with a smile*)—only somewhat bewildered.

87 **Proctor** (*laughing bitterly*). Oh, Elizabeth, your justice would freeze beer![1] (*He turns suddenly toward a sound outside. He starts for the door as* Mary Warren *enters. As soon as he sees her, he goes directly to her and grabs her by her cloak, furious.*) How do you go to Salem when I forbid it? Do you mock me? (*shaking her*) I'll whip you if you dare leave this house again! (*Strangely, she doesn't resist him, but hangs limply by his grip.*)

88 **Mary Warren.** I am sick, I am sick, Mr. Proctor. Pray, pray, hurt me not. (*Her strangeness throws him off, and her evident pallor and weakness. He frees her.*) My insides are all shuddery; I am in the proceedings all day, sir.

89 **Proctor** (*with draining anger—his curiosity is draining it*). And what of these proceedings here? When will you proceed to keep this house, as you are paid nine pound a year to do—and my wife not wholly well?

90 (*As though to compensate,* Mary Warren *goes to* Elizabeth *with a small rag doll.*)

91 **Mary Warren.** I made a gift for you today, Goody Proctor. I had to sit long hours in a chair, and passed the time with sewing.

[1] **your justice . . . beer:** Alcoholic beverages freeze at very low temperatures, so Proctor is sarcastically calling his wife cold-hearted.

92 **Elizabeth** (*perplexed, looking at the doll*). Why, thank you, it's a fair poppet.[2]

93 **Mary Warren** (*with a trembling, decayed voice*). We must all love each other now, Goody Proctor.

94 **Elizabeth** (*amazed at her strangeness*). Aye, indeed we must.

95 **Mary Warren** (*glancing at the room*). I'll get up early in the morning and clean the house. I must sleep now. (*She turns and starts off.*)

96 **Proctor.** Mary. (*She halts.*) Is it true? There be fourteen women arrested?

97 **Mary Warren.** No, sir. There be thirty-nine now—(*She suddenly breaks off and sobs and sits down, exhausted.*)

98 **Elizabeth.** Why, she's weepin'! What ails you, child?

99 **Mary Warren.** Goody Osburn—will hang!

100 (*There is a shocked pause, while she sobs.*)

101 **Proctor.** Hang! (*He calls into her face.*) Hang, y'say?

102 **Mary Warren** (*through her weeping*). Aye.

103 **Proctor.** The Deputy Governor will permit it?

104 **Mary Warren.** He sentenced her. He must. (*to ameliorate it*) But not Sarah Good. For Sarah Good confessed, y'see.

105 **Proctor.** Confessed! To what?

106 **Mary Warren.** That she—(*in horror at the memory*)—she sometimes made a compact with Lucifer, and wrote her name in his black book—with her blood—and bound herself to torment Christians till God's thrown down—and we all must worship Hell forevermore.

107 (*pause*)

108 **Proctor.** But—surely you know what a jabberer she is. Did you tell them that?

109 **Mary Warren.** Mr. Proctor, in open court she near to choked us all to death.

110 **Proctor.** How, choked you?

111 **Mary Warren.** She sent her spirit out.

112 **Elizabeth.** Oh, Mary, Mary, surely you—

113 **Mary Warren** (*with an indignant edge*). She tried to kill me many times, Goody Proctor!

114 **Elizabeth.** Why, I never heard you mention that before.

115 **Mary Warren.** I never knew it before. I never knew anything before. When she come into the court I say to myself, I must not accuse this woman, for she sleep in ditches, and so very old and poor. But then—

[2] **fair poppet:** pretty doll.

then she sit there, denying and denying, and I feel a misty coldness climbin' up my back, and the skin on my skull begin to creep, and I feel a clamp around my neck and I cannot breathe air; and then (*entranced*) I hear a voice, a screamin' voice, and it were my voice—and all at once I remembered everything she done to me!

116 **Proctor.** Why? What did she do to you?

117 **Mary Warren** (*like one awakened to a marvelous secret insight*). So many time, Mr. Proctor, she come to this very door, beggin' bread and a cup of cider—and mark this: whenever I turned her away empty, she *mumbled.*

118 **Elizabeth.** Mumbled! She may mumble if she's hungry.

119 **Mary Warren.** But *what* does she mumble? You must remember, Goody Proctor. Last month—a Monday, I think—she walked away, and I thought my guts would burst for two days after. Do you remember it?

120 **Elizabeth.** Why—I do, I think, but—

121 **Mary Warren.** And so I told that to Judge Hathorne, and he asks her so. "Sarah Good," says he, "what curse do you mumble that this girl must fall sick after turning you away?" And then she replies (*mimicking an old crone*) "Why, your excellence, no curse at all. I only say my commandments;[3] I hope I may say my commandments," says she!

122 **Elizabeth.** And that's an upright answer.

123 **Mary Warren.** Aye, but then Judge Hathorne say, "Recite for us your commandments!" (*leaning avidly toward them*) and of all the ten she could not say a single one. She never knew no commandments, and they had her in a flat lie!

124 **Proctor.** And so condemned her?

125 **Mary Warren** (*now a little strained, seeing his stubborn doubt*). Why, they must when she condemned herself.

126 **Proctor.** But the proof, the proof!

127 **Mary Warren** (*with greater impatience with him*). I told you the proof. It's hard proof, hard as rock, the judges said.

128 **Proctor** (*pauses an instant, then*). You will not go to court again, Mary Warren.

129 **Mary Warren.** I must tell you, sir, I will be gone every day now. I am amazed you do not see what weighty work we do.

130 **Proctor.** What work you do! It's strange work for a Christian girl to hang old women!

Don't forget to **Notice & Note** as you read the text.

ANALYZE CHARACTERS

Annotate: Mark phrases in paragraphs 115–117 that express Mary's belief in the witch hunt.

Interpret: What does Mary's dialogue tell you about her character?

[3] **commandments:** the Ten Commandments in the Bible.

131 **Mary Warren.** But, Mr. Proctor, they will not hang them if they confess. Sarah Good will only sit in jail some time (*recalling*) and here's a wonder for you; think on this. Goody Good is pregnant!

132 **Elizabeth.** Pregnant! Are they mad? The woman's near to sixty!

133 **Mary Warren.** They had Doctor Griggs examine her, and she's full to the brim. And smokin' a pipe all these years, and no husband either! But she's safe, thank God, for they'll not hurt the innocent child. But be that not a marvel? You must see it, sir, it's God's work we do. So I'll be gone every day for some time. I'm—I am an official of the court, they say, and I—(*She has been edging toward offstage.*)

134 **Proctor.** I'll official you! (*He strides to the mantel, takes down the whip hanging there.*)

135 **Mary Warren** (*terrified, but coming erect, striving for her authority*). I'll not stand whipping any more!

136 **Elizabeth** (*hurriedly, as* Proctor *approaches*). Mary, promise now you'll stay at home—

137 **Mary Warren** (*backing from him, but keeping her erect posture, striving, striving for her way*). The Devil's loose in Salem, Mr. Proctor; we must discover where he's hiding!

138 **Proctor.** I'll whip the Devil out of you! (*With whip raised he reaches out for her, and she streaks away and yells.*)

139 **Mary Warren** (*pointing at Elizabeth*). I saved her life today!

140 (*Silence. His whip comes down.*)

141 **Elizabeth** (*softly*). I am accused?

142 **Mary Warren** (*quaking*). Somewhat mentioned. But I said I never see no sign you ever sent your spirit out to hurt no one, and seeing I do live so closely with you, they dismissed it.

143 **Elizabeth.** Who accused me?

144 **Mary Warren.** I am bound by law, I cannot tell it. (*to Proctor*) I only hope you'll not be so sarcastical no more. Four judges and the King's deputy sat to dinner with us but an hour ago. I—I would have you speak civilly to me, from this out.

145 **Proctor** (*in horror, muttering in disgust at her*). Go to bed.

146 **Mary Warren** (*with a stamp of her foot*). I'll not be ordered to bed no more, Mr. Proctor! I am eighteen and a woman, however single!

147 **Proctor.** Do you wish to sit up? Then sit up.

148 **Mary Warren.** I wish to go to bed!

149 **Proctor** (*in anger*). Good night, then!

150 **Mary Warren.** Good night. (*Dissatisfied, uncertain of herself, she goes out. Wide-eyed, both, Proctor and Elizabeth stand staring.*)

151 **Elizabeth** (*quietly*). Oh, the noose, the noose is up!

Don't forget to **Notice & Note** as you read the text.

152 **Proctor.** There'll be no noose.

153 **Elizabeth.** She wants me dead. I knew all week it would come to this!

154 **Proctor** (*without conviction*). They dismissed it. You heard her say—

155 **Elizabeth.** And what of tomorrow? She will cry me out until they take me!

156 **Proctor.** Sit you down.

157 **Elizabeth.** She wants me dead, John, you know it!

158 **Proctor.** I say sit down! (*She sits, trembling. He speaks quietly, trying to keep his wits.*) Now we must be wise, Elizabeth.

159 **Elizabeth** (*with sarcasm, and a sense of being lost*). Oh, indeed, indeed!

160 **Proctor.** Fear nothing. I'll find Ezekiel Cheever. I'll tell him she said it were all sport.

161 **Elizabeth.** John, with so many in the jail, more than Cheever's help is needed now, I think. Would you favor me with this? Go to Abigail.

162 **Proctor** (*his soul hardening as he senses . . .*). What have I to say to Abigail?

163 **Elizabeth** (*delicately*). John—grant me this. You have a faulty understanding of young girls. There is a promise made in any bed—

164 **Proctor** (*striving against his anger*). What promise!

165 **Elizabeth.** Spoke or silent, a promise is surely made. And she may dote on it now—I am sure she does—and thinks to kill me, then to take my place.

166 (Proctor*'s anger is rising; he cannot speak.*)

167 **Elizabeth.** It is her dearest hope, John, I know it. There be a thousand names; why does she call mine? There be a certain danger in calling such a name—I am no Goody Good that sleeps in ditches, nor Osburn, drunk and half-witted. She'd dare not call out such a farmer's wife but there be monstrous profit in it. She thinks to take my place, John.

168 **Proctor.** She cannot think it! (*He knows it is true.*)

169 **Elizabeth** (*"reasonably"*). John, have you ever shown her somewhat of contempt? She cannot pass you in the church but you will blush—

170 **Proctor.** I may blush for my sin.

171 **Elizabeth.** I think she sees another meaning in that blush.

172 **Proctor.** And what see you? What see you, Elizabeth?

173 **Elizabeth** (*"conceding"*). I think you be somewhat ashamed, for I am there, and she so close.

174 **Proctor.** When will you know me, woman? Were I stone I would have cracked for shame this seven month!

ANALYZE CHARACTERS

Annotate: Mark stage directions in paragraphs 169–173 that explain the way Elizabeth delivers her statements.

Interpret: Why does Miller set these stage directions in quotation marks? What is revealed about the character of Elizabeth in these moments?

175 **Elizabeth.** Then go and tell her she's a whore. Whatever promise she may sense—break it, John, break it.

176 **Proctor** (*between his teeth*). Good, then. I'll go. (*He starts for his rifle.*)

177 **Elizabeth** (*trembling, fearfully*). Oh, how unwillingly!

178 **Proctor** (*turning on her, rifle in hand*). I will curse her hotter than the oldest cinder in hell. But pray, begrudge me not my anger!

179 **Elizabeth.** Your anger! I only ask you—

180 **Proctor.** Woman, am I so base? Do you truly think me base?

181 **Elizabeth.** I never called you base.

182 **Proctor.** Then how do you charge me with such a promise? The promise that a stallion gives a mare I gave that girl!

183 **Elizabeth.** Then why do you anger with me when I bid you break it?

184 **Proctor.** Because it speaks deceit, and I am honest! But I'll plead no more! I see now your spirit twists around the single error of my life, and I will never tear it free!

185 **Elizabeth** (*crying out*). You'll tear it free—when you come to know that I will be your only wife, or no wife at all! She has an arrow in you yet, John Proctor, and you know it well!

186 (*Quite suddenly, as though from the air, a figure appears in the doorway. They start slightly. It is* Mr. Hale. *He is different now—drawn a little, and there is a quality of deference, even of guilt, about his manner now.*)

187 **Hale.** Good evening.

188 **Proctor** (*still in his shock*). Why, Mr. Hale! Good evening to you, sir. Come in, come in.

189 **Hale** (*to* Elizabeth). I hope I do not startle you.

190 **Elizabeth.** No, no, it's only that I heard no horse—

191 **Hale.** You are Goodwife Proctor.

192 **Proctor.** Aye; Elizabeth.

193 **Hale** (*nods, then*). I hope you're not off to bed yet.

194 **Proctor** (*setting down his gun*). No, no. (*Hale comes further into the room. And Proctor, to explain his nervousness.*) We are not used to visitors after dark, but you're welcome here. Will you sit you down, sir?

195 **Hale.** I will. (*He sits.*) Let you sit, Goodwife Proctor.

196 (*She does, never letting him out of her sight. There is a pause as* Hale *looks about the room.*)

197 **Proctor** (*to break the silence*). Will you drink cider, Mr. Hale?

198 **Hale.** No, it rebels[4] my stomach; I have some further traveling yet tonight. Sit you down, sir. (*Proctor sits.*) I will not keep you long, but I have some business with you.

199 **Proctor.** Business of the court?

200 **Hale.** No—no, I come of my own, without the court's authority. Hear me. (*He wets his lips.*) I know not if you are aware, but your wife's name is—mentioned in the court.

201 **Proctor.** We know it, sir. Our Mary Warren told us. We are entirely amazed.

202 **Hale.** I am a stranger here, as you know. And in my ignorance I find it hard to draw a clear opinion of them that come accused before the court. And so this afternoon, and now tonight, I go from house to house—I come now from Rebecca Nurse's house and—

203 **Elizabeth** (*shocked*). Rebecca's charged!

204 **Hale.** God forbid such a one be charged. She is, however—mentioned somewhat.

205 **Elizabeth** (*with an attempt at a laugh*). You will never believe, I hope, that Rebecca trafficked with the Devil.

206 **Hale.** Woman, it is possible.

207 **Proctor** (*taken aback*). Surely you cannot think so.

208 **Hale.** This is a strange time, Mister. No man may longer doubt the powers of the dark are gathered in monstrous attack upon this village. There is too much evidence now to deny it. You will agree, sir?

209 **Proctor** (*evading*). I—have no knowledge in that line. But it's hard to think so pious a woman be secretly a Devil's bitch after seventy year of such good prayer.

210 **Hale.** Aye. But the Devil is a wily one, you cannot deny it. However, she is far from accused, and I know she will not be. (*pause*) I thought, sir, to put some questions as to the Christian character of this house, if you'll permit me.

211 **Proctor** (*coldly, resentful*). Why, we—have no fear of questions, sir.

212 **Hale.** Good, then. (*He makes himself more comfortable.*) In the book of record that Mr. Parris keeps, I note that you are rarely in the church on Sabbath Day.

213 **Proctor.** No, sir, you are mistaken.

214 **Hale.** Twenty-six time in seventeen month, sir. I must call that rare. Will you tell me why you are so absent?

215 **Proctor.** Mr. Hale, I never knew I must account to that man for I come to church or stay at home. My wife were sick this winter.

[4] **rebels:** upsets.

Don't forget to **Notice & Note** as you read the text.

ANALYZE CHARACTERS

Annotate: Mark the stage direction in paragraph 200 that suggests Hale's feelings.

Infer: What does this stage direction suggest about Hale's emotional state at the moment?

216 **Hale.** So I am told. But you, Mister, why could you not come alone?

217 **Proctor.** I surely did come when I could, and when I could not I prayed in this house.

218 **Hale.** Mr. Proctor, your house is not a church; your theology must tell you that.

219 **Proctor.** It does, sir, it does; and it tells me that a minister may pray to God without he have golden candlesticks upon the altar.

220 **Hale.** What golden candlesticks?

221 **Proctor.** Since we built the church there were pewter candlesticks upon the altar; Francis Nurse made them, y'know, and a sweeter hand never touched the metal. But Parris came, and for twenty week he preach nothin' but golden candlesticks until he had them. I labor the earth from dawn of day to blink of night, and I tell you true, when I look to heaven and see my money glaring at his elbows—it hurt my prayer, sir, it hurt my prayer. I think, sometimes, the man dreams cathedrals, not clapboard meetin' houses.

222 **Hale** (*thinks, then*). And yet, Mister, a Christian on Sabbath Day must be in church. (*pause*) Tell me—you have three children?

223 **Proctor.** Aye. Boys.

224 **Hale.** How comes it that only two are baptized?

225 **Proctor** (*starts to speak, then stops, then, as though unable to restrain this*). I like it not that Mr. Parris should lay his hand upon my baby. I see no light of God in that man. I'll not conceal it.

226 **Hale.** I must say it, Mr. Proctor; that is not for you to decide. The man's ordained, therefore the light of God is in him.

227 **Proctor** (*flushed with resentment but trying to smile*). What's your suspicion, Mr. Hale?

228 **Hale.** No, no, I have no—

229 **Proctor.** I nailed the roof upon the church, I hung the door—

230 **Hale.** Oh, did you! That's a good sign, then.

231 **Proctor.** It may be I have been too quick to bring the man to book,[5] but you cannot think we ever desired the destruction of religion. I think that's in your mind, is it not?

232 **Hale** (*not altogether giving way*). I—have—there is a softness in your record, sir, a softness.

233 **Elizabeth.** I think, maybe, we have been too hard with Mr. Parris. I think so. But sure we never loved the Devil here.

234 **Hale** (*nods, deliberating this. Then, with the voice of one administering a secret test*). Do you know your Commandments, Elizabeth?

[5] **bring the man to book:** judge the man.

Don't forget to **Notice & Note** as you read the text.

235 **Elizabeth** (*without hesitation, even eagerly*). I surely do. There be no mark of blame upon my life, Mr. Hale. I am a covenanted Christian woman.

236 **Hale.** And you, Mister?

237 **Proctor** (*a trifle unsteadily*). I—am sure I do, sir.

238 **Hale** (*glances at her open face, then at* John, *then*). Let you repeat them, if you will.

239 **Proctor.** The Commandments.

240 **Hale.** Aye.

241 **Proctor** (*looking off, beginning to sweat*). Thou shalt not kill.

242 **Hale.** Aye.

243 **Proctor** (*counting on his fingers*). Thou shalt not steal. Thou shalt not covet thy neighbor's goods, nor make unto thee any graven image. Thou shalt not take the name of the Lord in vain; thou shalt have no other gods before me. (*with some hesitation*) Thou shalt remember the Sabbath Day and keep it holy. (*Pause. Then.*) Thou shalt honor thy father and mother. Thou shalt not bear false witness. (*He is stuck. He counts back on his fingers, knowing one is missing.*) Thou shalt not make unto thee any graven image.

244 **Hale.** You have said that twice, sir.

245 **Proctor** (*lost*). Aye. (*He is flailing for it.*)

246 **Elizabeth** (*delicately*). Adultery, John.

247 **Proctor** (*as though a secret arrow had pained his heart*). Aye. (*trying to grin it away—to Hale*) You see, sir, between the two of us we do know them all. (*Hale only looks at Proctor, deep in his attempt to define this man. Proctor grows more uneasy.*) I think it be a small fault.

ANALYZE CHARACTERS

Annotate: Mark stage directions in paragraphs 237–247 that describe how Proctor feels.

Evaluate: Is Proctor's weakness in this scene believable? Why or why not?

248 **Hale.** Theology, sir, is a fortress; no crack in a fortress may be accounted small. (*He rises; he seems worried now. He paces a little, in deep thought.*)

249 **Proctor.** There be no love for Satan in this house, Mister.

250 **Hale.** I pray it, I pray it dearly. (*He looks to both of them, an attempt at a smile on his face, but his misgivings are clear.*) Well, then—I'll bid you good night.

251 **Elizabeth** (*unable to restrain herself*). Mr. Hale. (*He turns.*) I do think you are suspecting me somewhat? Are you not?

252 **Hale** (*obviously disturbed—and evasive*). Goody Proctor, I do not judge you. My duty is to add what I may to the godly wisdom of the court. I pray you both good health and good fortune. (*to John*) Good night, sir. (*He starts out.*)

253 **Elizabeth** (*with a note of desperation*). I think you must tell him, John.

254 **Hale.** What's that?

255 **Elizabeth** (*restraining a call*). Will you tell him?

256 (*Slight pause.* Hale *looks questioningly at* John.)

257 **Proctor** (*with difficulty*). I—I have no witness and cannot prove it, except my word be taken. But I know the children's sickness had naught to do with witchcraft.

258 **Hale** (*stopped, struck*). Naught to do—?

259 **Proctor.** Mr. Parris discovered them sportin' in the woods. They were startled and took sick.

260 (*pause*)

261 **Hale.** Who told you this?

262 **Proctor** (*hesitates, then*). Abigail Williams.

263 **Hale.** Abigail!

264 **Proctor.** Aye.

265 **Hale** (*his eyes wide*). Abigail Williams told you it had naught to do with witchcraft!

266 **Proctor.** She told me the day you came, sir.

267 **Hale** (*suspiciously*). Why—why did you keep this?

268 **Proctor.** I never knew until tonight that the world is gone daft with this nonsense.

269 **Hale.** Nonsense! Mister, I have myself examined Tituba, Sarah Good, and numerous others that have confessed to dealing with the Devil. They have *confessed* it.

270 **Proctor.** And why not, if they must hang for denyin' it? There are them that will swear to anything before they'll hang; have you never thought of that?

271 **Hale.** I have. I—I have indeed. (*It is his own suspicion, but he resists it. He glances at Elizabeth, then at John.*) And you—would you testify to this in court?

272 **Proctor.** I—had not reckoned with goin' into court. But if I must I will.

273 **Hale.** Do you falter here?

274 **Proctor.** I falter nothing, but I may wonder if my story will be credited in such a court. I do wonder on it, when such a steady-minded minister as you will suspicion such a woman that never lied, and cannot, and the world knows she cannot! I may falter somewhat, Mister; I am no fool.

275 **Hale** (*quietly—it has impressed him*). Proctor, let you open with me now, for I have a rumor that troubles me. It's said you hold no belief that there may even be witches in the world. Is that true, sir?

Don't forget to **Notice & Note** as you read the text.

276 **Proctor** (*He knows this is critical, and is striving against his disgust with* Hale *and with himself for even answering*). I know not what I have said, I may have said it. I have wondered if there be witches in the world—although I cannot believe they come among us now.

277 **Hale.** Then you do not believe—

278 **Proctor.** I have no knowledge of it; the Bible speaks of witches, and I will not deny them.

279 **Hale.** And you, woman?

280 **Elizabeth.** I—I cannot believe it.

281 **Hale** (*shocked*). You cannot!

282 **Proctor.** Elizabeth, you bewilder him!

283 **Elizabeth** (*to* Hale). I cannot think the Devil may own a woman's soul, Mr. Hale, when she keeps an upright way, as I have. I am a good woman, I know it; and if you believe I may do only good work in the world, and yet be secretly bound to Satan, then I must tell you, sir, I do not believe it.

284 **Hale.** But, woman, you do believe there are witches in—

285 **Elizabeth.** If you think that I am one, then I say there are none.

286 **Hale.** You surely do not fly against the Gospel, the Gospel—

287 **Proctor.** She believe in the Gospel, every word!

288 **Elizabeth.** Question Abigail Williams about the Gospel, not myself!

(Hale *stares at her.*)

289 **Proctor.** She do not mean to doubt the Gospel, sir, you cannot think it. This be a Christian house, sir, a Christian house.

290 **Hale.** God keep you both; let the third child be quickly baptized, and go you without fail each Sunday in to Sabbath prayer; and keep a solemn, quiet way among you. I think—

291 (Giles Corey *appears in doorway.*)

292 **Giles.** John!

293 **Proctor.** Giles! What's the matter?

294 **Giles.** They take my wife.

295 (Francis Nurse *enters.*)

296 **Giles.** And his Rebecca!

297 **Proctor** (*to* Francis). Rebecca's in the *jail!*

298 **Francis.** Aye, Cheever come and take her in his wagon. We've only now come from the jail, and they'll not even let us in to see them.

299 **Elizabeth.** They've surely gone wild now, Mr. Hale!

300 **Francis** (*going to* Hale). Reverend Hale! Can you not speak to the Deputy Governor? I'm sure he mistakes these people—

ANALYZE PLOT

Annotate: Mark dialogue in paragraphs 294–304 that tells what happened to the wives of Francis and Giles.

Interpret: Explain whether this event is a plot complication that makes the main conflict more difficult to resolve.

301 **Hale.** Pray calm yourself, Mr. Nurse.

302 **Francis.** My wife is the very brick and mortar of the church, Mr. Hale (*indicating Giles*) and Martha Corey, there cannot be a woman closer yet to God than Martha.

303 **Hale.** How is Rebecca charged, Mr. Nurse?

304 **Francis** (*with a mocking, half-hearted laugh*). For murder, she's charged! (*mockingly quoting the warrant*) "For the marvelous and supernatural murder of Goody Putnam's babies." What am I to do, Mr. Hale?

305 **Hale** (*turns from* Francis, *deeply troubled, then*). Believe me, Mr. Nurse, if Rebecca Nurse be tainted, then nothing's left to stop the whole green world from burning. Let you rest upon the justice of the court; the court will send her home, I know it.

306 **Francis.** You cannot mean she will be tried in court!

307 **Hale** (*pleading*). Nurse, though our hearts break, we cannot flinch; these are new times, sir. There is a misty plot afoot so subtle we should be criminal to cling to old respects and ancient friendships. I have seen too many frightful proofs in court—the Devil is alive in Salem, and we dare not quail to follow wherever the accusing finger points!

308 **Proctor** (*angered*). How may such a woman murder children?

309 **Hale** (*in great pain*). Man, remember, until an hour before the Devil fell, God thought him beautiful in Heaven.

310 **Giles.** I never said my wife were a witch, Mr. Hale; I only said she were reading books!

311 **Hale.** Mr. Corey, exactly what complaint were made on your wife?

312 **Giles.** That bloody mongrel Walcott charge her. Y'see, he buy a pig of my wife four or five year ago, and the pig died soon after. So he come dancin' in for his money back. So my Martha, she says to him, "Walcott, if you haven't the wit to feed a pig properly, you'll not live to own many," she says. Now he goes to court and claims that from that day to this he cannot keep a pig alive for more than four weeks because my Martha bewitch them with her books!

313 (*Enter* Ezekiel Cheever. *A shocked silence.*)

314 **Cheever.** Good evening to you, Proctor.

315 **Proctor.** Why, Mr. Cheever. Good evening.

316 **Cheever.** Good evening, all. Good evening, Mr. Hale.

317 **Proctor.** I hope you come not on business of the court.

318 **Cheever.** I do, Proctor, aye. I am clerk of the court now, y'know.

319 (*Enter* Marshal Herrick, *a man in his early thirties, who is somewhat shamefaced at the moment.*)

Don't forget to **Notice & Note** as you read the text.

320 **Giles.** It's a pity, Ezekiel, that an honest tailor might have gone to Heaven must burn in Hell. You'll burn for this, do you know it?

321 **Cheever.** You know yourself I must do as I'm told. You surely know that, Giles. And I'd as lief[6] you'd not be sending me to Hell. I like not the sound of it, I tell you; I like not the sound of it. (*He fears Proctor, but starts to reach inside his coat.*) Now believe me, Proctor, how heavy be the law, all its tonnage I do carry on my back tonight. (*He takes out a warrant.*) I have a warrant for your wife.

322 **Proctor** (*to* Hale). You said she were not charged!

323 **Hale.** I know nothin' of it. (*to Cheever*) When were she charged?

324 **Cheever.** I am given sixteen warrant tonight, sir, and she is one.

325 **Proctor.** Who charged her?

326 **Cheever.** Why, Abigail Williams charge her.

327 **Proctor.** On what proof, what proof?

328 **Cheever** (*looking about the room*). Mr. Proctor, I have little time. The court bid me search your house, but I like not to search a house. So will you hand me any poppets that your wife may keep here?

329 **Proctor.** Poppets?

330 **Elizabeth.** I never kept no poppets, not since I were a girl.

331 **Cheever** (*embarrassed, glancing toward the mantel where sits* Mary Warren's *poppet*). I spy a poppet, Goody Proctor.

332 **Elizabeth.** Oh! (*going for it*) Why, this is Mary's.

333 **Cheever** (*shyly*). Would you please to give it to me?

334 **Elizabeth** (*handing it to him, asks* Hale). Has the court discovered a text in poppets now?

335 **Cheever** (*carefully holding the poppet*). Do you keep any others in this house?

336 **Proctor.** No, nor this one either till tonight. What signifies a poppet?

337 **Cheever.** Why, a poppet—(*He gingerly turns the poppet over.*) a poppet may signify—Now, woman, will you please to come with me?

338 **Proctor.** She will not! (*to Elizabeth*) Fetch Mary here.

339 **Cheever** (*ineptly reaching toward* Elizabeth). No, no, I am forbid to leave her from my sight.

340 **Proctor** (*pushing his arm away*). You'll leave her out of sight and out of mind, Mister. Fetch Mary, Elizabeth. (*Elizabeth goes upstairs.*)

341 **Hale.** What signifies a poppet, Mr. Cheever?

[6] **as lief** (lēf): rather.

342 **Cheever** (*turning the poppet over in his hands*). Why, they say it may signify that she—(*He has lifted the poppet's skirt, and his eyes widen in astonished fear.*) Why, this, this—

343 **Proctor** (*reaching for the poppet*). What's there?

344 **Cheever.** Why (*He draws out a long needle from the poppet.*) it is a needle! Herrick, Herrick, it is a needle!

345 (Herrick *comes toward him.*)

346 **Proctor** (*angrily, bewildered*). And what signifies a needle!

ANALYZE LITERARY DEVICES

Annotate: Remember that **dramatic irony** is a contrast between what a character knows and what the reader or audience knows. Mark an example of dramatic irony in the section about the poppet.

Interpret: Why is this an example of dramatic irony?

347 **Cheever** (*his hands shaking*). Why, this go hard with her, Proctor, this—I had my doubts, Proctor, I had my doubts, but here's calamity. (*to Hale, showing the needle*) You see it, sir, it is a needle!

348 **Hale.** Why? What meanin' has it?

349 **Cheever** (*wide-eyed, trembling*). The girl, the Williams girl, Abigail Williams, sir. She sat to dinner in Reverend Parris's house tonight, and without word nor warnin' she falls to the floor. Like a struck beast, he says, and screamed a scream that a bull would weep to hear. And he goes to save her, and, stuck two inches in the flesh of her belly, he draw a needle out. And demandin' of her how she come to be so stabbed, she (*to Proctor now*) testify it were your wife's familiar spirit[7] pushed it in.

350 **Proctor.** Why, she done it herself! (*to Hale*) I hope you're not takin' this for proof, Mister!

351 (Hale, *struck by the proof, is silent.*)

352 **Cheever.** 'Tis hard proof! (*to Hale*) I find here a poppet Goody Proctor keeps. I have found it, sir. And in the belly of the poppet a needle's stuck. I tell you true, Proctor, I never warranted to see such proof of Hell, and I bid you obstruct me not, for I—

353 (*Enter* Elizabeth *with* Mary Warren. Proctor, *seeing* Mary Warren, *draws her by the arm to* Hale.)

354 **Proctor.** Here now! Mary, how did this poppet come into my house?

355 **Mary Warren** (*frightened for herself, her voice very small*). What poppet's that, sir?

356 **Proctor** (*impatiently, pointing at the doll in* Cheever*'s hand*). This poppet, this poppet.

357 **Mary Warren** (*evasively, looking at it*). Why, I—I think it is mine.

358 **Proctor.** It is your poppet, is it not?

359 **Mary Warren** (*not understanding the direction of this*). It—is, sir.

360 **Proctor.** And how did it come into this house?

[7] **familiar spirit:** the spirit or demon, most usually in the form of an animal, such as a black cat, that was a companion and helper to a witch.

361 **Mary Warren** (*glancing about at the avid faces*). Why—I made it in the court, sir, and—give it to Goody Proctor tonight.

Don't forget to **Notice & Note** as you read the text.

362 **Proctor** (*to* Hale). Now, sir—do you have it?

363 **Hale.** Mary Warren, a needle have been found inside this poppet.

364 **Mary Warren** (*bewildered*). Why, I meant no harm by it, sir.

365 **Proctor** (*quickly*). You stuck that needle in yourself?

366 **Mary Warren.** I—I believe I did, sir, I—

367 **Proctor** (*to* Hale). What say you now?

368 **Hale** (*watching* Mary Warren *closely*). Child, you are certain this be your natural memory? May it be, perhaps, that someone conjures you even now to say this?

369 **Mary Warren.** Conjures me? Why, no, sir, I am entirely myself, I think. Let you ask Susanna Walcott—she saw me sewin' it in court. (*or better still*) Ask Abby, Abby sat beside me when I made it.

370 **Proctor** (*to* Hale, *of* Cheever). Bid him begone. Your mind is surely settled now. Bid him out, Mr. Hale.

371 **Elizabeth.** What signifies a needle?

372 **Hale.** Mary—you charge a cold and cruel murder on Abigail.

373 **Mary Warren.** Murder! I charge no—

374 **Hale.** Abigail were stabbed tonight; a needle were found stuck into her belly—

375 **Elizabeth.** And she charges me?

376 **Hale.** Aye.

377 **Elizabeth** (*her breath knocked out*). Why—! The girl is murder! She must be ripped out of the world!

378 **Cheever** (*pointing at* Elizabeth). You've heard that, sir! Ripped out of the world! Herrick, you heard it!

379 **Proctor** (*suddenly snatching the warrant out of* Cheever's *hands*). Out with you.

380 **Cheever.** Proctor, you dare not touch the warrant.

381 **Proctor** (*ripping the warrant*). Out with you!

382 **Cheever.** You've ripped the Deputy Governor's warrant, man!

383 **Proctor.** Damn the Deputy Governor! Out of my house!

384 **Hale.** Now, Proctor, Proctor!

385 **Proctor.** Get y'gone with them! You are a broken minister.

386 **Hale.** Proctor, if she is innocent, the court—

387 **Proctor.** If *she* is innocent! Why do you never wonder if Parris be innocent, or Abigail? Is the accuser always holy now? Were they born this morning as clean as God's fingers? I'll tell you what's walking

Salem—vengeance is walking Salem. We are what we always were in Salem, but now the little crazy children are jangling the keys of the kingdom, and common vengeance writes the law! This warrant's vengeance! I'll not give my wife to vengeance!

388 **Elizabeth.** I'll go, John—

389 **Proctor.** You will not go!

390 **Herrick.** I have nine men outside. You cannot keep her. The law binds me, John, I cannot budge.

391 **Proctor** (*to* Hale, *ready to break him*). Will you see her taken?

392 **Hale.** Proctor, the court is just—

393 **Proctor.** Pontius Pilate! God will not let you wash your hands of this![8]

ANALYZE CHARACTERS

Annotate: Mark the stage direction in paragraph 394 that describes Proctor's behavior.

Interpret: What is the motivation for this behavior? Cite evidence in your response.

394 **Elizabeth.** John—I think I must go with them. (*He cannot bear to look at her.*) Mary, there is bread enough for the morning; you will bake, in the afternoon. Help Mr. Proctor as you were his daughter—you owe me that, and much more. (*She is fighting her weeping. To Proctor.*) When the children wake, speak nothing of witchcraft—it will frighten them. (*She cannot go on.*)

395 **Proctor.** I will bring you home. I will bring you soon.

396 **Elizabeth.** Oh, John, bring me soon!

397 **Proctor.** I will fall like an ocean on that court! Fear nothing, Elizabeth.

398 **Elizabeth** (*with great fear*). I will fear nothing. (*She looks about the room, as though to fix it in her mind.*) Tell the children I have gone to visit someone sick.

399 (*She walks out the door,* Herrick *and* Cheever *behind her. For a moment,* Proctor *watches from the doorway. The clank of chain is heard.*)

400 **Proctor.** Herrick! Herrick, don't chain her! (*He rushes out the door. From outside.*) Damn you, man, you will not chain her! Off with them! I'll not have it! I will not have her chained!

401 (*There are other men's voices against his.* Hale, *in a fever of guilt and uncertainty, turns from the door to avoid the sight;* Mary Warren *bursts into tears and sits weeping.* Giles Corey *calls to* Hale.)

402 **Giles.** And yet silent, minister? It is fraud, you know it is fraud! What keeps you, man?

403 (Proctor *is half braced, half pushed into the room by two deputies and* Herrick.)

404 **Proctor.** I'll pay you, Herrick, I will surely pay you!

---

[8] **Pontius Pilate** (pŏn′chəs pī′lət) **. . . hands of this:** the Roman official who presided over the trial and sentencing of Christ. Pilate publicly washed his hands to absolve himself of responsibility for Christ's death.

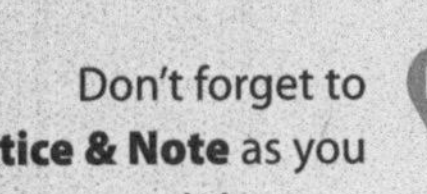

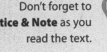

405 **Herrick** (*panting*). In God's name, John, I cannot help myself. I must chain them all. Now let you keep inside this house till I am gone! (*He goes out with his deputies.*)

406 (Proctor *stands there, gulping air. Horses and a wagon creaking are heard.*)

407 **Hale** (*in great uncertainty*). Mr. Proctor—

408 **Proctor.** Out of my sight!

409 **Hale.** Charity, Proctor, charity. What I have heard in her favor, I will not fear to testify in court. God help me, I cannot judge her guilty or innocent—I know not. Only this consider: the world goes mad, and it profit nothing you should lay the cause to the vengeance of a little girl.

410 **Proctor.** You are a coward! Though you be ordained in God's own tears, you are a coward now!

411 **Hale.** Proctor, I cannot think God be provoked so grandly by such a petty cause. The jails are packed— our greatest judges sit in Salem now—and hangin's promised. Man, we must look to cause proportionate. Were there murder done, perhaps, and never brought to light? Abomination? Some secret blasphemy that stinks to Heaven? Think on cause, man, and let you help me to discover it. For there's your way, believe it, there is your only way, when such confusion strikes upon the world. (*He goes to Giles and Francis.*) Let you counsel among yourselves; think on your village and what may have drawn from heaven such thundering wrath upon you all. I shall pray God open up our eyes.

412 (Hale *goes out.*)

413 **Francis** (*struck by* Hale's *mood*). I never heard no murder done in Salem.

414 **Proctor** (*He has been reached by* Hale's *words*). Leave me, Francis, leave me.

415 **Giles** (*shaken*). John—tell me, are we lost?

416 **Proctor.** Go home now, Giles. We'll speak on it tomorrow.

417 **Giles.** Let you think on it. We'll come early, eh?

418 **Proctor.** Aye. Go now, Giles.

419 **Giles.** Good night, then.

420 (Giles Corey *goes out. After a moment.*)

421 **Mary Warren** (*in a fearful squeak of a voice*). Mr. Proctor, very likely they'll let her come home once they're given proper evidence.

422 **Proctor.** You're coming to the court with me, Mary. You will tell it in the court.

423 **Mary Warren.** I cannot charge murder on Abigail.

424 **Proctor** (*moving menacingly toward her*). You will tell the court how that poppet come here and who stuck the needle in.

425 **Mary Warren.** She'll kill me for sayin' that! (*Proctor continues toward her.*) Abby'll charge lechery on you, Mr. Proctor!

426 **Proctor** (*halting*). She's told you!

427 **Mary Warren.** I have known it, sir. She'll ruin you with it, I know she will.

428 **Proctor** (*hesitating, and with deep hatred of himself*). Good. Then her saintliness is done with. (*Mary backs from him.*) We will slide together into our pit; you will tell the court what you know.

429 **Mary Warren** (*in terror*). I cannot, they'll turn on me—

430 (Proctor *strides and catches her, and she is repeating, "I cannot, I cannot!"*)

431 **Proctor.** My wife will never die for me! I will bring your guts into your mouth but that goodness will not die for me!

432 **Mary Warren** (*struggling to escape him*). I cannot do it, I cannot!

ANALYZE PLOT

Annotate: Mark striking details in Proctor's speech.

Interpret: What is the meaning of this speech? How does it relate to the central conflict of the play?

433 **Proctor** (*grasping her by the throat as though he would strangle her*). Make your peace with it! Now Hell and Heaven grapple on our backs, and all our old pretense is ripped away—make your peace! (*He throws her to the floor, where she sobs, "I cannot, I cannot . . ." And now, half to himself, staring, and turning to the open door.*) Peace. It is a providence, and no great change; we are only what we always were, but naked now. (*He walks as though toward a great horror, facing the open sky.*) Aye, naked! And the wind, God's icy wind, will blow!

434 (*And she is over and over again sobbing, "I cannot, I cannot, I cannot," as the curtain falls.*)

Don't forget to **Notice & Note** as you read the text.

COLLABORATIVE DISCUSSION

With a partner, discuss why John Proctor hesitates instead of immediately going to Salem and revealing what he knows? What will he lose if the truth is known? Support your ideas with details from the play.

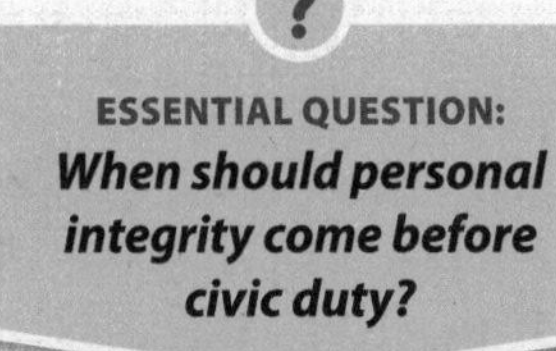
ESSENTIAL QUESTION:
When should personal integrity come before civic duty?

Review your notes and add your thoughts to your **Response Log.**

Assessment Practice

Answer these questions before moving on to the **Analyze the Text** section on the following page.

1. Why is Proctor reluctant to testify that Abigail said the dancing was not part of a witches' spell?

- (A) He wants to protect Abigail.
- (B) He wants to protect Elizabeth.
- (C) He wants to hide the fact he was alone with Abigail.
- (D) He wants to make sure people accused of witchcraft are punished.

2. Why does Mary Warren become more demanding of the Proctors?

- (A) Her need for their help has become greater.
- (B) She is being victimized by Abigail and her friends.
- (C) She knows more than they do about how witchcraft works.
- (D) She has more power over them due to her position in the court.

3. Who is the source of conflict between Abigail and Elizabeth?

- (A) Hale
- (B) Parris
- (C) Proctor
- (D) Rebecca

Test-Taking Strategies

Analyze the Text

Support your responses with evidence from the text.

NOTICE & NOTE

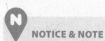

Review what you **noticed and noted** as you read the text. Your annotations can help you answer these questions.

1. **CITE EVIDENCE** How do the events in Act Two affect how readers perceive the situation in which Proctor and the others find themselves?

2. **DRAW CONCLUSIONS** Reread paragraphs 70–87. How does John and Elizabeth Proctor's relationship introduce a plot complication?

3. **ANALYZE** Why is Proctor struck by Hale's declaration that "some secret blasphemy" has caused all of the confusion? How does Hale's statement relate to Proctor's later words to Mary Warren that he and Abigail will "slide together into our pit; you will tell the court what you know"?

4. **ANALYZE** What does Mary Warren's behavior in Act Two foreshadow about her testimony in court? Explain.

5. **DRAW CONCLUSIONS** Often, characters in a drama act as foils for other characters. These characters—often minor ones—contrast strikingly with a main character, clarifying characteristics of the main character. Reread paragraphs 112–123. How could Mary be seen as a foil for Elizabeth?

Choices

Here are some other ways to demonstrate your understanding of Act Two.

Writing

↳ Support an Opinion

During the anti-Communist hearings, Arthur Miller said, "I saw accepted the notion that conscience was no longer a private matter but one of state administration."

Do you believe this comment applies to the Salem witch trials? If so, how? If not, why not? Write a short essay stating and supporting your opinion.

Media

↳ Presentation

In a group, research the McCarthy-era trials of the 1950s to create a media presentation that shows how the trials parallel events depicted in the play.

1. Use reliable sources and cite your findings.
2. Try to include charts, outlines, and illustrations in your organizational format.
3. Practice your presentation to make sure all the elements are in place. When you are ready, present your findings to the class.

Don't forget to **Notice & Note** as you read the text.

ACT THREE

1 (*The vestry room of the Salem meeting house, now serving as the anteroom*[1] *of the General Court.*

2 *As the curtain rises, the room is empty, but for sunlight pouring through two high windows in the back wall. The room is solemn, even forbidding. Heavy beams jut out, boards of random widths make up the walls. At the right are two doors leading into the meeting house proper, where the court is being held. At the left another door leads outside.*

3 *There is a plain bench at the left, and another at the right. In the center a rather long meeting table, with stools and a considerable armchair snugged up to it.*

4 *Through the partitioning wall at the right we hear a prosecutor's voice,* Judge Hathorne's, *asking a question; then a woman's voice,* Martha Corey's, *replying.*)

5 **Hathorne's Voice.** Now, Martha Corey, there is abundant evidence in our hands to show that you have given yourself to the reading of fortunes. Do you deny it?

6 **Martha Corey's Voice.** I am innocent to a witch. I know not what a witch is.

7 **Hathorne's Voice.** How do you know, then, that you are not a witch?

8 **Martha Corey's Voice.** If I were, I would know it.

9 **Hathorne's Voice.** Why do you hurt these children?

10 **Martha Corey's Voice.** I do not hurt them. I scorn it!

11 **Giles' Voice** (*roaring*). I have evidence for the court!

12 (*Voices of townspeople rise in excitement.*)

13 **Danforth's Voice.** You will keep your seat!

14 **Giles' Voice.** Thomas Putnam is reaching out for land!

15 **Danforth's Voice.** Remove that man, Marshal!

16 **Giles' Voice.** You're hearing lies, lies!

17 (*A roaring goes up from the people.*)

18 **Hathorne's Voice.** Arrest him, excellency!

19 **Giles' Voice.** I have evidence. Why will you not hear my evidence?

20 (*The door opens and* Giles *is half carried into the vestry room by* Herrick.)

21 **Giles.** Hands off, damn you, let me go!

22 **Herrick.** Giles, Giles!

23 **Giles.** Out of my way, Herrick! I bring evidence—

ANALYZE CHARACTERS

Annotate: Mark dialogue that explains what Giles thinks is behind the witch hunt.

Interpret: How does this dialogue suggest a motivation for Putnam's behavior?

[1] **vestry room . . . anteroom:** A vestry room is a room in a church used for nonreligious meetings or church business. An anteroom is a waiting room or a room that leads into another.

24 **Herrick.** You cannot go in there, Giles; it's a court!

25 (*Enter* Hale *from the court.*)

26 **Hale.** Pray be calm a moment.

27 **Giles.** You, Mr. Hale, go in there and demand I speak.

28 **Hale.** A moment, sir, a moment.

29 **Giles.** They'll be hangin' my wife!

30 (Judge Hathorne *enters. He is in his sixties, a bitter, remorseless Salem judge.*)

31 **Hathorne.** How do you dare come roarin' into this court! Are you gone daft, Corey?

32 **Giles.** You're not a Boston judge yet, Hathorne. You'll not call me daft!

33 (*Enter* Deputy Governor Danforth *and, behind him,* Ezekiel Cheever *and* Parris. *On his appearance, silence falls.* Danforth *is a grave man in his sixties, of some humor and sophistication that does not, however, interfere with an exact loyalty to his position and his cause. He comes down to* Giles, *who awaits his wrath.*)

34 **Danforth** (*looking directly at* Giles). Who is this man?

35 **Parris.** Giles Corey, sir, and a more contentious—

36 **Giles** (*to* Parris). I am asked the question, and I am old enough to answer it! (*to* Danforth, *who impresses him and to whom he smiles through his strain*) My name is Corey, sir, Giles Corey. I have six hundred acres, and timber in addition. It is my wife you be condemning now. (*He indicates the courtroom.*)

37 **Danforth.** And how do you imagine to help her cause with such contemptuous riot?[2] Now be gone. Your old age alone keeps you out of jail for this.

38 **Giles** (*beginning to plead*). They be tellin' lies about my wife, sir, I—

39 **Danforth.** Do you take it upon yourself to determine what this court shall believe and what it shall set aside?

40 **Giles.** Your Excellency, we mean no disrespect for—

41 **Danforth.** Disrespect indeed! It is disruption, Mister. This is the highest court of the supreme government of this province, do you know it?

42 **Giles** (*beginning to weep*). Your Excellency, I only said she were readin' books, sir, and they come and take her out of my house for—

43 **Danforth** (*mystified*). Books! What books?

44 **Giles** (*through helpless sobs*). It is my third wife, sir; I never had no wife that be so taken with books, and I thought to find the cause of it,

[2] **contemptuous** (kən-tĕmp´cho͞o-əs) **riot:** disrespectful, outrageous behavior.

d'y'see, but it were no witch I blamed her for. (*He is openly weeping.*) I have broke charity with the woman, I have broke charity with her. (*He covers his face, ashamed.* Danforth *is respectfully silent.*)

Don't forget to **Notice & Note** as you read the text.

45 **Hale.** Excellency, he claims hard evidence for his wife's defense. I think that in all justice you must—

46 **Danforth.** Then let him submit his evidence in proper affidavit. You are certainly aware of our procedure here, Mr. Hale. (*to* Herrick) Clear this room.

47 **Herrick.** Come now, Giles. (*He gently pushes* Corey *out.*)

48 **Francis.** We are desperate, sir; we come here three days now and cannot be heard.

49 **Danforth.** Who is this man?

50 **Francis.** Francis Nurse, Your Excellency.

51 **Hale.** His wife's Rebecca that were condemned this morning.

52 **Danforth.** Indeed! I am amazed to find you in such uproar. I have only good report of your character, Mr. Nurse.

53 **Hathorne.** I think they must both be arrested in contempt, sir.

54 **Danforth** (*to* Francis). Let you write your plea, and in due time I will—

55 **Francis.** Excellency, we have proof for your eyes; God forbid you shut them to it. The girls, sir, the girls are frauds.

56 **Danforth.** What's that?

57 **Francis.** We have proof of it, sir. They are all deceiving you.

58 (Danforth *is shocked, but studying* Francis.)

59 **Hathorne.** This is contempt, sir, contempt!

60 **Danforth.** Peace, Judge Hathorne. Do you know who I am, Mr. Nurse?

61 **Francis.** I surely do, sir, and I think you must be a wise judge to be what you are.

62 **Danforth.** And do you know that near to four hundred are in the jails from Marblehead to Lynn,[3] and upon my signature?

63 **Francis.** I—

64 **Danforth.** And seventy-two condemned to hang by that signature?

65 **Francis.** Excellency, I never thought to say it to such a weighty judge, but you are deceived.

66 (*Enter* Giles Corey *from left. All turn to see as he beckons in* Mary Warren *with* Proctor. Mary *is keeping her eyes to the ground;* Proctor *has her elbow as though she were near collapse.*)

[3] **Marblehead . . . Lynn:** two coastal towns in Massachusetts, near Salem.

67 **Parris** (*on seeing her, in shock*). Mary Warren! (*He goes directly to bend close to her face.*) What are you about here?

68 **Proctor** (*pressing* Parris *away from her with a gentle but firm motion of protectiveness*). She would speak with the Deputy Governor.

69 **Danforth** (*shocked by this, turns to* Herrick). Did you not tell me Mary Warren were sick in bed?

70 **Herrick.** She were, Your Honor. When I go to fetch her to the court last week, she said she were sick.

71 **Giles.** She has been strivin' with her soul all week, Your Honor; she comes now to tell the truth of this to you.

72 **Danforth.** Who is this?

73 **Proctor.** John Proctor, sir. Elizabeth Proctor is my wife.

ANALYZE CHARACTERS

Annotate: Mark phrases in paragraphs 74–84 that show Parris attempting to undermine Proctor.

Analyze: How do these lines help you determine who is the protagonist and who is the antagonist in the play?

74 **Parris.** Beware this man, Your Excellency, this man is mischief.

75 **Hale** (*excitedly*). I think you must hear the girl, sir, she—

76 **Danforth** (*who has become very interested in* Mary Warren *and only raises a hand toward* Hale). Peace. What would you tell us, Mary Warren?

77 (Proctor *looks at her, but she cannot speak.*)

78 **Proctor.** She never saw no spirits, sir.

79 **Danforth** (*with great alarm and surprise, to* Mary). Never saw no spirits!

80 **Giles** (*eagerly*). Never.

81 **Proctor** (*reaching into his jacket*). She has signed a deposition, sir—

82 **Danforth** (*instantly*). No, no, I accept no depositions. (*He is rapidly calculating this; he turns from her to* Proctor.) Tell me, Mr. Proctor, have you given out this story in the village?

83 **Proctor.** We have not.

84 **Parris.** They've come to overthrow the court, sir! This man is—

85 **Danforth.** I pray you, Mr. Parris. Do you know, Mr. Proctor, that the entire contention of the state in these trials is that the voice of Heaven is speaking through the children?

86 **Proctor.** I know that, sir.

87 **Danforth** (*thinks, staring at* Proctor, *then turns to* Mary Warren). And you, Mary Warren, how came you to cry out people for sending their spirits against you?

88 **Mary Warren.** It were pretense, sir.

89 **Danforth.** I cannot hear you.

90 **Proctor.** It were pretense, she says.

91 **Danforth.** Ah? And the other girls? Susanna Walcott, and—the others? They are also pretending?

Don't forget to **Notice & Note** as you read the text.

92 **Mary Warren.** Aye, sir.

93 **Danforth** (*wide-eyed*). Indeed. (*Pause. He is baffled by this. He turns to study* Proctor's *face.*)

94 **Parris** (*in a sweat*). Excellency, you surely cannot think to let so vile a lie be spread in open court!

95 **Danforth.** Indeed not, but it strike hard upon me that she will dare come here with such a tale. Now, Mr. Proctor, before I decide whether I shall hear you or not, it is my duty to tell you this. We burn a hot fire here; it melts down all concealment.

96 **Proctor.** I know that, sir.

97 **Danforth.** Let me continue. I understand well, a husband's tenderness may drive him to extravagance in defense of a wife. Are you certain in your conscience, Mister, that your evidence is the truth?

98 **Proctor.** It is. And you will surely know it.

99 **Danforth.** And you thought to declare this revelation in the open court before the public?

100 **Proctor.** I thought I would, aye—with your permission.

101 **Danforth** (*his eyes narrowing*). Now, sir, what is your purpose in so doing?

102 **Proctor.** Why, I—I would free my wife, sir.

103 **Danforth.** There lurks nowhere in your heart, nor hidden in your spirit, any desire to undermine this court?

104 **Proctor** (*with the faintest faltering*). Why, no, sir.

105 **Cheever** (*clears his throat, awakening*). I—Your Excellency.

106 **Danforth.** Mr. Cheever.

107 **Cheever.** I think it be my duty, sir—(*kindly, to* Proctor) You'll not deny it, John. (*to* Danforth) When we come to take his wife, he damned the court and ripped your warrant.

108 **Parris.** Now you have it!

109 **Danforth.** He did that, Mr. Hale?

110 **Hale** (*takes a breath*). Aye, he did.

111 **Proctor.** It were a temper, sir. I knew not what I did.

112 **Danforth** (*studying him*). Mr. Proctor.

113 **Proctor.** Aye, sir.

114 **Danforth** (*straight into his eyes*). Have you ever seen the Devil?

115 **Proctor.** No, sir.

116 **Danforth.** You are in all respects a Gospel Christian?

117 **Proctor.** I am, sir.

118 **Parris.** Such a Christian that will not come to church but once in a month!

119 **Danforth** (*restrained—he is curious*). Not come to church?

120 **Proctor.** I—I have no love for Mr. Parris. It is no secret. But God I surely love.

121 **Cheever.** He plow on Sunday, sir.

122 **Danforth.** Plow on Sunday!

123 **Cheever** (*apologetically*). I think it be evidence, John. I am an official of the court, I cannot keep it.

124 **Proctor.** I—I have once or twice plowed on Sunday. I have three children, sir, and until last year my land give little.

125 **Giles.** You'll find other Christians that do plow on Sunday if the truth be known.

126 **Hale.** Your Honor, I cannot think you may judge the man on such evidence.

127 **Danforth.** I judge nothing. (*Pause. He keeps watching* Proctor, *who tries to meet his gaze.*) I tell you straight, Mister—I have seen marvels in this court. I have seen people choked before my eyes by spirits; I have seen them stuck by pins and slashed by daggers. I have until this moment not the slightest reason to suspect that the children may be deceiving me. Do you understand my meaning?

128 **Proctor.** Excellency, does it not strike upon you that so many of these women have lived so long with such upright reputation, and—

129 **Parris.** Do you read the Gospel, Mr. Proctor?

130 **Proctor.** I read the Gospel.

131 **Parris.** I think not, or you should surely know that Cain were an upright man, and yet he did kill Abel.[4]

ANALYZE CHARACTERS

Annotate: Mark Danforth's response to Proctor's claim that Mary will admit to lying to the court.

Infer: What is Danforth's reason for telling Proctor that his wife is pregnant?

132 **Proctor.** Aye, God tells us that. (*to* Danforth) But who tells us Rebecca Nurse murdered seven babies by sending out her spirit on them? It is the children only, and this one will swear she lied to you.

133 (Danforth *considers, then beckons* Hathorne *to him.* Hathorne *leans in, and he speaks in his ear.* Hathorne *nods.*)

134 **Hathorne.** Aye, she's the one.

135 **Danforth.** Mr. Proctor, this morning, your wife send me a claim in which she states that she is pregnant now.

136 **Proctor.** My wife pregnant!

137 **Danforth.** There be no sign of it—we have examined her body.

138 **Proctor.** But if she say she is pregnant, then she must be! That woman will never lie, Mr. Danforth.

[4] **Cain . . . Abel:** According to the book of Genesis in the Bible, Cain and Abel were the sons of Adam and Eve, the first humans.

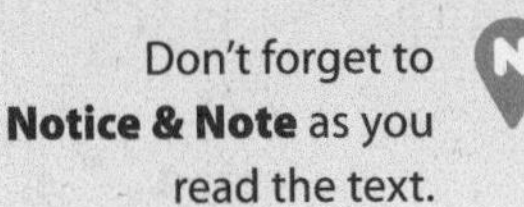

Don't forget to **Notice & Note** as you read the text.
N

139 **Danforth.** She will not?

140 **Proctor.** Never, sir, never.

141 **Danforth.** We have thought it too convenient to be credited. However, if I should tell you now that I will let her be kept another month; and if she begin to show her natural signs, you shall have her living yet another year until she is delivered—what say you to that? (John Proctor *is struck silent.*) Come now. You say your only purpose is to save your wife. Good, then, she is saved at least this year, and a year is long. What say you, sir? It is done now. (*In conflict,* Proctor *glances at* Francis *and* Giles.) Will you drop this charge?

142 **Proctor.** I—I think I cannot.

143 **Danforth** (*now an almost imperceptible hardness in his voice*). Then your purpose is somewhat larger.

144 **Parris.** He's come to overthrow this court, Your Honor!

145 **Proctor.** These are my friends. Their wives are also accused—

146 **Danforth** (*with a sudden briskness of manner*). I judge you not, sir. I am ready to hear your evidence.

147 **Proctor.** I come not to hurt the court; I only—

148 **Danforth** (*cutting him off*). Marshal, go into the court and bid Judge Stoughton and Judge Sewall declare recess for one hour. And let them go to the tavern, if they will. All witnesses and prisoners are to be kept in the building.

149 **Herrick.** Aye, sir. (*very deferentially*) If I may say it, sir, I know this man all my life. It is a good man, sir.

150 **Danforth** (*It is the reflection on himself he resents*). I am sure of it, Marshal. (Herrick *nods, then goes out.*) Now, what deposition do you have for us, Mr. Proctor? And I beg you be clear, open as the sky, and honest.

151 **Proctor** (*as he takes out several papers*). I am no lawyer, so I'll—

152 **Danforth.** The pure in heart need no lawyers. Proceed as you will.

153 **Proctor** (*handing* Danforth *a paper*). Will you read this first, sir? It's a sort of testament. The people signing it declare their good opinion of Rebecca, and my wife, and Martha Corey. (Danforth *looks down at the paper.*)

154 **Parris** (*to enlist* Danforth*'s sarcasm*). Their good opinion! (*But* Danforth *goes on reading, and* Proctor *is heartened.*)

155 **Proctor.** These are all landholding farmers, members of the church. (*delicately, trying to point out a paragraph*) If you'll notice, sir—they've known the women many years and never saw no sign they had dealings with the Devil.

156 (Parris *nervously moves over and reads over* Danforth*'s shoulder.*)

157 **Danforth** (*glancing down a long list*). How many names are here?

158 **Francis.** Ninety-one, Your Excellency.

159 **Parris** (*sweating*). These people should be summoned. (Danforth *looks up at him questioningly.*) For questioning.

160 **Francis** (*trembling with anger*). Mr. Danforth, I gave them all my word no harm would come to them for signing this.

161 **Parris.** This is a clear attack upon the court!

162 **Hale** (*to* Parris, *trying to contain himself*). Is every defense an attack upon the court? Can no one—?

163 **Parris.** All innocent and Christian people are happy for the courts in Salem! These people are gloomy for it. (*to* Danforth *directly*) And I think you will want to know, from each and every one of them, what discontents them with you!

164 **Hathorne.** I think they ought to be examined, sir.

165 **Danforth.** It is not necessarily an attack, I think. Yet—

166 **Francis.** These are all covenanted Christians, sir.

167 **Danforth.** Then I am sure they may have nothing to fear. (*hands* Cheever *the paper*) Mr. Cheever, have warrants drawn for all of these—arrest for examination. (*to* Proctor) Now, Mister, what other information do you have for us? (Francis *is still standing, horrified.*) You may sit, Mr. Nurse.

ANALYZE PLOT

Annotate: Mark details in paragraph 169 that tell you Danforth feels certain he is doing the right thing.

Analyze: Explain whether Danforth is justified in feeling this way.

Close Read Screencast

Listen to a modeled close read of this text.

168 **Francis.** I have brought trouble on these people; I have—

169 **Danforth.** No, old man, you have not hurt these people if they are of good conscience. But you must understand, sir, that a person is either with this court or he must be counted against it, there be no road between. This is a sharp time, now, a precise time—we live no longer in the dusky afternoon when evil mixed itself with good and befuddled the world. Now, by God's grace, the shining sun is up, and them that fear not light will surely praise it. I hope you will be one of those. (Mary Warren *suddenly sobs.*) She's not hearty,[5] I see.

170 **Proctor.** No, she's not, sir. (*to* Mary, *bending to her, holding her hand, quietly*) Now remember what the angel Raphael said to the boy Tobias.[6] Remember it.

171 **Mary Warren** (*hardly audible*). Aye.

172 **Proctor.** "Do that which is good, and no harm shall come to thee."

173 **Mary Warren.** Aye.

174 **Danforth.** Come, man, we wait you.

175 (Marshal Herrick *returns, and takes his post at the door.*)

176 **Giles.** John, my deposition, give him mine.

---

[5] **hearty:** well.

[6] **what the angel Raphael said . . . Tobias:** In the Book of Tobit in the Apocrypha, Tobit's son Tobias cured his father's blindness with the help of the angel Raphael.

Don't forget to **Notice & Note** as you read the text.

177 **Proctor.** Aye. (*He hands* Danforth *another paper.*) This is Mr. Corey's deposition.

178 **Danforth.** Oh? (*He looks down at it. Now* Hathorne *comes behind him and reads with him.*)

179 **Hathorne** (*suspiciously*). What lawyer drew this, Corey?

180 **Giles.** You know I never hired a lawyer in my life, Hathorne.

181 **Danforth** (*finishing the reading*). It is very well phrased. My compliments. Mr. Parris, if Mr. Putnam is in the court, will you bring him in? (Hathorne *takes the deposition, and walks to the window with it.* Parris *goes into the court.*) You have no legal training, Mr. Corey?

182 **Giles** (*very pleased*). I have the best, sir—I am thirty-three time in court in my life. And always plaintiff, too.

183 **Danforth.** Oh, then you're much put-upon.

184 **Giles.** I am never put-upon; I know my rights, sir, and I will have them. You know, your father tried a case of mine—might be thirty-five year ago, I think.

185 **Danforth.** Indeed.

186 **Giles.** He never spoke to you of it?

187 **Danforth.** No, I cannot recall it.

188 **Giles.** That's strange, he give me nine pound damages. He were a fair judge, your father. Y'see, I had a white mare that time, and this fellow come to borrow the mare—(*Enter* Parris *with* Thomas Putnam. *When he sees* Putnam, Giles' *ease goes; he is hard.*) Aye, there he is.

189 **Danforth.** Mr. Putnam, I have here an accusation by Mr. Corey against you. He states that you coldly prompted your daughter to cry witchery upon George Jacobs that is now in jail.

190 **Putnam.** It is a lie.

191 **Danforth** (*turning to* Giles). Mr. Putnam states your charge is a lie. What say you to that?

192 **Giles** (*furious, his fists clenched*). A fart on Thomas Putnam, that is what I say to that!

193 **Danforth.** What proof do you submit for your charge, sir?

194 **Giles.** My proof is there! (*pointing to the paper*) If Jacobs hangs for a witch he forfeit up his property—that's law! And there is none but Putnam with the coin to buy so great a piece. This man is killing his neighbors for their land!

195 **Danforth.** But proof, sir, proof.

196 **Giles** (*pointing at his deposition*). The proof is there! I have it from an honest man who heard Putnam say it! The day his daughter cried out on Jacobs, he said she'd given him a fair gift of land.

197 **Hathorne.** And the name of this man?

198 **Giles** (*taken aback*). What name?

199 **Hathorne.** The man that give you this information.

200 **Giles** (*hesitates, then*). Why, I—I cannot give you his name.

201 **Hathorne.** And why not?

202 **Giles** (*hesitates, then bursts out*). You know well why not! He'll lay in jail if I give his name!

203 **Hathorne.** This is contempt of the court, Mr. Danforth!

204 **Danforth** (*to avoid that*). You will surely tell us the name.

205 **Giles.** I will not give you no name. I mentioned my wife's name once and I'll burn in hell long enough for that. I stand mute.

206 **Danforth.** In that case, I have no choice but to arrest you for contempt of this court, do you know that?

207 **Giles.** This is a hearing; you cannot clap me for contempt of a hearing.

208 **Danforth.** Oh, it is a proper lawyer![7] Do you wish me to declare the court in full session here? Or will you give me good reply?

209 **Giles** (*faltering*). I cannot give you no name, sir, I cannot.

210 **Danforth.** You are a foolish old man. Mr. Cheever, begin the record. The court is now in session. I ask you, Mr. Corey—

211 **Proctor** (*breaking in*). Your Honor—he has the story in confidence, sir, and he—

212 **Parris.** The Devil lives on such confidences! (*to* Danforth) Without confidences there could be no conspiracy, Your Honor!

213 **Hathorne.** I think it must be broken, sir.

214 **Danforth** (*to* Giles). Old man, if your informant tells the truth let him come here openly like a decent man. But if he hide in anonymity I must know why. Now sir, the government and central church demand of you the name of him who reported Mr. Thomas Putnam a common murderer.

215 **Hale.** Excellency—

216 **Danforth.** Mr. Hale.

217 **Hale.** We cannot blink it more. There is a prodigious fear of this court in the country—

218 **Danforth.** Then there is a prodigious guilt in the country. Are *you* afraid to be questioned here?

219 **Hale.** I may only fear the Lord, sir, but there is fear in the country nevertheless.

---

[7] **Oh, . . . lawyer:** Oh, he thinks he is a real lawyer.

Don't forget to **Notice & Note** as you read the text.

220 **Danforth** (*angered now*). Reproach me not with the fear in the country; there is fear in the country because there is a moving[8] plot to topple Christ in the country!

221 **Hale.** But it does not follow that everyone accused is part of it.

222 **Danforth.** No uncorrupted man may fear this court, Mr. Hale! None! (*to* Giles) You are under arrest in contempt of this court. Now sit you down and take counsel with yourself, or you will be set in the jail until you decide to answer all questions.

223 (Giles Corey *makes a rush for* Putnam. Proctor *lunges and holds him.*)

224 **Proctor.** No, Giles!

225 **Giles** (*over* Proctor*'s shoulder at* Putnam). I'll cut your throat, Putnam, I'll kill you yet!

226 **Proctor** (*forcing him into a chair*). Peace, Giles, peace. (*releasing him*) We'll prove ourselves. Now we will. (*He starts to turn to* Danforth.)

227 **Giles.** Say nothin' more, John. (*pointing at* Danforth) He's only playin' you! He means to hang us all!

228 (Mary Warren *bursts into sobs.*)

229 **Danforth.** This is a court of law, Mister. I'll have no effrontery here!

230 **Proctor.** Forgive him, sir, for his old age. Peace, Giles, we'll prove it all now. (*He lifts up* Mary*'s chin.*) You cannot weep, Mary. Remember the angel, what he say to the boy. Hold to it, now; there is your rock. (Mary *quiets. He takes out a paper, and turns to* Danforth.) This is Mary Warren's deposition. I—I would ask you remember, sir, while you read it, that until two week ago she were no different than the other children are today. (*He is speaking reasonably, restraining all his fears, his anger, his anxiety.*) You saw her scream, she howled, she swore familiar spirits choked her; she even testified that Satan, in the form of women now in jail, tried to win her soul away, and then when she refused—

231 **Danforth.** We know all this.

232 **Proctor.** Aye, sir. She swears now that she never saw Satan; nor any spirit, vague or clear, that Satan may have sent to hurt her. And she declares her friends are lying now.

233 (Proctor *starts to hand* Danforth *the deposition, and* Hale *comes up to* Danforth *in a trembling state.*)

234 **Hale.** Excellency, a moment. I think this goes to the heart of the matter.

235 **Danforth** (*with deep misgivings*). It surely does.

236 **Hale.** I cannot say he is an honest man; I know him little. But in all justice, sir, a claim so weighty cannot be argued by a farmer. In God's

ANALYZE PLOT

Annotate: Mark the stage directions in paragraphs 223–228.

Analyze: What do the stage directions describe? How do they impact your understanding of events?

[8] **moving:** active.

name, sir, stop here; send him home and let him come again with a lawyer—

237 **Danforth** (*patiently*). Now look you, Mr. Hale—

238 **Hale.** Excellency, I have signed seventy-two death warrants; I am a minister of the Lord, and I dare not take a life without there be a proof so immaculate no slightest qualm of conscience may doubt it.

239 **Danforth.** Mr. Hale, you surely do not doubt my justice.

240 **Hale.** I have this morning signed away the soul of Rebecca Nurse, Your Honor. I'll not conceal it, my hand shakes yet as with a wound! I pray you, sir, this argument let lawyers present to you.

241 **Danforth.** Mr. Hale, believe me; for a man of such terrible learning you are most bewildered—I hope you will forgive me. I have been thirty-two year at the bar, sir, and I should be confounded were I called upon to defend these people. Let you consider, now—(*to* Proctor *and the others*) And I bid you all do likewise. In an ordinary crime, how does one defend the accused? One calls up witnesses to prove his innocence. But witchcraft is *ipso facto*,[9] on its face and by its nature, an invisible crime, is it not? Therefore, who may possibly be witness to it? The witch and the victim. None other. Now we cannot hope the witch will accuse herself; granted? Therefore, we must rely upon her victims—and they do testify, the children certainly do testify. As for the witches, none will deny that we are most eager for all their confessions. Therefore, what is left for a lawyer to bring out? I think I have made my point. Have I not?

242 **Hale.** But this child claims the girls are not truthful, and if they are not—

243 **Danforth.** That is precisely what I am about to consider, sir. What more may you ask of me? Unless you doubt my probity?[10]

244 **Hale** (*defeated*). I surely do not, sir. Let you consider it, then.

245 **Danforth.** And let you put your heart to rest. Her deposition, Mr. Proctor.

ANALYZE PLOT

Annotate: Mark the stage directions in paragraphs 246–248.

Analyze: Explain how these stage directions move the plot forward by revealing the feelings and attitudes of the characters. Cite evidence from the text in your response.

246 (Proctor *hands it to him.* Hathorne *rises, goes beside* Danforth, *and starts reading.* Parris *comes to his other side.* Danforth *looks at* John Proctor, *then proceeds to read.* Hale *gets up, finds position near the judge, reads too.* Proctor *glances at* Giles. Francis *prays silently, hands pressed together.* Cheever *waits placidly, the sublime official, dutiful.* Mary Warren *sobs once.* John Proctor *touches her head reassuringly. Presently* Danforth *lifts his eyes, stands up, takes out a kerchief and blows his nose. The others stand aside as he moves in thought toward the window.*)

247 **Parris** (*hardly able to contain his anger and fear*). I should like to question—

[9] ***ipso facto* (Latin):** by that very fact.
[10] **doubt my probity:** question my integrity.

Don't forget to **Notice & Note** as you read the text.

248 **Danforth** (*his first real outburst, in which his contempt for* Parris *is clear*). Mr. Parris, I bid you be silent! (*He stands in silence, looking out the window. Now, having established that he will set the gait.*) Mr. Cheever, will you go into the court and bring the children here? (Cheever *gets up and goes out upstage.* Danforth *now turns to* Mary.) Mary Warren, how came you to this turnabout? Has Mr. Proctor threatened you for this deposition?

249 **Mary Warren.** No, sir.

250 **Danforth.** Has he ever threatened you?

251 **Mary Warren** (*weaker*). No, sir.

252 **Danforth** (*sensing a weakening*). Has he threatened you?

253 **Mary Warren.** No, sir.

254 **Danforth.** Then you tell me that you sat in my court, callously lying, when you knew that people would hang by your evidence? (*She does not answer.*) Answer me!

255 **Mary Warren** (*almost inaudibly*). I did, sir.

256 **Danforth.** How were you instructed in your life? Do you not know that God damns all liars? (*She cannot speak.*) Or is it now that you lie?

257 **Mary Warren.** No, sir—I am with God now.

258 **Danforth.** You are with God now.

259 **Mary Warren.** Aye, sir.

260 **Danforth** (*containing himself*). I will tell you this—you are either lying now, or you were lying in the court, and in either case you have committed perjury and you will go to jail for it. You cannot lightly say you lied, Mary. Do you know that?

261 **Mary Warren.** I cannot lie no more. I am with God, I am with God.

262 (*But she breaks into sobs at the thought of it, and the right door opens, and enter* Susanna Walcott, Mercy Lewis, Betty Parris, *and finally* Abigail. Cheever *comes to* Danforth.)

263 **Cheever.** Ruth Putnam's not in the court, sir, nor the other children.

264 **Danforth.** These will be sufficient. Sit you down, children. (*Silently they sit.*) Your friend, Mary Warren, has given us a deposition. In which she swears that she never saw familiar spirits, apparitions, nor any manifest of the Devil. She claims as well that none of you have seen these things either. (*slight pause*) Now, children, this is a court of law. The law, based upon the Bible, and the Bible, writ by Almighty God, forbid the practice of witchcraft, and describe death as the penalty thereof. But likewise, children, the law and Bible damn all bearers of false witness. (*slight pause*) Now then. It does not escape me that this deposition may be devised to blind us; it may well be that Mary Warren has been conquered by Satan, who sends her here to distract our sacred purpose. If so, her neck will break for it. But if she speak true, I bid you now drop your guile and confess your pretense,

for a quick confession will go easier with you. (*pause*) Abigail Williams, rise. (Abigail *slowly rises.*) Is there any truth in this?

265 **Abigail.** No, sir.

266 **Danforth** (*thinks, glances at* Mary, *then back to* Abigail). Children, a very auger bit[11] will now be turned into your souls until your honesty is proved. Will either of you change your positions now, or do you force me to hard questioning?

267 **Abigail.** I have naught to change, sir. She lies.

268 **Danforth** (*to* Mary). You would still go on with this?

269 **Mary Warren** (*faintly*). Aye, sir.

270 **Danforth** (*turning to* Abigail). A poppet were discovered in Mr. Proctor's house, stabbed by a needle. Mary Warren claims that you sat beside her in the court when she made it, and that you saw her make it and witnessed how she herself stuck her needle into it for safe-keeping. What say you to that?

271 **Abigail** (*with a slight note of indignation*). It is a lie, sir.

272 **Danforth** (*after a slight pause*). While you worked for Mr. Proctor, did you see poppets in that house?

273 **Abigail.** Goody Proctor always kept poppets.

274 **Proctor.** Your Honor, my wife never kept no poppets. Mary Warren confesses it was her poppet.

275 **Cheever.** Your Excellency.

276 **Danforth.** Mr. Cheever.

277 **Cheever.** When I spoke with Goody Proctor in that house, she said she never kept no poppets. But she said she did keep poppets when she were a girl.

278 **Proctor.** She has not been a girl these fifteen years, Your Honor.

279 **Hathorne.** But a poppet will keep fifteen years, will it not?

280 **Proctor.** It will keep if it is kept, but Mary Warren swears she never saw no poppets in my house, nor anyone else.

281 **Parris.** Why could there not have been poppets hid where no one ever saw them?

282 **Proctor** (*furious*). There might also be a dragon with five legs in my house, but no one has ever seen it.

283 **Parris.** We are here, Your Honor, precisely to discover what no one has ever seen.

284 **Proctor.** Mr. Danforth, what profit this girl to turn herself about? What may Mary Warren gain but hard questioning and worse?

[11] **auger** (ô´gər) **bit:** drill.

Don't forget to **Notice & Note** as you read the text.

285 **Danforth.** You are charging Abigail Williams with a marvelous cool plot to murder, do you understand that?

286 **Proctor.** I do, sir. I believe she means to murder.

287 **Danforth** (*pointing at* Abigail, *incredulously*). This child would murder your wife?

288 **Proctor.** It is not a child. Now hear me, sir. In the sight of the congregation she were twice this year put out of this meetin' house for laughter during prayer.

289 **Danforth** (*shocked, turning to* Abigail). What's this? Laughter during—!

290 **Parris.** Excellency, she were under Tituba's power at that time, but she is solemn now.

291 **Giles.** Aye, now she is solemn and goes to hang people!

292 **Danforth.** Quiet, man.

293 **Hathorne.** Surely it have no bearing on the question, sir. He charges contemplation of murder.

294 **Danforth.** Aye. (*He studies* Abigail *for a moment, then.*) Continue, Mr. Proctor.

295 **Proctor.** Mary. Now tell the Governor how you danced in the woods.

296 **Parris** (*instantly*). Excellency, since I come to Salem this man is blackening my name. He—

297 **Danforth.** In a moment, sir. (*to* Mary Warren, *sternly, and surprised*) What is this dancing?

298 **Mary Warren.** I—(*She glances at* Abigail, *who is staring down at her remorselessly. Then, appealing to* Proctor.) Mr. Proctor—

299 **Proctor** (*taking it right up*). Abigail leads the girls to the woods, Your Honor, and they have danced there naked—

300 **Parris.** Your Honor, this—

301 **Proctor** (*at once*). Mr. Parris discovered them himself in the dead of night! There's the "child" she is!

302 **Danforth** (*It is growing into a nightmare, and he turns, astonished, to* Parris). Mr. Parris—

303 **Parris.** I can only say, sir, that I never found any of them naked, and this man is—

304 **Danforth.** But you discovered them dancing in the woods? (*Eyes on* Parris, *he points at* Abigail.) Abigail?

305 **Hale.** Excellency, when I first arrived from Beverly, Mr. Parris told me that.

306 **Danforth.** Do you deny it, Mr. Parris?

307 **Parris.** I do not, sir, but I never saw any of them naked.

308 **Danforth.** But she have *danced*?

309 **Parris** (*unwillingly*). Aye, sir.

310 (Danforth, *as though with new eyes, looks at* Abigail.)

311 **Hathorne.** Excellency, will you permit me? (*He points at* Mary Warren.)

312 **Danforth** (*with great worry*). Pray, proceed.

313 **Hathorne.** You say you never saw no spirits, Mary, were never threatened or afflicted by any manifest of the Devil or the Devil's agents.

314 **Mary Warren** (*very faintly*). No, sir.

315 **Hathorne** (*with a gleam of victory*). And yet, when people accused of witchery confronted you in court, you would faint, saying their spirits came out of their bodies and choked you—

316 **Mary Warren.** That were pretense, sir.

317 **Danforth.** I cannot hear you.

318 **Mary Warren.** Pretense, sir.

319 **Parris.** But you did turn cold, did you not? I myself picked you up many times, and your skin were icy. Mr. Danforth, you—

320 **Danforth.** I saw that many times.

321 **Proctor.** She only pretended to faint, Your Excellency. They're all marvelous pretenders.

ANALYZE PLOT

Annotate: Mark what is asked of Mary Warren and how she responds to the request.

Analyze: Consider what you have learned about Mary Warren up to this point. Why is placing great importance upon her testimony an effective way of creating suspense?

322 **Hathorne.** Then can she pretend to faint now?

323 **Proctor.** Now?

324 **Parris.** Why not? Now there are no spirits attacking her, for none in this room is accused of witchcraft. So let her turn herself cold now, let her pretend she is attacked now, let her faint. (*He turns to* Mary Warren.) Faint!

325 **Mary Warren.** Faint?

326 **Parris.** Aye, faint. Prove to us how you pretended in the court so many times.

327 **Mary Warren** (*looking to* Proctor). I—cannot faint now, sir.

328 **Proctor** (*alarmed, quietly*). Can you not pretend it?

329 **Mary Warren.** I—(*She looks about as though searching for the passion to faint.*) I—have no *sense* of it now, I—

330 **Danforth.** Why? What is lacking now?

331 **Mary Warren.** I—cannot tell, sir, I—

332 **Danforth.** Might it be that here we have no afflicting spirit loose, but in the court there were some?

333 **Mary Warren.** I never saw no spirits.

334 **Parris.** Then see no spirits now, and prove to us that you can faint by your own will, as you claim.

Don't forget to **Notice & Note** as you read the text.

335 **Mary Warren** (*stares, searching for the emotion of it, and then shakes her head*). I—cannot do it.

336 **Parris.** Then you will confess, will you not? It were attacking spirits made you faint!

337 **Mary Warren.** No, sir, I—

338 **Parris.** Your Excellency, this is a trick to blind the court!

339 **Mary Warren.** It's not a trick! (*She stands.*) I—I used to faint because I—I thought I saw spirits.

340 **Danforth.** *Thought* you saw them!

341 **Mary Warren.** But I did not, Your Honor.

342 **Hathorne.** How could you think you saw them unless you saw them?

343 **Mary Warren.** I—I cannot tell how, but I did. I—I heard the other girls screaming, and you, Your Honor, you seemed to believe them, and I—It were only sport in the beginning, sir, but then the whole world cried spirits, spirits, and I—I promise you, Mr. Danforth, I only thought I saw them but I did not.

344 (Danforth *peers at her.*)

345 **Parris** (*smiling, but nervous because* Danforth *seems to be struck by* Mary Warren*'s story*). Surely Your Excellency is not taken by this simple lie.

346 **Danforth** (*turning worriedly to* Abigail). Abigail. I bid you now search your heart and tell me this—and beware of it, child, to God every soul is precious and His vengeance is terrible on them that take life without cause. Is it possible, child, that the spirits you have seen are illusion only, some deception that may cross your mind when—

347 **Abigail.** Why, this—this—is a base question, sir.

348 **Danforth.** Child, I would have you consider it—

349 **Abigail.** I have been hurt, Mr. Danforth; I have seen my blood runnin' out! I have been near to murdered every day because I done my duty pointing out the Devil's people—and this is my reward? To be mistrusted, denied, questioned like a—

350 **Danforth** (*weakening*). Child, I do not mistrust you—

351 **Abigail** (*in an open threat*). Let *you* beware, Mr. Danforth. Think you to be so mighty that the power of Hell may not turn *your* wits? Beware of it! There is—(*Suddenly, from an accusatory attitude, her face turns, looking into the air above—it is truly frightened.*)

352 **Danforth** (*apprehensively*). What is it, child?

353 **Abigail** (*looking about in the air, clasping her arms about her as though cold*). I—I know not. A wind, a cold wind, has come. (*Her eyes fall on* Mary Warren.)

354 **Mary Warren** (*terrified, pleading*). Abby!

355 **Mercy Lewis** (*shivering*). Your Honor, I freeze!

356 **Proctor.** They're pretending!

357 **Hathorne** (*touching* Abigail*'s hand*). She is cold, Your Honor, touch her!

358 **Mercy Lewis** (*through chattering teeth*). Mary, do you send this shadow on me?

359 **Mary Warren.** Lord, save me!

360 **Susanna Walcott.** I freeze, I freeze!

361 **Abigail** (*shivering visibly*). It is a wind, a wind!

362 **Mary Warren.** Abby, don't do that!

363 **Danforth** (*himself engaged and entered by* Abigail). Mary Warren, do you witch her? I say to you, do you send your spirit out?

364 (*With a hysterical cry* Mary Warren *starts to run.* Proctor *catches her.*)

365 **Mary Warren** (*almost collapsing*). Let me go, Mr. Proctor, I cannot, I cannot—

366 **Abigail** (*crying to Heaven*). Oh, Heavenly Father, take away this shadow!

Don't forget to **Notice & Note** as you read the text.

367 (*Without warning or hesitation,* Proctor *leaps at* Abigail *and, grabbing her by the hair, pulls her to her feet. She screams in pain.* Danforth, *astonished, cries, "What are you about?" and* Hathorne *and* Parris *call, "Take your hands off her!" and out of it all comes* Proctor*'s roaring voice.*)

368 **Proctor.** How do you call Heaven! Whore! Whore!

369 (Herrick *breaks* Proctor *from her.*)

370 **Herrick.** John!

371 **Danforth.** Man! Man, what do you—

372 **Proctor** (*breathless and in agony*). It is a whore!

373 **Danforth** (*dumbfounded*). You charge—?

374 **Abigail.** Mr. Danforth, he is lying!

375 **Proctor.** Mark her! Now she'll suck a scream to stab me with, but—

376 **Danforth.** You will prove this! This will not pass!

377 **Proctor** (*trembling, his life collapsing about him*). I have known her, sir. I have known her.

ANALYZE PLOT

Annotate: Mark the climax of the play.

Predict: How might Proctor's confession change the outcome of the plot?

378 **Danforth.** You—you are a lecher?

379 **Francis** (*horrified*). John, you cannot say such a—

380 **Proctor.** Oh, Francis, I wish you had some evil in you that you might know me! (*to* Danforth) A man will not cast away his good name. You surely know that.

381 **Danforth** (*dumbfounded*). In—in what time? In what place?

382 **Proctor** (*his voice about to break, and his shame great*). In the proper place—where my beasts are bedded. On the last night of my joy, some eight months past. She used to serve me in my house, sir. (*He has to clamp his jaw to keep from weeping.*) A man may think God sleeps, but God sees everything, I know it now. I beg you, sir, I beg you—see her what she is. My wife, my dear good wife, took this girl soon after, sir, and put her out on the highroad. And being what she is, a lump of vanity, sir—(*He is being overcome.*) Excellency, forgive me, forgive me. (*Angrily against himself, he turns away from the* Governor *for a moment. Then, as though to cry out is his only means of speech left.*) She thinks to dance with me on my wife's grave! And well she might, for I thought of her softly. God help me, I lusted, and there *is* a promise in such sweat. But it is a whore's vengeance, and you must see it; I set myself entirely in your hands. I know you must see it now.

383 **Danforth** (*blanched, in horror, turning to* Abigail). You deny every scrap and tittle[12] of this?

384 **Abigail.** If I must answer that, I will leave and I will not come back again!

[12] **every scrap and tittle:** every tiny bit.

385 (Danforth *seems unsteady.*)

386 **Proctor.** I have made a bell of my honor! I have rung the doom of my good name—you will believe me, Mr. Danforth! My wife is innocent, except she knew a whore when she saw one!

387 **Abigail** (*stepping up to* Danforth). What look do you give me? (Danforth *cannot speak.*) I'll not have such looks! (*She turns and starts for the door.*)

388 **Danforth.** You will remain where you are! (Herrick *steps into her path. She comes up short, fire in her eyes.*) Mr. Parris, go into the court and bring Goodwife Proctor out.

389 **Parris** (*objecting*). Your Honor, this is all a—

390 **Danforth** (*sharply to* Parris). Bring her out! And tell her not one word of what's been spoken here. And let you knock before you enter. (Parris *goes out.*) Now we shall touch the bottom of this swamp. (*to* Proctor) Your wife, you say, is an honest woman.

391 **Proctor.** In her life, sir, she have never lied. There are them that cannot sing, and them that cannot weep—my wife cannot lie. I have paid much to learn it, sir.

392 **Danforth.** And when she put this girl out of your house, she put her out for a harlot?[13]

393 **Proctor.** Aye, sir.

394 **Danforth.** And knew her for a harlot?

395 **Proctor.** Aye, sir, she knew her for a harlot.

396 **Danforth.** Good then. (*to* Abigail) And if she tell me, child, it were for harlotry, may God spread His mercy on you! (*There is a knock. He calls to the door.*) Hold! (*to* Abigail) Turn your back. Turn your back. (*to* Proctor) Do likewise. (*Both turn their backs*—Abigail *with indignant slowness.*) Now let neither of you turn to face Goody Proctor. No one in this room is to speak one word, or raise a gesture aye or nay. (*He turns toward the door, calls.*) Enter! (*The door opens.* Elizabeth *enters with* Parris. Parris *leaves her. She stands alone, her eyes looking for* Proctor.) Mr. Cheever, report this testimony in all exactness. Are you ready?

397 **Cheever.** Ready, sir.

398 **Danforth.** Come here, woman. (Elizabeth *comes to him, glancing at* Proctor*'s back.*) Look at me only, not at your husband. In my eyes only.

399 **Elizabeth** (*faintly*). Good, sir.

400 **Danforth.** We are given to understand that at one time you dismissed your servant, Abigail Williams.

401 **Elizabeth.** That is true, sir.

[13] **for a harlot:** as a woman of low morals.

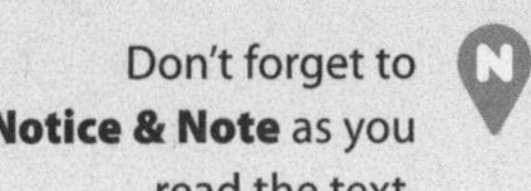

402 **Danforth.** For what cause did you dismiss her? (*Slight pause. Then* Elizabeth *tries to glance at* Proctor.) You will look in my eyes only and not at your husband. The answer is in your memory and you need no help to give it to me. Why did you dismiss Abigail Williams?

403 **Elizabeth** (*not knowing what to say, sensing a situation, wetting her lips to stall for time*). She—dissatisfied me. (*pause*) And my husband.

404 **Danforth.** In what way dissatisfied you?

405 **Elizabeth.** She were—(*She glances at* Proctor *for a cue.*)

406 **Danforth.** Woman, look at me! (Elizabeth *does.*) Were she slovenly? Lazy? What disturbance did she cause?

407 **Elizabeth.** Your Honor, I—in that time I were sick. And I—My husband is a good and righteous man. He is never drunk as some are, nor wastin' his time at the shovelboard, but always at his work. But in my sickness—you see, sir, I were a long time sick after my last baby, and I thought I saw my husband somewhat turning from me. And this girl—(*She turns to* Abigail.)

408 **Danforth.** Look at me.

409 **Elizabeth.** Aye, sir. Abigail Williams—(*She breaks off.*)

410 **Danforth.** What of Abigail Williams?

411 **Elizabeth.** I came to think he fancied her. And so one night I lost my wits, I think, and put her out on the highroad.

412 **Danforth.** Your husband—did he indeed turn from you?

413 **Elizabeth** (*in agony*). My husband—is a goodly man, sir.

414 **Danforth.** Then he did not turn from you.

415 **Elizabeth** (*starting to glance at* Proctor). He—

416 **Danforth** (*reaches out and holds her face, then*). Look at me! To your own knowledge, has John Proctor ever committed the crime of lechery? (*In a crisis of indecision she cannot speak.*) Answer my question! Is your husband a lecher!

ANALYZE PLOT

Annotate: Mark dialogue during Elizabeth's interrogation that tells you she is trying to protect Proctor.

Analyze: Explain how the interrogation of Elizabeth presents a plot complication.

417 **Elizabeth** (*faintly*). No, sir.

418 **Danforth.** Remove her, Marshal.

419 **Proctor.** Elizabeth, tell the truth!

420 **Danforth.** She has spoken. Remove her!

421 **Proctor** (*crying out*). Elizabeth, I have confessed it!

422 **Elizabeth.** Oh, God! (*The door closes behind her.*)

423 **Proctor.** She only thought to save my name!

424 **Hale.** Excellency, it is a natural lie to tell; I beg you, stop now before another is condemned! I may shut my conscience to it no more—private vengeance is working through this testimony! From the beginning this man has struck me true. By my oath to Heaven, I believe him now, and I pray you call back his wife before we—

425 **Danforth.** She spoke nothing of lechery, and this man has lied!

426 **Hale.** I believe him! (*pointing at* Abigail) This girl has always struck me false! She has—

427 (Abigail, *with a weird, wild, chilling cry, screams up to the ceiling.*)

428 **Abigail.** You will not! Begone! Begone, I say!

429 **Danforth.** What is it, child? (*But* Abigail, *pointing with fear, is now raising up her frightened eyes, her awed face, toward the ceiling—the girls are doing the same—and now* Hathorne, Hale, Putnam, Cheever, Herrick, *and* Danforth *do the same.*) What's there? (*He lowers his eyes from the ceiling, and now he is frightened; there is real tension in his voice.*) Child! (*She is transfixed—with all the girls, she is whimpering open-mouthed, agape at the ceiling.*) Girls! Why do you—?

430 **Mercy Lewis** (*pointing*). It's on the beam! Behind the rafter!

431 **Danforth** (*looking up*). Where!

432 **Abigail.** Why—? (*She gulps.*) Why do you come, yellow bird?

433 **Proctor.** Where's a bird? I see no bird!

434 **Abigail** (*to the ceiling*). My face? My face?

435 **Proctor.** Mr. Hale—

436 **Danforth.** Be quiet!

437 **Proctor** (*to* Hale). Do you see a bird?

438 **Danforth.** Be quiet!!

439 **Abigail** (*to the ceiling, in a genuine conversation with the "bird," as though trying to talk it out of attacking her*). But God made my face; you cannot want to tear my face. Envy is a deadly sin, Mary.

440 **Mary Warren** (*on her feet with a spring, and horrified, pleading*). Abby!

441 **Abigail** (*unperturbed, continuing to the "bird"*). Oh, Mary, this is a black art[14] to change your shape. No, I cannot, I cannot stop my mouth; it's God's work I do.

442 **Mary Warren.** Abby, I'm *here!*

443 **Proctor** (*frantically*). They're pretending, Mr. Danforth!

444 **Abigail** (*Now she takes a backward step, as though in fear the bird will swoop down momentarily*). Oh, please, Mary! Don't come down.

445 **Susanna Walcott.** Her claws, she's stretching her claws!

446 **Proctor.** Lies, lies.

447 **Abigail** (*backing further, eyes still fixed above*). Mary, please don't hurt me!

448 **Mary Warren** (*to* Danforth). I'm not hurting her!

[14] **a black art:** sorcery.

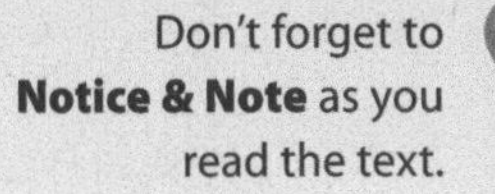

449 **Danforth** (*to* Mary Warren). Why does she see this vision?

450 **Mary Warren.** She sees nothin'!

451 **Abigail** (*now staring full front as though hypnotized, and mimicking the exact tone of* Mary Warren*'s cry*). She sees nothin'!

452 **Mary Warren** (*pleading*). Abby, you mustn't!

453 **Abigail and All the Girls** (*all transfixed*). Abby, you mustn't!

454 **Mary Warren** (*to all the* Girls). I'm here, I'm here!

455 **Girls.** I'm here, I'm here!

456 **Danforth** (*horrified*). Mary Warren! Draw back your spirit out of them!

457 **Mary Warren.** Mr. Danforth!

458 **Girls** (*cutting her off*). Mr. Danforth!

ANALYZE CHARACTERS

Annotate: Mark examples of repetition in paragraphs 450–471.

Analyze: Why do the other girls mimic Mary's dialogue?

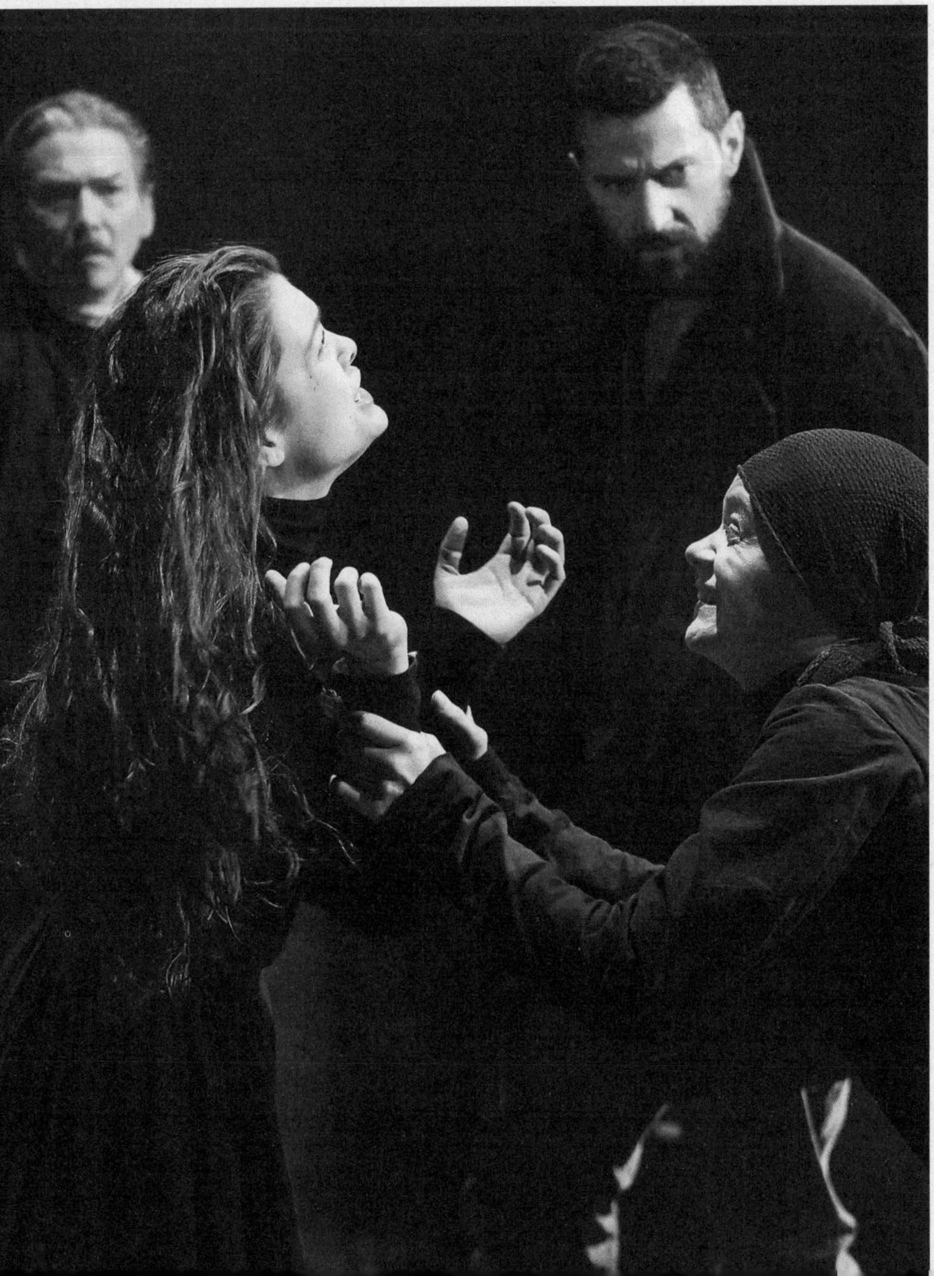

459 **Danforth.** Have you compacted with the Devil? Have you?

460 **Mary Warren.** Never, never!

461 **Girls.** Never, never!

462 **Danforth** (*growing hysterical*). Why can they only repeat you?

463 **Proctor.** Give me a whip—I'll stop it!

464 **Mary Warren.** They're sporting.[15] They—!

465 **Girls.** They're sporting!

466 **Mary Warren** (*turning on them all hysterically and stamping her feet*). Abby, stop it!

467 **Girls** (*stamping their feet*). Abby, stop it!

468 **Mary Warren.** Stop it!

469 **Girls.** Stop it!

470 **Mary Warren** (*screaming it out at the top of her lungs, and raising her fists*). Stop it!!

471 **Girls** (*raising their fists*). Stop it!!

472 (Mary Warren, *utterly confounded, and becoming overwhelmed by* Abigail's*—and the girls'—utter conviction, starts to whimper, hands half raised, powerless, and all the girls begin whimpering exactly as she does.*)

473 **Danforth.** A little while ago you were afflicted. Now it seems you afflict others; where did you find this power?

474 **Mary Warren** (*staring at* Abigail). I—have no power.

475 **Girls.** I have no power.

476 **Proctor.** They're gulling you,[16] Mister!

477 **Danforth.** Why did you turn about this past two weeks? You have seen the Devil, have you not?

478 **Hale** (*indicating* Abigail *and the girls*). You cannot believe them!

479 **Mary Warren.** I—

480 **Proctor** (*sensing her weakening*). Mary, God damns all liars!

481 **Danforth** (*pounding it into her*). You have seen the Devil, you have made compact with Lucifer, have you not?

482 **Proctor.** God damns liars, Mary!

483 (Mary *utters something unintelligible, staring at* Abigail, *who keeps watching the "bird" above.*)

484 **Danforth.** I cannot hear you. What do you say? (Mary *utters again unintelligibly.*) You will confess yourself or you will hang! (*He turns*

[15] **sporting:** playing a game.
[16] **gulling you:** deceiving you.

her roughly to face him.) Do you know who I am? I say you will hang if you do not open with me!

Don't forget to **Notice & Note** as you read the text.

485 **Proctor.** Mary, remember the angel Raphael—do that which is good and—

486 **Abigail** (*pointing upward*). The wings! Her wings are spreading! Mary, please, don't, don't—!

487 **Hale.** I see nothing, Your Honor!

488 **Danforth.** Do you confess this power! (*He is an inch from her face.*) Speak!

489 **Abigail.** She's going to come down! She's walking the beam!

490 **Danforth.** Will you speak!

491 **Mary Warren** (*staring in horror*). I cannot!

492 **Girls.** I cannot!

493 **Parris.** Cast the Devil out! Look him in the face! Trample him! We'll save you, Mary, only stand fast against him and—

494 **Abigail** (*looking up*). Look out! She's coming down!

495 (*She and all the girls run to one wall, shielding their eyes. And now, as though cornered, they let out a gigantic scream, and Mary, as though infected, opens her mouth and screams with them. Gradually* Abigail *and the girls leave off, until only* Mary *is left there, staring up at the "bird," screaming madly. All watch her, horrified by this evident fit.* Proctor *strides to her.*)

496 **Proctor.** Mary, tell the Governor what they—(*He has hardly got a word out, when, seeing him coming for her, she rushes out of his reach, screaming in horror.*)

497 **Mary Warren.** Don't touch me—don't touch me! (*At which the girls halt at the door.*)

498 **Proctor** (*astonished*). Mary!

499 **Mary Warren** (*pointing at* Proctor). You're the Devil's man! (*He is stopped in his tracks.*)

500 **Parris.** Praise God!

501 **Girls.** Praise God!

502 **Proctor** (*numbed*). Mary, how—?

503 **Mary Warren.** I'll not hang with you! I love God, I love God.

504 **Danforth** (*to* Mary). He bid you do the Devil's work?

505 **Mary Warren** (*hysterically, indicating* Proctor). He come at me by night and every day to sign, to sign, to—

506 **Danforth.** Sign what?

507 **Parris.** The Devil's book? He come with a book?

508 **Mary Warren** (*hysterically, pointing at* Proctor, *fearful of him*). My name, he want my name. "I'll murder you," he says, "if my wife hangs! We must go and overthrow the court," he says!

509 (Danforth*'s head jerks toward* Proctor, *shock and horror in his face.*)

510 **Proctor** (*turning, appealing to* Hale). Mr. Hale!

511 **Mary Warren** (*her sobs beginning*). He wake me every night, his eyes were like coals and his fingers claw my neck, and I sign, I sign . . .

512 **Hale.** Excellency, this child's gone wild!

513 **Proctor** (*as* Danforth*'s wide eyes pour on him*). Mary, Mary!

514 **Mary Warren** (*screaming at him*). No, I love God; I go your way no more. I love God, I bless God. (*Sobbing, she rushes to* Abigail.) Abby, Abby, I'll never hurt you more! (*They all watch, as* Abigail, *out of her infinite charity, reaches out and draws the sobbing* Mary *to her, and then looks up to* Danforth.)

515 **Danforth** (*to* Proctor). What are you? (Proctor *is beyond speech in his anger.*) You are combined with anti-Christ,[17] are you not? I have seen your power; you will not deny it! What say you, Mister?

---

[17] **anti-Christ:** in the New Testament, Christ's great enemy, expected to spread evil before Christ conquers him and the world ends (1 John 2:18).

Don't forget to **Notice & Note** as you read the text. 

NOTICE & NOTE

CONTRASTS AND CONTRADICTIONS

When you notice a sharp contrast between what you would expect and what the character actually does, you've found a **Contrasts and Contradictions** signpost.

Notice & Note: Mark a surprising detail in paragraph 514 about Abigail's response to Mary Warren's screaming.

Analyze: Explain whether this detail is intended to convey a genuine change in Abigail's behavior.

516 **Hale.** Excellency—

517 **Danforth.** I will have nothing from you, Mr. Hale! (*to* Proctor) Will you confess yourself befouled with Hell, or do you keep that black allegiance yet? What say you?

518 **Proctor** (*his mind wild, breathless*). I say—I say—God is dead!

519 **Parris.** Hear it, hear it!

520 **Proctor** (*laughs insanely, then*). A fire, a fire is burning! I hear the boot of Lucifer, I see his filthy face! And it is my face, and yours, Danforth! For them that quail to bring men out of ignorance, as I have quailed, and as you quail now when you know in all your black hearts that this be fraud—God damns our kind especially, and we will burn, we will burn together!

521 **Danforth.** Marshal! Take him and Corey with him to the jail!

522 **Hale** (*starting across to the door*). I denounce these proceedings!

523 **Proctor.** You are pulling Heaven down and raising up a whore!

524 **Hale.** I denounce these proceedings, I quit this court! (*He slams the door to the outside behind him.*)

525 **Danforth** (*calling to him in a fury*). Mr. Hale! Mr. Hale!

526 (*The curtain falls.*)

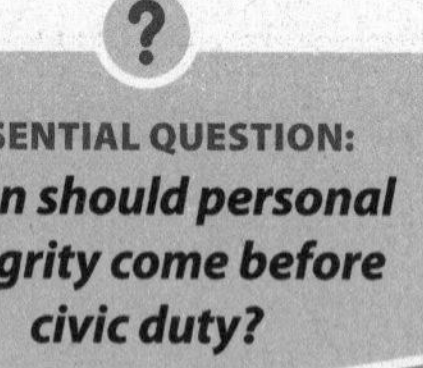
?
ESSENTIAL QUESTION:
When should personal integrity come before civic duty?

Review your notes and add your thoughts to your **Response Log.**

COLLABORATIVE DISCUSSION

With a partner, discuss why the judges are taken in by Abigail's faked terror. What are the implications for them if they are proven wrong about the girls? Support your ideas with examples from the play.

Assessment Practice

Answer these questions before moving on to the **Analyze the Text** section on the following page.

1. What is the setting for this act of the play?

- (A) a jail
- (B) a schoolhouse
- (C) a room in Proctor's home
- (D) a room in the meeting house

2. What proof does the judge require to show Mary is telling the truth?

- (A) Mary must faint convincingly.
- (B) Mary must produce an eyewitness.
- (C) Mary must give testimony against Abigail.
- (D) Mary must admit that she herself is a witch.

3. Why does Proctor confess to adultery?

- (A) to protect himself
- (B) to protect his wife
- (C) to protect Abigail
- (D) to protect his reputation

Test-Taking Strategies

Analyze the Text

Support your responses with evidence from the text.

NOTICE & NOTE

Review what you **noticed and noted** as you read the text. Your annotations can help you answer these questions.

1. **ANALYZE** Mary Warren might be seen as the foil for Abigail. Explain how she is used to emphasize some of Abigail's traits.

2. **ANALYZE** What does Danforth's reaction to Giles's outburst at the beginning of the act suggest about his character?

3. **ANALYZE** Elizabeth faces a moral dilemma regarding her husband's relationship with Abigail. What motivates her decision to lie to Danforth?

4. **INTERPRET** Why does the court debate whether Proctor plows on Sunday? What is the significance of this debate?

5. **ANALYZE** What might explain the **Contrasts and Contradictions** in Proctor's actions since the beginning of the play? What do his actions in this act reveal about his character?

Choices

Here are some other ways to demonstrate your understanding of Act Three.

Writing

↳ Literary Analysis

The real Abigail Williams was eleven years old in 1692 and had not had an illicit relationship with John Proctor. Write an analysis in which you discuss why Miller presents a different version of history.

- Identify how the relationship between Proctor and Abigail affects the plot of the play.
- Analyze how the play would change without the relationship.
- Discuss how the relationship relates to Miller's view of witch hunts.
- Cite details from the play to support your ideas.

Speaking & Listening

↳ Class Poll

Should writers be historically accurate when writing about true events, or should they feel free to change the details? You may use *The Crucible* for this activity, or other historical stories, movies, or shows that you know.

1. Conduct research about the work you chose and how events are presented.
2. Evaluate why the writer changed events and how this affected your understanding.
3. Take a poll on whether writers should change historical details in their works. Cite evidence to support your ideas.

ACT FOUR

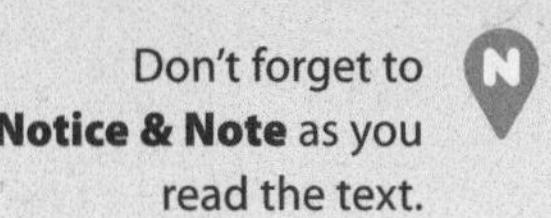

1 (*A cell in* Salem *jail, that fall.*

2 *At the back is a high barred window; near it, a great, heavy door. Along the walls are two benches.*

3 *The place is in darkness but for the moonlight seeping through the bars. It appears empty. Presently footsteps are heard coming down a corridor beyond the wall, keys rattle, and the door swings open.* Marshal Herrick *enters with a lantern.*

4 *He is nearly drunk, and heavy-footed. He goes to a bench and nudges a bundle of rags lying on it.*)

ANALYZE PLOT

Annotate: Mark details in Miller's stage directions about the setting that affect the mood of the scene.

Analyze: How does the mood reflect recent plot events?

5 **Herrick.** Sarah, wake up! Sarah Good! (*He then crosses to the other bench.*)

6 **Sarah Good** (*rising in her rags*). Oh, Majesty! Comin', comin'! Tituba, he's here, His Majesty's come!

7 **Herrick.** Go to the north cell; this place is wanted now.

8 (*He hangs his lantern on the wall.* Tituba *sits up.*)

9 **Tituba.** That don't look to me like His Majesty; look to me like the marshal.

10 **Herrick** (*taking out a flask*). Get along with you now, clear this place. (*He drinks, and* Sarah Good *comes and peers up into his face.*)

11 **Sarah Good.** Oh, is it you, Marshal! I thought sure you be the Devil comin' for us. Could I have a sip of cider for me goin'-away?

12 **Herrick** (*handing her the flask*). And where are you off to, Sarah?

13 **Tituba** (*as* Sarah *drinks*). We goin' to Barbados, soon the Devil gits here with the feathers and the wings.

14 **Herrick.** Oh? A happy voyage to you.

15 **Sarah Good.** A pair of bluebirds wingin' southerly, the two of us! Oh, it be a grand transformation, Marshal! (*She raises the flask to drink again.*)

16 **Herrick** (*taking the flask from her lips*). You'd best give me that or you'll never rise off the ground. Come along now.

17 **Tituba.** I'll speak to him for you, if you desires to come along, Marshal.

18 **Herrick.** I'd not refuse it, Tituba; it's the proper morning to fly into Hell.

19 **Tituba.** Oh, it be no Hell in Barbados. Devil, him be pleasure-man in Barbados, him be singin' and dancin' in Barbados. It's you folks—you riles him up 'round here; it be too cold 'round here for that Old Boy. He freeze his soul in Massachusetts, but in Barbados he just as sweet and—(*A bellowing cow is heard, and* Tituba *leaps up and calls to the window.*) Aye, sir! That's him, Sarah!

20 **Sarah Good.** I'm here, Majesty! (*They hurriedly pick up their rags as* Hopkins, *a guard, enters.*)

21 **Hopkins.** The Deputy Governor's arrived.

22 **Herrick** (*grabbing* Tituba). Come along, come along.

23 **Tituba** (*resisting him*). No, he comin' for me. I goin' home!

24 **Herrick** (*pulling her to the door*). That's not Satan, just a poor old cow with a hatful of milk. Come along now, out with you!

25 **Tituba** (*calling to the window*). Take me home, Devil! Take me home!

26 **Sarah Good** (*following the shouting* Tituba *out*). Tell him I'm goin', Tituba! Now you tell him Sarah Good is goin' too!

27 (*In the corridor outside* Tituba *calls on—"Take me home, Devil; Devil take me home!" and* Hopkins' *voice orders her to move on.* Herrick *returns and begins to push old rags and straw into a corner. Hearing footsteps, he turns, and enter* Danforth *and* Judge Hathorne. *They are in greatcoats and wear hats against the bitter cold. They are followed in by* Cheever, *who carries a dispatch case*[1] *and a flat wooden box containing his writing materials.*)

28 **Herrick.** Good morning, Excellency.

29 **Danforth.** Where is Mr. Parris?

30 **Herrick.** I'll fetch him. (*He starts for the door.*)

31 **Danforth.** Marshal. (Herrick *stops.*) When did Reverend Hale arrive?

32 **Herrick.** It were toward midnight, I think.

33 **Danforth** (*suspiciously*). What is he about here?

34 **Herrick.** He goes among them that will hang, sir. And he prays with them. He sits with Goody Nurse now. And Mr. Parris with him.

35 **Danforth.** Indeed. That man have no authority to enter here, Marshal. Why have you let him in?

36 **Herrick.** Why, Mr. Parris command me, sir. I cannot deny him.

37 **Danforth.** Are you drunk, Marshal?

38 **Herrick.** No, sir; it is a bitter night, and I have no fire here.

39 **Danforth** (*containing his anger*). Fetch Mr. Parris.

40 **Herrick.** Aye, sir.

41 **Danforth.** There is a prodigious stench in this place.

42 **Herrick.** I have only now cleared the people out for you.

43 **Danforth.** Beware hard drink, Marshal.

44 **Herrick.** Aye, sir. (*He waits an instant for further orders. But* Danforth, *in dissatisfaction, turns his back on him, and* Herrick *goes out. There is a pause.* Danforth *stands in thought.*)

45 **Hathorne.** Let you question Hale, Excellency; I should not be surprised he have been preaching in Andover[2] lately.

[1] **dispatch case:** a case for carrying documents.
[2] **Andover:** a town in Massachusetts, northwest of Salem.

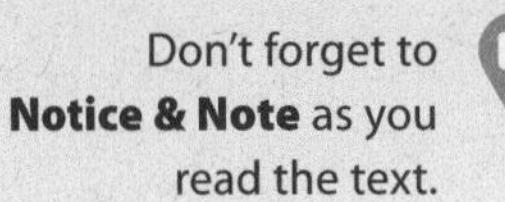

46 **Danforth.** We'll come to that; speak nothing of Andover. Parris prays with him. That's strange. (*He blows on his hands, moves toward the window, and looks out.*)

47 **Hathorne.** Excellency, I wonder if it be wise to let Mr. Parris so continuously with the prisoners. (Danforth *turns to him, interested.*) I think, sometimes, the man has a mad look these days.

48 **Danforth.** Mad?

49 **Hathorne.** I met him yesterday coming out of his house, and I bid him good morning—and he wept and went his way. I think it is not well the village sees him so unsteady.

50 **Danforth.** Perhaps he have some sorrow.

51 **Cheever** (*stamping his feet against the cold*). I think it be the cows, sir.

52 **Danforth.** Cows?

53 **Cheever.** There be so many cows wanderin' the highroads, now their masters are in the jails, and much disagreement who they will belong to now. I know Mr. Parris be arguin' with farmers all yesterday—there is great contention, sir, about the cows. Contention make him weep, sir; it were always a man that weep for contention. (*He turns, as do* Hathorne *and* Danforth, *hearing someone coming up the corridor.* Danforth *raises his head as* Parris *enters. He is gaunt, frightened, and sweating in his greatcoat.*)

54 **Parris** (*to* Danforth, *instantly*). Oh, good morning, sir, thank you for coming, I beg your pardon wakin' you so early. Good morning, Judge Hathorne.

55 **Danforth.** Reverend Hale have no right to enter this—

56 **Parris.** Excellency, a moment. (*He hurries back and shuts the door.*)

57 **Hathorne.** Do you leave him alone with the prisoners?

58 **Danforth.** What's his business here?

59 **Parris** (*prayerfully holding up his hands*). Excellency, hear me. It is a providence. Reverend Hale has returned to bring Rebecca Nurse to God.

60 **Danforth** (*surprised*). He bids her confess?

61 **Parris** (*sitting*). Hear me. Rebecca have not given me a word this three month since she came. Now she sits with him, and her sister and Martha Corey and two or three others, and he pleads with them, confess their crimes and save their lives.

62 **Danforth.** Why—this is indeed a providence. And they soften, they soften?

63 **Parris.** Not yet, not yet. But I thought to summon you, sir, that we might think on whether it be not wise, to—(*He dares not say it.*) I had thought to put a question, sir, and I hope you will not—

64 **Danforth.** Mr. Parris, be plain, what troubles you?

ANALYZE CHARACTERS

Annotate: Mark words in paragraphs 46–50 that describe Parris.

Analyze: What change in Parris is suggested by these details?

65 **Parris.** There is news, sir, that the court—the court must reckon with. My niece, sir, my niece—I believe she has vanished.

66 **Danforth.** Vanished!

67 **Parris.** I had thought to advise you of it earlier in the week, but—

68 **Danforth.** Why? How long is she gone?

69 **Parris.** This be the third night. You see, sir, she told me she would stay a night with Mercy Lewis. And next day, when she does not return, I send to Mr. Lewis to inquire. Mercy told him she would sleep in *my* house for a night.

70 **Danforth.** They are both gone?!

71 **Parris** (*in fear of him*). They are, sir.

72 **Danforth** (*alarmed*). I will send a party for them. Where may they be?

73 **Parris.** Excellency, I think they be aboard a ship. (Danforth *stands agape.*) My daughter tells me how she heard them speaking of ships last week, and tonight I discover my—my strongbox is broke into. (*He presses his fingers against his eyes to keep back tears.*)

74 **Hathorne** (*astonished*). She have robbed you?

75 **Parris.** Thirty-one pound is gone. I am penniless. (*He covers his face and sobs.*)

76 **Danforth.** Mr. Parris, you are a brainless man! (*He walks in thought, deeply worried.*)

77 **Parris.** Excellency, it profit nothing you should blame me. I cannot think they would run off except they fear to keep in Salem any more. (*He is pleading.*) Mark it, sir, Abigail had close knowledge of the town, and since the news of Andover has broken here—

78 **Danforth.** Andover is remedied.[3] The court returns there on Friday, and will resume examinations.

ANALYZE PLOT

Annotate: Mark details that tell what is happening in Andover.

Interpret: Why might what is happening in Andover be a plot complication?

79 **Parris.** I am sure of it, sir. But the rumor here speaks rebellion in Andover, and it—

80 **Danforth.** There is no rebellion in Andover!

81 **Parris.** I tell you what is said here, sir. Andover have thrown out the court, they say, and will have no part of witchcraft. There be a faction here, feeding on that news, and I tell you true, sir, I fear there will be riot here.

82 **Hathorne.** Riot! Why at every execution I have seen naught but high satisfaction in the town.

83 **Parris.** Judge Hathorne—it were another sort that hanged till now. Rebecca Nurse is no Bridget that lived three year with Bishop before she married him. John Proctor is not Isaac Ward that drank his family

[3] **remedied:** no longer a problem.

to ruin. (*to* Danforth) I would to God it were not so, Excellency, but these people have great weight yet in the town. Let Rebecca stand upon the gibbet[4] and send up some righteous prayer, and I fear she'll wake a vengeance on you.

84 **Hathorne.** Excellency, she is condemned a witch. The court have—

85 **Danforth** (*in deep concern, raising a hand to* Hathorne). Pray you. (*to* Parris) How do you propose, then?

86 **Parris.** Excellency, I would postpone these hangin's for a time.

87 **Danforth.** There will be no postponement.

88 **Parris.** Now Mr. Hale's returned, there is hope, I think—for if he bring even one of these to God, that confession surely damns the others in the public eye, and none may doubt more that they are all linked to Hell. This way, unconfessed and claiming innocence, doubts are multiplied, many honest people will weep for them, and our good purpose is lost in their tears.

89 **Danforth** (*after thinking a moment, then going to* Cheever). Give me the list.

90 (Cheever *opens the dispatch case, searches.*)

91 **Parris.** It cannot be forgot, sir, that when I summoned the congregation for John Proctor's excommunication[5] there were hardly thirty people come to hear it. That speak a discontent, I think, and—

92 **Danforth** (*studying the list*). There will be no postponement.

93 **Parris.** Excellency—

94 **Danforth.** Now, sir—which of these in your opinion may be brought to God? I will myself strive with him[6] till dawn. (*He hands the list to* Parris, *who merely glances at it.*)

95 **Parris.** There is not sufficient time till dawn.

96 **Danforth.** I shall do my utmost. Which of them do you have hope for?

97 **Parris** (*not even glancing at the list now, and in a quavering voice, quietly*). Excellency—a dagger— (*He chokes up.*)

98 **Danforth.** What do you say?

99 **Parris.** Tonight, when I open my door to leave my house—a dagger clattered to the ground. (*Silence.* Danforth *absorbs this. Now* Parris *cries out.*) You cannot hang this sort. There is danger for me. I dare not step outside at night!

100 (Reverend Hale *enters. They look at him for an instant in silence. He is steeped in sorrow, exhausted, and more direct than he ever was.*)

Don't forget to **Notice & Note** as you read the text.

---

[4] **gibbet** (jĭb´ĭt): gallows.

[5] **excommunication:** banishment from a church. For the Puritans in New England, this punishment resulted in the loss of church privileges.

[6] **strive with him:** struggle with him through prayer.

101 **Danforth.** Accept my congratulations, Reverend Hale; we are gladdened to see you returned to your good work.

102 **Hale** (*coming to* Danforth *now*). You must pardon them. They will not budge.

103 (Herrick *enters, waits.*)

104 **Danforth** (*conciliatory*). You misunderstand, sir; I cannot pardon these when twelve are already hanged for the same crime. It is not just.

105 **Parris** (*with failing heart*). Rebecca will not confess?

106 **Hale.** The sun will rise in a few minutes. Excellency, I must have more time.

107 **Danforth.** Now hear me, and beguile yourselves no more. I will not receive a single plea for pardon or postponement. Them that will not confess will hang. Twelve are already executed; the names of these seven are given out, and the village expects to see them die this morning. Postponement now speaks a floundering on my part; reprieve or pardon must cast doubt upon the guilt of them that died till now. While I speak God's law, I will not crack its voice with whimpering. If retaliation is your fear, know this—I should hang ten thousand that dared to rise against the law, and an ocean of salt tears could not melt the resolution of the statutes. Now draw yourselves up like men and help me, as you are bound by Heaven to do. Have you spoken with them all, Mr. Hale?

108 **Hale.** All but Proctor. He is in the dungeon.

109 **Danforth** (*to* Herrick). What's Proctor's way now?

110 **Herrick.** He sits like some great bird; you'd not know he lived except he will take food from time to time.

111 **Danforth** (*after thinking a moment*). His wife—his wife must be well on with child now.

112 **Herrick.** She is, sir.

113 **Danforth.** What think you, Mr. Parris? You have closer knowledge of this man; might her presence soften him?

114 **Parris.** It is possible, sir. He have not laid eyes on her these three months. I should summon her.

115 **Danforth** (*to* Herrick). Is he yet adamant? Has he struck at you again?

116 **Herrick.** He cannot, sir, he is chained to the wall now.

117 **Danforth** (*after thinking on it*). Fetch Goody Proctor to me. Then let you bring him up.

118 **Herrick.** Aye, sir. (Herrick *goes. There is silence.*)

119 **Hale.** Excellency, if you postpone a week and publish to the town that you are striving for their confessions, that speak mercy on your part, not faltering.

120 **Danforth.** Mr. Hale, as God have not empowered me like Joshua to stop this sun from rising,[7] so I cannot withhold from them the perfection of their punishment.

121 **Hale** (*harder now*). If you think God wills you to raise rebellion, Mr. Danforth, you are mistaken!

122 **Danforth** (*instantly*). You have heard rebellion spoken in the town?

123 **Hale.** Excellency, there are orphans wandering from house to house; abandoned cattle bellow on the highroads, the stink of rotting crops hangs everywhere, and no man knows when the harlots' cry will end his life—and you wonder yet if rebellion's spoke? Better you should marvel how they do not burn your province!

124 **Danforth.** Mr. Hale, have you preached in Andover this month?

125 **Hale.** Thank God they have no need of me in Andover.

126 **Danforth.** You baffle me, sir. Why have you returned here?

127 **Hale.** Why, it is all simple. I come to do the Devil's work. I come to counsel Christians they should belie themselves. (*His sarcasm collapses.*) There is blood on my head! Can you not see the blood on my head!!

128 **Parris.** Hush! (*For he has heard footsteps. They all face the door.* Herrick *enters with* Elizabeth. *Her wrists are linked by heavy chain, which* Herrick *now removes. Her clothes are dirty; her face is pale and gaunt.* Herrick *goes out.*)

129 **Danforth** (*very politely*). Goody Proctor. (*She is silent.*) I hope you are hearty?

130 **Elizabeth** (*as a warning reminder*). I am yet six month before my time.

131 **Danforth.** Pray be at your ease, we come not for your life. We—(*uncertain how to plead, for he is not accustomed to it.*) Mr. Hale, will you speak with the woman?

132 **Hale.** Goody Proctor, your husband is marked to hang this morning. (*pause*)

133 **Elizabeth** (*quietly*). I have heard it.

134 **Hale.** You know, do you not, that I have no connection with the court? (*She seems to doubt it.*) I come of my own, Goody Proctor. I would save your husband's life, for if he is taken I count myself his murderer. Do you understand me?

135 **Elizabeth.** What do you want of me?

136 **Hale.** Goody Proctor, I have gone this three month like our Lord into the wilderness.[8] I have sought a Christian way, for damnation's doubled on a minister who counsels men to lie.

Don't forget to **Notice & Note** as you read the text.

ANALYZE PLOT

Annotate: Mark stage directions that show what life has been like for Elizabeth Proctor since she was last seen in Act Three.

Analyze: How does this description help the reader understand her situation?

---

[7] **like Joshua . . . rising:** According to the Bible, Joshua became leader of the Israelites after Moses died. He led the people to the Promised Land while the sun stood still.

[8] **like our Lord . . . wilderness:** According to the New Testament, Jesus spent 40 days wandering in the desert while fasting.

137 **Hathorne.** It is no lie, you cannot speak of lies.

138 **Hale.** It is a lie! They are innocent!

139 **Danforth.** I'll hear no more of that!

140 **Hale** (*continuing to* Elizabeth). Let you not mistake your duty as I mistook my own. I came into this village like a bridegroom to his beloved, bearing gifts of high religion; the very crowns of holy law I brought, and what I touched with my bright confidence, it died; and where I turned the eye of my great faith, blood flowed up. Beware, Goody Proctor—cleave to no faith when faith brings blood. It is mistaken law that leads you to sacrifice. Life, woman, life is God's most precious gift; no principle, however glorious, may justify the taking of it. I beg you, woman, prevail upon your husband to confess. Let him give his lie. Quail not before God's judgment in this, for it may well be God damns a liar less than he that throws his life away for pride. Will you plead with him? I cannot think he will listen to another.

141 **Elizabeth** (*quietly*). I think that be the Devil's argument.

142 **Hale** (*with a climactic desperation*). Woman, before the laws of God we are as swine! We cannot read His will!

143 **Elizabeth.** I cannot dispute with you, sir; I lack learning for it.

144 **Danforth** (*going to her*). Goody Proctor, you are not summoned here for disputation. Be there no wifely tenderness within you? He will die with the sunrise. Your husband. Do you understand it? (*She only looks at him.*) What say you? Will you contend with him? (*She is silent.*) Are you stone? I tell you true, woman, had I no other proof of your unnatural life, your dry eyes now would be sufficient evidence that you delivered up your soul to Hell! A very ape would weep at such calamity! Have the Devil dried up any tear of pity in you? (*She is silent.*) Take her out. It profit nothing she should speak to him!

145 **Elizabeth** (*quietly*). Let me speak with him, Excellency.

146 **Parris** (*with hope*). You'll strive with him? (*She hesitates.*)

147 **Danforth.** Will you plead for his confession or will you not?

148 **Elizabeth.** I promise nothing. Let me speak with him.

149 *(A sound—the sibilance of dragging feet on stone. They turn. A pause.* Herrick *enters with* John Proctor. *His wrists are chained. He is another man, bearded, filthy, his eyes misty as though webs had overgrown them. He halts inside the doorway, his eye caught by the sight of* Elizabeth. *The emotion flowing between them prevents anyone from speaking for an instant. Now* Hale, *visibly affected, goes to* Danforth *and speaks quietly.)*

150 **Hale.** Pray, leave them, Excellency.

151 **Danforth** (*pressing* Hale *impatiently aside*). Mr. Proctor, you have been notified, have you not? (Proctor *is silent, staring at* Elizabeth.) I see light in the sky, Mister; let you counsel with your wife, and may God help you turn your back on Hell. (Proctor *is silent, staring at* Elizabeth.)

152 **Hale** (*quietly*). Excellency, let—

153 (Danforth *brushes past* Hale *and walks out.* Hale *follows.* Cheever *stands and follows,* Hathorne *behind.* Herrick *goes.* Parris, *from a safe distance, offers.*)

154 **Parris.** If you desire a cup of cider, Mr. Proctor, I am sure I—(Proctor *turns an icy stare at him, and he breaks off.* Parris *raises his palms toward* Proctor.) God lead you now. (Parris *goes out.*)

155 (*Alone.* Proctor *walks to her, halts. It is as though they stood in a spinning world. It is beyond sorrow, above it. He reaches out his hand as though toward an embodiment not quite real, and as he touches her, a strange soft sound, half laughter, half amazement, comes from his throat. He pats her hand. She covers his hand with hers. And then, weak, he sits. Then she sits, facing him.*)

156 **Proctor.** The child?

157 **Elizabeth.** It grows.

158 **Proctor.** There is no word of the boys?

159 **Elizabeth.** They're well. Rebecca's Samuel keeps them.

160 **Proctor.** You have not seen them?

161 **Elizabeth.** I have not. (*She catches a weakening in herself and downs it.*)

162 **Proctor.** You are a—marvel, Elizabeth.

163 **Elizabeth.** You—have been tortured?

164 **Proctor.** Aye. (*Pause. She will not let herself be drowned in the sea that threatens her.*) They come for my life now.

165 **Elizabeth.** I know it.

166 (*pause*)

167 **Proctor.** None—have yet confessed?

168 **Elizabeth.** There be many confessed.

169 **Proctor.** Who are they?

170 **Elizabeth.** There be a hundred or more, they say. Goody Ballard is one; Isaiah Goodkind is one. There be many.

171 **Proctor.** Rebecca?

172 **Elizabeth.** Not Rebecca. She is one foot in Heaven now; naught may hurt her more.

173 **Proctor.** And Giles?

174 **Elizabeth.** You have not heard of it?

175 **Proctor.** I hear nothin', where I am kept.

176 **Elizabeth.** Giles is dead.

177 (*He looks at her incredulously.*)

178 **Proctor.** When were he hanged?

Don't forget to **Notice & Note** as you read the text.

ANALYZE LITERARY DEVICES

Annotate: Mark the figurative language in paragraphs 154 and 164.

Evaluate: How does the use of figurative language reveal Proctor and Elizabeth's emotional states?

179 **Elizabeth** (*quietly, factually*). He were not hanged. He would not answer aye or nay to his indictment; for if he denied the charge they'd hang him surely, and auction out his property. So he stand mute, and died Christian under the law. And so his sons will have his farm. It is the law, for he could not be condemned a wizard without he answer the indictment, aye or nay.

180 **Proctor.** Then how does he die?

181 **Elizabeth** (*gently*). They press him, John.

182 **Proctor.** Press?

183 **Elizabeth.** Great stones they lay upon his chest until he plead aye or nay. (*with a tender smile for the old man*) They say he give them but two words. "More weight," he says. And died.

184 **Proctor** (*numbed—a thread to weave into his agony*). "More weight."

185 **Elizabeth.** Aye. It were a fearsome[9] man, Giles Corey.

186 (*pause*)

187 **Proctor** (*with great force of will, but not quite looking at her*). I have been thinking I would confess to them, Elizabeth. (*She shows nothing.*) What say you? If I give them that?

188 **Elizabeth.** I cannot judge you, John.

189 (*pause*)

190 **Proctor** (*simply—a pure question*). What would you have me do?

191 **Elizabeth.** As you will, I would have it. (*slight pause*) I want you living, John. That's sure.

192 **Proctor** (*pauses, then with a flailing of hope*). Giles' wife? Have she confessed?

193 **Elizabeth.** She will not.

194 (*pause*)

195 **Proctor.** It is a pretense, Elizabeth.

196 **Elizabeth.** What is?

ANALYZE CHARACTERS

Annotate: Mark what Proctor says about his honesty.

Analyze: Why does he feel this way about his honesty?

197 **Proctor.** I cannot mount the gibbet like a saint. It is a fraud. I am not that man. (*She is silent.*) My honesty is broke, Elizabeth; I am no good man. Nothing's spoiled by giving them this lie that were not rotten long before.

198 **Elizabeth.** And yet you've not confessed till now. That speak goodness in you.

199 **Proctor.** Spite only keeps me silent. It is hard to give a lie to dogs. (*Pause. For the first time he turns directly to her.*) I would have your forgiveness, Elizabeth.

200 **Elizabeth.** It is not for me to give, John, I am—

[9] **fearsome:** courageous.

Don't forget to **Notice & Note** as you read the text.

201 **Proctor.** I'd have you see some honesty in it. Let them that never lied die now to keep their souls. It is pretense for me, a vanity that will not blind God nor keep my children out of the wind. (*pause*) What say you?

202 **Elizabeth** (*upon a heaving sob that always threatens*). John, it come to naught that I should forgive you, if you'll not forgive yourself. (*Now he turns away a little, in great agony.*) It is not my soul, John, it is yours. (*He stands, as though in physical pain, slowly rising to his feet with a great immortal longing to find his answer. It is difficult to say, and she is on the verge of tears.*) Only be sure of this, for I know it now: Whatever you will do, it is a good man does it. (*He turns his doubting, searching gaze upon her.*) I have read my heart this three month, John. (*pause*) I have sins of my own to count. It needs a cold wife to prompt lechery.

203 **Proctor** (*in great pain*). Enough, enough—

204 **Elizabeth** (*now pouring out her heart*). Better you should know me!

205 **Proctor.** I will not hear it! I know you!

206 **Elizabeth.** You take my sins upon you, John—

207 **Proctor** (*in agony*). No, I take my own, my own!

208 **Elizabeth.** John, I counted myself so plain, so poorly made, no honest love could come to me! Suspicion kissed you when I did; I never knew how I should say my love. It were a cold house I kept! (*In fright, she swerves, as* Hathorne *enters.*)

209 **Hathorne.** What say you, Proctor? The sun is soon up.

210 (Proctor, *his chest heaving, stares, turns to* Elizabeth. *She comes to him as though to plead, her voice quaking.*)

211 **Elizabeth.** Do what you will. But let none be your judge. There be no higher judge under Heaven than Proctor is! Forgive me, forgive me, John—I never knew such goodness in the world! (*She covers her face, weeping.*)

212 (Proctor *turns from her to* Hathorne; *he is off the earth, his voice hollow.*)

213 **Proctor.** I want my life.

214 **Hathorne** (*electrified, surprised*). You'll confess yourself?

215 **Proctor.** I will have my life.

216 **Hathorne** (*with a mystical tone*). God be praised! It is a providence! (*He rushes out the door, and his voice is heard calling down the corridor.*) He will confess! Proctor will confess!

217 **Proctor** (*with a cry, as he strides to the door*). Why do you cry it? (*In great pain he turns back to her.*) It is evil, is it not? It is evil.

218 **Elizabeth** (*in terror, weeping*). I cannot judge you, John, I cannot!

219 **Proctor.** Then who will judge me? (*suddenly clasping his hands*) God in Heaven, what is John Proctor, what is John Proctor? (*He moves as*

ANALYZE PLOT

Annotate: Mark words in paragraphs 217–222 that show Proctor's inner conflict.

Analyze: How do Proctor's thoughts and actions reflect his internal conflict? How do they drive the action of the play at this point?

an animal, and a fury is riding in him, a tantalized search.) I think it is honest, I think so; I am no saint. (*As though she had denied this he calls angrily at her.*) Let Rebecca go like a saint; for me it is fraud!

220 (*Voices are heard in the hall, speaking together in suppressed excitement.*)

221 **Elizabeth.** I am not your judge, I cannot be. (*as though giving him release*) Do as you will, do as you will!

222 **Proctor.** Would you give them such a lie? Say it. Would you ever give them this? (*She cannot answer.*) You would not; if tongs of fire were singeing you you would not! It is evil. Good, then—it is evil, and I do it!

223 (Hathorne *enters with* Danforth, *and, with them,* Cheever, Parris, *and* Hale. *It is a businesslike, rapid entrance, as though the ice had been broken.*)

224 **Danforth** (*with great relief and gratitude*). Praise to God, man, praise to God; you shall be blessed in Heaven for this. (Cheever *has hurried to the bench with pen, ink, and paper.* Proctor *watches him.*) Now then, let us have it. Are you ready, Mr. Cheever?

225 **Proctor** (*with a cold, cold horror at their efficiency*). Why must it be written?

226 **Danforth.** Why, for the good instruction of the village, Mister; this we shall post upon the church door! (*to* Parris, *urgently*) Where is the marshal?

227 **Parris** (*runs to the door and calls down the corridor*). Marshal! Hurry!

228 **Danforth.** Now, then, Mister, will you speak slowly, and directly to the point, for Mr. Cheever's sake. (*He is on record now, and is really dictating to* Cheever, *who writes.*) Mr. Proctor, have you seen the Devil in your life? (Proctor*'s jaws lock.*) Come, man, there is light in the sky; the town waits at the scaffold; I would give out this news. Did you see the Devil?

229 **Proctor.** I did.

230 **Parris.** Praise God!

231 **Danforth.** And when he come to you, what were his demand? (Proctor *is silent.* Danforth *helps.*) Did he bid you to do his work upon the earth?

232 **Proctor.** He did.

233 **Danforth.** And you bound yourself to his service? (Danforth *turns, as* Rebecca Nurse *enters, with* Herrick *helping to support her. She is barely able to walk.*) Come in, come in, woman!

234 **Rebecca** (*brightening as she sees* Proctor). Ah, John! You are well, then, eh?

235 (Proctor *turns his face to the wall.*)

236 **Danforth.** Courage, man, courage—let her witness your good example that she may come to God herself. Now hear it, Goody Nurse! Say on, Mr. Proctor. Did you bind yourself to the Devil's service?

237 **Rebecca** (*astonished*). Why, John!

238 **Proctor** (*through his teeth, his face turned from* Rebecca). I did.

239 **Danforth.** Now, woman, you surely see it profit nothin' to keep this conspiracy any further. Will you confess yourself with him?

240 **Rebecca.** Oh, John—God send his mercy on you!

241 **Danforth.** I say, will you confess yourself, Goody Nurse?

242 **Rebecca.** Why, it is a lie, it is a lie; how may I damn myself? I cannot, I cannot.

243 **Danforth.** Mr. Proctor. When the Devil came to you did you see Rebecca Nurse in his company? (Proctor *is silent.*) Come, man, take courage—did you ever see her with the Devil?

244 **Proctor** (*almost inaudibly*). No.

245 (Danforth, *now sensing trouble, glances at* John *and goes to the table, and picks up a sheet—the list of condemned.*)

246 **Danforth.** Did you ever see her sister, Mary Easty, with the Devil?

247 **Proctor.** No, I did not.

248 **Danforth** (*his eyes narrow on* Proctor). Did you ever see Martha Corey with the Devil?

249 **Proctor.** I did not.

250 **Danforth** (*realizing, slowly putting the sheet down*). Did you ever see anyone with the Devil?

251 **Proctor.** I did not.

252 **Danforth.** Proctor, you mistake me. I am not empowered to trade your life for a lie. You have most certainly seen some person with the Devil. (Proctor *is silent.*) Mr. Proctor, a score of people have already testified they saw this woman with the Devil.

253 **Proctor.** Then it is proved. Why must I say it?

254 **Danforth.** Why "must" you say it! Why, you should rejoice to say it if your soul is truly purged of any love for Hell!

255 **Proctor.** They think to go like saints. I like not to spoil their names.

256 **Danforth** (*inquiring, incredulous*). Mr. Proctor, do you think they go like saints?

257 **Proctor** (*evading*). This woman never thought she done the Devil's work.

258 **Danforth.** Look you, sir. I think you mistake your duty here. It matters nothing what she thought—she is convicted of the unnatural murder of children, and you for sending your spirit out upon Mary

ANALYZE CHARACTERS

Annotate: Mark words that suggest a contrast between Rebecca and Proctor.

Analyze: How is Rebecca a foil for Proctor? Which of Proctor's traits are highlighted in comparison to Rebecca?

Warren. Your soul alone is the issue here, Mister, and you will prove its whiteness or you cannot live in a Christian country. Will you tell me now what persons conspired with you in the Devil's company? (Proctor *is silent.*) To your knowledge was Rebecca Nurse ever—

259 **Proctor.** I speak my own sins; I cannot judge another. (*crying out, with hatred*) I have no tongue for it.

260 **Hale** (*quickly to* Danforth). Excellency, it is enough he confess himself. Let him sign it, let him sign it.

261 **Parris** (*feverishly*). It is a great service, sir. It is a weighty name; it will strike the village that Proctor confess. I beg you, let him sign it. The sun is up, Excellency!

262 **Danforth** (*considers; then with dissatisfaction*). Come, then, sign your testimony. (*to* Cheever) Give it to him. (Cheever *goes to* Proctor, *the confession and a pen in hand.* Proctor *does not look at it.*) Come, man, sign it.

263 **Proctor** (*after glancing at the confession*). You have all witnessed it—it is enough.

264 **Danforth.** You will not sign it?

265 **Proctor.** You have all witnessed it; what more is needed?

266 **Danforth.** Do you sport with me? You will sign your name or it is no confession, Mister! (*His breast heaving with agonized breathing,* Proctor *now lays the paper down and signs his name.*)

267 **Parris.** Praise be to the Lord!

268 (Proctor *has just finished signing when* Danforth *reaches for the paper. But* Proctor *snatches it up, and now a wild terror is rising in him, and a boundless anger.*)

269 **Danforth** (*perplexed, but politely extending his hand*). If you please, sir.

270 **Proctor.** No.

271 **Danforth** (*as though* Proctor *did not understand*). Mr. Proctor, I must have—

272 **Proctor.** No, no. I have signed it. You have seen me. It is done! You have no need for this.

ANALYZE LITERARY DEVICES

Annotate: Mark examples of repetition in paragraphs 273–284.

Analyze: What does this repetition tell the audience about Proctor?

273 **Parris.** Proctor, the village must have proof that—

274 **Proctor.** Damn the village! I confess to God, and God has seen my name on this! It is enough!

275 **Danforth.** No, sir, it is—

276 **Proctor.** You came to save my soul, did you not? Here! I have confessed myself; it is enough!

277 **Danforth.** You have not con—

Don't forget to **Notice & Note** as you read the text. 

278 **Proctor.** I have confessed myself! Is there no good penitence but it be public? God does not need my name nailed upon the church! God sees my name; God knows how black my sins are! It is enough!

279 **Danforth.** Mr. Proctor—

280 **Proctor.** You will not use me! I am no Sarah Good or Tituba, I am John Proctor! You will not use me! It is no part of salvation that you should use me!

281 **Danforth.** I do not wish to—

282 **Proctor.** I have three children—how may I teach them to walk like men in the world, and I sold my friends?

283 **Danforth.** You have not sold your friends—

284 **Proctor.** Beguile me not! I blacken all of them when this is nailed to the church the very day they hang for silence!

285 **Danforth.** Mr. Proctor, I must have good and legal proof that you—

286 **Proctor.** You are the high court, your word is good enough! Tell them I confessed myself; say Proctor broke his knees and wept like a woman; say what you will, but my name cannot—

287 **Danforth** (*with suspicion*). It is the same, is it not? If I report it or you sign to it?

288 **Proctor** (*He knows it is insane*). No, it is not the same! What others say and what I sign to is not the same!

289 **Danforth.** Why? Do you mean to deny this confession when you are free?

290 **Proctor.** I mean to deny nothing!

291 **Danforth.** Then explain to me, Mr. Proctor, why you will not let—

292 **Proctor** (*with a cry of his whole soul*). Because it is my name! Because I cannot have another in my life! Because I lie and sign myself to lies! Because I am not worth the dust on the feet of them that hang! How may I live without my name? I have given you my soul; leave me my name!

293 **Danforth** (*pointing at the confession in* Proctor*'s hand*). Is that document a lie? If it is a lie I will not accept it! What say you? I will not deal in lies, Mister! (Proctor *is motionless.*) You will give me your honest confession in my hand, or I cannot keep you from the rope. (Proctor *does not reply.*) Which way do you go, Mister?

294 (*His breast heaving, his eyes staring,* Proctor *tears the paper and crumples it, and he is weeping in fury, but erect.*)

295 **Danforth.** Marshal!

ANALYZE LITERARY DEVICES

Annotate: Mark what Danforth says about himself in paragraph 293.

Analyze: What is ironic about Danforth's statements?

296 **Parris** (*hysterically, as though the tearing paper were his life*). Proctor, Proctor!

297 **Hale.** Man, you will hang! You cannot!

298 **Proctor** (*his eyes full of tears*). I can. And there's your first marvel, that I can. You have made your magic now, for now I do think I see some shred of goodness in John Proctor. Not enough to weave a banner with, but white enough to keep it from such dogs. (Elizabeth, *in a burst of terror, rushes to him and weeps against his hand.*) Give them no tear! Tears pleasure them! Show honor now, show a stony heart and sink them with it! (*He has lifted her, and kisses her now with great passion.*)

299 **Rebecca.** Let you fear nothing! Another judgment waits us all!

300 **Danforth.** Hang them high over the town! Who weeps for these, weeps for corruption! (*He sweeps out past them.* Herrick *starts to lead* Rebecca, *who almost collapses, but* Proctor *catches her, and she glances up at him apologetically.*)

301 **Rebecca.** I've had no breakfast.

302 **Herrick.** Come, man.

303 (Herrick *escorts them out,* Hathorne *and* Cheever *behind them.* Elizabeth *stands staring at the empty doorway.*)

304 **Parris** (*in deadly fear, to* Elizabeth). Go to him, Goody Proctor! There is yet time!

305 (*From outside a drumroll strikes the air.* Parris *is startled.* Elizabeth *jerks about toward the window.*)

306 **Parris.** Go to him! (*He rushes out the door, as though to hold back his fate.*) Proctor! Proctor! (*again, a short burst of drums*)

307 **Hale.** Woman, plead with him! (*He starts to rush out the door, and then goes back to her.*) Woman! It is pride, it is vanity. (*She avoids his eyes, and moves to the window. He drops to his knees.*) Be his helper!—

What profit him to bleed? Shall the dust praise him? Shall the worms declare his truth? Go to him, take his shame away!

308 **Elizabeth** (*supporting herself against collapse, grips the bars of the window, and with a cry*). He have his goodness now. God forbid I take it from him!

309 (*The final drumroll crashes, then heightens violently.* Hale *weeps in frantic prayer, and the new sun is pouring in upon her face, and the drums rattle like bones in the morning air. The curtain falls.*)

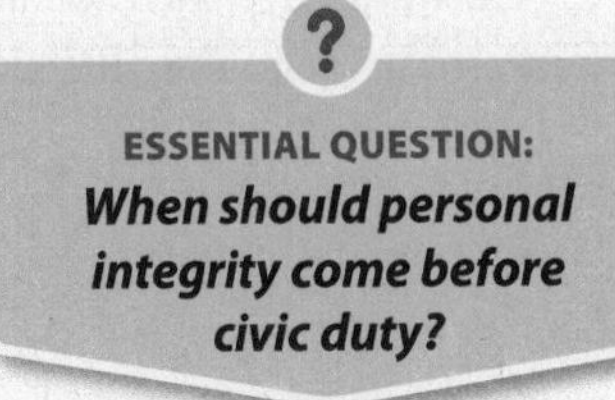
?
ESSENTIAL QUESTION:
When should personal integrity come before civic duty?

Review your notes and add your thoughts to your **Response Log.**

COLLABORATIVE DISCUSSION

With a partner, discuss what the last act reveals about the participants in the witch hunt. What is ironic about their circumstances? Support your ideas with examples from the text.

Assessment Practice

Answer these questions before moving on to the **Analyze the Text** section on the following page.

1. What is one effect of the witch hunt on people's everyday lives?

- (A) Crops cannot be harvested.
- (B) People are losing their jobs.
- (C) There are more robberies being committed.
- (D) The bank is repossessing many people's homes.

2. About how many people total stand accused of witchcraft?

- (A) about 30
- (B) about 50
- (C) about 80
- (D) about 100

3. How does the play end?

- (A) Abigail is sentenced to death.
- (B) Elizabeth is sentenced to death.
- (C) Rebecca and Proctor are sentenced to death.
- (D) Elizabeth and Proctor are sentenced to death.

Ed

Test-Taking Strategies

Analyze the Text

Support your responses with evidence from the text.

NOTICE & NOTE

Review what you **noticed and noted** as you read the text. Your annotations can help you answer these questions.

1 **INFER** Explain why each of the following characters wants Proctor and the other prisoners to confess: Danforth, Parris, and Hale. Cite evidence in support of your response.

2 **ANALYZE** Explain how Miller conveys a major theme of the play through Proctor's decision about whether to confess.

3 **INFER** What does the description of Giles Corey's death in Act Four, paragraphs 173–185, convey? Think of his earlier appearances in the play and infer what Giles Corey represents for Miller.

4 **INTERPRET** What does a crucible symbolize in this drama? How does a symbol suggest a theme? Use the chart below for your answer.

Definitions of a Crucible	What the Crucible Symbolizes	What Theme It Suggests
1. Severe test or trial **2.** Vessel in which materials are melted at high temperatures to produce a more refined substance		

5 **ANALYZE** Reread the passages identified in the list. What is the central paradox, or contradiction, of the trials? What truth is Miller hoping to reveal about these kinds of witch hunts by discussing this paradox?

- Act Two, paragraph 387
- Act Three, paragraph 169
- Act Three, paragraph 241

6 **SYNTHESIZE** Explain how the resolution of Proctor's conflict reveals a major theme of the play.

7 **DRAW CONCLUSIONS** Over the course of the play, characters change in surprising ways. What do these **Contrasts & Contradictions** suggest about the continuation of the Salem witch trials?

Choices

Here are some other ways to demonstrate your understanding of the ideas in this lesson.

Writing

↳ Literary Analysis

A constant thread running throughout the play is what qualities and behaviors define a person's moral compass. Reverends Parris and Hale have their own ideas, as does John Proctor. Using examples from the play, write an analysis that answers the following questions:

- How do Parris and Hale's ideas of moral behavior compare to Proctor's?
- How do those ideas evolve over the course of the play?
- Whose ideas of morality most conform with your own?

As you write and discuss, be sure to use the **Academic Vocabulary** words.

- contemporary
- global
- infinite
- simulated
- virtual

Media

↳ Infographic

The Salem witch trials are some of the most researched and documented witchcraft trials in the world. Create an infographic to show the scope of the hysteria. Include the following:

- the number of people tried
- the number of people executed and how they were put to death
- the number of orphaned children
- how far the trials spread beyond Salem

Speaking & Listening

↳ Group Discussion

Arthur Miller said that he wrote *The Crucible* with the conviction that "there were moments when an individual conscience was all that could keep the world from falling apart." Do you agree with this statement? In a small group, discuss examples in the play and/or in your own experience where someone's act of conscience stood out as a brave example of what ought to be done, even if it was not understood or appreciated at the time.

Vocabulary Strategy

↳ Determine the Meaning of Idioms

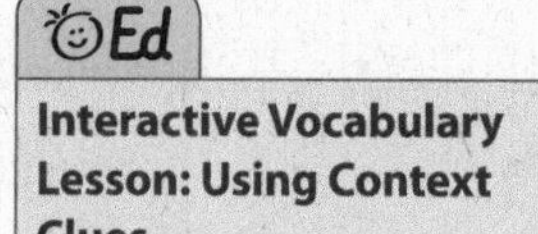

An **idiom** is a type of figurative language whose meaning is different from the literal meaning of its words. Idioms are common figures of speech and are often associated with certain time periods and locations.

Idiom	Meaning
Now I am undone. (Act One, paragraph 111)	This idiom means something similar to "I am ruined!"
I'll pay you, Herrick, I will surely pay you! (Act Two, paragraph 404)	This idiom is similar to the idiom "getting payback." It means something like "I will have revenge!"
Take it to heart, Mr. Parris. (Act One, paragraph 254)	This idiom is related to the heart being central and vital. It means something like "Consider it very important."
I think this goes to the heart of the matter. (Act Three, paragraph 234)	This idiom is also related to the heart being central and vital. It means something like "the most important part of the business."

PRACTICE AND APPLY

Find two idioms in the text. Read the idiom in context and infer its meaning. Then, check their meanings using an online idiom dictionary. Share your idioms, their context clues, and their meanings with the class.

Idiom	Inferred Meaning	Researched Meaning

Watch Your Language!

Dialogue

Dialogue is the foundation of drama. It can reveal a variety of character traits and motivations. In addition, it performs other important functions.

Dialogue moves the plot forward. Through characters' speech, readers learn about plot developments, the central conflict, and its impact. Danforth reveals important details about the witch trials in Act Four:

> **Twelve are already executed; the names of these seven are given out, and the village expects to see them die this morning.**

Dialogue conveys theme. Characters' speeches state ideas that help readers recognize the playwright's underlying message. In Act Four, when Proctor refuses to sign his name to a written confession, he cries out,

> **Because it is my name! Because I cannot have another in my life! Because I lie and sign myself to lies!**

This articulates an important message of the play: One's personal integrity is too high a price to pay for life. One's name—symbolically one's reputation and honor—cannot be sacrificed, not even to preserve life.

Dialogue conveys setting and character. How characters speak can bring authenticity to a historical setting. Miller's word choice and use of inverted sentences reflect the speech of 17th-century Salem.

> **Aye, sir, he have been searchin' his books since he left you, sir. But he bid me tell you, that you might look to unnatural things for the cause of it.**
> *(Act One, paragraph 32)*

Instead of *yes*, Miller uses *aye*, which was common in the 1600s but is not today. He uses "have been" instead of "has been," the verb form used in this context today.

PRACTICE AND APPLY

Read these examples of dialogue from Act Four. Tell whether each example advances the plot, helps create setting, or conveys theme.

1. **Danforth.** They are both gone?
   Parris (*in fear of him*). They are, sir.
2. Would you give them such a lie? . . . You would not; . . . It is evil.
3. Aye. It were a fearsome man, Giles Corey.

Get Ready

from The Crucible

Audio Excerpt from Act Three (paragraphs 352–423)
Production Images by **Walter Kerr Theatre, New York**

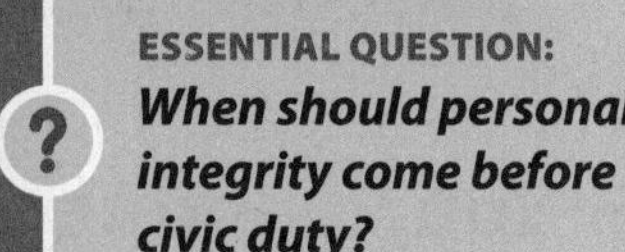

ESSENTIAL QUESTION:
When should personal integrity come before civic duty?

Engage Your Brain

Choose one or more of these activities to start connecting with the audio excerpt and the production images.

How to Make It Real

You have read Arthur Miller's *The Crucible*. Think about the lengthy explanations Miller included in the text. How might some of those ideas be presented in a staged version? Discuss your ideas with a partner.

There's Something About That Voice . . .

Have you ever heard it said that someone "makes reading the dictionary sound interesting"? Think of an actor or spokesperson who has a distinctive or compelling voice. What about this person's voice makes it instantly recognizable? Discuss your ideas in a small group.

Picture This!

What is your first impression of this image from the stage production of *The Crucible*? Write down your thoughts.

Analyze Text and Media

To analyze an audio recording or stage production of a play, you should think about how the cast and crew of a production present what the playwright set down in the script. Consider the following elements as you listen to the audio excerpt and view the production images.

Elements of a Dramatic Production	
Voice expression	Actors modulate their voice to evoke certain feelings. A low, deep voice may convey sadness or seriousness. A high voice may create feelings of stress, tension, happiness, or anxiety.
Volume, pace, and stress	Actors emphasize important lines of dialogue, speed up or slow down to convey emotion, or raise or lower the volume of their voices to express a character's reaction to another character.
Timing	Actors choose when to deliver lines of dialogue. They may employ dramatic pauses, interruptions, and/or simultaneous speech. These timing changes often reflect the playwright's punctuation and line arrangement but can be left open to interpretation.
Casting	Directors cast certain actors because their physical characteristics and acting styles impact the audience's perception of characters and plot.
Blocking	Actors' positions on stage, as well as their movements and gestures, are deliberately choreographed to reflect a character's emotions and relationship to other characters.
Lighting	Carefully positioned lights create mood, emphasize or explain characters' actions, and build suspense.
Set design and costuming	Sets and costumes create a sense of where and when the action takes place. Some interpretations use sets and costumes to maintain historical accuracy, while others use them to achieve other creative interpretations.

As you listen to the audio excerpt and look at the production images, note how the relevant dramatic aspects are interpreted. What choices did the actors, the director, and the designers make in their portrayals? What might they have done differently, and what would the effect have been had they chosen the alternative?

Focus on Genre
Audio Recording

- **is directed toward a listening audience**
- **may contain sound effects and music, as well as dialogue**
- **will showcase vocal techniques like timing, volume, pace, and stress**

Evaluate Interpretations of a Drama

The **script** of a play can be read and analyzed, but plays are meant to be performed. Performances can be presented in a variety of media. An audio recording should offer a compelling reading of dialogue that propels the plot forward and reveals the emotional lives of the characters. Images from a stage production can give the viewer an idea of the set, costumes, and cast, as well as some insight into the director's vision for his or her retelling.

Experiencing a drama through different media enables the audience to appreciate the text from different perspectives. For example, an audio recording allows listeners to concentrate on the characters' words without the distraction of visual elements. In production stills, costumes, staging, and lighting can draw you into the conflicts and bring the story to life. However, there are drawbacks to each medium, as well. In a recording, it may be difficult to identify who is speaking. In production images, some elements may distract from the essence of the drama.

As you listen to the audio and view the production images, keep in mind the advantages and disadvantages of each medium. To evaluate each interpretation, ask yourself the following questions:

- How closely do they reflect Arthur Miller's script?
- What do they reveal about the director's vision for the production?
- Which one most effectively conveys the themes of *The Crucible*?

Use the chart below to make notes about what you hear and see.

Elements to Evaluate	Audio Excerpt	Production Images
Theme		
Setting		
Characters		
Exposition		
Stage directions		

Focus on Genre
↳ **Production Images**

- **are used to promote a film or performance of a play**
- **convey key ideas about the work to an audience**
- **may reveal the artistic vision driving a production**

from
The Crucible

Audio Excerpt from Act Three (paragraphs 352–423)

Production Images by **Walter Kerr Theatre, New York**

BACKGROUND

There are several written versions of *The Crucible*, all of which Arthur Miller authored or co-authored. He wrote the play, which premiered in 1953 on Broadway and has been presented countless times since. Miller's play was later adapted for the opera in 1961, and Miller wrote the screenplay for the film in 1996. As you read the play, you saw images from a 2014 performance in London's Old Vic Theatre, which followed a somewhat true-to-history interpretation of the play in terms of sets, costumes, and casting.

The production stills you are about to see are from the 2016 Broadway production starring Ben Whishaw and Saoirse Ronan. Ivo van Hove is the Belgian director of the Toneelgroep Amsterdam theater company, but he is renowned on Broadway for his critically acclaimed avant-garde interpretations of well-known plays. This production of *The Crucible* furthered his acclaim. The characters and story follow the script, but these images reveal a fresh approach to set design, costumes, and lighting that does not strictly follow Miller's stage directions. In addition, the cast is a group of international actors who did not adopt a 17th-century American dialect in their portrayal of the characters. The play's essence, however, remains the same—a tale of mass hysteria and the fears and rationalizations of the people who succumb to it.

"The mission of the theater, after all, is to change, to raise the consciousness of people to their human possibilities."

—Arthur Miller

Listen as actors use different vocal techniques to bring the characters of *The Crucible* to life.

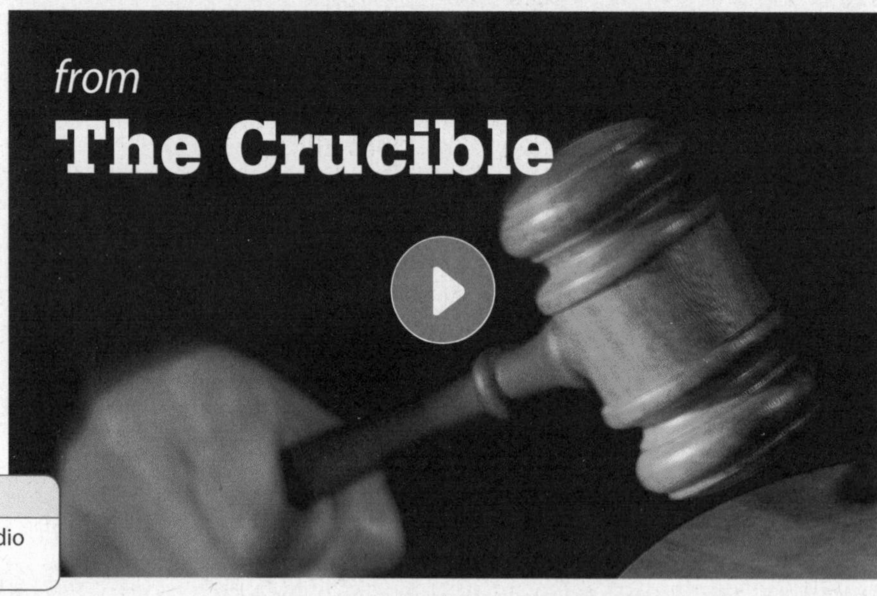

Audio

Listen to *The Crucible* audio excerpt in your ebook.

ESSENTIAL QUESTION:
When should personal integrity come before civic duty?

Review your notes and add your thoughts to your **Response Log.**

COLLABORATIVE DISCUSSION

With a partner, discuss which characters emerge most fully in this scene. What vocal techniques made the characters stand out? Use examples from the recording in your discussion.

Don't forget to **Notice & Note** as you read the text.

As you analyze these production images from *The Crucible,* think about how this staged production differs from the written script.

Act One

Reverend Parris's home. Abigail and Betty begin to accuse their neighbors of witchcraft, as Reverend Parris looks on.

EVALUATE INTERPRETATIONS OF A DRAMA

Annotate: List the elements of set design and lighting in this photo that conform to the setting Miller describes in the script of Act One. Create a separate list for those that break with the script.

Analyze: How do these similarities and differences affect your perceptions of the play?

ANALYZE TEXT AND MEDIA

Annotate: In this image, what observations can you make about the casting, set design, and costumes?

Draw Conclusions: What choices did the director and designers make? What effect do these choices have on your perception of the events and characters?

Act Three

Courtroom. John Proctor, Deputy Governor Danforth, Reverend Parris, Marshal Herrick, Judge Hathorne, and Ezekiel Cheever listen as Mary Warren testifies against Abigail.

Don't forget to **Notice & Note** as you read the text. 

Act Four

Prison. John Proctor recants his confession.

ANALYZE TEXT AND MEDIA

Annotate: Describe the lighting in relation to the actor's gestures and position on stage.

Interpret: What emotions do you think the actor is trying to portray? What does the lighting contribute to the scene?

Analyze Media

Support your responses with evidence from the play and the media versions.

1 **EVALUATE** If you only saw the production images, how would you describe John Proctor and Abigail Williams? Is your perception consistent with Miller's depiction of them in the play's script? Consider how multiple visual elements contribute to characterization, and use the chart below to help answer the questions.

Casting	Costumes	Props	Blocking	Lighting

2 **EVALUATE** If you could only listen to the recording, how close would you say this production is to Arthur Miller's script? What about this recording makes it effective or not so effective in portraying Miller's ideas? In your answer, consider how the following acting techniques affect the performance:

Timing	Voice Expression	Volume, Pace, Stress

3 **ANALYZE** What do the media reveal about the differences between the playwright's purpose and the directors' goals? How is the play's message about persecution and hysteria realized in each medium?

4 **ANALYZE** How are the relationships between John Proctor and Abigail portrayed in each medium? Are these consistent with the traditional interpretation of Miller's text? Explain.

5 **EVALUATE** How well do the production images represent the important moments in the play? Do the production images enhance the audio recording of Act Three? Why or why not?

6 **SYNTHESIZE** How do the production images and the text of the drama help you to understand the audio recording's version of the climactic Act Three? Which version of the scene was most powerful? Explain.

NOTICE & NOTE

Review the notes you took as you listened to the audio excerpt and viewed the production images. Your notes can help you answer these questions

Choices

Here are some other ways to demonstrate your understanding of the ideas in this lesson.

Writing

↳ Essay

Using an advantage/disadvantage essay structure, evaluate the strengths and weaknesses of the two media presentations of *The Crucible*. Choose a scene common to both the production images and the audio selection. Include the following in your evaluation:

- strengths and weaknesses of production images
- strengths and weaknesses of audio recordings
- specific details about dramatic techniques relevant to each medium: sets, costumes, sound design, vocal techniques, etc.
- a concluding statement that includes what meaning each medium helps you infer

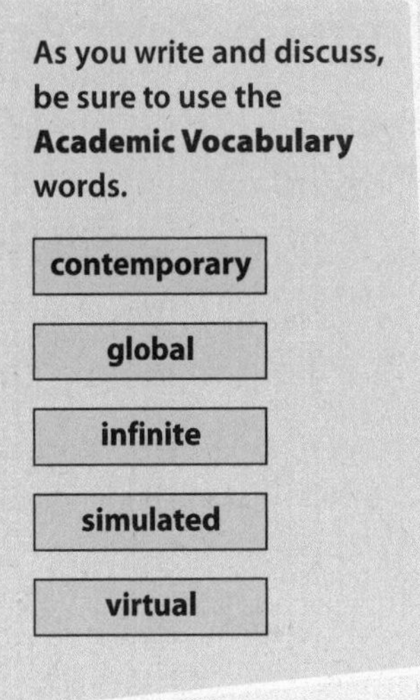
As you write and discuss, be sure to use the **Academic Vocabulary** words.
contemporary
global
infinite
simulated
virtual

Media

↳ Retelling

There are so many creative ways to recast *The Crucible*. Choose a new medium and retell the story. You can pick a comic book, a song, a poem, a news report—the possibilities are endless! When you are done, share your new story with your classmates or post it to a class web page.

Research

↳ Productions of *The Crucible*

Arthur Miller's play has been filmed and staged all over the world in productions large and small, and critics have had plenty to say about them. Do some research to find a critique of a production, then use it to answer the following questions:

- Who directed the performance? What does the critic say about the director's vision for the production?
- Who portrayed the main characters? Did the critic say what was noteworthy about the performance?
- How was the performance received by the public? Did the critic and the larger audience feel the same way about the production?

Get Ready

My Dungeon Shook: Letter to My Nephew

Open Letter by **James Baldwin**

ESSENTIAL QUESTION:
Can anyone achieve the American Dream?

Engage Your Brain

Choose one or more of these activities to start connecting with the letter you are about to read.

Baldwin's Lasting Power

The Fire Next Time—the book of essays that includes "My Dungeon Shook"—was published in 1963. Since its publication, critics have commented that the book has never lost its relevance.

Read the following quotation and think about whether it has anything to say about life in the United States today. "Privately, we cannot stand our lives and dare not examine them; domestically, we take no responsibility for (and no pride in) what goes on in our country; and, internationally, for many millions of people, we are an unmitigated disaster." Discuss your ideas in a small group.

The Role of a Writer

James Baldwin once said, "a writer is by definition a disturber of the peace." What do you think he meant by that? Can you think of any contemporary writer who acts as a "disturber of the peace"? Write your ideas in a paragraph.

City Living

Look at this photo of an urban landscape. What elements do you think are unique to a city? From your point of view, what challenges and opportunities does living in a city provide? Write or sketch your ideas.

Determine Central Ideas

In "My Dungeon Shook," the writer's central ideas may be stated directly or implied. To identify central ideas, look for places where Baldwin repeats words and phrases. As you read, pay attention to how the connotations of these words impact the meaning Baldwin conveys. Use the chart to trace Baldwin's repetition of key words and note changes in meaning.

Word	Appearance in Text	Changes in Meaning
Love		
Countrymen		
Innocence (innocents)		

Focus on Genre
↳ **Open Letter**

- addressed to a specific person but published for a wider readership
- generally written to present an idea, protest, or appeal
- may develop more than one idea

Analyze Rhetoric

Authors use **rhetorical devices** to capture attention, evoke emotion, or ignite critical thinking on the part of the reader. Baldwin uses the following rhetorical devices in the text.

- **Paradox**—a statement that appears contradictory or absurd, but when thought through, can suggest a possible truth. Baldwin uses this device to get his reader to think deeply about familiar ideas.

> **It is the innocence which constitutes the crime.**

- **Repetition**—the use of the same word, phrase, or sentence more than once for effect. Baldwin uses repetition to express deep emotion.

> **You must accept them and accept them with love.**

- **Allusion**—an indirect reference to a person, place, event, or literary work that the author believes readers will know and understand.

> **. . . your countrymen, have caused you to be born under conditions not very far removed from those described for us by Charles Dickens in the London of more than a hundred years ago.**

As you read, notice how Baldwin uses rhetorical devices to support his central ideas.

Annotation in Action

Here are one student's notes about Baldwin's use of repetition. As you read, look for examples of repetition and other rhetorical devices that emphasize a point or express a feeling.

Dear James,

I have begun this letter five times and torn it up five times. I keep seeing your face, which is also the face of your father and my brother. Like him, you are tough, dark, vulnerable, moody—with a very definite tendency to sound truculent because you want no one to think you are soft. You may be like your grandfather in this, I don't know, but certainly both you and your father resemble him very much physically.

Repetition shows the message is important so he wants to get it just right.

Expand Your Vocabulary

Put a check mark next to the vocabulary words that you feel comfortable using when writing or speaking.

truculent	☐
strive	☐
impertinent	☐
unassailable	☐

Then, turn to a partner and talk about a time when you offered advice to someone else. Use as many vocabulary words as you can in your discussion. As you read the text, use the definitions in the side column to learn the vocabulary words you don't already know.

Background

James Baldwin (1924–1987) During the racial and social unrest that characterized the 1950s and 1960s, James Baldwin profoundly influenced the ways in which both Black and white people perceived the plight of African Americans. He bluntly described the personal torments Black people endured, thus compelling Black people to overcome, and white people to acknowledge, the physical and psychological damage racism inflicts on individuals and on society.

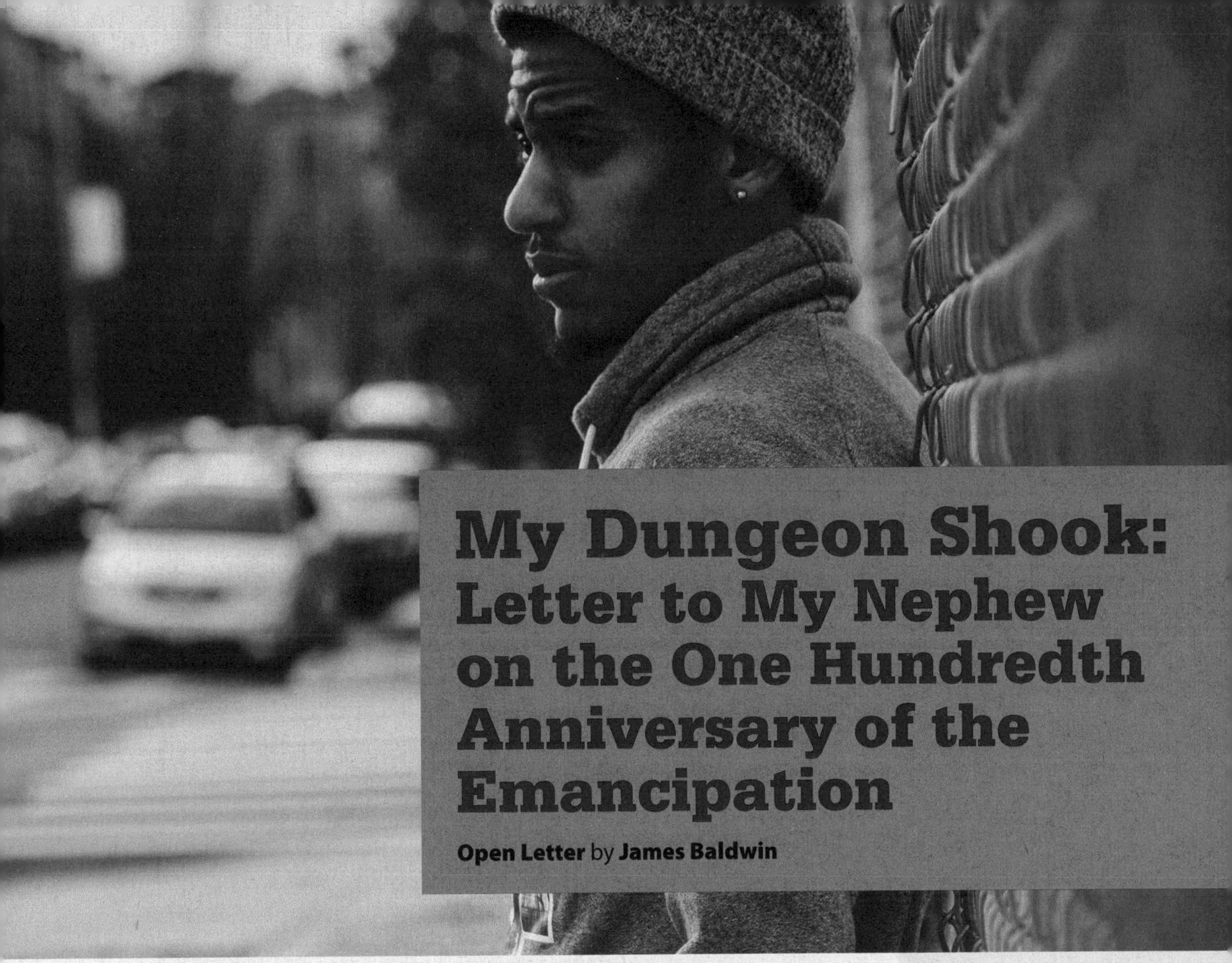

My Dungeon Shook: Letter to My Nephew on the One Hundredth Anniversary of the Emancipation

Open Letter by **James Baldwin**

Notice the points in the text where Baldwin tries to convince his nephew to believe in himself.

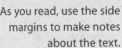

NOTICE & NOTE
As you read, use the side margins to make notes about the text.

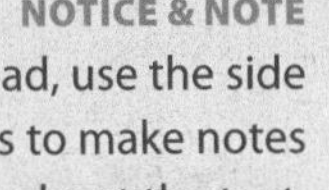

1 Dear James:

I have begun this letter five times and torn it up five times. I keep seeing your face, which is also the face of your father and my brother. Like him, you are tough, dark, vulnerable, moody—with a very definite tendency to sound **truculent** because you want no one to think you are soft. You may be like your grandfather in this, I don't know, but certainly both you and your father resemble him very much physically. Well, he is dead, he never saw you, and he had a terrible life; believed what white people said about him. This is one of the reasons that he became so holy.[1] I am sure that your father has told you something about all that. Neither you nor your father exhibit any tendency towards holiness: you really *are* of another era, part of what happened when the Negro left the land and came into what the late E. Franklin Frazier[2] called "the cities of destruction." You can only

truculent
(trŭk´yə-lənt) *adj.* eager for a fight; fierce.

DETERMINE CENTRAL IDEAS

Annotate: In paragraph 1, mark phrases that convey Baldwin's message to his nephew.

Analyze: Why might information about the grandfather be of interest to Baldwin's nephew?

[1] **so holy:** Baldwin's stepfather was a minister who raised his children in a strict, conservative, religious environment.

[2] **E. Franklin Frazier:** African American sociologist (1894–1962) who studied the structure of Black communities.

be destroyed by believing that you really are what the white world calls a *nigger*. I tell you this because I love you, and please don't you ever forget it.

ANALYZE RHETORIC

Annotate: In the last sentence of paragraph 2, mark the two contradictory words that make this sentence a paradox.

Interpret: Based on Baldwin's logic, how can this paradox be true?

2 I have known both of you all your lives, have carried your Daddy in my arms and on my shoulders, kissed and spanked him and watched him learn to walk. I don't know if you've known anybody from that far back; if you've loved anybody that long, first as an infant, then as a child, then as a man, you gain a strange perspective on time and human pain and effort. Other people cannot see what I see whenever I look into your father's face, for behind your father's face as it is today are all those other faces which were his. Let him laugh and I see a cellar your father does not remember and a house he does not remember and I hear in his present laughter his laughter as a child. Let him curse and I remember him falling down the cellar steps, and howling, and I remember, with pain, his tears, which my hand or your grandmother's so easily wiped away. But no one's hand can wipe away those tears he sheds invisibly today, which one hears in his laughter and in his speech and in his songs. I know what the world has done to my brother and how narrowly he has survived it. And I know, which is much worse, and this is the crime of which I accuse my country and my countrymen, and for which neither I nor time nor history will ever forgive them, that they have destroyed and are destroying hundreds of thousands of lives and do not know it and do not want to know it. One can be, indeed one must **strive** to become, tough and philosophical concerning destruction and death, for this is what most of mankind has been best at since we have heard of man. (But remember: *most* of mankind is not all of mankind.) But it is not permissible that the authors of devastation should also be innocent. It is the innocence which constitutes the crime.

strive
(strīv) *v.* to struggle or fight forcefully; contend.

NOTICE & NOTE
EXTREME OR ABSOLUTE LANGUAGE

When you notice language that leaves no doubt about a situation or allows no compromise, you've found an **Extreme or Absolute Language** signpost.

Notice & Note: In paragraph 3, mark language where Baldwin expresses certainty or an uncompromising position.

Infer: What is Baldwin's purpose for using this language?

3 Now, my dear namesake, these innocent and well-meaning people, your countrymen, have caused you to be born under conditions not very far removed from those described for us by Charles Dickens[3] in the London of more than a hundred years ago. (I hear the chorus of the innocents screaming, "No! This is not true! How *bitter* you are!"—but I am writing this letter to *you*, to try to tell you something about how to handle *them*, for most of them do not yet really know that you exist. I *know* the conditions under which you were born, for I was there. Your countrymen were *not* there, and haven't made it yet. Your grandmother was also there, and no one has ever accused her of being bitter. I suggest that the innocents check with her. She isn't hard to find. Your countrymen don't know that *she* exists, either, though she has been working for them all their lives.)

4 Well, you were born, here you came, something like fifteen years ago; and though your father and mother and grandmother, looking about the streets through which they were carrying you, staring at the walls into which they brought you, had every reason

[3] **described . . . by Charles Dickens:** Dickens (1812–1870) was a British novelist whose works frequently described the hardships suffered by the poor in London.

to be heavyhearted, yet they were not. For here you were, Big James, named for me—you were a big baby, I was not—here you were: to be loved. To be loved, baby, hard, at once, and forever, to strengthen you against the loveless world. Remember that: I know how black it looks today, for you. It looked bad that day, too, yes, we were trembling. We have not stopped trembling yet, but if we had not loved each other none of us would have survived. And now you must survive because we love you, and for the sake of your children and your children's children.

5 This innocent country set you down in a ghetto in which, in fact, it intended that you should perish. Let me spell out precisely what I mean by that, for the heart of the matter is here, and the root of my dispute with my country. You were born where you were born and faced the future that you faced because you were black and *for no other reason*. The limits of your ambition were, thus, expected to be set forever. You were born into a society which spelled out with brutal clarity, and in as many ways as possible, that you were a worthless human being. You were not expected to aspire to excellence: you were expected to make peace with mediocrity. Wherever you have turned, James, in your short time on this earth, you have been told where you could go and what you could do (and *how* you could do it) and where you could live and whom you could marry. I know your countrymen do not agree with me about this, and I hear them saying, "You exaggerate." They do not know Harlem, and I do. So do you. Take no one's word for anything, including mine—but trust your experience.

6 Know whence you came. If you know whence you came, there is really no limit to where you can go. The details and symbols of your life have been deliberately constructed to make you believe what white people say about you. Please try to remember that what they believe, as well as what they do and cause you to endure, does not testify to your inferiority but to their inhumanity and fear. Please try to be clear, dear James, through the storm which rages about your youthful head today, about the reality which lies behind the words *acceptance* and *integration*. There is no reason for you to try to become like white people and there is no basis whatever for their **impertinent** assumption that *they* must accept *you*. The really terrible thing, old buddy, is that *you* must accept *them*. And I mean that very seriously. You must accept them and accept them with love. For these innocent people have no other hope. They are, in effect, still trapped in a history which they do not understand; and until they understand it, they cannot be released from it. They have had to believe for many years, and for innumerable reasons, that black men are inferior to white men. Many of them, indeed, know better, but, as you will discover, people find it very difficult to act on what they know. To act is to be committed, and to be committed is to be in danger. In this case, the danger, in the minds of most white Americans, is the loss of their identity. Try to imagine how you would feel if you woke up one morning to find the sun shining and all the stars aflame. You would be frightened because it is out of the order of nature. Any upheaval in

Don't forget to **Notice & Note** as you read the text.

DETERMINE CENTRAL IDEAS

Annotate: In paragraph 4, mark words that are repeated at least twice.

Analyze: What effect does the use of repeated words have on the writer's central ideas?

VOCABULARY

Use Denotation and Connotation: In the second sentence of paragraph 5, mark the word *precisely*.

Analyze: Write down the **denotation,** or dictionary definition, of *precisely*. Then, write the **connotation,** or emotional response evoked by the same word.

impertinent (ĭm-pûr´tn-ənt) *adj.* rude; ill-mannered.

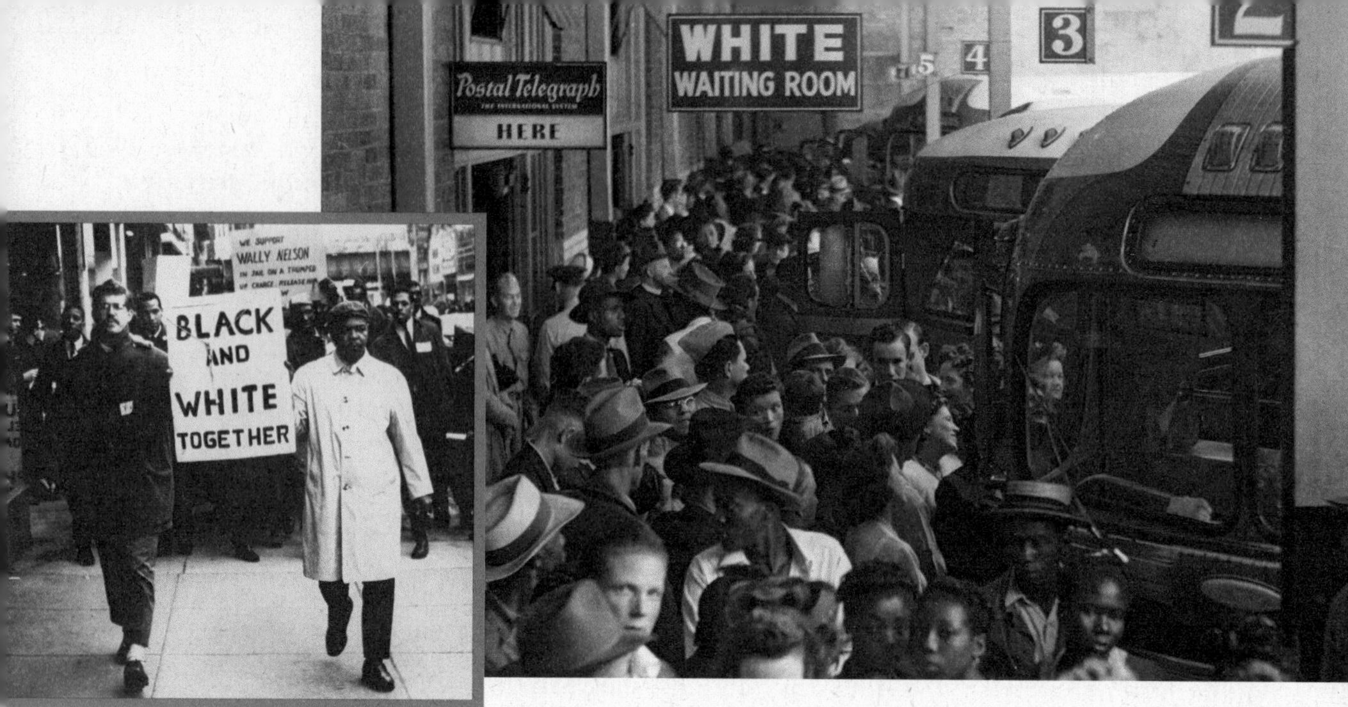

the universe is terrifying because it so profoundly attacks one's sense of one's own reality. Well, the black man has functioned in the white man's world as a fixed star, as an immovable pillar: and as he moves out of his place, heaven and earth are shaken to their foundations. You, don't be afraid. I said that it was intended that you should perish in the ghetto, perish by never being allowed to go behind the white man's definitions, by never being allowed to spell your proper name. You have, and many of us have, defeated this intention; and, by a terrible law, a terrible paradox, those innocents who believed that your imprisonment made them safe are losing their grasp of reality. But these men are your brothers—your lost, younger brothers. And if the word *integration* means anything, this is what it means: that we, with love, shall force our brothers to see themselves as they are, to cease fleeing from reality and begin to change it. For this is your home, my friend, do not be driven from it; great men have done great things here, and will again, and we can make America what America must become. It will be hard, James, but you come from sturdy, peasant stock, men who picked cotton and dammed rivers and built railroads, and, in the teeth of[4] the most terrifying odds, achieved an **unassailable** and monumental dignity. You come from a long line of great poets, some of the greatest poets since Homer. One of them said, *The very time I thought I was lost, My dungeon shook and my chains fell off.*[5]

unassailable
(ŭn-ə-sā´lə-bəl) *adj.* undeniable.

7 You know, and I know, that the country is celebrating one hundred years of freedom one hundred years too soon. We cannot be free until they are free. God bless you, James, and Godspeed.

Your uncle,
James

ANALYZE RHETORIC

Annotate: Recall that a **paradox** is a statement that appears contradictory but presents a possible truth. Mark two paradoxes in paragraph 7.

Analyze: How are these statements paradoxical? What insights on race in America do these two statements convey?

[4] **in the teeth of:** in spite of.

[5] ***The very time . . . fell off:*** a quotation from the traditional spiritual "My Dungeon Shook." It alludes to the biblical story of Paul and Silas (Acts 16), who were freed from an unjust imprisonment by the action of an earthquake.

COLLABORATIVE DISCUSSION

Did Baldwin appeal to his nephew's reasons or emotions? Discuss your ideas with a partner.

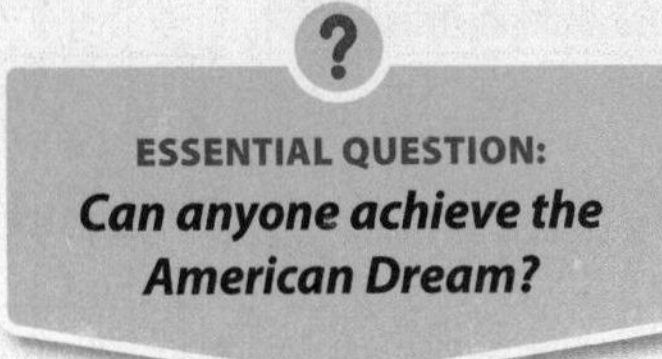
?
ESSENTIAL QUESTION:
Can anyone achieve the American Dream?

Review your notes and add your thoughts to your **Response Log.**

Assessment Practice

Answer these questions before moving on to the **Analyze the Text** section on the following page.

1. According to Baldwin, why did James's grandfather have a terrible life?

- (A) White people in the community ignored him.
- (B) He was unable to complete his education.
- (C) White business owners would not employ him.
- (D) He believed what white people said about him.

2. Baldwin says that James was born into a society that viewed him as —

- (A) a bitter man
- (B) a powerful survivor
- (C) a worthless human being
- (D) an ambitious student

3. What is Baldwin's advice to James about how to treat white people?

- (A) Accept them and accept them with love.
- (B) Feel sorry for them because of their ignorance.
- (C) Teach them that they are enslaved by their beliefs.
- (D) Convince them to accept African Americans.

Ed
Test-Taking Strategies

Analyze the Text

Support your responses with evidence from the text.

NOTICE & NOTE

Review what you **noticed and noted** as you read the text. Your annotations can help you answer these questions.

1. **INTERPRET** Explain how Baldwin refines the meaning of the word *innocence* over the course of the text. Does it carry a positive or negative connotation? Cite specific examples in your response.

2. **ANALYZE** What central ideas does Baldwin develop? How do these ideas change over the course of the letter? How is the reader able to trace these ideas as Baldwin builds his argument?

3. **EVALUATE** Baldwin uses **Extreme Language** to develop his ideas about race in America. How does this kind of language add strength to his argument?

4. **EVALUATE** Baldwin closes his letter by saying that the country is celebrating 100 years of emancipation too soon. Does his argument lead logically to this conclusion? Cite evidence from the text to support your answer.

5. **CITE EVIDENCE** Baldwin includes some details to provide an explanation to his nephew; he includes others to support a claim. Complete the chart below with details that support each purpose.

Explain	Support an Argument

6. **ANALYZE** The title of this letter, "My Dungeon Shook," is an allusion to a popular spiritual inspired by a biblical story. How does this allusion support Baldwin's claim that his nephew is worthy in his own right? How might it resonate with white Americans reading this letter?

Choices

Here are some other ways to demonstrate your understanding of the ideas in this lesson.

Writing

↳ An Open Letter

Over 60 years have passed since Baldwin wrote his letter to his 15-year-old nephew. Since that time civil rights were granted protection by law and racial equality improved to the point that Americans elected an African American president. However, there are still advances in this area to be made. Write an open letter to a friend or family member with your message about civil rights and racial equality. Remember, this will be an open letter, so your audience will include the public.

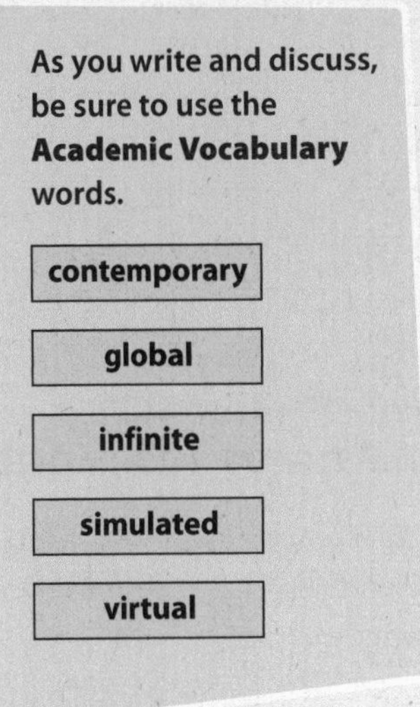
As you write and discuss, be sure to use the **Academic Vocabulary** words.
contemporary
global
infinite
simulated
virtual

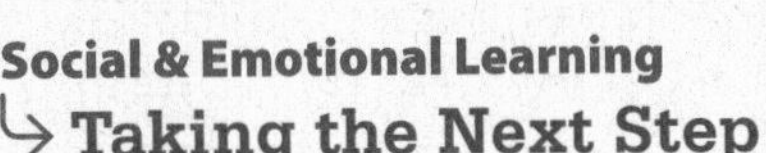

Social & Emotional Learning

↳ Taking the Next Step

While Baldwin's letter is for his nephew, an open letter is intended for everyone to read. Are you compelled to take a particular action based on anything Baldwin wrote? Write a paragraph in which you reflect on Baldwin's letter and discuss whether it will influence your behavior and interactions with others.

Speaking & Listening

↳ Role Model Behavior

Baldwin hopes that his advice will have a positive impact on his nephew's life. It is probable that Baldwin hopes to be a role model for his nephew. Have a group discussion about the importance and effectiveness of role models.

- In what ways is Baldwin an effective role model for his nephew? Cite specific examples from the text.
- What do you look for in a role model? Does Baldwin seem to have those characteristics?
- What is the most effective way for role models to communicate? What actions do you respond to?

Expand Your Vocabulary

PRACTICE AND APPLY

Choose the word that is closest in meaning to the vocabulary word.

1. **impertinent**
   - ○ insolent
   - ○ impossible
   - ○ unfriendly
2. **unassailable**
   - ○ unproven
   - ○ indisputable
   - ○ weakened
3. **truculent**
   - ○ belligerent
   - ○ rude
   - ○ civilized
4. **strive**
   - ○ attempt
   - ○ retreat
   - ○ wallow

Vocabulary Strategy

↳ Analyze Denotation and Connotation

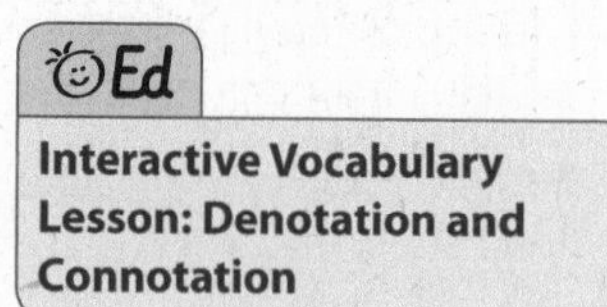

The literal meaning of a word, or **denotation,** can be found in a dictionary. A word also has a **connotation,** or an emotional response the word evokes.

In Baldwin's letter, he uses the word *unassailable* to describe "dignity." The denotation of *unassailable* is "impossible to dispute or disprove; undeniable." Baldwin did not use the word *undeniable* because people can attempt to deny or dispute someone's dignity. Instead, Baldwin deliberately chose a more intense word to indicate that dignity cannot successfully be taken away. If you consider the connotation of *unassailable,* you understand that it means "unquestionable, untouchable, cannot be revoked."

PRACTICE AND APPLY

Complete the chart by first writing the word's denotation. Then, identify the connotation associated with the word as it is used in the text.

Vocabulary Word	Denotation	Connotation
unassailable	undeniable	positive, intense
truculent		
strive		
impertinent		

Watch Your Language!

Interactive Grammar
Lesson: Sentence Structure

Varied Sentence Structure

An essential part of a writer's style is **syntax,** or how the writer arranges words to construct sentences. Effective writers employ varied sentence structure and length to create an engaging rhythm that holds the reader's interest.

There are many ways to vary sentence structure.

- Alternate long and short sentences to avoid monotony and produce rhythm.

I suggest that the innocents check with her. She isn't hard to find.

- Use short sentences to emphasize a point.

They do not know Harlem, and I do. So do you.

- Alternate subject-verb order with other introductory phrases or clauses.

Wherever you have turned, James, in your short time on this earth, you have been told where you could go. . . .

- Combine sentences into compound or complex sentences.

I tell you this because I love you, and please don't you ever forget it.

PRACTICE AND APPLY

Look for an opportunity to vary sentence structure in a piece of your own writing. When you have finished revising, share your sentences with a partner and compare your use of varied sentence structure.

Get Ready

The Latin Deli: An Ars Poetica

Poem by **Judith Ortiz Cofer**

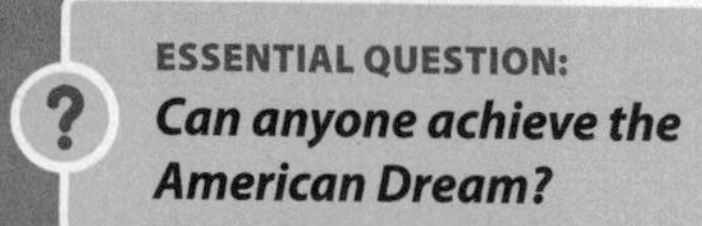
ESSENTIAL QUESTION:
Can anyone achieve the American Dream?

Engage Your Brain

Choose one or both of the following activities to start connecting with the poem you are about to read.

What Is Poetry?

An *ars poetica* is a poem about poetry. What does poetry mean to you? Is poetry a piece of writing or can poetry be found in other places? Freewrite your thoughts.

Where People Come Together

With a group, discuss the gathering places in your school or community. You might consider these questions:

- What places are considered gathering places?
- What about those places makes them appealing or special?
- What do people do when they go to one of those places?

Determine Themes

Themes are the truths about life that a writer wants to convey in her work. They are not usually stated directly, but they can be inferred from clues in the text. Details that reveal a theme can include the following:

- repeated words, phrases, or ideas
- powerful images or symbols
- events that have significance in a text
- a speaker's emotions or reactions

As you read, pay attention to the images and language, important statements and actions in the poem, the repetition of ideas, and the emotions and reactions of the owner of the deli. These elements of the poem help the reader to understand the theme.

Focus on Genre

Ars Poetica

- **explains or defines the "art of poetry"**
- **expresses the poet's ideas about poetry**
- **follows the tradition of Horace's original "Ars Poetica"**
- **uses the forms and techniques of poetry**

Analyze Figurative Language

Poets frequently use figurative language and imagery to communicate meaning.

- **Figurative language** has meaning beyond the literal words and often reveals a point of similarity between two things that are otherwise unlike each other.
- If the comparison is direct, using words such as *like* or *as*, it is a **simile**.
- If the comparison is indirect or implied, not using *like* or *as*, it is a **metaphor**.
- **Imagery** is language that helps readers experience sights, sounds, tastes, smells, and textures so they can understand something in a vivid way.

The chart shows an example of each type of figurative language from "The Latin Deli: An Ars Poetica."

Figurative Language	Example from "The Latin Deli: An Ars Poetica"
Simile: a comparison using *like* or *as*	". . . the green plantains hanging in stalks like votive offerings" (lines 5–6)
Metaphor: a comparison that does not use *like* or *as*	"who spends her days selling canned memories" (line 9)
Imagery: words and phrases that appeal to the senses	"the heady mix of smells from the open bins of dried codfish" (lines 4–5)

As you read "The Latin Deli: An Ars Poetica," look for instances of figurative language. Consider how the poet's use of this type of language contributes to the meaning of the poem.

Analyze Form

The poem you will read in this section is an ars poetica, which is a Latin phrase meaning "the art of poetry." An **ars poetica** is a poem that defines what a poem is and suggests how to best evaluate poetry.

- In the first century BCE, the Latin poet Horace wrote a poem titled "Ars Poetica," which outlines standards for poetry and the criticism of poetry.
- An ars poetica can take any form. There are no constraints on rhyming, line count, or meter.
- An ars poetica can address the principles of poetry, the techniques poets use, the relationship of the poet to the poem, and/or the act of writing a poem.

As you read "The Latin Deli: An Ars Poetica," pay attention to the form the poem takes. Think about the imagery and events, the sounds and feel of the poem, and what those elements imply about what makes a good poem.

Annotation in Action

Here are one student's notes on the figurative language in "The Latin Deli: An Ars Poetica." As you read, notice other instances of figurative language and the meaning they convey.

a woman of no-age who was never pretty, who spends her days selling canned memories	*metaphors compare a woman to a timeless being and canned food to memories*

Background

Judith Ortiz Cofer (1952–2016) traveled between Puerto Rico and the United States throughout her childhood. Themes related to her Puerto Rican and American identities appear in her work. She wrote across multiple genres, including poetry, fiction, creative nonfiction, and children's books. *The Latin Deli,* described as a combination of poetry, short fiction, and personal narrative, was nominated for a Pulitzer Prize.

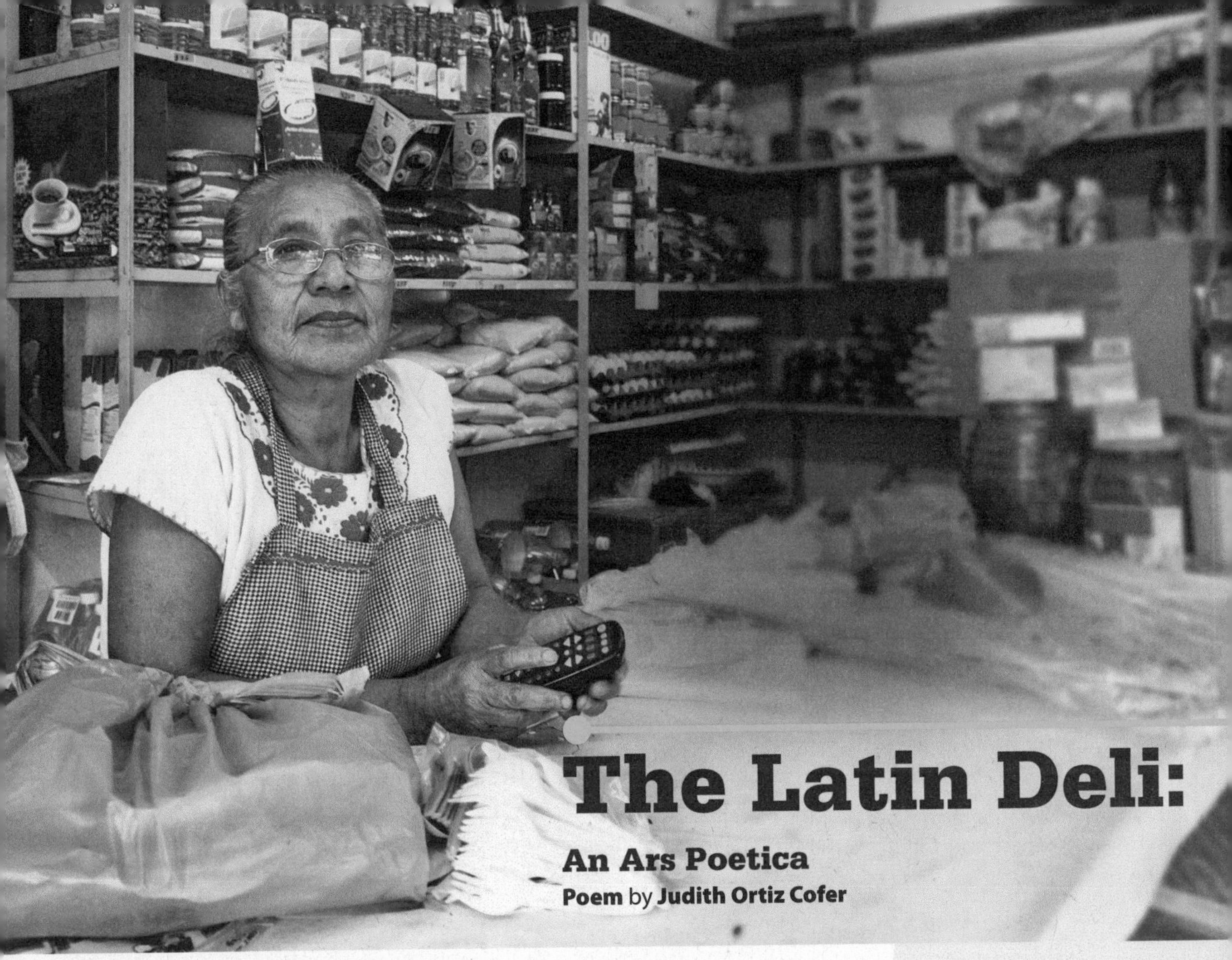

The Latin Deli:

An Ars Poetica

Poem by **Judith Ortiz Cofer**

Note details that show you how a place can be like a poem.

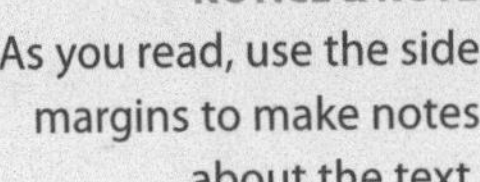

NOTICE & NOTE

As you read, use the side margins to make notes about the text.

Presiding over a formica counter,
plastic Mother and Child magnetized
to the top of an ancient register,
the heady mix of smells from the open bins
of dried codfish, the green plantains[1]
hanging in stalks like votive offerings,[2]
she is the Patroness of Exiles,
a woman of no-age who was never pretty,
who spends her days selling canned memories
while listening to the Puerto Ricans complain
that it would be cheaper to fly to San Juan
than to buy a pound of Bustelo coffee here,
and to Cubans perfecting their speech
of a "glorious return" to Havana—where no one
has been allowed to die and nothing to change until then;

ANALYZE FIGURATIVE LANGUAGE

Annotate: Mark sensory details in lines 1–9.

Analyze: Why do you think the author uses rich imagery in the opening lines of the poem?

[1] **plantains:** type of banana.

[2] **votive offerings:** sacrifices made to fulfill a vow or offered in devotion.

ANALYZE FORM

Annotate: Mark the words in lines 18–24 that suggest family or comfort.

Infer: What do these words imply about poetry?

DETERMINE THEMES

Annotate: Underline words and phrases in lines 29–38 that indicate the importance of the Latin deli to its customers.

Infer: What theme or themes can you infer from these words and phrases?

to Mexicans who pass through, talking lyrically[3]
of *dólares* to be made in El Norte—
all wanting the comfort
of spoken Spanish, to gaze upon the family portrait
of her plain wide face, her ample bosom
resting on her plump arms, her look of maternal interest
as they speak to her and each other
of their dreams and their disillusions—
how she smiles understanding,
when they walk down the narrow aisles of her store
reading the labels of packages aloud, as if
they were the names of lost lovers: *Suspiros,*[4]
Merengues,[5] the stale candy of everyone's childhood.
She spends her days
slicing *jamón y queso*[6] and wrapping it in wax paper
tied with string: plain ham and cheese
that would cost less at the A&P, but it would not satisfy
the hunger of the fragile old man lost in the folds
of his winter coat, who brings her lists of items
that he reads to her like poetry, or the others,
whose needs she must divine, conjuring up products
from places that now exist only in their hearts—
closed ports she must trade with.

---

[3] **lyrically:** highly enthusiastically.
[4] ***suspiros*** (so͞os-pē´rōs): type of small sponge cake.
[5] ***merengues*** (mā-rān´gās): candy made of meringue (mixture of egg whites and sugar).
[6] ***jamón y queso*** (hä-mōn ēkā´sō): Spanish for "ham and cheese."

COLLABORATIVE DISCUSSION

Pair up with a classmate and discuss the ways this poem suggests what all poems should be.

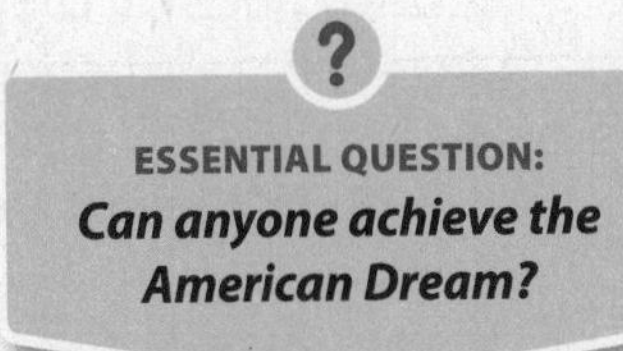
?
ESSENTIAL QUESTION:
Can anyone achieve the American Dream?

Review your notes and add your thoughts to your **Response Log.**

Assessment Practice

Answer these questions before moving on to the **Analyze the Text** section on the following page.

1. Who is the "Patroness of Exiles" (line 7)?

- (A) the poet
- (B) the plastic figurine on the register
- (C) the woman who runs the deli
- (D) one of the deli customers

2. How does the store owner respond to her customers' conversations?

- (A) by busying herself wrapping ham and cheese
- (B) with maternal interest and understanding
- (C) by gathering items on people's grocery lists
- (D) with disillusion and disinterest

3. Why do customers come to the Latin Deli?

- (A) The store owner is known for her fast service.
- (B) The Latin Deli has lower prices than the other stores.
- (C) The store owner knows the latest news from their home countries.
- (D) The Latin Deli has products that remind them of their childhood and homeland.

Ed **Test-Taking Strategies**

Analyze the Text

Support your responses with evidence from the text.

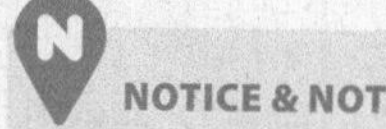

NOTICE & NOTE

Review what you **noticed and noted** as you read the text. Your annotations can help you answer these questions.

1. **SUMMARIZE** Reread and summarize lines 29–38. What does the owner of the deli provide her customers that other stores don't?

2. **CITE EVIDENCE** What types of imagery do you find that appeal to the five senses? How do they work together to suggest a theme? Find examples from the poem to support your ideas.

Sensory Imagery	Detail from Poem
Sight	
Sound	
Smell	
Touch	
Taste	
Possible Theme:	

3. **ANALYZE** Note that lines 18 and 29 are extremely indented. How do these oddities of form help to organize the ideas in the poem? Explain.

4. **EVALUATE** In addition to rich imagery, "The Latin Deli: An Ars Poetica" contains several similes and metaphors. Choose one simile or metaphor, and discuss how it contributes to the meaning of the poem.

5. **INFER** Look at the language Cofer uses to describe the owner of the Latin deli. What details in the poem equate her to a religious figure? Why would Cofer portray her as such?

6. **DRAW CONCLUSIONS** "The Latin Deli" is subtitled "An Ars Poetica," but poetry itself is only mentioned once and the poem does not directly analyze poetry as a form of writing. How might the subject of the poem be related to poetry? Does the author effectively express an idea about poetry in the poem? Explain.

Choices

Here are some other ways to demonstrate your understanding of the ideas in this lesson.

Writing

Poem

An *ars poetica* is anything you want it to be. Write a poem that embodies

- what you think poetry should look and sound like
- what techniques it should use
- what themes it should explore

Refer back to the Get Ready pages for the characteristics of an *ars poetica* or do some research on your own. After you've written your poem of poems, share it with your classmates.

As you write and discuss, be sure to use the **Academic Vocabulary** words.

contemporary

global

infinite

simulated

virtual

Media

Collage

Cofer's language in the poem is so real and vivid that it's easy to think of her poem as a collage in words. Think of a place you love and make a collage or painting using multiple images to represent it. As you put the images together, consider the mood that they create. Does this mood align with the way you want to represent this place?

Speaking & Listening

Group Discussion

Read the following quote from Judith Ortiz Cofer:

> **"Words have the power to transform you and give you the power to shape your life."**

How does this quote help you understand her idea of an *ars poetica*, given that she never specifically defines what a poem should be? Discuss your ideas in a small group.

Get Ready

Speech on the Vietnam War, 1967

Speech by **Martin Luther King, Jr.**

ESSENTIAL QUESTION:
When should personal integrity come before civic duty?

Engage Your Brain

Choose one or more of these activities to start connecting with the speech you're about to read.

I've Got Questions

In school, you've probably learned about Martin Luther King, Jr. over the years. What questions do you have that no one has answered yet? Write down two, then find a partner and take turns asking your questions. If neither of you has answers, do some research to see if you can get results.

Picture This!

Look at this image of a protest that occurred shortly after Martin Luther King, Jr. spoke out against the Vietnam War. Based on what you see, what ideas and arguments do you think King brings up in his speech? Discuss your ideas with a partner.

Two Truths and a Lie

Two of these statements are true, and one is false. Can you guess the false one?

1. The majority of U.S. troops who fought in Vietnam volunteered to fight, rather than being drafted.
2. The Vietnam War was fought between the North Vietnamese, the South Vietnamese, and the United States.
3. The Vietnam War didn't just take place in Vietnam.

Welcome to the
JEANNETTE
PEACE PARADE
END
THE WAR IN VIETNAM AND
SOCIAL CRISIS AT HOME!

Analyze Reasoning

To persuade readers, writers may rely on deductive or inductive reasoning to support their arguments. **Deductive reasoning** applies a general principle to a specific situation and provides relevant evidence to support a logical conclusion. For example, if all students in a class will graduate and Sarah is a member of that class, Sarah will graduate. **Inductive reasoning** starts with a body of facts or evidence and infers a logical conclusion. For example, since the sun has risen every morning, it will rise tomorrow.

Dr. Martin Luther King, Jr. primarily uses inductive reasoning in his speech. Use the chart to analyze his reasoning and evaluate his argument.

Is the evidence valid?	Evidence must be accurate and verifiable by sources such as eyewitness accounts, newspapers, or history books.
Is there enough evidence to draw a conclusion?	Evidence must be gathered from many sources, or the generalization drawn from them will be inaccurate.
Does the conclusion follow logically from the evidence?	Errors in logic occur when a complex issue is oversimplified or the evidence does not show how one event follows another.

Focus on Genre
Speech

- **presents evidence to support a position on an issue**
- **anticipates and addresses counterarguments**
- **includes rhetorical devices to emphasize ideas**

Evaluate Evidence

An effective argument contains a claim, reasons, and a conclusion drawn from evidence. The **claim** is the position that the writer is supporting. **Reasons** supporting the claim are sensible and presented in a logical order, and **evidence** proves that the reasons are valid and allows a conclusion to naturally follow. Examine the following excerpt from Dr. King's speech to understand how he uses these elements in his argument.

They must see Americans as strange liberators. The Vietnamese people proclaimed their own independence in 1954—in 1945 rather—after a combined French and Japanese occupation and before the communist revolution in China. They were led by Ho Chi Minh. Even though they quoted the American Declaration of Independence in their own document of freedom, we refused to recognize them. Instead, we decided to support France in its reconquest of her former colony.	**Claim**: American participation in the war is not easily explained. **Reason**: The Vietnamese people had already liberated themselves. **Evidence**: The Vietnamese wanted to follow the American example. **Conclusion**: Rather than support Vietnam, America contradicted its own principles for political expediency.

As you read, continue to evaluate the effectiveness of the evidence King provides.

Annotation in Action

Here is an example of notes a student made about King's evidence in this paragraph from "Speech on the Vietnam War, 1967." As you read, continue to analyze and evaluate King's evidence.

In 1957 a sensitive American official overseas said that it seemed to him that our nation was on the wrong side of a world revolution. During the past ten years we have seen emerge a pattern of suppression which has now justified the presence of U.S. military advisors in Venezuela. This need to maintain social stability for our investments accounts for the counter-revolutionary action of American forces in Guatemala. It tells why American helicopters are being used against guerillas in Cambodia and why American napalm and Green Beret forces have already been active against rebels in Peru.

starts with a claim, then lists examples; solid evidence that supports the claim.

Expand Your Vocabulary

Put a check mark next to the vocabulary words that you feel comfortable using when writing or speaking.

facile	☐
eviscerate	☐
indigenous	☐
extortionist	☐
insurgency	☐
reparations	☐
recalcitrant	☐
adamant	☐

Then, write a paragraph about whether individuals are obligated to speak out against injustice, using as many of the words as you can. As you read the speech, use the definitions in the side-column to learn the vocabulary words you don't already know.

Background

Martin Luther King, Jr. (1929–1968), a preacher and social activist, was the most prominent leader of the civil rights movement from the mid-1950s until his assassination in 1968. Committed to nonviolent protests, his efforts aided in the passage of the Civil Rights Act of 1964 and the Voting Rights Act of 1965. He became concerned about U.S. involvement in the Vietnam War, and gave this speech on April 4, 1967, at the Riverside Church in New York City.

Speech on the Vietnam War, 1967

Speech by **Martin Luther King, Jr.**

Look for connections between King's opposition to the war and his civil rights work.

NOTICE & NOTE
As you read, use the side margins to make notes about the text.

1 I come to this platform tonight to make a passionate plea to my beloved nation. This speech is not addressed to Hanoi or to the National Liberation Front.[1] It is not addressed to China or to Russia. Nor is it an attempt to overlook the ambiguity of the total situation and the need for a collective solution to the tragedy of Vietnam. Neither is it an attempt to make North Vietnam or the National Liberation Front paragons of virtue, nor to overlook the role they must play in the successful resolution of the problem. While they both may have justifiable reasons to be suspicious of the good faith of the United States, life and history give eloquent testimony to the fact that conflicts are never resolved without trustful give and take on both sides. Tonight, however, I wish not to speak with Hanoi and the National Liberation Front, but rather to my fellow Americans.

[1] **National Liberation Front:** also known as the Vietcong, revolutionary fighters in South Vietnam.

facile
(făs´əl) *adj.* achieved with little effort or difficulty.

eviscerate
(ĭ-vĭs´ə-rāt) *v.* to take away a vital or essential part of.

2 Since I am a preacher by calling, I suppose it is not surprising that I have seven major reasons for bringing Vietnam into the field of my moral vision. There is at the outset a very obvious and almost **facile** connection between the war in Vietnam and the struggle I and others have been waging in America. A few years ago there was a shining moment in that struggle. It seemed as if there was a real promise of hope for the poor, both black and white, through the poverty program.[2] There were experiments, hopes, new beginnings. Then came the buildup in Vietnam, and I watched this program broken and **eviscerated** as if it were some idle political plaything of a society gone mad on war. And I knew that America would never invest the necessary funds or energies in rehabilitation of its poor so long as adventures like Vietnam continued to draw men and skills and money like some demonic, destructive suction tube. So I was increasingly compelled to see the war as an enemy of the poor and to attack it as such.

ANALYZE REASONING

Annotate: Mark the phrases in paragraph 3 that are evidence of the treatment of the poor in the United States.

Evaluate: Does he arrive at his conclusion logically? Why or why not?

3 Perhaps a more tragic recognition of reality took place when it became clear to me that the war was doing far more than devastating the hopes of the poor at home. It was sending their sons and their brothers and their husbands to fight and to die in extraordinarily high proportions relative to the rest of the population. We were taking the black young men who had been crippled by our society and sending them eight thousand miles away to guarantee liberties in Southeast Asia which they had not found in southwest Georgia and East Harlem. So we have been repeatedly faced with the cruel irony of watching Negro and white boys on TV screens as they kill and die together for a nation that has been unable to seat them together in the same schools. So we watch them in brutal solidarity burning the huts of a poor village, but we realize that they would hardly live on the same block in Chicago. I could not be silent in the face of such cruel manipulation of the poor.

4 My third reason moves to an even deeper level of awareness, for it grows out of my experience in the ghettos of the North over the last three years, especially the last three summers. As I have walked among the desperate, rejected, and angry young men, I have told them that Molotov cocktails[3] and rifles would not solve their problems. I have tried to offer them my deepest compassion while maintaining my conviction that social change comes most meaningfully through nonviolent action. But they asked, and rightly so, "What about Vietnam?" They asked if our own nation wasn't using massive doses of violence to solve its problems, to bring about the changes it wanted. Their questions hit home, and I knew that I could never again raise my voice against the violence of the oppressed in the ghettos without having first spoken clearly to the greatest

[2] **poverty program:** legislation, often called the "War on Poverty," enacted in 1964 during Lyndon Johnson's administration.

[3] **Molotov cocktails:** homemade incendiary weapons made by filling breakable bottles with a flammable liquid, attaching and lighting wicks, and throwing them at a target.

purveyor of violence in the world today: my own government. For the sake of those boys, for the sake of this government, for the sake of the hundreds of thousands trembling under our violence, I cannot be silent.

5 For those who ask the question, "Aren't you a civil rights leader?" and thereby mean to exclude me from the movement for peace, I have this further answer. In 1957, when a group of us formed the Southern Christian Leadership Conference, we chose as our motto: "To save the soul of America." We were convinced that we could not limit our vision to certain rights for black people, but instead affirmed the conviction that America would never be free or saved from itself until the descendants of its slaves were loosed completely from the shackles they still wear. In a way we were agreeing with Langston Hughes, that black bard of Harlem, who had written earlier:

6 O, yes, I say it plain,
America never was America to me,
And yet I swear this oath—
America will be!

7 Now it should be incandescently clear that no one who has any concern for the integrity and life of America today can ignore the present war. If America's soul becomes totally poisoned, part of the autopsy must read "Vietnam." It can never be saved so long as it destroys the deepest hopes of men the world over. So it is that those

of us who are yet determined that "America will be" are led down the path of protest and dissent, working for the health of our land.

8 As if the weight of such a commitment to the life and health of America were not enough, another burden of responsibility was placed upon me in 1964. And I cannot forget that the Nobel Peace Prize[4] was also a commission, a commission to work harder than I had ever worked before for the brotherhood of man. This is a calling that takes me beyond national allegiances.

ANALYZE REASONING

Annotate: Underline the conclusions in paragraph 9 that Dr. King arrives at for why his ministry has led him to oppose the war.

Evaluate: Does he arrive at his conclusion logically? Why or why not?

9 But even if it were not present, I would yet have to live with the meaning of my commitment to the ministry of Jesus Christ. To me, the relationship of this ministry to the making of peace is so obvious that I sometimes marvel at those who ask me why I am speaking against the war. Could it be that they do not know that the Good News[5] was meant for all men—for communist and capitalist, for their children and ours, for black and for white, for revolutionary and conservative? Have they forgotten that my ministry is in obedience to the one who loved his enemies so fully that he died for them? What then can I say to the Vietcong[6] or to Castro or to Mao as a faithful minister of this one? Can I threaten them with death or must I not share with them my life?

10 Finally, as I try to explain for you and for myself the road that leads from Montgomery[7] to this place, I would have offered all that was most valid if I simply said that I must be true to my conviction that I share with all men the calling to be a son of the living God. Beyond the calling of race or nation or creed is this vocation of sonship and brotherhood. Because I believe that the Father is deeply concerned, especially for His suffering and helpless and outcast children, I come tonight to speak for them. This I believe to be the privilege and the burden of all of us who deem ourselves bound by allegiances and loyalties which are broader and deeper than nationalism and which go beyond our nation's self-defined goals and positions. We are called to speak for the weak, for the voiceless, for the victims of our nation, for those it calls "enemy," for no document from human hands can make these humans any less our brothers.

11 And as I ponder the madness of Vietnam and search within myself for ways to understand and respond in compassion, my mind goes constantly to the people of that peninsula. I speak now not of the soldiers of each side, not of the ideologies of the Liberation Front, not of the junta in Saigon, but simply of the people who have been living under the curse of war for almost three continuous decades now.

[4] **Nobel Peace Prize:** an annual award given to an individual who best promotes international friendship, reduces military forces, and fosters peaceful relations. King won the prize in 1964.

[5] **Good News:** the Gospels, or the written accounts of Jesus and his teachings.

[6] **Vietcong:** the National Liberation Front, South Vietnamese revolutionaries.

[7] **Montgomery:** Alabama city and site of the 1955 bus boycott, a civil rights protest that brought King to national prominence.

Don't forget to **Notice & Note** as you read the text.

I think of them, too, because it is clear to me that there will be no meaningful solution there until some attempt is made to know them and hear their broken cries.

12 They must see Americans as strange liberators. The Vietnamese people proclaimed their own independence in 1954—in 1945 rather—after a combined French and Japanese occupation and before the communist revolution in China. They were led by Ho Chi Minh. Even though they quoted the American Declaration of Independence in their own document of freedom, we refused to recognize them. Instead, we decided to support France in its reconquest of her former colony. Our government felt then that the Vietnamese people were not ready for independence, and we again fell victim to the deadly Western arrogance that has poisoned the international atmosphere for so long. With that tragic decision we rejected a revolutionary government seeking self-determination and a government that had been established not by China—for whom the Vietnamese have no great love—but by clearly **indigenous** forces that included some communists. For the peasants this new government meant real land reform, one of the most important needs in their lives.

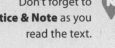

indigenous
(ĭn-dĭj´ə-nəs) *adj.* native to a land.

13 For nine years following 1945 we denied the people of Vietnam the right of independence. For nine years we vigorously supported the French in their abortive effort to recolonize Vietnam. Before the end of the war we were meeting 80 percent of the French war costs. Even before the French were defeated at Dien Bien Phu, they began to despair of their reckless action, but we did not. We encouraged them with our huge financial and military supplies to continue the war even after they had lost the will. Soon we would be paying almost the full costs of this tragic attempt at recolonization.

NOTICE & NOTE
NUMBERS AND STATS

When you notice the use of specific quantities or comparisons to depict the amount, size, or scale, you've found a **Numbers and Stats** signpost.

Notice & Note: In paragraph 13, mark the statistic King cites that explains how America supported the French against Vietnam.

Evaluate: How is this relevant to King's argument?

14 After the French were defeated, it looked as if independence and land reform would come again through the Geneva Agreement. But instead there came the United States, determined that Ho should not unify the temporarily divided nation, and the peasants watched again as we supported one of the most vicious modern dictators, our chosen man, Premier Diem.[8] The peasants watched and cringed as Diem ruthlessly rooted out all opposition, supported their **extortionist** landlords, and refused even to discuss reunification with the North. The peasants watched as all of this was presided over by United States influence and then by increasing numbers of United States troops who came to help quell the **insurgency** that Diem's methods had aroused. When Diem was overthrown they may have been happy, but the long line of military dictators seemed to offer no real change, especially in terms of their need for land and peace.

extortionist
(ĭk-stôr´shən-ĭst) *n.* one who obtains something by force or threat.

insurgency
(ĭn-sûr´jən-sē) *n.* rebellion or revolt.

15 The only change came from America as we increased our troop commitments in support of governments which were singularly corrupt, inept, and without popular support. All the while the people

[8] **Premier Diem** (dē-ĕm´)**:** Ngo Dinh Diem (1901–1963), the first president of South Vietnam in 1955, who was later killed in a military coup.

read our leaflets and received the regular promises of peace and democracy and land reform. Now they languish under our bombs and consider us, not their fellow Vietnamese, the real enemy. They move sadly and apathetically as we herd them off the land of their fathers into concentration camps where minimal social needs are rarely met. They know they must move on or be destroyed by our bombs.

16 So they go, primarily women and children and the aged. They watch as we poison their water, as we kill a million acres of their crops. They must weep as the bulldozers roar through their areas preparing to destroy the precious trees. They wander into the hospitals with at least twenty casualties from American firepower for one Vietcong inflicted injury. So far we may have killed a million of them, mostly children. They wander into the towns and see thousands of the children, homeless, without clothes, running in packs on the streets like animals. They see the children degraded by our soldiers as they beg for food. They see the children selling their sisters to our soldiers, soliciting for their mothers.

17 What do the peasants think as we ally ourselves with the landlords and as we refuse to put any action into our many words concerning land reform? What do they think as we test out our latest weapons on them, just as the Germans tested out new medicine and new tortures in the concentration camps of Europe? Where are the roots of the independent Vietnam we claim to be building? Is it among these voiceless ones?

EVALUATE EVIDENCE

Annotate: Underline one thing Dr. King concludes we have destroyed in paragraph 18.

Evaluate: What evidence does he provide that supports that conclusion?

18 We have destroyed their two most cherished institutions: the family and the village. We have destroyed their land and their crops. We have cooperated in the crushing of the nation's only noncommunist revolutionary political force, the unified Buddhist Church. We have supported the enemies of the peasants of Saigon. We have corrupted their women and children and killed their men.

19 Now there is little left to build on, save bitterness. Soon the only solid physical foundations remaining will be found at our military bases and in the concrete of the concentration camps we call "fortified hamlets." The peasants may well wonder if we plan to build our new Vietnam on such grounds as these. Could we blame them for such thoughts? We must speak for them and raise the questions they cannot raise. These, too, are our brothers.

20 Perhaps a more difficult but no less necessary task is to speak for those who have been designated as our enemies. What of the National Liberation Front, that strangely anonymous group we call "VC" or "communists"? What must they think of the United States of America when they realize that we permitted the repression and cruelty of Diem, which helped to bring them into being as a resistance group in the South? What do they think of our condoning the violence which led to their own taking up of arms? How can they believe in our integrity when now we speak of "aggression from the North" as if there were nothing more essential to the war? How can they trust us when now we charge them with violence after the murderous reign

of Diem and charge them with violence while we pour every new weapon of death into their land? Surely we must understand their feelings, even if we do not condone their actions. Surely we must see that the men we supported pressed them to their violence. Surely we must see that our own computerized plans of destruction simply dwarf their greatest acts.

Don't forget to **Notice & Note** as you read the text.

21 How do they judge us when our officials know that their membership is less than 25 percent communist, and yet insist on giving them the blanket name? What must they be thinking when they know that we are aware of their control of major sections of Vietnam, and yet we appear ready to allow national elections in which this highly organized political parallel government will not have a part? They ask how we can speak of free elections when the Saigon press is censored and controlled by the military junta. And they are surely right to wonder what kind of new government we plan to help form without them, the only party in real touch with the peasants. They question our political goals and they deny the reality of a peace settlement from which they will be excluded. Their questions are frighteningly relevant. Is our nation planning to build on political myth again, and then shore it up upon the power of a new violence?

22 Here is the true meaning and value of compassion and nonviolence, when it helps us to see the enemy's point of view, to hear his questions, to know his assessment of ourselves. For from his view we may indeed see the basic weaknesses of our own condition, and if we are mature, we may learn and grow and profit from the wisdom of the brothers who are called the opposition.

ANALYZE REASONING

Annotate: Mark the phrases that Dr. King uses to indicate the value of compassion and nonviolence.

Evaluate: Does he arrive at his conclusion logically? Why or why not?

23 So, too, with Hanoi. In the North, where our bombs now pummel the land, and our mines endanger the waterways, we are met by a deep but understandable mistrust. To speak for them is to explain this lack of confidence in Western words, and especially their distrust of American intentions now. In Hanoi are the men who led the nation to independence against the Japanese and the French, the men who sought membership in the French Commonwealth and were betrayed by the weakness of Paris and the willfulness of the colonial armies. It was they who led a second struggle against French domination at tremendous costs, and then were persuaded to give up the land they controlled between the thirteenth and seventeenth parallel as a temporary measure at Geneva. After 1954 they watched us conspire with Diem to prevent elections which could have surely brought Ho Chi Minh to power over a united Vietnam, and they realized they had been betrayed again. When we ask why they do not leap to negotiate, these things must be remembered.

24 Also, it must be clear that the leaders of Hanoi considered the presence of American troops in support of the Diem regime to have been the initial military breach of the Geneva Agreement concerning foreign troops. They remind us that they did not begin to send troops in large numbers and even supplies into the South until American forces had moved into the tens of thousands.

25 Hanoi remembers how our leaders refused to tell us the truth about the earlier North Vietnamese overtures for peace, how the president claimed that none existed when they had clearly been made. Ho Chi Minh has watched as America has spoken of peace and built up its forces, and now he has surely heard the increasing international rumors of American plans for an invasion of the North. He knows the bombing and shelling and mining we are doing are part of traditional pre-invasion strategy. Perhaps only his sense of humor and of irony can save him when he hears the most powerful nation of the world speaking of aggression as it drops thousands of bombs on a poor, weak nation more than eight hundred, or rather, eight thousand miles away from its shores.

26 At this point I should make it clear that while I have tried in these last few minutes to give a voice to the voiceless in Vietnam and to understand the arguments of those who are called "enemy," I am as deeply concerned about our own troops there as anything else. For it occurs to me that what we are submitting them to in Vietnam is not simply the brutalizing process that goes on in any war where armies face each other and seek to destroy. We are adding cynicism to the process of death, for they must know after a short period there that none of the things we claim to be fighting for are really involved. Before long they must know that their government has sent them into a struggle among Vietnamese, and the more sophisticated surely realize that we are on the side of the wealthy, and the secure, while we create a hell for the poor.

27 Somehow this madness must cease. We must stop now. I speak as a child of God and brother to the suffering poor of Vietnam. I speak for those whose land is being laid waste, whose homes are being destroyed, whose culture is being subverted. I speak for the poor of America who are paying the double price of smashed hopes at home, and dealt death and corruption in Vietnam. I speak as a citizen of the world, for the world as it stands aghast at the path we have taken. I speak as one who loves America, to the leaders of our own nation: The great initiative in this war is ours; the initiative to stop it must be ours.

28 This is the message of the great Buddhist leaders of Vietnam. Recently one of them wrote these words, and I quote:

> Each day the war goes on the hatred increases in the heart of the Vietnamese and in the hearts of those of humanitarian instinct. The Americans are forcing even their friends into becoming their enemies. It is curious that the Americans, who calculate so carefully on the possibilities of military victory, do not realize that in the process they are incurring deep psychological and political defeat. The image of America will never again be the image of revolution, freedom, and democracy, but the image of violence and militarism.
>
> Unquote.

NOTICE & NOTE

QUOTED WORDS

When you notice the author citing other people to provide support for a point, you've found a **Quoted Words** signpost.

Notice & Note: In paragraph 28, mark details in the quotation from the Buddhist leader that describe the effects of the Americans' behavior on the Vietnamese.

Draw Conclusions: How are these details relevant to King's argument?

29 If we continue, there will be no doubt in my mind and in the mind of the world that we have no honorable intentions in Vietnam. If we do not stop our war against the people of Vietnam immediately, the world will be left with no other alternative than to see this as some horrible, clumsy, and deadly game we have decided to play. The world now demands a maturity of America that we may not be able to achieve. It demands that we admit that we have been wrong from the beginning of our adventure in Vietnam, that we have been detrimental to the life of the Vietnamese people. The situation is one in which we must be ready to turn sharply from our present ways. In order to atone for our sins and errors in Vietnam, we should take the initiative in bringing a halt to this tragic war.

30 I would like to suggest five concrete things that our government should do immediately to begin the long and difficult process of extricating ourselves from this nightmarish conflict:

31 Number one: End all bombing in North and South Vietnam.

32 Number two: Declare a unilateral cease-fire in the hope that such action will create the atmosphere for negotiation.

33 Three: Take immediate steps to prevent other battlegrounds in Southeast Asia by curtailing our military buildup in Thailand and our interference in Laos.

34 Four: Realistically accept the fact that the National Liberation Front has substantial support in South Vietnam and must thereby play a role in any meaningful negotiations and any future Vietnam government.

35 Five: Set a date that we will remove all foreign troops from Vietnam in accordance with the 1954 Geneva Agreement. [*Sustained applause*]

36 Part of our ongoing [*Applause continues*], part of our ongoing commitment might well express itself in an offer to grant asylum to any Vietnamese who fears for his life under a new regime which included the Liberation Front. Then we must make what **reparations** we can for the damage we have done. We must provide the medical aid that is badly needed, making it available in this country if necessary. Meanwhile [*Applause*], meanwhile, we in the churches and synagogues have a continuing task while we urge our government to disengage itself from a disgraceful commitment. We must continue to raise our voices and our lives if our nation persists in its perverse ways in Vietnam. We must be prepared to match actions with words by seeking out every creative method of protest possible.

37 As we counsel young men concerning military service, we must clarify for them our nation's role in Vietnam and challenge them with the alternative of conscientious objection.[9] [*Sustained applause*] I am pleased to say that this is a path now chosen by more than seventy students at my own alma mater, Morehouse

Don't forget to **Notice & Note** as you read the text. 

ANALYZE REASONING

Annotate: In paragraph 29, mark the conclusion King reaches regarding the Vietnam War.

Draw Conclusions: How do King's proposals in paragraphs 31–35 affect his conclusion?

reparations
(rĕp-ə-rā´shəns) *n.* compensation or payment from a nation for damage or injury during a war.

[9] **conscientious objection:** the refusal to participate in military actions because of moral or religious beliefs.

College, and I recommend it to all who find the American course in Vietnam a dishonorable and unjust one. [*Applause*] Moreover, I would encourage all ministers of draft age to give up their ministerial exemptions and seek status as conscientious objectors. [*Applause*] These are the times for real choices and not false ones. We are at the moment when our lives must be placed on the line if our nation is to survive its own folly. Every man of humane convictions must decide on the protest that best suits his convictions, but we must all protest.

38 Now there is something seductively tempting about stopping there and sending us all off on what in some circles has become a popular crusade against the war in Vietnam. I say we must enter that struggle, but I wish to go on now to say something even more disturbing.

EVALUATE EVIDENCE

Annotate: Identify the phrase in paragraph 39 that states the focus of the next part of King's speech.

Analyze: How does the argument about ending the war in Vietnam relate to this idea? What evidence does King offer to support his assertion?

39 The war in Vietnam is but a symptom of a far deeper malady within the American spirit, and if we ignore this sobering reality [*Applause*], and if we ignore this sobering reality, we will find ourselves organizing "clergy and laymen concerned" committees for the next generation. They will be concerned about Guatemala and Peru. They will be concerned about Thailand and Cambodia. They will be concerned about Mozambique and South Africa. We will be marching for these and a dozen other names and attending rallies without end unless there is a significant and profound change in American life and policy. [*Sustained applause*] So such thoughts take us beyond Vietnam, but not beyond our calling as sons of the living God.

40 In 1957 a sensitive American official overseas said that it seemed to him that our nation was on the wrong side of a world revolution. During the past ten years we have seen emerge a pattern of suppression which has now justified the presence of U.S. military advisors in Venezuela. This need to maintain social stability for our investments accounts for the counter-revolutionary action of American forces in Guatemala. It tells why American helicopters are being used against guerrillas in Cambodia and why American napalm[10] and Green Beret forces have already been active against rebels in Peru.

41 It is with such activity in mind that the words of the late John F. Kennedy come back to haunt us. Five years ago he said, "Those who make peaceful revolution impossible will make violent revolution inevitable." [*Applause*] Increasingly, by choice or by accident, this is the role our nation has taken, the role of those who make peaceful revolution impossible by refusing to give up the privileges and the pleasures that come from the immense profits of overseas investments. I am convinced that if we are to get on the right side of the world revolution, we as a nation must undergo a radical revolution of values. We must rapidly begin [*Applause*], we must rapidly begin the shift from a thing-oriented society to a person-oriented society. When machines and computers, profit motives and

[10] **napalm:** an incendiary fuel used in U.S. bombs to burn Vietnamese opponents.

property rights, are considered more important than people, the giant triplets of racism, extreme materialism, and militarism are incapable of being conquered.

42 A true revolution of values will soon cause us to question the fairness and justice of many of our past and present policies. On the one hand we are called to play the Good Samaritan on life's roadside, but that will be only an initial act. One day we must come to see that the whole Jericho Road[11] must be transformed so that men and women will not be constantly beaten and robbed as they make their journey on life's highway. True compassion is more than flinging a coin to a beggar. It comes to see that an edifice which produces beggars needs restructuring. [*Applause*]

43 A true revolution of values will soon look uneasily on the glaring contrast of poverty and wealth. With righteous indignation, it will look across the seas and see individual capitalists of the West investing huge sums of money in Asia, Africa, and South America, only to take the profits out with no concern for the social betterment of the countries, and say, "This is not just." It will look at our alliance with the landed gentry of South America and say, "This is not just." The Western arrogance of feeling that it has everything to teach others and nothing to learn from them is not just.

44 A true revolution of values will lay hand on the world order and say of war, "This way of settling differences is not just." This business of burning human beings with napalm, of filling our nation's homes with orphans and widows, of injecting poisonous drugs of hate into the veins of peoples normally humane, of sending men home from dark and bloody battlefields physically handicapped and psychologically deranged, cannot be reconciled with wisdom, justice, and love. A nation that continues year after year to spend more money on military defense than on programs of social uplift is approaching spiritual death. [*Sustained applause*]

45 America, the richest and most powerful nation in the world, can well lead the way in this revolution of values. There is nothing except a tragic death wish to prevent us from reordering our priorities so that the pursuit of peace will take precedence over the pursuit of war. There is nothing to keep us from molding a **recalcitrant** status quo with bruised hands until we have fashioned it into a brotherhood.

46 This kind of positive revolution of values is our best defense against communism. [*Applause*] War is not the answer. Communism will never be defeated by the use of atomic bombs or nuclear weapons. Let us not join those who shout war and, through their misguided passions, urge the United States to relinquish its participation in the United Nations. These are days which demand wise restraint and calm reasonableness. We must not engage in a negative anticommunism, but rather in a positive thrust for

[11] **Jericho Road:** an ancient route between Jerusalem and Jericho. In the New Testament, the Good Samaritan stops on this road to help an injured robbery victim.

Don't forget to **Notice & Note** as you read the text.

ANALYZE REASONING

Annotate: Underline the three results Dr. King says will come of "a true revolution of values" in paragraphs 42–44.

Analyze: Choose one of those results, and find support for that conclusion earlier in the speech.

recalcitrant (rĭ-kăl´sĭ-trənt) *adj.* stubbornly resistant to and defiant of authority.

EVALUATE EVIDENCE

Annotate: Mark details in paragraphs 46–48 that support Dr. King's claim that a revolution of values is the best way to defeat communism.

Evaluate: Explain whether these details are effective support for the claim.

democracy [*Applause*], realizing that our greatest defense against communism is to take offensive action in behalf of justice. We must with positive action seek to remove those conditions of poverty, insecurity, and injustice, which are the fertile soil in which the seed of communism grows and develops.

47 These are revolutionary times. All over the globe men are revolting against old systems of exploitation and oppression, and out of the wounds of a frail world, new systems of justice and equality are being born. The shirtless and barefoot people of the land are rising up as never before. The people who sat in darkness have seen a great light. We in the West must support these revolutions.

48 It is a sad fact that because of comfort, complacency, a morbid fear of communism, and our proneness to adjust to injustice, the Western nations that initiated so much of the revolutionary spirit of the modern world have now become the arch antirevolutionaries. This has driven many to feel that only Marxism has a revolutionary spirit. Therefore, communism is a judgment against our failure to make democracy real and follow through on the revolutions that we initiated. Our only hope today lies in our ability to recapture the revolutionary spirit and go out into a sometimes hostile world declaring eternal hostility to poverty, racism, and militarism. With this powerful commitment we shall boldly challenge the status quo and unjust mores, and thereby speed the day when every valley shall be exalted, and every mountain and hill shall be made low [*Audience:*] (*Yes*); the crooked shall be made straight, and the rough places plain.[12]

49 A genuine revolution of values means in the final analysis that our loyalties must become ecumenical rather than sectional. Every nation must now develop an overriding loyalty to mankind as a whole in order to preserve the best in their individual societies.

EVALUATE EVIDENCE

Annotate: Underline a claim Dr. King makes in paragraph 50 about love.

Evaluate: Is his claim about love effective? Why or why not?

50 This call for a worldwide fellowship that lifts neighborly concern beyond one's tribe, race, class, and nation is in reality a call for an all-embracing and unconditional love for all mankind. This oft misunderstood, this oft misinterpreted concept, so readily dismissed by the Nietzsches[13] of the world as a weak and cowardly force, has now become an absolute necessity for the survival of man. When I speak of love I am not speaking of some sentimental and weak response. I'm not speaking of that force which is just emotional bosh. I am speaking of that force which all of the great religions have seen as the supreme unifying principle of life. Love is somehow the key that unlocks the door which leads to ultimate reality. This Hindu-Muslim-Christian-Jewish-Buddhist belief about ultimate reality is

[12] **every valley shall be . . . plain:** biblical quote from the Old Testament Book of Isaiah describing the arrival of the Messiah.

[13] **Nietzsches** (nē´chəz): a reference to the German philosopher Friedrich Nietzsche (1844–1900), who rejected Christianity and its associated morality.

beautifully summed up in the first epistle of Saint John: "Let us love one another (*Yes*), for love is God. (*Yes*) And every one that loveth is born of God and knoweth God. He that loveth not knoweth not God, for God is love. . . . If we love one another, God dwelleth in us and his love is perfected in us." Let us hope that this spirit will become the order of the day.

Don't forget to **Notice & Note** as you read the text.

51 We can no longer afford to worship the god of hate or bow before the altar of retaliation. The oceans of history are made turbulent by the ever-rising tides of hate. History is cluttered with the wreckage of nations and individuals that pursued this self-defeating path of hate. As Arnold Toynbee says: "Love is the ultimate force that makes for the saving choice of life and good against the damning choice of death and evil. Therefore the first hope in our inventory must be the hope that love is going to have the last word." Unquote.

52 We are now faced with the fact, my friends, that tomorrow is today. We are confronted with the fierce urgency of now. In this unfolding conundrum of life and history, there is such a thing as being too late. Procrastination is still the thief of time. Life often leaves us standing bare, naked, and dejected with a lost opportunity. The tide in the affairs of men does not remain at flood—it ebbs. We may cry out desperately for time to pause in her passage, but time is **adamant** to every plea and rushes on. Over the bleached bones and jumbled residues of numerous civilizations are written the pathetic words, "Too late." There is an invisible book of life that faithfully records our vigilance or our neglect. Omar Khayyam[14] is right: "The moving finger writes, and having writ moves on."

adamant
(ăd´ə-mənt) *adj.* inflexible and insistent, unchanging.

53 We still have a choice today: nonviolent coexistence or violent coannihilation. We must move past indecision to action. We must find new ways to speak for peace in Vietnam and justice throughout the developing world, a world that borders on our doors. If we do not act, we shall surely be dragged down the long, dark, and shameful corridors of time reserved for those who possess power without compassion, might without morality, and strength without sight.

54 Now let us begin. Now let us rededicate ourselves to the long and bitter, but beautiful, struggle for a new world. This is the calling of the sons of God, and our brothers wait eagerly for our response. Shall we say the odds are too great? Shall we tell them the struggle is too hard? Will our message be that the forces of American life militate against their arrival as full men, and we send our deepest regrets? Or will there be another message—of longing, of hope, of solidarity with their yearnings, of commitment to their cause, whatever the cost? The choice is ours, and though we might prefer it otherwise, we must choose in this crucial moment of human history.

EVALUATE EVIDENCE

Annotate: Mark the call to action in paragraph 54.

Evaluate: Explain whether King effectively conveys the importance of taking action.

[14] **Omar Khayyam:** (1048–c. 1132) influential Persian poet and scholar.

55 As that noble bard of yesterday James Russell Lowell eloquently stated:

Once to every man and nation comes a moment to decide,
In the strife of Truth and Falsehood, for the good or evil side;
Some great cause, God's new Messiah offering each the bloom or
  blight,
And the choice goes by forever 'twixt that darkness and that light.
Though the cause of evil prosper, yet 'tis truth alone is strong
Though her portions be the scaffold, and upon the throne be
  wrong
Yet that scaffold sways the future, and behind the dim unknown
Standeth God within the shadow, keeping watch above his own.

56 And if we will only make the right choice, we will be able to transform this pending cosmic elegy into a creative psalm of peace. If we will make the right choice, we will be able to transform the jangling discords of our world into a beautiful symphony of brotherhood. If we will but make the right choice, we will be able to speed up the day, all over America and all over the world, when justice will roll down like waters, and righteousness like a mighty stream. [*Sustained applause*]

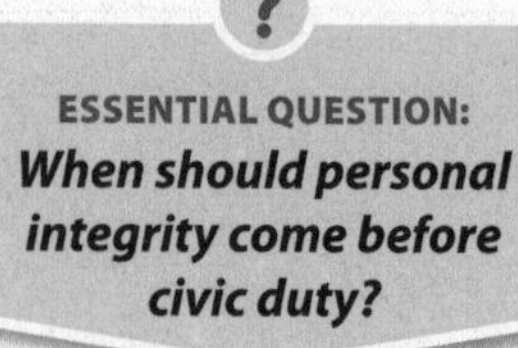

?
ESSENTIAL QUESTION:
When should personal integrity come before civic duty?

Review your notes and add your thoughts to your **Response Log.**

COLLABORATIVE DISCUSSION

What conclusion does King draw in the last paragraph of his speech? Has he provided enough evidence to support this conclusion? Discuss your ideas with a partner.

A man visits the Vietnam War Memorial in Washington, DC.

Assessment Practice

Answer these questions before moving on to the **Analyze the Text** section on the following page.

1. What does King describe as a "real promise of hope for the poor"?
   - (A) the rehabilitation of the poor
   - (B) the buildup in Vietnam
   - (C) the War on Poverty
   - (D) the National Liberation Front

2. What is the main focus of King's thoughts as he considers the "madness of Vietnam"?
   - (A) the people of Vietnam
   - (B) the government in Saigon
   - (C) the soldiers on each side
   - (D) the Liberation Front

3. King says he is convinced that we as a nation must undergo a radical revolution of —
   - (A) materialism
   - (B) technology
   - (C) capitalism
   - (D) values

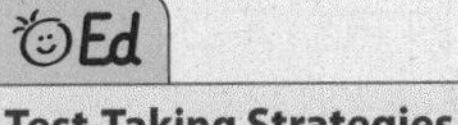

Test-Taking Strategies

Analyze the Text

Support your responses with evidence from the text.

> **NOTICE & NOTE**
> Review what you **noticed and noted** as you read the text. Your annotations can help you answer these questions.

1. **ANALYZE** How does Dr. King's explanation for speaking out against the war at the beginning of his speech lend authority to his argument?

2. **EVALUATE** In paragraph 12, Dr. King suggests that the United States is not really acting to liberate the Vietnamese people. Explain whether Dr. King uses inductive or deductive reasoning to make this point.

3. **ANALYZE** In paragraphs 17 and 20, Dr. King poses several rhetorical questions. Use the chart to identify the rhetorical questions and to explain the effect they have on King's audience.

Rhetorical Questions	Effect

4. **INTERPRET** Why does Dr. King help his audience understand the enemy in paragraphs 20–25? Consider details such as historical events, **Numbers and Stats**, and other evidence in your response.

5. **INTERPRET** What two things are contrasted in the quotation from John F. Kennedy in paragraph 41? What effect does Dr. King hope it will have on his audience?

6. **EVALUATE** Dr. King concludes that the United States should take part in a "positive revolution of values." Does this conclusion logically follow from the evidence he has presented? Why or why not?

7. **DRAW CONCLUSIONS** What words with strongly positive connotations does Dr. King use in paragraphs 54–56? Is his use of this loaded language an effective way to conclude the speech? Explain your response.

Choices

Here are some other ways to demonstrate your understanding of the ideas in this lesson.

Writing

Evaluate a Speech

Throughout his speech, Dr. King makes a connection between his civil rights work and his opposition to the war in Vietnam. Write an evaluation of this aspect of the speech. As you write, consider the following questions:

- How well does Dr. King connect the two movements?
- Does the connection strengthen his overall point about the war?

As you write and discuss, be sure to use the **Academic Vocabulary** words.

- contemporary
- global
- infinite
- simulated
- virtual

Research

How Did People React?

Do research to discover how the public received this particular speech by Dr. King and what happened because of his speech.

Question	Answer
What response from the public did Dr. King receive after his speech?	
What events happened because of Dr. King's speech?	

Media

Timeline

With a small group, create a multimedia timeline about Dr. Martin Luther King, Jr.'s life and work.

1. Choose six to eight landmark events in Dr. King's life. Conduct some research to help you decide.
2. Consider how you might present these events. You might choose to illustrate an event with a photograph or present an audio recording of Dr. King's voice.
3. Assemble what you have gathered into a multimedia timeline. You might find an online tool to help you create it.
4. Present your timeline to the class.

Expand Your Vocabulary

PRACTICE AND APPLY

Use your understanding of the vocabulary words to answer each question.

1. If you're an **extortionist** who is **adamant** about payment, are you less or more likely to get your money?
2. If you **eviscerate** an **insurgency,** are you helping or hurting the rebels?
3. If making **reparations** is a **facile** move for a government, will they be less or more likely to go through with the payments?
4. If the **indigenous** population is **recalcitrant** about allowing corporations to harvest their natural resources, are they happy or unhappy about gaining corporate partners?

Vocabulary Strategy

Suffixes

Interactive Vocabulary Lesson: Common Roots, Prefixes, and Suffixes

Several vocabulary words derive their meaning by adding **suffixes**, or endings. The suffix *-ous* means "relating to or having the quality of." This suffix forms an adjective, as with the word *continuous*. Knowing suffixes and the part of speech they form help you define unfamiliar words.

PRACTICE AND APPLY

In the chart, identify the base word without the suffix. Then define the base word. Finally, write a sentence using the nouns formed by each suffix. An example is provided.

Word/Base Word	Definition of Base Word	Sentence
Word: domination Suffix: *-tion (action, state)* Base word: dominate	to control, govern, or rule by superior authority	The emperor was amassing an army to achieve his goal of world domination.
Word: cynicism Suffix: *-ism (belief)* Base word:		
Word: interference Suffix: *-ence (state or quality of)* Base word:		

Watch Your Language!

Imperative Mood

Interactive Grammar Lesson: Correct Use of Verbs

The **mood** of a verb shows the way in which a thought or idea is expressed. The **imperative mood** is used to give orders, make requests, or issue advice. In the imperative mood, the subject is not typically stated but is understood. For comparison, this chart shows examples expressed in both the imperative mood and the indicative mood. A verb in the **indicative mood** expresses a fact or asks a question. Verbs in most sentences are in the indicative mood.

Indicative Mood	Imperative Mood
We must stop attacking the countryside.	Stop attacking the countryside.
We urge the government to sign the peace treaty.	Sign the peace treaty.
Returning soldiers should be given jobs.	Give jobs to returning soldiers.

Read this sentence from the speech.

End all bombing in North and South Vietnam.

Martin Luther King, Jr. could have said the sentence in this way instead:

The government should end all bombing in North and South Vietnam.

In the second sentence, notice that by adding a subject and a helping verb the mood changes from imperative to indicative. In the indicative sentence, the emphasis on the verb, or the action, is diluted. As a result, the intensity of the original version is lost, making the sentence less effective in conveying urgency, emotion, and meaning.

PRACTICE AND APPLY

Rewrite the following paragraph, changing some of the sentences to the imperative mood.

These are tips that I have found helpful for successful speech-giving. First, it is important to make sure you have prepared a set of speaking notes. Your main ideas and most important details should be written on large index cards. You should be able to see your notes at a glance. Second, you should practice in front of a mirror by yourself, incorporating gestures and working on eye contact. Third, it is a good idea to ask a friend or family member to listen to your speech. Finally, you should get a good night's sleep before the big day. If you are well rested, you will be able to do your best.

Get Ready

Ambush

Short Story by **Tim O'Brien**

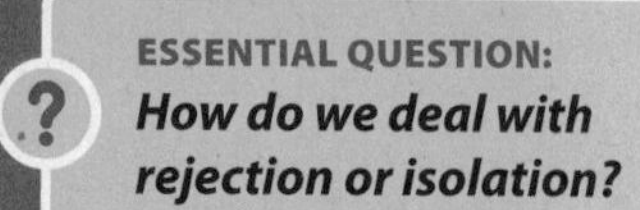
ESSENTIAL QUESTION:
How do we deal with rejection or isolation?

Engage Your Brain

Choose one or more of these activities to start connecting with the short story you're about to read.

If I Had It to Do Over Again

Think about a time when you regretted or second-guessed a decision you made. Write down what made you rethink the decision and how it feels when you look back on what happened.

Gut Reaction

Read the first line from the short story you're going to read.

"When she was nine, my daughter Kathleen asked if I had ever killed anyone."

Based on the quote, what do you think the story will be about? Discuss your ideas with a partner.

Nature Is Not Kind

The Vietnam War was complicated not only because of politics and history, but also because the natural environment was challenging. Do some research to learn more about what soldiers faced.

Vegetation	
Temperatures	
Rainfall	
Poisonous wildlife	

Analyze Character

Characterization refers to the techniques a writer uses to develop characters. There are four basic methods of characterization:

- A writer may use physical description.
- The character's own actions, words, thoughts, and feelings might be presented.
- The actions, words, thoughts, and feelings of other characters provide another means of developing a character.
- The narrator's own direct comments also serve to develop a character.

When a story is told from a first-person perspective, readers learn the main character's thoughts and gain insight into their motivations. These thoughts and motivations often contribute to **internal conflicts,** or struggles that take place within a character. As you read, note how these elements interact to help you gain an understanding of the main character.

Focus on Genre
Short Story

- usually centers on one main conflict
- may use several techniques to portray characters
- may use a frame story in which a story in the past is told within a second story

Analyze Structure

A story's **structure** is the way that it is put together—the arrangement of its parts. Tim O'Brien's short story "Ambush" includes a **frame story,** a device in which one story is told inside another story. The story opens with a frame—the narrator describes a time when his daughter asked him about the war. In a flashback, he then recounts an experience he'd had earlier, as a soldier in war. Use a chart to keep track of the events in the outer and inner story.

Story 1	Story 2
Beginning: End:	Beginning: Middle: End:

As you read, pay attention to the structure of the story and think about how using this structure has an impact on the meaning the author conveys.

Annotation in Action

Here are one student's notes on a character's thoughts and feelings in "Ambush." As you read, note the way the writer reveals character.

> When she was nine, my daughter Kathleen asked if I had ever killed anyone. She knew about the war; she knew I'd been a soldier. "You keep writing these war stories," she said, "so I guess you must've killed somebody." It was a difficult moment, but I did what seemed right, which was to say, "Of course not," and then to take her onto my lap and hold her for a while. Someday, I hope, she'll ask again.

His answer reflects his concern for his daughter rather than his concern for the truth.

Expand Your Vocabulary

Put a check mark next to the vocabulary words that you feel comfortable using when speaking or writing.

- platoon ☐
- grope ☐
- sliver ☐
- ponder ☐
- peril ☐
- gape ☐

With a partner, write a few sentences about someone escaping a dangerous situation, using as many of the vocabulary words as you can. As you read "Ambush," use the definitions in the side column to learn the vocabulary words you don't already know.

Background

Tim O'Brien (b. 1946) served in Vietnam, and his military experience provides much of the material for his fiction and personal narratives. In 1990, O'Brien published *The Things They Carried*, a remarkable fictional memoir about the Vietnam War and its human effects. The book is made up of interconnected stories narrated by a character named Tim O'Brien, who, the author says, is not himself. "Ambush" comes from that collection.

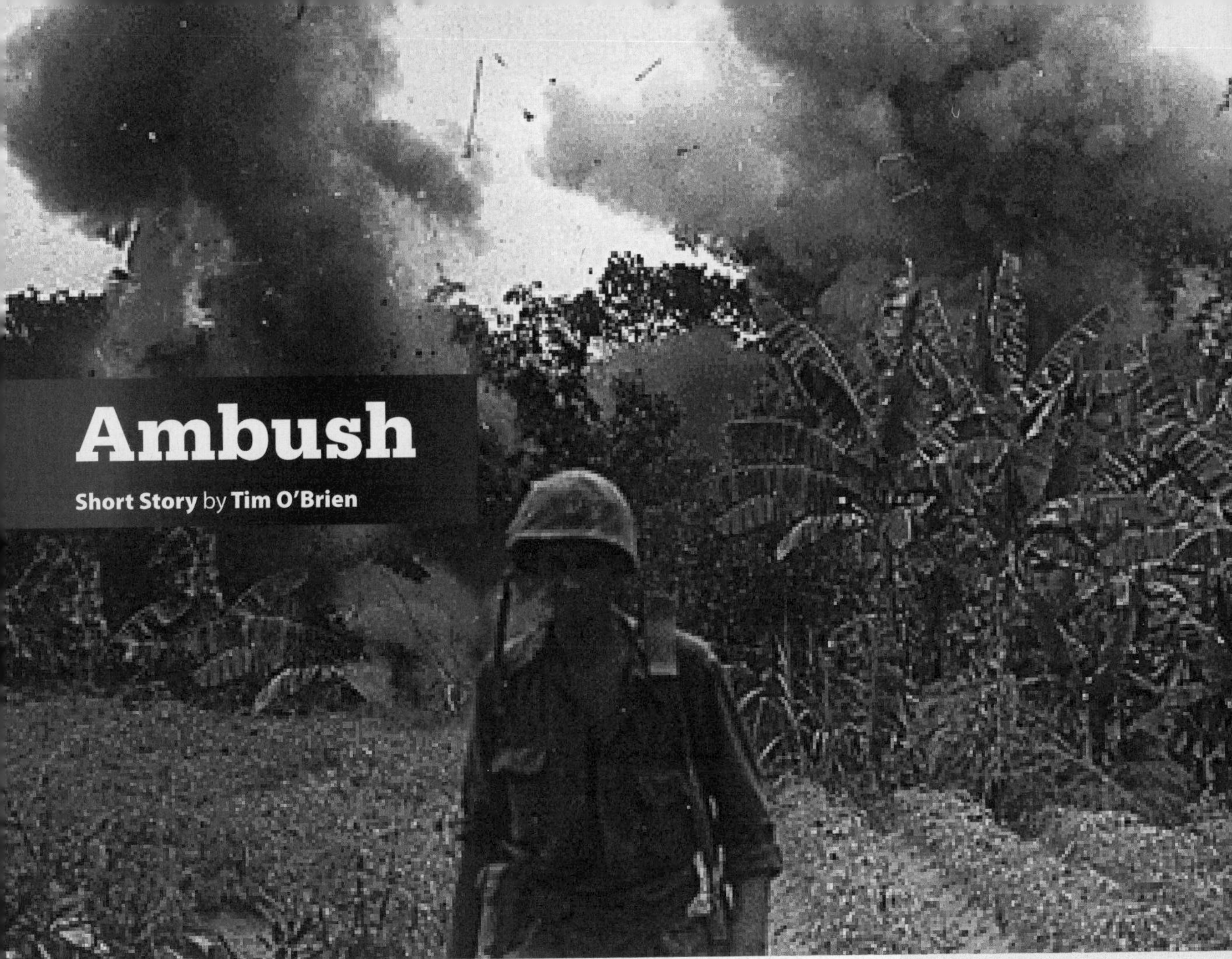

Ambush

Short Story by **Tim O'Brien**

Look for how O'Brien uses the narrator's internal conflict to shape the plot of "Ambush."

NOTICE & NOTE
As you read, use the side margins to make notes about the text.

1 When she was nine, my daughter Kathleen asked if I had ever killed anyone. She knew about the war; she knew I'd been a soldier. "You keep writing these war stories," she said, "so I guess you must've killed somebody." It was a difficult moment, but I did what seemed right, which was to say, "Of course not," and then to take her onto my lap and hold her for a while. Someday, I hope, she'll ask again. But here I want to pretend she's a grown-up. I want to tell her exactly what happened, or what I remember happening, and then I want to say to her that as a little girl she was absolutely right. This is why I keep writing war stories:

2 He was a short, slender young man of about twenty. I was afraid of him—afraid of something—and as he passed me on the trail I threw a grenade that exploded at his feet and killed him.

3 Or to go back:

4 Shortly after midnight we moved into the ambush site outside My Khe. The whole **platoon** was there, spread out in the dense brush along the trail, and for five hours nothing at all happened. We were working in two-man teams—one man on guard while the other slept,

platoon
(plə-to͞on′) *n.* a subdivision of a company of troops consisting of two or more squads or sections and usually commanded by a lieutenant.

grope
(grōp) *v.* to reach about uncertainly; feel one's way.

sliver
(slĭv´ər) *n.* a small narrow piece, portion, or plot.

ANALYZE CHARACTER

Annotate: In paragraph 4, mark the narrator's thoughts and feelings about killing the young man.

Draw Conclusions: What do these details tell you about the narrator's motivation for throwing the grenade?

ponder
(pŏn´dər) *tr. v.* to think about (something) with thoroughness and care.

switching off every two hours—and I remember it was still dark when Kiowa shook me awake for the final watch. The night was foggy and hot. For the first few moments I felt lost, not sure about directions, **groping** for my helmet and weapon. I reached out and found three grenades and lined them up in front of me; the pins had already been straightened for quick throwing. And then for maybe half an hour I kneeled there and waited. Very gradually, in tiny **slivers**, dawn began to break through the fog, and from my position in the brush I could see ten or fifteen meters up the trail. The mosquitoes were fierce. I remember slapping at them, wondering if I should wake up Kiowa and ask for some repellent, then thinking it was a bad idea, then looking up and seeing the young man come out of the fog. He wore black clothing and rubber sandals and a gray ammunition belt. His shoulders were slightly stooped, his head cocked to the side as if listening for something. He seemed at ease. He carried his weapon in one hand, muzzle down, moving without any hurry up the center of the trail. There was no sound at all—none that I can remember. In a way, it seemed, he was part of the morning fog, or my own imagination, but there was also the reality of what was happening in my stomach. I had already pulled the pin on a grenade. I had come up to a crouch. It was entirely automatic. I did not hate the young man; I did not see him as the enemy; I did not **ponder** issues of morality

or politics or military duty. I crouched and kept my head low. I tried to swallow whatever was rising from my stomach, which tasted like lemonade, something fruity and sour. I was terrified. There were no thoughts about killing. The grenade was to make him go away—just evaporate—and I leaned back and felt my head go empty and then felt it fill up again. I had already thrown the grenade before telling myself to throw it. The brush was thick and I had to lob it high, not aiming, and I remember the grenade seeming to freeze above me for an instant, as if a camera had clicked, and I remember ducking down and holding my breath and seeing little wisps of fog rise from the earth. The grenade bounced once and rolled across the trail. I did not hear it, but there must have been a sound, because the young man dropped his weapon and began to run, just two or three quick steps, then he hesitated, swiveling to his right, and he glanced down at the grenade and tried to cover his head but never did. It occurred to me then that he was about to die. I wanted to warn him. The grenade made a popping noise—not soft but not loud either—not what I'd expected—and there was a puff of dust and smoke—a small white puff—and the young man seemed to jerk upward as if pulled by invisible wires. He fell on his back. His rubber sandals had been blown off. He lay at the center of the trail, his right leg beneath him, his one eye shut, his other eye a huge star-shaped hole.

Don't forget to **Notice & Note** as you read the text. 

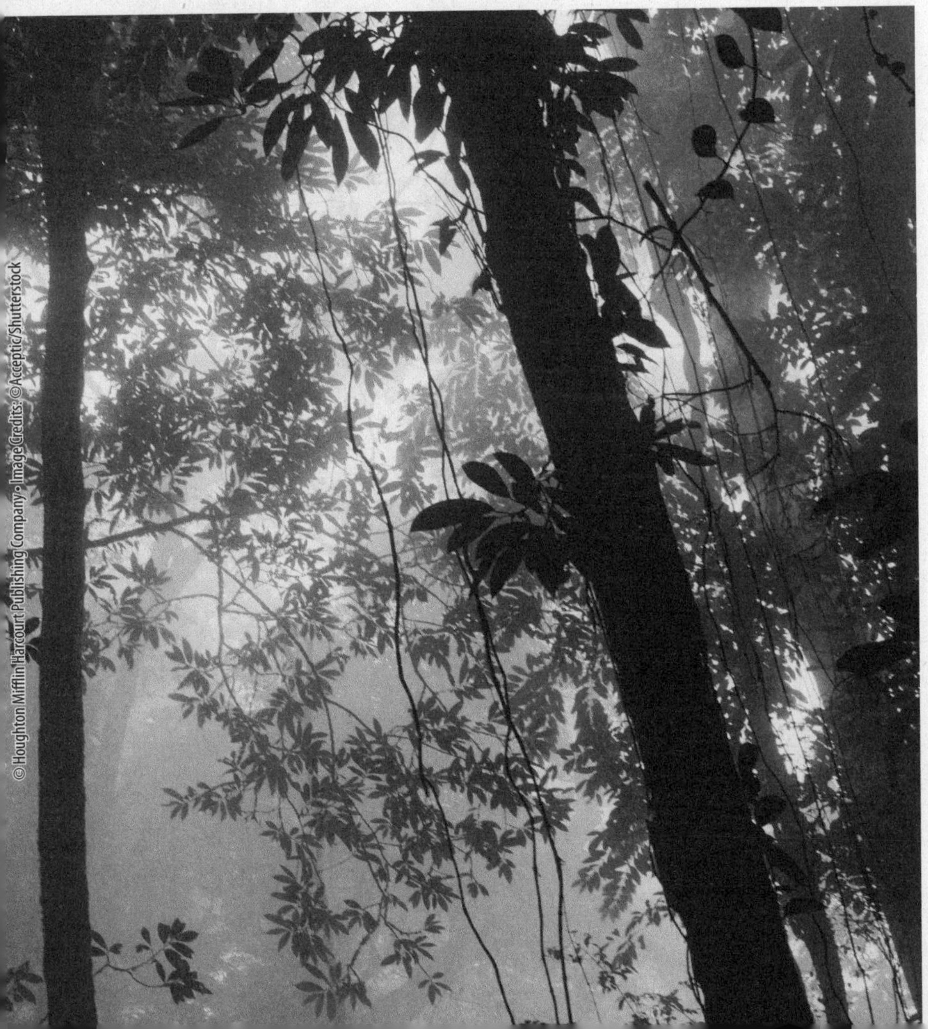

peril
(pĕr´əl) *n.* imminent danger.

NOTICE & NOTE
WORDS OF THE WISER

When you notice a wiser character giving advice about life to the main character, you've found a **Words of the Wiser** signpost.

Notice & Note: In paragraph 6, what does Kiowa tell the narrator about his actions?

Infer: What do Kiowa's words tell you about the narrator's immediate reaction to killing the young man?

gape
(gāp) *intr.v.* to stare wonderingly or stupidly, often with the mouth open.

5 For me, it was not a matter of live or die. I was in no real **peril**. Almost certainly the young man would have passed me by. And it will always be that way.

6 Later, I remember Kiowa tried to tell me that the man would've died anyway. He told me that it was a good kill, that I was a soldier and this was a war, that I should shape up and stop staring and ask myself what the dead man would've done if things were reversed.

7 None of it mattered. The words seemed far too complicated. All I could do was **gape** at the fact of the young man's body.

8 Even now I haven't finished sorting it out. Sometimes I forgive myself, other times I don't. In the ordinary hours of life I try not to dwell on it, but now and then, when I'm reading a newspaper or just

sitting alone in a room, I'll look up and see the young man step out of the morning fog. I'll watch him walk toward me, his shoulders slightly stooped, his head cocked to the side, and he'll pass within a few yards of me and suddenly smile at some secret thought and then continue up the trail to where it bends back into the fog.

ANALYZE STRUCTURE

Annotate: In paragraph 8, mark the story the narrator tells about the young man.

Analyze: Is this part of the main story or the frame story? Explain.

COLLABORATIVE DISCUSSION

With a partner, discuss whether knowing the narrator's thoughts helps you understand his situation.

?

ESSENTIAL QUESTION:

How do we deal with rejection or isolation?

Review your notes and add your thoughts to your **Response Log.**

Assessment Practice

Answer these questions before moving on to the **Analyze the Text** section on the following page.

1. What is the lie that the narrator tells his daughter?

- (A) that he did not fight in the war
- (B) that he killed someone because he was in danger
- (C) that he didn't kill anyone in the war
- (D) that he doesn't remember what happened

2. What was the narrator doing on the night he threw the grenade?

- (A) moving along the trail with his whole platoon
- (B) clearing dense brush in a two-man team
- (C) straightening the pins on three grenades
- (D) standing guard for the final watch of the night

3. Why does Kiowa think that the narrator did the right thing?

- (A) The young man would have died anyway.
- (B) The young man was there as a spy.
- (C) The young man was a threat.
- (D) The platoon was in peril.

Test-Taking Strategies

Respond

Analyze the Text

Support your responses with evidence from the text.

NOTICE & NOTE

Review what you **noticed and noted** as you read the text. Your annotations can help you answer these questions.

1. **INTERPRET** How does the narrator's prior behavior create an internal conflict when he is speaking with his daughter? Is this conflict adequately resolved in the story? Explain.

2. **INTERPRET** What does the narrator mean when he says in paragraph 5 that "it will always be that way"?

3. **ANALYZE** In paragraph 8, what does the story about the young man tell the reader about the narrator's character? How does this help develop the theme?

4. **EVALUATE** How does the **frame story** contribute to the meaning of the text? Consider what the first and last paragraphs add to your understanding of events.

Paragraph	What It Adds to the Story
Paragraph 1	
Paragraph 8	

5. **INTERPRET** Kiowa tells his comrade that "it was a good kill." How effective are Kiowa's **Words of the Wiser** in helping the narrator overcome his internal conflict?

6. **EVALUATE** Which method of characterization did O'Brien use to make characters come to life? Cite text evidence in your response.

Choices

Here are some other ways to demonstrate your understanding of the ideas in this lesson.

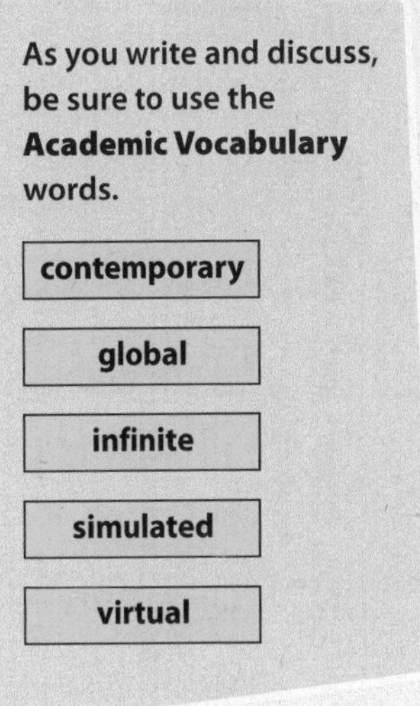
As you write and discuss, be sure to use the **Academic Vocabulary** words.
contemporary
global
infinite
simulated
virtual

Writing

↳ An Alternate Perspective

In "Ambush," the narrator describes the brutal killing of a Vietnamese soldier with a grenade. Consider the perspective of the Vietnamese soldier, and write a paragraph or two about this encounter from his perspective. Think about what he probably felt, saw, heard, smelled, etc. Use descriptive words to communicate what it was like for him.

Media

↳ Create a Soundtrack

Create a soundtrack or playlist for the story that reflects the characters' motivations and conflicts. Compile your soundtrack with those of your classmates and post it in your classroom or online. Be able to explain why you chose the tracks you did and how they relate to the story.

Social & Emotional Learning

↳ Seeking Help

Consider what it would be like for the narrator of "Ambush" to talk about his situation with a counselor. Write a dialogue between the narrator and a counselor in which you include the following:

- a clear relating of events
- an expression of how the narrator feels
- advice on what the narrator can do to manage his stress and the guilt
- details from the text in your conversation as needed

Expand Your Vocabulary

PRACTICE AND APPLY

Complete the sentences with one of the vocabulary words.

platoon	grope	sliver
ponder	peril	gape

1. She was disappointed to find only a small ______________ of cheese.
2. After the accident, all I could do was ______________ at the smashed-up car.
3. After the war, my grandfather corresponded with a man who had been in his ______________.
4. They seemed at ease, unaware of the ______________ they were really in.
5. Before falling asleep, I lie in bed and ______________ the events of the day.
6. When the power went out, I had to ______________ for the flashlight.

Vocabulary Strategy

↳ Connotation and Denotation

Interactive Vocabulary Lesson: Connotation and Denotation

A word's dictionary meaning is called its **denotation.** The images or feelings you connect to a word add a finer shade of meaning, called **connotation.** The connotation of a word goes beyond the word's basic dictionary definition. Writers use connotations of words to communicate positive or negative feelings. As in this sentence from "The Ambush," it is important to consider the denotation and connotation of words you use in your writing.

> **None of it mattered. The words seemed far too complicated. All I could do was <u>gape</u> at the fact of the young man's body.**

The word *gape* means the same thing as *stare*, but gape has a negative connotation. This particular usage evokes a sense of shock and horror.

PRACTICE AND APPLY

Work with a partner to explore words with different connotations. Follow these steps:

- List five words from the story that have a strong positive or negative connotation.
- Use a dictionary and a thesaurus to find definitions and synonyms of the words.
- Discuss how using synonyms with different connotations would affect meaning.

Watch Your Language!

Transitions

Authors use **transitions** to help clarify meaning, organize their writing, improve their style, or signal structural shifts to the reader. When used to signal a shift, transitions tell readers the direction a text is taking, such as another time, location, or point of view. Transitions help readers follow a story, especially when the narrative moves around in time rather than progressing in a strictly linear fashion, which occurs when authors use structural devices such as flashbacks and frame stories. Transitions can be in the form of time and place phrases, punctuation, formatting, section breaks, and chapter breaks.

Interactive Grammar Lesson: Using Transitions

In "Ambush," Tim O'Brien uses transitions to guide readers through the story frame structure.

But here I want to pretend she's a grown-up. I want to tell her exactly what happened, or what I remember happening, and then I want to say to her that as a little girl she was absolutely right. <u>This is why I keep writing war stories:</u>

He was a short, slender young man of about twenty. I was afraid of him—afraid of something—and as he passed me on the trail I threw a grenade that exploded at his feet and killed him.

The colon (:) at the end of the first paragraph signals a shift to a war story from the past.

From paragraph 7 to paragraph 8, the author shifts from the past time of the flashback to present time.

None of it mattered. The words seemed far too complicated. All I could do was gape at the fact of the young man's body.

<u>Even now</u> I haven't finished sorting it out. Sometimes I forgive myself, other times I don't.

The phrase *even now* signals to the reader that the story is shifting back to present time from the flashback.

PRACTICE AND APPLY

Write a paragraph in which you begin to tell someone about an event in the past. Be sure to include transitions that show the shift in time and place.

Get Ready

The Universe as Primal Scream

Poem by Tracy K. Smith

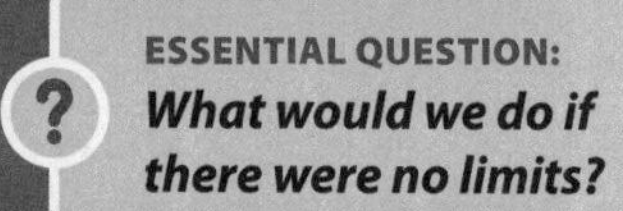
ESSENTIAL QUESTION:
What would we do if there were no limits?

Engage Your Brain

Choose one or more of these activities to start connecting with the poem you're about to read.

With a Rebel Yell

A *primal scream* is a form of therapy for releasing pent-up anger and frustration. If you were to let forth with a primal scream, what would you yell? (No cursing, please!) Share your yell—quietly—with a classmate.

The Dawn of Man

In the poem you are about to read, the writer refers to a scene from the movie *2001: A Space Odyssey* entitled "The Dawn of Man." Based on the name of the movie and scene, what would you expect to see in this scene? Discuss with a partner or small group.

Is This All There Is?

For all we know, life on this planet, in this solar system, in this galaxy, in all the universe, is the only known life there is. Chew on that and freewrite for five minutes.

Analyze Literary Devices

To understand the message of "The Universe as Primal Scream," we must analyze the language the author has used, including figurative language and other literary devices. These help give the poem meaning by setting tone and mood, revealing information about the speaker, and by triggering associations in the minds of the reader. Use this chart to analyze the literary devices Smith uses in her poem.

Literary Devices	Analyzing Meaning
An **idiom** is an informal expression that means something other than the literal meaning of its individual words. Line 1: "5pm on the nose."	What does the use of idioms suggest about the speaker? What image does the idiom convey? How does this affect the tone and mood?
Imagery is the use of words that appeal to the senses. Line 2: a sound that is "high, shrill and metallic."	What **connotations,** or emotional associations, do these words convey? What sound, or what mental picture, does the description create in the reader's imagination?
An **allusion** is a brief reference to a historic, literary, popular, or mythical person, place, or event. Lines 14–15: "we'll ride to glory / Like Elijah."	Consider what this allusion reveals about the speaker's state of mind, frame of reference, thoughts, or mood. How does the allusion connect to the global subject of the poem?
Personification is a type of figurative language that gives human traits to objects, animals, or abstract ideas. Line 18: "Let the heaven we inherit approach."	What picture does this create in the reader's mind? What does this comparison to a person reveal about the speaker's attitude toward the infinite and unknowable?

Focus on Genre
↳ **Poetry**

- **consists of lines and stanzas**
- **may be rhymed or unrhymed depending on style**
- **includes literary devices such as allusions, personification, and images that appeal to the senses**

Analyze Structure

The line is a core unit of a poem, and line length is an essential element of the poem's meaning and rhythm. A **line break,** or where a line of poetry ends, may occur at the end of a sentence. It may also occur in the middle of a sentence, creating a pause or emphasis. Smith even uses a line break to lead into a new stanza.

As you read the poem, use a chart like this to help you analyze the effects of line breaks on the meaning and rhythm of the poem.

Line Breaks	Effects

Annotation in Action

Here are one student's notes about imagery in "The Universe as Primal Scream." As you read, note the effect of imagery and other literary devices in the poem.

5pm on the nose. They open their mouths
And it rolls out: high, shrill and metallic.

imagery appeals to sense of sound

Background

Tracy K. Smith (b. 1972) was born in Falmouth, Massachusetts. This poem is from her collection *Life on Mars*, for which she won the 2012 Pulitzer Prize. In her poems, Smith delves into ideas about the universe and the future. Her influences include science fiction, movies (such as *2001: A Space Odyssey*), and even music (the collection's title is borrowed from a David Bowie song). She describes the book as an elegy for her late father, who was an engineer for the Hubble Telescope and spent many years exploring the mysteries of the universe.

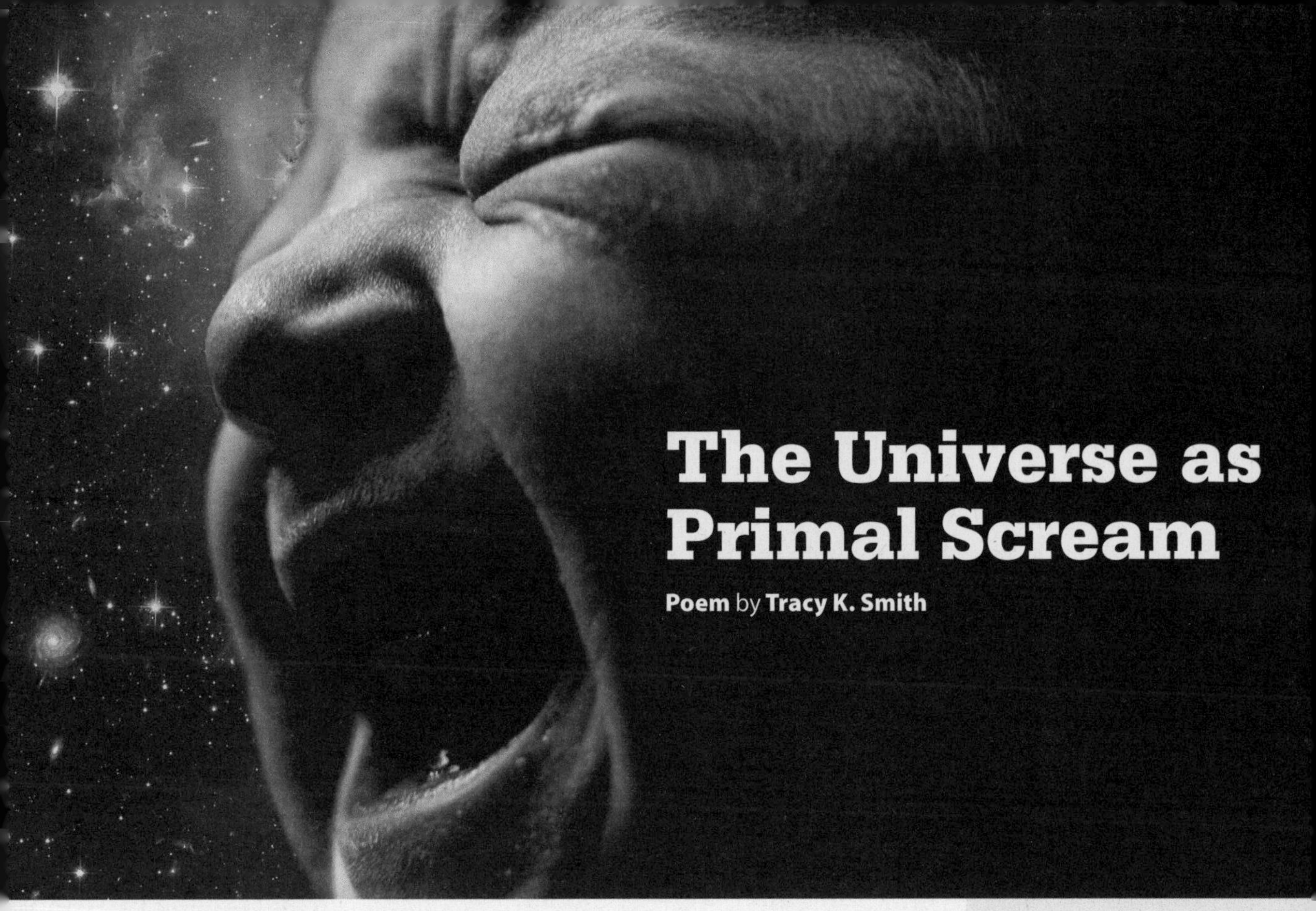

The Universe as Primal Scream

Poem by **Tracy K. Smith**

Note how one idea leads to another as the speaker builds her ideas about life and death.

NOTICE & NOTE 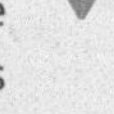
As you read, use the side margins to make notes about the text.

5pm on the nose. They open their mouths
And it rolls out: high, shrill and metallic.
First the boy, then his sister. Occasionally,
They both let loose at once, and I think
Of putting on my shoes to go up and see
Whether it is merely an experiment
Their parents have been conducting
Upon the good crystal, which must surely
Lie shattered to dust on the floor.

Maybe the mother is still proud
Of the four pink lungs she nursed
To such might. Perhaps, if they hit
The magic decibel, the whole building
Will lift-off, and we'll ride to glory
Like Elijah.[1] If this is it—if this is what
Their cries are cocked toward—let the sky
Pass from blue, to red, to molten gold,
To black. Let the heaven we inherit approach.

ANALYZE STRUCTURE

Annotate: Mark where sentences end in the first stanza.

Analyze: What is surprising about where the sentences end in relation to the line breaks? Why might the poet have chosen to break the lines as she did?

[1] **Elijah** (ĭ-lī′jə): biblical prophet who ascended to Heaven in a burning chariot.

ANALYZE LITERARY DEVICES

Annotate: Mark examples of personification in lines 21–26.

Analyze: What is being personified in these lines?

Whether it is our dead in Old Testament robes,
Or a door opening onto the roiling infinity of space.
Whether it will bend down to greet us like a father,
Or swallow us like a furnace. I'm ready
To meet what refuses to let us keep anything
For long. What teases us with blessings,
Bends us with grief. Wizard, thief, the great
Wind rushing to knock our mirrors to the floor,
To sweep our short lives clean. How mean[2]

Our racket seems beside it. My stereo on shuffle.
The neighbor chopping onions through a wall.
All of it just a hiccough against what may never
Come for us. And the kids upstairs still at it,
Screaming like the Dawn of Man,[3] as if something
They have no name for has begun to insist
Upon being born.

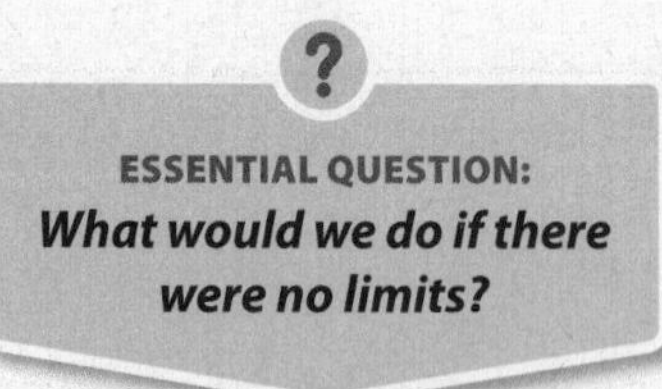
?
ESSENTIAL QUESTION:
What would we do if there were no limits?

Review your notes and add your thoughts to your **Response Log.**

[2] **mean:** inferior or shabby.

[3] **Screaming like the Dawn of Man:** an allusion to the opening segment of the 1968 film *2001: A Space Odyssey*, which features shouting, ape-like creatures.

COLLABORATIVE DISCUSSION

What insights about the cycle of life does Smith express? Discuss your thoughts with a partner.

Assessment Practice

Answer these questions before moving on to the **Analyze the Text** section on the following page.

1. In the first stanza, what causes the speaker to think that crystal must "surely" be "shattered"?

- (A) the volume of the children's crying
- (B) the clink of crystal falling to the floor
- (C) the knowledge of the crystal experiment
- (D) the sound of parents yelling at the children

2. What is described in the third stanza?

- (A) stormy weather
- (B) space flight
- (C) the afterlife
- (D) time travel

3. What noises in the last stanza are made by the kids upstairs?

- (A) hiccoughing
- (B) screaming
- (C) chopping onions
- (D) sweeping

Test-Taking Strategies

Analyze the Text

Support your responses with evidence from the text.

NOTICE & NOTE

Review what you **noticed and noted** as you read the text. Your annotations can help you answer these questions.

1. **INFER** Why did Smith choose "5pm" as the time for the events of this poem? What might be the connection between this time and her theme?

2. **ANALYZE** Consider Smith's **diction**, or word choice, in the first stanza. What do the words *metallic, experiment,* and *conducting* suggest about the speaker?

3. **DRAW CONCLUSIONS** Reread lines 10–18 and the accompanying footnote describing the biblical prophet Elijah. How does the allusion to Elijah relate to the subject of the poem?

4. **ANALYZE** What is the speaker hoping for in the third stanza (lines 19–27)? What does the careful list of possible scenarios reveal about the speaker's doubts and anxieties?

5. **INFER** Why does the poet break the sentence in lines 27–28 across two stanzas? What function does this line break serve?

6. **EVALUATE** What is the effect of Smith's use of imagery in the poem? In the chart, note examples of imagery, the sense each image appeals to, and each image's impact on the meaning of the poem.

Image	Sense	Meaning

Choices

Here are some other ways to demonstrate your understanding of the ideas in this lesson.

Writing

Breaking Up

Review the poem, keeping in mind what you learned about line breaks in poetry. Indicate in the poem at least five or six places you think there could or should be another line break, or indicate where you think lines could be combined. For each one, be sure to write a brief explanation why you think the line break is necessary or unnecessary and what it adds to the poem by putting it in or taking it away.

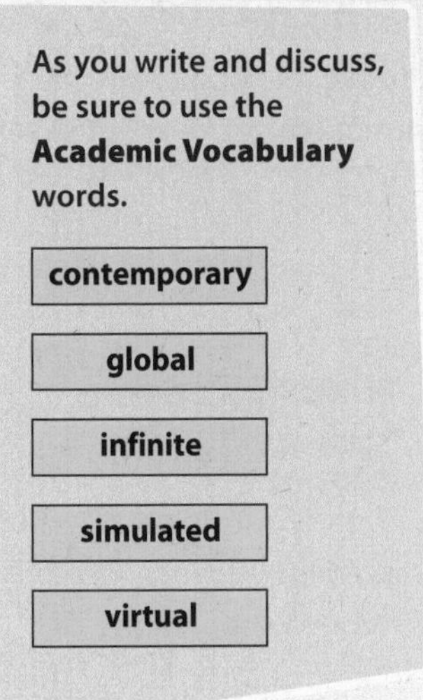
As you write and discuss, be sure to use the **Academic Vocabulary** words.
contemporary
global
infinite
simulated
virtual

Media

Postcards from the Edge

Imagine you took a trip to the end of the universe. Send a postcard back to a friend or family member and describe in a short paragraph what you've discovered about the origins of life, the universe, and so on. Describe what you've seen, felt, and realized. You might include drawings as well as words to create a unique postcard.

Speaking & Listening

Dramatic Reading

Present a dramatic reading of the poem to the class. Follow these tips as you work to create a compelling presentation.

- Note the line breaks and literary devices in how you read the poem and what you're trying to communicate to the audience.
- Include background music, sound effects, and other effects as you see fit.
- Be physical: include hand gestures and body language to convey meaning.
- Change your tone of voice as appropriate.

Get Ready

First Verse

Poem by **Tim Seibles**

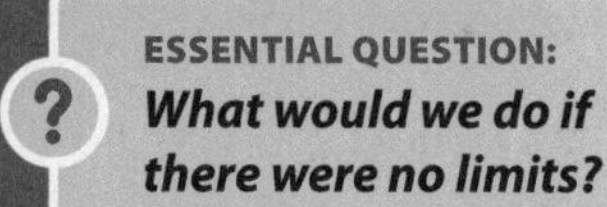
ESSENTIAL QUESTION:
What would we do if there were no limits?

Engage Your Brain

Choose one or more of these activities to connect with poem you're about to read.

Hindsight Being Twenty-Twenty

There's a saying that "hindsight is twenty-twenty," which suggests something like "looking back, clearly this was the better choice." Think about a time when you struggled to make a decision, but now it seems so clear what you should have done. Talk about your experience with a classmate.

Does It Spark Joy?

What little, seemingly unimportant things make you smile? List five things that bring you joy and explain why.

The Face of the Earth

In the poem you're about to read, the poet says:

> I see now
> the Earth itself *does*   have a face.

What does the face of the Earth look like to you? Use a separate sheet of paper to draw your vision of the Earth.

Analyze Imagery

Imagery is language that appeals to the senses. Poets use imagery to bring places, events, and feelings to life for readers. Follow these steps to notice how imagery in a poem helps readers experience sights, sounds, tastes, smells, and textures:

- Identify vivid images. Look for words and phrases that help you visualize what the writer is describing.
- Notice the specific sense or senses the language appeals to: sight, hearing, taste, smell, touch.
- Consider the effect of the image. How does it influence your response to the ideas in the poem?

Focus on Genre
↳ **Free Verse Poetry**

- **includes lines and stanzas**
- **does not have regular rhyme or meter patterns**
- **often sounds like everyday speech**

Use the chart to analyze images.

Imagery	Sense(s)	Effect

Analyze Tone

Tone is the attitude a writer expresses toward a subject. A writer communicates tone through words, details, and style choices.

- Tone can be described with an adjective, such as *serious*, *playful*, *sarcastic*, *dismissive*, or *angry*.
- An author's tone in writing is similar to someone's tone of voice when speaking. Read a poem aloud to identify the author's tone. Listen for how the author's choices reflect an attitude about the topic of the poem.

Analyze Theme

A **theme** is an underlying message that a writer wants the reader to understand. All of the elements in a poem work together to communicate themes.

- Consider how the images of the poem build and relate to each other. Do they create a single, unified impression? Are there contrasting images? Is the overall message clear, or is it a little uncertain?
- Also think about how the author's tone connects to the poem's central ideas. What does the poet's attitude help you understand about the topic—and about life?

Annotation in Action

Here is an example of notes a student made about imagery in "First Verse." As you read, mark examples of imagery that stand out to you.

Some mornings
I take myself away from the television
and go outside where the only news comes
as fresh air folding over the houses.

fresh air seems comforting, a relief

Background

Tim Seibles (b. 1955) writes poetry that addresses contemporary political, social, and personal issues. His direct yet questioning style echoes the improvisational riffs of a jazz musician. "Writing is like playing an instrument," he explains. "My instrument is English."

Seibles often finds fresh ways to look at familiar issues, helping readers engage with important subjects such as racial tension, class conflict, and the environment. For example, the poem "First Verse" was originally published in Seibles's collection *Buffalo Head Solos* (2004). Later, the poem was included in anthologies that focus on protecting the environment, such as *The Ecopoetry Anthology* (2013) and *Here: Poems for the Planet* (2019).

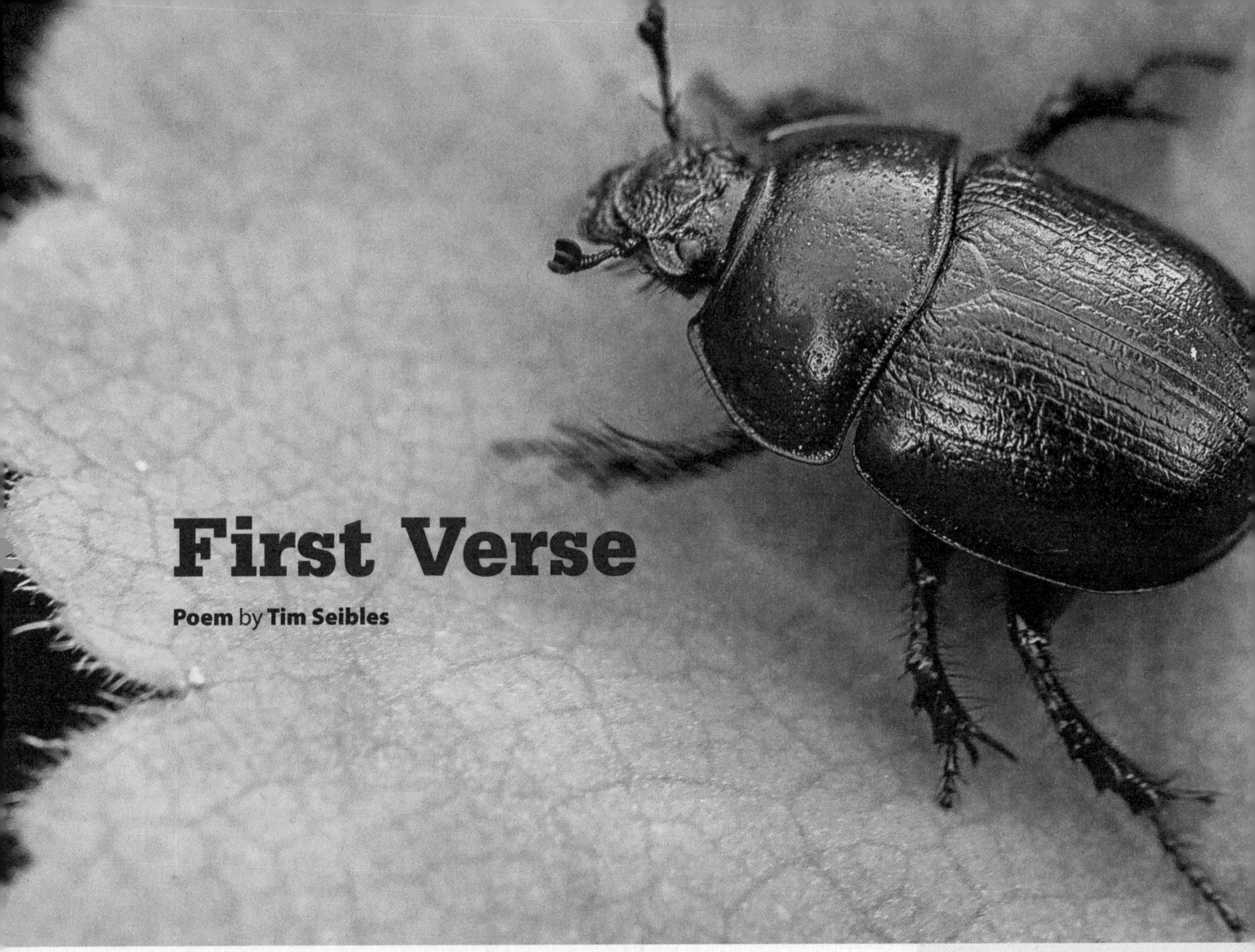

First Verse

Poem by **Tim Seibles**

Note the words and images that suggest the writer's tone, or attitude, toward his subject.

NOTICE & NOTE
As you read, use the side margins to make notes about the text.

I admit the world remains almost beautiful.
The dung beetles snap on their iridescent jackets
despite the canine holiness of the Vatican
and, despite the great predatory surge of industry,
two human hands still mate like butterflies
when buttoning a shirt.
                                        Some mornings
I take myself away from the television
and go outside where the only news comes
as fresh air folding over the houses.
And I feel glad for an hour in which race
and power and all the momentum of history
add up to nothing.

As if from all the mad grinding
in my brain, a single blue lily had grown —
my skull open like a lake. I can hear
an insect   sawing itself into what must be
a kind of speech.

ANALYZE IMAGERY

Annotate: Mark words that appeal to the senses in lines 14–18.

Compare: How do the images in this stanza create surprising contrasts?

ANALYZE TONE

Annotate: In lines 27–34, mark words that show how the author feels about humans and their choices.

Apply: How would you describe the author's attitude in these lines?

ANALYZE THEME

Annotate: In lines 35–39, mark the sentences that give advice about how we should live.

Analyze: What is the central message communicated by this advice?

I know there is little
mercy to be found among us, that we have
already agreed to go down fighting, but
I should be more amazed: look
at the blood   and guess who's holding
the knives. Shouldn't we be *more*
amazed? Doesn't the view
just blister your eyes?

To have come this long way, to stand
on two legs, to be   not tarantulas
or chimpanzees   but soldiers of our own
dim-witted enslavement. To utterly miss the door
to the enchanted palace. To see *myself*
coined into a stutter. To allow the money
to brand us   and the believers
to blindfold our lives.
In the name
of what? If that old book was true
the first verse would say   *Embrace*

the world.   Be friendly.   The forests
are glad you breathe.

I see now
the Earth itself *does*   have a face.
If it could say *I*   it would
plead with the universe, the way
dinosaurs once growled
at the stars.
It's like
the road behind us is stolen
completely   so the future can
never arrive.   So, look at this: look
what we've *done*. With all
we knew.
With all we knew
that we knew.

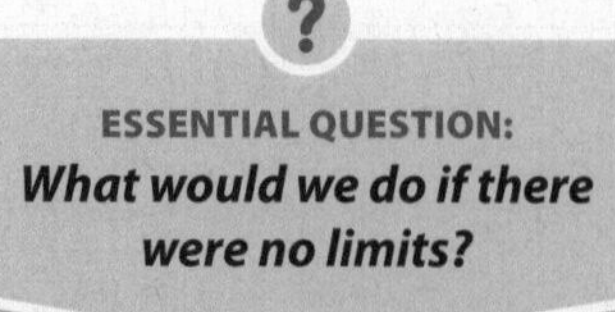
?
ESSENTIAL QUESTION:
What would we do if there were no limits?

Review your notes and add your thoughts to your **Response Log.**

COLLABORATIVE DISCUSSION

What image from the poem is most memorable to you? What feeling did this image convey? Discuss your ideas with a partner.

Assessment Practice

Answer these questions before moving on to the **Analyze the Text** section on the following page.

1. How does the speaker feel about the world?

Ⓐ People have forever destroyed the world's appearance.

Ⓑ The world will always be able to protect itself from harm.

Ⓒ Our physical world is not as important as our emotions.

Ⓓ Beauty remains in the world, despite people's actions.

2. The speaker celebrates the amazing qualities of –

Ⓐ industry

Ⓑ nature

Ⓒ religion

Ⓓ history

3. Which image from the poem suggests hopefulness?

Ⓐ two human hands still mate like butterflies / when buttoning a shirt (lines 5–6)

Ⓑ all the momentum of history / add up to nothing (lines 12–13)

Ⓒ I know there is little / mercy to be found among us (lines 19–20)

Ⓓ the road behind us is stolen / completely (lines 47–48)

Ed

Test-Taking Strategies

Analyze the Text

Support your responses with evidence from the text.

NOTICE & NOTE

Review what you **noticed and noted** as you read the text. Your annotations can help you answer these questions.

1. **INTERPRET** What idea about beauty does the poet introduce in the first line of the poem? Explain.

2. **COMPARE** Reread lines 7–18. How does the speaker compare and contrast imagery that describes the natural world with imagery that describes human experiences? Use the chart to complete your response.

	Nature Imagery	Human Imagery
Examples		
Overall Effect		

3. **CITE EVIDENCE** What is the author's tone, or attitude, about human behavior? Cite specific words and phrases that reflect this tone.

4. **INFER** Reread lines 35–39. What is the significance of the "first verse"? How does it connect to the text?

5. **ANALYZE** What theme about the natural world does the poet develop? How do the imagery and tone of the poem support the theme?

6. **CONNECT** How do the final lines of the poem relate to the first stanza?

Choices

Here are some other ways to demonstrate your understanding of the ideas in this lesson.

Writing

↳ Your Own First Verse

The first verse referred to in the title of the poem includes a few phrases that offer advice on and motivation for having a positive impact on the world: *Embrace the world. Be friendly. The forests are glad you breathe.*

What would your own "first verse" be? Write a poem in which you express your first verse. Consider the following as you write:

- Decide what your first verse is about. Seibles wrote about the connection between humanity and nature. What topic is most important to you?
- Your poem should be brief—no more than a few lines. Try writing one or two sentences and then adding line breaks. How will you emphasize what is most important?
- Include at least one vivid image so that your message comes alive to readers. How does this image express what you value?

As you write and discuss, be sure to use the **Academic Vocabulary** words.

contemporary

global

infinite

simulated

virtual

Media

↳ Make It Visual

Create a visual representation of "First Verse" that captures the feeling of the poem. You may decide to make a collage, slideshow, painting, or any other medium you prefer.

Will you decide to show concrete images or convey the ideas in the poem in an abstract way? As you capture the essence of the poem, try to be as creative as possible.

Speaking & Listening

↳ Take a Stance

Is the message of the poem ultimately optimistic or pessimistic? Gather evidence from the poem to help you decide. Then hold a discussion about the poem with a small group. Be sure to cite evidence in your conversation.

Collaborate & Compare

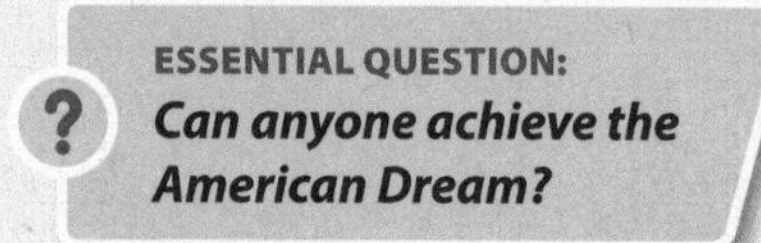

Compare Ideas Across Genres

The two nonfiction texts you're about to read look at race relations in the United States from slightly different perspectives. As you read, determine the main idea in each text. Then, look for ways that ideas in the two texts relate to each other or express different perspectives.

MENTOR TEXT

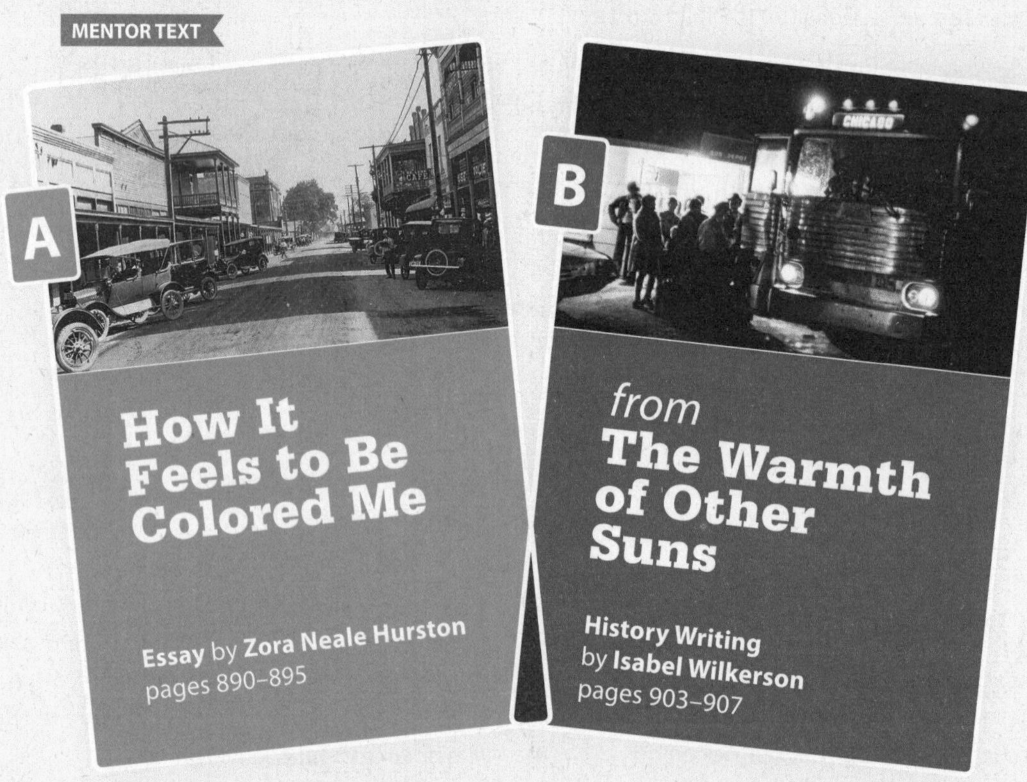

A
How It Feels to Be Colored Me
Essay by Zora Neale Hurston
pages 890–895
B
from
The Warmth of Other Suns
History Writing
by Isabel Wilkerson
pages 903–907

After you read both selections, you will collaborate with a small group on a final project. You will follow these steps:

- Review the texts
- Evaluate the ideas
- Present a debate

How It Feels to Be Colored Me

Essay by **Zora Neale Hurston**

Engage Your Brain

Choose one or more of these activities to start connecting with the essay you're about to read.

A Sunny Disposition

In a small group, have a discussion about the images, colors, and phrases people use to describe emotions. Consider the following in your discussion:

- Brainstorm words and phrases that come to mind.
- Explain why someone might use the phrases you came up with. For example: "a sunny disposition" would describe someone who is cheerful and happy.
- Are there any phrases that are especially memorable or effective?
- Are there some that don't make sense or that you don't like? How would you improve them?

Depends on How You Look at It

In the essay you're about to read, author Zora Neale Hurston says: "The front porch might seem a daring place for the rest of the town, but it was a gallery seat to me." Based on the quote, how do you think she views the world? What kind of person do you think she is? Compare your answers with a partner's.

I'd Like to Teach the World to Sing

It's been said that music is the universal language. Do you agree? Why or why not? Take five minutes to freewrite your response.

Analyze Development of Ideas

In an essay, the **main idea** is the most important point an author makes about a topic.

- The main idea can be **explicit,** or stated outright.
- More often, the main idea is indirectly stated, or **implicit.** That means reader must infer the author's main idea from key details in the text.

The essay's organizational structure may suggest the main idea. For example, is the author presenting two opposing views on a topic or arguing a specific viewpoint? As you read, note important details and what they suggest about the main idea.

Focus on Genre
Autobiographical Essay

- often told from first-person point of view
- usually focuses on a single subject
- reveals the main idea through explanations, personal examples, and anecdotes
- uses diction, imagery, and figurative language to reveal tone

Analyze Perspective

The ideas, values, feelings, and beliefs that influence the way a writer approaches a topic make up the **author's perspective.** Most authors will not reveal their perspective directly. You can often infer it from the author's tone.

Tone is the attitude a writer expresses toward a subject, and can be described as intimate, humorous, ironic, or earnest. In this essay, Hurston's tone and perspective are revealed through diction, imagery, and figurative language.

Literary Element	Example from Text	Tone
Diction	There is no great sorrow dammed up in my soul, nor lurking behind my eyes.	By taking a firm stance against "great sorrow," Hurston strikes a resilient tone.
Imagery	The native whites rode dusty horses, the Northern tourists chugged down the sandy village road in automobiles.	The vivid description contributes to a thoughtful tone.
Figurative language	. . . I whoop; I shake my assegai above my head, I hurl it true to the mark *yeeeeooww!*	The imitation of a yell (onomatopoeia) brings out a joyful tone.

As you read "How It Feels to Be Colored Me," ask yourself: What is the overall tone? How does it help you identify the author's perspective?

Annotation in Action

Here are one student's notes on the author's perspective. As you read, pay attention to details that give you insight into the author's values and beliefs.

The front porch might seem a daring place for the rest of the town, but it was a gallery seat to me. My favorite place was atop the gate-post. Proscenium box for a born first-nighter. Not only did I enjoy the show, but I didn't mind the actors knowing that I liked it. I actually spoke to them in passing. I'd wave at them and when they returned my salute, I would say something like this: "Howdy-do-well-I-thank-you-where-you-goin'?"

Details reveal that she enjoyed being on the front porch because she liked to talk to people as they passed by.

Expand Your Vocabulary

Put a check mark next to the vocabulary words that you feel comfortable using when speaking or writing.

extenuating	☐
exclusive	☐
specter	☐
narcotic	☐
miscellany	☐

Then, use these words to talk about having a conversation in a music venue. As you read "How It Feels to Be Colored Me," use the definitions in the side-column to learn the vocabulary words you don't already know.

Background

Zora Neale Hurston (1891–1960) grew up in the all-Black town of Eatonville, Florida. In 1925 she moved to New York City to study anthropology. After World War I, a huge migration north brought African Americans to the New York City neighborhood called Harlem. Hurston joined other Black artists, writers, and musicians who became part of a great cultural movement known as the Harlem Renaissance. She returned to the South to collect African American folklore, which she published in the collection *Mules and Men.* Sadly, her work fell out of favor in the 1940s, and Hurston died poor and nearly forgotten.

How It Feels to Be Colored Me

Essay by **Zora Neale Hurston**

NOTICE & NOTE

As you read, use the side margins to make notes about the text.

One woman maintains her sense of self, even as others want her to conform to their ideas of who she is.

extenuating
(ĭk-stĕn´yo͞o-ā´ting) *adj.* lessening the severity of a fault, partially excusing.

exclusive
(ĭk-sklo͞o´sĭv) *adj.* not allowing something else.

1 I am colored but I offer nothing in the way of **extenuating** circumstances except the fact that I am the only Negro in the United States whose grandfather on the mother's side was *not* an Indian chief.

2 I remember the very day that I became colored. Up to my thirteenth year I lived in the little Negro town of Eatonville, Florida. It is **exclusively** a colored town. The only white people I knew passed through the town going to or coming from Orlando. The native whites rode dusty horses, the Northern tourists chugged down the sandy village road in automobiles. The town knew the Southerners and never stopped cane chewing when they passed. But the Northerners were something else again. They were peered at

cautiously from behind curtains by the timid. The more venturesome would come out on the porch to watch them go past and got just as much pleasure out of the tourists as the tourists got out of the village.

3 The front porch might seem a daring place for the rest of the town, but it was a gallery seat to me. My favorite place was atop the gate-post. Proscenium box for a born first-nighter.[1] Not only did I enjoy the show, but I didn't mind the actors knowing that I liked it. I actually spoke to them in passing. I'd wave at them and when they returned my salute, I would say something like this: "Howdy- do-well-I-thank-you-where-you-goin'?" Usually automobile or the horse paused at this, and after a queer exchange of compliments, I would probably "go a piece of the way" with them, as we say in farthest Florida. If one of my family happened to come to the front in time to see me, of course negotiations would be rudely broken off. But even so, it is clear that I was the first "welcome-to-our-state" Floridian, and I hope the Miami Chamber of Commerce will please take notice.

4 During this period, white people differed from colored to me only in that they rode through town and never lived there. They liked to hear me "speak pieces" and sing and wanted to see me dance the parse-me-la,[2] and gave me generously of their small silver for doing these things, which seemed strange to me for I wanted to do them so much that I needed bribing to stop. Only they didn't know it. The colored people gave no dimes. They deplored any joyful tendencies in me, but I was their Zora nevertheless. I belonged to them, to the nearby hotels, to the county—everybody's Zora.

5 But changes came in the family when I was thirteen, and I was sent to school in Jacksonville. I left Eatonville, the town of the oleanders,[3] as Zora. When I disembarked from the riverboat at Jacksonville, she was no more. It seemed that I had suffered a sea change.[4] I was not Zora of Orange County any more, I was now a little colored girl. I found it out in certain ways. In my heart as well as in the mirror, I became a fast brown—warranted not to rub nor run.

6 But I am not tragically colored. There is no great sorrow dammed up in my soul, nor lurking behind my eyes. I do not mind at all. I do not belong to the sobbing school of Negrohood who hold that nature somehow has given them a low-down dirty deal and whose feelings are all hurt about it. Even in the helter-skelter skirmish that is my life, I have seen that the world is to the strong regardless of a little pigmentation more or less. No, I do not weep at the world—I am too busy sharpening my oyster knife.[5]

7 Someone is always at my elbow reminding me that I am the granddaughter of slaves. It fails to register depression with me.

Don't forget to **Notice & Note** as you read the text.

VOCABULARY

Synonyms and Antonyms: Mark the word *joyful* in paragraph 4. You can change the meaning of a word to its opposite by changing the suffix in a word. For example, replacing *-ful* with *-less* gives us *joyless*, the antonym of *joyful*.

Analyze: Why would Hurston say that colored people condemned her "joyful tendencies"? If she were joyless, what would their reaction be?

ANALYZE DEVELOPMENT OF IDEAS

Annotate: Mark the sentence that expresses the main idea of paragraph 6.

Infer: How do the details support the main idea?

---

[1] **Proscenium . . . first-nighter:** A proscenium box is a box near the stage. A first-nighter is a person who attends the opening night of a performance.

[2] **parse-me-la:** a dance movement popular with Southern African Americans of the period.

[3] **oleanders:** evergreen shrubs with fragrant flowers.

[4] **sea change:** a complete transformation.

[5] **oyster knife:** a reference to the saying "The world is my oyster," implying that the world contains treasure waiting to be taken, like the pearl in an oyster.

Slavery is sixty years in the past. The operation was successful and the patient is doing well, thank you. The terrible struggle that made me an American out of a potential slave said "On the line!" The Reconstruction said "Get set!"; and the generation before said "Go!" I am off to a flying start and I must not halt in the stretch to look behind and weep. Slavery is the price I paid for civilization, and the choice was not with me. It is a bully adventure and worth all that I have paid through my ancestors for it. No one on earth ever had a greater chance for glory. The world to be won and nothing to be lost. It is thrilling to think—to know that for any act of mine, I shall get twice as much praise or twice as much blame. It is quite exciting to hold the center of the national stage, with the spectators not knowing whether to laugh or to weep.

specter
(spĕk´tər) *n.* a ghostly apparition; a phantom.

8 The position of my white neighbor is much more difficult. No brown **specter** pulls up a chair beside me when I sit down to eat. No dark ghost thrusts its leg against mine in bed. The game of keeping what one has is never so exciting as the game of getting.

ANALYZE PERSPECTIVE

Annotate: Mark details in paragraphs 9–10 that reveal the author's overall attitude about her subject.

Summarize: How would you describe Hurston's sense of self in these paragraphs?

9 I do not always feel colored. Even now I often achieve the unconscious Zora of Eatonville before the Hegira.[6] I feel most colored when I am thrown against a sharp white background.

10 For instance at Barnard. "Beside the waters of the Hudson"[7] I feel my race. Among the thousand white persons, I am a dark rock surged upon, overswept by a creamy sea. I am surged upon and overswept, but through it all, I remain myself. When covered by the waters, I am; and the ebb but reveals me again.

narcotic
(när-kŏt´ĭk) *adj.* inducing sleep or stupor.

11 Sometimes it is the other way around. A white person is set down in our midst, but the contrast is just as sharp for me. For instance, when I sit in the drafty basement that is The New World Cabaret with a white person, my color comes. We enter chatting about any little nothing that we have in common and are seated by the jazz waiters. In the abrupt way that jazz orchestras have, this one plunges into a number. It loses no time in circumlocutions, but gets right down to business. It constricts the thorax and splits the heart with its tempo and **narcotic** harmonies. This orchestra grows rambunctious, rears on its hind legs and attacks the tonal veil with primitive fury, rending it, clawing it until it breaks through to the jungle beyond. I follow those heathen—follow them exultingly. I dance wildly inside myself; I yell within, I whoop; I shake my assegai[8] above my head, I hurl it true to the mark *yeeeeooww!* I am in the jungle and living in the jungle way. My face is painted red and yellow, and my body is painted blue. My pulse is throbbing like a war drum. I want to slaughter something—

[6] **Hegira:** journey (from the name given to Muhammad's journey from Mecca to Medina in 622).

[7] **Barnard . . . Hudson:** Barnard is the college in New York City from which Hurston graduated in 1928. "Beside the water . . ." is a reference to the first line of the college song. The college is located near the Hudson River.

[8] **assegai:** a type of light spear used in southern Africa.

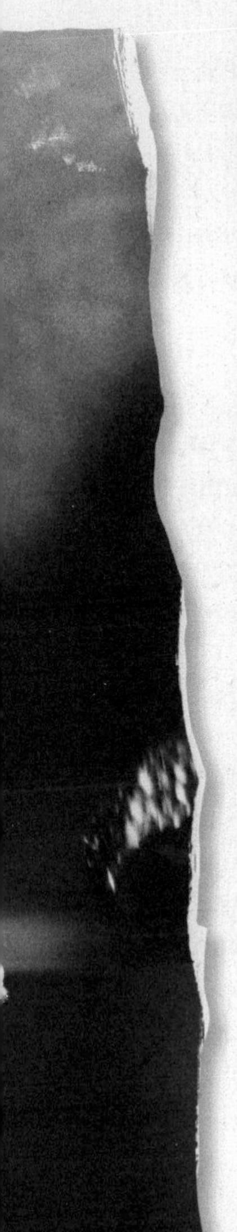

Don't forget to **Notice & Note** as you read the text.

give pain, give death to what, I do not know. But the piece ends. The men of the orchestra wipe their lips and rest their fingers. I creep back slowly to the veneer we call civilization with the last tone and find the white friend sitting motionless in his seat, smoking calmly.

12 "Good music they have here," he remarks, drumming the table with his fingertips.

13 Music! The great blobs of purple and red emotion have not touched him. He has only heard what I felt. He is far away and I see him but dimly across the ocean and the continent that have fallen between us. He is so pale with his whiteness then and I am *so* colored.

14 At certain times I have no race, I am *me*. When I set my hat at a certain angle and saunter down Seventh Avenue, Harlem City, feeling as snooty as the lions in front of the Forty-Second Street Library, for instance. So far as my feelings are concerned, Peggy Hopkins Joyce

ANALYZE DEVELOPMENT OF IDEAS

Annotate: Mark the details in paragraphs 12–13 that suggest a contrast.

Analyze: What difference between Hurston and the white man do these details suggest?

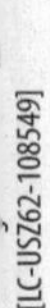
[LC-USZ62-108549]

on the Boule Mich[9] with her gorgeous raiment, stately carriage, knees knocking together in a most aristocratic manner, has nothing on me. The cosmic Zora emerges. I belong to no race nor time, I am the eternal feminine with its string of beads.

15 I have no separate feeling about being an American citizen and colored. I am merely a fragment of the Great Soul that surges within the boundaries. My country, right or wrong.

16 Sometimes, I feel discriminated against, but it does not make me angry. It merely astonishes me. How *can* any deny themselves the pleasure of my company! It's beyond me.

17 But in the main, I feel like a brown bag of **miscellany** propped against a wall. Against a wall in company with other bags, white, red, and yellow. Pour out the contents, and there is discovered a jumble of small things priceless and worthless. A first-water[10] diamond, an empty spool, bits of broken glass, lengths of string, a key to a door long since crumbled away, a rusty knife-blade, old shoes saved for a road that never was and never will be, a nail bent under the weight of things too heavy for any nail, a dried flower or two, still a little fragrant. In your hand is the brown bag. On the ground before you is the jumble it held—so much like the jumble in the bags, could they be emptied, that all might be dumped in a single heap and the bags refilled without altering the content of any greatly. A bit of colored glass more or less would not matter. Perhaps that is how the Great Stuffer of Bags filled them in the first place—who knows?

miscellany
(mĭs´ə-lā-nē) *n.* a collection of various items, parts, or ingredients, especially one composed of diverse literary works.

ANALYZE PERSPECTIVE

Annotate: Mark the simile in paragraph 17 that explains how Hurston feels.

Evaluate: Hurston extends the comparison to conclude the essay. How does she develop her conclusion and what perspective does it express?

[9] **Peggy . . . Boule Mich:** a wealthy woman of Hurston's day, walking along the Boulevard Saint-Michel in Paris.

[10] **first-water:** of the highest quality or purity.

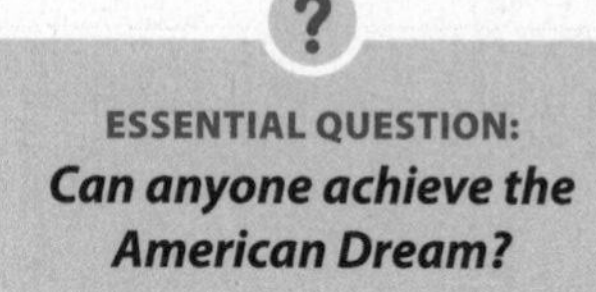
?
ESSENTIAL QUESTION:
Can anyone achieve the American Dream?

Review your notes and add your thoughts to your **Response Log.**

COLLABORATIVE DISCUSSION

With a partner, summarize Hurston's views on race. Discuss whether you think her perspective is similar to that of her peers.

Assessment Practice

Answer these questions before moving on to the **Analyze the Text** section on the following page.

1. When does Hurston first realize she is a colored girl?

(A) when she attends Barnard

(B) when she moves to Jacksonville

(C) when she performs for the Northerners

(D) when she goes to the jazz club in New York

2. What metaphor does Hurston use to convey she does not accept the self-pitying role of a victim?

(A) *My favorite place was atop the gate-post.*

(B) *It is a bully adventure and worth all that I have paid.*

(C) *No, I do not weep at the world—I am too busy sharpening my oyster knife.*

(D) *They liked to hear me "speak pieces" and sing and wanted to see me dance.*

3. What does Hurston think of herself in comparison to Peggy Hopkins Joyce?

(A) She feels bad for herself.

(B) She feels an air of superiority.

(C) She aspires to be more like Joyce.

(D) She thinks that she and Joyce are similar.

Test-Taking Strategies

Analyze the Text

Support your responses with evidence from the text.

NOTICE & NOTE

Review what you **noticed and noted** as you read the text. Your annotations can help you answer these questions.

1. **CITE EVIDENCE** Use the graphic to identify evidence in the text that helps to shape Hurston's perspective on race and race relations. Use that evidence to state what her perspective is on the topic.

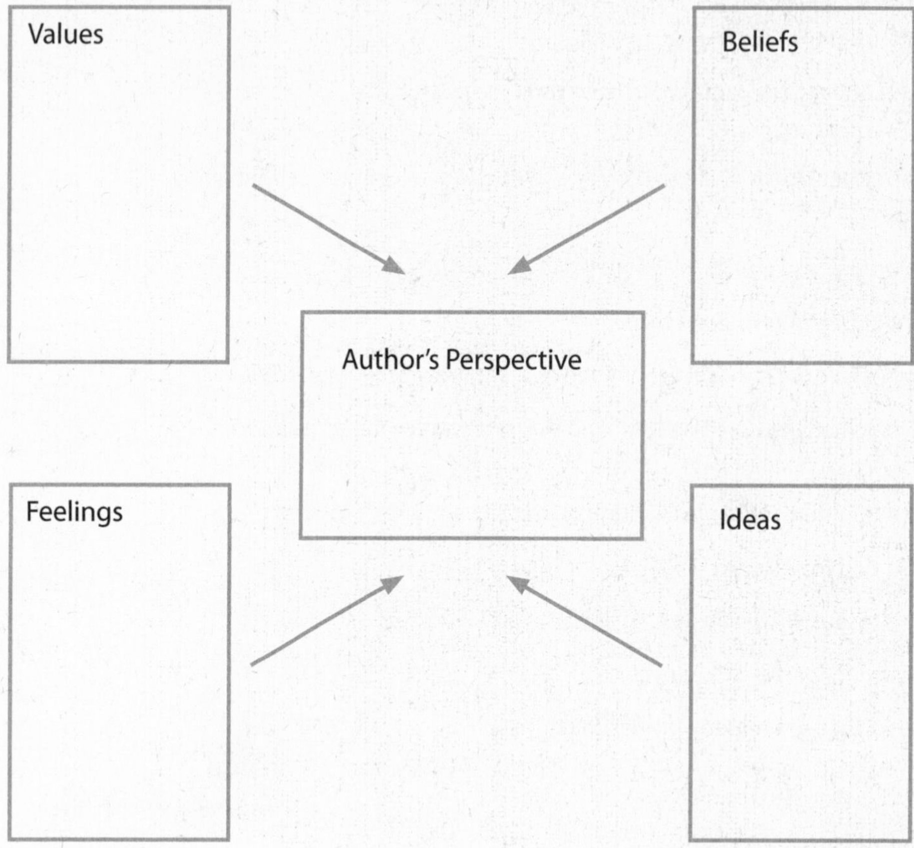

2. **EVALUATE** What is the most important idea Hurston expresses in paragraph 4? What details in the paragraph support this idea?

3. **INFER** What important word does Hurston repeat in paragraph 7? What key idea does this repetition convey?

4. **INFER** Judging from the anecdotes Hurston includes in her essay, what experiences and traits does she consider distinctly African American? Give examples from the text.

5. **INTERPRET** In paragraph 8, the author says, "The position of my white neighbor is much more difficult." What tone is expressed through this description of her circumstances?

6. **INTERPRET** What do the details in paragraph 16 suggest about the author's perspective? Cite text evidence in your response.

7. **DRAW CONCLUSIONS** What is the main idea of the essay? Is it explicitly or implicitly stated? Cite details that support this idea in your response.

Choices

Here are some other ways to demonstrate your understanding of the ideas in this lesson.

Writing

↳ Literary Criticism

The author Alice Walker, a great admirer of Hurston, said she sometimes finds Hurston's views "exasperating." In this essay, Walker believes that Hurston presents negative and stereotypical images of African Americans. Do you agree with Walker's critique? Why or why not? Cite evidence from the text in your response.

As you write and discuss, be sure to use the Academic Vocabulary words.

- contemporary
- global
- infinite
- simulated
- virtual

Media

↳ Vlog

Imagine Zora Neale Hurston finds herself living in the 21st century. She has a significant social media following and posts daily about her life and activities. With a group, recast the essay in the form of a vlog. Discuss the following questions for your vlog.

- What ideas from the essay would she include? What would she leave out?
- What should the scenery look like?
- What sound or visual effects would she use?

Speaking & Listening

↳ Group Discussion

Reread Zora Neale Hurston's comments about jazz music. How do you think she'd feel about more contemporary music like rap and hip hop? In a small group, infer what you think her views would be. Feel free to use specific songs to make your case.

Expand Your Vocabulary

PRACTICE AND APPLY

Fill in the blanks with the vocabulary words. One sentence uses two words.

extenuating	narcotic	exclusive	miscellany	specter

1. The dancer uses a(n) ________________ line of makeup for professional artists.
2. When Isabel recounted her dream of a(n) ________________ haunting the house, her sister said it was caused by the ________________ effects of eating too much pizza.
3. James was excused from class due to the ________________ circumstances that caused him to miss the bus.
4. When Emy's grandpa hoarded a(n) ________________ of junk, she was too shy to ask him to discard it, even though she hated the clutter.

Ed
Interactive Vocabulary Lesson: Synonyms and Antonyms

Vocabulary Strategy

Synonyms and Antonyms

To increase your understanding of a word, you sometimes need to understand its **antonym**, or opposite, or its **synonym**, a word with a similar meaning. It is possible to create synonyms or antonyms by adding or changing prefixes. Changing prefixes changes the meaning of a word. In the selection, the word *exclusive*, which means "with limited access," can be changed to its antonym *inclusive*, which means "to include all," by replacing the prefix *ex-* with *in-* . If you add the prefix *non-* to *narcotic*, the result is its antonym, *non-narcotic*. Consulting a dictionary will help you verify the meaning of words you change.

PRACTICE AND APPLY

For each of the following words, identify a synonym or an antonym by adding or changing a prefix.

Vocabulary Word	Synonym or Antonym
impel	
extenuate	
essential	
extrinsic	

Watch Your Language!

Sentence Variety

You have seen that diction and **syntax** help a writer develop a distinctive tone. In "How It Feels to Be Colored Me," Hurston varies sentence length and structure to create an informal, conversational style that hums with energy. To do so, she combines **simple** and **compound sentences**, as well as fragments. She also uses **parallelism**, similar grammatical structures, to express ideas of similar meaning or importance. Here is an example from the selection.

Interactive Grammar Lesson: Sentence Structure

> **It is exclusively a colored town. The only white people I knew passed through the town going to or coming from Orlando. The native whites rode dusty horses, the Northern tourists chugged down the sandy village road in automobiles. The town knew the Southerners and never stopped cane chewing when they passed. But the Northerners were something else again.**

The first sentence is a short, simple sentence that emphasizes its content. In the sentences that follow, Hurston uses parallel structure by starting each thought with the word *The*. This repetition helps tie together the separate sentences about the different people who passed through and the town's residents. If you look at the syntax, there is a simple sentence with added descriptive phrases, a compound sentence, and another simple sentence with a compound predicate. The final sentence is a short fragment, which grabs the reader's attention by emphasizing the residents' opinion of Northerners. The sentence variety allows the text to flow smoothly and keeps the reader engaged.

PRACTICE AND APPLY

Write a short paragraph about something you used to do when you were younger that you enjoyed tremendously. Use a variety of sentence types to develop a conversational style and unique tone.

from The Warmth of Other Suns

History Writing by **Isabel Wilkerson**

Engage Your Brain

Choose one or more of these activities to start connecting with the text you're about to read.

The Great Migration

For over 50 years, African Americans left the South and headed north and west to seek a better life. How much do you know about that era? Tell whether the following statements are true or false.

1. In 1916, when the Great Migration started, the situation for African Americans had improved substantially since Emancipation and the end of the Civil War.
2. Southern whites had grown used to living on equal footing with African Americans.
3. Segregation was a way of life in the South.
4. Southern whites liked segregation because it was more economical to keep the races separate.
5. In some states, it was illegal for African Americans to spend their leisure time doing things with white people.

As you read, check whether your answers were correct. How many did you get right?

Scavenger Hunt

How good are you at finding information? Use your best sleuthing skills to answer the following questions.

1. How many years did Isabel Wilkerson take to write *The Warmth of Other Suns*?
2. How many interviews did Wilkerson conduct as she was writing the book?
3. Where does the name of the book come from?
4. Which train routes were available to the families who decided to leave, and where did they go?
5. What artistic movement, named after a neighborhood in New York, came out of the Great Migration?

But I Like It Here!

Think about the reasons you like living where you do. What would have to change for you to want to move away? Share your ideas with a partner.

Analyze Development of Ideas

In informational writing, authors usually introduce their main idea at the beginning. They develop the idea in subsequent paragraphs with supporting details, such as facts, quotations, historical evidence, anecdotes, and examples. To determine the main idea of a passage, read it carefully and identify the most important details.

Even in an excerpt from a work, authors convey a main idea. In this excerpt from *The Warmth of Other Suns,* the author mentions a generation in the United States at the turn of the 20th century that was "unlike any other in the South." The details that follow describe the characteristics and circumstances of a generation living fifty years after the end of slavery. Use the chart to identify important ideas and the supporting details.

Important Idea	Supporting Details
A generation came into the world of the early 20th century unlike any other in the South.	

Focus on Genre
History Writing

- discusses significant individuals or events that occurred in the past
- features an organizational structure that supports the writer's purpose
- supports important ideas with carefully selected details
- often includes information from credible primary and secondary sources

Analyze Structure

History writing is a kind of informational text that deals with events in the past. Historical narratives cover a specific time period, event, or person in history. As with many informational texts, authors support their ideas with evidence, examples, and their own commentary.

Authors choose an organizational structure, or structures, that best support their purpose and the development of ideas. In this excerpt, Wilkerson lists examples from historical laws or events and makes an implied comparison between time periods. As you identify the main idea in the excerpt, pay attention to how the structure of the text supports that idea.

Annotation in Action

Here's an example of a student's notes about a main idea and supporting details in this excerpt from *The Warmth of Other Suns*. As you read, notice details that develop the author's ideas.

In the years leading up to and immediately following the turn of the twentieth century, a generation came into the world unlike any other in the South. It was made up of young people with no personal recollection of slavery—they were two generations removed from it.

This may hint at the central idea—something about this new generation. This detail tells me how this generation is different.

Expand Your Vocabulary

Put a check mark next to the vocabulary words that you feel comfortable using when speaking or writing.

- **subservience** ☐
- **sentiment** ☐
- **conceivable** ☐
- **conventional** ☐

Then, use these words to describe an unequal relationship. As you read this excerpt from *The Warmth of Other Suns*, use the definitions in the side column to learn the vocabulary words you don't already know.

Background

"The Great Migration" was the term given to the mass exodus of over 6 million African Americans from the southern states during the period from 1916 to 1970. **Isabel Wilkerson** (b. 1961) was born in Washington, D.C., to parents who had participated in the Great Migration, moving north during the civil rights era. Their journey would later inspire her award-winning historical epic of the Great Migration, *The Warmth of Other Suns.* Wilkerson has spoken and taught at universities across the United States.

B

from The Warmth of Other Suns

History Writing by **Isabel Wilkerson**

NOTICE & NOTE
As you read, use the side margins to make notes about the text.

For African Americans living in the South at the turn of the 20th century, daily life was different than that of their white counterparts.

1 In the years leading up to and immediately following the turn of the twentieth century, a generation came into the world unlike any other in the South. It was made up of young people with no personal recollection of slavery—they were two generations removed from it. The colored members of this generation were free but not free, chafing under Jim Crow and resisting the studied **subservience** of their slave parents and grandparents. They had grown up without the contrived intimacy that once bound the two races. And it appeared that young whites, weaned on a formal kind of supremacy, had grown more hostile to blacks than even their slaveholding ancestors had been.

subservience
(səb-sûr´vē-əns) *n.* the condition of being subordinate in capacity or function.

2 "The **sentiment** is altogether different now," William C. Oates, the old-guard former governor of Alabama, said in 1901 of the newer generation of white southerners. "When the Negro is doing no harm, why, the people want to kill him and wipe him from the face of the earth."

sentiment
(sĕn´tə-mənt) *n.* a thought, view, or attitude, especially one based mainly on emotion instead of reason.

3 The colored people of this generation began looking for a way out. "It is too much to expect that Negroes will indefinitely endure their severe limitations in the South when they can escape most of them in a ride of 36 hours," the Labor Department warned. "Fifty

ANALYZE DEVELOPMENT OF IDEAS

Annotate: Mark the sentence in paragraph 3 that expresses its main idea.

Analyze: What supporting evidence for this idea does the paragraph contain?

years after the Civil War, they should not be expected to be content with the same conditions which existed at the close of the war."

4 Younger blacks could see the contradictions in their world—that, sixty, seventy, eighty years after Abraham Lincoln signed the Emancipation Proclamation, they still had to step off the sidewalk when a white person approached, were banished to jobs nobody else wanted no matter their skill or ambition, couldn't vote, but could be hanged on suspicion of the pettiest infraction.

5 *These were the facts of their lives:*

6 There were days when whites could go to the amusement park and a day when blacks could go, if they were permitted at all. There were white elevators and colored elevators (meaning the freight

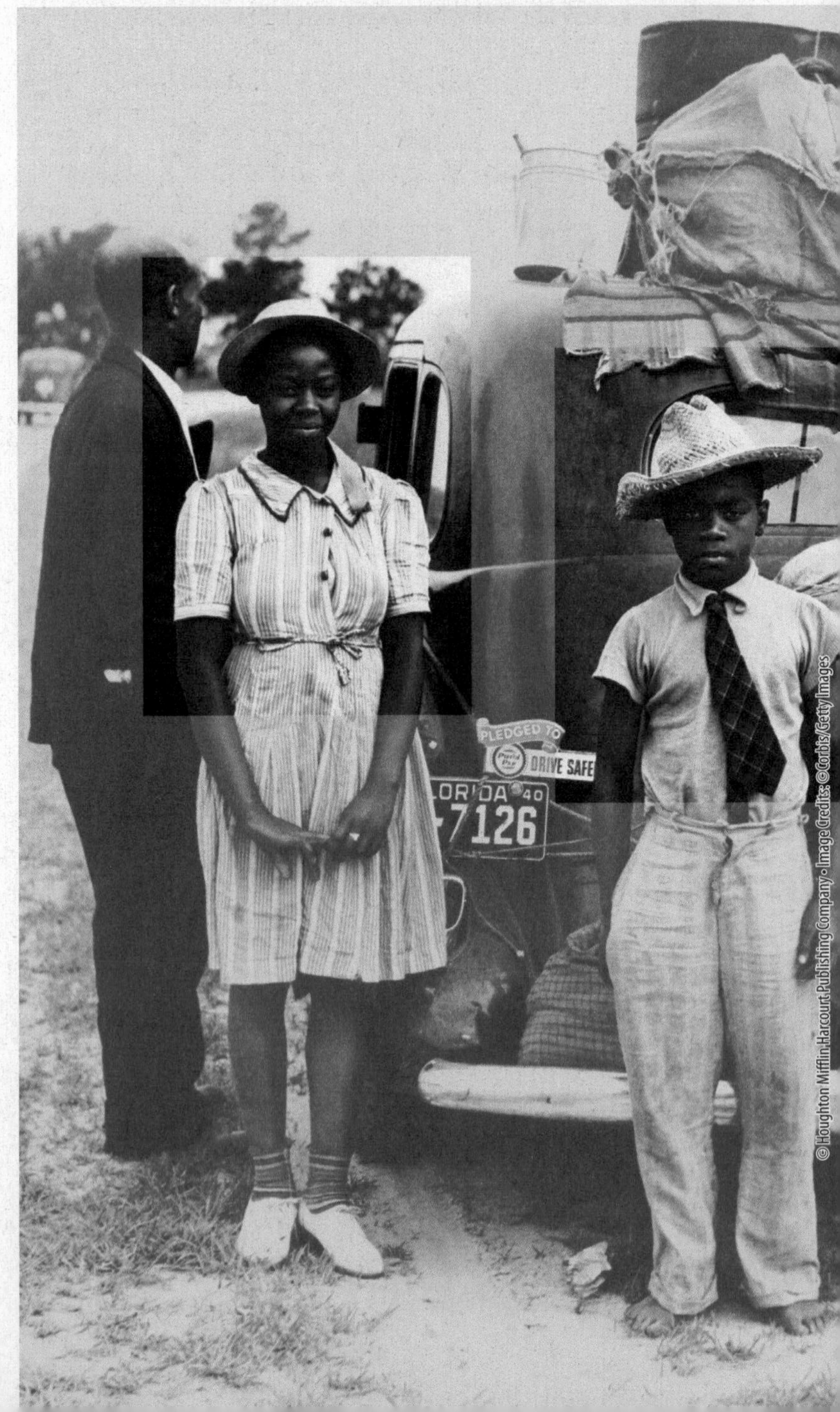

elevators in back); white train platforms and colored train platforms. There were white ambulances and colored ambulances to ferry the sick, and white hearses and colored hearses for those who didn't survive whatever was wrong with them.

7 There were white waiting rooms and colored waiting rooms in any **conceivable** place where a person might have to wait for something, from the bus depot to the doctor's office. A total of four restrooms had to be constructed and maintained at significant expense in any public establishment that bothered to provide any for colored people: one for white men, one for white women, one for colored men, and one for colored women. In 1958, a new bus station went up in Jacksonville, Florida, with two of everything, including

NOTICE & NOTE
QUESTIONING STANCE

When you read informational texts, you should take a **Questioning Stance,** which means that you engage with the information the author provides rather than accept it without thinking.

Notice & Note: Mark any details in paragraphs 4–6 that help you answer this **Big Question**: What challenged, changed, or confirmed what I already knew about the lives of African Americans in the decades after the Civil War?

conceivable
(kən-sēv´ə-bəl) *adj.* formed or developed in the mind.

NOTICE & NOTE

QUOTED WORDS

When you notice the author has quoted the opinions of someone who was a witness to an event, you've found a **Quoted Words** signpost.

Notice & Note: Mark the sentences in paragraph 7 that indicate the author is citing other people.

Infer: How do these quotations support Wilkerson's point? Are they adequate support for the point she's making?

two segregated cocktail lounges, "lest the races brush elbows over a martini," *The Wall Street Journal* reported. The president of Southeastern Greyhound told the *Journal*, "It frequently costs fifty percent more to build a terminal with segregated facilities." But most southern businessmen didn't dare complain about the extra cost. "That question is dynamite," the president of a southern theater chain told the *Journal*. "Don't even say what state I'm in."

8 There was a colored window at the post office in Pensacola, Florida, and there were white and colored telephone booths in Oklahoma. White and colored went to separate windows to get their license plates in Indianola, Mississippi, and to separate tellers to make their deposits at the First National Bank of Atlanta. There were taxicabs for colored people and taxicabs for white people in Jacksonville, Birmingham, Atlanta, and the entire state of Mississippi. Colored people had to be off the streets and out of the city limits by 8 P.M. in Palm Beach and Miami Beach.

conventional (kən-vĕn´shə-nəl) *adj.* based on or in accordance with general agreement, use, or practice; customary.

9 Throughout the South, the **conventional** rules of the road did not apply when a colored motorist was behind the wheel. If he reached an intersection first, he had to let the white motorist go ahead of him. He could not pass a white motorist on the road no matter how slowly the white motorist was going and had to take extreme caution to avoid an accident because he would likely be blamed no matter who was at fault. In everyday interactions, a black person could not contradict a white person or speak unless spoken to first. A black person could not be the first to offer to shake a white person's hand. A handshake could occur only if a white person so gestured, leaving many people having never shaken hands with a person of the other race. The consequences for the slightest misstep were swift and brutal. Two whites beat a black tenant farmer in Louise, Mississippi, in 1948, wrote the historian James C. Cobb, because the man "asked for a receipt after paying his water bill."

ANALYZE STRUCTURE

Notice: In paragraph 10, mark each instance of the words *white* and *colored*.

Analyze: Why does Wilkerson repeat these two contrasting words? What effect does this have on her writing?

10 It was against the law for a colored person and a white person to play checkers together in Birmingham. White and colored gamblers had to place their bets at separate windows and sit in separate aisles at racetracks in Arkansas. At saloons in Atlanta, the bars were segregated: Whites drank on stools at one end of the bar and blacks on stools at the other end, until the city outlawed even that, resulting in white-only and colored-only saloons. There were white parking spaces and colored parking spaces in the town square in Calhoun City, Mississippi. In one North Carolina courthouse, there was a white Bible and a black Bible to swear to tell the truth on.

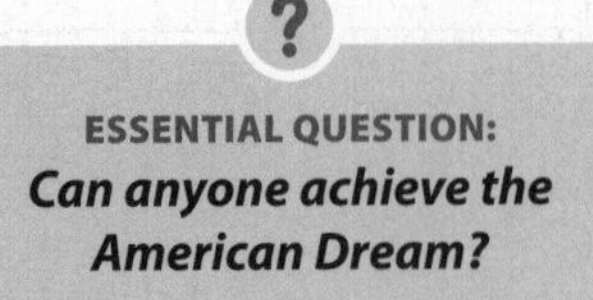
?
ESSENTIAL QUESTION:
Can anyone achieve the American Dream?

Review your notes and add your thoughts to your **Response Log.**

COLLABORATIVE DISCUSSION

Which detail from the text was the most memorable or powerful? Discuss your ideas with a partner.

Assessment Practice

Answer these questions before moving on to the **Analyze the Text** section on the following page.

1. How had the lives of African Americans in the South changed since the signing of the Emancipation Proclamation?

   (A) They were able to vote.

   (B) They saved money in a new bank.

   (C) They used the same waiting rooms as whites.

   (D) They were no longer held as slaves.

2. An African American could visit an amusement park

   (A) only on even days of the week

   (B) only on odd days of the week

   (C) on days reserved for African Americans only

   (D) on days reserved for whites

3. According to the author, what would happen if an African American motorist and a white motorist got into a car accident in the South?

   (A) The African American had to accept the blame for the accident.

   (B) The new laws protected anyone who got into an accident.

   (C) The motorists reported the accident to different police officers.

   (D) The African American could only drive on certain roads.

Test-Taking Strategies

Analyze the Text

Support your responses with evidence from the text.

Review what you **noticed and noted** as you read the text. Your annotations can help you answer these questions.

1. **CRITIQUE** In paragraph 1, Wilkerson states that "young whites . . . had grown more hostile to blacks than even their slaveholding ancestors had been." Using examples from the text, explain whether Wilkerson supports this idea adequately or not.

2. **ANALYZE** Is the comparison-and-contrast organizational structure an appropriate choice for Wilkerson to use? How does this structure support the development of her main idea? Use the graphic to help answer the question.

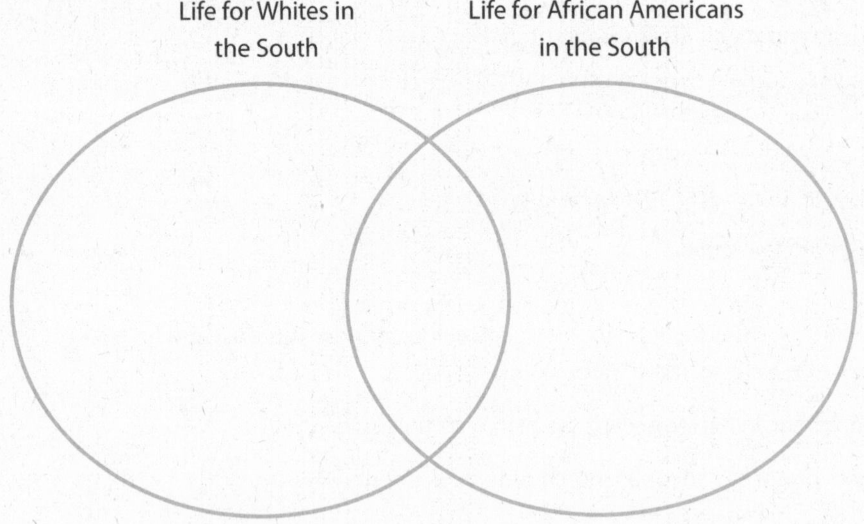

3. **EVALUATE** In paragraph 5, Wilkerson states clearly: "These were the facts of their lives." How do the remaining paragraphs (6–10) of the excerpt elaborate on this statement and contribute to the overall structure?

4. **INFER** In paragraph 7, the author states that although building segregated facilities was more expensive, "southern businessmen didn't dare complain about the extra cost." How does the author's use of this detail amplify the claim of segregation, no matter the cost?

5. **ANALYZE** How do the author's choices about structure affect the message she wants to impart? How would her message change if she used a different organizational structure?

6. **EVALUATE** How does Wilkerson's use of **Quoted Words** affect your perception of her main idea—that after two generations of freedom, younger African Americans could see contradictions in their world?

Choices

Here are some other ways to demonstrate your understanding of the ideas in this lesson.

Writing

↳ Blog Entries

You're researching the Great Migration and blogging about what you learn. Follow these steps to start writing:

1. Pick a catchy headline. It should draw readers in and give them a taste of what to expect.
2. Pick an aspect of the Great Migration that interests you. Then anticipate a question your audience might have, and plan to answer it. Get organized by creating an outline.
3. Draft your post. Hook your readers with an enticing introduction. Keep the text manageable by breaking it into sections with subheads. Write paragraphs that are similar in length and don't vary your style from paragraph to paragraph. Closing with a good conclusion leaves readers wanting to know more.
4. Add images. Your readers are more likely to keep reading if you have good visual elements.
5. Read your post out loud, then revise it to make your language smooth and clear. Check your spelling and grammar.
6. Post your final version.

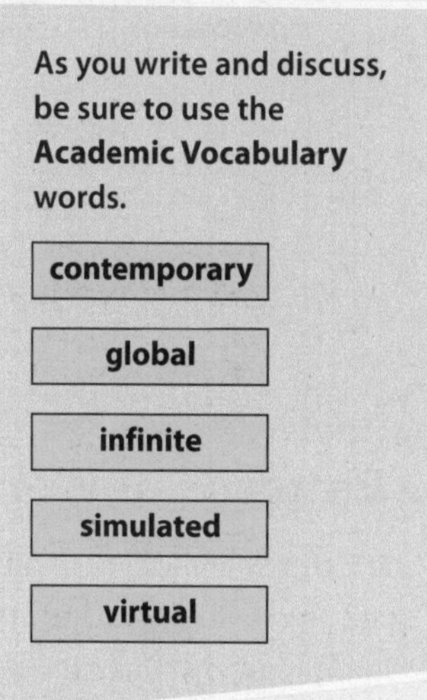
As you write and discuss, be sure to use the **Academic Vocabulary** words.
contemporary
global
infinite
simulated
virtual

Media

↳ Sketchnote

Sometimes it's easier to process information visually. Create a sketchnote of this excerpt from *The Warmth of Other Suns*. Mix and match words and visuals to summarize main ideas and supporting details for each paragraph.

Research

↳ Infographic

Research the answers to these questions and present your findings to the class in the form of an infographic.

- Why did so many African Americans move from southern to northern states during this time?
- How did this mass migration affect American culture?
- Did the lives of the people who migrated improve substantially?

Expand Your Vocabulary

PRACTICE AND APPLY

With a partner, discuss and write an answer to each of the following questions. Then, work together to write a sentence for each vocabulary word.

subservience	conventional	sentiment	conceivable

1. What word relates to inequality?
2. What word relates to customary practices?
3. What two words are related to mental and emotional thinking?

Interactive Vocabulary Lesson: Analyzing Word Structure

Vocabulary Strategy

↳ Patterns of Word Change

When affixes are added to a root word, certain **patterns of word change** emerge. For example, adding affixes to the Latin root *greg*, meaning "group" or "herd," creates a word family by connecting different affixes to the same root. Adding the prefix *se-*, meaning "apart," and the suffix *-ate*, meaning "state or quality of," to the root creates the word *segregate*, meaning "to isolate or separate from the group." However, adding the prefix *a-* (a variant of *ad-*), meaning "toward," creates the word *aggregate*, meaning "to bring together."

Learning the meanings of prefixes and suffixes will help you trace the patterns of words. Identifying common prefixes and suffixes helps you determine changes in word meanings.

PRACTICE AND APPLY

Use a word web like the one below to determine the root of each vocabulary word, and identify the affixes (prefix or suffix or both). Cite at least two more words that share the same root. Check your work in a dictionary or with an online reference tool.

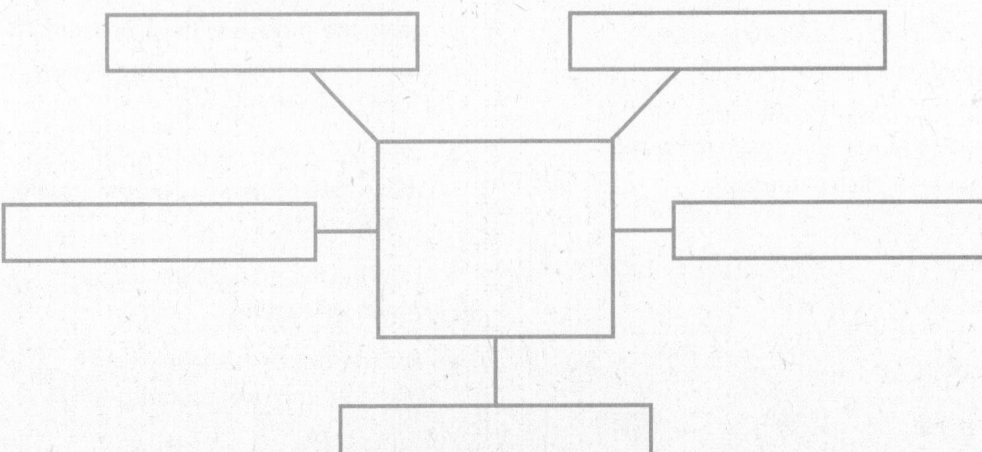

Watch Your Language!

Spelling

It is important to spell all words correctly when you communicate your ideas in writing. Learning basic spelling rules and checking your spelling in a dictionary will help you spell words that you may not use frequently.

Some spelling rules are for words ending in a consonant or for forming plural nouns.

Spelling Rule: In words of more than one syllable, double the final consonant when (1) the word ends with one consonant preceded by one vowel and (2) the word is accented on the last syllable.

Interactive Grammar Lesson: Spelling

Example: be-gin′ + ing = be-gin′ning

Spelling Rule: When a singular noun ends in *y* with a consonant before it, change the *y* to *i* and add *-es*.

Example: army = armies

Being familiar with the basic rules of spelling will help you learn to spell unknown words. Remember that the best way to check your spelling is by using a print or online dictionary.

PRACTICE AND APPLY

Draft a paragraph in which you express your opinion on the excerpt from *The Warmth of Other Suns*. Use as many of the vocabulary words as possible. Check your paragraph for spelling, and use a dictionary to look up the spelling of any words you are unsure of. Then, exchange your paragraph with a partner. Edit each other's paragraphs, correcting any spelling errors.

Compare Ideas Across Genres

In "How It Feels to Be Colored Me," Hurston presents her unique perspective on facing the social and racial restrictions imposed on African Americans in the 1920s. In the excerpt from *The Warmth of Other Suns*, contemporary journalist Wilkerson details the circumstances African Americans faced that led to the Great Migration.

Autobiographical essays and history writing are types of informational texts that use different elements of style and present information to the audience in a distinct way. However, both texts contain similarities as well. For example, both types of writing use first-hand accounts as evidence to support their main idea.

In a small group, complete the Venn diagram with similarities and differences.

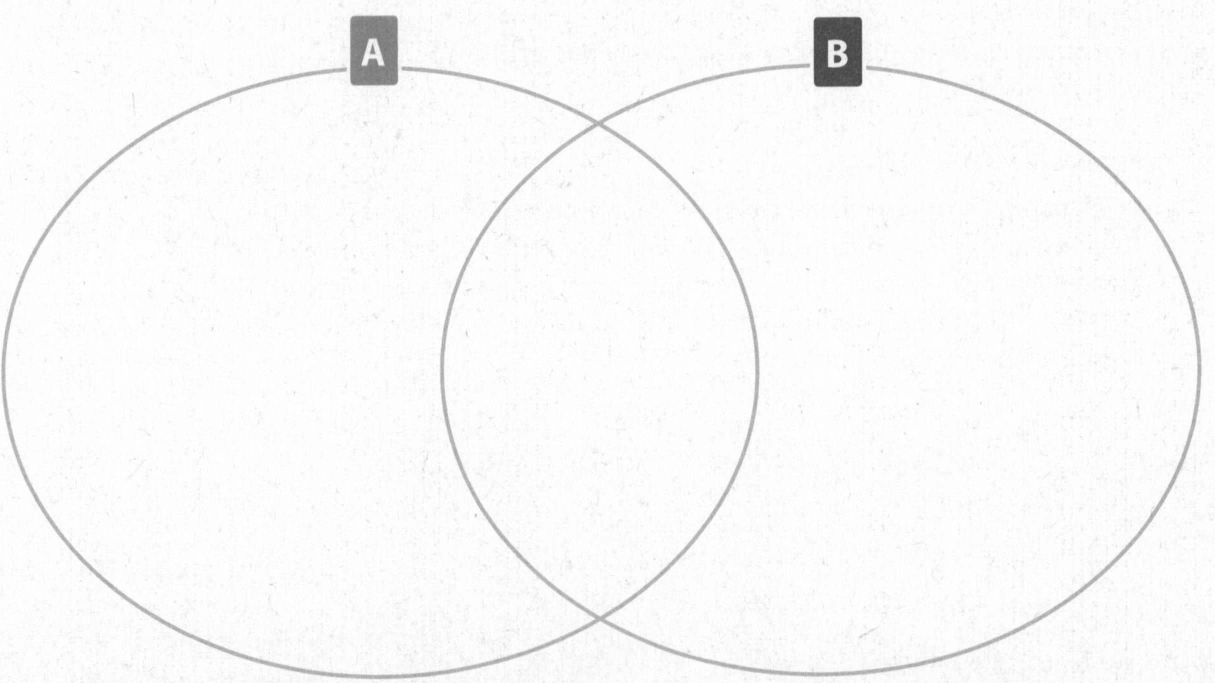

"How It Feels to Be Colored Me" **BOTH** from *The Warmth of Other Suns*

Analyze the Texts

Discuss these questions in your group.

1. **COMPARE** What are the differences between Wilkerson's and Hurston's descriptions of life in the South for African Americans? What ideas are emphasized in each text?

2. **EVALUATE** Which of these texts would be more effective at convincing people that the treatment of African Americans during this time period was unacceptable? Explain your answer.

3. **ANALYZE** How do the Hurston essay and the excerpt from *The Warmth of Other Suns* address the difficulties of life for African Americans?

4. **CONTRAST** Contrast the experience of the man who asked for the receipt in paragraph 9 from *The Warmth of Other Suns* to Hurston's experience with town passersby in paragraphs 2–3 of "How It Feels to Be Colored Me." How do these passages relate to the message of each text?

Collaborate and Debate

Your group can continue exploring the ideas in these texts by debating the effectiveness of the message each author presents. Follow these steps:

1. **REVIEW THE TEXTS** Reread "How It Feels to Be Colored Me" and the excerpt from *The Warmth of Other Suns*. Use the chart to record and synthesize the key information from each text. Determine the author's purpose, then summarize the main idea and list key supporting details.

Selection	Author's Purpose	Main Idea	Key Details
from *The Warmth of Other Suns*			
"How It Feels to Be Colored Me"			

2. **EVALUATE THE IDEAS** Determine which author had the better message and why by asking the following questions:

- Did the organizational structure make it clear?
- Were the key ideas easy to identify?
- Did the details support the message?
- How effective was the language?

3. **PRESENT A DEBATE** Decide which author your group members will defend. As you present your opinions, use evidence and examples from the text to support your argument. Listen to the arguments from the other side. Think of evidence that will help you respectfully rebut the claims the other side makes.

Reader's Choice

Continue your exploration of the Essential Questions for this unit by doing some independent reading. Read the titles and descriptions shown. Then, mark the texts that interest you.

ESSENTIAL QUESTION:
Review the four Essential Questions for this unit on page 641.

Short Reads

Available on 

These texts are available in your ebook. Choose one to read and rate. Then defend your rating to the class.

Poems of the Harlem Renaissance

Poems by **Langston Hughes, Jean Toomer, Countee Cullen, and Arna Bontemps**

What concerned the writers of the Harlem Renaissance? Read poems by four of its prominent members.

Rate It 

Martin Luther King Jr.: He Showed Us the Way

Essay by **César Chávez**

Find out why César Chávez believes that King's form of protest is the only way to achieve meaningful change.

Rate It 

Ten Kliks South

Short Story by **Phil Klay**

Follow a young Lance Corporal in the Marines as he sees action for the first time in Iraq.

Rate It

Poetry

Poem by **Marianne Moore**

Can you define poetry? Read along as one poet tries to put into words just what poetry is.

Rate It

YouTube Stars Stress Out, Just Like the Rest of Us

Article by **Neda Ulaby**

Discover why life as a YouTube celebrity is not all it's cracked up to be.

Rate It

Long Reads

Here are a few recommended books that connect to this unit. For additional options, ask your teacher, school librarian, or peers. Which titles spark your interest?

One Hundred Years of Solitude

Novel by **Gabriel García Márquez**

The isolated, mythical town of Macondo is founded by the Buendía family. It rises and falls over the course of 100 years.

They Called Us Enemy

Graphic Memoir by **George Takei**

How does a young boy emerge from the Japanese internment camps and go on to be a world-famous actor?

The Things They Carried

Fiction by **Tim O'Brien**

Danger, love, grief, and brotherhood are just some of the things these soldiers shipped to Vietnam during the war experience.

Extension

↳ Connect & Create

PERCHANCE TO DREAM In 1931, James Truslow Adams coined the term "the American Dream." He defined it as: "that dream of a land in which life should be better and richer and fuller for everyone, with opportunity for each according to ability or achievement." How does this definition apply to the text you chose? Discuss your ideas with others who read the same text you did or create an online poll to see what your classmates think.

ADVICE TO THE DISCONNECTED The opening quote for this unit states that everything is connected. Is this true for the text that you read? Are the characters in the text connected to their families and communities or are they somehow isolated? Or conversely, are the characters too connected, such that they've lost their personal identity? Have one character write an advice column on what it means to be connected in the modern world.

NOTICE & NOTE

- Pick one of the texts and annotate the **Notice & Note** signposts you find.
- Then use the **Notice & Note Writing Frames** to help you write about the significance of the signposts.
- Compare your findings with those of other students who read the same text.

Notice & Note Writing Frames

Write a Personal Narrative

Writing Prompt

Write a personal narrative for your school anthology. Describe an experience that shaped your identity.

Manage your time carefully so that you can

- reflect on a meaningful experience in your life;
- plan your personal narrative;
- write a draft of your narrative;
- revise and edit your work.

Be sure to

- develop a clear sequence of events;
- use descriptive details and sensory language; and
- reflect on how the event shaped your identity.

Review the Mentor Text

For an example of a well-written personal essay that you can use as an inspiration for your narrative, review

- **"How It Feels to Be Colored Me"** (pages 890–895)

Review your notes and annotations and think about the techniques the author uses to bring her story to life.

Consider Your Sources

Review the list of texts in the unit and consider which ones might provide ideas and inspiration for your personal narrative.

As you review selections, consult the notes you made in your **Response Log** and make additional notes about ideas that might be useful as you write your personal narrative. In particular, consider how the writers used language, included descriptive details, and employed other narrative techniques.

UNIT 6 SOURCES

- ☐ **A Rose for Emily**
- ☐ **Mending Wall**
- ☐ *from* **They Called Us Enemy**
- ☐ **The Crucible**
- ☐ **Audio and Production Images** *from* **The Crucible** MEDIA
- ☐ **My Dungeon Shook**
- ☐ **The Latin Deli: An Ars Poetica**
- ☐ **Speech on the Vietnam War, 1967**
- ☐ **Ambush**
- ☐ **The Universe as Primal Scream**
- ☐ **First Verse**
- ☐ **How It Feels to Be Colored Me**
- ☐ *from* **The Warmth of Other Suns**

Analyze the Prompt

Review the prompt to make sure you understand the assignment.

1. Mark the sentence in the prompt that identifies the topic of your personal narrative. Rephrase the sentence in your own words.
2. Then, look for words that indicate the purpose and audience of your narrative. Write a sentence describing each.

What is my topic? What is my writing task?

What is my purpose?

Who is my audience?

Consider Your Audience

As you respond, ask yourself:

- Who will read my personal narrative?
- What common experience do my readers and I share?
- What information will my readers need to understand my experience?

Review the Rubric

Your personal narrative will be scored using a rubric. As you write, focus on the characteristics of a high-scoring essay as described in the chart. You will learn more about these characteristics as you work through the lesson.

Purpose, Focus, and Organization	Evidence and Elaboration	Conventions of Standard English
The response includes: • An engaging introduction • A well-developed plot structure • Use of transitions to convey sequence and connect ideas • Logical sequence of events • A conclusion that follows from the narrated events	The response includes: • Use of descriptive details • Effective use of narrative techniques • Use of sensory language	The response may include: • Some minor errors in usage but no patterns of errors • Correct punctuation, capitalization, sentence formation, and spelling • Command of basic conventions

1 PLAN YOUR PERSONAL NARRATIVE

Choose a Significant Experience

Recall significant events in your life. Ask yourself:

- What made these events meaningful?
- How did the events shape who I am?

Complete the chart with details about one experience you want to write about.

Personal experience:
Significance of the experience:
How the experience shaped my identity:

Establish Your Point of View

In a personal narrative, you are the narrator.

- Write in the first-person point of view, using the pronouns *I, me,* and *my*.
- Develop an attitude, or tone, that will reflect your unique personality.

Identify Narrative Elements

A personal narrative tells a story.

- Set the scene. Where and when did the incident happen?
- Introduce the characters. Who was there besides you?
- Develop the conflict. What problem did you face?

Use the chart to recall elements from your life event.

Help with Planning

Consult **Interactive Writing Lesson: Writing Narratives**

Context or Setting:
Characters:
Conflict or Problem:

Use Logical Order

Most personal narratives are written in **chronological order**. Use this chart to recall events and list them in the order they occurred.

First: ↓
Then: ↓
Next: ↓
After that: ↓
Finally:

Flashbacks and Foreshadowing

Two alternatives to chronological order are flashbacks and foreshadowing.

- Start with a key moment and tell the events leading to it as a **flashback**.
- Withhold information, but offer clues as **foreshadowing**. Then, reveal the important information at a crucial moment in the story.

Organize Ideas

Now organize your personal narrative in a way that will clarify relationships between events. Use the chart to organize your ideas and create coherence.

INTRODUCTION	• Begin with interesting dialogue or a surprising detail to grab your reader's attention. • Introduce your setting, conflict, and characters to establish the context.
BODY PARAGRAPHS	• Tell what happened. • Include sensory details and vivid description to bring the incident to life. • Use realistic dialogue to reveal your characters' personalities.
TRANSITIONS	• Use transitions to create coherence between your ideas. • Develop a clear progression of events using transitional words and phrases.
CONCLUSION	• End your personal narrative by resolving the conflict and reflecting on how the incident changed you. • Tell how the experience shaped your identity.

2 DEVELOP A DRAFT

Now it is time to draft your narrative. Examine how professional writers craft their narratives. You can use similar techniques to develop your own writing skills.

Use Descriptive Details

How It Feels to Be Colored Me

EXAMINE THE MENTOR TEXT

Notice how the author of "How It Feels to Be Colored Me" uses vivid description, figurative language, and dialogue to help the reader visualize scenes.

This orchestra grows rambunctious, rears on its hind legs and attacks the tonal veil with primitive fury, rending it, clawing it until it breaks through to the jungle beyond. I follow those heathen—follow then exultingly. I dance wildly inside myself; I yell within, I whoop . . . *yeeeooww!* . . . My pulse is throbbing like a war drum. . . . But the piece ends. The men of the orchestra wipe their lips and rest their fingers. I creep back slowly to the veneer we call civilization with the last tone and find the white friend sitting motionless in his seat, smoking calmly.

"Good music they have here," he remarks, drumming the table with his fingertips.

The author uses **figurative language** to describe music and the emotions it invokes.

The author uses **vivid description** to provide contrast.

She uses **dialogue** to convey character.

APPLY TO YOUR DRAFT

Use this frame to practice using descriptive details for your draft. Recall specific details about one event.

Sensory Details What did you see, hear, smell, or taste? What physical sensations did you experience?	
Dialogue What did people say? What did their words reveal about their personalities or motivations?	
Figurative Language What did people or events remind you of?	

Develop Your Style and Voice

EXAMINE THE MENTOR TEXT

An author's writing style is expressed through word choice and sentence construction. Notice how Hurston uses syntax and style to establish a unique perspective and tone.

Drafting Online

Check your assignment list for a writing task from your teacher.

> The front porch might seem a daring place for the rest of the town, but it was a gallery seat to me. My favorite place was atop the gate-post. Proscenium box for a born first-nighter. Not only did I enjoy the show, but I didn't mind the actors knowing that I liked it. I actually spoke to them in passing. I'd wave at them and when they returned my salute, I would say something like this: "Howdy-do-well-I-thank-you-where-you-goin'?" . . .
>
> Sometimes, I feel discriminated against, but it does not make me angry. It merely astonishes me. How *can* any deny themselves the pleasure of my company! It's beyond me.

The author uses a fragment to create a **casual voice** and a **lively tone**.

The **light, informal tone** contrasts with the seriousness of discrimination.

APPLY TO YOUR DRAFT

Let your personality shine through your writing as you draft your personal narrative. Also, look for ways to establish your unique style.

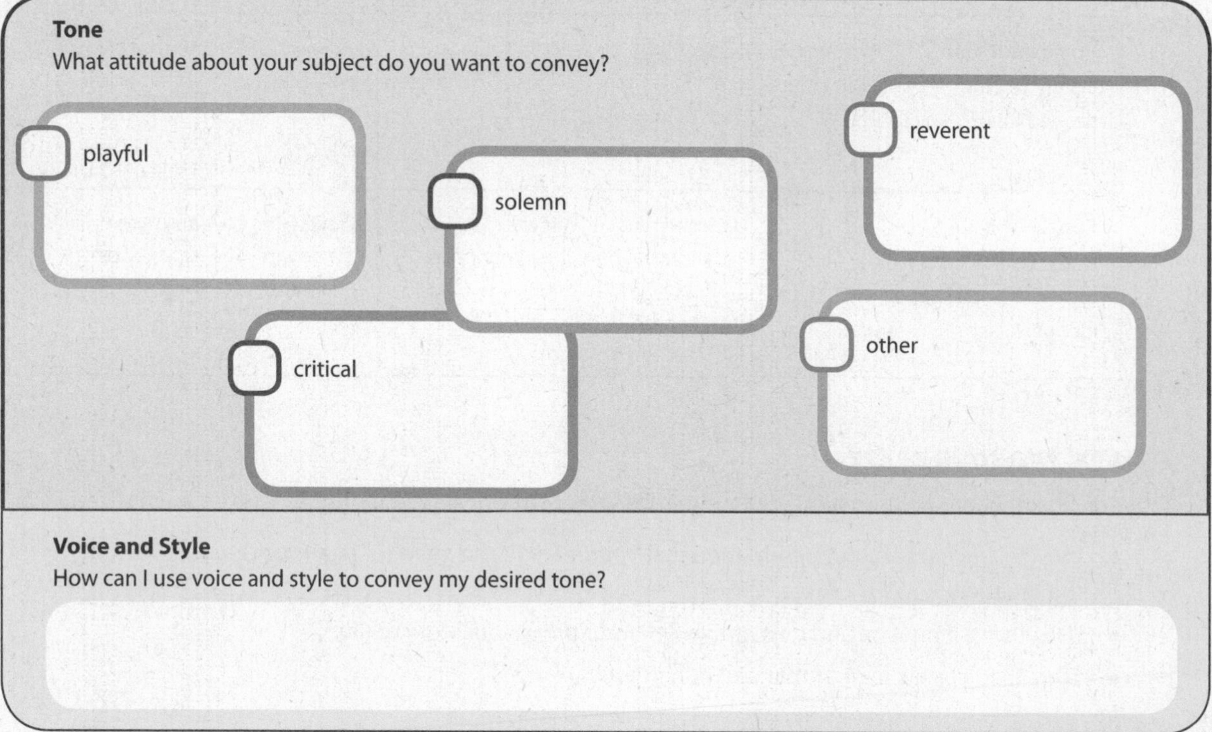

Tone
What attitude about your subject do you want to convey?
playful
solemn
reverent
critical
other
Voice and Style
How can I use voice and style to convey my desired tone?

3 REVISE YOUR PERSONAL NARRATIVE

Experienced writers know the importance of revision. Review your narrative and consider how it can be improved. Use the guide to help you revise your personal narrative.

Help with Revision

Find a **Peer Review Guide** and **Student Models** online.

REVISION GUIDE		
Ask Yourself	**Prove It**	**Revise It**
Introduction Does my introduction engage the reader and provide context?	**Underline** the sentence that grabs the audience's attention.	**Add** details to hook your reader.
Organization Are events organized logically?	**Highlight** each event in the narrative.	**Reorder** events if needed to clarify order.
Transitions Have I used transitions to connect events?	**Circle** transitions that connect events.	**Add** transitions to clarify event sequence.
Descriptive Details Do my details vividly show what's happening in my story?	**Underline** sensory details. **Circle** dialogue.	**Add** images, sounds, smells, tastes, or texture. **Add** dialogue.
Voice and Style Do my voice and style reflect my desired tone?	**Highlight** sentences that reveal your attitude.	**Rework** sentences that are not consistent with your desired tone.
Conclusion Does my conclusion show how the experience shaped my identity?	**Circle** parts of your conclusion that reveal how the experience affected you.	**Revise** the conclusion to reflect on how the life experience shaped who you are.

APPLY TO YOUR DRAFT

Consider the following as you look for opportunities to improve your writing:

- Provide any background information that your readers will need to understand the situation.
- Use precise language and descriptive details to bring your story to life.
- Correct any errors in grammar and punctuation.

Peer Review in Action

Once you have finished revising your personal narrative, you will exchange papers with a partner in a **peer review.** During a peer review, you will give suggestions to improve your partner's draft.

Read the introduction from a student's draft and examine the comments made by his peer reviewer.

First Draft

"A Life-saving Letter"
By Nadege Agwé, Leeward High School

On the last day of school last year, a guy gave me a letter. Then he just ran away. I unfolded the letter and read, "Thank you for saving my life." I was confused. What did I do to save his life? I couldn't remember anything. But that letter did something strange. It changed me.

This quote would make a great hook at the very beginning.

Rather than telling what the boy did and how you reacted, use precise details to "show" it.

Now read the revised introduction. Notice how the writer has improved his draft by revising based on his peer reviewer's comments.

Revision

"A Life-saving Letter"
By Nadege Agwé, Leeward High School

"Thank you for saving my life" was all the letter said. Just moments before, a timid kid from my Chemistry class had pushed the letter into my hand and scurried off. Over the next few days, I scoured my brain, searching desperately for some memory, some worthy act, some kind words, that might have been meaningful to him. Nothing came to mind. Still, that letter did something extraordinary—It saved *my* life.

Good job! Now I can really picture this kid and feel your confusion.

Great! Your introduction grabs the reader's interest from the first sentence.

Nice! I like the word *saved.* It's a nice connection back to the letter.

APPLY TO YOUR DRAFT

During your peer review, give each other specific suggestions for how to make your narratives more effective. Use your revision guide to help you.

When receiving feedback from your partner, listen attentively and ask questions to make sure you fully understand the revision suggestions.

4 EDIT YOUR PERSONAL NARRATIVE

Edit your final draft for proper use of standard English conventions and to correct any misspellings or grammatical errors.

Watch Your Language!

SENSORY LANGUAGE

Sensory language enlivens your writing with images of sight, sound, smell, taste, and texture. Zora Neale Hurston, as part of the Harlem Renaissance, was particularly conscious of the power of language to create an impact on her reader.

Read the following sentences from "How It Feels to Be Colored Me."

> I am a **dark** rock surged upon, overswept by a **creamy** sea.
> The **great blobs of purple and red emotion** have not touched him.
> The men of the orchestra **wipe their lips** and **rest their fingers**.

Authors use sensory language to heighten the effects of their descriptions and to create strong imagery. The way that authors use imagery may become a hallmark of their writing technique.

APPLY TO YOUR DRAFT

Now apply what you have learned about sensory language to your own work.

1. Read your paper aloud. Listen to your descriptions of setting and characters.
2. Add sensory language to help describe sights, sounds, tastes, smells, or physical sensations.
3. Consider using onomatopoeia or synesthesia to establish your voice and style.

Use Sensory Language

Sensory language may include **onomatopoeia** and **synesthesia**.

- Onomatopoeia is the use of words that mimic the sound they describe, such as *buzz*, *hiss*, or *whirr*.
- Synesthesia is the use of one sense to evoke another, such as "I feel most colored when I am *thrown against a sharp white background*."

Using these literary devices can add interest to your writing.

5 PUBLISH YOUR PERSONAL NARRATIVE

Share It!

Finalize your personal narrative for your school writing anthology. You may also use your narrative as inspiration for other projects.

Ways to Share

- **Give a class presentation** during which you read (or act out) your narrative.
- **Write a blog post** on a class or school website.
- **Create a media version** of your narrative. Consider a documentary, a visual timeline, or even a song.

Reflect & Extend

Here are some other ways to show your understanding of the ideas in Unit 6.

Reflect on the **Essential Questions**

Think about the Essential Question you identified as most intriguing on page 642. Has your answer to the question changed after reading the texts in the unit? Discuss your ideas.

You can use these sentence starters to help you reflect on your learning:

- **The text that influenced my thinking about . . . is . . .**
- **I think differently now because . . .**
- **One question I still have is . . .**

Project-Based Learning

↳ Create a Song

With a group of classmates, create a song that addresses a problem faced by a person or a group of people during this period.

Here are some questions to get you started:

- What familiar songs can you use as models? What stories do they tell?
- What melody or beat will invoke emotions representative of the problem you are writing about?
- Which significant words or phrases from the unit can you use in your verses, chorus, or refrain?
- Will you perform the song live or record it to share with your classmates?

Media Projects

To find help with this task online, access **Create a Song.**

Writing

↳ Write an Argument

Many of the texts in this unit are about people who may not have opportunities to act or speak out on their own behalf. Write an argument in support of a group of people who are persecuted or marginalized in society today. In your argument be sure to include

- a clear claim
- reasons and evidence that support your claim
- an action that you'd like your readers to take

Resources

HMH *Into Literature* Resources

For more instruction and practice, access the *Into Literature* Resources and Interactive Lessons.

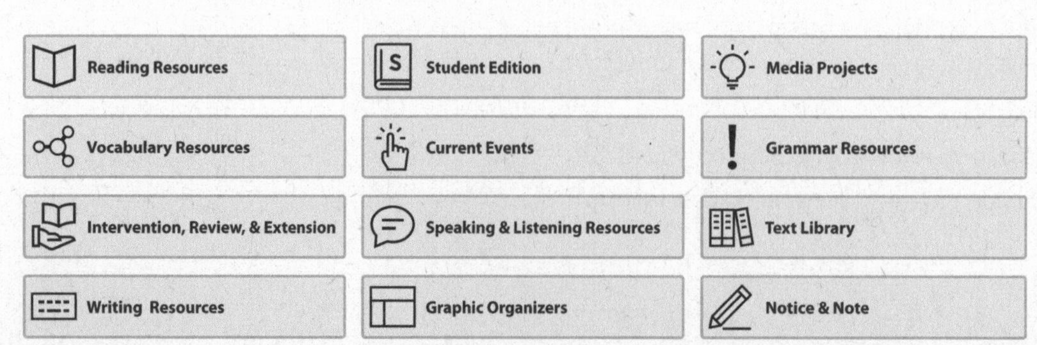

UNIT 1

Response Log

Use this Response Log to record information from the texts that relates to or comments on the **Essential Questions** in Unit 1.

? Essential Question	Details from Texts
What connects people to certain places?	
What values and beliefs shape who we are?	
What does it mean to be a stranger in a strange land?	
What happens when cultures collide?	

UNIT 2

Response Log

Use this Response Log to record information from the texts that relates to or comments on the **Essential Questions** in Unit 2.

? Essential Question	Details from Texts
What does oppression look like?	
How do we gain our freedom?	
How can we share power and build alliances?	
How do we reach our goals?	

UNIT 3

Response Log

Use this Response Log to record information from the texts that relates to or comments on the **Essential Questions** in Unit 3.

? Essential Question	Details from Texts
How can we be true to ourselves?	
How do we relate to the world around us?	
What do we secretly fear?	
When should we stop and reflect on our lives?	

UNIT 4

Response Log

Use this Response Log to record information from the texts that relates to or comments on the **Essential Questions** in Unit 4.

? Essential Question	Details from Texts
When is self-determination possible?	
What causes divisions between people?	
How do we respond to defeat?	
What is the price of progress?	

UNIT 5

Response Log

Use this Response Log to record information from the texts that relates to or comments on the **Essential Questions** in Unit 5.

? Essential Question	Details from Texts
How much do we control our lives?	
Why do humans cause harm?	
What are the consequences of change?	
What makes a place unique?	

UNIT 6

Response Log

Use this Response Log to record information from the texts that relates to or comments on the **Essential Questions** in Unit 6.

? Essential Question	Details from Texts
How do we deal with rejection or isolation?	
Can anyone achieve the American Dream?	
When should personal integrity come before civic duty?	
What would we do if there were no limits?	

Using a Glossary

A glossary is an alphabetical list of vocabulary words. Use a glossary just as you would a dictionary—to determine the meanings, parts of speech, pronunciation, and syllabification of words. (Some technical, foreign, and more obscure words in this book are defined for you in the footnotes that accompany many of the selections.)

Many words in the English language have more than one meaning. This glossary gives the meanings that apply to the words as they are used in the selections in this book.

The following abbreviations are used to identify parts of speech of words:

adj. adjective *adv.* adverb *n.* noun *v.* verb

Each word's pronunciation is given in parentheses. A guide to the pronunciation symbols appears in the Pronunciation Key below. The stress marks in the Pronunciation Key are used to indicate the force given to each syllable in a word. They can also help you determine where words are divided into syllables.

For more information about the words in this glossary or for information about words not listed here, consult a dictionary.

Pronunciation Key

Symbol	Examples
ă	**pat**
ā	**pay**
ä	**father, hard**
âr	**care**
b	**bib**
ch	**church**
d	**deed, milled**
ĕ	**pet**
ē	**bee**
f	**fife, phase, rough**
g	**gag**
h	**hat**
hw	**which**
ĭ	**pit**
ī	**pie, by**
îr	**pier**
j	**judge**
k	**kick, cat, pique**
l	**lid, needle*** (nēd′l)

Symbol	Examples
m	**mum**
n	**no, sudden*** (sŭd′n)
ng	**thing**
ŏ	**pot**
ō	**toe**
ô	**caught, paw**
oi	**noise**
o͝o	**took**
o͞o	**boot**
o͝or	**lure**
ôr	**core**
ou	**out**
p	**pop**
r	**roar**
s	**sauce**
sh	**ship, dish**
t	**tight, stopped**
th	**thin**
th	**this**
ŭ	**cut**

Symbol	Examples
ûr	**urge, term, firm, word, heard**
v	**valve**
w	**with**
y	**yes**
z	**zebra, xylem**
zh	**vision, pleasure, garage**
ə	**about, item, edible, gallop, circus**
ər	**butter**

Sounds in Foreign Words

Symbol	Examples
KH	*German* **ich, ach**; *Scottish* **loch**
N	*French* **bon** (bôN)
œ	*French* **feu, œuf**; *German* **schön**
ü	*French* **tu**; *German* **über**

*In English the consonants *l* and *n* often constitute complete syllables by themselves.

Stress Marks

The strongest, or primary, stress of a word is indicated by a mark (′). Syllables with weaker stress and words of one syllable show no stress mark.

Glossary of Academic Vocabulary

adapt (ə-dăpt´) *v.* to make something suitable for a particular situation; to adjust to an environment.

ambiguous (ăm-bĭg´yo͞o-əs) *adj.* open to more than one interpretation.

analogy (ə-năl´ə-jē) *n.* a similarity in some respects between things that are otherwise dissimilar or a comparison based on such similarity.

clarify (klăr´ə-fī) *v.* to make clear or easier to understand.

coherent (kō-hîr´ənt) *adj.* holding together in an orderly, logical, or consistent way.

confirm (kən-fûrm´) *v.* to support or establish the certainty or validity of; to verify.

contemporary (kən-tĕm´pə-rĕr-ē) *adj.* belonging to the same period of time; of about the same age; current or modern.

contrary (kŏn´trĕr-ē) *adj.* opposite or opposed in character or purpose.

definitely (dĕf´ə-nĭt-lē) *adv.* in a clearly defined manner; explicitly; precisely; decidedly.

denote (dĭ-nōt´) *v.* to mark; to indicate; to serve as a symbol or name for the meaning of; to signify.

deny (dĭ-nī´) *v.* to declare untrue; to assert to be false; to refuse to believe.

device (dĭ-vīs´) *n.* something made for a specific purpose; a literary technique used to achieve a certain effect.

displace (dĭs-plās´) *v.* to move or force from one place or position to another.

dynamic (dī-năm´ĭk) *adj.* characterized by change, movement, or activity.

format (fôr´măt) *n.* a plan for the organization and arrangement of a specified production.

founder (foun´dər) *n.* someone who sets up, establishes, or provides the basis for something.

global (glō´bəl) *adj.* spherical in shape; worldwide; total.

ideological (ī-dē-ə-lŏj´ĭ-kəl) *adj.* based on ideas, beliefs, or doctrines.

implicit (ĭm-plĭs´ĭt) *adj.* implied or understood though not directly expressed.

infinite (ĭn´fə-nĭt) *adj.* having no boundaries or limits; immeasurably great or large.

publication (pŭb-lĭ-kā´shən) *n.* the act of making public in printed or electronic form; the product of this act.

quote (kwōt) *v.* to repeat or copy words from a source such as a book, usually with an acknowledgment of the source; to give a quotation; *n.* a quotation.

revise (rĭ-vīz´) *v.* to alter or edit; to reconsider and change or modify.

revolution (rĕv-ə-lo͞o´shən) *n.* the overthrow and replacement of a government, often through violent means.

simulated (sĭm´yə-lā-tĭd) *adj.* made in resemblance of or as a substitute for another; performed or staged in imitation of a real event or activity.

somewhat (sŭm´wŏt, -hwŏt, -wŭt, -hwŭt) *adv.* to some extent or degree.

topic (tŏp´ĭk) *n.* the subject of a speech, essay, discussion, or conversation.

unify (yo͞o´nə-fī) *v.* to make into or become a unit; to consolidate.

unique (yo͞o-nēk´) *adj.* being the only one of its kind; remarkable or extraordinary.

virtual (vûr´cho͞o-əl) *adj.* existing or resulting in essence or effect though not in actual form; existing in the mind.

Glossary of Critical Vocabulary

abandonment (ə-băn´dən-mĕnt) *n.* a lack of restraint or inhibition.

abdicate (ăb´dĭ-kāt) *v.* to relinquish or cede responsibility for.

abhor (ăb-hôr´) *v.* to regard with horror or loathing; to detest.

abhorrence (ăb-hôr´əns) *n.* a feeling of repugnance or loathing.

abject (ăb´jĕkt) *adj.* miserable and submissive.

abstraction (ăb-străk´shən) *n.* something that is not part of the concrete, material world.

acrid (ăk´rĭd) *adj.* unpleasantly sharp, pungent, or bitter to the taste or smell.

adamant (ăd´ə-mənt) *adj.* inflexible and insistent, unchanging.

affect (ə-fĕkt´) *v.* to cause or influence.

affluence (ăf´lo͞o-əns) *n.* wealth.

aghast (ə-găst´) *adj.* struck by shock, terror, or amazement.

anomalous (ə-nŏm´ə-ləs) *adj.* unusual.

apprehension (ăp-rĭ-hĕn´shən) *n.* fear or anxiety; dread.

archaic (är-kā´ĭk) *adj.* relating to, being, or characteristic of a much earlier period.

artifice (är´tə-fĭs) *n.* a clever means to an end.

atrocious (ə-trō´shəs) *adj.* evil or brutal.

augment (ôg-mĕnt´) *v.* to make (something already developed or well underway) greater, as in size, extent, or quantity.

automation (ô-tə-mā´shən) *n.* the automatic operation or control of equipment, a process, or a system.

belatedly (bĭ-lā´tĭd-lē) *adv.* done too late or when overdue.

bravado (brə-vä´dō) *n.* a show of bravery or defiance, often in order to make a false impression or mislead someone.

cabal (kə-băl´) *n.* a group united in a secret plot.

calamity (kə-lăm´ĭ-tē) *n.* an event that brings terrible loss or lasting distress.

caliber (kăl´ə-bər) *n.* level of ability.

capacity (kə-păs´ĭ-tē) *n.* ability to hold or have something; function or role.

cardinal (kär´dn-əl) *adj.* most important; prime.

catalyst (kăt´l-ĭst) *n.* a substance, usually used in small amounts relative to the reactants, that modifies and increases the rate of a reaction without being consumed in the process.

cede (sēd) *v.* to yield or give away.

circumlocution (sûr-kəm-lō-kyo͞o´shən) *n.* the use of unnecessarily wordy language.

circumvent (sûr-kəm-vĕnt´) *v.* to avoid or get around by artful maneuvering.

clave (klāv) *v. Archaic* past tense of ***cleave:*** to cling; to adhere.

codify (kŏd´ ĭ-fī) *v.* to arrange or systematize.

compelled (kəm-pĕld´) *v.* forced (a person) to do something; drove or constrained.

composed (kəm-pōzd´) *adj.* self-possessed; calm.

conceivable (kən-sēv´ə-bəl) *adj.* able to be formed or developed in the mind.

configuration (kən-fĭg-yə-rā´shən) *n.* arrangement of parts or elements.

conjure (kŏn´jər) *v.* to influence or effect by or as if by magic.

conquistador (kŏng-kē´stə-dôr, kŏn-kwĭs´tə-dôr) *n.* a 16th-century Spanish soldier-explorer who took part in the defeat of the Indian civilizations of Mexico, Central America, or Peru.

consolation (kŏn-sə-lā´shən) *n.* act of giving comfort.

constitute (kŏn´stĭ-to͞ot) *v.* to amount to; to equal.

contrive (kən-trīv´) *v.* to plan skillfully; to design.

contrived (kən-trīvd´) *adj.* obviously planned or calculated; not spontaneous or natural.

conventional (kən-vĕn´shə-nəl) *adj.* based on or in accordance with general agreement, use, or practice; customary.

copious (kō´pē-əs) *adj.* extensive.

defection (dē-fĕkt´shŭn) *n.* the abandonment of one social or political group in favor of another.

delicacy (dĕl´ĭ-kə-sē) *n.* something pleasing and appealing, especially a choice food.

delinquency (dĭ-lĭng´kwən-sē) *n.* shortcoming or misbehavior.

delinquent (dĭ-lĭng´kwənt) *adj.* failing to do what law or duty requires.

demeanor (dĭ-mē´nər) *n.* the way in which a person behaves; deportment.

demurred (dĭ-mûrd´) *v.* disagreed politely or politely refused to accept a request or suggestion.

deprecate (dĕp´rĭ-kāt) *v.* to express disapproval.

deprive (dĭ-prīv´) *v.* to keep from possessing or enjoying; to deny.

diligence (dĭl´ə-jəns) *n.* consistent, thorough effort and dedication.

discord (dĭs´kôrd) *n.* disagreement or conflict.

disposed (dĭ-spōzd´) *adj.* having a preference, disposition, or tendency.

disposition (dĭs-pə-zĭsh´ən) *n.* character or temperament.

distinction (dĭ-stĭngk´shən) *n.* difference in quality.

divers (di´vərz) *adj.* various; several.

efface (ĭ-fās´) *v.* to rub or wipe out; to erase.

elusive (ĭ-lo͞o´sĭv) *adj.* difficult to define.

emblem (ĕm´bləm) *n.* an identifying mark or symbol.

engross (ĕn-grōs´) *v.* to completely engage the attention or interest.

eradicate (ĭ-răd´ĭ-kāt) *v.* to tear up by the roots; to eliminate.

establish (ĭ-stăb´lĭsh) *v.* to formally set up; to institute.

estrangement (ĭ-strānj´mənt) *n.* the condition of being detached or withdrawn; alienation.

eviscerate (ĭ-vĭs´ə-rāt) *v.* to remove the necessary or important parts of.

exclusive (ĭk-sklo͞o´sĭv) *adj.* not allowing something else.

expedience (ĭk-spē´dē-əns) *n.* a self-interested means to an end.

extenuating (ĭk-stĕn´yo͞o-ā-tĭng) *adj.* serving to make a fault or an offense seem less serious.

extortionist (ĭk-stôr´shən-ĭst) *n.* one who obtains something by force or threat.

extremity (ĭk-strĕm´ĭ-tē) *n.* the outermost or farthest point or portion; the hand or foot.

façade (fə-säd´) *n.* false or misleading appearance.

facile (făs´əl) *adj.* easy to make or understand.

felicity (fĭ-lĭs´ĭ-tē) *n.* great happiness.

ferry (fĕr´ē) *v.* to transport (people or goods) by vehicle.

fixed (fĭkst) *adj.* firmly in position; stationary.

formidable (fôr´mĭ-də-bəl) *adj.* difficult and intimidating.

frantically (frăn´tĭk-lē) *adv.* excitedly, with strong emotion or frustration.

gape (gāp, găp) *v.* to stare wonderingly or stupidly, often with the mouth open.

grope (grōp) *v.* to reach about uncertainly; to feel one's way.

illumination (ĭ-lo͞o-mə-nā´shən) *n.* awareness or enlightenment.

imperative (ĭm-pĕr´ə-tĭv) *adj.* of great importance; essential.

impertinent (ĭm-pûr´tn-ənt) *adj.* rude; ill-mannered.

impunity (ĭm-pyo͞o´nĭ-tē) *n.* exemption from punishment, penalty, or harm.

inclination (ĭn-klə-nā´shən) *n.* a characteristic disposition or tendency to act in a certain way; a propensity.

incorrigible (ĭn-kôr´ĭ-jə-bəl) *adj.* incapable of being reformed or corrected.

indigenous (ĭn-dĭj´ə-nəs) *adj.* native to a land.

induced (ĭn-do͞ost´) *v.* led or moved, as to a course of action, by influence or persuasion.

ineffable (ĭn-ĕf´ə-bəl) *adj.* beyond description; inexpressible.

infinitesimal (ĭn-fĭn-ĭ-tĕs´ə-məl) *adj.* immeasurably or incalculably minute.

infraction (ĭn-frăk´shən) *n.* the act or instance of infringing, as of a law or rule; a violation.

ingenious (ĭn-jēn´yəs) *adj.* having great inventive skill and imagination.

inhumanity (ĭn-hyo͞o-măn´ĭ-tē) *n.* lack of pity or compassion.

insurgency (ĭn-sûr´jən-sē) *n.* rebellion or revolt.

intangible (ĭn-tăn´jə-bəl) *adj.* unable to be defined or understood.

interminable (ĭn-tûr´mə-nə-bəl) *adj.* seemingly endless.

internalize (ĭn-tûr´nə-līz) *v.* to take in and make an integral part of one's attitudes or beliefs.

invest (ĭn-vĕst´) *v.* to grant or endow.

malign (mə-līn´) *v.* to make evil, harmful, and often untrue statements about (someone).

metaphysical (mĕt-ə-fĭz´ĭ-kəl) *adj.* based on speculative or abstract reasoning.

miscellany (mĭs´ə-lā-nē) *n.* a collection of various items, parts, or ingredients, especially one composed of diverse literary works.

mitigate (mĭt´ĭ-gāt) *v.* to lessen.

narcotic (när-kŏt´ĭk) *adj.* inducing sleep or stupor; causing narcosis.

noblesse oblige (nō-blĕs´ ō-blēzh´) *n.* the responsibility of people in a high social position to behave in a noble fashion.

oblige (ə-blīj´) *v.* to compel or require (someone) to do something.

obstinacy (ŏb´stə-nə-sē) *n.* stubbornness.

ostensibly (ŏ-stĕn´sə-blē) *adv.* apparently.

ostentatious (ŏs-tĕn-tā´shəs) *adj.* conspicuous and vulgar.

palpable (păl´pə-bəl) *adj.* capable of being handled, touched, or felt; tangible.

panic (păn´ĭk) *n.* sudden, overpowering feeling of fear.

parity (păr´ĭ-tē) *n.* equality; being equivalent.

patent (păt´nt) *n.* an official document granting ownership.

pathos (pā´thŏs) *n.* something that evokes pity or sympathy.

peril (pĕr´əl) *n.* imminent danger.

perturbation (pûr-tər-bā´shən) *n.* disturbance or agitation.

pigmentation (pĭg-mən-tā´shən) *n.* coloration of tissues by pigment.

platoon (plə-to͞on´) *n.* a subdivision of a company of troops consisting of two or more squads or sections and usually commanded by a lieutenant.

plausibility (plô-zə-bĭl´ĭ-tē) *n.* likelihood; believability.

pliable (plī´ə-bəl) *adj.* easily bent or shaped; easily influenced, persuaded, or controlled.

poignant (poin´yənt) *adj.* physically or mentally painful.

polarity (pō-lăr´ĭ-tē) *n.* separation to opposite sides.

ponder (pŏn´dər) *v.* to think about (something) with thoroughness and care.

posse (pŏs´ē) *n.* a group of civilians temporarily authorized by officials to assist in pursuing fugitives.

postulate (pŏs´chə-lāt) *v.* to assume or assert the truth, reality, or necessity of, especially as a basis of an argument.

presaging (prĕs´ĭj-ĭng) *adj.* predicting.

pristine (prĭs´tēn) *adj.* pure or unspoiled.

project (prə-jĕkt´) *v.* to communicate or put forth.

proposition (prŏp-ə-zĭsh´ən) *n.* a plan suggested for acceptance; a proposal.

protrude (prō-tro͞od´) *v.* to stick out or bulge.

provision (prə-vĭzh´ən) *n.* food supply.

provocation (prŏv-ə-kā´shən) *n.* the act of provoking or inciting.

recalcitrant (rĭ-kăl´sĭ-trənt) *adj.* uncooperative and resistant of authority.

reckless (rĕk´lĭs) *adj.* acting or done with a lack of care or caution.

reckoning (rĕk´ə-nĭng) *n.* a settlement of accounts.

recompense (rĕk´əm-pĕns) *n.* payment in return for something, such as a service.

regenerate (rĭ-jĕn´ə-rāt) *v.* to form, construct, or create anew.

regimen (rĕj´ə-mən) *n.* a system or organized routine of behavior.

remunerative (rĭ-myo͞o´nər-ə-tĭv) *adj.* bringing in money or profit.

reparations (rĕp-ə-rā´shəns) *n.* compensation or payment from a nation for damage or injury during a war.

rudiment (ro͞o´də-mənt) *n.* basic form.

sceptical (skĕp´tĭ-kəl) *adj.* marked by or given to doubt; questioning.

segregated (sĕg´rĭ-gāt-əd) *adj.* separated; isolated.

sentiment (sən´tə-mənt) *n.* a thought, view, or attitude, especially one based mainly on emotion instead of reason.

settlement (sĕt´l-mənt) *n.* a small community in a sparsely populated area.

sliver (slĭv´ər) *n.* a small narrow piece, portion, or plot.

sojourn (sō´jûrn´) *n.* a temporary stay; a brief period of residence.

specious (spē´shəs) *adj.* having the ring of truth or plausibility but actually fallacious.

specter (spĕk´tər) *n.* a ghostly apparition; a phantom.

stem (stĕm) *v.* to have or take origin or descent.

stoically (stō´ĭk-lē) *adv.* without showing emotion or feeling.

straits (strāts) *n.* a position of difficulty, distress, or extreme need.

strive (strīv) *v.* to struggle or fight forcefully; to contend.

subservience (səb-sûr´vē-əns) *n.* the condition of being subordinate in capacity or function.

summarily (sə-mĕr´ə-lē) *adv.* quickly and without ceremony.

sundry (sŭn´drē) *adj.* various or assorted.

superfluous (so͝o-pûr´flo͞o-əs) *adj.* unnecessary.

systematize (sĭs´tə-mə-tīz) *v.* to form something into an organized plan or scheme.

tableau (tăb´lō) *n.* a dramatic scene or picture.

tepid (tĕp´ĭd) *adj.* lukewarm; indifferent.

tidings (tī´dĭngs) *n.* information or news.

timid (tĭm´ĭd) *adj.* lacking self-confidence; shy.

transient (trăn´zē-ənt) *adj.* temporary; short-term.

transition (trăn-zĭsh´ən) *n.* process of change.

trifling (trī´flĭng) *adj.* frivolous; inconsequential.

truculent (trŭk´yə-lənt) *adj.* eager for a fight; fierce.

tyrannical (tĭ-răn´ĭ-kəl) *adj.* characteristic of a tyrant or tyranny; despotic and oppressive.

unalienable (ŭn-āl´yə-nə-bəl) *adj.* impossible to be taken away.

unassailable (ŭn-ə-sā´lə-bəl) *adj.* undeniable.

undulation (ŭn-jə-lā´shən) *n.* a regular rising and falling or movement to alternating sides; movement in waves.

unfathomed (ŭn-făth´əmd) *adj.* located at the deepest place.

unimpeded (ŭn-ĭm-pēd´əd) *adj.* not delayed or obstructed in its progress.

unremitting (ŭn-rĭ-mĭt´ĭng) *adj.* constant; never stopping.

vacant (vā´kənt) *adj.* blank, expressionless.

vanquish (văng´kwĭsh) *v.* to defeat in a contest or conflict.

venture (vĕn´chər) *v.* to risk or dare.

vindicate (vĭn´dĭ-kāt) *v.* to demonstrate or prove the validity of; to justify.

virtuous (vûr´cho͞o-əs) *adj.* having or showing virtue, especially moral excellence.

virulent (vîr´yə-lənt) *adj.* extremely hostile or malicious.

volatile (vŏl´ə-tl) *adj.* evaporating readily at normal temperatures and pressures.

watershed (wô´tər-shĕd) *n.* a turning point; a crucial dividing line.

wring (rĭng) *v.* to obtain through force or pressure.

Index of Skills

N

O

P

Q

R

S

Index of Titles and Authors

Acknowledgments

Excerpt from *1491: New Revelations of the Americas Before Columbus* by Charles C. Mann, map by Nick Springer and Tracy Pollack of Springer Cartographics LLC. Text and illustration copyright © 2005, 2006, 2011 by Charles C. Mann. Reprinted by permission of Alfred A. Knopf, an imprint of the Knopf Doubleday Publishing Group, a division of Penguin Random House LLC, Granta Publications, and Roam Agency on behalf of Charles C. Mann.

"Ambush" from *The Things They Carried* by Tim O'Brien. Text and audio copyright © 1990 by Tim O'Brien. Reproduced by permission of Houghton Mifflin Harcourt Publishing Company, HarperCollins Publishers Ltd, and Janklow and Nesbit Associates.

Excerpts from *The American Heritage Dictionary of The English Language, Fifth Edition.* Text copyright © 2016 by Houghton Mifflin Harcourt Publishing Company. Reprinted by permission of Houghton Mifflin Harcourt Publishing Company.

"Balboa" from *Tales of the New World* by Sabina Murray. Text copyright © 2011 by Sabina Murray. Reprinted by permission of Grove/Atlantic, Inc. Any third-party use of this material, outside of this publication, is prohibited.

"Because I could not stop for Death," "Much Madness is divinest Sense," "The Soul selects her own Society," and "Tell all the Truth but tell it slant" from *The Poems of Emily Dickinson* edited by Thomas H. Johnson. Text copyright © 1951, 1955, renewed 1979, 1983 by the President and Fellows of Harvard College. Text copyright 1914, 1918, 1919, 1924, 1929, 1930, 1932, 1935, 1937, 1942 by Martha Dickinson Bianchi. Text copyright © 1952, 1957, 1958, 1963, 1965 by Mary L. Hampson. Reprinted by permission of The Belknap Press of Harvard University Press, Cambridge, Mass.

"Building the Transcontinental Railroad" from *The Chinese in America: A Narrative History* by Iris Chang. Text copyright © 2003 by Iris Chang. Reprinted by permission of Viking Books, an imprint of Penguin Publishing Group, a division of Penguin Random House LLC. All rights reserved. Any third-party use of this material, outside of this publication, is prohibited. Interested parties must apply directly to Penguin Random House LLC for permission.

"Casualties and Costs of the Civil War" by The Gilder Lehrman Institute of American History. Copyright © 2017. Reprinted by permission of The Gilder Lehrman Institute of American History.

The Crucible by Arthur Miller. Text copyright © 1952, 1953, 1954 by Arthur Miller, renewed © 1980, 1981, 1982 by Arthur Miller. Reprinted by permission of Viking Books, an imprint of Penguin Publishing Group, a division of Penguin Random House LLC and The Wylie Agency LLC.

"A Desperate Trek Across America" by Andrés Reséndez from *American Heritage*, Fall 2008, Vol. 58, Issue 5. Text copyright © 2008 by American Heritage Publishing. Reprinted by permission of American Heritage Publishing via Copyright Clearance Center.

Excerpt from *Fast Food Nation* by Eric Schlosser. Text copyright © 2001 by Eric Schlosser. Reprinted by permission of Houghton Mifflin Harcourt, Penguin Books Ltd, Random House Audio Publishing Group, a division of Penguin Random House LLC, and Janklow & Nesbit Associates on behalf of the author.

"First Verse" from *Buffalo Head Solos* by Tim Seibles. Text copyright © 2002 by Tim Seibles. Reprinted by permission of the author.

"The Fourth Industrial Revolution Is Here: Are You Ready?" (retitled from "Why Everyone Must Get Ready for the 4th Industrial Revolution") by Bernard Marr from Forbes.com, April 5, 2016. Text copyright © 2016 by Bernard Marr. Reprinted by permission of Bernard Marr.

"In the Season of Change" by Teresa Palomo Acosta. Text copyright © 1994 by Teresa Palomo Acosta. Reproduced by permission of the author.

From "Introduction" from *Last Child in the Woods* by Richard Louv. Text copyright © 2005 by Richard Louv. Reprinted by permission of Algonquin Books of Chapel Hill. All rights reserved.

"The Latin Deli: An Ars Poetica" by Judith Ortiz Cofer from *The Americas Review,* vol. 19, no. 1. Text Copyright © 1991 by Arte Público Press – University of Houston. Reprinted by permission of Arte Público Press – University of Houston.

Excerpt from *Lean In: Women, Work, and the Will to Lead* by Sheryl Sandberg. Text copyright © 2013 by Lean In Foundation. Reprinted by permission of Alfred A. Knopf, an imprint of the Knopf Doubleday Publishing Group, a division of Penguin Random House LLC, William Morris Endeavor Entertainment, LLC, and The Random House Group Limited.

"The Lowest Animal" from *Letters from the Earth* by Mark Twain, edited by Bernard DeVoto. Text copyright © 1938, 1944, 1946, 1959, 1962 by The Mark Twain Company. Copyright 1942 by The President and Fellows of Harvard College. Reprinted by permission of HarperCollins Publishers.

"My Dungeon Shook: Letter to My Nephew on this One Hundredth Anniversary of the Emancipation" by James Baldwin. Text copyright © 1962, 1963 by James Baldwin. Copyright renewed. Originally published in *The Progressive.* Collected in *The Fire Next Time,* published by Vintage Books. Reprinted by arrangement with the James Baldwin Estate.

"My Friend Walt Whitman" from *Blue Pastures* by Mary Oliver. Text copyright © 1995 by Mary Oliver. Reprinted by permission of Houghton Mifflin Harcourt.

"New Orleans" from *She Had Some Horses* by Joy Harjo. Text copyright © 2008, 1983 by Joy Harjo. Reprinted by permission of W. W. Norton & Company, Inc.

From *Of Plymouth Plantation 1620–1647* by William Bradford, edited by Samuel Eliot Morison, New York: Alfred A. Knopf, 1952.

"One Today: A Poem for Barack Obama's Presidential Inauguration Jan. 21, 2013" from *One Today: A Poem for Barack Obama's Presidential Inauguration January 21, 2013* by Richard Blanco. Text copyright © 2013. Reprinted by permission of the University of Pittsburgh Press.

Acknowledgments

"A Rose for Emily" from *Collected Stories of William Faulkner* by William Faulkner. Text copyright 1930, renewed 1958 by William Faulkner. Reprinted by permission of Random House, an imprint and division of Penguin Random House LLC, W. W. Norton & Company, Inc., and Curtis Brown Ltd, London on behalf of The Estate of William Faulkner.

"Runagate Runagate" from *Collected Poems of Robert Hayden* by Robert Hayden, edited by Frederick Glaysher. Text copyright © 1966 by Robert Hayden. Reprinted by permission of Liveright Publishing Corporation.

"A Soldier for the Crown" from *Soulcatcher and Other Stories* by Charles Johnson. Text copyright © 1998 by Charles Johnson. Reprinted by permission of the WGBH Educational Foundation.

Excerpt from "Speech on the Vietnam War, New York City, April 4, 1967" by Martin Luther King, Jr. Text copyright © 1967 by Dr. Martin Luther King, Jr., renewed © 1991 by Coretta Scott King. Reprinted by permission of Writers House on behalf of the Heirs of the Estate of Martin Luther King, Jr.

Excerpt from *They Called Us Enemy* by George Takei. Copyright © 2019 by George Takei. Reprinted by permission of Top Shelf Productions / IDW Publishing.

"Thomas Jefferson: The Best of Enemies" from *Time Magazine*, July 5, 2004, by Ron Chernow. Text copyright © 2004 by TIME, Inc. Reprinted by permission of TIME, Inc. All rights reserved.

"The Universe as Primal Scream" from *Life on Mars* by Tracy K. Smith. Text copyright © 2011 by Tracy K. Smith. Reprinted with the permission of The Permissions Company, Inc. on behalf of Graywolf Press, Minneapolis, Minnesota. www.graywolfpress.org.

Excerpt from *The Warmth of Other Suns: The Epic Story of America's Great Migration* by Isabel Wilkerson. Text copyright © 2010 by Isabel Wilkerson. Reprinted by permission of Random House, an imprint and division of Penguin Random House LLC, and ICM Partners.

"World, in hounding me, what do you gain?" by Sor Juana Inés de la Cruz, from *A Sor Juana Anthology*, translated by Alan S. Trueblood. Copyright © 1988 by the President and Fellows of Harvard College. Published by Harvard University Press, Cambridge, MA. Reprinted by permission of the publisher.

"World on the Turtle's Back" from *The Great Tree and the Longhouse: The Culture of the Iroquois* by Hazel W. Hertzberg. Text copyright © 1966 by American Anthropological Association. Not for sale or further reproduction. Reprinted by permission of American Anthropological Association.